Captain Cook's Journal

First Voyage Round

in H. M. Bark "End...

James Cook

(Editor: W. J. L. Wharton)

Alpha Editions

This edition published in 2024

ISBN : 9789364734585

Design and Setting By
Alpha Editions
www.alphaedis.com
Email : info@alphaedis.com

As per information held with us this book is in Public Domain.
This book is a reproduction of an important historical work. Alpha Editions uses the best technology to reproduce historical work in the same manner it was first published to preserve its original nature. Any marks or number seen are left intentionally to preserve its true form.

Contents

PREFACE. ....- 1 -
SKETCH OF CAPTAIN COOK'S LIFE. ....- 7 -
PERSONS WHO LEFT ENGLAND IN H.M.S.
ENDEAVOUR, 26TH AUGUST, 1768. ....- 41 -
A JOURNAL OF THE PROCEEDINGS OF HIS MAJESTY'S
BARK ENDEAVOUR, ON A VOYAGE ROUND THE
WORLD, BY LIEUTENANT JAMES COOK,
COMMANDER, COMMENCING THE 25TH OF
MAY, 1768. ....- 42 -
CHAPTER 1. ENGLAND TO RIO JANEIRO. ....- 43 -
CHAPTER 2. RIO JANEIRO TO TAHITI. ....- 73 -
CHAPTER 3. TAHITI. ....- 107 -
CHAPTER 4. TAHITI TO NEW ZEALAND.....................- 154 -
CHAPTER 5. EXPLORATION OF NORTH ISLAND
OF NEW ZEALAND. ....- 178 -
CHAPTER 6. EXPLORATION OF MIDDLE ISLAND OF
NEW ZEALAND..- 229 -
CHAPTER 7. PASSAGE FROM NEW ZEALAND TO
NEW HOLLAND. ....- 280 -
CHAPTER 8. EXPLORATION OF EAST COAST OF
AUSTRALIA. ....- 284 -
CHAPTER 9. FROM TORRES STRAIT TO BATAVIA. ...- 372 -
CHAPTER 10. BATAVIA TO CAPE OF GOOD HOPE.....- 412 -
CHAPTER 11. CAPE OF GOOD HOPE TO ENGLAND. ..- 434 -

PREFACE.

STRANGE it must appear that the account of perhaps the most celebrated and, certainly to the English nation, the most momentous voyage of discovery that has ever taken place--for it practically gave birth to the great Australasian Colonies--has never before been given to the world in the very words of its great leader. It has fallen out in this wise.

After the return of the Endeavour it was decided that a full and comprehensive account of the voyage should be compiled. COOK'S JOURNAL dealt with matters from the point of view of the seaman, the explorer, and the head of the expedition, responsible for life, and for its general success. The Journals of Mr. Banks and Dr. Solander looked from the scientific side on all that presented itself to their enthusiastic observation.

What could be better than to combine these accounts, and make up a complete narrative from them all?

The result, however, according to our nineteenth-century ideas, was not altogether happy. Dr. Hawkesworth, into whose hands the Journals were put, not only interspersed reflections of his own, but managed to impose his own ponderous style upon many of the extracts from the united Journals; and, moreover, as they are all jumbled together, the whole being put into Cook's mouth, it is impossible to know whether we are reading Cook, Banks, Solander, or Hawkesworth himself.

The readers of the day were not, however, critical. Hawkesworth's book,* (* "Hawkesworth's Voyages" 3 volumes quarto 1773.) which undoubtedly contains all the most generally interesting passages of the three writers, gave a clear description of the events of the voyage in a connected manner, and was accepted as sufficient; and in the excitement of devouring the pages which introduced so many new lands and peoples, probably few wished for more, and the Journals were put away as dealt with.

Since that time it has been on several occasions in contemplation to publish Mr. (after Sir Joseph) Banks' Journal; but this has never been accomplished.

Cook's Journal was in triplicate. The Admiralty Orders of the day enjoined that the captain should keep a journal of proceedings, a copy of which was to be forwarded to the Admiralty every six months, or as soon after as possible. In the case of this voyage the ship was two and a half years from England before any opportunity of sending this copy occurred. The ship was the whole of this time in new and savage lands. When Batavia was reached the duplicate of Cook's Journal was sent home, and six months later, when the ship arrived in England, the full Journal of the voyage was deposited at the Admiralty.

The Secretary of the Admiralty, Sir Philip Stephens, a personal friend and appreciator of Cook, appears to have appropriated the Batavia duplicate, as we find it in the hands of his descendants, and passing thence by sale, first to Mr. Cosens in 1868, and then in 1890 to Mr. John Corner.

The other and complete copy is still in possession of the Admiralty, though in some unexplained manner it was absent for some years, and was only recovered by the exertions of Mr. W. Blakeney, R.N.

A third copy of the Journal also terminates a few days before reaching Batavia. It is in the possession of Her Majesty the Queen, and from its appearance was kept for, and probably presented to, George III, who took great interest in the voyage.

Neither private possessors nor the Admiralty have felt moved to publish this interesting document until Mr. Corner acquired his copy, when, being an enthusiastic admirer of Captain Cook, he determined to do so, and was making preliminary arrangements, when he suddenly died, after a few hours' illness. His son, anxious to carry out his father's wishes, which included the devotion of any proceeds to the restoration of Hinderwell Church--the parish church of Staithes, whence Cook ran away to sea--has completed these arrangements, and the present volume is the result.

The text is taken from Mr. Corner's copy so far as it goes, paragraphs from the Admiralty copy, which do not appear in the former, being added, with a notation of their source.

The last portion, from October 23rd, 1770, which is only given in the Admiralty copy, is necessarily taken from it.

The three copies are, practically, identical, except for the period August 13th to 19th, 1770, during which the wording is often different, though the events are the same.

It is not very difficult to account for this.

The two first-mentioned Journals are in the handwriting of an amanuensis, Mr. Orton, the clerk. No autograph journal is, so far as is known, in existence, but some rough original must have been kept, as both copies bear internal evidence of having been written up after the lapse of an interval after the events described.

This is markedly the case in the Australian part of the Journal.

It is known that Botany Bay was at first called by Cook, Stingray Bay, on account of the number of rays caught there; but after Banks had examined his collection, and found all his plants new to science, Cook determined to call it Botany Bay. It is, however, called Botany Bay from the first in the Journals.

The name, "New South Wales," was not bestowed without much consideration, and apparently at one stage New Wales was the appellation fixed upon, for in Mr. Corner's copy it is so called throughout, whereas the Admiralty copy has "New South Wales."

It would therefore seem that about the period of the discrepant accounts Mr. Corner's copy was first made, and that Cook, in the Admiralty copy, which for this part is fuller, revised the wording of his description of this very critical portion of the voyage.

The Queen's Copy has been written with especial care, and by several different hands. It was evidently the last in point of time.

In reading COOK'S JOURNAL of his First Voyage it must be remembered that it was not prepared for publication. Though no doubt the fair copies we possess were revised with the care that characterises the man, and which is evidenced by the interlineations and corrections in his own hand with which the pages are dotted, it may be supposed, from the example we have in the published account of his Second Voyage, which was edited by himself, that further alterations and additions would have been made, to make the story more complete, had he contemplated its being printed.

This does not, however, in any way detract from the interest of a transcript of his record on the spot; and though many circumstances recorded in Hawkesworth, from Banks or others, will not be found, it is probable that an exact copy of the great navigator's own impressions, and the disentanglement of them from the other interpolated matter, will be welcome.

In printing this Journal the only alterations that have been made are the breaking-up into chapters, with modern headings; the addition of punctuation; and in the form of the insertion of the daily record of wind, weather, and position of the ship. These in the original are on the left hand page in log form. To save space they have been placed at the end of every day's transactions.

The eccentricities in the spelling have been preserved. A good many of these would seem to be due to Mr. Orton, the transcriber, as Cook's own letters are generally correct in their orthography. The use of the capital letter was usual at the time.

References will be found to sketches and plans which have not been reproduced.

Cook's knack of finding names for localities was peculiarly happy. Those who have had to do this, know the difficulty. Wherever he was able to ascertain the native name, he adopts it; but in the many cases where this was impossible, he manages to find a descriptive and distinctive appellation for each point, bay, or island.

He seems to have kept these names very much to himself, as it is seldom the officers' logs know anything of them; and original plans, still in existence, in many cases bear different names to those finally pitched upon.

Cook's names have rarely been altered, and New Zealand and Australian places will probably for all time bear those which he bestowed.

In the orthography of his native names he was not so successful. The constant addition of a redundant "o" has altered many native sounds, such as Otaheite for Tahiti, Ohwhyhee for Hawaii; while his spelling generally has been superseded by more simple forms. This is a matter, however, in which great difficulties are found to the present day by Englishmen, whose language presents no certain laws for rendering any given sound into a fixed combination of letters.

Cook's language is unvarnished and plain, as a sailor's should be. His incidents, though often related with circumstance, are without exaggeration; indeed if any fault is to be found, it is that he takes occurrences involving much labour and hardship as such matters of course, that it is not easy for the reader, especially if he be a landsman, to realise what they really entail.

Cook was assiduous in obtaining observations to ascertain the Variation of the compass--i.e., the difference between the direction shown by the magnetic needle and the true north. He is constantly puzzled by the discrepancies in these observations made at short intervals. These arose from the different positions of the ship's head, whereby the iron within a certain distance of the compass is placed in different positions as regards the needle working the compass card, the result being that the needle is attracted from its correct direction in varying degree. This is known as the Deviation of the compass. The cause of this, and of the laws which govern it, were only discovered by Captain Flinders in 1805. Happily for the navigators of those days, little iron entered into the construction of ships, and the amount of the Deviation was not large, though enough to cause continual disquiet and wonderment.

Cook's longitudes in this voyage are all given as west of Greenwich, not divided into east and west, as is usual at this day. The latter system again has only been adopted universally since his time.

Though Cook himself gives, at the beginning of the Journal, a note of the method of reckoning days adopted, it may not be amiss to give further explanation here.

It was the usual custom on board ships to keep what was known as Ship time--i.e., the day began at noon BEFORE the civil reckoning, in which the day commences at midnight. Thus, while January 1st, as ordinarily reckoned, is from midnight to midnight, in ship time it began at noon on December 31st and ended at noon January 1st, this period being called January 1st. Hence the peculiarity all through the Journal of the p.m. coming before the a.m. It results that any events recorded as occurring in the p.m. of January 1st in the log, would, if translated into the ordinary system, be given as happening in the p.m. of December 31st; while occurrences in the a.m. of January 1st would be equally in the a.m. of January 1st in both systems.

This puzzling mode of keeping the day at sea continued to a late period, and was common to seamen of all nations.

The astronomical day, again, begins at noon AFTER the midnight at which the civil day begins, and hence is a whole day later than the ship's day. This does not enter into Cook's Journal, but one of the logs of the Endeavour, extant, that of Mr. Green the astronomer, was kept in this time, and the events of say Thursday, June 24th, of Cook's Journal, are therein given as happening on Wednesday, June 23rd. These differences of reckoning have been a fertile source of confusion in dates in many voyages.

Besides Cook's Journals there are other Journals and Logs of the voyage extant. Perhaps it may be necessary to state that a Log is the official document in which the progress of the ship from hour to hour is recorded, with such official notes as the alteration in sail carried, expenditure of provisions and stores, etc. A Journal contains this information in a condensed form, with such observations as the officer keeping it may feel inclined to insert.

The ship's Log Book of the Endeavour is in the British Museum. Mr. R.M. Hudson of Sunderland possesses Cook's own log, not autograph however, presented by Cook to Sir Hugh Palliser, the ancestor of his wife.

The Journals of all the officers of the Endeavour are preserved at the Public Record Office. There is, however, nothing to be got out of them, as they are mainly copies one of the other, founded on the ship's log.

The portion of Mr. Molineux's, the Master's, Log that exists (at the Admiralty) is a most beautifully kept and written document, enriched with charts and sketches that attest the accuracy of Cook's remark, that he was a "young man of good parts."

The log kept by Mr. Green, however, does contain a few original remarks, some of which have been made use of. This book contains a mass of astronomical observations, and witnesses to the zeal of this gentleman in his especial duty.

He records in one place, when far away from land, his disgust that the officers were unwilling to aid him in lunar observations. No doubt they saw no particular use in them when there was no coast to fix; but there is ample proof that he received every aid when Cook thought it necessary.

Sufficient charts have been placed in this book to enable the reader to follow the more interesting parts of the voyage; some being reproductions of Cook's own charts, others modern publications. In the case of the coast of East Australia, the coast-line as laid down by Cook, and as now known, are given side by side for comparison.

It must be understood, that although this book is styled CAPTAIN COOK'S JOURNAL, he was on this voyage only a Lieutenant in Command, and therefore only Captain by courtesy.

W.J.L. WHARTON.

FLORYS, WIMBLEDON PARK,

April 7th, 1893.

SKETCH OF CAPTAIN COOK'S LIFE.

CAPTAIN COOK'S life, or the account of so much of it as is recoverable, has been so often recounted that there is no occasion to insert more in this publication than is necessary as a reference to the reader, to enable him to realise the career and character of the man.

Cook's first biographer, Andrew Kippis, wrote in 1788, and his work has recently been republished.* (* "A Narrative of the Voyage round the World, performed by Captain James Cook, with an Account of His Life" by A. Kippis, D.D., F.R.S. London: Bickers & Son 1889.)

The latest and best life is by Walter Besant,* (* "Captain Cook" by Walter Besant: "English Men of Action" London, Macmillan & Co. 1890.) whose graceful pen has given us a fascinating, interesting, and, as far as is possible, complete picture of this great Englishman. Many details of Cook's private life are lost, but enough has been collected by Mr. Besant to place our hero vividly before us, and a perusal of his work is strongly recommended.

Many things in the following sketch are taken from Mr. Besant, to whom I wish to tender my acknowledgments.

James Cook rose from nearly the lowest ranks. The second son of James Cook, a Yorkshire labourer, and Grace his wife, he was born on the edge of the Cleveland Hills on February 27th, 1728, in the little village of Marton, which lies about four miles south-south-east of Middlesbrough, and five miles west of the well-known hill and landmark, Roseberry Topping. Eight years later his father removed to Great Ayton, which lies close under Roseberry Topping.

At the age of thirteen Cook, who, it is recorded, had had some elementary schooling both at Marton and Great Ayton, was apprenticed to one Sanderson, a draper and grocer of Staithes, a fishing village on the coast, about fourteen miles from Ayton and nine north-west of Whitby.

A year later Cook went, or ran away, to sea, shipping at Whitby on board the Freelove, a collier belonging to the brothers Walker.

In this hard school Cook learnt his sailor duties. No better training could have been found for his future responsibilities. Here he learnt to endure the utmost rigours of the sea. Constant fighting with North Sea gales, bad food, and cramped accommodation, taught him to regard with the indifference that afterwards distinguished him, all the hardships that he had to encounter, and led him to endure and persevere where others, less determined or more easily daunted by difficulties, would have hurried on, and left their work incomplete.

All details of Cook's life during his thirteen years in the merchant service are lost: what voyages he made, how he fared, whether he advanced in general knowledge, all is gone. The only fact known is that in May 1755, when Cook was twenty-seven years of age, and mate of a vessel of Messrs. Walker, then in the Thames, he, to avoid the press, then active on account of the outbreak of the war with France, volunteered on board H.M.S. Eagle, of 60 guns, as an able seaman.

Captain Hugh Palliser, who succeeded to the command of this ship in October, was certainly Cook's warmest patron, and it would appear that Cook did work superior to that of an able seaman in the Eagle. Be that as it may, all that is absolutely known is that that ship took her share of the fighting at the taking of Louisbourg and elsewhere on the North American and West Indian Station, and returned to England in 1759.

By Palliser's interest Cook was now appointed master of the Mercury. It is therefore evident that his qualifications as a navigator recommended themselves to Palliser.

The Mercury went to North America, and here Cook did his first good service recorded, namely, taking soundings in the St. Lawrence, to enable the fleet then attacking Quebec to take up safe positions in covering the army under Wolfe. This he accomplished with great skill, under many difficulties, in the face of the enemy, much of it being done at night. He was immediately employed in making a survey of the intricate channels of the river below Quebec, and for many years his chart was the guide for navigation. Cook was indeed a born surveyor. Before his day charts were of the crudest description, and he must have somehow acquired a considerable knowledge of trigonometry, and possessed an intuitive faculty for practically applying it, to enable him to originate, as it may truly be said he did, the art of modern marine surveying.

The expedition to Quebec concluded, Cook was appointed master of the Northumberland, bearing Admiral Lord Colville's flag, and during that ship's winter at Halifax he applied himself to further study of mathematics and astronomy.

In 1762, the Northumberland being at Newfoundland during the capture of that island from the French, Cook again was employed in surveys. This attracted the attention of Captain Graves, the Governor, who conceived a high opinion of his abilities in this respect.

In the latter part of 1762 Cook returned to England and married Elizabeth Batts, daughter of a man in business at Wapping; but a few months afterwards he was called upon by Captain Graves to go again to Newfoundland to make marine surveys.

In this important work he was engaged until 1767, Captain Palliser, who succeeded Captain Graves as Governor, being only too glad to avail himself of Cook's services.

The charts he made during these years in the schooner Grenville were admirable. The best proof of their excellence is that they are not yet wholly superseded by the more detailed surveys of modern times. Like all first surveys of a practically unknown shore, and especially when that shore abounds in rocks and shoals, and is much indented with bays and creeks, they are imperfect, in the sense of having many omissions; but when the amount of the ground covered, and the impediments of fogs and bad weather on that coast is considered, and that Cook had at the most only one assistant, their accuracy is truly astonishing. The originals of these surveys form part of the most precious possessions of the Hydrographic Office of the Admiralty.

We now approach the crowning achievements of Cook's life.

After many years' neglect the exploration of the Pacific was awaking interest. This great ocean, which very few, even to this day, realise occupies nearly one half of the surface of the globe, had been, since the first voyage of Magellan, crossed by many a vessel.

Notwithstanding, very little was known of the islands occupying its central portion.

For this there were two reasons. First, the comparatively small area covered by islands; secondly, the fact that nearly all who traversed it had followed Magellan's track, or, if they started, as many did, from Central America, they made straight for Magellan's discovery, the Ladrone Islands. For this, again, there was a reason.

Few sailed for the purpose of exploration pure and simple; and even those who started with that view found, when embarked on that vast expanse, that prudence dictated that they should have a moderate certainty of, by a certain time, falling in with a place of sure refreshment. The provisions they carried were bad at starting, and by the time they had fought their way through the Straits of Magellan were already worse; water was limited, and would not hold out more than a given number of days. Every voyage that is pursued tells the same story--short of water, and eagerly looking out for an opportunity of replenishing it. The winds were found to blow in fixed directions, and each voyager was fearful of deviating from the track on which it was known they would be fair, for fear of delays. And ever present in each captain's mind was the dread of the terrible scourge, scurvy. Every expedition suffered from it. Each hoped they would be exempt, and each in turn was reduced to impotence from its effects.

It was the great consideration for every leader of a protracted expedition, How can I obviate this paralyzing influence? And one after another had to confess his failure.

It is yearly becoming more difficult for us to realise these obstacles.

The prevailing winds and currents in each part of the ocean are well known to us: the exact distance and bearing from one point to another are laid down in the chart; steam bridges over calm areas, and in many cases conducts us on our entire journey at a speed but little inferior to that of land travelling by railroad; modern science preserves fresh and palatable food for an indefinite period; and, in a word, all the difficulties and most of the dangers of long voyages have disappeared.

Take one element alone in long voyages--the time required. The average progress of a ship in the eighteenth century was not more than fifty miles a day. Nowadays we may expect as much as four hundred miles in a full powered steamer, and not less than one hundred and fifty in a well-fitted sailing ship.

But navigation, and more especially the navigation of the unknown Pacific, was very different in Cook's days, when all the obstacles above mentioned impeded the explorers, and impelled them to follow a common track.

There were a few who had deviated from the common track.

The Spaniards, Mendana, Quiros, Torres, in the latter part of the sixteenth century, starting first from their colonies in Peru, had ventured along the central line of the Pacific, discovering the Marquesas, certain small coral islands, the Northern New Hebrides, and the Solomon Islands; but their voyages, mainly for fear of Drake and his successors, were kept so secret that no one quite knew where these islands lay.

Abel Tasman, in 1642, coming across the Indian Ocean from the westward, had touched at Tasmania, or, as he called it, Van Diemen's Land, had skirted the western coast of the north island of New Zealand without landing, and had stretched away to the north-east, and found the Tonga Group.

The English Buccaneers were not among these discoverers; Dampier, Woods Rogers, and others, all went from Acapulco to the Ladrones, looking out for the valuable Spanish galleons from Manila, and they added little or nothing to the knowledge of the Pacific and what it contained.

It was not therefore strange that the imagination of geographers ran riot amongst the great unknown areas. They were impressed, as they looked at the globes of the day, with the fact that, while the northern hemisphere contained much land, the southern showed either water or blank spaces; and starting with the ill-founded idea that the solid land in either hemisphere should balance, they conceived that there must be a great unknown continent in the southern part of the Pacific to make up the deficiency. This was generally designated Terra Australis Incognita, and many is the ancient chart that shows it, sketched with a free and uncontrolled hand, around the South Pole. It was held by many that Tasman had touched it in New Zealand; that Quiros had seen it near his island of Encarnacion, and again at Espiritu Santo (New Hebrides), but no one had been to see.

In George III's reign the desire to know more of this unknown ocean arose in England. The king himself took great interest in it, and for the first time since Queen Elizabeth's age, when Davis, Frobisher, Drake, Narborough, and others, had gone on voyages of discovery, the pursuit was renewed.

In 1764 the Dolphin and Tamor, under the command of Commodore Byron and Captain Mouat, sailed on a voyage round the world. They spent some time, as ordered, in exploring the Falkland Islands, and, after a two months' passage through Magellan Strait, they stood across the Pacific. They, however, also followed near the well-beaten track, and passing north of the Paumotus, of which they sighted a few small islands, they too made for the Ladrones. As usual, they suffered much from scurvy, and the one idea was to get to a known place to recover. Byron returned in May 1766, having added but little to the knowledge of the Pacific, and the Dolphin was again sent in the August of the same year, with the Swallow, under the command of Captains Wallis and Carteret, on a similar voyage.

They did somewhat better. After the usual struggle through the long and narrow Strait of Magellan, against the strong and contrary winds that continually blow, and which occupied four months, they got into the Pacific.

As they passed out they separated, the Dolphin outsailing the Swallow, and a dispassionate reader cannot well escape the conclusion that the senior officers unnecessarily parted company.

The Dolphin kept a little south of the usual route, fell in with some of the Paumotu Group, and finally discovered Tahiti, where she anchored at Royal Bay, after grounding on a reef at its entrance, with her people, as usual, decimated by scurvy. They were almost immediately attacked by the natives, who, however, received such a reception that they speedily made friends, and fast friends too. The remainder of the month of the Dolphin stay was marked with the most friendly intercourse, and she sailed with a high opinion of Tahiti and the Tahitians; the Queen, Cook's Obereia, being especially well disposed to them. Their communication with the natives must, however, have been limited, as they remained too short a time to learn the language, and we gather little of the manners and customs from the account of the voyage.

After sailing from Tahiti we hear the same tale--sickness, want of water, doubt of what was before them. After sailing by several small islands, and an attempt to water at one, course was steered as before for the Ladrones. Let Wallis tell his own story. He says:--

"I considered that watering here would be tedious and attended with great fatigue; that it was now the depth of winter in the southern hemisphere; that the ship was leaky, that the rudder shook in the stern very much, and that what other damage she might have received in her bottom could not be known. That for these reasons she was very unfit for the bad weather which she would certainly meet with, either in going round Cape Horn or through the Streight of Magellan; that if she should get safely through the streight or round the Cape, it would be absolutely necessary to refresh in some port; but in that case no port would be in her reach. I therefore determined to make the best of my way to Tinian, Batavia, and so to Europe by the Cape of Good Hope.

"By this rout, as far as we could judge, we should sooner be at home; and if the ship should prove not to be in a condition to make the whole voyage, we should still save our lives, as from this place to Batavia we should probably have a calm sea, and be not far from a port."

These are scarcely the sentiments of a bold explorer, and we shall look in vain for any similar ideas on the part of Cook. Here was a ship just a year from England, just come from a convenient and friendly island, where every refreshment and opportunity for refit were to be found, and the only thought is how to get home again!

It was the vastly different conduct of Cook's voyages; the determination that nothing should stop the main object of the expedition; his resource in every difficulty and danger; that caused, and rightly caused, him to be hailed as a born leader of such expeditions.

Wallis followed nearly on Byron's track: went from the Ladrones, through the China Sea, to Batavia, and so home, arriving in May 1768.

The Swallow, under Captain Carteret, was navigated in a different spirit. She was badly fitted out for such a voyage, had not even a forge, and all the articles for trade were on board the Dolphin. But Carteret was not easily daunted. He might, under the circumstances, when he found himself alone, have abandoned the voyage; but he boldly went forward. Passing from the Strait of Magellan, he touched at Juan Fernandez, and steering somewhat south of Wallis's line, he passed south of Tahiti, discovering Pitcairn's Island on his way, and some of the islands south of the Paumotus.

By this time his people were severely afflicted with scurvy, and his ship in a bad state; but Carteret only thought of getting to some place of refreshment, from which he might afterwards pass on his voyage towards the south, in the hope of falling in with the great southern Continent.

In this he was not fortunate. Missing all other islands, he fell across the Santa Cruz Group, and hoping that he had found what he wanted, he anchored and tried to water. The party were, however, attacked by the natives, and several, including the master, were wounded and died by poisoned arrows. All hope of a quiet refit was over, and his ship's company being in a wretched condition, no forge or tools on board to enable him to effect his many repairs, Carteret, who was himself very ill, was obliged to give up all intention of exploration to the southward. He got enough water to last him, and sailed on toward the Solomon Islands. These he also just missed, but fell in with New Britain, and passing between it and New Ireland, demonstrated for the first time that these two large islands were not one, as had been supposed. He here managed to do something to repair his leaky vessel, heeling and caulking her, but got little but fruit for his scurvy-stricken crew. He was attacked by the fierce islanders, and was altogether unable to do as much as he evidently earnestly desired towards examining the islands.

Thence they struggled on by Mindanao to Makassar in Celebes, delayed by contrary winds, disappointed of refreshments at every place they tried, and losing men from scurvy. At Makassar they met with but an inhospitable reception from the Dutch, who refused to permit them to receive refreshments there, and after waiting at Bonthain, a place in Celebes, several months, for the monsoon to change, they at last arrived at Batavia, the only port in the Dutch Indies really open to ships, in June 1768. Thence, after heaving down and a thorough repair, they reached home, via the Cape, on March 20th, 1769.

Of all the voyages before Cook's, Carteret's showed most determination and true spirit of enterprise; and had his ship been better supplied, and more suited to the exigencies of such a long cruise, he would, but for one thing, have accomplished far more. This was the fatal disease, which no captain had as yet succeeded in warding off, and which hampered and defeated the efforts of the most enthusiastic. No man could go beyond a certain point in disregarding the health of his crew.

These, then, were the kind of voyages, with their scanty fruits, to which the English people were getting accustomed, and they were not such as to encourage repetition.

In all the years that had elapsed since the Spaniards first sailed on the Pacific, but little real knowledge of the lands in it had been gained.

Let us attempt to give a picture of what was known.

The Marquesas and Santa Cruz Group were known to exist; but of the Solomons grave doubts were felt, as no man had seen them but Mendana, and they were, if placed on a map at all, shown in very different longitudes.

Several voyagers had sighted different members of the extensive Paumotu Group, but the varying positions caused great confusion.

Tahiti had been found by Wallis.

Tasman had laid down the south point of Tasmania, the western coast of the North Island of New Zealand, and the Tonga Islands. Dampier and Carteret had shown that New Britain and New Ireland were separate islands, lying north-east of New Guinea. Quiros had found the northern island of the New Hebrides.

But of none of these lands was anything really known. Those who had visited them had merely touched. In no case had they gone round them, or ascertained their limits, and their descriptions, founded on brief experience, were bald and much exaggerated.

Let us turn to what was unknown.

This comprises the whole of the east coast of Australia, or New Holland, and whether it was joined to Tasmania on the south, and New Guinea to the north; the dimensions of New Zealand; New Caledonia and the New Hebrides, with the exception of the fact that the northern island of the latter existed; the Fiji Islands; Sandwich Islands; the Phoenix, Union, Ellice, Gilbert, and Marshall Groups, with innumerable small islands scattered here and there; the Cook Islands, and all the Society Islands except Tahiti. The majority of the Paumotu Group. The coast of North America north of 45 degrees north was unknown, and there was the great, undefined, and imaginary southern Continent to disprove.

Whether other voyages of exploration would have been undertaken one cannot say; but in 1768 the Royal Society put in a word.

A transit of Venus over the sun's disc was to occur in 1769, and astronomers were anxious to take advantage of it, the object of the observation being to ascertain the distance of the earth from the sun, the fundamental base line in all astronomical measurements, and which was very imperfectly known.

The Central Pacific afforded a favourable position, and the Royal Society memorialised the king to send a ship for the purpose. The request was granted, and at first Alexander Dalrymple, who had conducted marine surveys in the East Indies, and was known as a scientific geographer, was selected as observer. As, however, it was found that he also expected to command the ship, the Admiralty positively refused to have anything to do with him, and after some discussion James Cook was selected.

This says volumes for Cook's reputation at the time. To have risen absolutely from the ranks was a great deal, but to be chosen as a master, to command a ship, and undertake a scientific observation of this importance, was a most exceptional occurrence, and speaks well for the judgment of those who had the selection.

It seems that Mr. Stephens, the Secretary to the Admiralty, had much to do with it. How Stephens had become acquainted with Cook history does not relate, but doubtless his personal visits to the Admiralty in connection with the completion of his charts of Newfoundland, from which he returned every winter, had brought him into contact with the Secretary, who had clearly formed a high opinion of him.

Cook, we may be sure, jumped at the chance, and his pride must have been great when he found he was to receive a commission as Lieutenant.

This in itself was a most unusual step. The occasions on which a master had been transferred to the executive line of the Royal Navy were very rare, and many an admiral used his influence in favour of some deserving officer in vain.

This was not without good reason, as the whole training of the Master of those days was unfavourable to success in command of ships or men. The exception was, however, in this case amply justified.

Cook was allowed to choose his vessel, and bearing in mind the dangers of grounding in unknown seas, he pitched upon his old friends, the stoutly-built, full-bottomed colliers of the North Sea trade.

His ship, the Endeavour, was a Whitby built vessel of three hundred and seventy tons, and was known as H.M. Bark Endeavour, there being another vessel, a cutter, of the same name in the Royal Navy. She was brought to the dockyard at Deptford to fit out. Her appearance was, of course, wholly different from that of a vessel built as a man-of-war, and we shall see that this caused trouble at Rio Janeiro, where the combination of merchant build and officers in uniform in an armed ship, aroused suspicions in the mind of the Portuguese Viceroy.

It is nowhere directly stated whether the Endeavour was sheathed with copper or not; but as Cook in the account of his second voyage expresses himself as adverse to this method of protecting ships' bottoms, and the operation is recorded of heeling and boot topping, which was cleaning and greasing the part of the ship just below waterline, it may be concluded that her sheathing was wood.

She proved a most suitable vessel. The log states she was a little crank, but an admirable sea-boat. Her rate of sailing was of course, with her build, slow, but her strength and flat bottom stood her in good stead when she made acquaintance with a coral reef.

She mounted ten small carriage guns and twelve swivels.

Mr. Banks, a scientific botanist, afterwards well known as Sir Joseph Banks, and for a long time President of the Royal Society, a gentleman of private means, volunteered to accompany Cook, and took with him a staff of his own, of artists and others.

He also induced Dr. Solander, a Swedish naturalist, afterwards attached to the British Museum, to accompany him.

Mr. Charles Green, one of the assistants at the Royal Observatory at Greenwich, was sent as astronomer.

This scientific staff added much to the success of the expedition.

Banks and Solander, both men of observation, were able to collect specimens of natural history, and study the manners and customs of the natives with whom they came in contact, which neither the time at Cook's disposal nor his training enabled him to undertake; and though the Journal of the former has never yet been published, and cannot at the present time be traced, many interesting remarks were extracted by Dr. Hawkesworth from it and went far to make his account of the voyage complete.

Mr. Green also demands special notice.

One great question of the day amongst seamen and geographers was the discovering of some ready and sure method of ascertaining the longitude. Half the value of the explorations made up to this time had been lost from this want. The recognised means of finding longitude was by the observation of lunars; that is, accurately measuring the angular distance between the centres of the moon and of the sun, or of the moon and some star.

The motion of the moon is so rapid that this angular distance changes from second to second, and thereby, by previous astronomical calculation, the time at Greenwich at which its distance from any body is a certain number of degrees can be ascertained and recorded.

By well-known calculations the local time at any spot can be obtained, and when this is ascertained, at the precise moment that the angular distance of sun and moon is observed, the difference gives the longitude.

This seems simple enough, but there is a good deal of calculation to go through before the result is reached, and neither the observation nor the calculation is easy, especially with the astronomical tables of those days, and there were very few sailors who were capable of, or patient enough to make them, nor was the result, as a rule, very accurate. For one thing, the motions of the moon, which are extremely complicated, were not enough known to allow her calculated position in the heavens to be very accurate, and a very small error in this position considerably affects the time, and therefore the longitude.

Luckily for Cook, the Nautical Almanac had just been started, and contained tables of the moon which had not previously been available, and which much lightened the calculations.

The great invention of the chronometer, that is, a watch that can be trusted to keep a steady rate for long periods, was at this time completed by Harrison; but very few had been manufactured, and astronomers and sailors were slow to believe in the efficacy of this method of carrying time about with a ship. Thus Cook had no chronometer supplied to him.

Green had accompanied Mr. Maskelyne, afterwards Astronomer Royal, to Barbados in 1763 in H.M.S. Princess Louisa, in order to test Harrison's timekeeper, and also a complicated chair, from which it was supposed observations of Jupiter's satellites could be observed on board ship; and as this trial afforded the final triumph of the new method, one would have thought that on a voyage of circumnavigation he would have made every effort to get one of these watches.

Be this as it may, the Endeavour had no chronometer, and lunars were the mainstay of the expedition.

In these observations Green was indefatigable. Cook, an excellent observer himself frequently took part in them; but it was Green's especial business, and no doubt to him is due the major part of the determinations of accurate longitude, which is one of the very remarkable points of this voyage.

Green's log, which is extant, is filled with lunar observations, and the extraordinary coincidence between different observations attests the care with which they were made. I dwell upon this because, while full of admiration for Cook's knowledge, and his untiring zeal in every detail of his expedition, it is evident, from a study of the original documents, that without Green many opportunities of getting longitude would have been lost, Cook having no time to spare to make use of them. Let us give honour to whom honour is due.

The final results of the observations are not equally good, but this arises from the errors, before referred to, in the moon's place in the heavens as given in the almanac, which would vary with her position, and affect the longitude accordingly. The astonishing thing is, not that some longitudes are considerably in error, but that the majority of them are so near the truth.

The Endeavour sailed from the Thames on June 30th, 1768, and was in Plymouth Sound from July 14th to the 26th, when she finally sailed, Banks and the scientific staff having joined here.

She carried a complement, all told, of ninety-four, and very close stowage it must have been.

A list is given in this book, immediately before the "Journal," of every person on board when the ship sailed from Plymouth.

The draught of the ship was 13 feet 6 inches, and her provisions were calculated to last eighteen months. The original intention had been that the transit of Venus should be observed at the Marquesas; but the Dolphin's return before Cook sailed, with the news of the discovery of Tahiti and its friendly inhabitants, caused this island to be finally selected.

The exact text of Cook's orders cannot be given. They were secret orders; but, curiously enough, while the covering letter, which enjoined him to show them to nobody, which is dated July 30th, 1768, is duly entered in Admiralty Records, the orders themselves, which should follow in the letter book, are omitted. They have never been published. Nevertheless, we can gather what they were.

Cook, in the published account of his Second Voyage, says he had instructions to proceed directly to Tahiti, and afterwards to prosecute the design of making discoveries in the Pacific by proceeding southward to the latitude of 40 degrees, and if he did not find land to continue his voyage to the west till he fell in with New Zealand, which he was directed to explore, and thence to return to England by such route as he should judge most convenient.

Precautions against the terrible scourge, scurvy, had not been forgotten.

Besides the supply of all anti-scorbutics then known, a special letter was written to Cook directing him to take a quantity of malt to sea, for the purpose of being made into wort, as a cure for scorbutic disorders, as recommended by Dr. McBride.

The directions for its use were as follows:--

"The malt must be ground under the direction of the surgeon, and made into wort, fresh every day, in the following manner:--

"1. Take one quart of ground malt, and pour on it three quarts of boiling water. Stir them well, and let the mixture stand close covered up for three or four hours, after which strain off the liquor.

"2. The wort, so prepared, is then to be boiled into a panada, with sea biscuit or dried fruits generally carried to sea.

"3. The patient must make at least two meals a day of the said panada, and should drink a quart or more of the fresh infusion as it may agree with him, every twenty-four hours.

"4. The surgeon is to keep an exact account of its effects."

Though it is somewhat anticipating events, it is convenient to record here the result of these efforts to defeat the hitherto unconquerable enemy. Mr. Perry's report at the termination of the voyage is as follows:--

"Sour krout, mustard, vinegar, wheat, inspissated orange and lemon juices, saloup, portable soup, sugar, molasses, vegetables (at all times when they could be got) were, some in constant, others in occasional use. These were of such infinite service to the people in preserving them from a scorbutic taint, that the use of the malt was (with respect to necessity) almost entirely precluded.

"Again cold bathing was encouraged and enforced by example; the allowance of salt beef and pork was abridged from nearly the beginning of the voyage, and the sailors' usual custom of mixing the salt beef fat with their flour, etc., was strictly forbad.

"Upon our leaving England, also, a stop was put to our issuing butter and cheese, and throughout the voyage raisins were served with the flour instead of pickled suet. At Tierra del Fuego we collected wild celery, and every morning our breakfast was made with this herb, with ground wheat and portable soup.

"We passed Cape Horn, all our men as free from scurvy as on our sailing from Plymouth.

"Three slight cases of scorbutic disorders occurred before arriving at Otaheite. Wort was given, with apparently good effect, and the symptoms disappeared.

"No other cases occurred during the voyage, but the wort was served out at sea as a regular article of diet."

To this it may be added, that no opportunity was, as appears by the Journal, ever lost of getting wild celery and any other wild herb that presented itself.

The personal washing is mentioned by Mr. Perry, and the tradition in the Navy is, that the men's deck was more constantly scrubbed than had then been usual; in fact, that unusual attention was paid to cleanliness. Stoves were used to dry the decks below even in hot weather.

As this voyage forms the subject of this book, its events may be passed over briefly.

Calling at Madeira--where the log records that the Endeavour was fired upon by the fort on the Loo Rock through some misapprehension while shifting berth, though Cook passes this by in silence--and Rio Janeiro, Cook proceeded to double Cape Horn. His predecessors had struggled through the Strait of Magellan, losing much time and wearing out their men with the continual anchoring and weighing in that long and narrow passage, rendered necessary by the constant foul and strong winds that prevail. The idea was to avoid the heavy seas and gales of the open sea; but Cook's action was amply justified by a more rapid passage without any danger. Discovering several of the low coral atolls of the Paumotu Group, he arrived at Tahiti on April 13th, 1769.

On July 13th, the transit of Venus having been observed under favourable conditions on June 1st, he left Tahiti, exploring and mapping the Society Islands immediately to the westward, never before visited, and then stood to the southward. It may here be mentioned that it is only during the last decade that Cook's charts of the Society Group have been superseded by more elaborate surveys by the French.

Cook went to 40 degrees south, discovering one of the Austral Group on his way, when, finding no sign of the hypothetical southern Continent, and getting into very dirty weather, he first gained a more northern latitude and favourable winds, and then stood for New Zealand.

On October 7th he arrived at Poverty Bay, and during the next six months he completely circumnavigated and mapped the islands of New Zealand. He had received on board at Tahiti a native, one Tupia, formerly the high priest, and a man of much intelligence. Tupia proved to be of the utmost service, as, to their astonishment and delight, they found that the languages were sufficiently identical to enable him to act as a most efficient interpreter; which made it possible to obtain information, and establish relations with the New Zealanders which they could never have succeeded in doing without him.

Cook now, after consideration, determined to explore the unknown east coast of New Holland. The health of his ship's company, and the good order on board, permitted him to make this good use of his time, instead of hurrying on to a civilised port, as all his forerunners had had to do.

He struck Australia at its south-east point, and followed the whole coast to the northward, mapping it as he went.

When nearing the northern end the voyage nearly came to a premature conclusion by the ship grounding on a coral reef, twenty miles from the land. Cook's seamanship was, however, equal to the occasion. The ship was got off, much damaged and leaking severely, and carried into a little port they discovered not far off. Here she was cleared out and laid upon the ground, the tide sufficing to dry enough of her bottom to let the carpenters repair it.

The wisdom of Cook's choice of a ship of the build of the Endeavour was here very apparent. It was not every ship that could be safely beached in this way without danger of falling over. After long delay she proceeded on her voyage, and soon had a second narrow escape. The long line of coral reefs that front the northern part of Eastern Australia, for a distance of 1200 miles, approach the coast about the place where the ship had grounded. The passage between the outer reef and the land is strewn with shoals, and finding his further progress much impeded by them, and fearful of a repetition of his disaster, Cook with some difficulty found a channel to seaward, and gained the open ocean. He was, however, yet determined to follow the land he was exploring, and more especially to solve the great question as to whether Australia was joined to New Guinea or no; and three days after his escape from the line of reefs he found himself with a light wind, embayed on the outer side of them, with the reefs close to him, and the ship drifting slowly but surely on them, the heavy swell of the great ocean breaking mountains high on their outer edge.

Here again calmness and promptitude saved him, and the ship was pushed through a narrow channel in these terrible reefs into the smooth, though reef-dotted, waters within. No event in the voyage is more dramatically narrated, though without any exaggeration, than this hair-breadth escape.

With the caution born of recent dangers, Cook now slowly found his way through the maze of reefs, by a route that no one has again followed, to the northern point of Australia, and was rewarded for his pertinacity by finding the channel now known as Torres Strait, which led him between New Guinea and Australia.

Thus far Cook's enthusiasm in adventure and desire to explore had been fully shared by his companions; but it is apparent that at this point they fell short of his high standard. Cook, having secured his direct passage to Batavia, and having still a little provision left, was anxious to do still more in the way of discovery, and stood over to the little-known New Guinea shore. It is evident, however, from Cook's expressions, though he does not complain, that his people were pining for fresh food and civilisation. Australia had produced them little but occasional fish and a few turtle. The salt provisions of those days were most unpalatable, and the effect of their continued hard work and inadequate food for so long, for they were now over two years from England, with no communication of any kind with the outer world, were telling on them, though they were still free from scurvy.

Cook, therefore, after landing once in New Guinea, unwillingly turned his ship's head towards Batavia.

The complaints grew louder as he passed by Timor without attempting to communicate, and falling in with the island of Savu, he yielded to importunity, and touched there to get refreshments.

Thence he went by the south shore of the chain of islands to Sunda Strait and Batavia.

So far all had gone well. It was undoubtedly far the most successful voyage ever made. Much had been done--more than his orders directed--to explore unknown lands, and the dire enemy of seamen, scurvy, had been conquered.

But his luck was not to last.

It was absolutely necessary to remain some time at Batavia, while the roughly repaired damage to the ship was made good in the Dutch dockyard.

Two months and a half in the sickly climate of Batavia, during a bad time of the year, wrought a sad change in his ship's company. The port they so much desired proved but the door of the grave to many of them, and Cook sailed for England on December 27th, 1770, with dysentery pervading the ship. The surgeon had already died of it; so had the poor Tahitian, Tupia, with two seamen, and one of Mr. Banks' artists.

Worse was, however, to follow. Day by day, as the ship slowly found her way over the Indian Ocean towards the Cape, against the wet and unhealthy north-west monsoon, the sick list grew larger. Man after man succumbed, and before half the distance to Capetown was traversed twenty-two more were carried off. Green, the astronomer, two more of Banks' staff, two midshipmen, the boatswain and carpenter were among the number. The crew was more than decimated.

The ship touched at the Cape, and war with France being expected, the Endeavour joined the East India convoy, under H.M.S. Portland, at St. Helena. The heavy-sailing, collier-built craft was not, however, when the ships had crossed the line and got upon a wind, able to keep up with them, and she once more found herself alone on her way.

Two more officers, the First Lieutenant, Mr. Hicks, and the Master, Mr. Molineux, died after leaving the Cape, but not of dysentery, and the ship finally reached England on June 12th, 1771.

Ninety-four persons left England in the Endeavour, of whom fifty-four returned. Thirty-eight died on the voyage, out of which number thirty-one died after reaching Batavia, most of them from fever and dysentery contracted at that place.

After paying off in August 1771, the Endeavour was sold in 1775, and for many years sailed as a collier in the North Sea.

This voyage gave a new impetus to discovery, and the immediate thought was to resume it, under this heaven-born leader.

Cook was given little leisure, as it was nearly at once decided to send him out again, and he was appointed to command the Resolution on November 28th, 1771, the interval having been occupied in considering what ships should be employed.

Cook's experience of the qualities of the Endeavour caused him to uphold the selection of similar vessels, for there were to be two, and the Resolution and Adventure, of 462 and 336 tons respectively, both Whitby built colliers, were bought for the voyage. Cook was promoted to Commander, and Tobias Furnaux, in the Adventure, was placed under his command. It was not, however, until April 1772 that they sailed.

It was originally intended that Banks should again accompany Cook, and with a view to his better accommodation a poop was added to the Resolution. The short trip, however, from Deptford to Sheerness proved to Cook that the ship was dangerously over-weighted, and the poop was removed, with the consequence that Banks did not sail. The alteration delayed final departure until June 22nd from Sheerness, and July 13th from Plymouth.

The naturalists on this voyage were two Forsters, Germans, father and son; and as astronomers Mr. Wales sailed in the Resolution, and Mr. Bayley in the Adventure. Two of Cook's former companions sailed as Lieutenants: Clerke, who was Lieutenant, and Pickersgill, who was master of the Endeavour when she reached England. This witnesses to the confidence and enthusiasm that Cook inspired amongst those under him. There were also other Endeavours amongst the junior officers.

The main object of the voyage was the settlement of the great question of the southern Continent. Cook was directed to explore the whole region about the South Pole, starting from the Cape of Good Hope, and working eastward. The winter of the southern hemisphere was to be employed as Cook thought fit.

This voyage brought Cook's qualities as a seaman and commander more prominently to view even than the former. The conditions were very different. Instead of mapping coasts and islands, the principal duty was exploration of tempestuous seas in high latitudes, amongst ice, searching in vain for the illusive southern land.

Cook carried it out thoroughly. No gales, no temperatures deterred him from searching wherever the ships would safely sail, and it was only ice in dense masses that turned him back.

What his people thought of it we do not know, but the Forsters have given a piteous account of the privations and hardships of an exploration that gave them little chance of exercising their special knowledge.

Cook was better provided with instruments for the determination of longitude than before, and the ships carried four chronometric timekeepers; but the proper method of making use of them was scarcely yet realised, and the course of his voyage did not permit them to be of much service.

Mindful of his former success in combating scurvy, and making use of his experience, Cook carried with him all his former anti-scorbutics, and redoubled his general precautions as to cleanliness, both of person and ship. The result was complete immunity from more than symptoms of scurvy. He was able to say, when he returned, that no man had died not only of this disease, but of any other, due to the exposures of the voyage. Three lost by accidents, and one from a complaint contracted before leaving England, were the sole losses on a voyage lasting three years, and during which the exposure to heat, cold, rain, and all the hardships of a sea life was probably never surpassed.

Leaving the Cape on November 22nd, Cook stood at once to the southward, intending to pass over a spot in latitude 54 degrees South, where in 1739 M. Bouvet sighted land that was generally supposed to be a part of the Southern Continent, and which he had been especially directed to examine. Gales, however, drove him from his course, and to this day Bouvet's Islands (for Cook proved they could be nothing else) are doubtfully shown upon charts.* (* They were again reported in 1825 by the Sprightly, an English whaler, but Sir James Ross searched for them in 1840 without success.) Cook soon got into the ice, and fought with it and gales of wind, in snow and sleet and fog, working gradually eastwards from the longitude of the Cape for four months. The ship penetrated to 67 degrees South at one point, and kept as high a latitude as ice permitted everywhere, but without discovering any land. Cook found to his great joy that the ice yielded good fresh water, and replenished his water casks in this manner, without any fear of falling short. With all his power of communicating his enthusiasm to others, it may be doubted if they shared his pleasure at finding that the search in these inclement regions need not be curtailed from lack of this necessary.

At last, in the longitude of Tasmania, Cook hauled to the northward, and headed for New Zealand, where, after sailing over eleven thousand miles since leaving the Cape without once sighting land, he anchored in Dusky Bay on March 26th, 1774, with the Resolution only, the Adventure having parted company in thick weather on February 9th. Moving on to Queen Charlotte's Sound, his old anchorage at the north end of Middle Island, he found the Adventure there on May 18th. Captain Furneaux had, after vainly searching for his consort, run for Tasmania, and explored the east coast. He did not, however, clear up the point for which he states he visited this coast, namely, whether it joined New Holland or not, as strong winds from the eastward made him fearful of closing what he thought was a deep bay, though really the Strait, and he sailed for the rendezvous in New Zealand under the impression that Tasmania and Australia were one.

The ships left New Zealand on June 7th, 1773, and, after making a wide circuit to the south and east in search of land, arrived at Tahiti on August 16th. A good many of the Adventure's people were ill with scurvy, and Cook is much puzzled to know the reason why they were attacked while his own crew were free. He puts it down to the greater trouble he had taken to make all his men use wild celery and other herbs in New Zealand, and no doubt this had its effect; but one cannot but suspect that the constant care on his part to keep the ship clean and sweet below had much to do with it. The Adventure had the same anti-scorbutics, and Cook especially mentions that they were in use; but the personal efforts of the captain in the direction of general sanitary precautions were, we know, exercised in one case, while we know nothing of the other.

After a month's stay at Tahiti and the Society Islands, where the crews were much benefited by fresh provisions, the ships sailed for the Friendly Islands, never visited since Tasrnan's time, and touched at Eoa and Tongatabu, or, as Tasman had called them, Middleburg and Amsterdam. These were finally left on October 7th for New Zealand, which was made on the 21st, and from this day to November 2nd the time was spent in fruitless endeavours to get into Cook's Strait. Gale succeeded gale--no uncommon thing here--and in one of them the Adventure parted company never again to rejoin. Cook anchored in Queen Charlotte's Sound on November 2nd, and waited until the 25th for his consort in vain. Whilst here they gained further and indisputable proof of the cannibalistic tendencies of the Maoris, some of the natives eating human flesh before them. Cook has been much blamed for permitting this scene, which took place on board; but there had been so much disputing in England as to the possibility of the fact, that he could not resist the opportunity of putting it beyond a doubt.

It was, however, to be shortly proved in a much more horrible manner, for the Adventure, which only arrived at Queen Charlotte's Sound after the Resolution left, had a boat's crew attacked, overpowered, and eaten by the natives. The circumstances were never wholly known, as not a man escaped; but the cooked remains were found, the natives decamping as the search-party approached.

Cook sailed south on November 25th, 1773, and was soon again battling with the ice, into which he pushed as far as was safe with as much hardihood as if he had still had the second ship with him. He gained the latitude of 67 degrees south, and worked eastward, searching religiously for land--which, needless to say, he never found--his ropes frozen, and sails like, as he says, plates of metal. Whatever the feelings of others on board were, Cook never flinched from every effort to get south, penetrating in one place to 71 degrees south, where he was stopped by dense pack, until he found himself nearly in the longitude of Tierra del Fuego, when, satisfied that no Southern Continent existed in the Pacific, he, on February 6th, steered north, to continue exploration in more genial weather and more profitable latitudes. All this time there was no scurvy, and very little sickness of any kind; an indisputable proof of the untiring supervision Cook exercised over the health of his men. The object of his voyage, so far as the Southern Pacific was concerned, was now accomplished, and Cook might have rounded Cape Horn, and made for the Cape of Good Hope, completing his tour of the world in southern latitudes; but such was not his idea of his duty. His own nervous words will explain his feelings best:--

"We undoubtedly might have reached the Cape of Good Hope in April, and so have put an end to the expedition so far as related to the finding of a continent, which indeed was the first object of the voyage; but for me at this time to have quitted this Southern Pacific Ocean with a good ship expressly sent out on discoveries, a healthy crew, and not in want either of stores or provisions, would have betrayed not only a want of perseverance, but of judgment, in supposing the South Pacific Ocean to be so well explored that nothing remained to be done in it. This, however, was not my opinion; for, although I had proved there was no continent but what must lie far to the south, there remained, nevertheless, room for very large islands in places wholly unexamined, and many of those which were formerly discovered are but imperfectly explored, and their situation as imperfectly known. I was, besides, of opinion that my remaining in this sea some time longer would be productive of improvements in navigation and geography, as well as other sciences."

Cook mentions that, on communicating his intentions to his officers, they all heartily concurred; and he adds, "Under such circumstances it is hardly necessary to say that the seamen were always obedient and alert, and they were so far from wishing the voyage at an end that they rejoiced at the prospect of its being prolonged another year." This, be it remembered, without a prospect of news from home or contact with civilisation, for Cook's design was to pass again through the breadth of the Pacific searching for islands as far as Quiros' discovery of Espiritu Santo, which lay due north of New Zealand, and then to return through the tempestuous regions they were now quitting to Cape Horn. Perhaps the charms of Tahiti reconciled them.

This design Cook triumphantly carried out; though shortly after leaving southern latitudes he was so ill of what he describes as a bilious cholic, that his life was despaired of. He first searched for, and visited, Davis' discovery of Easter Island, where he examined and described the wonderful colossal, though rude, statues there found. He then went to the Marquesas, a group but little known, where, after the usual attempt of the natives to appropriate sundry articles, and the consequent necessity of firing upon them, peaceful relations were established, and a brisk trade in much-wanted refreshments was set up. This did not last long, however, as the market was spoiled by some red feathers, obtained at the Friendly Islands, being given for a pig; after which nothing would buy provisions but these same red feathers, and these being scarce, trade ceased. Cook therefore sailed once more for Tahiti.

On his way he touched at some of the coral atolls of the innumerable Paumotu Group, and arrived at Matavai on April 22nd, again with not a sick man on board.

Three weeks were spent here with much satisfaction to all. Provisions were in plenty, the king and people very friendly, and all went well. The islanders were preparing for an attack on Eimeo, a neighbouring island, and a gathering of the fleets gave Cook an opportunity of learning much of their naval power and manner of conducting war. He observed that the general prosperity of Tahiti seemed to be at a much higher point than on his former visit.

After another three weeks' stay at Huaheine, and Ulietea, also amongst old friends, the Resolution sailed on June 4th to the west.

Discovering Palmerston and Savage Islands on the way, she called at Namuka, one of the Friendly Group, thus extending the knowledge of those islands gained the year before. Thence Cook sailed west, discovering Turtle Island, but just passing out of sight to the southward of the large Fiji Group, and thus lost the chance of adding them to his other finds.

He was now bound for the New Hebrides, of which the northern island had been discovered by Quiros. Bougainville, the French explorer, had, in 1768, passed just south of Quiros' Island, and named one or two others he sighted, but had made no stay, and knew nothing of the extent of the Group.

This was not Cook's fashion. He explored and circumnavigated the whole Group, which extends in a long line for three hundred and fifty miles. He touched first at Mallicolo, where, after a temporary disagreement, friendship was formed. Passing Sandwich Island, Erromanga was landed upon; but the suspicion of the natives here impelled them to attack the boats, and no intercourse was established.

The ship then anchored in the convenient harbour of Resolution Bay in the island of Tanna, and remained a fortnight, wooding and watering. Observations on the hot springs that gush from the side of the volcano bordering the harbour were made, and the relations with the natives were altogether friendly. Sighting Anityeum, the southern member of the New Hebrides, and making sure there was nothing beyond it, Cook returned along the west side of the islands, passing eastward of them again, between Mallicolo and Espiritu Santo. The latter island was closely followed round its whole extent, and Quiros' Bay of St. Philip and St. James identified in the great inlet in the northern side. Having laid down the whole of this extensive group of islands, and very accurately fixed the longitude by many lunar observations, Cook, on August 31st, sailed to the westward to search for more lands.

His chart of the New Hebrides is still, for some of the islands, the only one; and wherever superseded by more recent surveys the general accuracy of his work, both in outline and position, is very remarkable. On several occasions up to the present year (1893) Cook's recorded positions have saved the adoption of so-called amendments reported by passing ships, which would have been anything but amendments in reality.

Four days after leaving the New Hebrides Cook discovered New Caledonia. He explored the whole of the eastern side of this large island, which is three hundred miles in length, anchoring in one harbour inside the reefs which border it, and making friends with the natives. Other attempts to get inside the reefs were, however, unsuccessful, and after several narrow escapes from shipwreck Cook gave up, to his regret, a complete circumnavigation of the island. The summer approaching, he wished to refit and recruit in New Zealand before once more standing south.

Norfolk Island was discovered and landed upon on the way, and Queen Charlotte's Sound was once more reached on October 19th.

The Adventure's visit was ascertained from the Maoris, but Cook was much puzzled by incompletely understood accounts of white men having been killed. As far as could be gathered a ship had been lost on the coast, and Cook was led to believe that this disaster had no reference to the Adventure.

It was found that pigs and fowls left here on the former visit were still in existence, and presumably thriving. It may here be mentioned, that wherever Cook touched he invariably, so far as his stock allowed, left animals to stock the country, and that New Zealand was, when the settlers eventually came, found to be well supplied with pigs.

After a stay of three weeks the Resolution sailed, on November 10th, for Cape Horn. She kept farther north than on the last occasion, the object being to pass over new ground, and more completely disprove the existence of any land.

The western part of Tierra del Fuego being reached, Cook followed the shore to the south-east, mapping the outside of this dangerous and inhospitable archipelago. On December 20th he put in to what he afterwards called Christmas Sound, where large numbers of kelp geese were obtained, giving the crew what Cook describes as a dainty Christmas feast, though the flesh of these birds is as tough, fishy, and unpalatable as can well be imagined; on this occasion, however, the seamen seemed to have concurred in the verdict of their omnivorous commander, to whom nothing ever came amiss. Be it remembered, however, how long they had been on salt provisions, and that the South Sea Islands, though pleasant in many respects, produced but little solid food--no beef, mutton, or flesh of any quadruped but pigs, and those in not very great plenty--while New Zealand gave them nothing but fish.

Rounding Cape Horn, he passed through the Strait Le Maire, and followed the north shore of Staten Island, anchoring at one place to obtain seals and birds.

Whilst praising the flavour of a young seal cub, Cook is compelled to admit that the flesh of an old sea lion is abominable; a remarkable statement as coming from him.

Leaving Staten Island, Cook steered east and discovered South Georgia, named after the king. He followed the north coast of this desolate and ice-clad island, obtaining more refreshment in the shape of seals, penguins, and shags--unpalatable, but welcome food to men who had so long subsisted on bad salt meat. From South Georgia the ship's head was once more turned southwards, and before many days ice was again encountered. In stormy and thick weather the Resolution made her way, disproving the existence of a great tract of land laid down by speculative geographers, until January 31st, 1775, when Sandwich Land was discovered in about latitude 60 degrees south. This ice-covered group of islands was sketched under great difficulties from gales, fogs, snow, and numerous icebergs; and Cook then bore away along their parallel, to seek once more for Bouvet's Islands to the eastward.

He found nothing, and on February 26th steered for the Cape of Good Hope, even he being glad to leave this trying, tempestuous latitude. On March 23rd he anchored in Table Bay, having learnt from some vessels outside of the safe arrival of the Adventure in England the year before, and of her boat's crew having been eaten by the Maoris, which cleared up the mystery of the wrecked ship.

The Resolution finally arrived at Spithead on July 29th, 1775, after an absence of three years and eighteen days.

Captain Furneaux had, on leaving New Zealand, sailed straight for Cape Horn, the Cape of Good Hope, and England, arriving just a year before the Resolution.

Cook speaks most warmly of Captain Furneaux; but one cannot help contrasting his action with Cook's. Left, by the separation, his own master, he might have continued exploration, as did Cook. His ship was staunch, his provisions in much the same condition as the Resolution's; but he went straight home. His crew had suffered from scurvy, whereas Cook's had not; but he says not one word of this, nor does he give any reason why he gave up any further thought of the objects of the voyage, except a search for Bouvet's Islands, which he also looked for on his way.

It was the indomitable perseverance that led Cook to act so differently that raised his reputation so far above all other leaders.

Thus ended this very remarkable voyage. Never was a ship's crew exposed to more continual hardships, with so little to keep up interest and excitement, as the people of the Resolution; and yet Cook is able to record, with allowable pride, that only four lives had been lost, and only one by a sickness contracted before leaving England.

Once more the scurvy was defeated; and, without a doubt, owing to the intelligent action and untiring supervision of the captain. He gives a full description of the measures adopted, and while giving full acknowledgment to the anti-scorbutics with which he was supplied, he is of opinion that the general sanitary precautions formed the best prevention. Cleanliness of persons, bedding, clothes, and ship, were continually enforced. All these were foreign to the sailors of the time, and extraordinary it is that it was a man born in the lower rank of life, and brought up in a collier, who had the sense to perceive that in these lay the surest preventatives against this paralysing scourge.

Cook was promoted to captain--a proud position for the collier boy--and elected a Fellow of the Royal Society; perhaps even a greater distinction for a man of his bringing up. He contributed papers on his methods of preventing scurvy, and on the tides of the Pacific.

He also employed himself in publishing the account of his recent voyage, the only one which he himself edited.

He was not, however, long at rest. The Admiralty wished to send an expedition to explore the north-western coasts of North America, and to examine the Polar Sea from the Bering Straits side, with a view of the discovery of a north-west passage. Cook seems to have volunteered for the command without being actually asked, and, needless to say, was at once accepted.

In February he once more received his commission to command the Resolution, this time accompanied by the Discovery, a vessel very similar to the Adventure, his consort during the last voyage. Clerke, a master's mate in the Endeavour, and second lieutenant in the Resolution, was appointed as commander to the Discovery. He, like Cook, was fated not to return from this third journey to the great Pacific.

Others who had sailed with Cook before were ready to accompany him, once more to encounter privations and find new lands.

Cook's orders were long and detailed, but were to the effect that he was to proceed by way of the Cape of Good Hope to search in the Indian Ocean for the land recently seen by M. Kerguelen; thence via Tahiti, on to the coast of North America in about latitude 45 degrees, which he was to follow to latitude 65 degrees, searching especially for any channel which might lead to the north-east, as it was supposed there might be a passage communicating with Hudson's Bay. He was further to look for any passage north of North America to the Atlantic, and to make such other explorations as might seem fit to him. A money reward of 20,000 pounds was also offered in case of success in finding such a passage.

Chronometers were again carried, and more confidence in them being felt, more use was made of them.

Cook took with him Omai, a young Society islander, who had induced Captain Furneaux to take him to England, and whom Cook now engaged to return to his native country.

The ships sailed on July 11th, 1776, and arrived at Table Bay on October 18th.

Sailing thence on November 30th, he passed and roughly mapped Prince Edward's, Marion, and Croset's Islands, all of which had been discovered by Marion de Fresne. He then struck Kerguelen's Land, spent Christmas Day in one of its harbours, and mapped the eastern side of this large but desolate island. He was unaware that Kerguelen had visited this island a second time, and had gained much more information about it than he did in his first voyage.

Cook had taken on board at the Cape as many cattle, horses, bulls, cows, goats, and sheep as he could stow, with a view of landing them at Tahiti or elsewhere, and it is without surprise that we learn that after several weeks in these stormy seas a good many of them had died. When we consider the size of the ships the wonder is where they found room for these animals.

On January 26th the ships arrived in Tasmania, and anchored in Adventure Bay, principally with a view of getting fodder for the remaining cattle. Pigs were left here, according to Cook's usual custom.

After four days the ships sailed, and arrived in Queen Charlotte's Sound, New Zealand, on February 12th, 1777. Here Cook learnt the history of the attack on the Adventure's boat's crew from the chief who led it, but made no attempt at reprisals, although urged by many other natives to kill him. He seems to have been guided by the consideration that, as related by the natives, it was a dishonest act of barter on the part of one of the sailors which commenced the disturbance; and that occurring so long before, no good purpose would be served by punishment. It says much for his humane treatment of natives.

On leaving this, Cook records that he had at different times left about a dozen pigs in New Zealand. These increased, and stocked the whole island by the time the English settlers arrived.

On the way to Tahiti Cook fell across several islands belonging to what was afterwards called after him, the Cook Group. He visited Mangaia, Atiu, Takutea,* (* Spelt by Cook Mangeea, Wateeo, and Otakootaia.) and the Hervey Islands. Relations were established with the natives, and Cook was much interested at finding on Atiu three natives of the Society Islands, the survivors of twelve, who had been blown away in a canoe, and landed on this island, five hundred miles distant. As he remarks, this throws great light on the manner in which the different islands of the Pacific have been peopled.

Cook now made up his mind that he was too late to prosecute discovery this year on the American Continent, it being well into April, and being anxious to save the remaining cattle that he wished to land at Tahiti, and which had been taken on board especially for this purpose, the island being still far to windward, he bore away for the Friendly Islands for fodder and refreshments. He landed on Palmerston on the way--an island discovered last voyage--and arrived at Namuka* (* Cook's Anamooka.) on May 1st, with not a sick man in the ships.

The ships remained in the Friendly Group for two months and a half, visiting and mapping the different islands, and learning much of the manners of this interesting race, seeing their great concerted dances, and the ceremonies of coming of age of the heir to the throne. Cook here first became acquainted with the mysterious rite of Tabu, which was closely connected with his own death. A selection of useful animals, including horses, were left at Tongatabu.

While at the Friendly Islands Cook heard of the Fiji Group, and saw some of the natives, who had come over in a canoe. The intelligence he was able to gather concerning them was imperfect, and he saw no reason to justify a long detour to leeward to search for them, when his object was to stock the Society Islands with the animals he had. Had he known their size and importance, his course might possibly have been different. As it was, he sailed for Tahiti, and discovering Tubuai, one of the Austral Group, on his passage, arrived there on August 13th, 1777.

Six weeks were spent here, and the old friendships further cemented. Bulls and cows and other animals were presented to the king. Cook also attended at several ceremonies consequent on war being declared against Eimeo, which included the offering of the dead body of a man, previously killed for the purpose, to the war god. He positively refused to aid in this war, which very shortly came to an end.

Eimeo was next visited, and here the theft of a goat, which Cook intended to land at Huaheine, induced him to take severe measures to get it back. Several war canoes and houses were destroyed before it was returned. At Huaheine, Omai was established, with many valuable European articles in his possession. Here again Cook acted with considerable severity in the case of a thief cutting off his ears, and confining him on board. His action has been questioned, but considering his humane character, and the judgment that he always displayed in these questions, we are justified in believing that he had good reason for departing from his ordinary custom of mild treatment of natives. At Ulietea, or Raiatea, next visited, a midshipman and a seaman of the Discovery deserted. Cook took his usual step of confining some natives of importance, and informing their relatives that they would be retained until the deserters were returned. In this case he impounded the king's son and daughter, with the desired effect, as the stragglers were soon brought back from Bolabola, whither they had gone; but both Cook and Captain Clerke were nearly captured by the natives when on shore in the interval.

It is only surprising that more of Cook's people did not attempt to remain in these pleasant islands. The hardships of the sea press much on certain natures, and the allurements of the easy and careless life of a tropical island offered such a contrast, that it scarcely required the desire of the natives to get white men with their superior knowledge, and above all superior arms, to remain with them, to induce them to desert. This last, however, made desertion more easy, and had not Cook taken strong measures, no doubt the epidemic would have spread.

After visiting Bolabola, Cook sailed north, to prosecute the main object of his voyage, the exploration of the north-west coast of America. On December 24th he fell in with Christmas Island, which he so named from the season. After mapping it, and getting many turtle, he continued his course to the north, and discovered Atooi or Kauai, the western island of the Sandwich Group.

Communicating with this island and another, he finally left on February 3rd, 1778, and on March 7th made the coast of North America, a little south of the Columbia River. Gales ensued, and Cook missed the entrance of Juan de Fuca Strait, making the land again a little north of it.

Anchoring first in Nootka Sound in Vancouver Island--though Cook did not know it was an island--the ships continued their exploration to the north-west, skirting the coast as near as stormy weather permitted them, and calling at various places until the north-west extremity of the Alaska Peninsula was reached. In one place, afterwards called Cook's River, it was hoped that the desired passage eastward was found; but it was soon discovered that it was merely an inlet.

Passing through the Aleutian Chain, east of Unalaska, Cook visited that island, and continued his voyage through the Bering Sea, clinging to the land as much as possible, and finally got into Bering Strait. Here he had both continents in sight, and communicated with both sides.

Standing further north, he, in latitude 70 degrees 30 minutes north, came across the icy barrier of the Arctic Sea. After vainly trying for a passage in fog and strong wind, surrounded by loose ice, and after mapping a good deal of the shores on both sides, the ships again turned south at the end of August, exploring as they went first on the Asiatic side, and afterwards on the American, especially examining Norton Sound. In the beginning of October they once more arrived at Unalaska, and the Resolution having sprung a dangerous leak, the opportunity was taken to stop it.

On October 26th the ships sailed for the Sandwich Islands, where Cook had determined to winter, for the double purpose of refreshing his crew, gaining more knowledge of the Group, and being in a convenient position for resuming his exploration in the spring.

The voyage just accomplished was very remarkable, whether for the amount of coast mapped, which extended for between three and four thousand miles, or for the determination with which it was prosecuted in tempestuous and thick weather, on a most dangerous and inhospitable coast, part of the time in ice. The crews were perfectly healthy, with no sign of scurvy, and he brought both his ships off without any damage.

Maui, another of the Sandwich Group, was made on November 26th, and after communicating, the ships stood over to Owhyhee (Hawaii). Wind was against them, and it was not until January 17th that the two ships, having passed along the north side of the island to the eastward, at last anchored in Kealakekua Bay, on the south-west side.

The events which followed the arrival of the ships at Hawaii, which terminated in Captain Cook's death, were not understood at the time, but have been elucidated by the inquiries of the early missionaries, which throw much light upon the beliefs of the islanders.

It appears that a tradition existed that a chief of earlier times, one Rono, Orono, or Lono (the R and the L in the Pacific languages are almost interchangeable), had, after killing his wife, become frantically insane, and after travelling through the islands boxing and wrestling with all he met, had departed in a canoe, prophesying that he would some day return in an island with trees, hogs, and dogs. He was deified, and temples erected in his honour.

When Cook's ships arrived it was believed that the prophecy was fulfilled. Rono had returned as he had said, and the natives flocked to do him honour. When Cook landed he was received with adoration, the crowds prostrating themselves, and the priests escorting him with much ceremony. Led to a temple, he was clothed with red cloth, had pigs offered to him, and was generally treated in a manner which, though satisfactory as showing the friendly feelings of the natives, was puzzling to the Europeans. This continued throughout their stay, presents of all kinds being showered upon them. The officers, however, observed that the warrior chiefs were not so enthusiastic as the priests and common people. The death of a seaman, who was buried on shore in the presence of a large concourse, would seem to have been the first circumstance that threw doubts upon the godlike character of the visitors; but the ready way in which the fence of a Morai or sacred inclosure, which included various images, was granted for fuel, shows that the priests still held to their idea. The king, Taraiopu (or Terreooboo, as his name was written by Captain King), arrived shortly after the ships anchored, and showed himself to be as much impressed with the public belief as any of his subjects.

Thus matters continued during the eighteen days the ships remained; but towards the end of this time the natives began to show anxiety that they should be gone. The drain of hogs and other provisions, which were poured upon the visitors, doubtless led to anxious thoughts as to how long this was to last; and probably those members of the community who were less amenable to the influence of the priests, and were jealous of their own authority, were by no means so certain that the popular opinion of the supernatural nature of the white men was correct.

The ships sailed on February 4th, but, as ill-luck had it, the Resolution sprung her foremast in a gale, and Cook resolved to return to Kealakekua Bay for repairs. Here they again anchored on the 11th.

Their reception was, however, very different.

No crowd of canoes round the ship; no enthusiastic mass of natives on shore. Everything was silence.

What had happened was that the king had departed, leaving the bay under "tabu," i.e., a sacred interdict.

The priests, however, received them with as much friendliness as before, and the Morai was given up to them as a place of repairs for the damaged mast.

The king hurried back on hearing of the return of the ships, and removed the tabu; but the native disposition was changed. Some of the party on shore had persuaded women to break the tabu.

Whether this affected relations is uncertain, but the inhabitants generally exhibited considerable hostility, and headed by some chiefs, showed an inclination to attack a watering party. Thefts followed, and the capture of a canoe as a reprisal caused a scuffle on the beach, in which the Englishmen were worsted by the crowd, though a friendly chief soon restored order.

Instructions were now given to the party on shore at the Morai to permit no natives to approach in the night, and a musket was fired at one of them who came near.

On the morning of February 14th the Discovery's cutter was found to have been stolen.

Cook at once decided to have recourse to his usual practice, and get either the king or some principal chief on board, as a hostage till it was returned. He at the same time gave orders to prevent any canoes from leaving the bay, in order that he might, if necessary, seize them, and sent his boats to carry this out. Guns were fired from the ships at two large canoes that attempted to pass. Cook himself landed with a small armed force, and went in search of the king, who at once consented to come on board. The conduct of Taraiopu throughout showed that he had perfect confidence in Cook, and was entirely friendly, whether he still believed in the Rono theory or not.

While walking down to the boat, the natives, who were momentarily increasing in numbers, implored the king not to go. His wife joined her entreaties. Taraiopu hesitated. At this moment a man ran up and cried, "It is war; they have killed a chief!" One of the guard boats had, in fact, fired at a canoe attempting to leave the bay, and killed a man. The natives at once ran to arms, and Cook, seeing his intentions frustrated, walked towards the boat. A native attacked him with a spear, and Cook shot him with his gun. Still, no further attack was made, but the men in the boats hearing Cook's shot, and seeing the excited crowd, commenced to fire without orders. Cook still moved to the shore, calling to his men to cease firing; but whilst so doing, and with his back to the exasperated natives, he was stabbed in the back with a dagger, and fell with his face in the water.

There was then general confusion. The boats were a little way from the beach, and several of the marines were also killed, before they could reach them. Cook's body was at once dragged off by the natives.

The boats returned on board amid general consternation, and it is mentioned that a general silence reigned on board when it was known that their beloved commander had fallen.

The party at the Morai were shortly after attacked, but beat off the assailants, and reinforcements were sent from the ships. Lieutenant King, a favourite officer of Cook's, behaved with great discretion, and assisted by some of the priests, made a truce, during which the mast and other articles on shore for repairs were got off.

The sailors were mad for reprisals, but Captain Clerke, on whom the command devolved, decided on pacific measures, and every attempt was made to recover Cook's body. All that was obtained, however, were some of his bones, which were brought down with much solemnity by a chief, and delivered wrapped up in new cloth and red feathers.

It was known in after years that Cook's body had been instantly cut up; the flesh was burnt, as was the custom with great chiefs and many of the bones were preserved with great honour in a Morai dedicated to Rono.

It seems clear that Cook's death was due to a revulsion of feeling on the part of some of the natives, who no longer believed in his divine character, but that many regarded the outrage with horror. When the first Europeans came to reside on the island, and learnt the story from the native side, they found universal regret prevailing at this untoward occurrence.

Cook left officers imbued with his own noble sentiments. No general attack was made in revenge for what they saw was the result of misunderstanding, although they were ignorant of the exact circumstances which led, first to the uncommon and extraordinary veneration with which he had been treated, and then to the sudden change in the native behaviour.

It was found necessary to fire on the natives who prevented the watering party from working, and some of the sailors on this duty burnt some houses; but before the ships left, friendly relations were again established, and many natives visited them.

After Cook's remains had been committed to the sea, the prosecution of the voyage was determined upon, although Captain Clerke was in the last stage of consumption, and as soon as the Resolution's mast could be repaired, the two vessels once more departed, on February 22nd, 1779.

Cook's intentions were carried out as if he had still been in command. The remainder of the Sandwich Group was mapped, and the ships proceeded once more to the north. Calling at Petropavlovsk in Avatcha Bay, Kamtchatka, they again passed through Bering Strait, and sought in vain for a passage either to the north-east or north-west, being everywhere baffled by dense masses of ice. Captain Clerke at last abandoned the struggle, and repassed Bering Strait on his way south on August 1st.

On August 22nd Captain Clerke died.

This officer had accompanied Captain Cook in all his voyages, and had also circumnavigated the globe in the Dolphin with Captain Byron before. No man had seen more of the Pacific, and he proved himself, during his short period of command, a worthy successor of Cook.

Captain Gore, who had been with Cook on his First Voyage, now succeeded, King being put as Commander into the Discovery, and the two ships made the best of their way home, via Macao and the Straits of Sunda, arriving at the Nore on October 4th, 1780, after an absence of four years and two months. During the whole of this voyage not the slightest symptom of scurvy appeared in either ship, so completely were Cook's precautions successful.

Cook had six children. Three died young. Of the others, all boys, the eldest, James, entered the Navy, and lived to be a Commander, when, in 1794, he was drowned. The second, Nathaniel, also in the Navy, was lost in a hurricane in 1780. The third died when at Cambridge. They none of them lived to be married, and no descendant of the great navigator has perpetuated his race.

Of Cook's private life during his brief intervals at home we know nothing. A man rising from the ranks, and of his reserved character, would have but few friends, when he had such short time to make them in his new sphere. He lived at Mile End when at home, but after his death his widow removed to Clapham, living there for forty years, at first with her cousin, Isaac Smith, who had served with Cook in the Endeavour and Resolution. She died in 1835, at the great age of ninety-three.

Of Cook's character, none could be a better judge than Captain King, who writes as follows, after describing his death:--

"Thus fell our great and excellent commander. After a life of so much distinguished and successful enterprise, his death, as far as regards himself, cannot be considered premature, since he lived to finish the great work for which he seems to have been designed. How sincerely his loss was felt and lamented, by those who had so long found their general security in his skill and conduct, and every consolation in their hardships in his tenderness and humanity, it is neither necessary nor possible for me to describe. The constitution of his body was robust, inured to labour, and capable of undergoing the severest hardships. His stomach bore without difficulty the coarsest and most ungrateful food. Indeed, temperance with him was scarcely a virtue, so great was the indifference with which he submitted to every kind of self-denial. The qualities of his mind were of the same hardy, vigorous kind with those of his body. His understanding was strong and perspicacious. His judgment in whatever related to the service he was engaged in quick and sure. His designs were bold and manly, and both in the conception and in the mode of execution bore evident marks of a great original genius. His courage was cool and determined, and accompanied by an admirable presence of mind in the moment of danger. His manners were plain and unaffected. His temper might, perhaps, have been justly blamed as subject to haughtiness and passion, had not these been disarmed by a disposition the most benevolent and humane. Those intervals of recreation, which sometimes unavoidably occurred, and were looked for by us with a longing that persons who have experienced the fatigues of service will readily excuse, were submitted to by him with a certain impatience whenever they could not be employed in making further provision for the more effectual prosecution of his designs."

This is a pretty complete picture, and of a great man; a man who had before him continually his duty, and who had in an eminent degree the capacity to carry it out.

Though, under his determination to do this, he drove his people hard; though he tried them with his irascibility; their conviction of his greatness, their confidence in his leadership and in his justice, led them to love him. He had no sympathy with the ordinary foibles and weaknesses of his men. The charms of Tahiti, the paradise of the sailor, were no charms for him; he hardly notices the attractive ladies of that island; the attractions of the place to him were the abundance of provisions, as a means of fitting his expedition for further exploration and hardship. The strongest proof of his capacity as a commander is the devotion of his officers. Those who know the Navy know how difficult it is for any man who rises from the ranks to be successful in command. But Cook was a gentleman born; he had the intuition of great minds for fitting themselves to every position to which they may rise, and there is never a whisper of disinclination to submit to the rule of the once collier boy, the son of a labourer.

His intelligence is remarkably shown in his greatest triumph, the suppression of scurvy. That it should be left to a man of little education to discern the combination of means by which this enemy of long voyages could be conquered, is the most remarkable thing about this remarkable man. He himself notices the disinclination of the sailor to any new article of food, especially when not particularly palatable; but he soon found the means to induce them to understand that their lives greatly depended upon these rather nasty messes. Sour krout; the unsavoury portable soups of that day; the strange greens that Cook insisted on hunting up at every land he visited, and boiling with their ordinary food; the constant washing between decks; the drying below with stoves, even in the hottest weather; the personal baths; the change of wet clothing; the airing of bedding, were all foreign and repugnant to the notions of the seamen of the day, and it required constant supervision and wise management to enforce the adoption of these odd foods and customs.

It is evident that it is to Cook's personal action the success was due. Wallis and Byron had anti-scorbutics, but they suffered from scurvy; Furneaux, sailing with Cook in the second voyage, under precisely similar circumstances, suffered from scurvy. It was only in Cook's ships, and in the Discovery, commanded and officered by men who had sailed with Cook, and seen his methods, that exemption occurred.

Cook did more, incomparably more, than any other navigator to discover new lands. This was only accomplished by dint of hard work; and yet his men suffered less than in any ships, British or foreign, or similar expeditions. Though his tracks were in new and unknown waters, we never hear of starvation; he always manages to have an abundant supply of water.

The completeness and accuracy of his accounts and charts are no less remarkable.

M. de La Perouse, one of the foremost of the great French navigators, told Captain Phillip, the founder of the Colony of New South Wales, that "Cook had left him nothing but to admire." This was all but literally true; wherever Cook went he finished his work, according to the requirements of navigation of his time. He never sighted a land but he determined its dimensions, its shape, its position, and left true guides for his successors. His charts are still for some parts unsuperseded, and his recorded observations still save us from hasty and incorrect alterations desired by modern navigators.

Well may Englishmen be proud that this greatest of navigators was their countryman.

PERSONS WHO LEFT ENGLAND IN H.M.S. ENDEAVOUR, 26TH AUGUST, 1768.

Name.	Rank or Rating.	Disposal.	Date.
James Cook	Lieut. in Command		
Zachary Hicks	Lieut.	Died	25 May, 1771
John Gore	"		
Robert Molineux	Master	Died	15 Apr., 1771
Rich. Pickersgill	Mast. Mate		
Chas. Clerke	Master, 26 Ap., 1771 Mast. Mate A.B., 29 Aug., 1768 Mast. Mate, 27 Ap., 1771 Lieut. 26 May, 1771		
Francis Wilkinson	A.B. Mast. Mate, 20 Aug., 1768		
John Bootie	Mid.	Died	4 Feb., 1771
Jonathan Monkhouse	"	Died	6 Feb., 1771
Patrick Saunders	A.B., 24 May, 1770	Deserted	25 Dec., 1770
Isaac Smith	Mid., 24 May, 1770 Mast. Mate, 27 May, 1771		
Wm. Harvey	Lieut.'s Servant Mid., 8 Feb., 1771		
Jno. Magra	A.B. Mid., 27 May, 1771		
Isaac Manley	Master's Servant Mid., 5 Feb., 1771		
Wm. B. Monkhouse	Surgeon	Died	5 Nov., 1770
Wm. Perry	Surgeon's Mate Surgeon, 6 Nov., 1770		
Rich. Orton	Clerk		
Stephen Forwood	Gunner		
John Gathrey	Boatswain	Died	4 Feb., 1771
John Satterly	Carpenter	Died	12 Feb., 1771
John Thompson	Cook	Died	31 Jan., 1771
Sam Evans	Quarter Master Boatswain, 6 Feb., 1771		
Alex. Weir	Quarter Master	Drowned	14 Sept., 1768
Thos. Hardman	Boatswain's Mate A.B., 26 Mar., 1769 Sailmaker, 8 Feb., 1771		

Name.	Rank or Rating.	Disposal.	Date.
John Reading	Boatswain's Mate	Died	29 Aug., 1769
Benjamin Jordan	Carpenter's Mate	Died	31 Jan., 1771
John Ravenhill	Sailmaker	Died	27 Jan., 1771
George Nowell	A.B. Carpenter, 14 Feb., 1771		
Isaac Parker	A.B. Boatswain's Mate, 26 Nov., 1769		
Robt. Anderson	A.B. Quarter Master, 16 Sept., 1768		
James Gray	A.B. Quarter Master, 6 Feb., 1771		
Robert Taylor	Armourer	Died	1 Aug., 1771
Rich. Hutchins	A.B. Boatswain's Mate, 1 Sept., 1769		
Joseph Childs	A.B. Cook, 1 Feb., 1771		
Peter Flowers	A.B.	Drowned	2 Dec., 1768
Timothy Reardon	"	Died	24 Dec., 1770
John Ramsay	"		
Wm. Dawson	"		
Francis Haite	"	Died	1 Feb., 1771
Sam Jones	"		
James Nicholson	"	Died	31 Jan., 1771
Forby Sutherland	"	Died	30 Apr., 1770
Thomas Simmonds	"		
Rich. Hughes	Carpenter's Mate, 24 Feb., 1771		
Sam Moody	A.B.	Died	31 Jan., 1771
Isaac Johnson	"		
Robt. Stainsby	"		
Wm. Collett	"		
Archibald Wolfe	"	Died	31 Jan., 1771
Matthew Cox	"		
Chas. Williams	"		
Alex. Sampson	"	Died	21 Feb., 1771
Thos. Knight	"		
Hy. Stevens	"		
Thos. Jones (2)	"		
Antony Ponto	"		
Jeh. Dozey	"	Died	7 Apr., 1771
Jas. Tunley	"		
Mich. Littleboy	"		
John Goodjohn	"		
John Woolworth	"	Died	24 Dec., 1770
Wm. Peckover	"		
Robt. Littleboy	"		
Henry Jeffs	"	Died	27 Feb., 1771
Wm. Howson	Captain's Servant	Died	30 June, 1771
Nathl. Morey	Lieut.'s Servant		
Thos. Jones	Surgeon's Servant		
Ed. Terrell	Carpenter's Servant A.B., 1 Sept., 1769	Discharged	5 Nov., 1770
Thos. Jordan	Boatswain's Servant		
Thos. Matthews	Cook's Servant		
Danl. Roberts	Gunner's Servant	Died	2 Feb., 1771
John Thurmand (Pressed at Madeira)	A.B.	Died	3 Feb., 1771

MARINES.

Name.	Rank or Rating.	Disposal.	Date.
John Edgecombe	Sergeant R.M.		
John Truslove	Corporal	Died	24 Jan., 1771
Thos. Rossiter	Drummer		
Wm. Judge	Private		
Hy. Paul	"		
Danl. Preston	"	Died	16 Feb., 1771
Wm. Wiltshire	"	Drowned	6 Apr., 1769
Wm. Greenslade	"		
Saml. Gibson	"		
Thos. Dunster	Corporal, 26 Jan., 1771	Died	25 Jan., 1771
Clement Webb	Private		
John Bowles	"		

CIVILIANS AND STAFF.

Name.	Rank or Rating.	Disposal.	Date.
Joseph Banks, Esq.	Naturalist		
Charles Solander	Astronomer		
Charles Green	"	Died	29 Jan., 1771
John Reynolds	Artist	Died	18 Dec., 1770
Sydney Parkinson	"	Died	26 Jan., 1771
Alexander Buchan	"	Died	17 Apr., 1769
Herman Sporing	Servant	Died	24 Jan., 1771
James Roberts	"		
Peter Briscoe	Negro Servant	Frozen to death	16 Jan., 1769
Thomas Richmond	"		
George Dorlton	"		

TOTAL LOSS.

1768.—Drowned		2
1769.—Drowned		1
" Frozen		2
" Died		2
1770.—Died		5
1771.—Died		26
		38

- 41 -

A JOURNAL OF THE PROCEEDINGS OF HIS MAJESTY'S BARK ENDEAVOUR, ON A VOYAGE ROUND THE WORLD, BY LIEUTENANT JAMES COOK, COMMANDER, COMMENCING THE 25TH OF MAY, 1768.

EXPLANATION (FROM JOURNAL).

IT is necessary to premise by way of explanation, that in this Journal (except while we lay at George's Island) the day is supposed to begin and end at noon, as for instance, Friday the 27th May, began at noon on Thursday 26th, and ended the following noon according to the natural day, and all the courses and bearings are the true courses and bearings according to the Globe, and not by Compass. The longitude is counted West from the meridian of Greenwich where no other place is particularly mentioned. The proportional length of the log-line to the half minute glass, by which the ships run was measured, is as thirty seconds is to thirty feet.

While the ship lay in port or was coasting in sight of land, or sailing in narrow seas, this Journal is not kept in the usual form, but the degrees of Latitude and Longitude the ship passes over are put down at the top of each page, by which together with the notes in the margin* an easy reference will be had to the Chart. (* These notes in the margin have not been printed. ED.)

CHAPTER 1.
ENGLAND TO RIO JANEIRO.

REMARKABLE OCCURRENCES ON BOARD HIS MAJESTY'S BARK ENDEAVOUR.

1768.

[May to July 1768.]

RIVER THAMES, Friday, May 27th, to Friday, July 29th. Moderate and fair weather; at 11 a.m. hoisted the Pendant, and took charge of the Ship, agreeable to my Commission of the 25th instant, she lying in the Bason in Deptford Yard. From this day to the 21st of July we were constantly employed in fitting the Ship, taking on board Stores and Provisions, etc. The same day we sailed from Deptford and anchored in Gallions reach, were we remained until the 30th. The transactions of Each Day, both while we lay here and at Deptford, are inserted in the Log Book, and as they contain nothing but common Occurrences, it was thought not necessary to insert them here.

[July to August 1768.]

July 30th to August 7th. Saturday, July 30th, Weighed from Gallions, and made sail down the River, the same day Anchored at Gravesend, and the next Morning weighed from thence, and at Noon Anchored at the Buoy of the Fairway. On Wednesday, 3rd of August, Anchored in the Downs in 9 fathoms of water, Deal Castle North-West by West. On Sunday, 7th, I joined the Ship, discharged the Pilot, and the next day saild for Plymouth.

Monday, 8th. Fresh Breezes and Cloudy weather the most part of these 24 hours. At 10 a.m. weighed and came to sail; at Noon the South Foreland bore North-East 1/2 North, distant 6 or 7 Miles. Wind West by North, North-West.

Tuesday, 9th. Gentle breezes and Cloudy weather. At 7 p.m. the Tide being against us, Anchored in 13 fathoms of Water; Dungeness South-West by West. At 11 a.m. Weighed and made Sail down Channel; at Noon, Beachy Head, North by East 1/2 East, distant 6 Leagues, Latitude observed 50 degrees 30 minutes North. Wind North-West to North.

Wednesday, 10th. Variable: light Airs and Clear weather. At 8 p.m. Beachy Head North-East by East, distant 4 Leagues, and at 8 a.m. it bore North-East by North, 9 Leagues. Found the Variation of the Compass to be 23 degrees West; at Noon the Isle of Wight North-West by North. Wind West by North, North-East by East.

Thursday, 11th. Light Airs and Clear weather. At 8 p.m. Dunnose North by West 5 Leagues, and at 4 a.m. it bore North-North-East 1/2 East, distant 5 Leagues. Wind Variable.

Wednesday, 12th. Light Airs and Calms all these 24 Hours. At Noon the Bill of Portland bore North-West 1/2 West, distant 3 Leagues. Latitude Observed 50 degrees 24 minutes North. Wind Easterly.

Thursday, 13th. Ditto weather. At Noon the Start Point West 7 or 8 miles. Latitude Observed 50 degrees 12 minutes North, which must be the Latitude of the Start, as it bore West.* (* This is correct.) Wind Variable.

Sunday, 14th. Fine breezes and Clear weather. At 1/2 past 8 p.m. Anchored in the Entrance of Plymouth Sound in 9 fathoms water. At 4 a.m. weighed and worked into proper Anchoring ground, and Anchored in 6 fathoms, the Mewstone South-East, Mount Batten North-North-East 1/2 East, and Drake's Island North by West. Dispatched an Express to London for Mr. Banks and Dr. Solander to join the Ship, their Servants and Baggage being already on board. Wind North-Easterly.

Monday, 15th. First and latter parts Moderate breezes and fair; Middle squally, with heavy showers of rain. I this day received an order to Augment the Ship's Company to 85 Men, which before was but 70. Received on board fresh Beef for the Ship's Company. Wind South-West to South-East.

Tuesday, 16th. First part moderate and Hazey; Middle hard Squalls with rain; the Latter moderate and fair. Received on board a supply of Bread, Beer, and Water. A Sergeant, Corporal, Drummer, and 9 Private Marines as part of the Complement. Wind South-South-East to North-East.

Wednesday, 17th. Little wind and Hazey weather. Sent some Cordage to the Yard in order to be Exchanged for Smaller. Several Shipwrights and Joiners from the Yard Employed on board refitting the Gentlemen's Cabins, and making a Platform over the Tiller, etc. Wind South-East to East by South.

Thursday, 18th. Little wind and Cloudy. Struck down 4 guns into the Hold. Received on board 4 More, with 12 Barrels of Powder and several other Stores. Shipwrights and Joiners Employed on board. Wind Easterly.

Friday, 19th. Former part little wind with rain; remainder fair weather; a.m. Read to the Ship's Company the Articles of War and the Act of Parliament, they likewise were paid two Months' Wages in advance. I also told them that they were to Expect no additional pay for the performance of our intended Voyage; they were well satisfied, and Expressed great Cheerfulness and readiness to prosecute the Voyage. Received on board another Supply of Provisions, Rum, etc. Wind North-West to South-West.

Saturday, 20th. First part little wind with rain; remainder fresh Gales and thick rainy weather. Employed making ready for Sea. Wind West-South-West.

Sunday, 21st. Fresh Gales and Ditto Weather. The Shipwrights having finished their Work, intended to have sailed, instead of which was obliged to let go another Anchor. Wind South-West, West-South-West.

Monday, 22nd. Fresh Gales, with heavy squalls of Wind and Rain all this 24 hours. Wind South-West.

Tuesday, 23rd. Ditto weather. Struck Yards and Topmasts; Anchored between the Island and the Main His Majesty's Ship Gibraltar. Wind West by South.

Wednesday, 24th. Fresh Gales and Hazey weather; a.m. hove up the Small Bower Anchor and got Topmasts and Yards. Wind West by South.

Thursday, 25th. Moderate and Cloudy weather; a.m. received on Board a supply of Beer and Water, and returned all our Empty Casks. Loosed the Topsails as a Signal for Sailing. Wind West, North by West, North-West by West.

[Sailed from Plymouth.]

Friday, 26th. First part fresh Breezes and Cloudy, remainder little wind and Clear. At 2 p.m. got under Sail and put to Sea, having on board 94 Persons, including Officers, Seamen, Gentlemen, and their Servants; near 18 Months' Provisions, 10 Carriage Guns, 12 Swivels, with good Store of Ammunition and Stores of all kinds. At 8 the Dodman Point West-North-West, distant 4 or 5 Leagues; at 6 a.m. the Lizard bore West-North-West 1/2 West, 5 or 6 Leagues distant. At Noon Sounded and had 50 fathoms, Grey sand with small Stones and broken Shells. Wind North by West, North-West, West by South; course South 21 degrees East; distance 23 miles; latitude 49 degrees 30 minutes North, longitude 5 degrees 52 minutes West; at noon, Lizard North 21 degrees West distant 23 miles.

Saturday, 27th. First part Light Airs and Clear weather, remainder fresh breezes and Cloudy. Berthed the Ship's Company, Mustered the Chests and Stove all that were unnecessary. Wind North-West, North-East, South-East; course South-West; distance 77 miles; latitude 48 degrees 42 minutes North, longitude 6 degrees 49 minutes West; at noon, Lizard North 29 degrees East, 80 miles.

Sunday, 28th. Former part fresh Gales and Hazey with rain; remainder a Moderate breeze and Cloudy. Wind Easterly; course South 48 degrees West; distance 130 miles; latitude 47 degrees 16 minutes North, longitude 9 degrees 7 minutes West; at noon Lizard North 40 degrees 5 minutes East; 69 leagues.

Monday, 29th. Light Airs and Hazey the Most part of these 24 hours with some Rain. Wind North-Westerly; course South 21 degrees West; distance 41 miles; latitude 46 degrees 38 minutes North, longitude 9 degrees 29 minutes West; at noon, Lizard North 37 degrees 45 minutes East, 86 leagues.

Tuesday, 30th. Fresh Gales all these 24 Hours. At 1/2 past 1 p.m. Spoke with His Majesty's Ship Guardaloupe; at 6 Close Reeft the Topsails, and got down the Top Gallant Yards. Wind Westerly; course South 27 degrees West; distance 33 miles; latitude 46 degrees 9 minutes North, longitude 9 degrees 52 minutes West; at noon, Lizard North 36 degrees East, 96 leagues.

Wednesday, 31st. First and Middle parts, Moderate breezes and Clear; Latter, fresh Gales and Cloudy. At 6 p.m. loosed the 2nd Reef out of the Topsails, and at 8 a.m. took them in again; at Noon Tacked and stood to the North-West, having stood before to the Southward. Wind West to South-West; course South 36 degrees East; distance 82 miles; latitude 45 degrees 3 minutes North, longitude 8 degrees 43 minutes West; at noon, Lizard North-North-East, 105 leagues.

[September 1768. Plymouth to Madeira.]

Thursday, September 1st. Very hard gales, with some heavy showers of Rain, the most part of these 24 Hours, which brought us under our two Courses, Broke one of our Main Topmast phuttock Plates, washed overboard a small Boat belonging to the Boatswain, and drowned between 3 and 4 Dozen of our Poultry, which was worst of all. Towards Noon it moderated, so that we could bear our Maintopsail close Reefd. At Midnight wore and stood to the Southward. Wind Westerly; course South 70 degrees West; distance 20 miles; latitude 44 degrees 56 minutes North, longitude 9 degrees 9 minutes West; at noon, Lizard North 28 degrees 15 minutes West, 109 leagues.

Friday, 2nd. Fresh Gales and Cloudy the most part of these 24 hours. P.M. got up the spare Mainsail to dry, it being Wet by the Water getting into the Sail room, occasioned by the Ship being very Leakey in her upper works. At 5 a.m. loosed 2 Reefs out of each Topsail, and saw the Land, which we judged to be Cape Finister and Cape Ortugal. At 10 Tackt, being about 4 miles off Shore, and stood to the North-West; at Noon, Cape Ortugal bore East by South, distance about 8 Leagues. Wind North by West, West, South-West, West-South-West; course South by West; distance 64 miles; latitude 43 degrees 53 minutes North, longitude 9 degrees 26 minutes West; at noon, Lizard North-North-East, 130 leagues.

Saturday, 3rd. First part little wind and Hazey, with rain; remainder strong Gales with hard squalls, which brought us under our close Reeft Topsails, and obliged us to strike Topgallant Yards. At 8 a.m. wore ship and stood to the Southward. Wind South-West and West; course South 68 degrees 45 minutes West; distance 44 miles; latitude 44 degrees 9 minutes North, longitude 10 degrees 20 minutes West; at noon, Lizard North 29 1/2 degrees East, 138 leagues.

Sunday, 4th. Fore part fresh Gales and Clear; remainder light Airs and Calm. At 6 a.m. Cape Finister bore South by West 1/2 West, distance 10 or 11 leagues. Loosed all the Reefs out of the Topsails, and got Topgallant Yards across. Wind Westerly, Calm; at noon, Island of Cyserga,* (* Sisarga, near Coruna.) East-South-East 3 leagues.

Monday, 5th. Light breezes and Calm all these 24 hours. At 2 p.m. had an Observation of the Sun and Moon, which gave the Longitude 8 degrees 42 minutes West from Greenwich. At 6 Cape Finister bore South by West 1/2 West, 6 Leagues. Variation of the Compass per Azimuth 18 degrees 42 minutes West. At Noon, Cape Finister South by East, distant 4 leagues; latitude observed 43 degrees 4 minutes, therefore Cape Finister must lay in latitude 42 degrees 53 minutes North.* (* This is correct.) Wind Westerly, North-West, Calm.

Tuesday, 6th. Moderate breezes and Clear weather these 24 Hours. A.M. found the Variation by the Mean of 5 Azimuth to be 21 degrees 40 minutes West, 3 Degrees more than what it was found Yesterday, which I cannot account for,* (* Cook, as all other navigators of his time, was unaware of the deviation of the compass caused by the iron of the ship.) as both Observations appeared to me to be equally well made. At 10.28 had an Observation of the sun and moon, which gave the Longitude 9 degrees 40 minutes West from Greenwich. By this Observation Cape Finister must lay in 8 degrees 52 minutes, and by that made yesterday in 8 degrees 40 minutes. The Mean of the two is 8 degrees 46 minutes West of Greenwich the Longitude of the Cape,* (* The correct longitude is 9 degrees 15 minutes West.) its latitude being 42 degrees 53 minutes North. Wind North-West; course South 42 degrees West; distance 70 miles; latitude 42 degrees 1 minute North, longitude 9 degrees 50 minutes West; at noon, Cape Finister North 42 degrees East, 70 miles.

Wednesday, 7th. Moderate breezes and Clear weather; found the Variation to be 21 degrees 4 minutes West. Wind West-North-West; course South by West; distance 92 miles; latitude 40 degrees 29 minutes North, longitude 10 degrees 11 minutes West; at noon, Cape Finister North 13 degrees East, 49 leagues.

Thursday, 8th. Fresh Gales and Cloudy weather. A.M. Past by 2 Sail, which were standing to the North-East. Wind West-North-West to West by South; course South 4 degrees East; distance 111 miles; latitude 38 degrees 33 minutes North, longitude 10 degrees West; at noon, Cape Finister North 12 degrees East, 88 leagues.

Friday, 9th. First part fresh Gales; remainder moderate breezes and fine, Clear weather. Set up the Topmast rigging, and found the Variation to be 19 degrees 50 minutes West. Wind West by North to North-East; course South 40 degrees West; distance 116 miles; latitude 37 degrees 4 minutes North, longitude 11 degrees 33 minutes West; at noon, Cape Finister North 20 degrees East, 124 leagues.

Saturday, 10th. A steady, fresh breeze and fine Clear weather. Found the Variation of the Compys by the Evening and Morning Amplitude and by 2 Azimuth to be 20 degrees 59 minutes West. Wind North-East by East; course South 36 minutes West; distance 130 miles; latitude 35 degrees 20 minutes North, longitude 13 degrees 28 minutes West; at noon, Cape Finister North 24 degrees East, 166 leagues.

Sunday, 11th. The same Winds and weather Continue. Found the Variation to be this Evening 18 degrees 54 minutes, and in the Morning 17 degrees 58 minutes West, they both being the mean result of several good Observations. Wind North-East by East, North by East; course South 32 degrees West; distance 94 miles; latitude 34 degrees 1 minute North, longitude 14 degrees 29 minutes West; at noon, Cape Finister North 26 1/2 degrees East, 198 leagues.

Monday, 12th. Moderate breezes and fine Clear weather. At 6 a.m. the Island of Porto Santo bore North-West by West, distance 9 or 10 leagues. Hauld the Wind to the westward at noon, the Deserters extending from West-South-West to South-West by South, the Body of Madeira West 1/2 South, and Porto Santo North-North-West 1/2 West. Wind North-North-West; course South 40 degrees West; distance 102 miles; latitude 32 degrees 43 minutes North, longitude 15 degrees 53 minutes West.

Tuesday, 13th. Fresh breezes and clear weather. At 8 p.m. anchored in Funchal Road in 22 fathoms. Found here His Majesty's Ship Rose and several Merchants' Vessels. In the Morning new berthed the Ship, and Moor'd with the Stream Anchor, half a Cable on the Best Bower and a Hawser and a half on the Stream Wind North-West.

MOORED IN FUNCHAL ROAD, MADEIRA, Wednesday, 14th. First part fine, Clear weather, remainder Cloudy, with Squals from the land, attended with Showers of rain. In the Night the Bend of the Hawsers of the Stream Anchor Slip'd owing to the Carelessness of the Person who made it fast. In the Morning hove up the Anchor in the Boat and carried it out to the Southward. In heaving the Anchor out of the Boat Mr. Weir, Master's Mate, was carried overboard by the Buoy rope and to the Bottom with the Anchor. Hove up the Anchor by the Ship as soon as possible, and found his Body intangled in the Buoy rope. Moor'd the Ship with the two Bowers in 22 fathoms Water; the Loo Rock West and the Brazen Head East. Saild His

Majesty's Ship Rose. The Boats employed carrying the Casks a Shore for Wine, and the Caulkers caulking the Ship Sides. Wind Easterly.

Thursday, 15th. Squals of Wind from the Land, with rain the most part of these 24 Hours. Received on board fresh Beef and Greens for the Ship's Company, and sent on shore all our Casks for Wine and Water, having a Shore Boat employed for that purpose. Wind North-East to South-East.

Friday, 16th. The most part fine, Clear weather. Punished Henry Stevens, Seaman, and Thomas Dunster, Marine, with 12 lashes each, for refusing to take their allowance of Fresh Beef. Employed taking on board Wine and Water. Wind Easterly.

Saturday, 17th. Little wind, and fine Clear weather. Issued to the whole Ship's Company 20 pounds of Onions per Man. Employed as Yesterday. Wind Westerly.

Sunday, 18th. Ditto Weather. P.M. received on board 270 pounds of fresh Beef, and a Live Bullock charged 613 pounds. Compleated our Wine and Water, having received of the former 3032 Gallons, of the Latter 10 Tuns. A.M. unmoor'd and prepar'd for Sailing. Funchall, in the Island of Madeira, by Observations made here by Dr. Eberton, F.R.S., lies in the latitude of 32 degrees 33 minutes 33 seconds North and longitude West from Greenwich 16 degrees 49 minutes,* (* Modern determination is 32 degrees 38 minutes North, 16 degrees 54 minutes West.) the Variation of the Compass 15 degrees 30 minutes West, decreasing as he says, which I much doubt;* (* Cook was right: the variation was increasing.) neither does this Variation agree with our own Observations. The Tides flow full, and Change North and South, and rise Perpendicular 7 feet at Spring Tides and 4 feet at Niep tides. We found the North point of the Diping Needle, belonging to the Royal Society, to Dip 77 degrees 18 minutes. The Refreshments for Shipping to be got at this place are Wine, Water, Fruit of Several Sorts, and Onions in Plenty, and some Sweatmeats; but Fresh Meat and Poultry are very Dear, and not to be had at any rate without Leave from the Governour. Wind southerly, East-South-East, South-West.

[Sailed from Madeira.]

Monday, 19th. Light breezes and fine Clear weather. At Midnight Sailed from Funchall. At 8 a.m. the high land over it bore North 1/2 East. Unbent the Cables, stow'd the Anchors, and issued to the Ship's Company 10 pounds of Onions per Man. Ship's Draught of Water, Fore 14 feet 8 inches; Aft 15 feet 1 inch. Wind East-South-East; latitude 31 degrees 43 minutes North; at noon, High land over Funchall North 7 degrees East, 49 miles.

Tuesday, 20th. Light Airs and Clear weather. P.M. took several Azimuth, which gave the Variation 16 degrees 30 minutes West. Put the Ship's

Company to three Watches. Wind variable; course South 21 degrees 30 minutes West; distance 28 miles; latitude 31 degrees 17 minutes, longitude 17 degrees 19 minutes West; at noon, Funchall, Island of Madeira, North 13 degrees East, 76 miles.

Wednesday, 21st. First part light Airs, remainder fresh Breezes and Clear weather. Served Hooks and Lines to the Ship's Company, and employed them in the day in making Matts, etc., for the Rigging. Wind South-West to South-West by West; course South 60 degrees East; distance 60 miles; latitude 30 degrees 46 minutes North, longitude 16 degrees 8 minutes South; at noon, Funchall North 10 degrees West, 113 miles.

Thursday, 22nd. Genteel breezes and Clear weather. At 4 p.m. saw the Salvages bearing South; at 6, the Body of the Island bore South 1/2 West, distant about 5 leagues. Found the Variation of the Compass by an Azimuth to be 17 degrees 50 minutes West. At 10 the Isles of Salvages bore West by South 1/2 South, distance 2 leagues. I make those Islands to be in latitude 30 degrees 11 minutes South, and South 16 degrees East, 58 leagues from Funchall, Madeira. Wind South-West; course South 35 degrees 30 minutes East; distance 73 miles; latitude 29 degrees 40 minutes North, longitude 15 degrees 31 minutes West; at noon, Funchall North 21 degrees West, 62 leagues.

Friday, 23rd. Light breezes and Clear weather. At 6 a.m. saw the Peak of Teneriff bearing West by South 1/2 South, and the Grand Canaries South 1/2 West. The Variation of the Compass from 17 degrees 22 minutes to 16 degrees 30 minutes, Wind South-West, North-East; course South 26 degrees West; distance 54 miles; latitude 28 degrees 51 minutes North, longitude 15 degrees 50 minutes West; at noon, Funchal North 12 degrees 45 minutes West, 77 leagues.

Saturday, 24th. A fresh Breeze and Clear weather the most part of these 24 Hours. I take this to be the North-East Trade we have now got into. At 6 p.m. the North-East end of the Island of Teneriff West by North, distance 3 or 4 Leagues. Off this North-East point lies some Rocks high above the water. The highest is near the point, and very remarkable. By our run from Yesterday at Noon this end of the Island must lie in the latitude of 28 degrees 27 minutes and South 7 degrees 45 minutes East, distance 83 leagues from Funchal, and South 18 degrees West, 98 miles from the Salvages. At 1 a.m. the Peak of Teneriff bore West-North-West. Found the Variation to be this morning 16 degrees 14 minutes West. The Peak of Teneriff (from which I now take my departure) is a very high Mountain upon the Island of the same name--one of the Canary Islands. Its perpendicular higth from Actual Measurement is said to be 15,396 feet.* (* The received height is 12,180 feet. Latitude 28 degrees 16 minutes North, Longitude 16 degrees 38 minutes

West.) It lies in the Latitude of 28 degrees 13 minutes North, and Longitude 16 degrees 32 minutes from Greenwich. Its situation in this respect is allowed to be pretty well determined. Wind North-East by East; latitude 27 degrees 10 minutes North; at noon Peak of Teneriff North 18 degrees 45 minutes, 74 miles.

Sunday, 25th. A Steady Trade Wind and Clear Weather. The Variation by the Amplitude this Evening was 14 degrees 58 minutes West. Wind East by North, East-North-East; course South 41 degrees West; distance 126 miles; latitude 25 degrees 36 minutes North; at noon Peak of Teneriff North 33 degrees 15 minutes East, 61 leagues.

Monday, 26th. Fresh breezes and somewhat Hazey. Variation by this Evening Amplitude 15 degrees 1 minute West. Wind North-East by East; course South 22 degrees 15 minutes West; distance 122 miles; latitude 23 degrees 43 minutes North; at noon Peak of Teneriff North 29 degrees East, 317 miles.

Tuesday, 27th. Ditto weather. Served Wine to the Ship's Company, the Beer being all Expended but 2 Casks, which I intend to keep some time Longer, as the whole has proved very good to the last Cask. At Noon found the Ship by Observation 10 miles a Head of the Log, which I suppose may be owing to a Current setting in the same direction of the Trade Wind. Wind North-East; course South 19 degrees West; distance 145 miles; latitude 21 degrees 26 minutes North; at noon, Peak of Teneriff, North 26 degrees East, 154 leagues.

Wednesday, 28th. A Fresh Trade wind and Hazey weather. The Variation of the Compass by the mean of Several Azimuth taken this Evening 12 degrees 46 minutes, and in the Morning by the same Method 12 degrees 43 minutes West. This day's Log and Observed Latitude agree, which is not reconcilable to Yesterday. Exercised the People at Small Arms. Wind North-East, East-North-East; course South 12 degrees 30 minutes West; distance 150 miles; latitude 18 degrees 59 minutes North; at noon, Peak of Teneriff North 23 degrees 15 minutes East, 204 leagues.

Thursday, 29th. Fresh breezes and Hazey weather. The Variation 12 degrees 33 minutes West; the Observed Latitude ahead of that given by the Log 10 miles. Wind North-East by North; course South 14 degrees West; distance 90 miles; latitude 17 degrees 32 minutes North; at noon Peak of Teneriff, North 33 degrees East, 236 leagues.

[Off Cape de Verd Islands.]

Friday, 30th. A Steady breeze and Pleasant weather. At 6 a.m. saw the Island of Bonavista (one of the Cape de Verd islands), Extending from South by East to South-West by South, distance 3 or 4 Leagues. Ranged the East side of this Island at the Distance of 3 or 4 miles from the Shore, until we were obliged to Haul Off to avoid a Ledge of Rocks which stretched out South-West by West from the Body or South-East Point of the Island 1 1/2 leagues. Had no ground with 40 fathoms a Mile without this Ledge. The Island of Bonavista is in Extent from North to South about 5 leagues, is of a very uneven and hilly Surface, with low sandy beaches on the East side. The South-East part of the Island, from which I take my Departure, by an Observation this day at Noon lies in the latitude of 16 degrees North, and according to our run from Madeira in the longitude of 21 degrees 51 minutes West from Greenwich, and South 21 degrees West; 260 leagues from Tenerriff. Drawings Numbers 1 and 2 represent the appearance of the East side of this Island, where (2) is the South-East point, with the hill over it, which is high, of a round Figure, and the southermost on the Island. Wind North-East; course South 12 degrees 30 minutes West; distance 97 miles; latitude 15 degrees 37 minutes North per observation; Teneriffe, North 20 degrees 43 minutes East, 262 1/3 leagues; at noon the hill on the South-East Point of the Island Bonavista North 69 degrees West, distant from the shore 3 leagues.

[October 1768.]

Saturday, October 1st. A steady gale and somewhat Hazey. Variation by very good Azimuths this Evening 10 degrees 37 minutes, and by the same in the Morning 10 degrees 0 minutes West; at Noon found the ship a Head of the Log 5 Miles. Wind North, North-North-East; course South 12 degrees 12 minutes West; distance 114 miles; latitude 14 degrees 6 minutes North, longitude 22 degrees 10 minutes West; at noon Island of Bonavista, South-East point, North 9 degrees West, 116 miles.

Sunday, 2nd. First part a Steady breeze and pleasant weather, remainder light breezes and Cloudy. At noon found the Ship by Observation ahead of the Log 7 miles. Wind North by East, North-North-West; course South 1 degree West; distance 92 miles; latitude 12 degrees 34 minutes North, longitude 22 degrees 10 minutes West; at noon Bonavista, South-East point, North 5 degrees 45 minutes East, 69 leagues.

Monday, 3rd. Cloudy weather, with light winds and Calms. Variation by this Evening Amplitude South 8 degrees 49 minutes West. A.M. hoisted out a Boat to try if there was any Current; found one setting to the South-East at the rate of 3/4 of a Mile per hour. Wind North, calm, South-South-West 1/2 West; course South 3 degrees 30 minutes East; distance 20 miles; latitude 12 degrees 14 minutes North, longitude 22 degrees 10 minutes West; at noon, Bonavista, South-East point, North 5 degrees East, 76 leagues.

Tuesday, 4th. Calm for the Greatest part of the 24 Hours. By an Observation we had this Morning of the Sun and Moon found our Selves in the Longitude of 22 degrees 32 minutes 30 seconds West from Greenwich; that by account is 21 degrees 58 minutes, the Difference being 34 miles Westerly, which does not agree with the Setting of the Current, for having try'd it twice to-day and found it set to the East-South-East 1 Mile per Hour, and at the same time found the Ship to the Southward of the Log by the Noon Observation 10 miles. Served Portable soup and Sour kroutt to the Ship's Company. Wind variable; course South 53 degrees West; distance 17 miles; latitude 11 degrees 53 minutes North, longitude 22 degrees 33 minutes West; at noon, Bonavista, South-East point, North 2 degrees East, 82 leagues.

Wednesday, 5th. Light breezes of Wind, sometimes Clear and sometimes Cloudy weather. Variation 6 degrees 10 minutes West by an Amplitude and Azimuth this evening. At noon found the Ship by the Observed Latitude 7 Miles to the Southward of the Log, and by the Observed Longitude 30 degrees to the Eastward of Yesterday's Observations; and as these Observations for finding the Longitude (if carefully observed with good Instrument) will generally come within 10 or 15 Miles of each other, and very often much nearer, it therefore can be no longer in Doubt but that there is a Current setting to the Eastward;* (* This was the Counter Equatorial Current.) yet we cannot have had this Current long, because the Longitude by account and that by Observation agree to-day, but Yesterday she was 28 miles to the Westward of the Observation. Wind calm, North-East, East; course South 29 degrees East; distance 57 miles; latitude 10 degrees 56 minutes North, longitude 22 degrees 3 minutes West; at noon, Bonavista, South-East point, North 2 degrees East, 101 leagues.

Thursday, 6th. First part light Breezes and Cloudy; Middle frequent heavy Squalls, with rain, till towards Noon when we had again little wind. Found the Variation by the mean of 3 Azimuth, taken this Morning, to be 8 degrees 52 minutes West, which makes the Variation found Yesterday doubtful. Wind North-East, South-East, Southerly; course South 10 degrees 30 minutes West; distance 77 miles; latitude 9 degrees 40 minutes North, longitude 22 degrees 28 minutes West; at noon, Bonavista, South-East point, North 4 degrees East, 128 leagues.

Friday, 7th. Variable light Airs and Calm all these 24 Hours. At Noon found the Current to set South-East 1/4 South one Mile per hour, and yet by Observation at Noon I find the Ship 12 Miles to the Northward of Account, a Circumstance that hath not hapned for many days, and which I believe to be owing to the heavy Squalls we had Yesterday from the South-East, which obliged us to put frequently before the Wind. Wind Southerly, calm, Northerly; course South 5 degrees West; distance 10 miles; latitude 9 degrees 42 minutes North, longitude 22 degrees 19 minutes West; at noon, Bonavista, South-East point, North 4 degrees East, 127 leagues.

[Between Cape de Verd Islands and Equator.]

Saturday, 8th. First part, light Airs and Clear weather; Middle, Squally, with Thunder and Lightning all round; latter part, Moderate breezes and Clear weather. Had several Azimuths both in the Evening and Morning, which gave the Variation South 8 degrees 30 minutes West. At Noon found by Observation that the Ship had outrun the Log 20 Miles, a Proof that there is a Current setting to the Southward. Wind North-East by North to East-South-East; course South by East; distance 78 miles; latitude 8 degrees 25 minutes North, longitude 22 degrees 4 minutes West; at noon, Bonavista, South-East point, North 1 degree 45 minutes East, 152 leagues.

Sunday, 9th. Light Airs and fine Clear weather. Found the Variation by a great Number of Azimuth made this Afternoon to be 8 degrees 21 minutes 30 seconds West, and by the Morning Amplitude 7 degrees 48 minutes. At Noon try'd the Current, and found it set North-North-West 3/4 West, 1 1/8 miles per hour. The Shifting of the Current was conformed by the Observed Latitude Wind East-South-East; course South 16 degrees West; distance 29 miles; latitude 7 degrees 58 minutes North, longitude 22 degrees 13 minutes West; at noon, Bonavista, South-East point, North 2 degrees 40 minutes, 161 leagues.

Monday, 10th. First part, light breezes and Clear weather; Middle, squally, with heavy Showers of Rain; latter, Variable, light Airs and Calm and dark gloomy weather. At 3 p.m. found the Current to set North-North-East 1/4 East, 1 1/4 Mile per Hour, and at Noon found it to set North-East 3/4 North at the same rate, and the Variation to be 8 degrees 39 minutes West by the Mean of Several Azimuth. Wind South-East by East, Southerly; course South; distance 10 miles; latitude 7 degrees 48 minutes North; longitude 22 degrees 13 minutes West; at noon, Bonavista, South-East point, North 3 degrees East, 164 leagues.

Tuesday, 11th. Very Variable weather, with frequent Squalls rain, and Lightning. By the Observed Latitude at Noon I find the Ship hath only made 22 Miles Southing since the last Observation two days ago, whereas the Log gives 55 Miles, a Proof that there is a Current setting to the Northward. Wind South-East; course South 52 degrees West; distance 18 miles; latitude 7 degrees 36 minutes North, longitude 22 degrees 8 minutes West; at noon, Bonavista, South-East point, North 3 degrees East, 168 leagues.

Wednesday, 12th. Much the same weather as Yesterday the first part, the remainder mostly Calm and cloudy weather. A.M. try'd the Current and found it set South by West 1/4 West, 1/2 Mile per Hour, which is not agreeable to yesterday's remark. Wind variable; course South 33 degrees 30 minutes West; distance 20 miles; latitude 7 degrees 21 minutes North, longitude 22 degrees 39 minutes West; at noon Bonavista North 5 degrees East, 174 leagues.

Thursday, 13th. Light Airs of Wind, with some heavy showers of rain. Variation by Azimuth and Amplitude this Evening 8 degrees 46 minutes West. At Noon try'd the Current, and found it set South 3/4 East, 1/3 of a Mile per Hour; but finding the Observation and Log agree, I am inclinable to think it hath had no effect upon the Ship. Wind South-West, West-South-West; course South 16 degrees 45 minutes East; distance 21 miles; latitude 7 degrees 1 minute North, longitude 22 degrees 32 minutes West; at noon, Bonavista, South-East point, North 5 degrees East, 181 leagues.

Friday, 14th. Dark, gloomy weather, with much rain, the Wind Variable from West-South-West to South-South-East, sometimes on one Tack and sometimes on the other. Wind West-South-West to South-South-East; course South 5 degrees East; distance 24 miles; latitude 6 degrees 38 minutes North, longitude 22 degrees 30 minutes West; at noon, Bonavista, South-East point, North 3 degrees 15 minutes, 188 leagues.

Saturday, 15th. First part, little wind and Cloudy; Middle, Squally, with rain; latter part, light Airs and Clear weather. A little before Noon took several Observations of the sun and moon, the mean result of which gave the Longitude to be 23 degrees 46 minutes West from Greenwich, which is 1 degree 22 minutes more Westerly than that by account carried on from the last Observation; and the Observed Latitude is 24 Miles more Northerly than the Log since the Last Observation 2 days ago, all of which shows that the North-Westerly Current hath prevailed for this some Days past. Wind South-South-West to South-East; course South 30 degrees East per log; distance 12 miles; latitude 6 degrees 50 minutes North; longitude 22 degrees 23 minutes West per account, 23 degrees 46 minutes per sun and moon; at noon, Bonavista, South-East point, North by East, 187 leagues.

Sunday, 16th. First part Calm, the remainder Gentle breezes and fine, Pleasant weather. At 3 hours 30 minutes 39 seconds Apparent time p.m. the observed distance of the sun and moon's nearest Limb was 52 degrees 42 minutes 30 seconds; the Altitude of the sun's lower limb 32 degrees 39 minutes; the Altitude of the moon's lower limb 58 degrees 36 minutes; the longitude of the Ship from the aforegoing Observations 23 degrees 33 minutes 33 seconds West from Greenwich, differing 13 minutes from those made this Morning or Yesterday, the Ship laying all the time becalmed. Variation of the Compass 8 degrees 45 minutes West. Wind South-East, variable, North-East; course South 2 degrees East; distance 72 miles; latitude 5 degrees 38 minutes North, longitude 23 degrees 45 minutes West; at noon, Bonavista, South-East point, North 5 degrees 15 minutes East, 208 leagues.

Monday, 17th. Variable, light Airs and Calm clear weather. 1/2 past 1 p.m. took two Distances of the sun and moon, the first of which gave the Longitude 23 degrees 45 minutes 56 seconds, and the last 23 degrees 44 minutes West, the difference being not quite two miles, which shows how near to one another these observations can be made. Wind South, South-East, variable; course South by West 1/2 West; distance 11 miles; latitude 5 degrees 17 minutes North, longitude 23 degrees 47 minutes West; at noon, Bonavista, South-East point, North 5 degrees 15 minutes East, 212 leagues.

Tuesday, 18th. Sometimes little wind, sometimes Squally, with rain and Lightning. Wind South to East-South-East; course South 48 degrees West; distance 45 miles; latitude 4 degrees 47 Minutes North, longitude 24 degrees 23 minutes West; at noon, Bonavista, South-East point, North 12 degrees East, 229 leagues.

Wednesday, 19th. Fresh breezes and Cloudy weather. The Observed Latitude to the Northward of that given by the Log 9 miles, which I suppose must be owing to a Current. Wind South by East to South-East by South; course South 42 degrees West; distance 88 miles; latitude 3 degrees 44 minutes North, longitude 25 degrees 23 minutes West; at noon, Bonavista, South-East point, North 14 degrees East, 253 leagues.

Thursday, 20th. A Genteel gale and Clear weather. At a little before 5 p.m. had an Observation of the sun and moon, which gave the Longitude 25 degrees 46 minutes West from Greenwich, which is more Westerly than that by account carried on from the last Observation; and the Observed latitude being again to the Northward shows that there must be a current setting between the North and West. Wind South by East to South-East by South; course South 52 degrees West; distance 48 miles; latitude 3 degrees 16 minutes North, longitude 26 degrees 20 minutes West; at noon, Bonavista, North 18 degrees 30 minutes East, 270 leagues.

[Crossing Equator.]

Friday, 21st. A moderate breeze, and for the most part clear weather. Longitude per the Mean of 2 Observations of the sun and moon made at 4 hours 45 minutes and at 4 hours 54 minutes p.m., 26 degrees 33 minutes West. Variation of the Compass 4 degrees 7 minutes West, and the Observed Latitude at Noon to the Northward of the Log 7 Miles. Wind South-East to South-South-East; course South 58 degrees West; distance 57 miles; latitude 2 degrees 46 minutes North, longitude 27 degrees 11 minutes West; at noon, Bonavista South-East point, North 21 degrees East, 281 leagues.

Saturday, 22nd. Moderate breezes and fine, pleasant weather. Variation 3 degrees 17 minutes West. Wind South-East by South; course South 43 degrees 15 minutes West; distance 87 miles; latitude 1 degree 40 minutes

North, longitude 28 degrees 12 minutes West; at noon, Bonavista, South-East point, North 23 degrees East, 312 leagues.

Sunday, 23rd. A moderate, Steady breeze and fine Clear weather. The Ship by Observation at Noon is 8 Miles to the Northward of the Log. Wind South-South-East; course South; distance 5 miles; latitude 1 degree 40 minutes North, longitude 28 degrees 12 West; at noon, Bonavista, South-East point, North 23 degrees East, 312 leagues.

Monday, 24th. First part ditto weather; remainder fresh Breezes and Cloudy, with some flying Showers of rain. Variation per Azimuth this morning 3 degrees West. At Noon by Observation found the Ship 11 Miles ahead of the Log. Wind South by East to South-East by South; course South 49 degrees West; distance 50 miles; latitude 1 degree 7 minutes North; longitude 28 degrees 50 minutes West; at noon, Bonavista, South-East point, North 25 degrees East, 328 leagues.

Tuesday, 25th. A Genteel breeze and Clear weather, with a Moist Air. Soon after sunrise found the Variation of the Compass to be 2 degrees 24 minutes West, being the Mean result of several very good Azimuths. This was just before we crossed the Line in the Longitude of 29 degrees 29 minutes West from Greenwich. We also try'd the Diping Needle belonging to the Royal Society, and found the North point to Dip 26 degrees below the Horizon; but this Instrument cannot be used at Sea to any great degree of accuracy on account of the Motion of the Ship, which hinders the Needle from resting. However, as the Ship was pretty steady, and by means of a Swinging Table I had made for that purpose, we could be Certain of the Dip to two Degrees at most. The Observed Latitude and that by account nearly Agree. Wind South-East to South-East by East; course South 30 degrees West; distance 95 miles; latitude 0 degrees 15 minutes South, longitude 29 degrees 30 minutes West; at noon, Bonavista, South-East point, North 26 degrees East, 358 leagues.

Wednesday, 26th. First part light Airs and Cloudy weather, the remainder a Moderate Breeze and Cloudy. After we had got an observation, and it was no longer Doubted that we were to the Southward of the Line, the Ceremony on this occasion practis'd by all Nations was not Omitted. Every one that could not prove upon the Sea Chart that he had before Crossed the Line was either to pay a Bottle of Rum or be Duck'd in the Sea, which former case was the fate of by far the Greatest part on board; and as several of the Men chose to be Duck'd, and the weather was favourable for that purpose, this Ceremony was performed on about 20 or 30, to the no small Diversion of the Rest. Wind South-East to South-South-East; course South 31 degrees West; distance 77 miles; latitude 1 degree 21 minutes South, longitude 30 degrees 18 minutes West; at noon, Bonavista, South-East point, North 25 degrees 30 minutes East, 385 leagues.

Thursday, 27th. Fresh Gales and Close Cloudy weather. Variation 2 degrees 48 minutes West. Wind South-South-East to South-East; course South 38 degrees 15 minutes West; distance 79 miles; latitude 2 degrees 23 minutes South, longitude 31 degrees 7 minutes West; at noon, Bonavista, South-East point, North 26 degrees East, 410 leagues.

Friday, 28th. Fresh Breeze and fine Clear weather. At a little past 1 a.m. Longitude in by the 3 following Observations--viz., by the Moon and the star Arietis, 32 degrees 27 minutes; by the Moon and Pollux, 32 degrees 0 minutes 15 seconds; by ditto, 31 degrees 48 minutes 32 seconds; the mean of the whole is 32 degrees 5 minutes 16 seconds West from Greenwich, which is 31 minutes more Westerly than the longitude by account carried on since the last Observation. The two first observations were made and computed by Mr. Green, and the last by myself. The star Arietis was on one side of the Moon and Pollux on the other. This day at Noon, being nearly in the latitude of the Island Ferdinand Noronha, to the Westward of it by some Charts and to the Eastward by others, was in Expectation of seeing it or some of those Shoals that are laid down in most Charts between it and the Main; but we saw neither one nor a Nother. We certainly passed to the Eastward of the Island, and as to the Shoals, I don't think they Exhist, grounding this my Opinion on the Journal of some East India Ships I have seen who were detain'd by Contrary winds between this Island and the Main, and being 5 or 6 Ships in Company, doubtless must have seen some of them did they lay as Marked in the Charts.* (* There is a very dangerous reef, As Rocas, 80 miles west of Fernando Noronha. The Endeavour passed 60 miles east of latter.) Wind South-East to South-East by East; course South 33 degrees West; distance 93 miles, latitude 3 degrees 41 minutes South, longitude 32 degrees 29 minutes West.

Saturday, 29th. Fresh Breezes and pleasant weather. Variation of the Compass 2 degrees 25 minutes West. Wind East-South-East; course South by West; distance 101 miles; latitude 5 degrees 25 minutes South, longitude 32 degrees 48" West.

Sunday, 30th. A Steady breeze, and for the most part close cloudy weather. Variation by several Azimuths 1 degree 31 minutes West. At noon the observed latitude 7 miles southward of account. Wind East-South-East; course South 3/4 West; distance 107 miles; latitude 7 degrees 8 minutes South, longitude 33 degrees 4 minutes West.

Monday, 31st. A Fresh breeze and Clear weather. Variation 0 degrees 15 minutes West. Observed Latitude again to the Southward of the Log. Wind

East to East-South-East; course, South 1/2 West; distance 114 miles; latitude 9 degrees 1 minute South, longitude 33 degrees 16 minutes West.

[November 1768. Between Equator and Rio.]

Tuesday, November 1st. Moderate breezes, for the most part Cloudy. Variation by the mean of Several Azimuths 0 degrees 58 minutes West in the Evening, and in the Morning found it to be 0 degrees 18 minutes West. Wind East-South-East; course South 3/4 West; distance 98 miles; latitude 10 degrees 38 minutes South.

Wednesday, 2nd. A Steady breeze and fine pleasant weather. This Afternoon, by the mean of Several Azimuths and the Amplitude, found the Variation to be 0 degrees 34 minutes East, from which it appears that about the aforegoing Noon we have Crossed the Line of no Variation in the Latitude of 10 degrees 38 minutes South, and, according to the following Observations, in 32 degrees 0 minutes West longitude from Greenwich. At 5 hours 5 minutes 0 seconds Apparent time a.m. the longitude of the Ship and the Observation of the moon and the star Aldebaran was found to be 32 degrees 0 minutes 45 seconds; at 8 hours 17 minutes 0 seconds, per sun and moon, 32 degrees 25 minutes 0 seconds; and at 9 hours 0 minutes 16 seconds, 32 degrees 19 minutes 0 seconds. The mean of the three is 32 degrees 14 minutes 55 seconds. And again at 7 hours 12 minutes 52 seconds, per sun and moon, 32 degrees 10 minutes 4 seconds; and at 7 hours 19 minutes 42 seconds, per sun and moon, 32 degrees 15 minutes 20 seconds. The mean of these two is 32 degrees 12 minutes 42 seconds, and the mean of the whole is 32 degrees 13 minutes 43 seconds West from Greenwich, which is less by a whole Degree than that by account, which is a Considerable Error to be made in 5 Days in these low Latitudes. One would think from this that we must have had a Current setting to the Eastward, which is not likely that it should set against the settled trade wind. The 3 first of these Observations were made by Mr. Green, and the 2 last by myself. Wind East-South-East, South; course South by West; distance 132 miles; latitude 12 degrees 48 minutes South, longitude 32 degrees 20 minutes West per Observation.

Thursday, 3rd. A Fresh Trade wind and fair weather. Variation per Azimuth this Evening 0 degrees 47 minutes East, and at a little past 9 a.m. longitude in per sun and moon 33 degrees 0 minutes West of Greenwich. Wind East by South-East; course South 15 degrees West; distance 128 miles; latitude 14 degrees 51 minutes South, longitude 33 degrees 7 minutes West.

Friday, 4th. A Steady Gale and fair weather. P.M. Variation per Azimuth 1 degree 29 minutes West, ditto 1 degree 28 minutes West, and by the Amplitude 1 degree 12 minutes West; mean 1 degree 23 minutes West, by which it appears that we have again Crossed the Line of no Variation. At 1/2 past 9 a.m. the longitude of the Ship, per Observation of the sun and moon,

33 degrees 26 minutes 30 seconds. Wind East by South; course South 19 degrees 30 minutes West; distance 125 miles; latitude 16 degrees 49 minutes South, longitude 33 degrees 37 minutes West.

Saturday, 5th. Fine pleasant weather. Variation per Azimuth this morning 3 degrees 21 minutes East, which makes me Doubtful of the Variation found yesterday, tho' at the time I had not the least room to doubt of the Accuracy of the Observations. Longitude per Observation 34 degrees 43 minutes 30 seconds West. Wind East to North-East; course South 30 degrees 35 minutes West; distance 109 miles; latitude 18 degrees 22 minutes South, longitude 34 degrees 50 minutes West.

Sunday, 6th. First and Latter part squally, with heavy Showers of rain; middle moderate and fair. I now determined to put into Rio de Janeiro in preferance to any other port in Brazil or Falkland Islands, for at this place I knew we could recruit our Stock of Provisions, several Articles of which I found we should in time be in want of, and at the same time procure Live Stock and refreshment for the People; and from the reception former Ships had met with here I doubted not but we should be well received. Wind North-North-East, variable, South; course South 55 degrees West; distance 74 miles; latitude 19 degrees 3 minutes South, longitude 35 degrees 50 minutes West.

Monday, 7th. Moderate breezes and Clear weather. P.M. found the Variation to be 4 degrees 49 minutes East. At 6 Sounded and had 32 fathoms Water; the Bottom Coral Rocks, fine Sand and Shells, which Soundings we carried upon a South-West 1/2 West Course 9 or 10 leagues, and then had no ground with 100 fathom. We were by our account and per run afterwards 54 Leagues East from the Coast of Brazil and to the Southward of the Shoals called Abrollos, as they are laid down in Most Charts. Wind South-East to North-East; course South 58 degrees West; distance 68 miles; latitude 19 degrees 46 minutes South, longitude 36 degrees 50 minutes West.

Tuesday, 8th. Fresh breezes and Cloudy weather. P.M. variation by the Mean of 12 Azimuths 5 degrees 26 minutes East, and by an Amplitude in the Morning 7 degrees 52 minutes. At 6 a.m. saw the Land of Brazil bearing North-West 1/2 North, distance 8 or 10 leagues. At 8 Sounded, had 37 fathoms, Coarse Sand, broken Shells, and Coral Rocks. At 9 brought too and Spoke with a Fishing Boat, who informed us that the land in sight lay to the Southward of Santo Espiritu. It appears high and Mountainous; the drawing Number (3) exhibits a View of this Land as it appeared from the Ship (A), being near to Santo Espiritu, and a remarkable hill (B) bore North-West 1/2 North, distance 7 or 8 leagues. Made Sail in Shore, the wind being Southerly. Had from the above Depth to 14 fathoms the same sort of Bottom. Found the Ship at Noon by Observation 10 Miles to the Southward of account, which I suppose to be occasioned by a Current setting between the South and West. Wind North-North-East, North by West, South-South-West to South by West; course South 50 degrees West; distance 140 miles; latitude 21 degrees 16 minutes South, longitude 37 degrees 35 minutes West.

Wednesday, 9th. First and Latter part Hazey, with a Moderate Breeze; Middle, fresh Gales, with Thunder, Lightning, and rain. At 3 p.m. tack't in 16 fathoms, distance from the Shore 5 Leagues, the land Extending from the North-West by West to North-East. At 5 took the 2nd Reef in the Topsails and got down Topgallant Yards, stood to the South-East until Midnight, then tack'd, Sounding from 16 to 55 fathoms. At 8 a.m. Loosed the Reefs out of the Topsails and got Topgallant Yards a Cross; unstowed the Anchors and bent the Cables. At Noon Latitude Observed 21 degrees 29 minutes South, the Land Extending from South-West by South to North-North-West, distance 4 leagues, Soundings from 55 to 10 fathoms. Wind South-South-East, South-South-West, South; course South 62 degrees 15 minutes West; distance 28 miles; latitude 21 degrees 29 minutes South.

[Nearing Rio Janeiro.]

Thursday, 10th. Moderate breezes and Hazey upon the Land. Stood in for the Shore South-West 1/2 West. Depth of water from 10 to 9 fathoms and from 9 to 16 fathoms, being then 4 Leagues from the Land. From 16 fathoms it shoalded gradually to 5 fathoms; then we tacked, being about 1 1/2 Leagues from the Shore. The extreams of the Land to the Southward, which we took for Cape St. Thomas, bore South 3/4 West, distance 4 leagues. The Land from Cape St. Thomas to the Northward lies North by East 1/2 East. Along the Shore is low land covered with Wood and Sandy Beaches, but inland are very high Mountains, the greatest part of them being hid in the Clouds. Stood off until 5 in the Morning East and East by South. Depth of Water 10, 20, 16, 23, and 30 fathoms. At Noon Latitude Observed 21 degrees 30 minutes; Depth of Water 14 fathoms; Grey sand with black Specks. Extreams of the Land from South-West by West to North-North-West; distance 12 or 14 leagues. Wind South-South-East, South-East by South, South by East; course East 1/4 South; distance 17 miles; latitude 21 degrees 30 minutes South, longitude 37 degrees 43 minutes West per account.

Friday, 11th. First and Latter parts, moderate breezes and fair, but Cloudy and Hazey over the Land; middle, a fresh breeze and Cloudy. At 8 tack'd and Stood to the North-East. Extream of the Land to the southward, which we took for Cape St. Thomas, South-West 1/2 South; distance 5 or 6 leagues; Depth of Water 13 fathoms, Grey sand. At 11 a.m. tack'd in 14 fathoms and Stood to the South-South-East, and at 3 a.m. Stood over a Shoal or Bank of 6 fathoms, afterwards the Depth increased to 30 fathoms, at Noon in 36 fathoms. Latitude Observed 22 degrees 37 minutes South, which is 10 miles to the Southward of the Log. No Land in sight. Wind South-East to East;

course South 5 degrees West; distance 67 miles; latitude 23 degrees 37 minutes South, longitude 37 degrees 49 minutes West.

Saturday, 12th. Genteel breezes and fine Clear weather. At 2 p.m. Sounded, but had no ground with 38 fathoms, and soon after sounded and had none at 50 fathoms, from which it appears that we are to the Southward of the Bank we have been upon this 2 days past. It Extends off from the Land between the Latitude 21 degrees and 22 degrees nor less than 18 or 20 Leagues, How much farther I know not. Standing in from Sea, the Depth of Water very soon diminisheth from 30 to 20 and 17 fathoms, afterwards gradually from 9, 8 and even to 6 fathoms; but between this Shoal Water and the Main, which is 6 or 7 leagues, you will have 10, 12 and even 16 fathoms, till you come within 2 or 3 leagues of the Shore. The Bottom is of Various kinds, sometimes Coral Rocks, Coral Rocks and broken Shells, Coarse sand and broken Shells, Small Stones and at other times fine Sand varying at almost every Cast of the Lead. At 5 p.m. saw the Land bearing North-West by West 1/2 West, distance 10 or 12 leagues, which proved to be the Island of Cape Frio; it appeared in two Hillocks, and from the Deck looked like two Islands. Took several Azimuth of the Sun, which gave the Variation 6 degrees 40 minutes East. At 8 a.m. the Isle of Cape Frio bore West by North 4 leagues. This Island is situated in the Latitude of 23 degrees 2 minutes South, and according to our Reckoning in the Longitude of 38 degrees 45 minutes West from Greenwich, but from many Circumstances I have good reason to think that our reckoning is wrong and that it lies in the Longitude 41 degrees 10 minutes West. It is not of a Large Circuit, but Tolerable high, with a hollow in the Middle, which makes it look like 2 Islands when it first makes its appearance out of the Water. It lays not far from the Main, which with the Island forms a right Angle, one side trending North and the other West. To the northward of the Island and between it and the Main there appears to lay several smaller Islands near each other. The Main land on the Sea Coast appears to be low, but inland are high Mountains. Drawing Number 4 exhibits a View of this Island when it bore West-North-West, distance 4 leagues. Wind North-East, East-North-East; course South 60 degrees 30 minutes West; distance 59 miles; latitude 23 degrees 6 minutes South; Isle of Cape Frio North 60 degrees East, 4 leagues.

Sunday, 13th. First and Latter parts a Genteel Sea breeze and Clear weather, the Middle Calm. P.M. standing along Shore for Rio De Janeiro observed that the land on the Sea Coast is high and Mountainous, and the shore forms some small Bays or Coves wherein are Sandy Beaches. At 8 Shortned Sail; the Sugar Loaf Hill at the West Entrance to Rio De Janeiro West-North-West, distant 4 or 5 leagues, at the same time was abreast of 2 Small rocky Islands, that lie about 4 Miles from the Shore. At 9 a.m. Sprung up a light breeze at South-East, at which time we made Sail for the Harbour, and sent the Pinnace with a Lieutenant before us up to the city of Rio De Janeiro, to acquaint the Vice Roy with the reason that induced us to put in here, which was to procure Water and other refreshments, and to desire the Assistance of a Pilot to bring us into proper Anchoring ground; at Noon Standing in for the Harbour.

[At Rio Janeiro.]

ARRIVAL AT RIO DE JANEIRO, Monday, 14th. Moderate Sea and Low breezes and fine pleasant weather. At 5 p.m. Anchored in 5 fathoms just above the Isle of Cobras, which lies before the City of Rio De Janeiro. A little before we Anchor'd the Pinnace return'd and informed me that the Vice Roy had thought proper to detain the Officer until I went ashore. Soon after we Anchored a Boat came on board bringing several of the Vice Roy's Officers, who asked many Questions in respect to the Ship: Cargo, from whence she came, Number of Guns, Men, etc., all of which was Answered to their satisfaction. They told me it was the Custom of the Port to Detain the first Officer that came from any Ship on her first Arrival until a Boat from the Vice Roy had Visited her; that my Officer would be sent on board as soon as they got on shore, which was accordingly done. About this time a Boat filled with Soldiers kept rowing about the Ship, which had orders, as I afterwards understood, not to Suffer any one of the Officers or Gentlemen, except myself, to go out of the Ship. In the Morning I waited upon the Vice Roy and obtained leave to purchase Provisions, Refreshments, etc., for the Ship, but obliged me to employ a person to buy them for me under a pretence that it was the Custom of the Place, and he likewise insisted (notwithstanding all I could say to the contrary), on putting a Soldier into the Boats that brought anything to or from the Ship, alledging that it was the Orders of his Court, and they were such as he could not Dispence with, and this indignity I was obliged to submit to, otherwise I could not have got the supplys I wanted; being willing, as much as in me lay, to avoid all manner of Disputes that might cause the least delay, and at the same time to Convince him that we did not come here to Trade, as I believe he imagined--for he Certainly did not believe a word about our being bound to the Southward to observe the Transit of Venus, but looked upon it only as an invented story to cover some other design we must be upon, for he could form no other Idea of that Phenomenon (after I had explained it to him), than the North Star Passing through the South Pole; these were his own words. He would not permit the Gentlemen to reside ashore during our Stay here, nor permit Mr. Banks to go into the country to gather plants, etc.; but not the least hint was given me at this time that no one of the Gentlemen was to come out of the Ship but myself, or that I was to be put under a Guard when I did come; but this I was soon Convinced of after I took my leave of His Excellency and found that an Officer was to attend upon me whereever I went, which at first the

Vice Roy pretended was only meant as a Complement, and to order me all the Assistance I wanted. This day the People were Employed in unbending the Sails, in fitting and rigging the Spare Topmasts in the room of the others, and getting on shore Empty Water Casks.

Tuesday, 15th. Fine pleasant weather. Received on board fresh Beef and Greens for the Ship's Company, with which they was served every Day During our Stay here. Got all the Empty Casks on shore, and set the Coopers to Work to repair them; Heeld and Boot Topt the Starboard side.

Wednesday, 16th. Set up the Forge to repair the Iron Work; the People employed in Heeling and Boot Topping the Larboard side, Blacking the Yards, etc.

Thursday, 17th. Set some People to repair the Sails and the Caulkers to Caulk the Ship; the rest of the People employed in the Hold and about the Rigging. For 3 days past I have remonstrated to the Vice Roy and his Officers against his putting a Guard into my Boat, thinking I could not Answer it to the Admiralty the tamely submitting to such a Custom, which, when practiced in its full force, must bring Disgrace to the British Flag. On the other hand, I was loath to enter into Disputes, seeing how much I was like to be delay'd and imbarrassed in getting the supplys I wanted, for it was with much difficulty that I obtained leave for one of my People to attend the Market to buy necessaries for my Table and to assist the Agent to buy the things for the Ship. Having gained this Point and settled everything with the Agent in regard to what was wanting for the Ship, I resolved, rather than be made a Prisoner in my own Boat, not to go any more ashore unless I could do it without having a Soldier put into the Boat, as had hitherto been done; and thinking that the Vice Roy might lay under some Mistake, which on proper Application might be clear'd up, I therefore drew up a Memorial stating the whole case and sent to the Vice Roy this afternoon; and thus a Paper War commenced between me and His Excellency, wherein I had no other Advantage than the racking his invention to find reasons for treating us in the manner he did, for he never would relax the least from any one point.

Friday, 18th. This day I received an Answer to my Memorial, wherein he tells me, amongst other things, that if I think it hard submitting to the Customs of this Port I may leave it when I please; but this did not suit my purpose at present, but I resolved to make my stay as short as possible. I must own that the Memorial of the Vice Roy's was well drawn up and very much to the Purpose, which is more than I can say of any of the subsequent ones.

Saturday, 19th. Close cloudy weather. Employed getting aboard Rum, Water, and other necessaries. Caulking and refitting the Ship. Punished John Thurman, Seaman, with 12 Lashes for refusing to assist the Sailmaker in repairing the Sails.

Sunday, 20th. First part cloudy weather; the Middle very hard Storms of Wind and Rain; the Latter moderate, with rain. This Afternoon sent Lieutenant Hicks in the Pinnace with an Answer to the Vice Roy's Memorial, with orders not to Suffer a Soldier to be put into the Boat; upon which the Guard Boat attended him to the Landing Place and reported it to the Vice Roy, who refused to receive the Memorial, and ordered Mr. Hicks on board Again; but in the Meantime they had put a Guard into the Boat, which Mr. Hicks insisted should be order'd out, that he might return on board in the same manner as he came, without a Guard; and upon his refusing to return other way, all the Crew were by Arm'd force taken out of the Boat (though they gave no provocation nor made the least resistance) and hurried to Prison, where they remained until the next day. Mr. Hicks was then put into one of their Boats, and brought on board under the Custody of a Guard. Immediately upon my hearing of this I wrote to the Vice Roy demanding my Boat and Crew and his Excellency's reason for detaining her, and inclosed the Memorial he had before refused to receive. This I sent by a petty Officer, as I had never objected against a Guard being put into any of my Boats wherein was no Commissioned Officer. He was admitted ashore and delivered the Letter, and was told an Answer would be sent the next day. This evening, between 8 and 9 o'Clock, came on an Excessive hard storm of Wind and Rain, the Longboat coming on board the same time with 4 Pipes of Rum in her. The rope they got hold of broke, and she went a Drift. The Yawl was immediately sent after her; but the Longboat filling with Water, they brought her to a Grapnel and left her, and the Yawl with the People got on board about 3 in the morning. Early this Morning I sent to the Vice Roy to acquaint him with the loss of our Boat, to desire leave and the Assistance of a Shore Boat to look after her, and at the same time to demand the Pinnace and her Crew. After some time the whole was granted, and we was so fortunate as to find the Longboat the same Day, and likewise the 4 Pipes of Rum; but every other thing that was in her was lost.

Monday, 21st. This Morning I received his Excellency's Answer to my last Memorial and Letter. In his Letter he owns there was some indecency in Detaining the Boat, but lays the Blame to my Officer, who only Executed the orders I gave him with Spirit. In one part of his Memorial he says that from the Built of the Ship and other Circumstances he Doubts that she is the King's. This I thought proper to Answer in Writing by telling his Excellency that I was ready to produce my Commission. Rain the most part of this Day.

Tuesday, 22nd. Moderate breezes, with frequent Showers of Rain. Employed getting on board Water, Provisions, etc. Caulking the Ship and repairing the Sails.

Wednesday, 23rd. Fine pleasant weather. Employed as before and setting up the Rigging. This day I received from the Vice-Roy an Answer to my last Memorial, wherein he still keeps up his Doubts that she is not a King's Ship, and accuseth my people of Smuggling, a thing I am very Certain they were not guilty of, and for which his Excellency could produce no proof, notwithstanding many Artful means were made use of to tempt such of our People as were admitted ashore to Trade by the Very Officers that were under His Excellency's own Roof. I thought it incumbent on me to Answer this Memorial, in which I desir'd His Excellency to take into Custody any one of my People that should be found trading even if it amounted to no more than one of the Sailors selling his Cloaths from off his Back for a Bottle of Rum--for what His Excellency called smuggling I was very certain amounted to no more, and even this was only Suspicions of my own.

Thursday, 24th. This day a Spanish Packet (a Small Brig) from Buenos Ayres put in here in her way to Spain. This Vessel belonged to his Catholic Majesty, and notwithstanding the Vice-Roy had all along pretended that the orders he had respecting Foreign Vessels were General, yet this Vessel meet with very Different Treatment from us. No Guard was put over her, and her Officers and Crew went wherever they pleased.* (* The build and general appearance of the Endeavour not being that of a man-of-war, the Portuguese authorities entertained suspicions regarding her true character, which is not altogether surprising, considering the times; but we can well understand Cook's indignation.)

Friday, 25th, Saturday, 26th. Employed getting on board Water as fast as the Coopers could set up and repair the Casks, setting up the rigging and Caulking the Ship's sides.

Sunday, 27th. Bent the Sails and Cleaned the Ship Fore and Aft.

Monday, 28th. Fine pleasant weather. The Caulkers having finished the sides, paid them with Tar. This day I unexpectedly received an Answer from my last Memorial, wherein were only a few weak Arguments to support His Excellency's Suspicions that the Ship did not belong to the King, and that my People Smugled. This Memorial I answered.

Tuesday, 29th. Employed Lashing the Casks that were on the upper Deck and between Decks and making ready for Sea.

Wednesday, 30th. Punished Robert Anderson, Seaman, and William Judge, Marine, with 12 Lashes Each, the former for leaving his Duty ashore and attempting to desert from the Ship, and the latter for using abusive language to the Officer of the Watch, and John Reading, Boatswain's Mate, with 12 lashes for not doing his Duty in punishing the above two Men. Sent a Shore to the Vice-Roy for a Pilot to Carry us to Sea, who sent one on board together with a Large Boat, which I did not want, but it is the Custom in this Port for the Pilots to have such a Boat to attend upon the Ship they Pilot out, and for which you must pay 10 shillings per day, besides the Pilot's fees, which is Seven pounds four Shillings Sterling.

[December 1768.]

Thursday, 1st December. Wind at South-East, which hinder'd us from Sailing as we intended. Received on board a large Quantity of fresh Beef, Greens and Yams for the Ship's Company.

Friday, 2nd. This morning sent a Packet for the Secretary of the Admiralty on board the Spanish Pacquet, containing copies of all the Memorials and Letters that have passed between the Vice-Roy and me, and likewise another Packet containing Duplicates thereof I left with the Vice-Roy to be by him forwarded to Lisbon. At 9 Weighed and came to Sail and turned down the Bay. Peter Flower, Seaman, fell overboard, and before any Assistance could be given him was drowned; in his room we got a Portugue.

Saturday, 3rd. First part, moderate breezes at South-East; remainder, fresh Gales at South with Rain. At 1 p.m. Anchored in 18 fathoms Water in the Great Road (see Plan).

Sunday, 4th. Fore and Middle parts fresh Gales at South-South-East with heavy rain; Latter, Variable Light Airs and fair weather. Hoisted in the Longboat and secured her.

Monday, 5th. First part, little wind and Cloudy; Middle, Thunder, Lightning and Rain; latter, little wind at South-West and fair. At 4 a.m. Weighed and tow'd down the Bay (being Calm) with an intent to go to Sea, but having 2 Shott fired at us from Santa Cruze Fort was obliged to come to an Anchor and to send a Boat to the Fort to know the Reason of their firing, who it seems had no orders to let us pass, without which no Ship can go to Sea. This surprized me not a little, as I had but this very morning received a very Polite Letter from the Vice-Roy (in answer to one I had wrote some days ago), wherein he wishes me a good voyage. I immediately dispatched a petty Officer to the Vice-Roy to know the reason why we was not permitted to pass the Fort; the Boat very soon return'd with an order to the Captain of the Fort to let us pass, which Order had been wrote some Days Ago, but either by Design or neglect had not been sent. At 11 weighed in order to put to Sea, but before we could heave up the Anchor, it got hold of a Rock, where it held fast in spite of all our endeavours to Clear it until the Sea Breeze set in.

Tuesday, 6th. The Sea breeze continued all this day. At 2 p.m. the Ship tended to the Wind, which cleared the Anchor. Hove it up and run higher up the Bay and Anchored in 15 fathoms, a little below the Isle or Church of Bon

Voyage; found the cable very much rubbed several fathoms from the Anchor.

Wednesday, 7th. First and latter part a Genteel breeze at South-East and East; the Middle, Calm. At 5 a.m. weighed and tow'd out of the Bay; at 8 Discharged the Pilot and his Boat. A breeze of Wind Springing up Easterly made Sail out to Sea, and sent a boat to one of the Islands laying before the Bay to cut Brooms, a thing we was not permitted to do while we lay in the Harbour; the Guard Boat which had constantly attended all the time we lay in the Bay and Harbour did not leave us until the Pilot was discharged. At noon the Sugar Loaf at the west Entrance of the Bay bore North by West 1/2 West, distance, 8 or 9 miles.

[Description of Rio Janeiro.]

A DESCRIPTION OF THE BAY OR RIVER OF RIO DE JANEIRO.

The few days' delay we met with in getting out of Rio de Janeiro gave me an opportunity of Drawing a Plan or Sketch of great part of the Bay, but the Strict watch that was kept over us during our whole stay hinder'd me from taking so accurate a Survey as I wisht to have done, and all the Observations I could make was taken from on board the Ship. This Plan hath no pretensions to accuracy, yet it will give a very good idea of the place, differing not much from the truth in what is Essential.

The Bay of Rio de Janeiro, by some called a River--which its Name Signifies--but this I think is improper, it being nothing more than a Deep inlet of the Sea, into which no considerable fresh water River Emptys itself that I could hear of. Be this as it will, it is Capacious and Capable of Containing a vast Number of Shipping where they may ride in perfect Security. The Entrance is Situated West by North 18 Leagues from Cape Frio, and may be known by a remarkable Hill in the Form of a Sugar Loaf, at the West Entrance of the Bay; but as all the Coast is exceeding high, terminating at the top in Peaked Hills, it is much better known by the Islands laying before it, one of which (called Rodonda) is high and round in form of a Hay Stack, and lies South by West 2 1/2 leagues from the Sugar Loaf or Entrance of the Bay. A little without the East Entrance of the Bay, and near the shore, lay 2 Islands near each other: 3 leagues from the Eastward and 4 miles from the Shore are 2 low Rocky Islands, which are the first you meet with in coming from the Eastward or from Cape Frio.

To sail into Rio de Janeiro there is not the least Danger until you are the length of the Fort of Santa Cruze, which stands on the point that forms the East Entrance of the Bay or River; on the West Entrance is Fort Lorio, built upon a Rock which lies close to the Main Land, the distance from one Fort to the other is 3/4 of a mile East and West, but the Channel for Shipping is not quite so broad by reason of Sunken Rocks laying off each of the Forts; these rocks may not be properly placed in the plan, being only laid down from the information of the Pilot. The Narrowness of the Channell here causeth the Tides both Flood and Ebb to run pretty strong, insomuch that you cannot Stem it without a fresh breeze of Wind, nor is it safe Anchoring because the bottom is foul and Rocky. By keeping in the Middle of the Channell you will not only avoid being forced to come to an Anchor, but all other Dangers. Being got within the entrance your Course up the Bay is North by West 1/2 West and North-North-West something more than one League; this brings you the length of the great Road, and North-West and West-North-West one league more carrys you the length of the Ilha dos Cobras, which lies before the City. Keep the North side of this Island close on board and Anchor above it in 5 fathoms of water, where you see most Convenient before the Monastery of Benedictines, which stands upon a hill at the North-West End of the City. Small Ships and Vessels generally lay between the Town and the Ilha dos Cobras, but in order to get there they must come round the North side of the Island.

I shall now give the best description I can of the Different Forts that are Erected for the Defence of the Bay. The first you meet with coming in from Sea is a Battery of 22 Guns, seated in the Bottom of a sandy Bay, which is on the South side of the Sugar Loaf, and can be designed for no other use than to hinder an Enemy from landing in that valley, from whence I suppose they may March up to the Town or round by the West side of the Sugar Loaf to attack the Forts that are on that side of the Entrance into the Bay, the first of which is Seated under the foot of the Sugar Loaf on a low Isthmus which joyns the Peninsula or point of the Bay with the Land of the Sugar Loaf. It appears to be a square of Stone Work without a Ditch, with Bastions and furnished with Cannon. A little within this fort are 2 battrys of 5 or 6 Guns each. They are designed to play upon Shipping, but neither these battrys or the Fort are out of reach of a Ship's Cannon. Hard by these batterys stands Fort Logie. It is an irregular hexagon, built of Stone upon a Small Rock standing at the west Entrance of the Bay, and is surrounded on all Sides by the Sea. It is mounted with 14 or 15 guns, which are placed so as to play upon Shipping going in and out of the Harbour. There is only one way to go into it, which is by Steps Leading up to a Sally Port on the North-West side. Opposite this is the Fort of Santa Cruze, built upon a low rocky point that forms the East Entrance of the Bay. It hath the Appearance of a Regular Fortification of Stone Work built upon the Slope of the Rock, on which account there are in some places 2 Tier of Guns. It hath no Ditch but on the Land side, where it is cut out of the Rock; in every other part the Sea washes up to its Walls. It seems everywhere to be well Mounted with Cannon Except on the land side, where none are wanting, because they could be of no use, the land being so very high above it. Yet, after all, neither this Fort nor those on the opposite shore do not appear to be of any great Strength, even against Shipping, for which they are wholly design'd, being the key of the Bay. They lay low, and Ships may come so near as to have them entirely within the reach of their Guns; but it would require 5 or 6 Sail of the line to insure Success. Between 2 and 3 Miles within the Entrance of the Bay, on the West Side, is the Isle Borghleone, upon the east point of which is Erected a Battry of Stone, and Mounted with 17 pieces of Cannon. Besides this, on the highest part of the Island, is a Battry of 6 Guns mounted on an Open Platform. These battrys are designed to play upon Shipping in the Bay, and seems not ill designed for that purpose; yet they would be Obliged to Submit to the Attack of Shipping or that of a Land force, there being nothing to hinder the latter from Landing on the Island behind the Battrys. Opposite to this Island, on the low point on the east side of the Bay, is the Battry of St. Dominica of 7 Guns. A little without this Battry, on the East side of the Bay, is a small but high Island, close to the Shore, on the Top of which is the Church of Bonn Voyage, about half-way down the Cliff. Below the Church is a Battry of 3 Guns. Neither the one nor the other of these battry's are of much Consequence. They serve, indeed, to force Shipping coming into the Bay between 2 Fires, and hinder them from Anchoring on that side until they are silenced. The next fortification is that on the Ilha dos Cobras, the east point and North side of which consists of a Rampart Bastion and a Parrapet faced with Stones and mounted with Cannon, but no Ditch, which is not much wanting, as the works are built on the Edge of the rising Ground. The other side next the Town hath no other inclosure but a plain wall without any Guns. It is said that the works on this Island are in bad repair, on account of being so Extensive that they would take more men to Defend them than they could spare, and, placing no Dependancy on their Strength, let them go to decay. The ground on which the Monastry of Benedictines Stands Commands the Works on the Island. Over the South end of the City stands the Castle of St. Sebastian; it is Seated upon a Hill, and Commands the whole Town; and this is all I know of it, only that it is not counted a place of any great Strength. For the Defence of these Forts and the Town the King of Portugal Maintains 7 Regiments of Regular Troops. Those I saw were well cloathed and in good Condition; but this, as I was told, was not the Case with the whole. Besides these Troops are 3 Regiments of Militia, 2 of Horse and one of foot. These consist of the principal inhabitants of the place, who serve without pay, Muster and Exercise in turns nine Months in the year, on which account they rank with the Regular Troops.

The City of Rio de Janeiro is in the Latitude of 22 degrees 50 minutes South and Longitude 42 degrees 15 minutes West from Greenwich.* (* Modern determination, 22 degrees 54 minutes South, 43 degrees 10 minutes West.) According to Observations made at Sea it is Seated on a plain close to the Shore on the West side of the Bay, at the foot of Several high Mountains. It is neither ill designed nor ill built. The Houses are mostly stone, generally one and two Storys high, with Balconys to most of them. The Streets are of a Convenient breadth, and Cross each other at right Angles, and the whole City may be about 3 miles in Compass. It is Govern'd by a Governor appointed by the King. The present Governor is Don Anto Mendoyaz Fastada, who is no Friend to the English. It likewise is the Residence of the Vice-Roy and Captain General of the States of Brazil, who is as absolute as any Monarch on Earth, and the people to all appearance as much Slaves. This City and Adjacent parts about the Bay are said to contain 100,000 Souls; but not above a twentieth part are Whites. The rest are blacks, many of whom are free, and seem to live in tolerable Circumstances.

The city of Rio de Janeiro is supplied with Water from 2 Different parts of the Adjacent Mountains. That which comes from the Southward is Convey'd a Cross a Deep Valley by an Acquiduct, which Consists of a great Number of Arches placed in 2 Rows, one upon the other; from thence in pipes to a fountain which stands in the Middle of the Square before the Vice-Roy's Palace. At another part of the City is a Reservoir, to which the water is conveyed much in the same manner. From these 2 places, but mostly from the former, the inhabitants fetch all they want, where there is always a Centinel to keep order: and it is likewise here that the Ships Water. They land their Casks upon a Smooth sandy beach about 100 yards from the Fountain, and upon application to the Vice-Roy you have a Centinel to look after them and to clear the way for to come to the fountain to fill water. Upon the whole, Rio de Janeiro is not a bad place for Ships to put in at that want refreshments, not only because the Harbour is safe and Commodious, but that Provision and all manner of Refreshments may be had in tolerable plenty. Bread and Flour are, however, Scarce and Dear, being brought hither from Europe, and are never the better for that Passage. In lieu of these are to be had Yams and Casada. All sorts of Grain--though it may be the produce of this Country--is Dear. Fresh Beef (tho' bad) is to be had in plenty at about 2 1/4 pence per pound, and Jurked Beef about the same price. This is cured with Salt, and dryd in the shade, the bones being taken out, and the Meat cut into large but very thin slices. It eats very well, and if kept in a dry place will remain good a long time at Sea. Rum, Sugar, and Molasses are all good and Cheap. Tobacco is Cheap, but not good. Mutton they have very little. Hogs and all sorts of Poultry are to be got, tho' in no great plenty, and of Course rather dear. Garden Stuff and Fruit in plenty, but none that will keep long at Sea except Pumpkins.

They have a Yard for building Shipping and a small Hulk for heaving down by, there being no other method to come at a Ship's bottom, as the Tides doth not rise above 6 or 7 feet. At the New and full Moon it is high Water at that time about 8 o'clock, when the Land and Sea breezes are regular, but when they are not the Course of Tides are alter'd. The Sea breeze begins to blow about 10 or 12 o'clock, and continues until sunset, when it dies away and is succeeded by the land breeze, which continues most part of the night. From a little after sunrise until the Sea breeze sets in it is generally Calm, and is then the Hotest and most Disagreeable part of the whole day.

CHAPTER 2.
RIO JANEIRO TO TAHITI.

REMARKABLE OCCURRENCES FROM RIO DE JANEIRO TOWARDS TERRA DEL FUEGO.

[December 1768. Rio to Strait Le Maire.]

THURSDAY, December 8th. Fore and Middle parts Moderate breezes and Cloudy; remainder, little wind and Clear weather. At 3 p.m. the Boat returned from the Island; hoisted her in and made Sail at 6. The Sugar Loaf at the west Entrance of Rio de Janeiro bore North 1/2 East, distance 7 leagues; it lies from the City of Rio de Janeiro, from which I take my Departure, South-West 4 miles. Wind East-North-East, North-East, North by East; course South 7 degrees 30 minutes West; distance 85 miles; latitude 24 degrees 17 minutes South, longitude 42 degrees 29 minutes West.

Friday, 9th. Genteel light breezes and Clear weather. At 3 a.m. the Fore top-gallant Mast broke short by the Cap; the Carpenter employed making another. Wind North, North-East, South-South-West; course South 22 degrees East; distance 32 miles; latitude 24 degrees 46 minutes South, longitude 42 degrees 16 minutes West.

Saturday, 10th. Moderate breezes with some flying showers of Rain the first part. Wind southerly; course, South-East 1/2 East; distance 75 miles; latitude 25 degrees 34 minutes South, longitude 41 degrees 12 minutes West.

Sunday, 11th. Little wind and Clear weather the Most part of this day. Serv'd Slops* (* Slops are materials for making clothes.) to the People. Wind southerly; course South 20 degrees East; distance 9 miles; latitude 25 degrees 43 minutes South, longitude 41 degrees 8 minutes West.

Monday, 12th. First part, light Airs; remainder, Genteel breezes and Clear weather. Found the variation of the Compass by the Evening Amplitude and an Azimuth in the Morning to be 8 degrees 30 minutes East, and the Observed Latitude at Noon to be short of that given by the Log 10 Miles. Exercised the People at Great Guns and Small Arms. Wind variable; course South-South-West; distance 34 miles; latitude 26 degrees 14 minutes South, longitude 41 degrees 23 minutes West.

Tuesday, 13th. First part Gentle breezes and Clear, remainder a Steady Gale. The weather a little hazey. Variation 8 degrees 23 minutes East. Wind North-East and North-North-East; course South 19 degrees 40 minutes West; distance 113 miles; latitude 28 degrees 0 minutes South, longitude 42 degrees 6 minutes West.

Wednesday, 14th. First and latter parts, fresh breezes and Cloudy; middle, little wind, with Thunder, Lightning and Rain. The Caulkers employed Caulking the Ship's Decks. Wind, North-West, West, South by West; course South 16 degrees East; distance 87 miles; latitude 29 degrees 24 minutes South, longitude 41 degrees 55 minutes West.

Thursday, 15th. The first part a fresh Gale and dark Cloudy weather; Remainder, little wind and clear; a large swell from South-West. Wind South-West by South, South, East-South-East; course South 14 degrees 15 minutes East; distance 45 miles; latitude 30 degrees 8 minutes South, longitude 41 degrees 39 minutes West.

Friday, 16th. Genteel breezes and Clear weather. Variation 9 degrees 36 minutes East. Wind East-North-East, North-West, North-East; course South 32 degrees West: distance 86 miles; latitude 31 degrees 21 minutes South, longitude 42 degrees 32 minutes West.

Saturday, 17th. Hazey with frequent Showers of Rain all the Fore and Middle part; latter, Clear weather with a Gentle breeze of wind. Wind, variable from North-West, South-West, to South-South-East; course South 14 degrees West; distance 56 miles; latitude 32 degrees 15 minutes South, longitude 42 degrees 48 minutes West.

Sunday, 18th. First part, light winds; remainder, fresh breezes and Clear weather. Variation 11 degrees 3 minutes East. Wind, South-East to North-East; course South 51 West; distance 43 miles; latitude 32 degrees 42 minutes South, longitude 43 degrees 27 minutes West.

Monday, 19th. A steady fresh breeze and fair weather. At half-past 5 p.m. Longitude in per Observation of the sun and moon 43 degrees 38 minutes West from Greenwich. Variation 11 degrees 3 minutes East. The Observed Latitude exceeds that given by the Log 7 Miles. Wind northerly; course South-West; distance 116 miles; latitude 34 degrees 4 minutes South, longitude 45 degrees 6 minutes West.

Tuesday, 20th. A fresh breeze of Wind and hazey. Variation 13 degrees 44 minutes East. Observed Latitude exceeds that given by the Log 11 miles. Wind north; course South-West 1/4 South; distance 160 miles; latitude 36 degrees 2 minutes South, longitude 47 degrees 14 minutes West.

Wednesday, 21st. Wind and weather Variable. Saw several black sheer Waters. Sounded twice this 24 Hours but found no ground with 90 fathoms. The Observed Latitude again ahead of the Log 16 miles. Wind variable; course South 42 degrees 45 minutes West; distance 90 miles; latitude 37 degrees 8 minutes South, longitude 48 degrees 30 minutes West.

Thursday, 22nd. Little wind the most part of this day. Variation 15 degrees 30 minutes East. Bent a New Suit of Sails. Wind southerly; course West; distance 40 miles; latitude 37 degrees 8 minutes South, longitude 49 degrees 1 minute West.

Friday, 23rd. Light Airs and Clear weather. Saw some Turtle upon the Water but could not catch any. Sounded no ground with 200 fathoms. Variation 15 degrees 40 minutes East. Wind southerly; course North 48 degrees West; distance 33 miles; latitude 36 degrees 46 minutes South, longitude 49 degrees 32 minutes West.

Saturday, 24th. First part Calm; remainder a Genteel breeze and fine Clear weather. This night had 2 Sets of Observations of the Moon and the Star Aldebaran, which gave the Longitude 49 degrees 54 minutes 15 seconds West; the first sett gave 49 degrees 55 minutes 15 seconds, and the Second 49 degrees 53 minutes 15 seconds. Wind calm, north-easterly; course South 50 degrees West; distance 39 miles; latitude 37 degrees 11 minutes South, longitude 50 degrees 32 minutes West.

Sunday, 25th. Fresh breezes and fine Clear weather. Wind North-East by North to North; course South 50 degrees West; distance 116 miles; latitude 38 degrees 37 minutes South, longitude 52 degrees 5 minutes West.

Monday, 26th. A Fresh breeze of Wind and Cloudy weather; passed by some Rock Weed. At noon the Observed latitude 26 Miles to the Southward of the Log, which I believe is chiefly owing to her being Generally steer'd to the Southward of her Course. Yesterday being Christmas Day the people were none of the Soberest. Wind North; course South-West; distance 158 miles; latitude 40 degrees 19 minutes South, longitude 54 degrees 30 minutes West.

Tuesday, 27th. Fresh breezes and Hazey with Squalls which Obliged us during the Night to take in the small Sails and 2 reefs in the Topsails which were let out in the Morning. Wind northerly; course South 50 degrees West; distance 123 miles; latitude 41 degrees 38 minutes South, longitude 56 degrees 15 minutes West.

Wednesday, 28th. First part Strong Gales and Cloudy, which Obliged us to get down Top-Gallant Yards. At 8 p.m. it blew a Storm of Wind with Rain which brought us under our Mainsail with her Head to the Westward. Sounded 50 fathoms, fine brown Sand; at midnight had 40 fathoms, the same bottom. At 4 a.m. had 46 fathoms Coral Rock. The weather being more Moderate, made Sail under the Courses and Set the Topsails with 2 Reefs in. Wind South-East to South; latitude 40 degrees 49 minutes South, longitude 58 degrees 29 minutes West.

Thursday, 29th. First part moderate breezes and Cloudy; remainder fresh breezes and Clear. P.M. loosed all the Reefs out, and got Topgallant Yards a

Cross. Variation per Azimuth 16 degrees 12 minutes, per Amplitude 16 degrees 32 minutes; Mean of the Two 16 degrees 22 minutes East. Between 9 and 10 a.m. took 7 sets of Observations between the sun and moon to find the Longitude of the Ship. Each set Consists of three Observations; the Mean of the whole gave 59 degrees 18 minutes 34 seconds West of Greenwich. The result of each set was as follows: viz., 1st set, 59 degrees 8 minutes; Second, 59 degrees 21 minutes; Third, 59 degrees 34 minutes; Fourth, 59 degrees 17 minutes; Fifth, 59 degrees 11 minutes 45 seconds; Sixth, 59 degrees 19 minutes 30 seconds; and the Seventh, 59 degrees 20 minutes 45 seconds. The greatest differance between any two--viz., the first and third--is but 26 minutes, and the mean of these two differ from the mean of the whole only 2 minutes 26 seconds. This shews to what degree of accuracy these observations can be made even by Different Persons, for four of these were made and computed by Mr. Green and the rest by myself. The Longitude given by the Ship, reckoning from the last Observation 5 Days ago, differs only 8 Miles from the Observation, which shews that we have not been in any Currents. Soundings from 40 to 47. Wind North-Easterly; course South 46 degrees 30 minutes West; distance 81 miles; latitude 41 degrees 45 minutes South, longitude 59 degrees 37 minutes West.

Friday, 30th. Little wind, and sometimes Calm; the first part Clear weather, remainder Foggy and Hazey. Soundings from 44 to 49 fathoms; Grey sandy Bottom. Caught both this Morning and last Night a great Number of insects. Some were upon the Wing, but the greater part were upon the water, and many of these alive and of such sort as cannot fly far; and yet at this Time we could not be less than 30 Leagues from Land. Wind variable; course South 30 degrees West; distance 54 miles; latitude 42 degrees 32 minutes South, longitude 60 degrees 15 minutes West.

Saturday, 31st. Cloudy weather, with some Lightning and a few showers of rain. Variation 18 degrees 36 minutes East. Soundings from 46 to 50 fathoms; fine dark sand. Wind South-Easterly; course South 18 degrees West; distance 43 miles; latitude 43 degrees 14 minutes South, longitude 60 degrees 26 minutes West.

[January 1769.]

Sunday, January 1st, 1769. First and Latter part, fresh breezes and Clear weather; in the Middle, light Airs and Calm. At Noon, longitude in per 4 Sets of Observations between the sun and moon 61 degrees 8 minutes 28 seconds west. The Difference between the least and Greatest of these sets was 8 minutes, and the mean of 2 differs from the Mean of the whole but 32 seconds. The Longitude by account carried on from the last Observations exactly agree with these Observations. Saw a great number of small Whales about the Ship. Wind South to West-South-West; course South 36 degrees

West; distance 39 miles; latitude 43 degrees 35 minutes South; longitude 61 degrees 8 minutes 28 seconds West.

Monday, January 2nd. The first part of this day a Genteel gale and Clear weather; middle, Squally, with Lightning and rain, and some showers of Large Hail Stones; towards Noon a Steady fresh breeze and Clear weather. At noon longitude in by 3 sets of Observations between the sun and moon 61 degrees 7 minutes 45 seconds, which is 43 seconds to the Eastward of yesterday's Observations. The Ship by the Log has made 4 minutes East. Wind Westerly; course South 2 degrees East; distance 92 miles; latitude 45 degrees 17 minutes South, longitude 61 degrees 7 minutes 45 seconds West.

Tuesday, 3rd. Fresh gales and clear weather; under Single Reef Topsails. P.M. Saw some Whales and Porpoises and small red Crawfish, some of which we Caught. At Noon saw several Birds of a light Grey Colour, like Pidgeons, but smaller; these are of the Mother Carey's kind. Longitude per Observation 61 degrees 29 minutes 45 seconds, which is 22 minutes to the westward of Yesterday, but the ship hath made 41 minutes, Consequently there is an Error of 19 minutes, which is not to be supposed to be in the Log in one Day's run; but, be it which way it will, it is not great. Wind West, Southerly; course South 11 degrees; distance 122 miles; latitude 47 degrees 17 minutes South, longitude 61 degrees 29 minutes 45 seconds West.

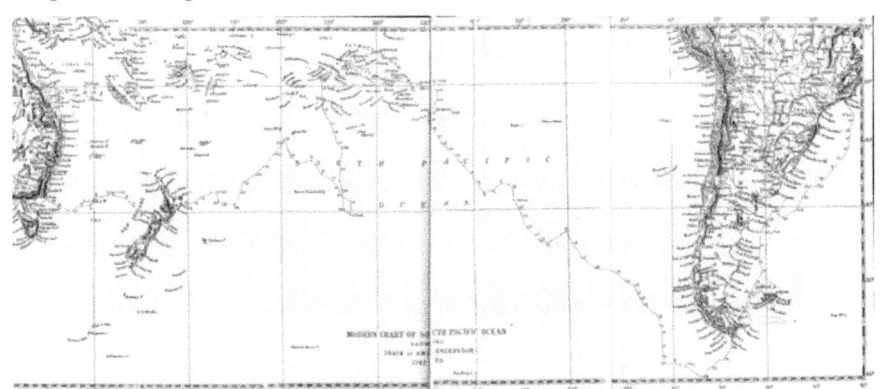

MODERN CHART OF SOUTH PACIFIC OCEAN SHOWING TRACK OF H.M.S. ENDEAVOUR, 1769 TO 1770.

Wednesday, 4th. First part, genteel breeze and Clear; latter, fresh gales, with heavy squalls of wind and rain, which brought us under our courses and main topsails close reefed. Soon after noon saw the appearance of Land to the Eastward, and being in the Latitude of Peypes Island, as it is lay'd down in some Charts, imagined it might be it.* (* Pepys' Island, placed on charts, from a report by Captain Cowley in 1683, about 230 miles north of Falkland

- 77 -

Islands, and long imagined to exist. It was eventually recognised, after the discovery of Cowley's manuscript Journal, that Cowley had sighted the Falklands.) Bore down to be Certain, and at 1/2 past 2 p.m. discovered our Mistake, and hauld the Wind again. At 6 sounded, and had 72 fathoms black sand and mud. Variation 19 degrees 45 minutes East. Wind West-North-West to South-West by South; course South 30 degrees East; distance 76 miles; latitude 48 degrees 28 minutes South, longitude 60 degrees 51 minutes West.

[Nearing Terra del Fuego.]

Thursday, 5th. Fore part, fresh Gales and Clear; Middle, light Airs; remainder, fresh Gales and a little hazey. P.M. found the Variation to be 20 degrees 4 minutes East; Soundings 75 and 73 fathoms. A great Number of Water Fowl about the Ship. Wind South-West, North-East, North-North-East; course South 28 degrees West; distance 92 miles; latitude 49 degrees 49 minutes South, longitude 61 degrees 67 minutes West.

Friday, 6th. Fresh gales, the Air very Sharp and Cold; frequent showers of rain and Squalls. Soundings 75 fathoms. Saw some Penguins. Gave to each of the People a Fearnought Jacket and a pair of Trowsers, after which I never heard one Man Complain of Cold, not but that the weather was cold enough. Wind West, Southerly; course South 8 degrees 45 minutes West; distance 92 miles; latitude 51 degrees 20 minutes South, longitude 62 degrees 19 minutes West.

Saturday, 7th. First part, Strong Gales, with excessive hard Squals, with rain. At 9 p.m. wore and brought too, her head to the Westward under the Mainsail, and Reef'd the Foresail for the first time. The Storm continued with a little intermission until a little towards Noon, when it abated, so we could set the Topsails close Reefed. Saw many Penguins and some Seals. Wind southerly: course South 62 degrees East; distance 14 miles; latitude 51 degrees 26 minutes South, longitude 61 degrees 59 minutes West.

Sunday, 8th. Wind and weather both Variable, but for the most part little wind. P.M. loosed the Reef out of the Foresail and 2 Reefs out of Each Topsail. A.M. got Top gallant Yards aCross and loosed all the Reefs out. Soundings from 80 to 75 fathoms. Wind South, South-West, West, North-West; course North 72 degrees West; distance 33 miles; latitude 51 degrees 16 minutes South; longitude 62 degrees 50 minutes West.

Monday, 9th. First and Latter parts, a moderate breeze and Clear weather; Middle, squally with rain. P.M. found the Variation by several azimuths to be 22 degrees 24 minutes East. Saw a great Number of Penguins and Seals.

Tuesday, 10th. Moderate breezes and fine clear weather. At 2 p.m. Sounded 86 fathoms; black sand and Small stones. Variation 21 degrees 57 minutes

East. At 1/2 past 10 Tackt having Stood south 12 Leagues. After standing to the Westward 14 Miles, sounded, and had 80 fathoms black grey sand; 3 Leagues farther 76, coarse black sand; Tack'd, and at noon had 70 fathoms black gravel and Small Stones of different Colours. Saw several flights of black Sheerwaters. Wind West-South-West, South-West; course South 18 degrees West; distance 38 miles; latitude 52 degrees 54 minutes South, longitude 63 degrees 10 minutes West.

Wednesday, 11th. A Steady Genteel breeze and clear weather. P.M. after standing 13 Leagues South-South-West Sounded 64 fathoms Gravel and small Stones; Standing South-West by South 11 leagues farther, had 46 fathoms, the same sort of bottom. At 8 a.m. saw the land of Terra del Fuego, extending from the west to the South-East by South, distance off shore between 3 and 4 Leagues; sounded and had 35 fathoms small, soft, Slate Stones. Variation 23 degrees 30 minutes East. In ranging along shore to the South-East at the distance of 2 or 3 leagues, had 27 and 26 fathoms muddy bottom. Saw some of the natives, who made a Smook in several places, which must have been done as a Signal to us as they did not continue it after we passed. By our Longitude we ought not to have been so far to the Westward as Statenland, as it is laid down in the Charts; but it appeared from Subsequent Observations that the Ship had got near a Degree of Longitude to the Westward of the Log, which is 35 Miles in these Latitudes. Probably this in part may be owing to a Small Current setting to the Westward, occasioned by the Westerly Current which comes round Cape Horn and through Strait La Maire, and the inDraught of the Streights of Magellan. Wind westerly; course South 30 degrees West; distance, 100 miles; latitude 54 degrees 20 minutes South, longitude 64 degrees 35 minutes West per log.

Thursday, 12th. First part, moderate breezes and Cloudy; remainder sometimes a fresh breeze, sometimes Calm, Hazey weather with rain. At 5 the wind coming to the Northward obliged us to Tack and Stood North-Westward, being then about 5 Miles from the Shore, and had 23 fathoms, sandy Bottom. At Midnight Tackt and Stood to the Eastward. At Noon the Land over the Entrance of Straits La Maire, East-North-East, distance, 7 leagues; Soundings from 28 to 38 fathoms. Wind North, North-North-East, variable, West-South-West; latitude 54 degrees 34 minutes South per observation.

Friday, 13th. The greatest part of this day little wind and Cloudy. At 8 p.m., Cape St. Diego, at the west entrance of Straits La Maire, East, distance about 5 leagues. Keept under an easey Sail until daylight, at which time we were abreast of Cape St. Diego, and then put into the Straits, but the Tide soon turned against us and obliged us to haul under the Cape again and wait until 9 a.m. when it shifted in our favour. Put into the Straits again with a Moderate breeze at South-West, which soon grew Boisterous with very heavy Squalls, with rain and hail, and obliged us to Close reef our Topsails. Wind North-East by East, West-South-West, South-West; latitude 54 degrees 39 minutes South; at noon, Cape St. Diego North 2 leagues.

[In Strait of Le Maire.]

Saturday, 14th. First part Strong Gales, and very heavy squalls with Hail and Rain; remainder more moderate but unsettled, sometimes a fresh breeze and Squally, and sometimes little wind. Kept plying in the Straits until 1/2 past 4 p.m., at which time the Tide had made strong against us, and the wind not abating, bore away, intending to have hauled under Cape St. Diego, but was prevented by the force of the Tide, which carried us past that Cape with surprising rapidity, at the same time caused a very great sea. At 6, the weather being Clear, took 9, or 3 sets of, Observations of the sun and moon in order to find the Longitude of the place, and as they perhaps are the first Observations of this kind that were ever made so near to the Extremity of South America, I have inserted them below just as they were taken, that everybody may judge for themselves.

COLUMN 1: NAME OF SET. COLUMN 2: TIME BY THE WATCH IN HOURS, MINUTES AND SECONDS. COLUMN 3: APPARENT TIME COMPUTED FROM IN HOURS, MINUTES AND SECONDS. COLUMN 4: OBSERVED DISTANCE. SUN AND MOON'S NEAREST LIMB IN DEGREES, MINUTES AND SECONDS. COLUMN 5: OBSERVED ALTITUDE. SUN'S LOWER LIMB IN DEGREES, MINUTES AND SECONDS. COLUMN 6: OBSERVED ALTITUDE. MOON'S UPPER LIMB IN DEGREES, MINUTES AND SECONDS. COLUMN 7: CORRECT ALTITUDE. SUN'S CENTER IN DEGREES, MINUTES AND SECONDS. COLUMN 8: CORRECT ALTITUDE. MOON'S CENTER IN DEGREES, MINUTES AND SECONDS. COLUMN 9: THE LONGITUDE RESULTING FROM BOTH SETS OF OBSERVATIONS IN DEGREES, MINUTES AND SECONDS.

-- : 8 27 15 : -- : 71 26 0 : 15 36 0 : 24 13 0 : -- : -- : --. -- : 8 30 30 : -- : 71 28 0 : 15 11 0 : 24 8 0 : -- : -- : --. -- : 8 32 15 : -- : 71 29 0 : 14 56 0 : 23 57 0 : -- : -- : --. -- -- : 25 30 00 : -- : - 83 0 : 45 43 0 : 72 18 0 : -- : -- : --. -- 1st set : 8 30 0 : 6 12 53 : 71 27 40 : 15 14 20 : 24 6 0 : 15 22 39 : 23 43 0 : 66 7 45. ----
--- ----------------

-- : 8 33 50 : -- : 71 30 0 : 14 43 0 : 23 38 0 : -- : -- : --. -- : 8 35 39 : -- : - 31 0 : 14 25 0 : 23 42 0 : -- : -- : --. -- : 8 37 46 : -- : - 30 30 : 14 10 0 : 23 32 0 : -- : -- : --. -- -- : 8 107 15 : -- : - 91 30 : 43 18 0 : 23 112 0 : -- : -- : --. -- 2nd set : 8 35 45 : 6 18 41 : 71 30 30 : 14 26 0 : 23 37 20 : 14 34 00 : 23 14 0 : 66 19

45. --- ---------------

-- : 8 39 10 : -- : 71 31 30 : 13 56 0 : 23 26 0 : -- : -- : --. -- : 8 41 20 : -- : - 32
00 : 13 40 0 : 23 20 0 : -- : -- : --. -- : 8 43 49 : -- : - 33 00 : 13 18 0 : 23 6 0 : -
- : -- : --. -- -- : 8 124 19 : -- : - 96 30 :
- 114 0 : - 52 0 : -- : -- : --. -- 3rd set :
8 41 26 : 6 24 26 : 71 32 10 : 13 38 0 : 23 17 20 : 13 46 0 : 22 55 0 : 66 0 45.
--- --------------------

N.B. The mean of the three sets is 66 degrees 9 minutes 25 seconds, and the mean of Mr. Green's Computations from the same Observations was 66 degrees 14 minutes 0 seconds, and the mean of his computations and mine will be 66 degrees 11 minutes 32 seconds, and therefore the Longitude of Cape St. Diego or the North-West entrance of Strait Le Maire will be 66 degrees 0 minutes 0 seconds West from Greenwich, and its Latitude 54 degrees 39 minutes South.* (* Modern determination is 54 degrees 40 minutes South, 65 degrees 8 minutes West.)

Note: The distance of the sun and moon was taken by Mr. Green alone, my Quadrant being out of Order.

Cape St. Diego bore at this time South by East about 4 Leagues Distant. At 1/2 past 7 Tackt and Stood to the South-East, Cape St. Diego bearing South by East, distance 5 Leagues. At 1 a.m., Squally, wore Ship, Staten Land extending from North to East. At 4, Moderate Weather, loosed a Reef out of each Topsail, the Cape of Good Success West by South, and Cape St. Diego North-North-West, being now in the Strait, but the Tide turning against us soon carried us out. The Violence of the Tide of Ebb rose such a Sea off Cape St. Diego, that it looked as if it was breaking Violently on the ledge of Rocks, and would be taken for such by any who know'd not the true cause. When the Ship was in this Torrent she frequently Pitched her Bowsprit in the Water. By Noon we got under the Land between Cape St. Diego and Cape St. Vincent, where I thought to have Anchored, but found the Bottom every where hard and Rocky; the Depth of Water from 30 to 12 fathoms. Sent the Master to Examine a small Cove which appeared to our View a little to the Eastward of Cape St. Vincent. Wind South-South-West and South-West by South.

Sunday, 15th. Moderate breezes at South and South-East, and cloudy weather, the greater part of this day. At 2 p.m. the Master return'd with an account that there was Anchorage in 4 fathoms Water and a good bottom close to the Eastward of the first black bluff point which is on the East side of Cape St. Vincent, at the very Entrance of the Cove we saw from the Ship (which I named Vincent Bay). Before this Anchoring ground lay several Rocky Ledges covered with Sea Weed: on these Ledges I was informed was not less than 8 or 9 fathoms, but in standing in with the Ship the first we came upon had only 4 fathoms upon it. I therefore thought that Anchoring here would be attended with some Risk, and that it would be better to Endeavour to find some Port in the Strait, and there Compleat our Wood and Water. However, I sent an Officer with a Boat on shore to attend to Mr. Banks and people who was very desirous of being on shore at any rate, while I keept plying as near the shore as possible with the Ship. At 9 they return'd on board bringing with them several Plants, Flowers, etc., most of them unknown in Europe, and in that Alone consisted their whole Value; they saw none of the Natives, but meet with several of their old Hutts. Hoisted the Boat in and made Sail into the Straits and at 3 a.m. Anchord in 12 1/2 fathoms Water (the bottom Coral rocks) before a small Cove which we took for Port Maurice, and near 1/2 a Mile from the shore Cape St. Diego South-South-West, and Cape St. Bartholomew (which is the south point of Staten Land) East-South-East.

Port Maurice appeared to afford so little Shelter for Shipping that I did not think it worth while to hoist a Boat out to Examine it; we saw here 2 of the Natives come down to the Shore, who stay'd sometime, then retir'd into the Woods againe. At 10 o'Clock got under Sail, Wind at South-East, and plyed to Windward.

[In Success Bay.]

Monday, 16th. A Fresh breeze of Wind at South and South-West, with frequent showers of Rain and Snow. At 2 p.m. Anchored in the Bay of Success in 9 fathoms, the bottom Owse and sand.* (* The Endeavour was three days and a half in getting through the Strait of Le Maire, as far as Success Bay. It is a difficult passage for a sailing vessel even in the present day, as the tides are strong and winds generally contrary, but experience has enabled good directions to be given as to the best way to pass the Strait. Cook himself gives capital advice farther on.) The south point of the Bay bore South-East and the north point East-North-East. This Bay I shall describe when I come to speake of the rest of the Coast. Hoisted out the Boats and moor'd with the Stream Anchor. While this was doing I went ashore accompanied by Mr. Banks and Dr. Solander to look for a Watering place and to speak with the Natives, who were assembled on the Beach at the Head of the Bay to the Number of 30 or 40. They were so far from being afraid or surprised at our coming amongst them that three of them came on board without the least hesitation. They are something above the Middle size, of a Dark Copper Colour with long black hair; they paint their Bodies in Streakes, mostly Red and Black. Their Cloathing consists wholy in a Guanacoe Skin or that of a Seal, in the same form as it came from the Animal's back.

The Women Wear a Piece of Skin over their Privy Parts, but the Men observe no such decency. Their Hutts are made like a behive, and open on one side where they have their fires; they are made of small Sticks and covered with branches of trees, long Grass, etc., in such a manner that they are neither Proof against Wind, Hail, rain or Snow, a sufficient proof that these People must be a very hardy race. They live chiefly on shell fish, such as Muscels, which they gather from off the Rocks along the Sea Shore, and this seems to be the Work of the Women. Their Arms are Bows and Arrows neatly made; their Arrows are bearded, some with glass and others with fine flint; several Pieces of the former we saw amongst them with other European things, such as rings, Buttons, Cloth, Canvas, etc., which I think proves that they must sometimes travel to the Northward, as we know of no Ship that hath been in these parts for many Years; besides, they were not at all surprised at our Fire Arms; on the Contrary, they seemed to know the use of them, by making signs to us to fire at Seals or Birds that might come in the way. They have no Boats that we saw or anything to go upon the Water with; their number doth not Exceed 50 or 60 young and old, and there are fewer Women than Men. They are Extreamly fond of any Red thing, and seemed to set more Value on Beads than anything we could give them; in this Consists their whole Pride, few, either Men or Women, are without a Necklace or String of Beads made of Small Shells or bones about their Necks. They would not taste any strong Liquor, neither did they seem fond of our Provisions. We could not discover that they had any Head or Chief or Form of Government, neither have they any useful or necessary Utensil except it be a Bag or Basket to gather their Muscels into. In a word they are perhaps as Miserable a sett of People as are this day upon Earth.* (* Cook's description of the natives of Tierra del Fuego is good to the present day, except that those who live farther westward are still more wretched. Those of the main island, in which the Bay of Good Success lies, are able to kill guanaco, and enjoy a better climate. They, as Cook observed, never go on the water, whereas those westward practically live in canoes.) Having found a convenient place on the south side of the Bay to Wood and Water at, we set about that Work in the Morning, and Mr. Banks with a Party went into the Country to gather Plants, etc.

Tuesday, 17th. Fresh Gales at South-South-West and West-South-West with rain and Snow, and, of Course, very cold weather; notwithstanding we kept geting on board Wood and Water, and finished the Survey of the Bay. Mr. Banks and his Party not returning this Evening as I expected, gave me great uneasiness, as they were not prepared for Staying out the Night. However, about Noon they returned in no very Comfortable Condition, and what was still worse 2 blacks, servants to Mr. Banks, had perished in the Night with Cold. Great part of the day they landed was spent before they got through the Woods, after which they advanced so far into the Country that they were so far from being able to return that night, and with much difficulty they got to a place of Tolerable Shelter where they could make a fire: these 2 men being Intrusted with great part of the Liquor (that was for the whole party) had made too free with it, and Stupified themselves to that degree that they either could or would not Travel, but laid themselves down in a place where there was not the least thing to Shelter them from the inclemency of the night. This was about 1/4 of a Mile from where the rest took up their Quarters, and notwithstanding their repeated Endeavours, they could not get them to move one Step farther, and the bad travelling made it impossible for any one to Carry them, so that they were Obliged to leave them, and the next morning they were both found dead.

Wednesday, 18th. All the Middle and Latter parts of this day it blow'd very strong from the South-South-West and South-West, attended with Snow, Hail and Rain, and brought such a Sea into the Bay, which rose the Surf to such a Height that no Boat could land. The same Stormy weather and Surf continued all

Thursday, 19th. All this time the Ship road very easy with her Broad side to the swell. The great Surf that always will be upon the Shore when the wind blows hard from the Southward makes Wooding and Watering tedious, notwithstanding there are great plenty of both close to high water Mark.

Friday, 20th. Moderate gales and Cloudy with frequent Showers of rain all this day. This Evening the Surf abated, and at 2 a.m. sent the People on shore to Wood and Water and cut Brooms, all of which we Completed this day. In this Service we lost our small Kedge Anchor, it having been laid off the Watering Place to ride the Long-boat by, and the Gale had broke away the Hawser and Buoy rope, and perhaps buried the Anchor in the Sand, for notwithstanding our utmost Endeavours we were not able to Hook it. Took up the Stream Anchor and made ready for Sailing.

[Sailed from Success Bay.]

Saturday, 21st. Wind from South-South-West to South-West; moderate breezes the first part; latter, fresh Gales with Showers of Rain. P.M. hoisted in the Boats, and made ready for Sailing; at 2 a.m. weighed and made Sail out of the Bay. At 1/2 past 4 the Cape of good Success bore West, and Cape Bartholomew East. Variation per Azimuth, 24 degrees 9 minutes East; at Noon the Cape of good Success bore North 36 degrees West; distance, 11 leagues.

Sunday, 22nd. Wind between the South and the West first and Latter part, fresh Gales and Squally, with rain; the Middle, little wind and rain. A.M. found the Variation by several Azimuths to be 20 degrees 4 minutes East. Unbent the Cables and Stowed the Anchors. At Noon, Latitude observed 56 degrees 7 minutes South, longitude, made from the Cape of Good Success, 42 minutes East.

Monday, 23rd. Winds variable from South-East round by the South-West to North-West. First part, a fresh breeze and Squally, the remainder moderate breezes and sometimes Calm and clear weather, which is more than we have had for several days past. At 4 a.m. saw the Land in the South-West Quarter, and a small Island bearing West; from this Time until 9 it was Calm, at which time the Ship drove very fast to the North-East by North. At 9 Sprung up a light breeze at North, loos'd all the Reefs out, and set the Steering sails. The Cape of good Success bore North-East by North; Staten land seen from the Deck bearing North-East; the Sugar Loaf on Terra Del Fuego North-North-East, and is the same Hill as is seen from the North-East side of the Land; it appears to stand but a little way in Land from the Shore; and the Mainland and Islands on the Coast extending from the Cape of good Success to the South by West. The Country Mountainous, of an indifferent height; the Tops were covered with Snow, which had lately fell, as it did not lay long. There appeared to be several Bays and inlets and Islands laying along the Coast; the 3rd view in the Chart exhibits the appearance of this Coast where g is new Island, c the Sugar Loaf, and h the Cape of good Success. At noon the West End of New Island bore North-West by West, 5 leagues. Latitude observed 55 degrees 25 minutes South, this Island I named New Island because it is not laid down in any Chart.* (* This island is still so called in the charts.)

Tuesday, 24th. The fore and Middle parts of these 24 Hours Moderate Gales and Cloudy with some Showers of Rain; the Latter, fresh gales with flying Showers. At 7 p.m. New Island bore North-West by North, and a small Island laying to the Westward of it bore West by North. Variation per Several Azimuths 21 degrees 0 minutes East, which is much less than we have yet found it upon this Coast; yet I am satisfied with the Goodness of the Observations. At 1/2 past 1 a.m. the Wind Shifted from South-South-West to East-South-East. Tackt and stood South-West; at 6 Saw the Land to the Westward making like several Islands. At 8 two Small Islands laying off a low Point of Land bore West by South, distant 3 Leagues, and the small Island we saw last night bore North-North-West. This I take to be the Island of Evouts, it is about one League in Circuit, and of a Moderate height and lies 4 Leagues from the Main. Near the South Point of it are some Peaked rocks pretty high above Water; the wind coming to the Southward we did but just weather this Island; in passing it, sounded and had 40 fathoms Water, sand, and broken Shells. At Noon it bore North-East distance one League, and the low point of land before mentioned South 17 degrees West distant 4 or 5 Leagues. Tackt and Stood to the South-East, wind at South-South-West. From this low Point the land trends to the North-West, about 4 Leagues, where it ends in a low point round which to the Westward appears to be a

Deep Bay, unless this land should prove to be an Island or Islands, which is most likely. It rises into high Craggy hills, and the Shore seems to form several Bays; if so, they must afford good Shelter for Shipping against Southerly and Westerly winds.

[Off Cape Horn.]

Wednesday, 25th. Winds from the South to the West-North-West, the first part fresh Gales and Squally with some Rain; Middle, little wind with Hail and Rain; latter, fresh Gales and Hazey, with Showers of Rain. At 8 p.m. the Island of Evouts North-West, distant 3 or 4 miles. Variation, per morning Amplitude 21 degrees 16 minutes East. At 8 a.m. the Southermost low point of land seen Yesterday Bore South 74 degrees West, and a remarkable Peaked Hill to the Southward of it South-West; and soon after we discovered that the land which we took Yesterday to be a part of the Main or an Island, was three Islands, which I take to be Hermites. At Noon the South Point of the Southermost Island bore North-West by West distant 3 leagues, having then 58 fathoms Peble Stones. This Point is pretty high and consists of Peaked Craggy rocks, and not far from it lay several others high above Water. It lies in the Latitude of 55 degrees 53 minutes South and South-West 26 Leagues from Straits La Mair, and by some on board thought to be Cape Horn; but I was of another Opinion, and with good reason, because we saw land to the Southward of it about 3 or 4 leagues. It appeared not unlike an Island with a very high round Hummock upon it; this I believe to be Cape Horn, for after we had stood about 3 Leagues the weather cleared up for about a quarter of an hour, which gave us a sight of the land bearing West-South-West, but we could see no land to the southward or Westward of it, and therefore conclude that it must be the Cape, but whether it be an Island of itself, a part of the Southermost of Hermits Islands, or a part of Terra del Fuego, I am not able to determine. However, this is of very little Consequence to Navigation: I only wished to be Certain whether or no it was the Southermost Land on or near to Terra del Fuego; but the thick foggy weather and the westerly winds which Carried us from the land prevented me from satisfying my Curiosity in this point, but from its Latitude and the reasons before given I think it must, and if so it must be Cape Horn, and lies in the latitude of 55 degrees 53 minutes South and Longitude 68 degrees 13 minutes West from the Meridian of Greenwich,* (* No doubt this was Cape Horn, but it lies in 55 degrees 58 minutes South, 67 degrees 16 minutes West.) being the Mean result of Several Observations of the sun and moon made the day after we left the land, and which agreed with those made at Straits Le Mair, allowing for the distance between one place and the other, which I found means very accurately to determine. As we are now about taking our departure from the Land, which we are not likely to fall in with again, I shall give a more full

Description of such parts of the Coasts of Terra del Fuego as hath fallen under my inspection.

We fell in with this Coast 21 Leagues to the Westward of Straits Le Mair, and ranged the coast from thence to the Strait within 2 or 3 Leagues of the Land, and had soundings all the way from 40 to 20 fathoms, a Gravelly and Sandy Bottom. The land near the Shore is in general low but hilly, the face of the Country appears Green and Woody, but in land are Craggy Mountains; they appeared to be of no great height, nor were they Covered with Snow. The most remarkable land on Terra Del Fuego is a high Mountain in form of a Sugar Loaf, situated not far from the sea on the South-West side of the Land, and 3 hills called the 3 Brothers. They lay near the Shore and nine Miles to the Westward of Cape St. Diego, which is a low point that forms the North-West Entrance of Strait Le Mair, and are Contiguous to Each other. The Sugar Loaf lies from these Hills South-South-West, and when it was in this situation the Appearances of the Land is represented in the first View in the Chart, but it must be observed that from this point of View the Three Brothers appear far more Conspicuous than from any other; these land Marks are by some Voyagers thought very necessary to know Strait Le Mair by, but whoever coasts Terra Del Fuego within sight of land cannot possibly miss the Strait, it being of itself so very Conspicuous; and Staten Land, which forms the East side, is still more so from its very rugged appearance. One League and a half to the Westward of Cape St. Diego lies Cape St. Vincent, between these two Capes lies Vincent's Bay,* (* Now called Thetis Bay, it is a very poor anchorage.) a Small Cove wherein is Wood and Water, and before which a Ship might Anchor with a Southerly or South-West wind, but the ground is none of the best, unless you go into the very Mouth of the Cove, which is on the East side of the first Bluff point from Cape St. Vincent, where there is Anchorage in 4 fathoms, a Sandy Bottom. In going in keep clear of the Sea Weed, and send a Boat Ahead to sound, and at best this is but a bad place for Shipping, and only recommended to such as are in want of Wood and Water, and have no Opportunity to put into the Strait, which in Prudence ought not to be attempted but with a fair wind or Moderate weather, and upon the very first of the Tide of Flood, which hapens here at the full and Change of the Moon about 1 or 2 o'clock, and then to keep as near to Terra Del Fuego Shore as the winds will permit. By using these Precautions you will be sure of either getting quite through the Straits in one Tide or to the Southward of Success Bay; and it may be more Prudent to put in there should the wind be Southerly, than to attempt to weather Staten Land with a Lee Wind and Current, for I believe this to be the Chief reason why Ships have run a Risk of being drove on that Island.

Strait Le Maire is formed on the West by part of Terra Del Fuego, and on the East by the West end of Staten Land or Island; its Length and Breadth is about 5 Leagues each; about the Middle of the Strait is Success Bay, on Terra Del Fuego side, and about a 1/4 of a League more to the Northwards is Port Maurice, a little Cove, before which we Anchored in 12 fathoms.

[Description of Strait of Le Maire.]

The Bay of Success is discovered immediately upon entring the Strait from the Northward; there is likewise a good Land Mark near the South head to know it by, which is a Mark on the land like a lane or broad road leading up from the Sea into the Country; this Bay is 1/2 a League Wide at the Entrance, and lies in West 2 1/2 Miles, and hath good Anchorage in every part of it, in 10, 8, and 7 fathoms clear ground, and affords plenty of exceeding good Wood and Water. The Wood is of the Birch kind, but of a diffrent Quality to that in England or North America; here are likewise of the Winter Bark tree and some few others, Wild Selary, some Berrys like Cranberrys, but growing on Bushes, very few Wild Fowls of any Sort, and no Fish Except Shell Fish, such as Muscels, Limpets, etc.; and what we saw of the interior parts of the Country is still more barren of the necessarys of Life than the Sea. The few days we stay'd here we had constant bad weather, the Winds from the South-West and West-South-West with rain, Hail and Snow. Snow generally fell on the Hills everywhere with these winds when we had rain in the Bay or upon the Sea Coast. I observed the same in respect to Staten Land, but as it never froze it did not lay long; yet it must render the Country Cold and barren, and unfit for Cultivation. The Tides in Success Bay flows at the full and Change of the Moon, about 4 or 5 o'Clock, and riseth between 5 and 6 feet Perpendicular, but in the Strait the flood runs 2 or 3 Hours longer, and there the Ebb or Southerly Current runs near Double the strength of the Flood or Northerly Current.

Staten Island lies nearest East and West, and from what I could see and judge of it may be about 12 Leagues in length and 5 in breadth. On the North side are the appearances of Bays or Harbours, and the land is not destitute of Wood and Verdure, nor covered with Snow any more than Terra del Fuego.

On the South-West side of the Cape of good Success (which forms the South-West entrance of Strait Le Mair, and is known by some rocks off it) lies Valentine's Bay, the entrance of which we only saw. From this Bay the land Trends to the West-South-West; for 20 or 30 Leagues it appears High and Mountainous, and forms several Bays and inlets South-West 1/2 South 14 Leagues from the Cape of good Success, and 2 or 3 Leagues from the Shore lies New Island; it is 2 leagues in length, North-East and South-West, the North-East end is terminated by a remarkable Hillock. South-West 7 Leagues from New Island lies the Isle Evouts, and South, a little Westerly from this island, lies Barnevelts, two small flatt Islands close to each other; they are partly Environ'd with rocks of Different height above water, and lay

South-West 24 leagues from Strait le Mair. From Barnevelts Island to the South-East point of Hermites island is South-West by South, distance 3 Leagues. These Islands lay South-East and North-West, and are pretty high, and will, from most points of view, be taken for one Island or a part of the Main; from the South-East point of Hermites Isles to Cape Horn, the Course is South-West by South, distance 3 Leagues. The Appearance of this Cape and Hermites Islands is represented in the last View in the chart which I have drawn of this Coast from our first making the land unto Cape Horn, in which is included Strait Le Mair and part of Staten Land. In this chart I have laid down no land nor figured out any Shore, but what I saw myself and thus far the Chart may be depended upon. The Bays and inlets are left voide, the openings of which we only see from the Ship. It cannot be doubted but what there is Anchorage, Wood and Water in those Bays, and it must have been in some of them that the Dutch Squadron commanded by Hermites put into in the year 1624. It was the Vice Admiral Chapenham, of this Squadron, who first discovered that the land of Cape Horn was consisted of a Number of Islands, but the account they have given of those parts is very short and imperfect, and that of Schouton and Le Maire still worse, that it is no wonder that the Charts hitherto published should be found incorrect, not only in laying down the Land, but in the Latitude and Longitude of the places they contain, but I can now venture to Assert that the Longitude of few parts of the World are better Ascertained than that of Strait Le Maire and Cape Horn, being determined by several Observations of the Sun and moon made both by myself and Mr. Green, the Astronomer.

We found the Variation of the Compass on this Coast to be from 23 to 25 degrees east, except near Barnevelts Islands and Cape Horn, where we found it less and unsettled; it is likely that it is here disturbed by the land, as the Dutch Squadron before mentioned found in this very place all their Compasses to differ from each other. The declination of the South point of the Dipping Needle when set up ashore in Success Bay was 68 degrees 15 minutes below the horizon. Between Strait Le Maire and Cape Horn we found a Current setting generally pretty strong to the North-East when we were in with the Shore, but when 15 or 20 Leagues off we were not sencible of any.

REMARKABLE OCCURRENCES IN JANUARY 1769. SOUTH SEAS.

[Off Cape Horn.]

Thursday, 26th. Fresh Gales and thick Hazey weather, with small rain. At 2 p.m., the weather clearing up a little, saw Cape Horn bearing West-South-West, distance about 6 leagues, and from which I take my departure. Its Latitude and Longitude have before been taken notice of. Wind South-West by West to West-North-West; course South 15 degrees West; distance, 63 miles; latitude 56 degrees 57 minutes South; longitude 68 degrees 13 minutes West; at noon, Cape Horn North, 58 miles.

Friday, 27th. First part, moderate breezes and thick Hazey weather; the Middle, fair and Cloudy; and the Latter, fresh Gales with some rain. At 8 a.m. took two Setts of Observations of the sun and moon; the first gave 68 degrees 15 minutes; the second, 68 degrees 9 minutes; the Mean of the 2 is 68 degrees 12 minutes West. The Longitude of the Ship at Noon by these Observations is 68 degrees 42 minutes less 14 minutes, the Longitude made from Cape Horn, equal to 68 degrees 28 minutes, the longitude of Cape Horn according to the Observation. A Great many large Albetrosses about the Ship. Wind, South-West, West and North; course, South and West; distance, 32 miles; latitude 57 degrees 2 minutes South, longitude 68 degrees 27 minutes West.

Saturday, 28th. Fresh Gales the most part of this day; first and Middle parts cloudy; latter, clear with a Sharp cold air. At 2 p.m. saw the land, bearing North, distant about 8 Leagues; it made in 2 Hummocks, and appeared to be an Island, which I take to be the Isle of Diego Ramirez. It lays in the Latitude of 56 degrees 38 minutes South and Longitude 68 degrees 47 minutes West from Greenwich.* (* Diego Ramirez is in 56 degrees 31 minutes South, 68 degrees 43 minutes West.) Found the Variation this Evening to be 22 degrees East. A.M. had 3 sets of Observations of the sun and moon, which gave the Longitude 69 degrees 7 minutes 15 seconds West. The Longitude of the Ship at Noon by the Observation is 69 degrees 24 minutes, from which take 1 degree 48 minutes, the longitude made from Cape Horn, the remainder is 67 degrees 36 minutes, the Longitude of the Cape, which is 52 minutes less than the result of Yesterday's Observations.* (* This was the best observation.) This difference may arise partly from the Observations and partly from the Ship's runs; the mean of the 2 gives 68 degrees 2 minutes and 68 degrees 24 minutes, the Longitude of the Cape from the Observations taken at Strait Maire 136 degrees 26 minutes/2 = 68 degrees 13 minutes West from Greenwich. The Longitude of Cape Horn being deduced from no less than 24 Observations taken at no very great distance from the Cape, and on both sides of it, and when the Sun was both to the East and West of the Moon; for in this case the Errors arising from the Observations are most likely to Correct one another. Wind, North and West by North to North-West by West; course, South 39 degrees West; distance, 80 miles; latitude 58 degrees 4 minutes South, longitude 70 degrees 1 minute West.

Sunday, 29th. First and Latter parts, fresh Gales and Squally, with flying Showers of rain and Hail; the Middle, strong Gales with heavy Squalls and showers of rain. At 8 p.m. took 2nd Reef Topsails, at 6 a.m. Close reefd the Foretopsails and took in the Mizen Topsl, and at 10 set it again and let the reef out of the Fore top-sails. Wind, West Northerly; course South-West;

distance, 79 miles; latitude 59 degrees 0 minutes South, longitude 72 degrees 48 minutes West.

Monday, 30th. Fore part, fresh Gales and Squally with Hail and rain, remainder moderate and Cloudy. At 6 a.m. loosed the 2nd reef out of the Topsails and set Top-gallant Sails. At 11 Longitude per 3 sets of Observations of the sun and moon, 1st set 73 degrees 38 minutes 15 seconds; second set 73 degrees 25 minutes 45 seconds; and 3rd, 73 degrees 19 minutes 30 seconds; the mean of the whole is 73 degrees 27 minutes 50 seconds West, and 35 minutes less than the Longitude by Dead reckoning, which is only 6 Leagues in this Latitude, and therefore not worth taking notice of. Latitude per Observation 60 degrees 4 minutes South. Wind West by North and West-North-West; course, South 33 degrees West; distance, 76 miles; latitude 60 degrees 4 minutes South, longitude 74 degrees 10 minutes West.

Tuesday, 31st. First part moderate and Cloudy, with some rain; in the night, little wind and Calm; towards Noon, fresh Gales and Cloudy. Between 7 and 8 p.m., being then in the Latitude of 60 degrees 10 minutes, which was the farthest south we were, and in the Longitude of 74 degrees 30 minutes found the Variation of the Compass by the mean of Azimuth to be 27 degrees 9 minutes East. At 3 a.m. wind at East-South-East, and Moderate breeze. Set the Steeringsails, and soon after 2 Birds like Penguins were seen by the Mate of the Watch. Wind West-North-West, calm, East-South-East, South-South-East; course North 71 degrees West; distance, 55 miles; latitude 59 degrees 46 minutes South, longitude 75 degrees 54 minutes West.

[February 1769.]

Wednesday, February 1st. First part, fresh Gales; latter, light Airs and Cloudy; P.M. found the Variation by several Azimuth to be 24 degrees 53 minutes East. At Noon sounded, but had no ground with 240 fathoms of line; hoisted a Boat out to try if there was any Current, but found none. The weather was such as to admit Mr. Banks to row round the Ship in a Lighterman's Skiff shooting birds. Wind, South-East by East, South-South-East, East; course, North-West by West; distance, 106 miles; latitude 58 degrees 46 minutes South, longitude 78 degrees 42 minutes West.

Thursday, 2nd. First part, light breezes and Cloudy; remainder, sometimes a fresh breeze and at other times little wind and hazey, rainy, Cold weather. Took in the Steeringsls and a reef in each Topsail. Wind variable, North-North-West, South-West and South; course, West by North; distance, 82 miles; latitude 58 degrees 30 minutes South, longitude 80 degrees 58 minutes West.

Friday, 3rd. Calm and Light Airs, and for the most part Cloudy and sometimes drizling rain. Variation 24 degrees 4 minutes East. Wind, West by

North, North-West by West; course South 82 West; distance 30 miles; latitude 58 degrees 33 minutes South, longitude 81 degrees 55 minutes West.

Saturday, 4th. Fore and Middle parts, little wind and dark cloudy weather; latter, fresh Gales and Cloudy with some rain. P.M. had a Boat out and Shott several sorts of Birds, one of which was an Albetross as large as a Goose, whose wings when Extended measured 10 feet 2 inches; this was grey, but there are of them all White except the very tip end of their Wings. Another sort, in size between an Albetross and a large Gull, of a grey Colour, with a white Spot above their Tail about the Breadth of one's hand, and several other sorts. Wind Westerly; course North 13 degrees West; distance 48 miles; latitude 57 degrees 45 minutes South, longitude 82 degrees 16 minutes West.

Sunday, 5th. Fresh gales with heavy squalls the first part; remainder, little wind and Cloudy. Very cold weather. Wind, West-South-West, West by North and South-West by West; course North; distance 49 miles; latitude 56 degrees 46 minutes South, longitude 82 degrees 16 minutes West.

Monday, 6th. A moderate breeze of Wind with some flying showers of hail and rain; close upon a Wind all this day. Wind South-West by West to West by North; course North 1/4 East; distance 86 miles; latitude 55 degrees 20 minutes South, longitude 82 degrees 23 minutes West.

Tuesday, 7th. A fresh breeze and dark cloudy weather, with some showers of rain; the wind, varying from West to North by West, obliged us to Tack several times. Wind North-West by West, West by South; course North 20 degrees West; distance 46 miles; latitude 54 degrees 40 minutes South, longitude 82 degrees 54 minutes West.

Wednesday, 8th. First part, cloudy with Squalls of wind and Showers of rain and hail; Latter part thick hazey weather, with frequent Showers. Wind, Westerly, South by West; course North 14 degrees 43 minutes West; distance 58 miles; latitude 53 degrees 36 minutes South, longitude 83 degrees 19 minutes West.

Thursday, 9th. Fresh gales all this day, sometimes squally with rain; under Double-reef Topsails in the night, and Single-reeft Topsail in the day. Wind Southerly; course North 55 degrees West: distance 130 miles; latitude 52 degrees 22 minutes South, longitude 86 degrees 17 minutes West.

Friday, 10th. The former part of this day had fresh breezes and Dark cloudy weather; in the night hard Squalls with rain, and afterwards hazy, rainy weather. Wind Westerly; course North 22 degrees West; distance 67 miles; latitude 51 degrees 16 minutes South, longitude 86 degrees 37 minutes West.

Saturday, 11th. Former part Light Airs with drizling rain; remainder, a Moderate breeze and Cloudy. Wind, variable, southerly; course, North 54 degrees West; distance 36 miles; latitude 50 degrees 55 minutes South, longitude 87 degrees 24 minutes West.

Sunday, 12th. First and Middle parts, fresh gales and cloudy; latter, little wind and clear. Having for some time past generally found the Ship by Observation to the Northward of the Log, which is not owing to a Current as I at first imagined, but to a wrong Division of the Log line, being 2 1/2 feet in each Knot--but this is now rectified. Wind South-West by South; course North 48 degrees West; distance 113 miles; latitude 49 degrees 41 minutes South, longitude 89 degrees 36 minutes West.

Monday, 13th. The first part of these 24 Hours, moderate breezes and Cloudy; remainder, fresh Gales and cloudy. P.M saw a great many Albetrosses and other Birds about the Ship; some were all white and about the size of Teal. Took several Observations of the sun and moon, the result of which gave 90 degrees 13 minutes West Longitude from Greenwich. The Variation of the Compass by the Mean of several Azimuths 17 degrees East. The Longitude by account is less than that by Observation, 37 minutes, which is about 20 Miles in these high Latitudes, and nearly equal to the Error of the Log line before mentioned. This near Agreement of the 2 Longitudes proves to a Demonstration that we have had no Western Current since we left the Land. Wind West, Northerly; course North 75 degrees West; distance 35 miles; latitude 49 degrees 35 minutes, longitude 90 degrees 37 minutes.

[Remarks on Passage round Cape Horn.]

From the Foregoing observations it will appear that we are now advanced about 12 degrees to the westward of the Strait of Magellan, and 3 1/2 degrees to the Northward of it, having been 33* (* N.B. 23 days only from Success Bay.) days in Doubling Cape Horn or the Land of Terra del Fuego, and Arriving into the Degree of Latitude and Longitude we are now in, and without being brought once under our close Reef'd Topsails since we left Strait Le Maire, a Circumstance that perhaps never hapned before to any ship in those Seas so much dreaded for Hard gales of Wind; in so much that the doubling of Cape Horn is thought by some to be a mighty thing, and others to this day prefer the Straits of Magellan. As I have never been in those Straits I can only form my Judgement on a Carefull Comparison of the Different Ships' Journals that have passed them, and those that have sail'd round Cape Horn, particularly the Dolphin's two last Voyages and this of ours, being made at the same season of the Year, when one may reasonable expect the same Winds to prevail. The Dolphin in her last Voyage was three Months in getting through the Straits, not reckoning the time she lay in Port Famine; and I am firmly perswaided from the Winds we have had, that had we come by that Passage we should not have been in these Seas, besides the fatiguing of our People, the damage we must have done to our Anchors, Cables, Sails, and Rigging, none of which have suffer'd in our passage round Cape Horn.

From what I have said it will appear that I am no advocate for the Straits of Magellan, but it should be expected that I should say something of Strait le Mair, through which we passed, and this is the more incumbant on me as it was by choice and contrary to the Advice given by Mr. Walter, the ingenious Author of Lord Anson's Voyage, who advised all Ships not to go through this Strait but to go to the Eastward of Staten Land, and likewise to stand to the Southward as far as 61 or 62 degrees south before any Endeavour is made to get to the Westward. With respect to the Passing of Strait le Mair or going round Staten Land, I look upon of little Consequence, and either one or the other to be pursued according to Circumstances; for if you happen to fall in with the land to the Westward of the Strait, and the winds favourable for going through, it certainly must be a piece of folly to lose time in going round Staten Land, for by paying a little Attention to the Directions I have already given no ill Consequences can attend; but on the Contrary if you should fall in with the land to the eastward of the Straits or the wind should prove Boisterous, or unfavourable, in any of these Cases the going to the eastward of Staten Land is the most Advisable. And next, as to running into the Latitude of 61 or 62 degrees South before any Endeavour is made to get to the Westward, is what I think no man will ever do that can avoid it, for it cannot be supposed that anyone will steer south mearly to get into a high Latitude, when at the same time he can steer west, for it is not Southing but Westing that is wanting. But this way you cannot Steer because the Wind blows almost Constantly from that Quarter, so that you have no other Choice but to stand to the Southward, close upon a Wind, and by keeping upon that Tack you not only make Southing but Westing also, and sometimes not a little when the wind Varies to the Northward of West; and the farther you advance to the Southward the better Chance you have of having the Winds from that Quarter or Easterly, and likewise of meeting with finer weather, both of which we ourselves Experienced. Prudence will direct every man when in those high Latitudes to make sure of sufficient Westing to double all the lands before he thinks of standing to the Northward. When the winds was Westerly the Mountains on Terra Del Fuego were generally covered with dense Clouds, formed, as one may reasonably suppose, by Westerly Exhalations and by Vapours brought thither by the Westerly winds. From that Quarter come frequent Showers of rain, hail, and Snow; and after we had left the land and were standing to the Southward, with the winds westerly, dark dence clouds were Continually forming in the Horizon, and rose to about 45 degrees, where they began to dissipate. These were generally attended with Showers of Rain, or hail, and Squals of Wind, but as we advanced to the Southward, these Clouds became less dence, and in the Latitude of 60 degrees 10 minutes, when we got the winds Easterly, the weather was more serene and Milder; again as we advanced to the Northward we had a constant Clouded sky and dark gloomy weather, the whole time exceeding Cold.

[Cape Horn to Tahiti.]

Tuesday, 14th. The first part, fresh Gales and Hazey with rain; the remainder moderate and Cloudy, with frequent rain. Wind, Westerly, South; course South-West; distance 32 miles; latitude 49 degrees 6 minutes South, longitude 91 degrees 12 minutes West.

Wednesday, 15th. Little wind and Cloudy the most part of this day. Variation per Azimuth in the Evening 12 degrees East, and in the morning both by an Amplitude and an Azimuth 11 degrees East. A.M. Shifted the Mainsail, Mizen, Fore, and Main topsail. Wind, South-South-West, South-West, West by North; course North 46 degrees West; distance 86 miles; latitude 48 degrees 27 minutes South, longitude 92 degrees 5 minutes West.

Thursday, 16th. The first part of this day had fresh Gales and Cloudy; in the night thick hazey weather with heavy squalls of wind and rain, which obliged us to close-reef our Topsails. In the morning and all the forenoon had strong gales and cloudy weather, and very heavy Seas from the South-South-West, one of which broke upon the Quarter and carried away the Driver Boom. Wind North-West, West, and South; course North 74 degrees West; distance 97 miles; latitude 48 degrees 0 minutes South, longitude 94 degrees 25 minutes West.

Friday, 17th. Strong Gales and Cloudy the most part of this day. Split the Maintopsail and unbent it, and bent another. Wind South-South-West; course North-West by West 1/2 West; distance 132 miles; latitude 46 degrees 48 minutes South, longitude 97 degrees 17 minutes West.

Saturday, 18th. Fresh gales all this day. The weather Variable, sometimes fair and Cloudy, other times hazey, with drizzling rain. Saw some Birds nearly as big as Albetrosses; they were all black, with Yellow Beaks. Wind South-West by West; course North 32 degrees 30 minutes West; distance 140 miles; latitude 44 degrees 50 minutes South, longitude 99 degrees 7 minutes West.

Sunday, 19th. First part, fresh Gales and Hazey; the Middle part, hazey, with drizling rain; the latter, gentle breezes and fine Clear weather, yet the Air is still Cold. Wind South-West by West to West by South; course North-North-West 3/4 West; distance 103 miles; latitude 43 degrees 21 minutes South, longitude 100 degrees 21 minutes West.

Monday, 20th. Moderate breezes and fine weather the greater part of this day, and the Sea very smooth. Found by repeated trials that the South point of the Dipping Needle Dip'd 65 degrees 52 minutes below the Horizon.

Wind Westerly; course South 65 degrees West; distance 58 miles; latitude 43 degrees 46 minutes South, longitude 101 degrees 34 minutes West.

Tuesday, 21st. Fresh breezes and pretty Clear weather. Variation 6 degrees 30 minutes East. Wind North-West; course South 62 degrees West; distance 115 miles; latitude 44 degrees 39 minutes South, longitude 103 degrees 54 minutes West.

Wednesday, 22nd. Hazey, rainy weather the most part of this Day. Wind North-Westerly; course South 86 degrees West; distance 91 miles; latitude 44 degrees 46 minutes South, longitude 106 degrees 1 minute West.

Thursday, 23rd. Little wind and Calm, and some Lightning, a thing we have not seen for some time past, and therefore suppose not common in these Seas in high Latitudes. Variation 5 degrees 34 minutes East. Wind North-West, calm; course North 30 degrees East; distance 13 miles; latitude 44 degrees 35 minutes South, longitude 105 degrees 52 minutes West.

Friday, 24th. First part, Calm; Middle, light breezes; latter, fresh breezes and hazey. P.M. had several Azimuths, all of which gave the Variation less than 4 degrees East, but they were a little doubtful on account of the Rowling of the Ship. What winds we have had this day hath been from the Eastward, and are the first we have had from that Quarter since we left the Latitude 58 degrees 46 minutes. Wind calm, East-North-East and East-South-East; course North 42 degrees 45 minutes West; distance 79 miles: latitude 43 degrees 37 minutes South, longitude 107 degrees 6 minutes West.

Saturday, 25th. First and Middle parts, fresh Gales and Cloudy, with some rain; the Latter, little Wind and Cloudy. Wind South-East by East, South-South-East; course North 48 degrees 30 minutes West; distance 112 miles; latitude 42 degrees 23 minutes South, longitude 109 degrees 0 minutes West.

Sunday, 26th. First part, Calm and light Airs; remainder, very strong gales and Squally, with Showers of rain, which at length brought us under our two Courses, and close-reefed Maintopsail. Wind calm, North-West and West-South-West; course North 26 degrees 15 minutes West; distance 88 miles; latitude 41 degrees 4 minutes South, longitude 109 degrees 52 minutes West.

Monday, 27th. First part, Strong Gales and Cloudy; the remainder, Gentle Breezes and clear weather. P.M. set the topsail one Reef out. A large swell from the South-West. Wind westerly; course North 18 degrees West; distance 85 miles; latitude 39 degrees 43 minutes South, 110 degrees 26 minutes West.

Tuesday, 28th. The former part little wind and fine clear weather; the Air full as warm as in the same Degree of North Latitude at the Correspondent Season of the Year. The South-West swells still keep up, notwithstanding the

Gale hath been over about 30 Hours, a proof that there is no land near in that Quarter.* (* These are instances of Cook's observation and seamanlike perspicacity. The prevailing belief of the time was in a great southern continent.) The remainder part of this day fresh breezes and clear. At 9 a.m. took 3 Sets of Observations of the sun and moon in order to find the Longitude of the Ship. Wind West to North-West; course North 13 degrees West; distance 42 miles; latitude 39 degrees 33 minutes 30 seconds South, longitude 110 degrees 38 minutes West.

[March 1769.]

Wednesday, March 1st. First part fresh breezes, the remainder moderate breezes and clear weather. The result of the Forementioned Observations gives 110 degrees 33 minutes West Longitude from Greenwich, and exactly agrees with the Longitude given by the Log from Cape Horn. This Agreement of the two Longitudes after a Run of 660 leagues is surprizing, and much more than could be expected; but, as it is so, it serves to prove, as well as the repeated trials we have made when the weather would permit, that we have had no Current that hath Affected the Ship since we came into these Seas. This must be a great Sign that we have been near no land of any extent, because near land are generally found Currents. It is well known that on the East side of the Continent in the North Sea we meet with Currents above 100 Leagues from the Land, and even in the Middle of the Atlantic Ocean, between Africa and America, are always found Currents; and I can see no reason why Currents should not be found in this Sea, supposing a Continent or lands lay not far West from us, as some have imaggin'd, and if such land was ever seen we cannot be far from it, as we are now 560 leagues West of the Coast of Chili.* (* These are instances of Cook's observation and seamanlike perspicacity. The prevailing belief of the time was in a great southern continent.) Wind West by South; course North 76 degrees West; distance 52 miles; latitude 38 degrees 44 minutes South, longitude 111 degrees 43 minutes West; at noon, Cape Horn South 60 degrees East 660 leagues.

Thursday, 2nd. Former part, fresh gales and hazey, with much rain; the remainder, a Strong fresh gale and pretty clear weather. Wind Westerly; course North by West; distance 87 miles; latitude 37 degrees 16 minutes South, longitude 112 degrees 5 minutes West.

Friday, 3rd. First part, moderate breezes; remainder, calm and clear weather. A.M. employed filling salt Water in the Fore Hold and airing all the Spare Sails. Wind West, calm; course North 17 degrees East; distance 31 miles; latitude 36 degrees 49 minutes South, longitude 111 degrees 34 minutes West.

Saturday, 4th. First part, Calm; remainder, a fine genteel breeze and clear weather. Variation per Azimuth and Amplitude this Evening 2 degrees 26 minutes East. The South-West swell still keeps up, notwithstanding it hath been Calm 24 hours. Wind calm, North-East, North; course North 50 degrees West; distance 58 miles; latitude 36 degrees 12 minutes South, longitude 112 degrees 50 minutes West.

Sunday, 5th. First and latter parts, fine Clear weather; the Middle, fresh gales and Hazey, with rain. Wind North-West by North and North-West; course South 81 degrees 40 minutes West; distance 64 miles; latitude 36 degrees 21 minutes South, longitude 114 degrees 9 minutes West.

Monday, 6th. Moderate breezes and Tolerable clear weather all this day. The wind a little Variable, which caused us to Tack several Times. Wind North-West by North to West-North-West; course South 57 degrees West; distance 20 miles; latitude 36 degrees 32 minutes South, longitude 114 degrees 30 minutes West.

Tuesday, 7th. A Moderate steady breeze and clear weather. Wind North-West; course South 64 degrees 15 minutes West; distance, 83 miles; latitude 37 degrees 8 minutes South, longitude 116 degrees 8 minutes West.

Wednesday, 8th. The first and Middle parts moderate breezes and Cloudy; the Latter Part Variable winds and much Rain. Wind North-West, variable; course South 78 degrees West; distance, 76 miles; latitude 37 degrees 24 minutes South, longitude 117 degrees 41 minutes West.

Thursday, 9th. First part, moderate and Hazey, with Drizling rain; the remainder fresh breezes and clear weather. Variation 4 degrees 41 minutes east. Wind South-West by West to South by East; course North 38 degrees West; distance 123 miles; latitude 35 degrees 47 minutes South, longitude 119 degrees 18 minutes West.

Friday, 10th. Moderate breezes and fine Pleasant weather. Wind South-East; course North 40 degrees West; distance 121 miles; latitude 34 degrees 14 minutes South, longitude 120 degrees 54 minutes West.

Saturday, 11th. A Steady gale and fine weather. Variation 4 degrees 12 minutes East. Wind South-East; course North 46 degrees 15 minutes West; distance 116 miles; latitude 32 degrees 54 minutes South, longitude 122 degrees 35 minutes West.

Sunday, 12th. Ditto weather. Variation 4 degrees 12 minutes East. Put the Ship's Company to three Watches, they having been at Watch and Watch since our first arrival on the coast of Terra del Fuego. Wind South-East; course North 49 degrees West; distance 122 miles; latitude 31 degrees 34 minutes South, longitude 124 degrees 25 minutes West.

Monday, 13th. First part a Steady, fresh Gale; the remainder, little wind and fine Clear weather. Wind South-East; course North 48 degrees 15 minutes West; distance 72 miles; latitude 30 degrees 46 minutes South, longitude 125 degrees 28 minutes West.

Tuesday, 14th. Little wind and fine Pleasant weather. At 3 p.m. took several Observations of the sun and moon; the mean result of which gave 126 degrees 20 minutes 45 seconds, the Longitude of the Ship West of Greenwich, and is 47 degrees Longitude West of account carried on from Cape Horn. Wind South, East-South-East, East-North-East; course North 50 degrees West; distance 47 miles; latitude 30 degrees 17 minutes South, longitude 126 degrees 10 minutes West.

Wednesday, 15th. Light breezes and clear weather. Variation, p.m. 3 degrees 45 minutes East, a.m. 3 degrees 22 minutes East. Saw a Tropic Bird. Wind, East-North-East and East-South-East; course, North 47 degrees 15 minutes West; distance, 50 miles; latitude 29 degrees 43 minutes South, longitude 126 degrees 53 minutes West.

Thursday, 16th. Light Airs next to a Calm and clear Weather. Variation by the mean result of 21 Azimuths, 1 degree 30 minutes East. This evening observed an Occultation of h by the [crescent],* (* h is Saturn, [crescent] the Moon.) Immersion at ---- hours ---- minutes and Emersion at ---- hours ---- minutes ---- seconds a.m.* (* Blanks in manuscript.) Variation per several Azimuths 2 degrees East. Wind East-South-East, South-South-East, South-West; course North-North-West; distance 34 miles; latitude 29 degrees 22 minutes South, longitude 127 degrees 8 minutes West.

Friday, 17th. Little wind and fine Pleasant weather. Variation, p.m. 3 degrees 27 minutes East. Wind, South-East by South; course, North 20 degrees West; distance, 55 miles; latitude 28 degrees 30 minutes South, longitude 127 degrees 29 minutes West.

Saturday, 18th. First part, little wind and Cloudy; latter, fresh gales and hard Squalls, with much rain. Took 2 Reefs in the Topsails. Wind North-East North; course North 60 degrees 45 minutes West; distance 78 miles; latitude 27 degrees 52 minutes South, longitude 128 degrees 44 minutes West.

Sunday, 19th. First part fresh Gales and Squally, with rain; remainder more moderate and cloudy. Variation, a.m. per Means of several Azimuths, 3 degrees 14 minutes East. Loosed the 2d reefs out of the Topsails. Wind between the North and West; course North 52 degrees West; distance 50 miles; latitude 27 degrees 21 minutes South, longitude 129 degrees 28 minutes West.

Monday, 20th. A Fine breeze and pleasant weather. Saw several Tropic Birds. Wind West; course North; distance 95 miles; latitude 25 degrees 44 minutes South, longitude 129 degrees 28 minutes West.

Tuesday, 21st. First part little wind, the remainder Calm. Variation, 3 degrees 43 minutes East. Saw some rock weed and a great many Tropic Birds. Wind West by North, calm; course North; distance 23 miles; latitude 25 degrees 21 minutes South, longitude 129 degrees 28 minutes West.

Wednesday, 22nd. First part Calm, in the night Squally, with rain. A.M. a fresh breeze and Cloudy. Variation per Amplitude 3 degrees 10 minutes East. Saw some Egg Birds. Wind North by East to North-North-West; course West; distance 57 miles; latitude 25 degrees 21 minutes South, longitude 129 degrees 52 minutes West.

Thursday, 23rd. Fresh gales and Squally, with rain, the first part; remainder fresh Gales and Cloudy. P.M. saw some Men-of-War Birds, and Egg Birds, and in the Morning saw more Egg Birds and Tropic Birds. The Man-of-War and Tropic Birds are pretty well known, but the Egg Bird (as it is called in the Dolphin's Journal) requires some discription to know it by that Name. It is a small slender Bird of the Gull kind, and all white, and not much unlike the small white Gulls we have in England, only not so big.* (* Terns.) There are also Birds in Newfoundland called Stearings that are of the same shape and Bigness, only they are of a Greyish Colour. These Birds were called by the Dolphin Egg Birds on account of their being like those known by that name by Sailors in the Gulph of Florida; neither they nor the Man-of-War Birds are ever reckoned to go very far from Land. Wind North by West to West by North: course North 13 degrees West; distance 49 miles; latitude 24 degrees 43 minutes South, longitude 130 degrees 8 minutes West.

[Passing Low Archipelago.]

Friday, 24th. Fresh Gales and Cloudy, with some rain in the forepart of this day. All the forepart of these 24 hours the Sea was smooth, but at 12 at night it was more so, and about 3 in the Morning one of the people saw, or thought he saw, a Log of Wood pass the Ship. This made us think that we were near some land,* (* The Endeavour was now passing to the northward of the easternmost islands of the Paumotu or Low Archipelago, though out of sight of them.) but at daylight we saw not the least appearance of any, and I did not think myself at liberty to spend time in searching for what I was not sure to find, although I thought myself not far from those Islands discovered by Quiros in 1606; and very probably we were not, from the birds, etc., we have seen for these 2 or 3 days past. Wind West-North-West to North-West; course North-East by North 1/4 East; distance 99 miles; latitude 22 degrees 23 minutes South, longitude 129 degrees 2 minutes West.

Saturday, 25th. First part dark cloudy weather, with rain and a fresh breeze of wind; remainder fair and Cloudy. Wind North-West by North, to West by North; course North-East 1/2 North; distance 95 miles; latitude 22 degrees 11 minutes South, longitude 127 degrees 55 minutes West.

Sunday, 26th. Squally weather, with rain. At 5 p.m. saw some sea Weed pass the Ship, and at 7 William Greenslade, Marine, either by Accident or design, went overboard and was Drowned. The following circumstances makes it appear as tho' it was done design'dly. He had been Centinel at the Steerage door between 12 and 4 o'clock, where he had taken part of a Seal Skin put under his charge, and which was found upon him. The other Marines thought themselves hurt by one of their party commiting a crime of this nature, and he being a raw young fellow, and, as very probable, made him resolve upon commiting this rash Action, for the Serjeant not being willing that it should pass over unknown to me, was about 7 o'clock going to bring him aft and have it inquired into, when he gave him the Slip between Decks, and was seen to go upon the Forecastle, and from that time was seen no more. I was neither made acquainted with the Theft or the Circumstances attending it, until the Man was gone. Wind, North-West to West; longitude 127 degrees 43 minutes West.

Monday, 27th. Variable winds and weather, with frequent showers of rain. At Noon saw a Bird like a Gannet. Wind variable; course North 1/4 East; distance 30 miles; latitude 21 degrees 2 minutes South, longitude 127 degrees 38 minutes West.

Tuesday, 28th. Little wind and Cloudy. Variation per Amplitude 3 degrees 56 minutes East. Wind Easterly; course North-North-West; distance 37 miles; latitude 20 degrees 38 minutes South, longitude 127 degrees 50 minutes West.

Wednesday, 29th. Little winds and Cloudy weather. Variation per Azimuth 2 degrees 27 minutes East. Saw a Bird like a Dove and several fish about the Ship. Employed worming the Best Br. Cable, repairing and Painting the Boats. Wind Easterly; course North 75 degrees West; distance 50 miles; latitude 20 degrees 14 minutes South, longitude 129 degrees 27 minutes West.

Thursday, 30th. First part, Calm and close Cloudy weather; in the night had Variable winds and weather, with rain. A.M. Genteel Breezes and Cloudy weather. Between 10 and 11 a.m. took several Observations of the sun and moon; the mean result of them gave the Longitude of the Ship at Noon to be 127 degrees 38 minutes, and is 1 degree 49 minutes East of the Longitude given by the Log; but on the 4th Instant the ship by Observation was 47 minutes West of the Log, therefore she must have lost 2 degrees 36 minutes of the Log since the last Observation--an Error too great to be accounted for. Wind calm, variable, South-South-East; course North 40 degrees West; distance 53 miles; latitude 19 degrees 34 minutes South, longitude 129 degrees 27 minutes West.

Friday, 31st. A Steady breeze and fine pleasant weather. A.M. took several Observations of the sun and moon, the mean result of them came within 8 Miles of Yesterday's Observations computed both by Mr. Green and myself, and yet cannot think so great an error can have been committed in the ship's run in so short a time as these observations seem to point out, and therefore I shall abide by the Longitude given by the Log unless from subsequent Observations this error should be found to be just. Wind South; course North 75 degrees 45 minutes West; distance 111 miles; latitude 19 degrees 7 minutes South, longitude 131 degrees 21 minutes West.

[April 1769.]

Saturday, April 1st. A steady fresh Trade and fine Weather. Variation per several Azimuths 2 degrees 32 minutes East. Wind South-East to East 1/2 North; course West; distance 122 miles; latitude 19 degrees 7 minutes South, longitude 133 degrees 28 minutes West.

Sunday, 2nd. A fresh Trade wind and fine pleasant weather. At Noon saw a Large flock of Birds; they had brown backs and white Bellies. They fly and make a noise like Stearings, and are shaped like them, only something larger. Saw likewise some black Sheerwaters and Several Man-of-War birds. Wind East; course North 86 degrees 30 minutes West; distance 118 miles; latitude 19 degrees 0 minutes South, longitude 135 degrees 33 minutes West.

Monday, 3rd. First and Latter parts a steady fresh Breeze and cloudy; the Middle, sometimes squally with rain, at other times little wind. P.M. saw 2 Birds like Albetrosses; they were all white except the Tip of their wings and Tails. Wind East; course North 82 degrees 45 minutes West; distance 110 miles; latitude 18 degrees 46 minutes South, longitude 137 degrees 29 minutes West.

Tuesday, 4th. A Steady fresh Trade and clear weather. At 1/2 past 10 a.m. saw land bearing south, distance 3 or 4 Leagues. Haul'd up for it, and soon found it to be an Island of about 2 Leagues in Circuit and of an Oval form, with a Lagoon in the Middle, for which I named it Lagoon Island. The Border of land Circumscribing this Lagoon is in many places very low and narrow, particularly on the south side, where it is mostly a Beach or Reef of rocks; it is the same on the North side in 3 places, and these disjoins the firm land and make it appear like so many Islands covered with wood. On the West end of the Island is a large Tree which looks like a large Tower, and about the Middle of the Island are two Cocoa Nutt Trees that appears above all the other wood, which as we approached the Island looked very much like a flag.

We approached the north side of this Island within a Mile, and found no Bottom with 130 fathoms of line, nor did there appear to be Anchorage about it. We saw several of the Inhabitants, the most of them men, and these Marched along the shore abreast of the Ships with long Clubs in their hands as tho' they meant to oppose our landing. They were all naked except their Privy parts, and were of a Dark Copper Colour with long black Hair, but upon our leaving the Island some of them were seen to put on a Covering, and one or two we saw in the Skirts of the Wood was Cloathed in White; these we supposed to be Women. This Island lies in the Latitude of 18 degrees 47 minutes and Longitude 139 degrees 28 minutes West from the Meridian of Greenwich;* (* This island is Vahitahi, one of the Paumotu or Low Archipelago.) variation 2 degrees 54 minutes East. Wind East, East by South; course North 88 degrees West; distance 114 miles; latitude 18 degrees 42 minutes South, longitude 139 degrees 29 minutes West.

Wednesday, 5th. A fresh steady gale and fine weather. At 1 p.m. made Sail to the Westward, and at 1/2 past 3 saw land to the North-West, which we got up with at Sun sett and proved to be a low woody Island of a Circular form, and not much above a Mile in Compass. This Island I called Thrum Cap* (* Akiaki. It is inhabited.); it lies in the Latitude of 18 degrees 35 minutes South and in the Longitude of 139 degrees 48 minutes West from Greenwich, and North 62 degrees West, 7 Leagues from Lagoon Island. We saw no inhabitants, nor the appearance of any, and yet we were within 1/2 a Mile of the Shore. I observed by the Shore that it was near low Water, and at Lagoon Island I observed that it was either high Water or else there was no Ebbing and flowing of the Sea. From these Circumstances I infer that a South by East or South Moon makes high Water. Here we caught a King Fish, being the first fish we have got in these Seas. Wind East; course North 77 degrees 30 minutes West; distance 79 miles; latitude 18 degrees 25 minutes South, longitude 140 degrees 51 minutes West.

Thursday, 6th. A fresh Trade and fine Pleasant weather. At 3 p.m. Saw land to the Westward, which proved to be an Island of about 12 or 15 Leagues in Compass; is very low and entirely drown'd in the Middle, forming there a large lake, into which there appeared to be no inlet. The border of land and Reef surrounding this lake like a wall appeared to be of a Bow-like figure, for which reason I named it Bow Island. The South side, along which we sail'd, was one continued low narrow Beach or Reef like a Causeway for 4 Leagues and upwards, and lies East by North and West by South. The East and West Ends and North side of this Island are wooded-in Groves, and the firm Land appeared disjoined and like a Number of Islands, and very probably is so. The North-West parts of the Island we only saw aCross the Lake, and not very distinct on account of its great extent, and night coming on before we had run the whole length of the Island. This description must be imperfect, and the whole Island may form a Different figure to what I have here described.* (* Hao. It is a large atoll, thirty miles in length. Cook only saw a portion of it.) The east end lies in the Latitude of 18 degrees 23 minutes South, and Longitude 141 degrees 12 minutes West from Greenwich. Variation 5 degrees 38 minutes East. This Island is Inhabited; we not only saw smook in Different Parts, but people also. At Noon saw Land to the Westward. Wind east; course North 85 degrees West; distance 94 miles; latitude 18 degrees 19 minutes South, longitude 142 degrees 29 minutes West.

Friday, 7th. Fresh Gales and Cloudy. At 1/2 past 2 p.m. got up with the East end of the Land seen yesterday at Noon, and which proved to be an assemblage of Islands join'd together by Reef, and extending themselves North-West by North and South-East by South in 8 or 9 Leagues and of various breadths; but there appeared to be a total Seperation in the middle by a Channell of half a Mile broad, and on this account they are called the two Groups.* (* Marokau and Ravahare. Two atolls close together.) The South Eastermost of them lies in the Latitude of 18 degrees 12 minutes and Longitude of 142 degrees 42 minutes West from Greenwich, and West 1/2 North distant 25 Leagues from the West end of Bow Island. We ranged along the South-West side of this Island, and hauled into a Bay which lies to the North-West of the Southermost point of them, and where there appeared to be Anchorage and the Sea was smooth and not much Surf on the Shore; but we found no ground with 100 fathoms 3/4 of a Mile from the Shore, and nearer we did not go. Here several of the Inhabitants assembled together with their Canoes, with a design, as we thought, to come off to us, as they hauld one of them over the reef seemingly for that purpose; but after waiting near 1/2 an hour, and they not attempting to come, we bore away and made Sail, and presentley the Canoe put off after us; but, as we did not stop, they soon went back again. They were in all respects like those we had seen on Lagoon Island, and Armed with Clubs and long Pikes like them. At 1/2 past 6 a.m. Saw a small Island to the Northward, hauled our wind for it, and soon got close in with it. It is about 3 or 4 Miles in Circuit, and very low, with a Pond in the Middle. There is some wood upon it, but no inhabitants but Birds, and for this reason is called Bird Island.* (* Reitoru.) It lies in the latitude 17 degrees 48 minutes and longitude 143 degrees 35 minutes West, and West 1/2 North 10 Leagues from the West end of the two Groups. The birds we saw were Men-of-War Birds and several other sorts. Wind East; course North 66 degrees West; distance 66 miles; latitude 17 degrees 48 minutes South, longitude 143 degrees 31 minutes West.

Saturday, 8th. Fresh Trade and pleasant weather, but about noon had a few flying showers of rain. Variation 6 degrees 32 minutes East. Wind East by

South and East; course North 87 degrees West; distance 100 miles; latitude 17 degrees 43 minutes South, longitude 145 degrees 16 minutes West.

Sunday, 9th. A steady fresh gale and pleasant weather. At 2 p.m. saw Land to the Northward, hauld up for it, and found it to be a double range of low woody islands joined together by reefs, by which means they make one Island in form of an Ellipsis or Oval, in the Middle of which is a Salt water lake. The small Islands and reefs circumscribes or bounds this lake like a Chain; it is therefore called Chain Island.* (* Anaa.) It is in length, North-West and South-East, about 5 Leagues, and in breadth about 5 Miles. The middle of it lies in the Latitude of 17 degrees 23 minutes South, and Longitude 145 degrees 54 minutes West, and West by North 45 Leagues from Bird Island. Variation per Several Azimuths 4 degrees 54 minutes East. Wind East by North to North by East; course West, Northerly; distance 81 miles; latitude 17 degrees 42 minutes South, longitude 146 degrees 40 minutes West.

Monday, 10th. P.M. moderate breezes and cloudy; in the Night, dark, cloudy, unsettled weather, with very much Thunder, Lightning, and rain. A.M. little wind and fair. P.M. variation per Several Azimuths 5 degrees 41 minutes East. At 8 a.m. saw Osnaburg Island* (* Maitea, the easternmost of the Society Islands, which are all high, and a great contrast to the low coral atolls of the Paumotus.) (so called by Captain Wallis, the first discoverer) bearing North-West by West, distance 4 or 5 Leagues. It is a high round Island, and appears to be not above a League in Circuit, and when it bears as above it looks like a high Crown'd Hatt, but when it bears North the Top is more like the roof of a House. It lies in the Latitude of 17 degrees 48 minutes South and Longitude 148 degrees 10 minutes West, and West by South, 44 Leagues, from Chain Island. Wind North-North-West, variable, North-West by North; course South 13 degrees West; distance 67 miles; latitude 18 degrees 00 minutes South, longitude 147 degrees 47 minutes West; at noon, Osnaburg Island North by West 1/2 West, 5 leagues.

[Arrive at Tahiti.]

Tuesday, 11th. First part, little wind and cloudy; the remainder, little wind and very Variable; unsettled weather, with some rain. P.M. took several Observations of the sun and moon, which gave the Longitude of the ship to be 148 degrees 18 minutes West, and differs but little from that given by the Log. At 6 a.m. saw King George's Island* (* So named by Captain Wallis. The native name was ascertained by Cook, who spelt it Otaheite. Now known as Tahiti. It is the chief island of the Society Group, and was annexed by the French in 1844.) Extending from West by South 1/2 South to West by North 1/2 North. It appeared very high and Mountainous. Wind variable; course North 66 degrees West; distance 54 miles; latitude 17 degrees 38 minutes South, longitude 148 degrees 39 minutes West; Osnaburg Island East 1/2 South, 13 leagues.

Wednesday, 12th. Variable, light Airs all these 24 Hours, and Hot sultry weather. At 5 p.m. King George's Island extending from North-West by West to South-West, distance 6 or 7 Leagues; and at 6 a.m. it bore from South-South-West to West by North, being little wind with Calms. Several of the Natives came off to us in their Canoes, but more to look at us than anything else. We could not prevail with any of them to come on board, and some would not come near the ship. Wind variable; course West; distance 18 miles; latitude 17 degrees 38 minutes South, longitude 148 degrees 58 minutes West; at noon, King George's Island, from South to West by North, 5 leagues.

Thursday, 13th. The first part Cloudy and Squally, with Showers of rain; remainder, genteel breezes and clear weather. At 4 p.m. the North-East point of Royal Bay West 1/2 North; run under an easy sail all night, and had soundings from 22 to 12 fathoms 2 or 3 Miles from the Shore. At 5 a.m. made sail for the bay, and at 7 anchored in 13 fathoms.* (* Matavai Bay.) At this time we had but very few men upon the sick list, and these had but slite complaints. The Ship's company had in general been very healthy, owing in a great measure to the Sour kroutt, Portable Soup and Malt; the two first were served to the People, the one on Beef Days and the other on Banyan Days. Wort was made of the Malt, and at the discretion of the Surgeon given to every man that had the least simptoms of Scurvy upon him. By this means, and the Care and Vigilance of Mr. Monkhouse, the Surgeon, this disease was prevented from getting a footing in the Ship. The Sour Kroutt, the Men at first would not eat it, until I put it in practice--a method I never once Knew to fail with seamen--and this was to have some of it dressed every day for the Cabin Table, and permitted all the Officers, without exception, to make use of it, and left it to the Option of the men either to take as much as they pleased or none at all; but this practice was not continued above a Week before I found it necessary to put every one on board to an allowance; for such are the Tempers and disposition of Seamen in general that whatever you give them out of the common way--altho' it be ever so much for their good--it will not go down, and you will hear nothing but murmurings against the Man that first invented it; but the moment they see their superiors set a value upon it, it becomes the finest stuff in the world and the inventor an honest fellow. Wind easterly.

CHAPTER 3.
TAHITI.

REMARKABLE OCCURRENCES, ETC., AT GEORGE'S ISLAND.

[At Tahiti.]

NOTE. The way of reckoning the day in Sea Journals is from Noon to Noon, but as the most material transaction at this Island must hapen in the Day time, this method will be attended with ill conveniences in inserting the transactions of each day; for this reason I shall during our stay at this Island, but no longer, reckon the day according to the Civil account that is to begin and end at Midnight.

We had no sooner come to an Anchor in Royal Bay, as before-mentioned, than a great number of the Natives in their Canoes came off to the Ship and brought with them Cocoa Nuts, etc.; these they seem'd to set a great value upon. Amongst those that came off to the Ship was an elderly man whose Name was Owhaa, him the Gentlemen that had been here before in the Dolphin* (* Lieutenant Gore and Mr. Molineux, the Master.) knew and had often spoke of as one that had been of Service to them. This man (together with some others) I took on board and made much of, thinking that he might on some occasions be of use to us. As our stay at this place was not likely to be very short, I thought it very necessary that some order should be observed in Traficking with the Natives, that such Merchandize as we had on board for that purpose might continue to bear a proper value, and not leave it to everyone's own particular fancy, which could not fail to bring on Confusion and Quarrels between us and the Natives, and would infallibly lessen the value of such Articles as we had to trafick with. In Order to prevent this, the following rules were ordered to be Observed; viz.:--

Rules to be observed by every person in or belonging to His Majesty's Bark the Endeavour for the better Establishing a regular and uniform Trade for Provisions, etc., with the Inhabitants of George's Island:--

1. To endeavour by every fair means to Cultivate a Friendship with the Natives, and to treat them with all imaginable humanity.

2. A Proper Person or Persons will be appointed to Trade with the Natives for all manner of Provisions, Fruits, and other Productions of the Earth; and no Officer or Seaman or other person belonging to the Ship, excepting such as are so appointed, shall Trade or offer to Trade for any sort of Provisions, Fruit or other Productions of the Earth, unless they have my leave so to do.

3. Every Person employ'd on shore on any duty whatsoever is strictly to attend to the same, and if by neglect he looseth any of His Arms or working Tools, or suffers them to be stole, the full value thereof will be charged against his pay, according to the Custom of the Navy in such Cases, and he shall receive such further punishment as the nature of the Offence may deserve.

4. The same Penalty will be inflicted upon every person who is found to Embezzle, Trade, or Offer to Trade with any of the Ship's Stores of what Nature so ever.

5. No sort of Iron or anything that is made of Iron, or any sort of Cloth or other useful or necessary Articles, are to be given in Exchange for anything but Provisions.

J.C.

As soon as the Ship was properly secured I went on shore, accompanied by Mr. Banks and the other Gentlemen,* (* Cook generally uses this term for the civilians on board.) with a Party of Men under Arms; we took along with us Owhaa--who took us to the place where the Dolphin watered, and made signs to us as well as we could understand that we might Occupy that ground, but it hapned not to be fit for our purpose. No one of the Natives made the least opposition at our landing, but came to us with all imaginable Marks of Friendship and Submission. We Afterwards made a Circuit through the Woods, and then came on board. We did not find the inhabitants to be numerous, and we imagin'd that several of them had fled from their habitations upon our Arrival in the Bay.

Friday, 14th. This morning we had a great many Canoes about the Ship; the most of them came from the Westward, and brought nothing with them but a few Cocoa Nuts, etc. Two that appeared to be Chiefs we had on board, together with several others, for it was a hard matter to keep them out of the Ship, as they Climb like Munkeys; but it was still harder to keep them from Stealing but everything that came within their reach; in this they are Prodigious Expert. I made each of these two Chiefs a present of a Hatchet, things that they seemed mostly to value. As soon as we had partly got clear of these People I took 2 Boats and went to the Westward, all the Gentlemen being along with me. My design was to see if there was not a more commodious Harbour, and to try the disposition of the Natives, having along with us the 2 Chiefs above mentioned; the first place we landed at was in great Canoe Harbour (so called by Captain Wallis); here the Natives Flocked about us in great numbers, and in as friendly a manner as we could wish, only that they show'd a great inclination to Pick our Pockets. We were conducted to a Chief, who for distinction sake we called Hurcules. After staying a short time with him, and distributing a few Presents about us, we proceeded farther, and came to a Chief who I shall call Lycurgus; this man entertained us with broil'd fish, Cocoa Nutts, etc., with great Hospitality, and all the time took great care to tell us to take care of our Pockets, as a great number of People had crowded about us. Notwithstanding the care we took, Dr. Solander and Dr. Monkhouse had each of them their Pockets picked: the one of his spy glass and the other of his snuff Box. As soon as Lycurgus was made acquainted with the Theft he dispers'd the people in a moment, and the method he made use of was to lay hold on the first thing that came in his way and throw it at them, and happy was he or she that could get first out of his way. He seem'd very much concern'd for what had hapned, and by way of recompence offered us but everything that was in his House; but we refused to accept of anything, and made signs to him that we only wanted the things again. He had already sent people out after them, and it was not long before they were return'd. We found the Natives very numerous wherever we came, and from what we could judge seemed very peacably inclin'd. About six o'Clock in the evening we return'd on board, very well satisfied with our little Excursion.

Saturday, 15th. Winds at East during the day, in the Night a light breeze off the land; and as I apprehend it be usual here for the Trade wind to blow during a great part of the day from the Eastern Board, and to have it Calm or light breezes from the land that is Southerly during the night with fair weather, I shall only mention the wind and weather when they deviate from this rule. This morning several of the Chiefs we had seen Yesterday came on board, and brought with them Hogs, Bread fruit, etc., and for these we gave them Hatchets, Linnen, and such things as they valued. Having not met with yesterday a more Convenient situation for every purpose we wanted than the place we now are, I therefore, without delay, resolved to pitch upon some spot upon the North-East point of the Bay, properly situated for observing the Transit of Venus, and at the same time under the command of the Ship's Guns, and there to throw up a small fort for our defence. Accordingly I went ashore with a party of men, accompanied by Mr. Banks, Dr. Solander, and Mr. Green. We took along with us one of Mr. Banks's Tents, and after we had fix'd upon a place fit for our purpose we set up the Tent and marked out the ground we intended to Occupy. By this time a number of the Natives had got collected together about us, seemingly only to look on, as not one of them had any weapon, either Offensive or defensive. I would suffer none to come within the lines I had marked out, excepting one who appeared to be a chief and old Owhaa--to these 2 men we endeavour'd to explain, as well as we could, that we wanted that ground to Sleep upon such a number of nights and then we should go away. Whether they understood us or no is uncertain, but no one appeared the least displeased at what we was about; indeed the Ground we had fixed upon was of no use to them, being part of the sandy Beach upon the shore of the Bay, and not near to any of their Habitations.

It being too late in the day to do anything more, a party with a petty officer was left to guard the Tent, while we with another party took a Walk into the woods, and with us most of the natives. We had but just crossed the River when Mr. Banks shott three Ducks at one shott, which surprised them so much that most of them fell down as though they had been shott likewise. I was in hopes this would have had some good effect, but the event did not prove it, for we had not been long from the Tent before the natives again began to gather about, and one of them more daring than the rest pushed one of the Centinels down, snatched the Musket out of his hand and made a push at him, and then made off, and with him all the rest. Immediately upon this the Officer ordered the party to fire, and the Man who took the musket was shot Dead before he had got far from the Tent, but the musquet was carried quite off when this hapned. I and Mr. Banks with the other party was about half a Mile off, returning out of the woods, upon hearing the firing of Muskets, and the Natives leaving us at the same time, we Suspected that something was the matter and hastened our march, but before we arrived the whole was over, and every one of the Natives fled except old Owhaa, who stuck by us the whole time, and I believe from the first he either knew or had some suspicion that the People would attempt something at the Tent, as he was very much against our going into the Woods out of sight of the Tent. However, he might have other reasons, for Mr. Hicks, being ashore the day before, the natives would not permit him to go into the Woods. This made me resolved to go and see whether they meant to prescribe bounds to us or no. Old Owhaa, as I have said before, was the only one of the Natives that stayed by us, and by his means we prevail'd on about 20 of them to come to the Tent and there sit down with us, and Endeavour'd by every means in our power to Convince them that the Man was kill'd for taking away the Musket, and that we still would be friends with them. At sunset they left us seemingly satisfied, and we struck our Tent and went on board.

Sunday, 16th. This day worked the Ship nearer the Shore and moored her in such a manner as to command all the shore of the North-East part of the Bay, but more particularly the place where we intended to Erect a Fort. Punished Richard Hutchins, seaman, with 12 lashes for disobeying commands. Several of the Natives came down to the shore of the Bay, but not one of them came off to the Ship during the whole day. In the evening I went on shore with only a Boat's crew and some of the Gentlemen. The Natives gathered about us to the Number of about 30 or 40, and brought us Cocoa Nuts, etc., and seemed as friendly as ever.

Monday, 17th. At two o'Clock this morning, departed this life, Mr. Alex Buchan, Landskip Draftsman to Mr. Banks, a Gentleman well skill'd in his profession and one that will be greatly missed in the Course of this Voyage. He had long been subject to a disorder in his Bowels, which had more than once brought him to the very point of Death, and was at one time subject to fits, of one of which he was taken on Saturday morning; this brought on his former disorder, which put a Period to his life. Mr. Banks thought it not so advisable to Inter the Body ashore in a place where we were utter strangers to the Custom of the Natives on such occasions; it was therefore sent out to sea and committed to that Element with all the decency the Circumstance of the place would admit of. This morning several of the Chiefs from the westward made us a Visit: they brought with them Emblems of Peace, which are Young Plantain Trees. These they put on board the Ship before they would venture themselves. They brought us a present of 2 Hogs (an Article we find here very Scarce) and some Bread Fruit; for these they had Hatchets and other things. In the afternoon we set up one of the Ship's Tents ashore, and Mr. Green and myself stay'd there the night to observe an eclipse of Jupiter's first Satilite, which we was hinder'd from seeing by Clouds.

Tuesday, 18th. Cloudy weather with some showers of rain. This morning took as many people out of the Ship as could possibly be spared, and set about Erecting a Fort. Some were employ'd in throughing up intrenchment, while others was cutting facines, Picquets, etc. The Natives were so far from hindering us that several of them assisted in bringing the Picquets and facines out of the woods, and seemed quite unconcern'd at what we was about. The wood we made use of for this occasion we purchased of them, and we cut no Tree down before we had first obtained their Consent. By this time all the Ship's sails were unbent and the Armourer's Forge set up to repair the Ironwork, etc. Served fresh Pork to the Ship's Company to-day for the first time. This is like to be a very scarce Article with us, but as to Bread fruit, Cocoa Nutts and Plaintains, the Natives supply us with as much as we can destroy.

Wednesday, 19th. This morning Lycurgus, whose real name is Toobouratomita, came with his family from the Westward in order, from what we could understand, to live near us. He brought with him the cover of a House, with several other Materials for building one. We intend to requite the confidence this man seems to put in us by treating him with all imaginable kindness. Got on shore some Empty Casks, which we placed in a double row along the Bank of the River, by way of a breast work on that side.

Thursday, 20th. Wind at South-East and Squally, with rain. All hands employ'd on shore, and nothing remarkable, excepting a Hog weighing about 90 pound was brought alongside the Ship for Sale, but those who brought it would not part with it for anything we could offer them but a Carpenter's broad axe, and this was what we could not part with; they carried it away. Thus we see those very People who but 2 years ago prefer'd a spike Nail to an Axe of any Sort, have so far learnt the use of them that they will not part with a Pig of 10 or 12 pounds weight for anything under a Hatchet, and even those of an inferior or small sort are of no great esteem with them, and small Nails such as 10 penny, 20 penny, or any under 40 penny, are of no value at all; but beads, particularly white cut glass beads, are much valued by them. Mr. Banks and Dr. Solander lays ashore to-night for the first time, their Markee's being set up within the Walls of the Fort and fit for their reception.

Friday, 21st. Got the Copper Oven ashore and fixed it in the bank of the breastwork. Yesterday, as Mr. Green and Dr. Monkhouse were taking a walk, they happened to meet with the Body of the Man we had shott, as the Natives made them fully understand; the manner in which the body was interred being a little extraordinary. I went to-day, with some others, to see it. Close by the House wherein he resided when living was built a small shed, but whether for the purpose or no I cannot say, for it was in all respects like some of the Sheds or Houses they live in. This shed was about 14 or 16 feet long, 10 or 12 broad, and of a proportionable height. One end was wholy open, the other end and two sides was partly inclosed with a kind of wicker'd work. In this Shed lay the Corps, upon a Bier or frame of wood, with a matted bottom, like a Cott frame used at Sea, and Supported by 4 Posts about 5 feet from the Ground. The body was cover'd with a Matt, and over that a white Cloth; alongside of the Body lay a wooden Club, one of their Weapons of War. The Head of the Corps lay next the close end of the Shed, and at this end lay 2 Cocoa Nutt Shells, such as they sometimes use to carry water in; at the other end of the Shed was a Bunch of Green leaves, with some dry'd twigs tied all together and stuck in the Ground, and a stone lying by them as big as a Cocoa Nutt. Near to these lay a young Plaintain Tree, such as they use as Emblems of Peace, and by it lay a stone Axe. At the open end of the Shed was stuck upwright in the ground the Stem of a Plaintain Tree about 5 feet high, on the Top of which stood a Cocoa Nutt shell full of fresh water, and on the side of the post hung a small Bag, wherein was a few pieces of Bread Fruit roasted ready for eating. Some of the pieces were fresh and others Stale. The Natives did not seem to like that we should go near the body, and stood at a little distance themselves while we examin'd these matters, and appeared to be pleased when we came away. It certainly was no very agreeable place, for it stunk intollerably, and yet it was not above 10 yards from the Huts wherein several of the living resided. The first day we landed we saw the Skeleton of a human being laying in this manner under a shade that was just big enough to cover it, and some days after that, when some of the Gentlemen went with a design to examine it more narrowly, it was gone. It was at this time thought that this manner of interring their Dead was not common to all ranks of People, as this was the first we had seen Except the Skeleton just mentioned; but various were the opinions concerning the Provisions, etc., laid about the Dead. Upon the whole, it should seem that these people not only believe in a Supreem being, but in a future state also, and this must be meant either as an Offering to some Deitie or for the use of the Dead in the other world; but this latter is not very probable, as there appeared to be no Priest Craft in the thing, for whatever Provisions were put there it appeared very plain to us that there it remain'd until it consumed away of itself. It is most likely that we shall see more of this before we leave the Island, but if it is a Religious ceremony we may not be able to understand it, for the Misteries of most Religions are very Dark and not easily understood, even by those who profess them.

Saturday, 22nd, to Thursday, 27th. Nothing worthy of Note Hapned. The people were Continually at work upon the Fort,* (* Near the site of this Fort is still a Tamarind Tree, planted by Captain Cook. All visitors to Tahiti go to see "Cook's Tamarind.") and the Natives were so far reconciled to us that they rather assisted us than not. This day we mounted 6 Swivels at the Fort, which was now nearly finished. This struck the Natives with some fear, and some fishermen who lived upon the point moved farther off, and old Owhaa told us by signs that after 4 days we should fire Great Guns from the Ship. There were some other Circumstances co-operated with this man's prophecy, whether an opinion hath prevailed amongst them that after that time we intend to fire upon them, or that they intend to Attack us, we know not: the first we do not intend unless the latter takes place, which is highly improbable.

Friday, 28th. This morning a great number of the natives came to us in their Canoes from differant parts of the Island, several of whom we had not seen before. One of these was the Woman called by the Dolphins the Queen of this Island; she first went to Mr. Banks's tent at the fort, where she was not known, till the Master, happening to go ashore, who knew her, and brought her on board with 2 Men and several Women, who seem'd to be all of her family. I made them all some presents or other, but to Oberiea (for that is this Woman's name) I gave several things, in return for which, as soon as I went on shore with her, she gave me a Hog and several Bunches of plaintains. These she caused to be carried from her Canoes up to the Fort in a kind of Procession, she and I bringing up the rear. This Woman is about 40 years of Age, and, like most of the other Women, very Masculine. She is head or chief of her own family or Tribe, but to all appearance hath no Authority over the rest of the Inhabitants, whatever she might have when the Dolphin was here. Hercules, whose real Name is Tootaha, is, to all appearance, the Chief Man of the Island, and hath generally visited us twice a week since we have been here, and came always attended by a number of Canoes and people; and at those times we were sure to have a supply, more or less, of everything the Island afforded, both from himself and from those that came with him, and it is a Chance thing that we get a Hog at any other time. He was with us at this Time, and did not appear very well pleased at the Notice we took of Oberiea.

Saturday, 29th. This day got the 4 guns out of the Hold, and Mounted 2 of them on the Quarter Deck and the other 2 in the Fort on the Bank of the River.

Sunday, 30th. This being the day that Owhaa told us that we should fire our Guns, no one of us went from the Fort; however, the day passed over without any Visible alteration in the behaviour of any one of the Natives.

[May 1769.]

Monday, 1st May. This morning Tootaha came on board the Ship, and was very Desireous of seeing into every Chest and Drawer that was in the Cabin. I satisfied his curiosity so far as to open most of those that belong'd to me. He saw several things that he took a fancy to, and collected them together; but at last he Cast his eyes upon the Adze I had from Mr. Stephens* (* The Secretary of the Admiralty.) that was made in imitation of one of their Stone Adzes or Axes.* (* The stone adzes of Tahiti were of excellent workmanship.) The Moment he lays his hands upon it he of his own accord put away everything he had got before, and ask'd me if I would give him that, which I very readily did, and he went away without asking for any one thing more, which I by experience knew was a sure sign that he was well pleased with what he had got.

This day one of the Natives, who appeared to be a Chief, dined with us, as he had done some days before; but then there were always some Women present, and one or another of them put the Victuals into his Mouth, but this day there hapned to be none to Perform that Office. When he was help'd to victuals and desir'd to eat, he sat in the Chair like a Statute, without once attempting to put a Morsel to his mouth, and would certainly have gone without his dinner if one of the Servants had not fed him. We have often found the women very officious in feeding us, from which it would seem that it is the Custom on some occasions for them to feed the Chiefs. However, this is the only instance of that kind we have seen, or that they could not help themselves as well as any of us.

This afternoon we set up the Observatory and took the Astronomical Quadrant ashore for the first time, together with some other Instruments, the fort being now finished and made as Tenantable as the time, Nature, and situation of the Ground and Materials we had to work upon would admit of. The North and South parts consisted of a Bank of Earth 4 1/2 feet high on the inside, and a Ditch without, 10 feet broad and 6 feet deep; on the West side facing the Bay a Bank of Earth 4 feet high, and Palisades upon that, but no Ditch, the works being at high-water mark. On the East side upon the Bank of the river was placed a double row of Casks, and, as this was the weakest side, the 2 four Pounders were planted there, and the whole was defended, beside these 2 Guns, with 6 Swivels, and generally about 45 Men with small Arms, including the Officers and Gentlemen who resided ashore. I now thought myself perfectly secure from anything these people would attempt.

Tuesday, 2nd. This morning, about 9 o'Clock, when Mr. Green and I went to set up the Quadrant, it was not to be found. It had never been taken out of the Packing Case (which was about 18 Inches square) since it came from Mr. Bird, the Maker; and the whole was pretty heavy, so that it was a matter of Astonishment to us all how it could be taken away, as a Centinal stood the whole night within 5 Yards of the door of the Tent, where it was put, together with several other Instruments; but none of them was missing but this. However, it was not long before we got information that one of the Natives had taken it away and carried it to the Eastward. Immediately a resolution was taken to detain all the large Canoes that were in the Bay, and to seize upon Tootaha and some others of the principal people, and keep them in Custody until the Quadrant was produced; but this last we did not think proper immediately to put in Execution, as we had only Oberiea in our power, and the detaining of her by force would have alarm'd all the rest. In the meantime, Mr. Banks (who is always very alert upon all occasions wherein the Natives are concern'd) and Mr. Green went into the Woods to enquire of Toobouratomita which way and where the Quadrant was gone. I very soon was inform'd that these 3 was gone to the Eastward in quest of it, and some time after I followed myself with a small party of Men; but before I went away I gave orders that if Tootaha came either to the Ship or the Fort he was not to be detain'd, for I found he had no hand in taking away the Quadrant, and that there was almost a Certainty of getting it again. I met Mr. Banks and Mr. Green about 4 miles from the Fort, returning with the Quadrant. This was about Sun set, and we all got back to the Fort about 8 o'Clock, where I found Tootaha in Custody, and a number of the Natives crowding about the Gate of the Fort. My going into the Woods with a party of Arm'd men so alarmed the Natives that in the evening they began to move off with their Effects, and a Double Canoe putting off from the Bottom of the Bay was observ'd by the Ship, and a Boat sent after her. In this Canoe hapned to be Tootaha, and as soon as our Boat came up with her, he and all the people that were in the Canoe jump'd overboard, and he only was taken up and brought on board the Ship, together with the Canoe; the rest were permitted to swim to the Shore. From the Ship Tootaha was sent to the Fort, where Mr. Hicks thought proper to detain him until I return'd. The Scene between Toobouratomita and Tootaha, when the former came into the Fort and found the latter in Custody, was really moving. They wept over each other for some time. As for Tootaha, he was so far prepossessed with the thought that he was to be kill'd that he could not be made sencible to the Contrary till he was carried out of the Fort to the people, many of whom Expressed their joy by embracing him; and, after all, he would not go away until he had given us two Hogs, notwithstanding we did all in our power to hinder him, for it is very certain that the Treatment he had meet with from us did not merit such a reward. However, we had it in our power to make him a present of equal value whenever we pleased.

Wednesday, 3rd. Very early this morning Tootaha sent for the Canoe we had detained yesterday, and in the Afternoon sent a man for an Axe and a Shirt in return for the Hogs he gave us last night; but as this man told us that Tootaha would not come near us himself in less than 10 days, we thought proper not to send them, to try if he would not come himself for them sooner.

Thursday, 4th. Some people came to the Fort to-day from York Island; one of them gave us an account of 22 Islands lying in this Neighbourhood. Set up the 2 Clocks; one in the Tent wherein Mr. Green and I lay, and the other in the Observatory. This evening Tootaha sent a man again for the Axe and Shirt, and we sent him word by the same man that Mr. Banks and I would come and see him to-morrow and bring them along with us, for it now became necessary that we should take some steps to reconcile this man to us in order to procure a sufficient supply of Bread fruit, and Cocoa Nuts, which we have not had for these 2 days past, owing, as we apprehend, to Tootaha not being reconciled to us, or otherwise the people take this method to shew their resentment of the Treatment their Chief meet with.

Friday, 5th. Early this morning Tootaha sent some of his people to put us in mind of our promise, and these seem'd very uneasy until we set out, which Mr. Banks, Dr. Solander, and myself did about 10 o'clock in the Pinnace, having one of these men with us. As soon as we came to Appara, the place where Tootaha resided, we saw a great number of People at the landing place near his House; one among them, who had a large Turban about his Head, and a long white stick in his Hand, drove the others from the landing place by beating them with his Stick, and throwing stones at them, and at the same time directed us whereabouts to land. After we had landed he conducted us to the Chief, but in this there was no order, everyone crowded upon us crying out "Tyo Tootaha," this Tootaha was our Friend. We found the chief setting in the shade under a large Tree, with a Circle of old men round him; he made us set down by him, and immediately asked for the Axe. I then gave him one, together with an upper Garment made of Broad Cloth after their Fashion, and a Shirt. The Garment he put on, but the Shirt he gave to the man who first received us at landing, who was now seated by us, and the Chief seemed desirous that we should take particular notice of him. By that Time Obaria, and several other women whom we knew, came and sat down by us. Tootaha did not stay long before he went away, as we thought to show himself to the people in his new Dress. He was not gone long before he return'd and took his seat again for a few minutes, then went away again, as we was told, to order something to be got for us to Eat, and at this time we gladly would have gone too, being almost Suffocated with the Crowd that was about us. However, here we remained for about 10 Minutes longer, when word was brought us that the Chief wanted us. We were then conducted to our own Boat, where we found him setting alone under the Awning. He made signs to us to come to him, which we did, and as many with us as the Boat would hold. Here he ordered some Bread fruit and Cocoa Nut to be brought, of both of which we tasted.

After we had set here sometime, a Message was brought to the Chief, who immediately went out of the Boat, and we was desired to follow, and was conducted to a large Aria or Court Yard on one side of his House, where we were entertained with Public wrestling. Tootaha seated himself at one end of the place, and several of his Principal men sat round him in a Semicircle. We were desir'd to sit down here likewise, but we rather chose to walk about. Everything being now ready, several men entered the Theater, 8, 10, or 12, sometimes more. These walked about in a Stooping Poster, with their left hand upon their right breast, and with their Right hand Open struck with a smack their left Arm and fore-arm. In this manner they walked about until one Challenged another, which was done by motion and jesture, without speaking one word. The 2 Antagonists would then meet and endeavour to seize each other by the thighs, but if that fail'd they would seize each other by the Hair of the Head or wherever they could, and then Wrestle together until by main Strength the one or the other was thrown on his back. This was always (Except once) followed by three Huzzas from some old men who sat in the House, and at the same time another Company of men would dance for about a Minute, the Wrestlers all the time continuing their game without taking the least notice of anything else. The only dexterity the Wrestlers seemed to make use of was in first seizing each other, for after they had closed it was all decided by Main strength. It would sometimes happen that neither the one nor the other could throw his Antagonist; in this Case they would either part by mutual consent or were parted by others. The Conqueror never exulted over the Conquer'd, neither did the Conquer'd ever repine at his ill luck, but the whole was carried on with great good Humour. There were present, Young and old, near 500 People. The women do not seem to partake of this diversion, only some few of the Principal ones were present, and that appeared to be owing to us being there.

After this was over we were given to understand that we were to go to Dinner, and were desired to follow Tootaha, who led us into our own Boat, and soon after came a small Pig ready roasted, with some Bread Fruit and Cocoa Nuts. Here we thought we were to have dined, but Tootaha, after waiting about 10 Minutes, made signs to us to put off the Boat and go a Board, which we did, and bring him and Toobouratomida along with us. As soon as we got on board we all dined on the Cheer the Chief had provided. We soon found the good effects of having made friends with this man, for it was no sooner known to the Natives that he was on board the Ship than they brought Bread Fruit, Cocoa Nuts, etc., to the Fort.

Saturday, 6th; Sunday, 7th. Nothing remarkable, only that the Natives supply us with as much bread fruits and Cocoa Nuts as we can destroy.

Monday, 8th. Early this morning the Master went to the Eastward in the Pinnace to try if he could procure some Hogs and Fowls from that Quarter; but he return'd in the evening without success. He saw but very few, and those the inhabitants pretended belonged to Tootaha; so great is this man's influence or authority over them that they dare part with nothing without his Consent, or otherwise they use his Name to Excuse themselves from parting with the few they have, for it is very certain these things are in no great plenty with them.

Tuesday, 9th; Wednesday, 10th; Thursday, 11th. Nothing remarkable hapned for these three days. Oberiea, the Dolphin's queen, made us a Visit for the first time since the Quadrant was Stolen. She introduced herself with a Small Pig, for which she had a Hatchet, and as soon as she got it she Lugg'd out a Broken Axe, and several pieces of Old Iron. These, I believe, she must have had from the Dolphin; the Axe she wanted to be mended, and Axes made of the old iron. I obliged her in the first, but excused myself in the latter: since the Natives had seen the Forge at work they have frequently brought pieces of Iron to be made into one sort of Tool or other, which hath generally been done whenever it did not hinder our own work--being willing to Oblige them in everything in my power. These Pieces of old Iron the Natives must have got from the Dolphin, as we know of no other Ship being here;* (* M. de Bougainville, in the French ships La Boudeuse and L'Etoile, had visited Tahiti the year before, after its discovery by the Dolphin. He was unfortunate in his choice of anchorage, and his ships lost anchors and got into various difficulties. The crews were also much afflicted with scurvy.) and very probable some from us, for there is no species of Theft they will not commit to get this Article, and I may say the same of the common Seamen when in these parts.

Friday, 12th. Cloudy weather with Showers of rain. This morning a Man and 2 Young Women, with some others, came to the Fort, whom we had not seen before, and as their manner of introducing themselves was a little uncommon, I shall insert it. Mr. Banks was as usual at the gate of the Fort trading with the people, when he was told that some Strangers were coming, and therefore stood to receive them. The Company had with them about a Dozen young Plantain Trees, and some other small Plants, these they laid down about 20 feet from Mr. Banks; the people then made a Lane between him and them. When this was done the Man (who appeared to be only a Servant to the two Women) brought the young Plantains singly, together with some of the other plants, and gave them to Mr. Banks, and at the delivery of each pronounced a Short sentence which we understood not. After he had thus disposed of all his plantain trees, he took several pieces of Cloth and spread them on the ground. One of the Young women then stepp'd upon the Cloth, and with as much innocency as one could possibly conceive, exposed herself, entirely naked, from the waist downwards; in this manner she turn'd herself once or twice round, I am not certain which, then stepped off the cloth, and dropp'd down her Cloaths. More Cloth was then spread upon the former, and she again performed the same Ceremony. The Cloth was then rowled up and given to Mr. Banks, and the two Young women went and Embraced him, which ended the Ceremony.

Saturday, 13th. Nothing worthy of Note hapned during the day; in the Night one of the Natives attempted to get into the Fort by Climbing over the Wall, but, being discovered by the Centinel, he made off. The Iron and Iron Tools daily in use at the Armourer's Forge are Temptations that these people cannot possibly withstand.

Sunday, 14th. This day we performed divine Service in one of the Tents in the fort, where several of the Natives attended and behaved with great decency the whole time. This day closed with an odd sceen at the Gate of the Fort, where a young Fellow above 6 feet high made love to a little Girl about 10 or 12 years of Age publickly before several of our people and a number of the Natives. What makes me mention this is because it appear'd to be done according to Custom, for there were several women present, particularly Obariea and several others of the better sort, and these were so far from showing the least disapprobation that they instructed the Girl how she should Act her part, who, young as she was, did not seem to want it.

Monday, 15th. Winds variable and cloudy weather. Last Night one of our Water Casks was taken away from the outside of the Fort, where they stood full of water. In the morning there was not one of the Natives but what knew it was gone; yet, Contrary to what we had always met with on these Occasions, not one of them would give us any information about it, and I thought it of too little Consequence to take any methods to Oblige them. In the evening Toobouratomida and his Wife, and a Man belonging to Tootaha, would needs lay all Night by the Casks to prevent any more from being taken away; but, as we had placed a Centinel there, this care of theirs became unnecessary, and they were prevailed upon to go home; but before they went away they made signs to the Centinel to keep his Eyes open. From this it should seem that they knew that an attempt would be made in the night to take away more, which would have been done had not the Centinel prevented it.

Tuesday, 16th. Winds Westerly. The morning cloudy, with heavy showers of rain; the Remainder of the day fair weather. From this day nothing remarkable hapned until

Monday, 22nd, which was usher'd in with thick Cloudy weather, and Excessive hard Showers of rain and very much Thunder and Lightning, which Continued the Greater part of the day.

Tuesday, 23rd. Wind Southerly and fair weather in the Forenoon, but in the Afternoon Showers. We have had a Scarcity of all sorts of Fruit for these 2 days past, which we immagine to be owing to the Wet weather.

Wednesday, 24th. Fine clear weather all this day. Having found the Long boat Leakey for these few days past, we hauld her ashore to-day to stop the leakes, when, to our great surprise, we found her bottom so much Eaten by the Worms that it was necessary to give her a new one, and all the Carpenters were immediately set to work upon her.

Thursday, 25th. Most part of these 24 hours Cloudy, with frequent Showers of Rain.

Friday, 26th. Some flying showers again. This morning we hauled the pinnace a Shore to examine her bottom, and had the Satisfaction to find that not one worm had touched it, notwithstanding she hath been in the water nearly as long as the Long Boat. This must be owing to the White Lead with which her bottom is painted, the Long boats being paid with Varnish of Pine, for no other reason can be assign'd why the one should be preserved and the other destroy'd, when they are both built on the Same sort of Wood and have been in equal use. From this Circumstance alone the Bottom of all Boats sent into Countrys where these worms are ought to be painted with White Lead, and the Ships supply'd with a good stock in order to give them a New Coat whenever it's necessary. By this means they would be preserved free from these destructive Vermin. The Long boat's Bottom being so much destroy'd appear'd a little extraordinary, as the Dolphin's Launch was in the Water at this very place full as long, and no such thing happened to her, as the Officers that were in the Dolphin say.

Saturday, 27th. Winds variable and fair weather.

Sunday, 28th. Winds Southerly and clear weather. This morning myself, Mr. Banks, and Dr. Solander set out in the Pinnace to pay Tootaha a Visit, who had moved from Apparra to the South-West part of the island. What induced us to make him this visit was a Message we had received from him some days ago importing that if we would go to him he would give us several Hogs. We had no great faith in this, yet we were resolved to try, and set out accordingly. It was Night before we reached the place where he was, and, as we had left the Boat about half-way behind us, we were obliged to take up our Quarters with him for the Night. The Chief received us in a Friendly manner, and a Pig was ordered to be killed and dressed for Supper; but we saved his Life for the present, thinking it would do us more service in another place, and we supped on Fruit and what else we could get. Here was, along with the Chief, Obariea and many more that we knowd. They all seem'd to be travellers like ourselves, for neither the Canoes they had along with them, nor the Houses where they were, were sufficient to contain the one half of them. We were in all Six of us, and after supper began to look out for Lodgings. Mr. Banks went to one place, Dr. Solander to another, while I and the other 3 went to a third. We all of us took as much care of the little we had about us as possible, knowing very well what sort of People we were among; yet, notwithstanding all the care we took, before 12 o'clock the most of us had lost something or other. For my own part I had my Stockings taken from under my head, and yet I am certain that I was not a Sleep the whole time. Obariea took charge of Mr. Banks's things, and yet they were stol'n from her, as she pretended. Tootaha was acquainted with what had hapned, I believe by Obariea herself, and both him and her made some stir about it; but this was all meer shew, and ended in nothing. A little time after this Tootaha came to the Hutt where I and those that were with me lay, and entertain'd us with a Consort of Musick consisting of 3 Drums, 4 Flutes, and Singing. This lasted about an Hour, and then they retir'd. The Music and Singing was so much of a piece that I was very glad when it was over. We stay'd with them till near noon the next day in hopes of getting some of our things again, and likewise some Hogs; but we were at last obliged to come away with the one we had saved out of the Fire last Night, and a promise from Tootaha that he would come to the Ship in a Day or two with more, and bring with him the things that are lost, a promise we had no reason to expect he would fulfill. Thus ended our Visit, and we got to the Fort late in the evening.

Tuesday, 30th. We are now very buisey in preparing our Instruments, etc., for the Observations, and Instructing such Gentlemen in the use of them, as I intend to send to other parts to observe, for fear we should fail here.

Wednesday, 31st. Late this Evening the Carpenters finished the Long boat.

[June 1769.]

Thursday, June 1st. This day I sent Lieutenant Gore in the Long boat to York Island* (* Eimeo, westward of, and near to Tahiti.) with Dr. Monkhouse and Mr. Sporing (a Gentleman belonging to Mr. Banks) to Observe the Transit of Venus, Mr. Green having furnished them with Instruments for that purpose. Mr. Banks and some of the Natives of this Island went along with them.

Friday, 2nd. Very early this morning Lieutenant Hicks, Mr. Clark, Mr. Pickersgill and Mr. Saunders went away in the Pinnace to the Eastward, with orders to fix upon some Convenient situation upon this Island, and there to Observe the Transit of Venus, they being likewise provided with Instruments for that purpose.

Saturday, 3rd. This day proved as favourable to our purpose as we could wish. Not a Cloud was to be seen the whole day, and the Air was perfectly Clear, so that we had every advantage we could desire in observing the whole of the Passage of the planet Venus over the Sun's Disk. We very distinctly saw an Atmosphere or Dusky shade round the body of the planet, which very much disturbed the times of the Contact, particularly the two internal ones. Dr. Solander observed as well as Mr. Green and myself, and we differ'd from one another in Observing the times of the Contact much more than could be expected. Mr. Green's Telescope and mine where of the same Magnifying power, but that of the Doctor was greater than ours. It was nearly calm the whole day, and the Thermometer Exposed to the Sun about the Middle of the day rose to a degree of heat we have not before met with.

FACSIMILE OF SATURDAY, 3RD JUNE, 1769.

Sunday, 4th. Punished Archd. Wolf with 2 Dozen lashes for Theft, having broken into one of the Storerooms and stol'n from thence a large quantity of Spike Nails; some few of them where found upon him. This evening the Gentlemen that were sent to observe the Transit of Venus, return'd with success; those that were sent to York Island were well received by the Natives. That Island appear'd to them not to be very fruitful.

Monday, 5th. Got some of the Bread ashore out of the Bread Room to dry and Clean. Yesterday being His Majesty's birthday, we kept it to-day and had several of the Chiefs to dine with us.

Tuesday, 6th. This day and for some days past we have been informd by several of the Natives that about 10 or 15 months ago Two Ships touched at this Island and stayed 10 days in a Harbour to the Eastward, called Ohidea, the Commander's name was Tootteraso,* (* M. de Bougainville, who laid at Hitiaa from April 6th to April 16th, 1768.)--so at least the Natives call him--and that one of the Natives, Brother to the Chief of Ohidea, went away with him. They likewise say these ships brought the venerial distemper to this Island, where it is now as Common as in any part of the world, and which the people bear with as little concern as if they have been accustom'd to it for Ages past. We had not been here many days before some of our People got this disease, and as no such thing hapned to any of the Dolphin's people while she was here, that I ever heard of, I had reason (notwithstanding the improbability of the thing) to think that we had brought it along with us, which gave me no small uneasiness, and did all in my power to prevent its progress, but all I could do was to little purpose, as I was obliged to have the most part of the Ship's Company ashore every day to work upon the Fort, and a Strong Guard every Night; and the Women were so very liberal with their favours--or else Nails, Shirts, etc., were temptations that they could not withstand, that this distemper very soon spread itself over the greatest part of the Ship's company, but now I have the satisfaction to find that the Natives all agree that we did not bring it here.

We have several times seen Iron tools and other Articles with these people that we suspected came not from the Dolphin, and these they now say they had from these two Ships.

Wednesday, 7th; Thursday, 8th; Friday, 9th. These three days we have been employ'd in Careening both sides of the Ship, and paying them with Pitch and Brimstone. We found her Bottom in good order, and that the worm had not got into it.

Saturday, 10th. Wind Variable, with very much rain all day and last night.

Sunday, 11th. Cloudy, with rain last night and this morning; the remainder of the day fair weather. This day Mr. Banks and I took Toobouratomita on board the Ship and shew'd him the print containing the Colours worne by the ships of Diffrent Nations, and very soon made him understand that we wanted to know which of them was worn by the ships that were at Ohidea. He at once pitched upon the Spanish Flag and would by no means admit of any other; this, together with several Articles we have lately seen amongst these people, such as Jackets, Shirts, etc., usually worn by Spanish Seamen, proves beyond doubt that they must have been Ships of that Nation, and come from some Port on the Coast of South America.* (* This was of course a mistake, as the ships were French.)

Monday, 12th. Yesterday Complaint was made to me by some of the Natives that John Thurman and James Nicholson, Seamen, had taken by force from them several Bows and Arrows and plaited Hair, and the fact being proved upon them they were this day punished with 2 dozen lashes each.

Tuesday, 13th. Some Showers of rain last night, but fair weather the most part of the day. Tootaha, whom we have not seen for some time past, paid us a Visit to-Day. He brought with him a Hog and some Bread Fruit, for which he was well paid.

Wednesday, 14th. Between 2 and 4 o'clock this morning, one of the Natives stole out of the Fort an Iron rake, made use of for the Oven. It hapned to be set up against the Wall, and by that means was Visible from the outside, and had been seen by them in the evening, as a man had been seen lurking about the Fort some Hours before the thing was Missed. I was informed by some others of the Natives that he watch'd an opportunity when the Centinel's back was turned, he hooked it with a long crooked stick, and haled it over the Wall. When I came to be informed of this theft in the Morning I resolved to recover it by some Means or other, and accordingly went and took possession of all the Canoes of any value I could meet with, and brought them into the River behind the Fort to the number of 22, and told the Natives then present (most of them being the owners of the Canoes) that unless the principal things they had stol'n from us were restored I would burn them every one: not that I ever intended to put this in execution, and yet I was very much displeased with them, as they were daily committing, or attempting to commit, one theft or other, when at the same time--contrary to the opinion of everybody, I would not suffer them to be fir'd upon, for this would have been putting it in the power of the Centinels to have fir'd upon them upon the most slitest occasions, as I had before experienced. And I have a great Objection to firing with powder only amongst People who know not the difference, for by this they would learn to despise fire Arms and think their own Arms superior, and if ever such an Opinion prevailed they would certainly attack you, the Event of which might prove as unfavourable to you as them. About Noon the rake was restored us, when they wanted to have their Canoes again; but now, as I had them in my possession, I was resolved to try if they would not redeem them by restoring what they had stol'n from us before. The Principal things which we had lost was the Marine Musquet, a pair of Pistols belonging to Mr. Banks, a Sword belonging to one of the Petty Officers, and a Water Cask, with some other Articles not worth mentioning. Some said that these things were not in the Island, others that Tootaha had them, and those of Tootaha's friends laid the whole to Obariea, and I believe the whole was between these two persons.

Thursday, 15th. We have been employed for some Days past in overhauling all the Sea Provisions, and stowing such as we found in a State of decay to hand, in order to be first expended; but having the people divided between the Ship and the Shore, this work, as well as refitting the Ship, goes on but slowly.

Friday, 16th; Saturday, 17th. Variable winds, with Showers of rain and Cloudy weather.

Sunday, 18th. Variable winds and Clear weather. This Night was observed the Moon totally Eclipsed.

Monday, 19th. Punished James Tunley with 12 lashes for taking Rum out of the Cask on the Quarter Deck.

Tuesday, 20th. Got all the Powder aShore to Air, all of which we found in a bad Condition, and the Gunner informs me that it was very little better when it came first on board. Last Night Obariea made us a visit, whom we have not seen for some time. We were told of her coming, and that she would bring with her some of the Stol'n things, which we gave Credit to because we know'd several of them were in her possession; but we were surprised to find this Woman put herself wholy in our power, and not bring with her one Article of what we had lost. The Excuse she made was that her Gallant, a man that used to be along with her, did Steal them, and she had beat him and turned him away, but she was so Sencible of her own Guilt that she was ready to drop down through fear, and yet she had resolution Enough to insist upon Sleeping in Mr. Banks's Tent all Night, and was with difficulty prevailed upon to go to her canoe, altho no one took the least notice of her. In the morning she brought her Canoe, with everything she had, to the Gate of the Fort, after which we could not help admiring her for her Courage and the Confidence she seem'd to place in us, and thought that we could do no less than to receive her into favour, and except the Present she had brought us, which consisted of a Hog, a Dog, some Bread Fruit and Plantains.

We refused to Except of the Dog, as being an Animal we had no use for; at which she seemed a little surprised, and told us it was very good eating, and we very soon had an opportunity to find that it was so, for Mr. Banks, having bought a Basket of Fruit in which was the Thigh of a Dog ready dressed, of this several of us tasted, and found that it was Meat not to be despised, and therefore took Obariea's Dog and had him immediately dressed by some of the Natives in the following manner: They first made a hole in the Ground about a foot Deep, in which they made a fire and heated some small Stones. While this was doing the Dog was strangled and the hair got off by laying him frequently on the fire, and as clean as if it had been scalded off with hot water. His Intrails was taken out, and the whole washed Clean, and as soon as the Stones and Hole was sufficiently heated the fire was put out and part of the Stones were left in the bottom of the hole. Upon these stones were laid green leafs, and upon them the Dog, together with the Intrails, these were likewise covered with leaves, and over them hot stones; and then the hole was close cover'd with mould. After he had laid here about 4 Hours, the Oven (for so I must call it) was op'ned, and the dog taken out, whole and well done, and it was the Opinion of every one who tasted it that they never eat sweater Meat, therefore we resolved for the future never to dispise Dog's flesh. It is in this manner that the Natives dress and Bake all their Victuals that require it--Flesh, fish, and Fruit. I now gave over all thoughts of recovering any of the things the Natives had stol'n from us, and therefore intend to give them up their Canoes whenever they apply for them.

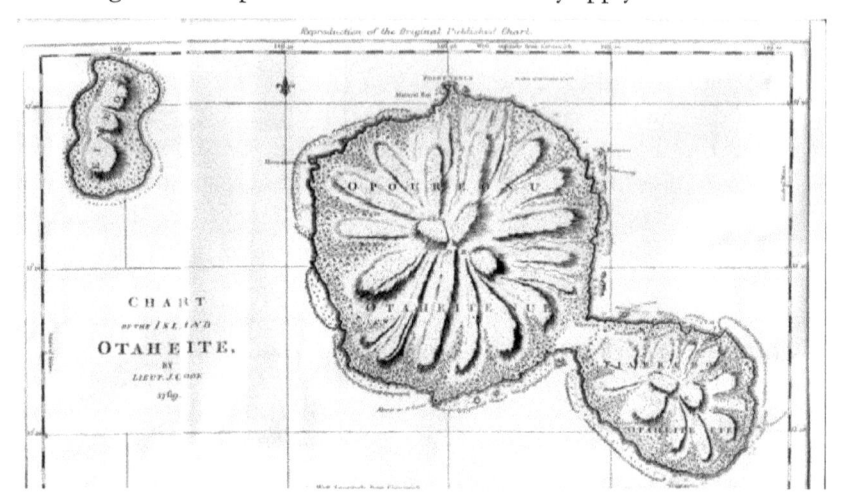

CHART OF THE ISLAND OTAHEITE, BY LIEUTENANT JAMES COOK, 1769. REPRODUCTION OF THE ORIGINAL PUBLISHED CHART.

Wednesday, 21st. Employed drying the Powder, or getting on board Wood, Water, etc. Confined Robert Anderson, Seaman, for refusing to obey the orders of the Mate when at work in the Hold. This morning a Chief, whose Name is Oamo, and one we had not seen before, came to the Fort. There came with him a Boy about 7 Years of Age and a Young Woman of about 18 or 20. At the Time of their coming Obariea and several others were in the fort. They went out to meet them, having first uncovered their Heads and Bodies as low as their Waists; and the same thing was done by all those that were on the outside of the Fort. As we looked upon this as a Ceremonial respect, and had not seen it paid to any one before, we thought that this Oamo must be some extraordinary person, and wondered to see so little notice taken of him after the Ceremony was over. The Young woman that came along with him could not be prevailed upon to come into the Fort, and the Boy was Carried upon a Man's back, altho' he was as able to walk as the Man who carried him. This Lead us to inquire who they were; and we was informed that the Boy was Heir Apparent to the Sovereignty of the Island, and the Young Woman was his Sister, and as such the respect was paid them which was due to no one else except the Arreedehi, which was not Tootaha, from what we could learn, but some other person who we had not seen, or like to do, for they say that he is no Friend of ours, and therefore will not come near us. The Young Boy above mentioned is son to Oamo by Obariea, but Oamo and Obariea do not at this time live together as Man and Wife, he not being able to endure with her troublesome disposition. I mention this because it shows that seperation in the Marriage state is not unknown to these people.* (* See note Notes on Tahiti below.)

Thursday, 22nd. This morning I released Robert Anderson from Confinement at the intercession of the Master and a promise of behaving better for the future.

Friday, 23rd. This morning Emanuel Parreyra, a Portugue, was Missing, and I had some reason to think that he was gone with an intent to stay here. It was not long before I was informed that he was at Apparra with Tootaha. The Man who gave us this information was one of Tootaha's Servants. He was Offer'd a Hatchet if he would go to Apparra and bring him to us. This was perhaps the very thing he came for, for he immediately set out and return'd with the Man in the Evening. The man said in his defence that as he was going to the Boat to go on board last night, he was taken away by force by 3 Men, and upon enquiring farther into this matter I found it to be so, and that Tootaha wanted to have kept him, only that he was perswaided to the contrary, or perhaps he thought that the Hatchet he would get by returning him would do him more service than the Man.

Saturday, 24th, Sunday, 25th. Nothing remarkable.

[Tahiti: Expedition round Island.]

Monday, 26th. Very early this morning I set out in the pinnace, accompanied by Mr. Banks, with an intent to make the Circuit of the Island in order to Examine and draw a Sketch of the Coast and Harbours thereof. We took our rout to the Eastward, and this night reached the Isthmus, which is a low neck of Land running across the Island, which divides it into two districts or Governments wholly independent of each other as we was informed. The first thing we saw which struck our attention in this day's rout was a small Pig that had not been roasted above a Day or 2 laid upon one of their Altars near to a place where lay the Body or Bones of a Dead Person. This Pig must have been put their as an offering to their God, but on what account we know not. The Coast from Royal Bay trends East by South and East-South-

East 10 miles South by East and South 11 miles to the Isthmus. In the first direction the Shore is mostly open to the Sea, but in the last it is cover'd by reefs of rocks; these forms several good Harbours, wherein are safe Anchorage for Shipping in 16, 18, 20, and 24 fathoms, with other Conveniences. It was in one of these Harbours the Spanish Ships before mentioned lay; the Natives shew'd us the place where they Pitched their Tent and the Brook they water'd at, otherways there was not the least signs of Shipping having been there.

Tuesday, 27th. Winds Easterly and fine weather. It was late last night before we reached the Isthmus, and all the Observations I could make this morning was that it appeared to be a Marshey flatt of about 2 miles in Extent aCross which the Natives Haul their Canoes partly by land and partly by water. From the Isthmus the land trends East Southerly near 3 Leagues, to the South-East point of the Great Bay which lies before the Isthmus. On the west side of this point is a Bay called Ohitepepa, which is in many respects similar to Royal Bay, and is situated in every bit as fertile and populous part of the Island. There are other places formed by the Reefs that lay along the Shore between this and the Isthmus, where Shipping can lay in perfect security. The Land then trends South-East and South to the South-East part of the Island, which is near 3 Leagues, and covered all the way by a Reef of Rocks, but no Harbour. We took up our Quarters at the East part of the Island, being conducted thither by a Young Chief we had Often seen on board the Ship, and the next morning proceeded round the South-East point of the Island, part of which is not cover'd by any reef, but lies wholy open to the Sea and here the Hills rise directly from the Shore. At the Southernmost part of the Island the Shore is again cover'd by a Reef, and there forms a very good Harbour, and the land about it very fertile. At this place we saw a Goose and a Turkey left at Royal Bay by the Dolphin; they were in possession of a Chief who came along with us in the Boat, and remain'd with us the remainder of the day, and conducted us over the Shoals we here meet with; and for this piece of service we lent him a Cloak to Sleep in in the night, but we had not been laid down above 10 minutes before he thought proper to move off with it, but both Mr. Banks and I pursued him so close that he was obliged to relinquish his prize, and we saw no more of him. When we returned to our Lodging we found the House, in which were not less than 2 or 300 people when we went away, intirely deserted, so that we had one of the Largest and best houses on the Island wholy to ourselves; but when they found that we meant them no harm the Chief and his Wife with some others came and Slept by us the remainder of the night. This place is situated on the South-West side of Tiarreboo,* (* Taiarapu.) the South-East district of the Island, and about 5 miles South-East from the Isthmus. Here is a large, safe, and Commodious Harbour, inferior to none on the whole Island, and the land about it Rich in Produce. We found that the people of this district had had little or no communication with us, yet we was everywhere well received by them. We found all this part of the Island very fertile and the Natives numerous, and had a great many large Double Canoes built and Ornamented uniformly. They were all halled ashore, and appeared to be going to decay for want of use. Their Mories or Burial places stood generally upon these points of land that projected into the Sea, and were both better built and Ornamented than those about Royal Bay--Tootaha's excepted. In general this district appear'd to be in a more flourishing state than the other, although it is not above one fourth part as big and cannot contain nothing near the Number of inhabitants.

Thursday, 29th. Squally weather with Showers of rain. This morning we left Tiaraboo and entered upon that of Opooreonoo, the North-West district of the Island. The first thing we met with worthy of note was at one of their Mories, where lay the scull bones of 26 Hogs and 6 Dogs. These all lay near to and under one of their Altars. These Animals must have been offer'd as a Sacrifice to their Gods either all at once or at different times, but on what account we could not learn. The next day we met with an Effigy or Figure of a Man made of Basket work and covered with white and Black feathers placed in such order as to represent the Colour of their Hair and Skins when Tattow'd or painted. It was 7 1/2 feet high and the whole made in due proportion; on its head were 4 Nobs not unlike the stumps of Large Horns--3 stood in front and one behind. We were not able to learn what use they made of this Monster; it did not at all appear to us that they paid it the least Homage as a God: they were not the least Scrupulous of letting us examine every part of it. I am inclinable to think that it is only used by way of diversion at their Hevas or public entertainments, as Punch is in a Puppet show.* (* Note by Cook in Admiralty copy: "Tupia informs us that this is a representation of one of the Second rank of Eatuas or Gods, called Mauwi, who inhabited the Earth upon the Creation of man. He is represented as an immense Giant who had seven heads, and was indued with immense strength and abilities. Many absurd stories are told of his Feats by Tupia.") We next passed through a Harbour, which is the only one on the south side of Opooreonoo fit for Shipping. It is situated about 5 Miles to the Westward of the Isthmus between 2 Small Islands that lay near the shore and a Mile from each other. In this Harbour is 11 and 12 fathoms of water and good Anchorage. About a League and a half to the Westward of this Harbour is the Morie of Oamo or Oberia, for some told us it belong'd to the one and some to the other; it far Exceeds every thing of this Kind upon the whole Island. It is a long square of Stonework built Pyramidically; its base is 267 feet by 87 feet; at the Top it is 250 feet by 8 feet. It is built in the same manner as we do steps leading up to a Sun Dial or fountain erected in the Middle of a Square where there is a flite of steps on each side. In this building there are 11 of such steps; each step is about 4 feet in height and the breadth 4 feet 7 inches, but they decreased both in height and breadth from the bottom to the Top. On the middle of the Top stood the Image of a Bird carved in Wood, near it lay the broken one of a Fish carved in stone. There was no hollow or Cavity in the inside, the whole being fill'd up with stones. The outside was faced partly with hewn stones and partly with others, and these were placed in such a manner as to look very agreeable to the Eye. Some of the hewn stones were 4 feet 7 inches by 2 feet 4 inches and 15 inches thick, and had been squared and Polished with some sort of an Edge Tool. On the East side was enclosed with a stone wall a piece of ground in form of a square, 360 feet by 354, in this was growing several Cypress trees and Plantains. Round about this Morie was several smaller ones all going to decay, and on the Beach between them and the Sea lay scatter'd up and down a great quantity of human bones. Not far from the Great Morie was 2 or 3 pretty large Altars, where lay the Scull bones of some Hogs and dogs. This Monument stands on the south side of Opooreonoo, upon a low point of land about 100 Yards from the Sea.* (* On map Morai-no te Oamo.) It appeared to have been built many Years, and was in a State of decay, as most of their Mories are. From this it would seem that this Island hath been in a more Flourishing state than it is at present, or that Religious Customs are (like most other Nations) by these people less observed. We took up our Quarters near this Morie for the night, and early in the Morning proceeded on our rout, and without meeting with anything remarkable, got on board the Ship on Saturday, the 1st of July, having made the Circuit of the whole Island, which I Estimated at something more than 30 Leagues.* (* A remarkably close estimate.) The Plan or Sketch which I have drawn, altho' it cannot be very accurate, yet it will be found sufficient to point out the Situation of the different Bays and Harbours and the true figure of the Island, and I believe is without any Material error. For the first 2 or 3 days we was out upon this excursion we labour'd under some difficulty for want of Provisions--particularly bread--an Article we took but little of with us--not doubting that we should get bread fruit, more than sufficient for a Boat's Crew at every place we went to, but, on the Contrary, we found the season for that fruit wholy over, and not one to be seen on the Trees, and all other fruit and roots were scarce. The Natives live now on Sour paist--which is made from bread fruit--and some bread fruit and plantains that they get from the Mountains where the season is Later, and on a Nut not unlike a chessnut which are now in Perfection; but all these Articles are at present very scarce, and therefore it is no wonder that the Natives have not supply'd us with these things of Late. [At Tahiti.] Upon my return to the Ship I found that the Provisions had been all examined and the Water got on board, amounting to 65 Tons. I now determind to get everything off from the Shore and leave the Place as soon as possible. The getting the several Articles on board, and

Scraping and paying the Ship's side, took us up the following Week without anything remarkable happening until

[July 1769. At Tahiti.]

Sunday, July 9th. When, sometime in the Middle Watch, Clement Webb and Saml. Gibson, both Marines and young Men, found means to get away from the Fort (which was now no hard matter to do) and in the morning were not to be found. As it was known to everybody that all hands were to go on board on the Monday morning, and that the ship would sail in a day or two, there was reason to think that these 2 Men intended to stay behind. However I was willing to stay one day to see if they would return before I took any step to find them.

Monday, 10th. The 2 Marines not returning this morning, I began to enquire after them, and was inform'd by some of the Natives that they were gone to the Mountains, and that they had got each of them a Wife and would not return; but at the same time no one would give us any certain intelligence where they were, upon which a resolution was taken to seize upon as many of the Chiefs as we could. This was thought to be the readiest method to induce the other natives to produce the 2 Men. We had in our custody Obariea, Toobouratomita, and 2 other Chiefs, but that I know'd Tootaha would have more weight with the Natives than all these put together, I dispatched Lieutenant Hicks away in the Pinnace to the place where Tootaha was, to endeavour to decoy him into the Boat and bring him on board, which Mr. Hicks performed without the least disturbance. We had no sooner taken the other Chiefs into Custody in Mr. Banks's Tent than they became as desirous of having the Men brought back has they were before of keeping them, and only desir'd that one of our people might be sent with some of theirs for them. Accordingly I sent a petty officer and the Corporal of Marines with 3 or 4 of their People, not doubting but they would return with the 2 Men in the evening; but they not coming as soon as I expected, I took all the Chiefs on board the ship for greater safety. About 9 o'Clock in the evening Webb, the Marine, was brought in by some of the natives and sent on board. He informed me that the Petty Officer and Corporal that had been sent in quest of them were disarm'd and seiz'd upon by the natives, and that Gibson was with them. Immediately upon getting this information I dispatch'd Mr. Hicks away in the Long boat with a strong party of men to rescue them but before he went Tootaha and the other Chiefs was made to understand that they must send some of their People with Mr. Hicks to shew him the place where our men were, and at the same time to send orders for their immediate releasement, for if any harm came to the men they (the Chiefs) would suffer for it; and I believe at this time they wished as much to see the Men return in safety as I did, for the guides conducted Mr. Hicks to the place before daylight, and he recovered the men without the least opposition, and return'd with them about 7 o'Clock in the morning of

Tuesday, 11th. I then told the Chiefs that there remain'd nothing more to be done to regain their liberty but to deliver up the Arms the People had taken from the Petty Officer and Corporal, and these were brought on board in less than half an Hour, and then I sent them all on shore. They made but a short stay with our people there before they went away, and most of the natives with them: but they first wanted to give us 4 Hogs. These we refused to except of them, as they would take nothing in return. Thus we are likely to leave these people in disgust with our behaviour towards them, owing wholy to the folly of 2 of our men, for it does not appear that the natives had any hand in inticing them away, and therefore were not the first Agressors. However, it is very certain that had we not taken this step we never should have recovered them. The Petty Officer whom I sent in quest of the deserters told me that the Natives would give him no intelligence where they were, nor those that went along with him, but, on the contrary, grew very troublesome, and, as they were returning in the evening, they were suddenly seized upon by a number of Armed men that had hid themselves in the wood for that purpose. This was after Tootaha had been seized upon by us, so that they did this by way of retaliation in order to recover their Chief; but this method did not meet with the approbation of them all. A great many condemn'd these proceedings, and were for having them set at liberty, while others were for keeping them until Tootaha was releas'd. The dispute went so far that they came from words to blows, and our people were several times very near being set at liberty; but at last the party for keeping them Prevailed, but, as they had still some friends, no insult was offer'd them. A little while after they brought Webb and Gibson, the two deserters, to them as Prisoners likewise; but at last they agreed that Webb should be sent to inform us where the others were. When I came to Examine these 2 Men touching the reasons that induced them to go away, it appeared that an acquaintance they had contracted with 2 Girls, and to whom they had strongly attached themselves, was the Sole reason of their attempting to stay behind. Yesterday we weighed the small Bower Anchor, the Stock of which was so much eaten by the worms as to break in heaving up, and to-day we hove up the best Bower, and found the Stock in the very same Condition. This day we got everything off from the Shore, and to-night everybody lays on board.

Wednesday, 12th. The Carpenter employ'd in stocking the Anchors and the Seamen in getting the Ship ready for Sea. This morning we found the Staves of the Cask the Natives stole from us some time ago laying at the Watering place; but they had been Sencible enough to keep the Iron Hoops, and only return what to them was of no use.

[Sail from Tahiti.]

Thursday, 13th. Winds Easterly, a light breeze. This morning we was visited by Obariea and several others of our acquaintance, a thing we did not expect after what had hapned but 2 days ago; but this was in some measures owing to Mr. Banks, Dr. Solander, and myself going to Apparra last night, where we so far convinc'd them of our Friendly disposition that several of them were in tears at our coming away. Between 11 and 12 o'Clock we got under Sail, and took our final leave of these People, after a stay of just three Months, the most part of which time we have been upon good terms with them. Some few differences have now and then hapned owing partly to the want of rightly understanding each other, and partly to their natural thievish disposition, which we could not at all times bear with or guard against; but these have been attended with no ill consequence to either side except the first, in which one of them was kill'd, and this I was very sorry for, because from what had hapned to them by the Dolphin I thought it would have been no hard matter to have got and keep a footing with them without bloodshed. For some time before we left this Island several of the Natives were daily offering themselves to go away with us; and as it was thought they must be of use to us in our future discoveries we resolved to bring away one whose name is Tupia, a Chief and a Priest. This man had been with us most part of the time we had been upon the Island, which gave us an opportunity to know something of him. We found him to be a very intelligent person, and to know more of the Geography of the Islands situated in these Seas, their produce, and the religion, laws, and Customs of the inhabitants, than any one we had met with, and was the likeliest person to answer our Purpose. For these reasons, and at the request of Mr. Banks, I received him on board, together with a young Boy, his Servant. For the first two Months we were at this Island the Natives supplied us with as much Bread fruit, Cocoa Nuts, etc., as we could well dispence with, and now and then a few Hogs, but of these hardly sufficient to give the Ship's company one and sometimes two fresh Meals a week. As to Fowls, I did not see above 3 dozen upon the whole Island, and fish they seldom would part with; but during the last Month we got little refreshment of any sort. The detaining of their Canoes broke off Trade at that time, and it never after was begun again with any Spirit. However, it was not wholy owing to this, but to a Scarcity. The Season for Bread fruit was wholy over, and what other Fruits they had were hardly sufficient for themselves; at least, they did not care to part with them. All sorts of Fruits we purchased with Beads and Nails, not less than 40-penny, for a nail under that size was of no value; but we could not get a Hog above 10 or 12 pounds weight for anything less than a Hatchet, not but that they set great value upon Spike Nails; but, as this was an Article many in the Ship are provided with, the Women soon found a much easier way at coming at them than by bringing Provisions. Our Traffick with this people was carried on with as much Order as in the best regulated Market in Europe. It was managed ashore chiefly by Mr. Banks, who took uncommon Pains to procure from the Natives every kind of refreshment that was to be got. Axes, Hatchets, Spikes, large Nails, looking Glasses, Knives, and Beads are all highly valued by this People, and nothing more is wanting to Traffick with them for everything they have to dispose of. They are likewise very fond of fine Linnen Cloth, both White and Printed, but an Axe worth half a Crown will fetch more than a Piece of Cloth worth Twenty Shillings.

Upon our arrival at Batavia we had certain information that the two ships that were at George's Island some time before our arrival there were both French ships.* (* In Admiralty copy.)

DESCRIPTION OF KING GEORGE'S ISLAND.

This Island is called by the Natives Otaheite, and was first discovered by Captain Wallis, in His Majesty's ship Dolphin, on June 19th, 1767, and to the Credit of him and his Officers, the Longitude of Royal Bay was by them settled to within half a degree of the Truth, and the whole figure of the Island not ill described. It is situated between the Latitude of 17 degrees 29 minutes and 17 degrees 53 minutes South, and between the Longitude of 149 degrees 10 minutes and 149 degrees 39 minutes West from the Meridian of Greenwich.* (* These latitudes are exact. The modern limits of longitude are 149 degrees 7 minutes to 149 degrees 36 minutes 30 seconds.) Point Venus, so called from the Observation being made there, is the Northern extremity of the Island, and lies in the Longitude of 149 degrees 30 minutes,* (* Now considered to be 149 degrees 29 minutes.) being the mean result of a Great number of Observations made upon the Spot. The Shores of this Island are mostly guarded from the Sea by reefs of coral rocks, and these form several excellent Bays and Harbours, wherein are room and depth of Water sufficient for the largest Ships.

Royal Bay, called by the Natives Matavie,* (* Matavai.) in which we lay, and the Dolphin before us, is not inferior to any on the Island, both in Point of conveniency and Situation. It may easily be known by a Prodigious high Mountain in the middle of the Island, which bears due south from Point Venus, which is the Eastern point of the Bay. To sail into it either keep the West point of the Reefs which lies before Point Venus close on board, or give it a berth of near half a Mile in order to avoid a small Shoal of Coral Rocks, whereon is but 2 1/2 fathoms of water. The best Anchoring is on the Eastern side of the Bay in 16 or 14 fathoms of water, owsey bottom. The Shore of the bay is all a fine sandy beach, behind which runs a river of Fresh Water, so that any Number of Ships might Water here without discommoding one another. The only wood for fuel upon the whole Island is fruit Trees, and these must be purchased of the Natives, if you mean to keep on good Terms with them. There are some Harbours to the Westward of this bay that have not been mentioned, but as they lay Contiguous to it, and are to be found in the plan, the description of them is unnecessary.

The land of this Island, except what is immediately bordering upon the Sea coast, is of a very uneven Surface, and rises in ridges which run up into the middle of the Island, and there form mountains, that are of a height Sufficient to be seen at the distance of 20 leagues. Between the foot of the ridges and the Sea is a border of low Land surrounding the whole Island, except in a few places where the ridge rises directly from the Sea. This low land is of Various Breadths, but nowhere exceeds a Mile and a half. The Soil is rich and fertile, being for the most part well stock'd with fruit Trees and small Plantations. and well water'd by a number of small Rivulets of Excellent Water which come from the adjacent hills. It is upon this low Land that the greatest part of the inhabitants live, not in Towns or Vilages, but dispersed everywhere round the whole Island; the Tops of most of the ridges and mountains are Barren and, as it were, burnt up with the sun, yet many parts of some of them are not without their produce, and many of the Valleys are fertile and inhabited.

[Produce of Tahiti.]

OF THE PRODUCE.

The produce of this Island is Bread Fruit, Cocoa Nuts, Bonanoes, Plantains, a fruit like an Apple, sweet Potatoes, Yams, a Fruit known by the name of Eag Melloa, and reck'ned most delicious; Sugar Cane which the inhabitants eat raw; a root of the Salop kind, called by the inhabitants Pea; the root also of a plant called Ether; and a fruit in a pod like a Kidney bean, which when roasted eats like a Chestnut, and is called Ahee; the fruit of a Tree which they call Wharra, something like a Pine Apple; the fruit of a Tree called by them Nano; the roots of a Fern and the roots of a plant called Thive. All these Articles the Earth almost Spontaniously produces, or, at least, they are raised with very little Labour. In the Article of food these people may almost be said to be exempt from the Curse of our Forefathers, scarcely can it be said that they Earn their bread with the sweat of their brow; benevolent Nature hath not only Supply'd them with necessarys, but with abundance of Superfluities. The Sea coast supplies them with vast Variety of most Excellent fish, but these they get not without some Trouble and Perseverance. Fish seems to be one of their greatest Luxuries, and they Eat it either raw or Dressed and seem to relish it one way as well as the other. Not only fish but almost everything that comes out of the Sea is Eat and Esteem'd by these People; Shell Fish, Lobsters, Crabs, and even sea insects, and what is commonly called blubbers of many kinds, conduce to their support.

For tame Animals they have Hogs, Fowls, and Dogs, the latter of which we learned to Eat from them, and few were there of us but what allow'd that a South Sea dog was next to an English Lamb. One thing in their favour is that they live intirely upon Vegetables; probably our Dogs would not Eat half so well. Little can be said in favour of their Fowles, but their pork is most Excellent, they have no beasts of Prey of any Sort, and Wild Fowls are scarce and confin'd to a few Species. When any of the Chiefs kill a Hog it seems to be almost equally divided among all his Dependents, and as these are generally very numerous, it is but a little that come to each person's share, so that their chief food is Vegetables, and of these they eat a large quantity.

Cookery seems to have been but little studied here; they have only 2 Methods of applying Fire--broiling and Baking, as we called it; the method this is done I have before described, and I am of Opinion that Victuals dressed this way are more juicy and more equally done than by any of our Methods, large Fish in particular, Bread Fruit, Bananoes. Plantains Cooked this way eat like boil'd Potatoes, and was much used by us by way of bread whenever we could get them. Of bread Fruit they make 2 or 3 dishes by beating it with a Stone Pestle till it makes a Paste, mixing Water or Cocoa Nut Liquor, or both, with it, and adding ripe Plantains, Bananoes, Sour Paste, etc.

This last is made from bread Fruit in the following manner. This fruit, from what I can find, remains in Season only 8 or 9 months in the year, and as it is the Chief support of the inhabitants a reserve of food must be made for those months when they are without it. To do this the Fruit is gathered when upon the point of ripening; after the rinde is scraped off it is laid in heaps and coverd close with leaves, where it undergoes a fermentation, and becomes soft and disagreeably sweet. The Core is then taken out, and the rest of the fruit thrown into a Hole dug for that purpose, the sides and bottom of which are neatly laid with grass. The whole is covered with leaves and heavy stones laid upon them; here it undergoes a second Fermentation and becomes sourish, in which condition they say it will keep good 10 or 12 months. As they want to use it they make it into balls, which they wrap up in leaves and bake in the same manner as they do the Fruit from the Tree; it is then ready for eating either hot or cold, and hath a sour and disagreeable taste. In this last State it will keep good a Month or 6 Weeks; it is called by them Mahai, and they seldom make a Meal without some of it, one way or another. To this plain diet Salt Water is the universal sauce, hardly any one sets down to a meal without a Cocoa Nut shell full of it standing by them, into which they dip most of what they Eat, especially Fish, drinking at Intervals large sops of it out of their Hands, so that a man may use half a Pint at a Meal.

It is not common for any 2 to eat together, the better sort hardly ever; and the women never upon any account eat with the Men, but always by themselves. What can be the reason of so unusual a custom it is hard to say; especially as they are a people, in every other instance, fond of Society and much so of their Women. They were often Asked the reason, but they never gave no other Answer, but that they did it because it was right, and Express'd much dislike at the Custom of Men and Women Eating together of the same Victuals. We have often used all the intreatys we were Masters of to invite the Women to partake of our Victuals at our Tables, but there never was an instance of one of them doing it publick, but they would Often goe 5 or 6 together into the Servants apartments, and there eat very heartily of whatever they could find, nor were they the least disturbed if any of us came in while they were dining; and it hath sometimes hapned that when a woman was alone in our company she would eat with us, but always took care that her own people should not know what she had don, so that whatever may be the reasons for this custom, it certainly affects their outward manners more than their Principle.

[Natives of Tahiti.]

PERSON OF THE NATIVES.

With respect to their persons the Men in general are tall, strong-limb'd, and well shaped. One of the tallest we saw measured 6 feet 3 inches and a half. The superior women are in every respect as large as Europeans, but the inferior sort are in General small, owing possibly to their early Amours, which they are more addicted to than their superiors. They are of various Colours: those of the inferior sort, who are obliged to be much exposed to the Sun and air, are of a very Dark brown; the superiors again, who spend most of their Time in their Houses under Shelter, are not browner than people who are born or reside longer in the West Indies; nay, some of the Women are almost as fair as Europeans. Their hair is almost universally black, thick, and Strong; this the Women wear short Cropt Round their Ears. The Men, on the other hand, wear it different ways: the better sort let it grow long, and sometimes tying it up on the Top of their Heads, or letting it hang loose over their Shoulders; but many of the inferiors, and such who, in the exercise of their professions, fishing, etc., are obliged to be much upon or in the Water, wear it cropt short like the women. They always pluck out a part of their beards, and keep what remains neat and Clean. Both Sexes eradicate every hair from under their Armpits, and look upon it as a mark of uncleanliness in us that we do not do the Same.

They have all fine white Teeth, and for the most part short flat Noses and thick lips; yet their features are agreeable, and their gaite graceful, and their behavior to strangers and to each other is open, affable, and Courteous, and, from all I could see, free from treachery, only that they are thieves to a man, and would steal but everything that came in their way, and that with such dexterity as would shame the most noted Pickpocket in Europe. They are very cleanly people, both in their persons and diet, always washing their hands and Mouth immediately before and after their Meals, and wash or Bathe themselves in fresh Water 3 times a day, morning, Noon, and Night.

The only disagreeable thing about them is the Oil with which they anoint their heads, Monoe, as they call it; this is made of Cocoanutt Oil, in which some sweet Herbs or Flowers are infused. The Oil is generally very rancid, which makes the wearer of it smell not very agreeable.* (* Other voyagers have, on the contrary, described the odour of this sweetened oil as agreeable.) Another custom they have that is disagreeable to Europeans, which is eating lice, a pretty good stock of which they generally carry about them. However, this custom is not universal; for I seldom saw it done but among Children and Common People, and I am perswaided that had they the means they would keep themselves as free from lice as we do; but the want of Combs in a Hot climate makes this hardly possible. There are some very fine men upon this Island whose skins are whiter than any European's, but of a Dead Colour, like that of the Nose of a White Horse; their Eyes, eyebrows, hair and beards are also White. Their bodys were cover'd, more or less, with a kind of White down. Their skins are spotted, some parts being much whiter than others. They are short-sighted, with their eyes oftimes full of rheum, and always look'd unwholesome, and have neither the Spirit nor the activity of the other Natives. I did not see above 3 or 4 upon the whole Island, and these were old men; so that I concluded that this difference of colour, etc., was accidental, and did not run in families, for if it did they must have been more Numerous. The inhabitants of this Island are Troubled with a sort of Leprosy, or Scab all over their bodys. I have seen Men, Women, and Children, but not many, who have had this distemper to that degree as not to be able to walk. This distemper, I believe, runs in familys, because I have seen both mother and Child have it.

Both sexes paint their Bodys, Tattow, as it is called in their Language. This is done by inlaying the Colour of Black under their skins, in such a manner as to be indelible. Some have ill-design'd figures of men, birds, or dogs; the women generally have this figure Z simply on every joint of their fingers and Toes; the men have it likewise, and both have other differant figures, such as Circles, Crescents, etc., which they have on their Arms and Legs; in short, they are so various in the application of these figures that both the quantity and Situation of them seem to depend intirely upon the humour of each individual, yet all agree in having their buttocks covered with a Deep black. Over this Most have Arches drawn one over another as high as their short ribs, which are near a Quarter of an inch broad. These Arches seem to be their great pride, as both men and Women show them with great pleasure.

Their method of Tattowing I shall now describe. The colour they use is lamp black, prepar'd from the Smoak of a Kind of Oily nut, used by them instead of Candles. The instrument for pricking it under the Skin is made of very thin flatt pieces of bone or Shell, from a quarter of an inch to an inch and a half broad, according to the purpose it is to be used for, and about an inch and a half long. One end is cut into sharp teeth, and the other fastened to a handle. The teeth are dipped into black Liquor, and then drove, by quick, sharp blows struck upon the handle with a Stick for that purpose, into the skin so deep that every stroke is followed with a small quantity of Blood. The part so marked remains sore for some days before it heals. As this is a painful operation, especially the Tattowing their Buttocks, it is perform'd but once in their Life times; it is never done until they are 12 or 14 years of Age.

[Clothing of Tahitians.]

Their Cloathing is either of Cloth or Matting of several different sorts; the dress of both Men and Women are much the same, which is a Piece of Cloth or Matting wrapp'd 2 or 3 times round their waist, and hangs down below their Knees, both behind and before, like a Pettycoat; another piece, or sometimes 2 or 3, about 2 yards or 2 1/2 yards long, with a hole in the Middle, through which they put their heads. This hangs over their Shoulders down behind and before, and is tied round their waist with a long piece of thin Cloth, and being open at the sides gives free liberty to their arms. This is the common dress of all ranks of people, and there are few without such a one except the Children, who go quite naked, the Boys until they are 6 or 7 years of Age, and the girls until 3 or 4. At these Ages they begin to cover what nature teaches them to hide. Besides the dress I have mentioned some of the better sort, such as can afford it, but more especially the Women, will one way or other wrap round them several pieces of Cloth, each 8 or 10 Yards long and 2 or 3 broad, so much that I have often wondered how they could bear it in so hot a climate. Again, on the other hand, many of the inferior sort during the heat of the Day, go almost naked, the women wearing nothing but the Petticoat aforementioned, and sometimes hardly that. The men wear a piece of Cloth like a Sack, which goes between their thighs, and brought up before and behind, and then wrapped round their waist. This every man wears always without exception, and it is no uncommon thing to see many of the better sort have nothing else on, as it is reckoned no shame for any part of the body to be exposed to View, except those which all mankind hide.

Both sexes sometimes shade their faces from the Sun with little Bonnets made of Cocoa-Nut leaves. Some have them of fine Matting, but this is less common. They sometimes wear Turbands, but their Chief Headdress is what they call Tomou, which is human Hair plaited scarce thicker than common thread. Of this I can safely affirm that I have seen pieces near a mile in length worked upon one end without a Knott. These are made and worn only by the women, 5 or 6 such pieces of which they will sometimes wind round their Heads, the effect of which, if done with taste, is very becoming. They have Earings by way of Ornament, but wear them only at one Ear. These are made of Shells, Stones, Berries, red pease, and some small pearls which they wear 3 tied together; but our Beads, Buttons, etc., very soon supply'd their places.

[Customs of Tahiti.]

MANNERS AND CUSTOMS.

After their meals in the Heat of the day they often Sleep, middle Aged people especially, the better sort of whom seem to spend most of their time in eating and Sleeping. Diversions they have but few, shooting with the Bow and Wrestling are the Chief; the first of which is confin'd almost wholy to the Chiefs; they shoot for distance only, kneeling upon one knee and dropping the Bow the instant of the Arrows parting from it. I have seen one of them shoot an Arrow 274 yards, yet he looked upon it as no Great Shotte.

Musick is little known to them, yet they are very fond of it; they have only 2 Instruments--the flute and the Drum. The former is made of hollow Bamboo about 15 inches long, in which are 3 Holes; into one of them they blow with one Nostril, stopping the other with the thumb of the left hand, the other 2 Holes they stop and unstop with their fingers, and by this means produce 4 Notes, of which they have made one Tune, which serves them upon all Occasions, to which they sing a number of songs generally consisting of 2 lines and generally in rhime. At any time of the day when they are Lazy they amuse themselves by singing these Couplets, but especially after dark when their candles are lighted, which are made of the Kernels of a Nutt abounding much in oil; these are stuck upon a Skewer of Wood one upon another, and give a very Tolerable light, which they often keep burning an hour after dark, and if they have strangers in the House much longer. Their drums are made of a hollow block of wood covered with Shark's Skin, and instead of Drumsticks they use their hands. Of these they make out 5 or 6 tunes and accompany the flutes.

The drums are Chiefly used at their Heivas, which are a set of Musicians, 2 or 3 Drums for instance, as many flutes and singers, which go about from House to House and play, and are always received and rewarded by the Master of the family, who gives them a Piece of Cloth or whatever he can spare, for which they will stay 3 or 4 hours, during which time his house will be crowded full, for the people are extravagantly fond of this diversion. The Young Girls whenever they can collect 8 or 10 Together dance a very indecent Dance, which they call Timorodee, singing most indecent songs and using most indecent actions, in the practice of which they are brought up from their earliest childhood; in doing this they keep time to a great nicety. This exercise is generally left off as soon as they arrive at Years of Maturity, for as soon as they have form'd a connection with man they are expected to leave off dancing Timorodee.

One amusement or custom more I must mention, though I confess I do not expect to be believed, it is founded upon a Custom so inhuman and contrary to the Principles of human nature. It is this: that more than one half of the better sort of the inhabitants have enter'd into a resolution of injoying free liberty in Love, without being Troubled or disturbed by its consequences. These mix and Cohabit together with the utmost freedom, and the Chilldren who are so unfortunate as to be thus begot are smother'd at the Moment of their Birth; many of these People contract intimacies and live together as man and wife for years, in the course of which the Children that are born are destroy'd. They are so far from concealing it that they look upon it as a branch of freedom upon which they Value themselves. They are called Arreoys, and have meetings among themselves, where the men amuse themselves with Wrestling, etc., and the Women in dancing the indecent dance before-mentioned, in the course of which they give full Liberty to their desires, but I believe keep up to the appearance of decency. I never see one of these meetings; Dr. Monkhouse saw part of one, enough to make him give Credit to what we had been told.

Both sexes express the most indecent ideas in conversation without the least emotion, and they delight in such conversation beyond any other. Chastity, indeed, is but little valued, especially among the middle people--if a Wife is found guilty of a breach of it her only punishment is a beating from her husband. The Men will very readily offer the Young Women to Strangers, even their own Daughters, and think it very strange if you refuse them; but this is done merely for the sake of gain.

The Houses or dwellings of these People are admirably calculated for the continual warmth of the Climate; they do not build them in Towns or Villages, but seperate each from the other, and always in the Woods, and are without walls, so that the air, cooled by the shade of the Trees, has free access in whatever direction it happens to blow. No country can boast of more delightful walks than this; the whole Plains where the Natives reside are covered with groves of Bread Fruit and Cocoa Nut Trees, without underwood, and intersected in all directions by the Paths which go from House to House, so that nothing can be more grateful in a Climate where the sun hath so powerful an influence. They are generally built in form of an Oblong square, the Roofs are supported by 3 Rows of Pillars or posts, and neatly covered with Thatch made of Palm leaves. A middle-siz'd house is about 24 feet by 12, extream heigth about 8 or 9, and heigth of the Eves 3 1/2 or 4. The floors are cover'd some inches deep with Hay, upon which, here and there, lay matts for the conveniency of sitting down; few houses has more than one Stool, which is only used by the Master of the family.

TAHITI: TYPES OF CANOES.

TAHITI: TYPES OF CANOES.

In their houses are no rooms or Partitions, but they all huddle and Sleep together; yet in this they generally observe some order, the Married people laying by themselves, and the unmarried each sex by themselves, at some small distance from each other. Many of the Eares or Chiefs are more private, having small movable houses in which they Sleep, man and Wife, which, when they go by Water from place to place, are tied upon their Canoes; these have walls made of Cocoa-Nut leaves, etc. I have said that the houses are without walls, but this is only to be understood in general, for many of them are walled with wickering, but not so close but to admit a free circulation of Air. The matts which serve them to sit upon in the daytime are also their beds in the night, and the Cloathes they wear in the day serve for covering, a little wood Stool, block of wood, or bundle of Cloth for a Pillow. Besides these common houses there are others much larger, 200 feet long and upwards, 30 broad, and 20 in heigth. There are generally 2 or 3 of these in every district, and seem'd not only built for the accommodation of the principal people, but common to all the inhabitants of that district, and raised and kept up by their joint Labour; these are always without walls, and have generally a large Area on one side neatly inclosed with low pallisades, etc.

[Tahitian Canoes.]

Their Canoes or Proes are built all of them very narrow, and some of the largest are 60 or 70 feet long. These consist of several pieces; the bottom is round and made of large logs hollow'd out to the thickness of about 3 Inches, and may consist of 3 or 4 pieces; the sides are of Plank of nearly the same thickness, and are built nearly perpendicular, rounding in a little towards the Gunwale. The pieces on which they are built are well fitted, and fastned or sewed together with strong platting something in the same manner as old China, Wooden Bowls, etc., are mended. The greatest breadth is at the after part, which is generally about 18 or 20 Inches, and the fore part about 1/3 Narrower; the heigth from the bottom to the Gunwale seldom exceeds 2 1/2 or 3 feet. They build them with high curv'd Sterns which are generally ornamented with carved work; the head or fore part curves little or nothing. The smaller Canoes are built after the same plan, some out of one, 2, or more trees according to their size or the use they are for. In order to prevent them from oversetting when in the Water, all those that go single, both great and Small, have what is called Outriggers, which are Pieces of Wood fastened to the Gunwale and project out on one side about 6, 8, or 10 feet, according to the size of the Boat. At the end is fastened in a Parrallel direction to the Canoe a long log of wood simply; or some have it Shaped in the form of a small Boat, but this is not common; this lays in the Water and Balances the Boat. Those that are for sailing have Outriggers only on the other side abreast of the Mast; these serves to fasten the Shrouds to, and are of use in Trimming the Boat when it blows fresh; the sailing proes have some one and some 2 masts; the sails are of Matting and are made narrow at the head and Square at the foot, something like a Shoulder of Mutton Sail, such as are generally used in Man-of-War Barges, etc.

I have mentioned above that the single Canoes have Outriggers, for those that go double--that is 2 together, which is very common--have no need of any; and it is done in this manner: 2 Canoes are placed in a parrallel direction to each other, about 3 or 4 feet asunder, securing them together by small Logs of Wood laid across and lashed to each of their gunwales; thus the one boat supports the other, and are not in the least danger of upsetting, and I believe it is in this manner that all their large Proes are used, some of which will carry a great number of Men, by means of a Platform made of Bamboo or other light wood and the whole length of the Proes and considerably broader, but I never saw but one fitted in this manner upon the whole Island. Upon the Forepart of all these large double Proes was placed an Oblong Platform about ten or twelve feet in length, and six or eight in Breadth, and supported about 4 feet above the Gunwale by stout Carved Pillars. The use of these Platforms, as we were told, are for the Club Men to stand and fight upon in time of Battle, for the large Canoes, from what I could learn, are built most, if not wholly, for war, and their method of fighting is to Graple one another and fight it out with Clubs, spears, and stones. I never saw but one of these sort of Canoes in the water, the rest was all hauled ashore and seemed to be going to decay, neither were there very many of them upon the Island.* (* The war canoes of Tahiti exist no longer. The others are still used, and merit all Cook's encomiums on their sailing qualities.)

The Chiefs and better sort of People generally go from one part of the island to another in small double Canoes which carry a little movable House, this not only Skreens them from the Sun by day, but serves them to Sleep in in the Night, and this way of Travelling is Extremely commodious about such Islands as are inclosed by a reef as this is; for as these Canoes draw but Little water they can always keep in the Reefs, and by that means are never in danger.

They have some few other Canoes, Pahees as they call them, which differ from those above discribed, but of these I saw but 6 upon the whole Island, and was told they were not built here. The 2 largest was each 76 feet long, and when they had been in use had been fastned together. These are built Sharp and Narrow at both Ends and broad in the Middle; the bottom is likewise Sharp, inclining to a Wedge, yet Buldges out very much and rounds in again very quick just below the Gunwale. They are built of several pieces of thick plank and put together as the others are, only these have timbers in the inside, which the others have not. They have high Curved Sterns, the head also Curves a little, and both are ornamented with the image of a man carved in wood, very little inferior work of the like kind done by common Ship Carvers in England.

When one Considers the Tools these people have one cannot help but admiring their workmanship; these are Adzes and small Hatchets made of a hard Stone, Chizels and Gouges made of human bones, generally the bones of the Forearm, but Spike Nails have pretty well supplyd the place of these. With these ordinary Tools, that a European would expect to break the first stroke, I have seen them work surprisingly fast. To plain or polish their work they rub upon it, with a small stone, Coral Beat small and Mixed with Water; this is done sometimes by scraping it with Shells, with which alone they perform most of their Small wood work.

Their Proes or Canoes, large and Small, are row'd and Steer'd with Paddles, and, notwithstanding the large ones appear to be very unweildy, they manage them very dexterously, and I believe perform long and distant Voyages in them, otherwise they could not have the knowledge of the Islands in these Seas they seem to have. They wear for Shew or Ornament at the Mast Head of most of their Sailing Canoes Pendants made of Feathers.

Having described their fighting Canoes I shall next describe their Arms with which they attack their Enemys, both by Sea and Land. These are Clubs, Spears or Lances, Slings and Stones which they throw by hand. The Clubs are made of a hard wood, and are about 8 or 9 feet long; the one half is made flatish with 2 Edges, and the other half is round and not thicker than to be easily grasped by the hand. The Lances are of various lengths, some from 12, 20 or 30 feet, and are generally Arm'd at the Small end with the Stings of

Sting-rays, which makes them very dangerous weapons. Altho' these people have Bows and Arrows--and those none of the worst--we are told that they never use them in their wars, which doubtless is very extraordinary and not easily accounted for. They have very Curious breastplates, made of small wickers, pieces of Matting, etc., and neatly Cover'd with Sharks' teeth, Pearl Oyster shells, birds' feathers, and dogs' hair. Thus much for their Arms, etc.

[Tahitian Cloth.]

I shall now describe their way of making Cloth, which, in my opinion, is the only Curious manufacture they have. All their Cloth is, I believe, made from the Bark of Trees; the finest is made from a plant which they Cultivate for no other purpose.* (* Broussonetia papyrifera. The manufacture is common to all Polynesia, and the ordinary name for it in the Pacific is Tapa. The Tahitians, however, called it Ahu.) Dr. Solander thinks it is the same plant the bark of which the Chinese make paper of. They let this plant grow till it is about 6 or 8 feet high, the Stem is then about as thick as one's Thum or thicker; after this they cut it down and lay it a Certain time in water. This makes the Bark strip off easy, the outside of which is scraped off with a rough Shell. After this is done it looks like long strips of ragged linnen; these they lay together, by means of a fine paist made of some sort of a root, to the Breadth of a yard more or less, and in length 6, 8 or 10 Yards or more according to the use it is for. After it is thus put together it is beat out to its proper breadth and fineness, upon a long square piece of wood, with wooden beaters, the Cloth being keept wet all the time. The beaters are made of hard wood with four square sides, are about 3 or 4 inches broad and cut into grooves of different fineness; this makes the Cloth look at first sight as if it was wove with thread, but I believe the principal use of the Groves is to facilitate the beating it out, in the doing of which they often beat holes in it, or one place thinner than another; but this is easily repair'd by pasting on small bits, and this they do in such a manner that the Cloth is not the least injured. The finest sort when bleached is very white and comes nearest to fine Cotton. Thick cloth, especially fine, is made by pasting two or more thickness's of thin cloth, made for that Purpose, together. Coarse thick cloth and ordinary thin cloth is made of the Bark of Bread fruit Trees, and I think I have been told that it is sometimes made from the Bark of other trees. The making of Cloth is wholy the work of the women, in which all ranks are employ'd. Their common colours are red, brown and yellow, with which they dye some pieces just as their fancy leads them. Besides Cloth they make several different sorts of matting, both better and finer than any we have in Europe; the stuff they make it on is the Produce of the Palm tree.

This Island produceth 2 or 3 sorts of plants, of which they make the rope they use in rigging their Canoes, etc.; the finest sort, such as fishing lines, saine twine, etc., is made of the Bark of a Tree, and some from the Kind of

Silk grass. Their fishing lines and saines are in Point of goodness preferable to any of ours. Their fishing Hooks are very curiously made of Tortoise, Pearl Oyster Shells, etc. They have a sort of Saine that is made of Coarse broad grass like flags; these are twisted and tied together in a loose manner until the whole is as thick as a large sack, and 60 or 80 fathoms long. This they haul in Shoal smooth water; its own weight keeps it so close to the ground that hardly the smallest fish can escape out.

I have before mentioned that the Island is divided into two districts or kingdoms, which are frequently at war with each other, as hapned about 12 Months ago, and each of these are again divided into smaller districts, Whennuas as they call them. Over each of the kingdoms is an Eare dehi, or head, whom we call a King, and in the Whennuas are Eares, or Chiefs. The King's power seems to be but very little; he may be reverenced as a father, but he is neither fear'd nor respected as a monarch, and the same may be said of the other Chiefs. However, they have a pre-eminence over the rest of the People, who pay them a kind of a Voluntary Obedience. Upon the whole, these people seem to enjoy liberty in its fullest extent--every man seems to be the sole judge of his own actions and to know no punishment but death, and this perhaps is never inflicted but upon a public enemy. There are 3 ranks of Men and Women: first, the Eares, or chiefs; second, the Manahoonas, or Middling sort; and lastly, the Toutous, which comprehend all the lower-class, and are by far the most numerous. These seem to live in some sort dependent on the Eares, who, together with the Manahoonas, own most, if not all the land. This is Hereditary in their families, and the moment the Heir is born he succeeds the Father, both in title and Estate; at least to the name, for its most likely that the latter must have the power during his Son or Daughter's Minority.

Note by Cook. Upon our arrival at Batavia, we were informed the two French Ships, commanded by the Monsieurs Beaugainvile, touched at that place in their way home from the South Seas two years ago. We were here told many circumstances of these two Ships, all tending to prove that they were the same ships that were at George's Island, which we judged were Spaniards; being led into this mistake by the Spanish Iron, etc., we saw among the natives, which is easy accounted for, for we are told that while Beaugainvile in the Frigate was delivering up that part of Falkland Islands possess'd by the French, to the Spaniards, the Store ship was trading with the Spaniards in the River Plate, where it is very probable she disposed of all her European goods, and purchased others to trade with the Islands in the South Seas. To confirm these last circumstances we were told that when they arrived at Batavia, the Frigate had on board a great quantity of Spanish Dollars.

[Religion of Tahiti.]

Having given the best account I can of the manners and Customs of these people, it will be expected that I should give some account of their religion, which is a thing I have learned so little of that I hardly dare to touch upon it, and should have passed it over in silence, was it not my duty as well as inclination to insert in this Journal every and the least knowledge I may obtain of a People, who for many Centuries have been shut up from almost every other part of the world.

They believe that there is one Supreem God whom they call Tane; from him sprung a number of inferior Deities, Eatuas as they call them--these they think preside over them and intermeddle in their affairs. To these they offer Oblations such as Hogs, Dogs, Fish, Fruit, etc., and invoke them on some particular occasions, as in time of real or Apparent Danger, the setting out of a long Voyage, sickness's, etc.; but the Ceremony made use of on these occasions I know not. The Mories, which we at first thought were burying places, are wholy built for Places of worship, and for the Performing of religious ceremonies in.* (* Cook did not apparently learn anything in this voyage of the human sacrifices offered in the Morais on many occasions, such as before war; at the coronation of the king; etc. The Tahitians were, however, never guilty of cannibalism.) The Viands are laid upon altars erected 8, 12, or 12 Feet high, by stout Posts, and the Table of the Altar on which the Viands lay, is generally made of Palm leaves; they are not always in the Mories, but very often at some Distance from them. Their Mories, as well as the Tombs of the Dead, they seem to hold sacred, and the women never enter the former, whatever they may do the latter. The Viands laid near the Tombs of the Dead are, from what I can learn, not for the deceased, but as an Offering to the Eatua made upon that Occasion who, if not, would distroy the body and not except of the soul--for they believe of a future state of rewards and punishments; but what their Ideas are of it I know not. We have seen in some few places small Houses set apart on purpose for the Oblations offer'd to the Eatua, which consists of small strips of Cloth, Viands, etc. I am of Opinion they offer to the Eatua a Strip or small piece of every piece of Cloth they make before they use it themselves, and it is not unlikely but what they observe the same thing with respect to their Victuals, but as there are but few of these houses this cannot be a common Custom; it may only be observ'd by the Priests and such families as are more religious than others.

Now I have mentioned Priests, there are men that Exercise that function, of which Numbers Tupia is one. They seem to be in no great repute, neither can they live wholy by their Profession, and this leads me to think that these People are no bigots to their religion. The Priests on some occasions do the Office of Physicians, and their prescriptions consists in performing some religious ceremony before the sick person. They likewise Crown the Eare dehi, or King, in the performing of which we are told much form and Ceremony is used, after which every one is at liberty to treat and play as many Tricks with the new King as he pleaseth during the remainder of the day.

There is a ceremony which they perform at or after the Funerals of the Dead which I had forgot to mention at the time; we hapned to see it sometime before we left the Island. An old Woman, a relation of Toobouratomita's, hapned to die and was interr'd in the Usual manner. For several successive evenings after, one of her relations dressed himself in a very odd dress, which I cannot tell how to describe or to convey a better Idea of it than to suppose a man dress'd with plumes of feathers, something in the same manner as those worn by Coaches, Hearses, Horses, etc., at the Funerals in London. It was very neatly made up of black or brown and white cloth, black and white feathers, and pearl Oyster Shells. It cover'd the head, face, and body, as low as the Calf of the Legs or lower, and not only looked grand but awful likewise. The man thus equip'd, and attended by 2 or 3 more men and Women with their faces and bodys besmear'd with soot, and a Club in their hands, would about sunset take a Compass of near a mile running here and there, and wherever they came the People would fly from them as tho' they had been so many hobgoblins, not one daring to come in their way. I know not the reason for their Performing this ceremony, which they call Heiva, a name they give to most of their divertisements.

They compute time by the Moon, which they call Malama, reckoning 30 days to each moon, 2 of which they say the moon is Mattee, that is, dead, and this is at the time of the new moon, when she cannot be seen. The day they divide into smaller Portions not less than 2 Hours. Their computations is by units, tens, and scores, up to ten score, or 200, etc. In counting they generally take hold on their fingers one by one, Shifting from one hand to the other, until they come to the number they want to express; but if it be a high number, instead of their fingers they use pieces of Leaves, etc.

In conversation one with another they frequently join signs to their words, in which they are so expressive that a stranger will very soon comprehend their meaning by their actions.

Having now done with the People, I must once more return to the Island before I quit it altogether, which, notwithstanding nature hath been so very bountiful to it, yet it does not produce any one thing of intrinsick value or that can be converted into an Article of Trade; so that the value of the discovery consists wholy in the refreshments it will always afford to shipping in their passage through those seas; and in this it may be greatly improved by transporting hither horned cattle, etc. Pumpkins have got quite a footing here, the seeds of which most probably were brought here by the Spaniards.* (* Bougainville.) We sowed of the seeds of Water and Musk Mellons, which grew up and throve very fast. We also gave of these seeds and the seeds of Pine Apples to several of the Natives, and it cannot be doubted but what they will thrive here, and will be a great addition to the fruits they already have. Upon our first arrival we sowed of all sorts of English garden seeds and grain, but not a single thing came up except mustard sallad; but this I know was not owing either to the Soil or Climate, but to the badness of the seeds, which were spoil'd by the length of the Passage.

[Winds at Tahiti.]

Altho' this Island lies within the Tropick of Capricorn, yet the Heat is not Troublesome, nor do the winds blow constantly from the East, but are subject to variations, frequently blowing a fresh gale from the South-West Quarter for two or three days together, but very seldom from the North-West. Whenever these variable winds happen they are always accompanied with a swell from the South-West or West-South-West, and the same thing happens whenever it is calm and the Atmosphere at the same time loaded with Clouds--sure indication that the winds are Variable or Westerly out at Sea, for clear weather generally attends the settled Trade.

The meeting of Westerly winds within the general Limits of the Easterly Trade is a little extraordinary, and has induced former Navigators, when they met with them, to think that they were caused by the nearness of some large Tracks of Land: but I rather think they were owing to another Cause. It hath been found both by the Dolphin and us that the trade winds in those parts of this Sea doth not extend further to the Southward than 20 degrees, and without which we generally meet with a wind from the westward. Now, is it not reasonable to suppose that when these winds blow strong they must encroach upon and drive back the Easterly winds as to cause the variable winds and South-Westerly swells I have been speaking of? It is well known that the Trade winds blow but faint for some distance within their limits, and are therefore easily stopt by a wind from the Contrary direction. It is likewise known that these limits are subject to vary several degrees, not only at different seasons of the Year, but at one and the same season. Another reason why I think that these South-West winds are not caused by the nearness of any large Track of land, is in their being always accompanied with a large swell from the same Quarter, and we find a much greater surf beating upon the Shores of the South-West sides of the Islands situated just within the Limits of the Trade winds than upon any other part of them.

The tides are perhaps as inconsiderable in these Seas as in any part of the world. A South or South by West moon makes high water in Royal Bay, but the water does not rise upon a perpendicular above 10 or 12 inches, except on some very Extraordinary occasions.

The variation of the Compass I found to be 4 degrees 46 minutes Easterly, this being the mean result of a great number of Trials made by 4 of Dr. Knight's needles belonging to the Azimuth Compasses, all of which I judged to be good ones, and yet when applied to the Meridian line I found them not only differ one from another sometimes a degree and a half; but the same needle would differ from itself more or less, the difference sometimes amounting to half a degree, both at the same time and on differant days. This will in a great measure account for the seeming errors that may, upon a nice examination, appear to have been made in observing the Variation inserted in the Course of this Journal. This variableness in Magnetick Needles I have many times and in many places experienced both ashore and on board of Ships, and I do not remember of ever finding two Needles that would agree exactly together at one and the same time and place, but I have often found the same Needle agree with itself for several Trials made immediately one after another.* (* These discrepancies result from imperfections in the suspension and mounting of the needles, and are only absent in instruments too delicate for ordinary sea service.) However, all this is of no sort of consequence to Navigation, as the Variation of the Compass can always be found to a degree of accuracy more than sufficient for all nautical Purposes.

I have before hinted that these People have an Extensive knowledge of the Islands situated in these Seas. Tupia, as well as several others, hath given us an account of upwards of 70; but, as the account they have given of their situation is so Vague and uncertain, I shall refer giving a list of them until I have learnt from Tupia the Situation of each island with a little more certainty. Four of these islands--viz., Huaheine, Ulietea, Otaha, and Bolabola* (* These islands are now known as Huaheine, Raiatea, Tahaa, and Borabora or Bolabola, and are under French sovereignty.)--we were informed, lay only one or two days' sail to the Westward of George's Island, and that we might there procure Hogs, Fowls, and other refreshments, Articles that we have been very sparingly supply'd with at this last Island, as the Ship's Company (what from the Constant hard duty they have had at this place, and the two free use of Woman) were in a worse state of health than they were on our first arrival, for by this Time full half of them had got the Venerial disease, in which Situation I thought they would be ill able to stand the Cold weather we might expect to meet with to the Southward at this Season of the Year, and therefore resolved to give them a little time to recover while we ran down to and explored the Islands before-mentioned.

Tupia informs us that in the Months of November, December, and January they have constant Westerly winds, with rain; also that the whole island can muster 6780 Fighting Men, by which some judgment can be formed of the number of inhabitants. Each district furnishes a certain number, which the chief is obliged to bring into the field when summoned by the Eare dehi, or

King of the Island, either to make war or repell an invasion.* (* This paragraph is added in Admiralty copy.)

[Historical Notes, Tahiti.]

Notes on Tahiti. The missionaries who came to Tahiti in 1797, in the missionary ship Duff, and settled at Matavai, gathered many details of the history and economy of the islands. It appears that the state of society, though in many respects savage, had attained a certain pitch of civilisation, especially with regard to government. There was generally a head chief or king of the whole island, who governed after the feudal manner by the sub-chiefs. The sovereignty was hereditary, with this peculiarity, that the eldest son of the king became from his birth the sovereign. The father governed henceforth as regent until the son was of an age to take the reins in his own hands, when the father retired. This was the idea; but, as may be imagined, it led to various complications and difficulties, and wars between the different parts of the island and the different chiefs were frequent.

When Wallis discovered the island, in June 1767, Amo was king, or Arii-rahi (called by Cook Eare-dehi), Bereia (Cook's Obereia) being his wife. The latter seems to have been a woman of much character, and to have practically governed the island. The two were separated, inasmuch that they had mutually contracted other alliances, but, according to the custom of the country, without affecting their friendship.

On Wallis's appearance the warlike Tahitians at once attacked the Dolphin, but were easily defeated, and the guns and small arms with which they then for the first time made acquaintance had such an effect upon them that they speedily made peace, and recognised the superiority of Europeans.

The defeat had, however, a great effect on the prestige of Amo, whose authority rapidly diminished. Tootaha, Amo's brother, and chief of the district of Matavai, where the Dolphin anchored, was much enriched by her visit, and became a greater man in the eyes of his compatriots. Bougainville also touched at Tootaha's district; and although his two ships only remained ten days, it was long enough to furnish this chief with many more valuable and coveted articles.

In about December 1768, or six months before Cook's visit, war broke out in the island, and Amo was totally defeated by the chief who governed the eastern peninsula. Cook saw at Papara, on the south side of the main island, the relics of this battle in the shape of many human bones. Tootaha, who had joined in the war against his brother, became regent for the son (Pomare) of another brother, Hapai, and was therefore the principal man in the island when Cook appeared. Notwithstanding, when Amo (whom Cook calls Oamo), came to visit the Europeans on 21st June, bringing his young son,

Temare, with him, the latter was carried on men's shoulders, which was one of the ceremonial observances due to the Otou, or young king, and the natives present recognised his royal character by uncovering their shoulders.

Tupia (or Tupaia), who left the island with Cook, was the chief priest of the island, and had been living with Bereia; but having shortly before conspired to kill Tootaha, it is probable that he felt his life was unsafe in the island.

Frequent wars raged in the island for many years after Cook's first visit. Tootaha was killed in one of these, and when Cook again arrived, in 1773, Pomare was king, though Cook only knew him by his title of Otou, which he apparently still retained, though there was no regent.

In 1789 Captain Bligh called at Tahiti in the Bounty, to export young breadfruit trees to the West Indies. The delights of Tahiti probably had their part in bringing about the well-known mutiny a few days after the ship left; and on the return of the Bounty with her crew of mutineers, sixteen of them remained on the island. These men took a leading part in the continual dissensions in the island, until, in 1791, they were carried off by the Pandora, sent with the object of capturing the mutineers.

English missionaries came to Tahiti in 1797; but after twelve years' residence, during which they made no progress, and were constantly in danger from the frequent wars, they retreated to Sydney, in New South Wales, leaving two only of their number in Huahine and Eimeo, two of the Society Islands. Two years later, on the invitation of Pomare II, who was, however, then expelled from Tahiti and living in Eimeo, some of them returned, and Pomare became the first convert. Christianity rapidly spread, and in 1815, Pomare having returned to Tahiti, he and his Christian followers were attacked. The battle ended in the complete victory of Pomare, and for the first time in the sanguinary history of the island no butchery of the vanquished followed, nor any devastation of the country. The principal idols were destroyed; and whether in consequence of the surprise the natives felt at finding that no retribution followed this sacrilege, or from gratitude at the clemency of the victors, opposition to the new religion ceased, the whole island soon became Christian, and the customs of the inhabitants were much changed. In 1827 the British Government declined to accede to a request to throw its protectorate over Tahiti.

In 1836 two French priests came to the island with the avowed intention of proselytising. They were expelled; and after several visits of French men-of-war, who came to obtain redress for this act, and an assurance of free entrance for French subjects, the island was taken possession of by a French squadron in 1843, and Queen Pomare, daughter of Pomare II, was de facto deposed. The island has been ever since under the dominion of France.

Tahiti is now in a flourishing condition, and exports a considerable quantity of cotton, cocoanuts, and vanilla.

The majority of the natives still profess the Protestant religion.

Papiete, a little westward of Matavai, is now the principal port and town of the island, the harbour possessing some advantages over the latter.

The Tahitians are marvellously fond of singing and dancing, and still retain their primitive and exceedingly free manners, and the custom of decorating themselves with flowers.

The beauty of the island, with its neighbouring western group, is probably unsurpassed, and, considering all the circumstances, it says much for the discipline of the Endeavour that only two of her crew attempted to remain in what seemed a Paradise.

Cook's efforts to make his men deal properly with the natives are well illustrated by the following extract from Mr. Molineux's Log, of the 29th April. The incident is not mentioned by Cook.

"Punished Hy. Jeffs, Seaman, with a dozen lashes for ill-behaviour on shore. He had been rude to a man's wife yesterday, of which the Indian complained, and Jeffs was confined immediately the Captain had the fact plainly proved, and next morning the Captain invited the offended Parties on board, who were ignorant of his intentions. All hands being called, and the Prisoner brought aft, the Captain explained the nature of his Crime in the most lively manner, and made a very Pathetick speech to the Ship's Company during his punishment. The woman was in the greatest agonies, and strongly interceded for him. The man's name was Tuburi and his wife's name Tamide. I remember them both last Voyage. I should have mentioned Tuburi being sorry to see Jeffs punished."

It is evident, from what Cook himself tells us (above), and from what is now well known of the laxity of Tahitian morals, that this punishment would seem excessive to the natives, and especially to the women, who were accustomed themselves to bear whatever blame was bestowed.

Note. For full description of original Tahitian manners and customs, see "Polynesian Researches," by W. Ellis (London, H.G. Bohn, 1853); "Iles Taiti," par MM. Vincendon-Dumoulin et Chas. Desgraz (Paris, 1844).

CHAPTER 4.
TAHITI TO NEW ZEALAND.

REMARKABLE OCCURRENCES AT SEA.

[July 1769.]

FRIDAY, July 14th. Gentle breezes at North-East and Clear weather. I have before made mention of our departure from Royal Bay on the preceeding forenoon, and likewise that I had determined to run down to Huaheine and Ulietea* (* Raiatea.) before we stood to the Southward; but having discovered, from the Hills of George's Island, an Island laying to the Northward, we first stood that way to take a nearer View of it. This Island is called Tethuroa.* (* Tetiaroa.) It lies North 1/2 West, distant 8 Leagues from Point Venus, and is a small, low, uninhabited Island, frequented by the people of George's Island for fish, with which it is said to abound. At 6 A.M. the Westermost part of York Island bore South-East 1/2 South and the body of George's Island East 1/2 South. Punished the 2 Marines who attempted to desert from us at George's Island with 2 Dozen lashes each, and then released them from Confinement. At Noon the body of York Island* (* Eimeo, or Murea.) bore East by South 1/2 South, Royal Bay South 70 degrees 45 minutes East, distant 61 Miles; and an Island which we took to be Saunder's Island, discovered by Captain Wallace (called by the Natives Topoamanan),* (* Tubuai Manu.) bore South-South-West Latitude observed, 17 degrees 9 minutes South. Saw land bearing North-West 1/2 West, which Tupia calls the Island of Huaheine.

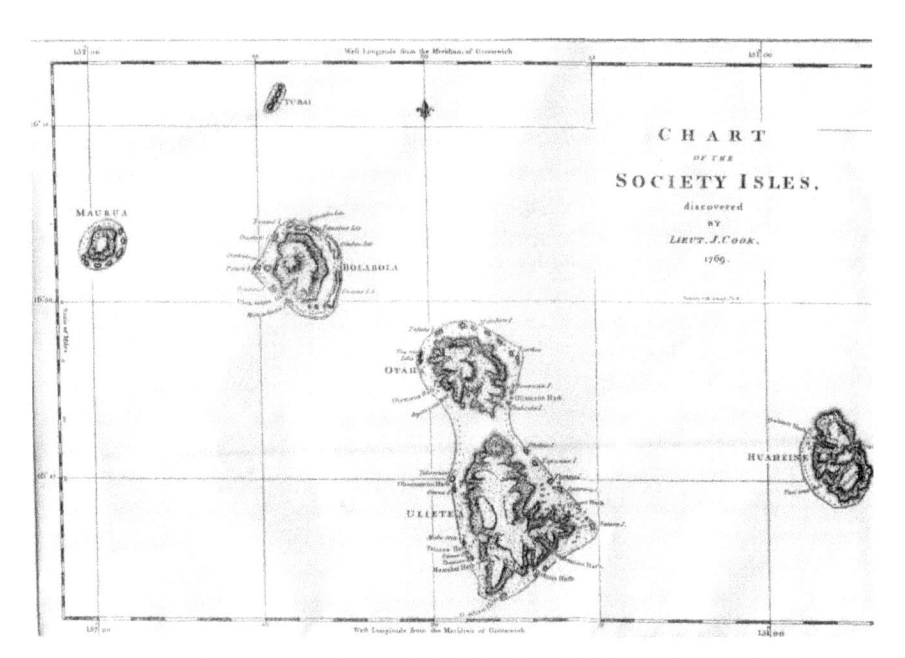

**CHART OF THE SOCIETY ISLES, DISCOVERED BY
LIEUTENANT JAMES COOK, 1769.
REPRODUCTION OF THE ORIGINAL PUBLISHED CHART.**

Saturday, 15th. Light airs and Variable between the North and West-South-West. Clear weather. At 6 p.m. York Island bore South-East, and Huaheine West-North-West, and at 7 a.m. it bore West. Latitude observed at Noon 16 degrees 50 minutes South. Royal Bay South 37 degrees 30 minutes East, distant 22 Leagues.

[At Huaheine.]

Sunday, 16th. Winds at South and South-South-East. A Gentle Breeze, with some few showers of rain. At 6 p.m. the Island of Huaheine West 1/2 South, distant 7 or 8 leagues. At 8 a.m., being close in with the North-West part of the Island, sounded, but had no ground with 80 fathoms. Some of the Natives came off to the Ship, but they were very shy of coming near until they discover'd Tupia; but after that they came on board without hesitation. Among those who came on board was the King of the Island, whose name is Oree. He had not been long on board before he and I exchanged Names, and we afterwards address'd each other accordingly.* (* The Tahitians called Cook Tootee, which was their idea of the sound of his name, with a vowel termination, none of their words ending in a consonant.) At noon the North end of the Island bore South by East 1/2 East, distant 72 Leagues. Latitude observed, 16 degrees 40 minutes South. Three other Islands in sight, namely,

Ulietea, Otaha, and Bolabola,* (* Tahaa and Borabora.) so called by the Natives.

Monday, 17th. Winds Southerly, fine pleasant weather. At 3 p.m. anchored in a small Harbour on the West side of the Island called by the Natives Owarhe, in 18 fathoms water, clear ground, and secure from all winds. Soon after, I went on shore, accompanied by Mr. Banks, Dr. Solander, and Dr. Monkhouse, Tupia, the King of the Island, and some others of the Natives, who had been on board since the morning. The Moment we landed Tupia stripped himself as low as his waist, and desir'd Mr. Monkhouse to do the same. He then sat down before a great number of the Natives that were collected together in a large Shed or House, the rest of us, by his own desire, standing behind; he then begun a long speach or prayer, which lasted near a Quarter of an Hour, and in the Course of this Speech presented to the People two Handkerchiefs, a black silk Neckcloth, some beads, and two very small bunches of Feathers. These things he had before provided for that purpose. At the same time two Chiefs spoke on the other side in answer to Tupia, as I suppose, in behalf of the People, and presented us with some young Plantains plants, and 2 small bunches of Feathers. These were by Tupia order'd to be carried on board the Ship. After the Peace was thus concluded and ratified, every one was at liberty to go where he pleased, and the first thing Tupia did was to go and pay his Oblations at one of the Mories. This seem'd to be a common ceremony with this people, and I suppose always perform'd upon landing on each other's Territories in a peaceable manner. It further appear'd that the things which Tupia gave away was for the God of this People, as they gave us a Hog and some Cocoanuts for our God, and thus they have certainly drawn us in to commit sacriledge, for the Hog hath already received sentence of Death, and is to be dissected to-morrow. A.M. I set about Surveying the Island, and Dr. Monkhouse, with some hands, went ashore to Trade with the Natives, while the Long boat was employ'd compleating our Water.

Tuesday, 18th. Gentle breezes at South and South-South-West. Clear weather. The Trading party had no Success to-day. The Natives pretend that they have not had time to collect their provisions from the Differant parts of the Island, but that on the Morrow we should have some; and as I had not seen so much of the Island as I desir'd, I resolved to stay one day longer to see if anything was to be got.

Wednesday, 19th. P.M. Variable light Airs and clear weather. The Trading party had better success to-day than Yesterday. A.M. a Gentle breeze at South-East. As it was known to the Natives that we intended to sail to-day, Oree, the Chief, and several more, came on board to take their leave of us. To the Chief was given a small plate on which was Stamp'd the following inscription--viz., "His Britannick Majesty's Ship, Endeavour, Lieutenant

Cook, Commander, 16th July, 1769, Huaheine." This was accompanied with some Medals, or Counters, of the English Coins, struck 1761, together with some other Presents. All these, but more particularly the Plate, the Chief promised never to part with. This we thought would prove as lasting a Testimony of our having first discover'd this Island as any we could leave behind. After this was done they were dismissed, and we began to prepare to leave the place. But as that falls out on the following day, I shall conclude this with a Discription of the Island, which is situated in the Latitude of 16 degrees 43 minutes South, and Longitude 150 degrees 52 minutes West from Greenwich and North 58 degrees West, distance, 31 leagues, from King George's Island, or Otaheite. It is about 7 Leagues in compass, and of a Hilly and uneven surface. It hath a safe and commodious Harbour, which lies on the West side, under the Northermost high land and within the North end of the Reef which lays along that side of the Island. Into this Harbour are 2 inlets, or openings in the Reef, about 1 1/2 Miles from each other. The Southermost is the Broadest, on the South side of which is a very small sandy Island. This Harbour is called by the Natives Ohwarhe. The produce of this Island is in all respects the same as King George's Island, and the Manner and Customs of the inhabitants much the same, only that they are not addicted to Stealing; and with respect to colour they are rather fairer than the natives of George's Island, and the whole more Uniformly of one Colour.

[At Raiatea.]

Thursday, 20th. Moderate breezes at East and East-North-East. Fair weather. At 1/2 past 2 p.m. weighed and made Sail for the Island of Ulietea, which lies South-West by West, Distance 7 or 8 leagues from Huaheine. At 1/2 past 6 we were within 3 Leagues of it, then shortened sail and stood off and on all night, and at daylight made Sail in shore, and soon after discover'd an opening in the Reef that lies along this side of the Island, within which, Tupia said, was a good Harbour. Upon this I hoisted out the Pinnace, and sent the Master in to Examine it, who soon made the Signal for the Ship to follow. Accordingly we stood in and Anchor'd in 22 fathoms, soft ground. Soon after we Anchor'd some of the Natives came on board the Ship with very little invitation.

Friday, 21st. Winds variable, and dark, cloudy weather, with frequent Showers of rain. At 1 p.m. I landed in Company with Mr. Banks and the other gentlemen. The first thing done was the performing of Tupia's ceremony in all respects as at Huaheine. I then hoisted an English jack, and took possession of the Island and those adjacent in the name of His Britannick Majesty, calling them by the same names as the natives do. A.M. sent the Master in the Long boat to examine the coast of the South part of the Island, and one of the Mates in the Yawl to sound the Harbour where the Ship lay, while I was employ'd in the Pinnace surveying the Northern part of the Island, and Mr. Monkhouse went ashore to trade with the Natives for such refreshments as were to be got.

Saturday, 22nd. P.M. the wind Variable with Showers of rain. A.M. strong Gales at South and hazey with rain, and which continued the most part of

Sunday, 23rd, in so much that I did not think it safe to break the Ship loose and put to sea as I intended.

Monday, 24th. Winds variable from South-South-East to North-East. At 8 a.m. got under sail and plyed to the Northward within the Reef, in order to go out at the Northern Channell, it being the broadest; but being little wind and meeting with Shoals we had not before discovered, we turned down but slowly.

Tuesday, 25th. First part, little wind at North-East; in the night calm, A.M. a fresh breeze at West-North-West, fair weather. At 3 p.m. Anchor'd in 22 fathoms Muddy bottom, the North Channell open bearing North-East 1/2 East, at 5 a.m. a breeze sprung up at North-West, weighed and put to Sea, and hauled to the Northward in order to take a View of the Island and Ataha and Bolabola; but before I proceed farther, I shall describe the Harbour we have been in.* (* It has no particular name, but extends the whole of the eastern side of Raiatea.) This Harbour, taken in its greatest Extent, is capable of holding any number of Shipping in perfect security, as it extends almost the whole length of this side of the Island, and is defended from the Sea by a reef of Coral rocks; the Southermost opening* (* Teava Moa Pass.) in this reef or Channell into the Harbour, which is not more than a Cable's length wide, is off the Eastermost point of the Island, and may be known by a small woody Island, which lies a little to the South-East of it. Between 3 and 4 miles North-West from this Island lies 2 other small Islands, and in the same direction as the reef, of which they are a part. Between these 2 Islands is another Channell* (* Iriru Pass.) into the Harbour that is a full Quarter of a Mile broad; still further to the North-West are some other small Islands, where, I am informed, is another small inlet, but this I did not see; but, as to the other 2, we enter'd the Harbour by the one and came out by the other.

The principal refreshments we have got here consists in Plantains, Cocoa nuts, some Yams and a few Hogs and fowls. This side of the Island is neither Populous nor Rich in Produce, if compared to George's Island, or even Huaheine; however, here is no want of refreshments for a ship who may put in here and stay but a short time; and wood and water may be got everywhere, tho' the latter is not very convenient to come at.

[Off Bolabola.]

Wednesday, 26th. Winds at West by North and West by South, but very Variable towards the Latter part. At 4 p.m. the North End of Ulietea South

75 degrees West, distance 2 leagues, and the south end of Otaha North 77 degrees West. About a League to the Northward of the South end of Otaha, on the East side of the Island, a mile or more from the Shore, lies 2 Small Islands. Between these Islands Tupia says there is a Channell into a very good harbour which lies within the Reef and it had all the appearance of such. Keept plying to Windward all night without getting any ground. At Noon the Peak on Bolabola West by South. Latitude observed 16 degrees 26 minutes South.

Thursday, 27th. Variable light Airs of wind in the South-West Quarter, and fair weather. Seeing that there is a broad Channell between Otaha and Bolabola, I intend to go through that way and not run to the Northward of all; but as the wind is right an end, and very Variable withall, we get little or no ground. Between 5 and 6 o'Clock p.m., as we were standing to the Northward, we discover'd a small low Island lying North by West or North-North-West distant 4 or 5 Leagues from Bolabola. This Island is called Tubai. Tupia says it produces nothing but a few Cocoa Nuts, that there are only 3 families live upon it, but that the people from these Islands resort thither to Catch fish. At Noon the peak of Bolabola bore North 25 degrees West, and the north end of Otaha North 80 degrees West, distant 3 Leagues. Latitude observed 16 degrees 38 minutes South.

Friday, 28th. Little wind and Variable between the South-West and North-West. At 6 a.m., being near the Entrance of the Harbour which lies on the East side of Otaha before mentioned,* (* Hamene Bay.) and finding that it might be examin'd without loosing time, I sent away the Master in the Long boat, with orders to sound the Harbour, and if the wind did not shift in our favour to land upon the Island and to Traffick with the Natives for such refreshments as were to be got. Mr. Banks and Dr. Solander went along with him.

Saturday, 29th. Little wind and Variable. Kept plying on and off this day, waiting for the return of the Long boat. At 1/2 past 5 not seeing anything of her, fir'd a Gun for her to return, and as soon as it was dark hoisted a light. At 1/2 past 8 heard the report of a musquet, which we answered with a Gun; and soon after the Boat came on board with 3 small Hogs, a few Fowls, and a large Quantity of Plantains, and some Yams. They found the Natives very Sociable and ready to part with anything they had, and the Harbour safe and Commodious, with a good Anchorage in 25, 20, and 16 fathoms clear ground. As soon as the Boat was hoisted in we made Sail to the Northward, and at 8 o'Clock a.m. were close under the Peak of Bolabola, but as we could not weather the Island, we Tack'd and stood off until near Noon, then Tack'd again and stood to the South-West. At Noon the Peak of Bolabola bore South 75 degrees West; we were then distant from the Shore under it 2 or 3 miles, and from the Peak about 5 miles. Latitude observed 16 degrees 29 minutes South.

Sunday, 30th. Wind in the South-East Quarter. At first a Gentle breeze, but afterwards freshned upon us. P.M. made several Trips before we could weather the South end of Bolabola, which at last we accomplished between 7 and 8 o'Clock, and stood off South-South-West until 12 at night, then Tack'd and stood in until 4 a.m., then stood off again; but meeting with a large swell from the Southward, against which the Ship made little or no way, at 8 we tack'd and stood in Shore again. At this time we discovered an Island which bore from us North 63 degrees West, distant about 8 Leagues: at the same time the Peak of Bolabola bore North 1/2 East, distance 3 or 4 Leagues. This Island Tupia calls Maurua, and according to his account it is but small, and surrounded by a Reef of Rocks, and hath no Harbour fit for Shipping. It is inhabited, and its produce is the same as the other Islands we have touched at. It riseth in a high round hill in the middle of the Island, which may be seen 10 Leagues. At noon the South end of Otaha bore North 80 degrees East, distance 4 Leagues. Latitude observed 16 degrees 39 minutes South.

Monday, 31st. Fresh Gales in the South-East Quarter, and close, cloudy weather. Plying to windward all this day, on the South-West side of Otaha, without gaining little or anything. In the middle watch was obliged to double reef our Topsails, but in the morning it fell moderate, and we crowded all the sail we could. At Noon the South end of Otaha bore East, distance 2 Leagues. Latitude observed 16 degrees 40 minutes South. Tupia told us there was a very good Harbour within the Reef which lies on this side of Otaha; but this Harbour I shall discribe in another place.

[August 1769. At Raiatea.]

Tuesday, August 1st. A fresh Gale at South-East the most part of this day. Keept plying to windward all the afternoon and night, and in the morning found ourselves nearly the length of the South end of Ulietea, and to windward of some Harbours that lay on the West side of this Island. Into one of them I intended to go with the Ship, in order to stop a Leak in the Powder room, which could not be easily done at Sea, and to take in more Ballast, as I found her too light to carry sail upon a wind. At Noon plying off one of the Harbour's mouth, the wind being right out.

Wednesday, 2nd. Moderate breezes at South-East and East, with some Showers of Rain. At 3 p.m. anchor'd in the Entrance of the Channell leading into the Harbour* (* Rautoanui.) in 14 fathoms water; found a tide setting pretty strong out, which was the reason that we could not work in; carried out the Kedge Anchor in order to warp into the Harbour, but after this was done we could not Trip the Bower Anchor with all the purchass we could make, and was therefore obliged to lay still all night, but in the morning we did it with Ease, and warped the Ship into a proper birth, and moor'd in 28 fathoms, a sandy bottom. A great many of the Natives came off to us both last night and this morning, and brought with them Hogs, Fowls, Plaintains, etc., which they parted with at a very easy rate.

Thursday, 3rd. Winds from East-South-East to North-East; very Hot weather this afternoon. I went ashore to look for a place to get stones for Ballast, and a watering place, both of which I found very convenient; and in the morning sent an Officer a Shore to Superintend the getting off the Ballast and Water, and I went in the Pinnace to the Northward to survey that part of the Island, accompanied by Mr. Banks and Dr. Solander, while the Carpenters were employ'd on board stopping the Leaks of the Powder room and Foresail room.

Friday, 4th. First and Latter parts, moderate breezes, at East-North-East; in the night, Calm, Hot, and sultry. In our rout to the Northward this afternoon we were entertained at one place with Musick and Dancing. The Musick consisted of 3 Drums, and the Dancing was mostly perform'd by 2 Young Women and one Man, and this seem'd to be their profession. The dress of the women was such as we had not seen before; it was neat, decent, and well chose, and in many respects not much unlike a European dress; only their Arms, Necks, and Shoulders were bare, and their headdress was the Tomow stuck with Flowers. They made very little use of their feet and Legs in Dancing, but one part or another of their bodies were in continual motion and in various postures, as standing, setting, and upon their Hands and knees, making strange Contorsions. Their Arms, hands, and Fingers they moved with great Agility and in a very Extraordinary manner, and altho' they were very exact in observing the same motion in all their movements, yet neither their Musick or Dancing were at all Calculated to please a European. There were likewise some men, who acted a kind of a Farce; but this was so short that we could gather nothing from it, only that it shew'd that these People have a Notion of Dramatick performances, and some of our Gentlemen saw them act a Farce the next day, wherein was 4 Acts, and it seem'd to them to represent a War between the Bolabola men and those of Ulietea, wherein the former triumph'd over the latter; but what might help them to draw this Conclusion was the knowing that such a thing has not long ago hapned between these 2 People, and that the Bolabola men at present possess most of the Lands on this Island. This is their grand Dramatick Heiva, and I believe is occasionally performed in all the Islands. Upon my return to the Ship in the evening I found that they had got on board 20 Tuns of Ballast, and this I thought would be sufficient. In the morning we sent all our water Casks on shore, and got them all off full by Noon. This morning I received a present from Opoony, the Eare dehi of Bolabola, who at this time was upon this Island. It consisted of 3 Hogs, some pieces of Cloth, Plantains, Cocoa Nuts, etc. These were sent by his Servants, and I was told that he would come the next day himself.

Saturday, 5th. This evening we bought as much Fish as the whole Ship's Company could destroy while good. In the morning I sent the Master to the North End of the Island with the Long boat to Traffick with the Natives for Provisions, as they did not bring it to the Ship, as they had hitherto done; and myself, accompanied by Mr. Banks and Dr. Solander, went in the Pinnace to the Southern part of the Island, partly on the same account and partly to Examine that part of the Island. In our rout we passed thro' 2 Harbours equally as good as the one in which the Ship lays, but the Country about them is poorer and but thinly inhabited, and we got no one thing worth bringing home with us, but the Master succeeded something better.

Sunday, 6th. Variable light Airs and fair weather. A.M. I sent the Master again to the Northward to procure refreshments, who return'd not unsuccessfull. Opoony, the Chief, sent some of his people this morning to me to get something in return for the present he sent the other day; he not choosing, as I suppose, to trust himself on board, or perhaps he thought the persons he sent (who were 3 very pretty young Girls) would succeed better than he should do. Be this as it may, they went away very well satisfied with what they got, altho' I believe that they were disappointed in some things.

Monday, 7th. Variable light Airs. P.M. some Showers of rain. Being desirous to see King Opoony, we made a party this afternoon and I went ashore for that purpose, carrying along with us a small present. Upon our landing he did not receive us setting, as all the other Chiefs had hitherto done, or in any manner of Form; this we attributed to his Stupidity, for such he appeared to be. However, he gave me a Hog in return for the present I made him, and this was paying us full as great a Complement. Before we took our leave we let him know that we should go to Otaha in the morning in our Boats, and would be glad to have him along with us, and he accordingly promised to accompany us thither. Accordingly, very early in the morning, I set out with both Pinnace and Long boat for Otaha, and some of the Gentlemen along with me; and in our way called upon Opoony, who was in his Canoe ready to set out. As soon as we landed on Otaha I made him a present of a Axe; this I thought would induce him to incourage his Subjects to bring us such Provisions as we wanted, but I believe we had already got all they intended us, for after staying with him until Noon we were obliged to go away without geting any one thing.

Tuesday, 8th. After leaving Opoony we proceeded towards the North point of the Island, and in our way pick'd up half a Dozen Hogs, as many Fowls, and some Plantains and Yams; and I had an opportunity to view and draw a

Sketch of the Harbour which lies on this Side of the Island, and which was the only thing that induced me to make this Excursion. After it was dark we met with the Longboat, which I had in the morning dispatch'd to another part of the Island; and we now made the best of our way to the Ship and got on board about 10 at night. The Carpenter having finished stopping the Leaks about the Powder Room and Sailroom I now intend to sail as soon as ever the wind will permit us to get out of the Harbour.

Wednesday, 9th. P.M. had a light breeze of wind at North; in the night had much rain. A.M. little wind and Variable, with some Showers of rain. At 11 a.m. a breeze of wind sprung up at East, which carried us out of the Harbour, and as soon as the Boats were hoisted in made Sail to the Southward. Since we have been about these Islands we have expended but little of our Sea Provisions, and have at this last place been very plentifully supply'd with Hogs, Fowls, Plantains, and Yams, which will be of very great use to us in case we should not discover any lands in our rout to the Southward, the way I now intend to Steer.

[Description of Society Islands.]

DESCRIPTION OF THE ISLANDS, ULIETEA, OTAHA AND BOLABOLA.

So called by the Natives, and it was not thought adviseable to give them any other Names; but these three, with Huaheine, Tuibai, and Maurua, as they lay contigious to one another, I have named Society Isles.

They are situated between the Latitude of 16 degrees 10 minutes and 16 degrees 55 minutes South and between the Longitude 151 degrees 00 minutes and 151 degrees 42 minutes West from the Meridian of Greenwich. Ulietea and Otaha lay close to each other, and are both inclosed within a Reef of Coral Rocks; and altho' the distance between the one and the other is near 2 Miles, yet there is no Passage for Shipping. By means of this reef are form'd several excellent Harbours. The entrance into them are but narrow, but when a Ship is once in nothing can hurt her. Those on the East side have been already described. On the West side of Ulietea, which is the largest Island of the 2, are 3, the Northermost of which, called Oraotanue,* (* Rautoanui.) we lay in, the Channell leading in is a 1/4 of a Mile wide and lies between 2 low sandy Islands, which are the Northermost small Islands on this side. You have good Anchorage between or just within the 2 Islands in 28 fathoms soft ground. This harbour, tho' but small, yet it is preferable to any on the Island, on account of the easy getting of fresh Water, and being seated in the most fertile part of the Island. The other 2 harbours lay to the Southward of this, and not far from the South end of the Island. In both of them are good Anchorage in 10, 12, and 14 fathoms water: they are readily known by 3 small woody Islands that lay at their entrance, the Southermost Harbour lies within and to the Southward of the Southermost Island, and the other lies between the Northermost. There are more Harbours at the South End of this Island, as I am inform'd, but these were not examind by us.

Otaha affords 2 very good Harbours, one on the East and the other on the West side; that on the East side called Ohamane* (* Hamene.) hath been already mentioned, the other is called Oharurua* (* Hurepiti.) and lies about the middle of the South-West side of the Island. It is pretty large, and affords good Anchorage in 20 and 25 fathoms, and there is no want of fresh Water. The breach in the Reef which forms a Channell into this harbour is 1/4 of a mile broad, steep too, on both sides, and the same may be said of all the others, and in general there is no danger but what is Visible.

The Island of Bolabola lies North-West by West from Otaha, distant 4 Leagues, it is incompassed by a reef of Rocks and several small Islands, and the Circuit of the whole appear'd to be about 8 Leagues. On the South-West side of the Islands (as I am inform'd) is an opening in the Reef which admits of a Channell into a very good Harbour. This Island is very remarkable on account of a high Craggy hill upon it, which Terminates at Top in 2 Peaks, one higher than the other; this hill is so perpendicular that it appears to be quite inaccessible. The land on Ulietea and Otaha is of a very hilly, broken, and uneven surface, except what borders upon the Sea Coast, and high withall, yet the Hills look green and pleasant and are in many places cloathed with woods.

The Produce of these Islands, and manners and Customs of the Natives are much the same as at King George's Island, only as the Bread fruit Tree is here in not such plenty, the natives to supply that deficiency plant and Cultivate a greater Quantity of Plantains and Yams of several sorts, and these they have in the greatest Perfection.

The inhabitants are rather of a fairer Colour than the Generality of the Natives of George's Island, but more especially the Women, who are much fairer and handsomer, and the Men are not so much Addicted to thieving, and are more Open and free in their behaviour.

The only differance we could see in their Religion was in the Houses of their Gods, which were very different to those we saw on George's Island. Those here were made about the Size and shape of a Coffin open at one End; they are laid upon a Number of small Wooden Arches, which are fram'd and fastned together like the Roof of a House, and these are generally supported about 3 or 4 feet above the ground by Posts. Over the box is a small roof or shade made of Palm thatch; in this Box are deposited the Oblations of the Gods, such as Pieces of Cloth, Human bone, etc., and these places they hold sacred, and some are placed in their Mories, and some not. They have a Custom of preserving the Sculls and under Jaw bones of the Dead, but wether of their Friends or Enemies I cannot pretend to say. Several of the Sculls, we observed, were broke, and its very probable that the owners of them had been kill'd in battle, as some of their Weapons are well Calculated for breaking of Heads; and from what we could learn it is a Custom with them to cut out the Lower jaw of their Enemies, but I believe not before they are kill'd, and these they keep as Trophies, and are sometimes hung up in their Houses.

The Chief or King of Bolabola hath of late Years Usurped the Sovereignty of the other two, and the Bolabola men at this time possess great part of the Lands on Ulietea and Otaha that they have taken from the Natives. The Lands adjoining to the Harbours of Oraotanue belong'd to Tupia, the Person we have on board, who is a Native of Ulietea. These people are very ingenious in building their Proes or Canoes, and seem to take as much Care of them, having large Shades or Houses to put them in, built for the purpose, and in these houses they likewise build and repair them, and in this they shew a great deal of ingenuity far more than one could expect. They are built full Bellied, and after the very same Model as those Six we saw on George's Island, which I have already described, and some of them are full as large; it is more than probable that these 6 Proes were built at some of these Islands. In these Proes, or Pahies as they call them, from all the accounts we can learn, these people sail in those Seas from Island to Island for several hundred Leagues, the Sun serving them for a Compass by day, and the Moon and Stars by night. When this comes to be proved, we shall be no longer at a loss to know how the Islands lying in those Seas came to be peopled; for if the inhabitants of Ulietea have been at Islands laying 2 or 300 Leagues to the Westward of them, it cannot be doubted but that the inhabitants of those Western Islands may have been at others as far to Westward of them, and so we may trace them from Island to Island quite to the East Indies.

Tupia tells us that during the months of November, December, and January Westerly winds, with rain, prevail; and as the inhabitants of the Islands know very well how to make the proper use of the winds, there will no difficulty arise in Trading or Sailing from Island to Island, even tho' they lie in an East and West direction.* (* This paragraph is from the Admiralty copy of Cook's Journal. This fact is now well known. The islands here described, the Society Islands of Cook, and now known as the Leeward Group of the Society Islands, were generally under the dominion of Tahiti. At the time of Cook's visit, the chief of Bolabola was supreme over most of the group, and their tie to Tahiti was but slight. They are all very beautiful and fertile. Within the last decade they have formally been recognised as belonging to France.)

[Sail from Society Islands.]

REMARKABLE OCCURRENCES IN THE SOUTH SEAS.

Thursday, August 10th. P.M., Light Airs and Calm, remainder fresh breezes and Cloudy. At 6 p.m. the South end of Ulietea South-East 1/2 East, distant 4 Leagues; but I take my departure from the Harbour, saild from in Latitude 16 degrees 46 minutes South, and Longitude 151 degrees 27 minutes West. At 7 a.m. found the Variation to be 5 degrees 50 minutes East. Wind Easterly; course South 16 degrees West; distance 50 miles; Latitude observed 17 degrees 34 minutes South, longitude 151 degrees 41 minutes West.

Friday, 11th. Fresh breezes and Clear weather. Wind East; course South 4 degrees West; distance 85 miles; latitude 18 degrees 59 minutes South, longitude 151 degrees 45 minutes West.

Saturday, 12th. Gentle breezes and fair weather. Wind East, East by North; course South 3/4 East; distance 77 miles; latitude 20 degrees 15 minutes South, longitude 151 degrees 36 minutes West.

Sunday, 13th. Moderate breezes and Clear weather. Variation 5 degrees 40 minutes East. Wind East by North; course South 16 degrees East; distance 96 miles; latitude 21 degrees 47 minutes South, longitude 151 degrees 9 minutes West.

Monday, 14th. Fresh breezes and fair weather. At 2 p.m. saw land bearing South-East, which Tupia calls the Island of Ohetiroa.* (* Rurutu, one of the Tubuai or Austral Group. They are now under French protectorate.) At 6 was within 2 or 3 Leagues of it, the Extreams bearing from South by East to South-East; shortned sail and stood off and on all night; at 6 a.m. made Sail and stood in for the Land and run to Leeward of the Island, keeping close in shore all the time, saw several of the Natives as we run along shore, but in no great numbers. At 9 hoisted out the Pinnace and sent Lieutenant Gore, Mr. Banks, and Tupia to Endeavour to land upon the Island, and to speak with the Natives, and to try if they could learn from them what lands lay to the Southward of us, and likewise to see if there was Anchorage in a Bay which appear'd to our View, not that I intended to Anchor or make any stay here. Wind North-North-East; latitude 22 degrees 26 minutes South, longitude 150 degrees 55 minutes West; at noon, Ohetiroa East 2 leagues.

Tuesday, 15th. Fresh breezes and fair weather. At 2 p.m. the Pinnace return'd on board without landing, not but what it was practicable, but they did not think it Altogether safe with only one Boat, as it would have been attended with some danger on account of the Surf and Rocks upon the Shore. The Natives were Arm'd, and Shewd no Signs either of fear or Friendship. Some of them came off to the Boat in a Canoe, and had some Nails and Beads given them; but with these they were not Satisfied, thinking they had a right to everything in the Boat, and at last grew so Troublesome that in order to get clear of them our People were obliged to fire some Musquets, but with no intent to hurt any of them; however, it so hapned that one Man was

Slightly wounded in the head. The firing had the desired effect, and they thought fit to retire. After this, as the Boat lay near the Shore, some of them waded off to her, and brought with them some Trifles which they parted with for small Nails, etc. They seem'd desirous that our people should land, but this was looked upon as a Piece of Policy in them to get the whole Boat's Crew in their power; however, this was not attempted, as I had given orders to run no Risk. The Bay they went into, which lies on the West side of the Island, had in it 25 fathoms Water, but the bottom was very foul and Rocky. We had now made the Circuit of the Island (which did not appear to the best advantage), and found that there was neither a Harbour or safe Anchorage about it, and therefore I thought the Landing upon it would be attended with no advantage either to ourselves or any future navigators; and from the Hostile and thievish disposition of the Natives it appear'd that we could have no friendly intercourse with them until they had felt the Smart of our fire Arms, a thing that would have been very unjustifiable in me at this Time; we therefore hoisted in the Boat, and made Sail to the Southward.

[Of the Austral Group.]

This Island is situated in the Latitude of 22 degrees 27 minutes South, and in the Longitude of 150 degrees 47 minutes West from the Meridian of Greenwich.* (* Latitude is correct. Longitude 151 degrees 20 minutes West.) It is 13 miles in Circuit, and tolerably high; it appears to be neither Populous nor fertile; its produce seem'd to be nearly the same as the other Islands we have touched at, and likewise the Stature, Colour, Habit, and Arms of the Natives, only that some of them wore Pieces of Cloth like broad belts, different both in Shape and Colour to anything of the kind we had seen before, and their Arms, and in general everything they had about them, much neater made, and shew'd great proofs of an ingenious fancy. Tupia says that their are several Islands laying at different directions from this--that is, from the South to the West and North-West--and that 3 days' sail to the North-East is an Island called Manua, that is Bird Island, and that it lies 4 days' sail from Ulietea, which is one day less than from Ulietea to Ohetiroa.* (* Tupia was right except with respect to Manua, as there is no island answering his description.) From this account I shall be able to find the Situation of Manua pretty well. Since we have left Ulietea Tupia hath been very desirous for us to steer to the Westward, and tells us if we will go that way we shall be with plenty of Islands: the most of them he himself hath been at, and from the discription he gives of two of them they must be those discover'd by Capt. Wallace, and by him called Boscawen and Keppel's Islands, and those do not lay less than 400 Leagues to the Westward of Ulietea. He says that they are 10 or 12 days in going thither, and 30 or more in coming Back, and that their Pahies--that is their large Proes--sails much faster than this Ship. All this I believe to be true, and therefore they may with Ease sail 40 Leagues a day or more.

The farthest Island to the Southward that Tupia hath been at, or knows anything of, lies but 2 days' Sail from Ohetiroa, and is called Moutou,* (* Tubuai.) but he says that his father once told him that there was Islands to the Southward of it; but we Cannot find that he either knows or ever heard of a Continent or large Track of Land. I have no reason to doubt Tupia's information of these Islands, for when we left Ulietea and steer'd to the Southward he told us that if we would keep a little more to the East (which the wind would not permit us to do) we should see Manua, but as we then steer'd we should see Ohetiroa, which hapned accordingly. If we meet with the Islands to the Southward he speaks off, it's well, but if not, I shall spend no more time searching for them, being now fully resolv'd to stand directly to the Southward in search of a Continent. Wind Northerly; course South 1/2 East; distance 94 miles; latitude 24 degrees 1 minute South, longitude 150 degrees 37 minutes West; at noon, Ohetiroa North 1/2 West, 31 leagues; variation 6 degrees 7 minutes East.

NOTE. As we advanced to the Southward into Cold weather, and a troubled Sea, the Hogs we got at Ulietea began to die apace. They cannot endure the least cold, nor will they hardly eat anything but vegetables, so that they are not at all to be depended upon at Sea. The fowls also have a complaint general among them which affects their heads, so that they continue holding it down betwixt their Legs until they die; this at least was the fate of most of ours. This is necessary to be known to those who come such Voyages as these, least they place too much dependance on the live stock they get at the Islands.

Wednesday, 16th. Fresh breezes and Cloudy the first part; in the night, Squally, with rain; remainder, moderate and fair weather. At 8 am, saw the Appearances of high land to the Eastward; bore up towards it, but at 10 we discover'd it to be only Clouds, at which we hauld our wind to the Southward. At Noon found the Ship by Observation 21 Miles to the Northward of the Log, which may in some measure be owing to a South-West swell we have had all the last 24 hours. Wind North by West, West, West by South; course South 15 degrees East; distance 62 miles; latitude 25 degrees 00 minutes South, longitude 150 degrees 19 minutes West.

Thursday, 17th. A Gentle breeze with some flying showers of rain. Had a large Swell from the South-West all this day, much larger than yesterday, and this must be the reason why the observ'd Latitude differ'd from the Log again to day 16 miles. Wind West by South to South-West by South; course South-South-East; distance 76 miles; latitude 26 degrees 10 minutes South, longitude 149 degrees 46 minutes West.

Friday, 18th. The first part Calm; remainder light breezes and Clear. Variation per Amplitude in the evening 8 degrees 8 minutes East; in the Morning 7 degrees 56 minutes East. Carpenters employed repairing the Boats. The South-West swell still Continues, but not so much as Yesterday, and the observed Latitude and Log agrees. Wind Calm, North; course South 18 degrees East; distance 38 miles; latitude 26 degrees 48 minutes South, longitude 149 degrees 42 minutes West.

Saturday, 19th. Little wind with much rain in the night, the South-West swell still Continues, from which I conclude that there is no land near us in that Quarter. Wind North-West; course South-East by South; distance 62 miles; latitude 27 degrees 40 minutes South; longitude 149 degrees 6 minutes West.

Sunday, 20th. Little wind all this day. Saw a large Albetross. Wind North-West; course South-East by South; distance 57 miles; latitude 28 degrees 24 minutes South, longitude 148 degrees 25 minutes West.

Monday, 21st. Fresh Gales and Hazey weather. Saw 2 Pintado Birds, the first I have seen this Voyage; they are larger than a Pidgeon and checquer'd black and white over their backs and wings, with white Bellies, Black heads, and the end of their Tails black.* (* Cape pigeons, Daption Capensis.) Wind North-North-West; course South by East; distance 80 miles; latitude 29 degrees 44 minutes South, longitude 148 degrees 22 minutes West.

[Society Islands to New Zealand.]

Tuesday, 22nd. First part Strong Gales with much rain, Thunder, and Lightning; remainder moderate and fair weather. About Noon saw some rock weed, an Albetross, and some Smaller Sea Birds. Wind North by West, South-West by West; course South 14 degrees East; distance 81 miles; latitude 31 degrees 3 minutes South, longitude 148 degrees 00 minutes West.

Wednesday, 23rd. Little wind for the most part, and pretty clear weather. In the night had some Showers of rain. Saw a Grampus, and several Pintado Birds. Wind South-West to West-South-West; course South-South-East; distance 68 miles; latitude 31 degrees 6 minutes South; longitude 147 degrees 29 minutes West.

Thursday, 24th. The first part light Airs and Calm; Middle, moderate breezes and Cloudy; latter part very squally with rain. A.M. Variation per Azimuth 7 degrees 18 minutes East. At Noon took in the Topsails and got down Topgallant yards. Saw a Water Spout in the North-West; it was about the breadth of a Rainbow, of a dark Colour, the Upper end of the Cloud from whence it came was about 8 degrees above the Horizon. Wind Variable; course South-South-East; distance 41 miles; latitude 32 degrees 44 minutes South, longitude 147 degrees 10 minutes West.

Friday, 25th. The first and middle part Strong Gales and Squally with rain, remainder moderate and Cloudy. P.M. Unbent the Maintopsail being Split and bent another; in the night lay too under the Foresail, and in the morning made sail under the Courses and Topsails with one reef only. Had a large Sea from the Southward, saw several Albetrosses, Pintado Birds, and Sheer Waters; some of the Albetrosses were small, such as we usually saw off Cape Horn; all these kinds of birds are generally seen at a great distance from land. Wind, Southerly; course North-West; distance 26 miles; latitude 32 degrees 26 minutes South; longitude 147 degrees 32 minutes West.

Saturday, 26th. Moderate and cloudy weather, a Swell from the South-West. By observation of the Sun and Moon made this morning, the Longitude of the Ship at Noon is 147 degrees 18 minutes 40 seconds, which differs but 11 minutes from that given by the Log. Wind South-West; course South 6 degrees East; South distance 13 miles; latitude 32 degrees 39 minutes South, longitude 147 degrees 30 minutes West.

Sunday, 27th. First part little wind and Cloudy; latter part, fresh Gales and Clear weather. Variation per Azimuth 6 degrees 40 minutes East. Saw several Albetrosses, Pintado Birds and Sheer Waters. Wind West, North-North-West; course South 5 degrees East; distance 55 miles; latitude 33 degrees 34 minutes, longitude 147 degrees 25 minutes.

Monday, 28th. Fresh Gales and Cloudy, with rain on the Latter part. At 10 departed this Life Jno. Rearden,* (* John Reading.) Boatswain's Mate; his Death was occasioned by the Boatswain out of mere good Nature giving him part of a Bottle of Rum last night, which it is supposed he drank all at once. He was found to be very much in Liquor last night, but as this was no more than what was common with him when he could get any, no farther notice was taken of him than to put him to Bed, where this morning about 8 o'clock he was found Speechless and past recovery. Wind Northerly; course South; distance 110 miles; latitude 35 degrees 34 minutes South, longitude 147 degrees 25 minutes West.

Tuesday, 29th. Fore and Middle parts fresh Gales and Dark, Hazey weather with some rain. At 5 a.m. saw a Comet in the North. Wind North-West to South-West; course South 1/4 East; distance 96 miles; latitude 37 degrees 0 minutes South, longitude 147 degrees 21 minutes West.

Wednesday, 30th. Fresh breeze and fair weather. At 1 a.m. saw the Comet a little above the Horizon in the East. It pass'd the Meridian about 1/2 past 4; the Tail of the Comet Subtended an Angle of 42 degrees. At 8 a.m. Variation per Azimuth 7 degrees 9 minutes East. Bent another suit of Sails. Saw a piece of Rock weed, Some Pintado birds and Sheer Waters and a Green bird something smaller than a Dove, but it was not near enough to distinguish whether it was a Sea or Land bird; it was only seen by one Person, and he probably was Mistaken in the Colour. A Swell from the South-West, Wind Westerly; course South 3/4 East; distance 81 miles; latitude 38 degrees 20 minutes South, longitude 147 degrees 6 minutes West.

Thursday, 31st. The first part a fresh breeze and cloudy. At 6 p.m. hauld the wind to the South-West and close reefd the Topsails. At 1 a.m. being very squally with rain, took in the Topsails and brought too under the Mainsail. At 6 made Sail under the Courses. Saw some seaweed, sounded, but had no ground at 65 fathoms of Line. Some Albetrosses, Sheer Waters, and a great many Pintado Birds about the Ship with some hundreds of Birds that were smaller than Pidgeons, their backs were grey, their Bellies white, and the ends of their Tails black, and have a blackish line along the upper parts of the wings from the Tip of one to the other. We saw birds very like those near Faulklands Islands on the Coast of Patagonia, only they had not the black streak along the wings; they fly low like sheer waters or mother Carys birds, and are perhaps of the same Tribe, for Distinction sake I shall call them Doves.* (* Probably petrels of the genus Prion.) Wind Westerly; course South 4 degrees 15 minutes East; distance 68 miles; latitude 39 degrees 28 minutes South, longitude 147 degrees 0 minutes West.

[September 1769.]

Friday, September 1st. Very strong Gales and heavy Squalls with rain; at 6 p.m. brought too under the Main Sail. At 6 a.m. set the Foresail, a Great Sea from the Westward. The same sort of Birds about the Ship as Yesterday, but not in such great Numbers. Wind, Westerly; Course, South 29 degrees East; distance 50 miles; latitude 40 degrees 12 minutes South, longitude 146 degrees 29 minutes West.

Saturday, 2nd. Very strong Gales, with heavy squalls of Wind, hail, and rain. At 4 p.m., being in the Latitude of 40 degrees 22 minutes South, and having not the least Visible signs of land, we wore, and brought too under the Foresail, and reef'd the Mainsail, and handed it. I did intend to have stood to the Southward if the winds had been Moderate, so long as they continued Westerly, notwithstanding we had no prospect of meeting with land, Rather than stand back to the Northward, on the same Track as we came, but as the weather was so very Tempestious I laid aside this design, and thought it more adviseable to stand to the Northward into better weather, least we should receive such Damage in our Sails and Rigging as might hinder the further Prosecutions of the Voyage.* (* This long excursion to the south is a fine instance of Cook's thoroughness and determination in exploration. The belief in a southern continent was strong amongst most geographers; but it rested on nothing more than the false idea that dry lands in the two hemispheres should balance one another. Cook himself did not share the general belief; and few others in his position would have struggled for 1500 miles out of his direct course into bad weather, simply to disprove an idea, when so much unexplored ocean lay before him to the westward, with a fair wind and fine weather.) Some Albetrosses, Pintado birds, and Doves about the Ship, and a Bird larger than a Duck, his plumage of a Dark Brown, with a Yellow beak. We saw of these Birds in our Passage to the Northward, after doubling Cape Horn. At Noon the weather was more moderate; set the Reefd Mainsail. A great Sea from the West-South-West. Wind West; Course North 54 degrees 30 minutes East; distance 46 miles; latitude 39 degrees 45 minutes South, longitude 145 degrees 39 minutes West.

Sunday, 3rd. The fore and Middle parts fresh gales, with hard Squalls; Latter more moderate. At 5 a.m. loos'd the Reef out of the Mainsail, and set the Topsail double reef'd, and before noon had all the Reefs out. Wind Westerly; course North; distance 50 miles; latitude 38 degrees 54 minutes South, longitude 145 degrees 39 minutes West.

Monday, 4th. First and latter parts, little wind and Cloudy; in the night Calm. Very few Birds about the Ship. Wind Westerly; course North by East; distance 26 miles; latitude 38 degrees 29 minutes South, longitude 145 degrees 32 minutes West.

Tuesday, 5th. Fresh breezes and Cloudy weather. At 2 p.m. saw a piece of rock Weed. Variation, per Azimuth 7 degrees 0 minutes East. Wind West to North-West; course North 32 West; distance 44 miles; latitude 37 degrees 52 minutes South, longitude 146 degrees 2 minutes West.

Wednesday, 6th. Fresh Gales and Squally, with rain. At Noon saw a Bird which was all white, except the Tip of each Wing; it was nearly as big as an Albetross. We saw 2 of these Birds in Latitude 19 degrees before we Arrived at George's Island. Wind Westerly; course South 87 degrees 30 minutes West; distance 70 miles; latitude 37 degrees 49 minutes South, longitude 147 degrees 30 West.

Thursday, 7th. Fresh Gales and hard squalls, with rain. At 3 p.m. saw something upon the Water, which must either have been a Billet of Wood or a Seal. At Noon a hard gale and Squally, which obliged us to take in the Topsails. Wind Westerly; course South 80 degrees West; distance 15 miles; latitude 37 degrees 52 minutes South, longitude 147 degrees 49 minutes West.

Friday, 8th. P.M. very strong gales and Squally. A.M. more moderate; set the Topsails. At Noon the Observed Latitude was 13 Miles to the North of the Log. This I take to be owing to the great Sea we have had constantly of Late from the South-West. Wind Westerly; course North 1/4 East; distance 76 miles; latitude 36 degrees 36 minutes South, longitude 147 degrees 40 minutes West.

Saturday, 9th. Moderate breezes and dark, cloudy weather, sometimes Hazey, with Drizling Rain. Wind South-East; course North 77 degrees West; distance 76 miles; latitude 36 degrees 19 minutes South, longitude 149 degrees 12 minutes West.

Sunday, 10th. Fresh breezes and cloudy. At 9 a.m. we thought the Colour of the Sea was paler than Usual, which occasioned us to sound, but had no ground with 100 fathoms. Wind South-West, West-South-West; course North 52 degrees West; distance 97 miles; latitude 35 degrees 19 minutes South, longitude 150 degrees 46 minutes West.

Monday, 11th. Fresh breezes, and for the most part thick, hazey weather, with rain. Wind South-West; course North 43 degrees West; distance 87 miles; latitude 34 degrees 15 minutes South, longitude 152 degrees 00 minutes West.

Tuesday, 12th. Fresh breezes and cloudy; a swell from the South-South-West. Some Albetrosses and Pintado Birds about the Ship. Wind Westerly; course North 30 degrees West; distance 73 miles; latitude 33 degrees 12 minutes South, longitude 152 degrees 44 minutes West.

Wednesday, 13th. Gentle breezes, with some flying Showers. At 6 p.m. Variation per Azimuth, 8 degrees 8 minutes East. Note, while we was between the Latitude of 37 and 40 degrees we had constantly blowing Tempestious weather, but since we have been to the Northward of 37 degrees, the weather hath been very moderate. Wind South-West and West-South-West; course North-North-West; distance 74 miles; latitude 32 degrees 3 minutes South, longitude 153 degrees 16 minutes West.

Thursday, 14th. Gentle breezes, and sometimes Calm. A Swell from the South-South-West. Wind Variable; course South 86 degrees West; distance 33 miles; latitude 32 degrees 5 minutes South, longitude 153 degrees 54 minutes West.

Friday, 15th. First part, moderate and Cloudy, remainder Strong Gales and Squally. Several Albetrosses, Pintado Birds, and Sheer Waters about the Ship; some of the Albetrosses were all White. Wind North-East to South-East; course South 77 West; distance 139 miles; latitude 32 degrees 36 minutes South, longitude 156 degrees 34 minutes West.

Saturday, 16th. First part very strong Gales and Squally; remainder more moderate, with a large Swell from the Southward. Wind South-South-East, South, West-South-West; course North 60 degrees West; distance 100 miles; latitude 31 degrees 45 minutes South, longitude 158 degrees 16 minutes West.

Sunday, 17th. Fresh Gales and Cloudy. Wind South-West; course North 25 West; distance 100 miles; latitude 31 degrees 14 minutes South, longitude 159 degrees 6 minutes West.

Monday, 18th. Moderate Gales and Cloudy, with a Swell from the Southward. Wind Westerly; course North by West 1/2 West; distance 78 miles; latitude 29 degrees 00 minutes South, longitude 159 degrees 32 minutes West.

Tuesday, 19th. Variable; light Airs and Calm. Variation per Amplitude at sunset, 8 degrees 36 minutes East; per Azimuth in the morning, 8 degrees 29 minutes East; mean, 8 degrees 32 1/2 minutes East. A large hollow swell from the Southward. Wind Variable; course East; distance 6 miles; latitude 29 degrees 00 minutes South, longitude 159 degrees 25 minutes West.

Wednesday, 20th. Light Airs and Calm. Wind Variable; course South-West by South; distance 20 miles; latitude 29 degrees 20 minutes South, longitude 159 degrees 47 minutes West.

Thursday, 21st. Most part Gentle breezes and clear weather. Wind South Easterly; course South 50 degrees West; distance 62 miles; latitude 30 degrees 00 minutes South, longitude 160 degrees 42 minutes West.

Friday, 22nd. Fresh breezes and Cloudy. The Southerly swell still Continues, from which I conjecture that there is no land near in that Direction. Wind South-East; course South 34 West; distance 81 miles; latitude 31 degrees 7 minutes South, longitude 161 degrees 35 minutes West.

Saturday, 23rd. Gentle breezes and Cloudy weather. Wind South-East; course South-West by South; distance 62 miles; latitude 31 degrees 59 minutes South, longitude 162 degrees 44 minutes West.

Sunday, 24th. Moderate breezes and Cloudy. At Noon saw some sea-Weed. The Southerly swell is now quite gone down. Wind South-East to North-East; course South 35 West; distance 97 miles; latitude 33 degrees 18 minutes South, longitude 162 degrees 51 minutes West.

Monday, 25th. Ditto weather. At 1 p.m. passed by a Piece of Wood, about 3 feet long and 7 or 8 Inches thick. Variation at 6 p.m. per Azimuth, 10 degrees 48 minutes East. A.M., got up all the Boatswain's Stores, to take an account of them. Wind North-East; course South 43 1/2 West; distance 103 miles; latitude 34 degrees 30 minutes South, longitude 165 degrees 10 minutes West.

Tuesday, 26th. Fresh breezes and fair weather. Wind North-North-East; course South-West; distance 136 miles; latitude 36 degrees 9 minutes South, longitude 167 degrees 14 minutes West.

Wednesday, 27th. Very strong Gales and hazey, with rain the First and Middle part; Latter, moderate and clear weather. In the evening took in the Topsails and Mainsail, and lay too with her head to the Westward under the Foresail. During the night, at 4 a.m., made Sail. Saw several Pieces of Sea Weed at different times this 24 Hours. Wind North by East, Westerly; course South 28 West; distance 95 miles; latitude 37 degrees 33 minutes South, longitude 168 degrees 10 minutes West.

Thursday, 28th. First and Middle parts, fresh gales and Cloudy; Latter part, very strong Gales and Squally. At 4 p.m. saw a Seal aSleep upon the Water, and some Weed. A.M. saw several bunches of Sea Weed and a few Albetrosses and Sheer Waters. Wind Westerly; course South 21 degrees West; distance 92 miles; latitude 38 degrees 59 minutes South, longitude 169 degrees 5 minutes West.

Friday, 29th. The first part strong Gales and Squally; remainder a fresh breeze and settled weather. At 1 p.m. was obliged to take in the Topsails, but set them again at 4. At 11 a.m. saw a Bird something like a Snipe, only it had a short bill; it had the appearance of a land bird. Several Albetrosses, Pintado birds, and Sheer Waters about the Ship, and a Number of Doves; of these we have seen more or less ever since the 31st of last Month, the day we first saw them. Wind South-West; course North 59 degrees West; distance 60 miles; latitude 38 degrees 30 minutes South, longitude 170 degrees 14 minutes West.

Saturday, 30th. Moderate breezes and Settled weather. Saw a dark brown bird as big as a Raven; it is a Sea Fowl, and are seen in great Numbers about the Faulkland Islands, as I am told. We likewise saw several pieces of Sea Weed. Wind South Easterly; course North 87 1/2 West; distance 90 miles; latitude 38 degrees 26 minutes South, longitude 172 degrees 20 minutes West.

[October 1769.]

Sunday, October 1st. Little Wind in the day time and Calm in the Night. At 8 a.m. sounded: no ground with 120 fathoms of line. Saw an immence number of Birds, the most of them were Doves; saw likewise a Seal aSleep upon the Water, which we at first took for a Crooked billet. These creatures, as they lay upon the Water, hold their fins up in a very odd manner, and very different to any I have seen before; we generally reckon that seals never go out of Soundings or far from Land, but the few we have seen in this Sea is certainly an exception to that rule. However, one would think that we were not far from some land, from the Pieces of Rock weed we see daily floating upon the Water. To-day we took up a small Piece of Stick, but to all appearance it had been a long time at Sea. The observ'd Latitude is considerable to the Northward of that given by the Log, in so much that I think there must be some Current seting from the Southward. Wind South to West by North; course North 16 degrees West; distance 43 miles; latitude 37 degrees 45 minutes South, longitude 172 degrees 36 minutes West.

Monday, 2nd. Little wind. At 3 p.m. hoisted out a Boat to try the Current, but found none. Saw several Grampusses. A.M. had a Boat in the Water, and Mr. Banks shott an Albetross which measured 10 feet 8 Inches from the tip of Wing to the other. He likewise shott 2 birds that were very much like Ducks, excepting their head and Bill; their plumage were dark brown. We first saw some of these birds in the Latitude of 40 degrees South, after our first coming into those Seas. Wind West-South-West, South-West; course North-North-West; distance 35 miles; latitude 37 degrees 10 minutes South, longitude 172 degrees 54 minutes West.

Tuesday, 3rd. Little wind and sometimes Calm. A.M. Variation per Azimuth 13 degrees 22 minutes East. Saw some fish like a Skip Jack, and a small sort that appeared very Transparent. Took up a very small piece of wood with Barnacles upon it, a proof that it hath been some time at Sea. Some very large Albetrosses about the Ship and other birds. The observed Latitude is 10 Miles to the Northward of that given by the Log, and it was the same Yesterday, which I think is a Proof that there must be a Current setting to the Northward, notwithstanding we did not find any when we try'd it. Wind Southerly; course North 60 degrees West; distance 28 miles; latitude 36 degrees 56 minutes South, longitude 173 degrees 27 minutes West.

Wednesday, 4th. Gentle breezes and Cloudy weather. P.M. Variation per Azimuth 12 degrees 48 minutes East; sounded twice, but found no ground, with 120 fathoms of line. Saw some rock weed, but not in such plenty as of late. Wind South-East; course South 52 1/2 West; distance 86 miles; latitude 37 degrees 43 minutes South, longitude 175 degrees 00 minutes West.

Thursday, 5th. Light, gentle breezes and Clear weather. P.M. saw one of the same sort of Birds as we saw last Saturday. These birds are of a dark brown or Chocolate Colour, with some white feathers under their wings, and are as big as Ravens. Mr. Gore says that they are in great plenty at Port Egmont in Faulklands Islands, and for that reason calls them Port Egmont Hens. Saw a great many Porpoisses, large and Small; the small ones had white bellies and Noses. A.M. saw 2 Port Egmont Hens, a Seal, some sea Weed, and a Piece of wood with Barnacles upon it. Wind South-East to East-North-East; course South 49 1/2 West; distance 63 miles; latitude 38 degrees 23 minutes South, longitude 176 degrees 3 minutes West.

Friday, 6th. Little wind, and fine pleasant weather. Saw some Seals, sea weed, and Port Egmont Hens. P.M. Variation per Azimuth 12 degrees 50 minutes East. Per Amplitude 12 degrees 40 minutes. A.M. per Azimuth 14 degrees 2 minutes East; the difference is 1 degree 3 minutes, and the Ship has only gone 9 Leagues in the Time. The Colour of the water appears to be paler than common, and hath been so for some days past; this makes us sound frequently, but can find no ground with 180 fathoms of Line. Wind East-North-East; course South-West; distance 62 miles; latitude 39 degrees 11 minutes South, longitude 177 degrees 2 minutes West.

[Make New Zealand.]

Saturday, 7th. Gentle breezes and settled weather. At 2 p.m. saw land* (* The North island of New Zealand.) from the Masthead bearing West by North, which we stood directly for, and could but just see it of the Deck at sunset. Variation per Azimuth and Amplitude 15 degrees 4 1/2 minutes East; by observation of the Sun and Moon made this afternoon the Longitude of the Ship is 180 degrees 55 minutes West, by the mean of these and Subsequent observations the Error of the Ship's account in Longitude from George's Island is 3 degrees 16 minutes; that is, so much to the Westward of the Longitude resulting from the Log, which is what is inserted in the Columns. At Midnight brought too and sounded, but had no ground with 170 fathoms. At daylight made sail in for the Land, at Noon it bore from South-West to North-West by North, distant 8 Leagues. Latitude observed 38 degrees 57 minutes South; Wind North-East, South-East, Variable; course South 70 degrees West; distance 41 miles; latitude 38 degrees 57 minutes observed South; longitude 177 degrees 54 minutes West.

Sunday, 8th. Gentle breezes and clear weather. At 5 p.m., seeing the opening of a Bay that appear'd to run pretty far inland, hauld our wind and stood in for it; but as soon as night came on we keept plying on and off until day light, when we found ourselves to leeward of the Bay, the wind being at North. By Noon we fetch'd in with the South-West point, but not being able to weather it we tacked and stood off. We saw in the Bay several Canoes, People upon the Shore, and some houses in the Country. The land on the Sea Coast is high, with Steep Cliffs; and back inland are very high Mountains. The face of the Country is of a hilly surface, and appears to be cloathed with wood and Verdure. Wind between the East-North-East and North.

CHAPTER 5. EXPLORATION OF NORTH ISLAND OF NEW ZEALAND.

[October 1769. At Poverty Bay, North Island, New Zealand.]

MONDAY, 9th October. Gentle breezes and Clear Weather. P.M. stood into the Bay and Anchored on the North-East side before the Entrance of a small River,* (* Tauranga nui. The township of Gisborne is now situated on its eastern bank.) in 10 fathoms, a fine sandy bottom. The North-East point of the Bay bore East by South 1/2 South, and the South-West point South, distance from the Shore half a League. After this I went ashore with a Party of men in the Pinnace and yawl accompanied by Mr. Banks and Dr. Solander. We landed abreast of the Ship and on the East side of the River just mentioned; but seeing some of the Natives on the other side of the River of whom I was desirous of speaking with, and finding that we could not ford the River, I order'd the yawl in to carry us over, and the pinnace to lay at the Entrance. In the mean time the Indians made off. However we went as far as their Hutts which lay about 2 or 300 Yards from the water side, leaving 4 boys to take care of the Yawl, which we had no sooner left than 4 Men came out of the woods on the other side the River, and would certainly have cut her off had not the People in the Pinnace discover'd them and called to her to drop down the Stream, which they did, being closely persued by the Indians. The coxswain of the Pinnace, who had the charge of the Boats, seeing this, fir'd 2 Musquets over their Heads; the first made them stop and Look round them, but the 2nd they took no notice of; upon which a third was fir'd and kill'd one of them upon the Spot just as he was going to dart his spear at the Boat. At this the other 3 stood motionless for a Minute or two, seemingly quite surprised; wondering, no doubt, what it was that had thus kill'd their Comrade; but as soon as they recovered themselves they made off, dragging the Dead body a little way and then left it. Upon our hearing the report of the Musquets we immediately repair'd to the Boats, and after viewing the Dead body we return'd on board. In the morning, seeing a number of the Natives at the same place where we saw them last night, I went on shore with the Boats, mann'd and arm'd, and landed on the opposite side of the river. Mr. Banks, Dr. Solander, and myself only landed at first, and went to the side of the river, the natives being got together on the opposite side. We called to them in the George's Island Language, but they answer'd us by flourishing their weapons over their heads and dancing, as we suppos'd, the War Dance; upon this we retir'd until the Marines were landed, which I order'd to be drawn up about 200 yards behind us. We went again to the river side, having Tupia, Mr. Green, and Dr. Monkhouse along with us. Tupia spoke to them in his own Language, and it was an agreeable surprize to us to find that they perfectly understood him. After some little conversation had passed one of them swam over to us, and after him 20 or 30 more; these last brought their Arms, which the first man did not. We made them every one presents, but this did not satisfy them; they wanted everything we had about us, particularly our Arms, and made several attempts to snatch them out of our hands. Tupia told us several times, as soon as they came over, to take care of ourselves for they were not our friends; and this we very soon found, for one of them snatched Mr. Green's hanger from him and would not give it up; this encouraged the rest to be more insolent, and seeing others coming over to join them, I order'd the man who had taken the Hanger to be fir'd at, which was accordingly done, and wounded in such a manner that he died soon after. Upon the first fire, which was only 2 Musquets, the others retir'd to a Rock which lay nearly in the middle of the River; but on seeing the man fall they return'd, probably to carry him off or his Arms, the last of which they accomplished, and this we could not prevent unless we had run our Bayonets into them, for upon their returning from off the Rock, we had discharged off our Peices, which were loaded with small shott, and wounded 3 more; but these got over the River and were carried off by the others, who now thought proper to retire. Finding nothing was to be done with the People on this side, and the water in the river being salt, I embarked with an intent to row round the head of the Bay in search of fresh water, and if possible to surprise some of the Natives and to take them on board, and by good Treatment and Presents endeavour to gain their friendship with this view.

Tuesday, 10th. P.M., I rowed round the head of the bay, but could find no place to land on account of the Great Surf which beat everywhere upon the Shore. Seeing 2 Boats or Canoes coming in from Sea I rowed to one of them, in order to Seize upon the People; and came so near before they took notice of us that Tupia called to them to come alongside and we would not hurt them; but instead of doing this they endeavour'd to get away, upon which I order'd a Musquet to be fir'd over their Heads, thinking this would either make them surrender, or jump overboard; but here I was mistaken, for they immediately took to their Arms or whatever they had in the Boat, and began to attack us. This obliged us to fire upon them, and unfortunately either 2 or 3 were kill'd and one wounded, and 3 jumped overboard. These last we took up and brought on board, where they was Cloathed and Treated with all imaginable kindness; and to the Surprise of everybody became at once as cheerful and as merry as if they had been with their own Friends. They were all 3 Young, the eldest not above 20 years of Age, and the youngest about 10 or 12. I am aware that most Humane men who have not experienced things of this nature will Censure my Conduct in firing upon the People in their Boat, nor do I myself think that the reason I had for seizing upon her will at all justify me; and had I thought that they would have made the Least Resistance I would not have come near them; but as they did, I was not to stand still and suffer either myself or those that were with me to be knocked on the head.

In the morning, as I intended to put our 3 Prisoners ashore, and stay here the day to see what effect it might have upon the other Natives, I sent an Officer ashore with the Marines and a party of men to cut wood, and soon after followed myself, accompanied by Mr. Banks, Dr. Solander, and Tupia, taking the 3 Natives with us, whom we landed on the West side of the River before mentioned. They were very unwilling to leave us, pretending that they should fall into the hands of their Enemies, who would kill and Eat them. However, they at last of their own accord left us and hid themselves in some bushes. Soon after this we discover'd several bodys of the Natives marching towards us, upon which we retir'd aCross the River, and joind the wooders; and with us came the 3 Natives we had just parted with, for we could not prevail upon them to go to their own people. We had no sooner got over the River than the others assembled on the other side to the Number of 150 or 200, all Arm'd. Tupia now began to Parly with them, and the 3 we had with us shew'd everything we had given them, part of which they laid and left upon the Body of the Man that was Kill'd the day before. These things seem'd so far to Convince them of our friendly intentions that one man came over to us, while all the others sat down upon the Sand. We everyone made this man a present, and the 3 Natives that were with us likewise presented him with such things as they had got from us, with which, after a short Stay, he retir'd aCross the River. I now thought proper to take everybody on board, to prevent any more Quarrels, and with us came the 3 Natives, whom we could not prevail upon to stay behind; and this appear'd the more strange as the man that came over to us was Uncle to one of them. After we had return'd on board we saw them Carry off the Dead Man; but the one that was Kill'd the first evening we Landed remain'd in the very spot they had left him.

[Leave Poverty Bay.]

Wednesday, 11th. In the P.M., as I intended to sail in the Morning, we put the 3 Youths ashore, seemingly very much against their inclination; but whether this was owing to a desire they had to remain with us, or the fear of falling into the hands of their Enemies, as they pretended, I know not. The latter, however, seemed to be ill-founded, for we saw them carried aCross the River in a Catamaran, and walk Leasurely off with the other Natives. At 6 a.m. we weighed and stood out of the Bay, which I have named Poverty Bay, because it afforded us no one thing we wanted (Latitude 38 degrees 42 minutes South, Longitude 181 degrees 36 minutes West).* (* Latitude correct. Longitude is 181 degrees 57 minutes West.) It is in the form of a Horse Shoe, and is known by an Island lying close under the North-East point. The 2 points which forms the Entrance are high, with Steap white

Cliffs, and lay a League and a half or 2 Leagues from Each other, North-East by East and South-West by West. The Depth of Water in this Bay is from 12 to 6 and 5 fathoms, a sandy bottom and good Anchorage, but you lay open to the winds between the South and East. Boats can go in and out of the river above mentioned at any time of Tide in fine weather; but as there is a Bar at the Entrance, on which the Sea Sometimes runs so high that no Boat can either get in or out, which hapned while we laid here; however, I believe that Boats can generally land on the North-East side of the river. The shore of this Bay, from a little within each Entrance, is a low, flat sand; but this is only a Narrow Slip, for the face of the Country appears with a variety of hills and Vallies, all cloathed with woods and Verdure, and to all appearance well inhabited, especially in the Vallies leading up from the Bay, where we daily saw Smoke at a great distance inland, and far back in the Country are very high Mountains. At Noon the South-West point of Poverty Bay, which I have named Young Nicks head (after the Boy who first saw this land),* (* In Mr. Molineux's Log, his name is given as Nicholas Young, but no such name appears in the official lists.) bore North by West, distance 3 or 4 leagues, being at this time about 3 Miles from the Shore, and had 25 fathoms Water, the Main Land extending from North-East by North to South. My intention is to follow the direction of the Coast to the Southward, as far as the Latitude of 40 or 41 degrees, and then to return to the Northward, in case we meet with nothing to incourage us to proceed farther.

[Off Portland Island, North Island, New Zealand.]

Thursday, 12th. Gentle breezes at North-West and North, with frequent Calms. In the Afternoon, while we lay becalm'd, several Canoes came off to the Ship, but kept at a distance until one, who appeared to come from a different part, came off and put alongside at once, and after her all the rest. The people in this boat had heard of the Treatment those had met with we had had on board before, and therefore came on board without hesitation; they were all kindly treated, and very soon entered into a Traffick with our People for George's Island Cloth, etc.; giving in Exchange their Paddles, having little else to dispose of, and hardly left themselves a sufficient number to paddle ashore; nay, the people in one Canoe, after disposing of their Paddles, offer'd to sell the Canoe. After a stay of about 2 hours they went away, but by some means or other 3 were left on board, and not one boat would put back to take them in, and, what was more surprizing, those aboard did not seem at all uneasy with their situation. In the evening a light breeze springing up at North-West, we steer'd along Shore, under an easy sail, until midnight, then brought too. Soon after it fell Calm, and continued so until 8 o'Clock a.m., when a breeze sprung up at North, with which we stood along shore South-South-West. At and after sunrise found the variation to be 14 degrees 46 minutes East. About this time 2 Canoes came off to the Ship, one of which was prevailed upon to come along side to take in the 3 people we had had on board all night, who now seem'd glad of the opportunity to get ashore. As the People in the Canoe were a little shy at first, it was observed that one Argument those on board made use on to intice the others alongside, was in telling them that we did not Eat men; from which it should seem that these people have such a Custom among them. At the time we made sail we were abreast of the Point of Land set yesterday at Noon, from which the Land trends South-South-West. This point I have named Cape Table, on account of its shape and figure. It lies 7 Leagues to the Southward of Poverty Bay, in the Latitude of 39 degrees 7 minutes South, longitude 181 degrees 36 minutes West, it is of a moderate height, makes in a sharpe Angle, and appears to be quite flat at Top. In steering along shore to the Southward of the Cape, at the distance of 2 or 3 miles off, our soundings were from 20 to 30 fathoms, having a Chain of Rocks that appears at different heights above water, laying between us and the Shore. At Noon, Cape Table bore North 20 degrees East, distant 4 Leagues, and a small Island (being the Southermost land in sight) bore South 70 degrees West, distant 3 miles. This Island I have named Isle of Portland, on account of its very great resemblance to Portland in the English Channel. It lies about a mile from a Point on the Main, but there appears to be a ledge of Rocks extending nearly, if not quite, aCross from the one to the other. North 57 degrees East, 2 Miles from the South point of Portland, lies a sunken rock whereon the sea breaks; we passed between this Rock and the land having 17, 18, and 20 fathom Water. We saw a great Number of the Natives assembled together on the Isle of Portland; we likewise saw some on the Main land, and several places that were Cultivated and laid out in square Plantations.

Friday, 13th. At 1 p.m. we discover'd land behind or to the Westward of Portland, extending to the Southward as far as we could see. In hauling round the South end of Portland we fell into Shoal Water and broken ground, which we, however, soon got clear of. At this time 4 Canoes came off to us full of People, and keept for sometime under our stern threatning of us all the while. As I did not know but what I might be obliged to send our Boats ahead to sound, I thought these Gentry would be as well out of the way. I order'd a Musquet shott to be fir'd close to one of them, but this they took no notice of. A 4 Pounder was then fir'd a little wide of them; at this they began to shake their Spears and Paddles at us, but notwithstanding this they thought fit to retire. Having got round Portland, we hauled in for the Land North-West, having a Gentle breeze at North-East, which died away at 5 o'Clock and obliged us to Anchor in 21 fathoms, a fine sandy bottom: the South Point of Portland bore South-East 1/2 South distant about 2 Leagues, and a low Point on the Main bore North 1/2 East. In this last direction there runs in a deep bay behind the Land on which is Table Cape, which makes this Land a Peninsula, joined to the Main by a low, narrow neck of land; the Cape is the North Point of the Peninsula, and Portland the South. While we lay at Anchor 2 Boats came off to us, and so near as to take up some things we throw'd them out of the Ship, but would not come alongside. At 5 a.m. a breeze springing northerly we weigh'd and steer'd in for the Land. The shore here forms a very large Bay, of which Portland is the North-East Point, and the Bay above mentioned is an Arm of it. I would gladly have examin'd this Arm, because there appear'd to be safe Anchorage in it, but as I was not certain of this, and the wind being right an End, I did not care to spend time in Turning up to it. At Noon Portland bore South 50 degrees East, and the Southermost land in sight bore South-South-West, distant 10 or 12 Leagues, being about 3 miles from the Shore, and in this situation had 12 fathoms water--24 fathoms have been the most Water we have had since we have been within Portland, every where clear ground. The land near the Shore is of a moderate height, with white Cliffs and Sandy beaches. Inland are several Pretty high Mountains, and the whole face of the Country appears with a very hilly surface, and for the most part Covered with wood, and hath all the appearances of a very pleasant and fertile Country.

Saturday, 14th. P.M. had Gentle breezes between the North-East and North-West. Kept running down along shore at the distance of 2 or 3 miles off. Our sounding was from 20 to 13 fathoms, an even sandy bottom. We saw some Canoes or Boats in shore, and several houses upon the Land, but no harbour or Convenient watering place--the Main thing we were looking for. In the night had little wind, and Sometimes Calm with Dirty, rainy weather. A.M. had Variable light Airs next to a Calm and fair weather. In the morning, being not above 2 Leagues from the South-West corner of the great Bay we have been in for the 2 days past, the Pinnace and Long boat were hoisted out in order to search for Fresh Water; but just as they were ready to put off we observed several Boats full of People coming off from the Shore, and for that reason I did not think it prudent to send our own from the Ship. The first that came were 5 in Number, in them were between 80 and 90 men. Every Method was tried to gain their Friendship, and several things were thrown overboard to them; but all we could do was to no purpose, neither would they accept of any one thing from us, but seem'd fully bent on attacking us. In order to prevent this, and our being obliged to fire upon them, I order'd a 4 Pounder Loaded with grape to be fir'd a little wide of them, letting them know at the same time by Means of Tupia what we were going to do; this had the desir'd effect, and not one of these would afterwards trust themselves abreast of the Ship. Soon after 4 more came off; one of these put what Arms they had into another Boat, and then came alongside so near as to take what things we gave them, and I believe might have been Prevailed upon to come on board had not some of the first 5 came up under our Stern and began again to threaten us, at which the people in this one Boat seem'd displeased; immediately after this they all went ashore. At Noon

Latitude in per Observation 39 degrees 37 minutes South. Portland bore by our run from it East by North, distant 14 Leagues; the Southermost land in sight, and which is the South point of the Bay, South-East by South, distant 4 or 5 Leagues; and a Bluff head lying in the South-West corner of the Bay South by West 2 or 3 Miles. On each side of this bluff head is a low narrow sand or stone beach; between these beaches and the Main land is a pretty large lake of Salt Water, as I suppose. On the South-East side of this head is a very large flatt, which seems to extend a good way inland to the Westward; on this flatt are Several groves of Streight, tall Trees, but there seems to be a great Probability that the lake above mentiond extends itself a good way into this flatt Country. Inland are a Chain of Pretty high Mountains extending North and South; on the Summits and Sides of these Mountains were many Patches of Snow, but between them and the Sea the Land is Cloathed with wood.* (* The Endeavour was now off what is called Ahuriri Bay. The bluff head is known as Ahuriri Bluff, and the town of Napier, of 8000 inhabitants, lies at the back of it. The large sheet of salt water is called Manganui-o-rotu. There was no sheltered harbour for a vessel in the Endeavour's situation, but at present, harbour works have improved the entrance to the lagoon into which vessels drawing 12 feet can enter. Produce of the value of over a million pounds per annum is now exported from Napier.)

[In Hawkes Bay, North Island, New Zealand.]

Sunday, 15th. P.M. stood over for the Southermost Land or South point of the Bay, having a light breeze at North-East, our soundings from 12 to 8 fathoms. Not reaching this point before dark, we stood Off and on all night, having Variable light Airs next to a Calm; depth of water from 8 to 7 fathoms; Variation 14 degrees 10 minutes East. At 8 a.m., being abreast of the South-West point of the Bay, some fishing Boats came off to us and sold us some stinking fish; however it was such as they had, and we were glad to enter into Traffick with them upon any Terms. These People behaved at first very well, until a large Arm'd boat, wherein were 22 Men, came alongside. We soon saw that this Boat had nothing for Traffick, yet as they came boldly alongside we gave them 2 or 3 pieces of Cloth, Articles they seem'd the most fond off. One Man in this Boat had on him a black skin, something like a Bear Skin, which I was desirous of having that I might be a better judge what sort of an Animal the first Owner was. I offer'd him for it a piece of Red Cloth, which he seem'd to jump at by immediately putting off the Skin and holding it up to us, but would not part with it until he had the Cloth in his possession and after that not at all, but put off the Boat and went away, and with them all the rest. But in a very short time they return'd again, and one of the fishing Boats came alongside and offer'd us some more fish. The Indian Boy Tiata, Tupia's Servant, being over the side, they seiz'd hold of him, pull'd him into the Boat and endeavoured to carry him off; this obliged us to fire upon them, which gave the Boy an opportunity to jump overboard. We brought the Ship too, lower'd a Boat into the Water, and took him up unhurt. Two or 3 paid for this daring attempt with the loss of their lives, and many more would have suffer'd had it not been for fear of killing the Boy. This affair occasioned my giving this point of land the name of Cape Kidnapper. It is remarkable on account of 2 White rocks in form of Haystacks standing very near it. On each side of the Cape are Tolerable high white steep Cliffs, Latitude 39 degrees 43 minutes South; Longitude 182 degrees 24 minutes West; it lies South-West by West, distant 13 Leagues from the Island of Portland. Between them is a large Bay wherein we have been for these 3 days past; this Bay I have named Hawkes Bay in Honour of Sir Edward, first Lord of the Admiralty; we found in it from 24 to 8 and 7 fathoms, everywhere good Anchoring. From Cape Kidnapper the Island Trends South-South-West, and in this direction we run along shore, keeping about a League off, having a steady breeze and Clear weather. At Noon the above Cape bore from us North 9 degrees East, distant 2 Leagues, and the Southermost land in sight South 25 degrees West Latitude in Per Observation 39 degrees 50 minutes South.

Monday, 16th. First and latter part, fresh breezes, Northerly; in the night, Variable and sometimes calm. At 2 p.m. passed by a Small but a Pretty high white Island lying close to the Shore. On this Island we saw a good many Houses, Boats, and Some People. We concluded that they must be fishers, because the Island was quite barren; we likewise saw several people upon the Shore in a small Bay on the Main within the Island. At 7 the Southermost land in sight bore South-West by South, and Cape Kidnapper North 3/4 East, distant 8 leagues, being then about 2 Leagues from the Shore, and had 55 fathoms. At 11 brought too until daylight, then made Sail along shore to the Southward. At 7 passed a pretty high point of Land, which lies South-South-West, 12 Leagues from Cape Kidnapper. From this point the Land Trends 3/4 of a point more to the Westward. At 10 saw more land appear to the Southward, at South-West by South. At Noon the Southermost land in sight bore South 39 degrees West, distant 8 or 10 Leagues, and a high Bluff head with Yellowish Cliffs bore West, distant 2 miles, Latitude observed 40 degrees 34 minutes South; depth of water 32 fathoms.

[Returning North from Cape Turnagain.]

Tuesday, 17th. P.M. winds at West, a fresh breeze; in the night, Variable light Airs and Calm; a.m. a Gentle breeze between the North-West and North-East. Seeing no likelyhood of meeting with a Harbour, and the face of the Country Visibly altering for the worse, I thought that the standing farther to the South would not be attended with any Valuable discovery, but would be loosing of Time, which might be better employ'd and with a greater Probability of success in examining the Coast to the Northward. With this

View, at 1 p.m. Tack'd and stood to the Northward, having the Wind at West, a fresh breeze.* (* If Cook had known the exact shape of New Zealand, he could scarcely have taken a better resolve, in view of saving time, than to turn northward again when he did.) At this time we could see the land extending South-West by South, at least 10 or 12 Leagues. The Bluff head or high point of land we were abreast off at Noon I have called Cape Turnagain because here we returned. It lies in the Latitude of 40 degrees 34 minutes South, Longitude 182 degrees 55 West, and 18 Leagues South-South-West and South-South-West 1/2 West from Cape Kidnapper. The land between them is of a very unequal height; in some places it is high, with White Cliffs next the Sea--in others low, with sandy beaches. The face of the Country is not nearly so well Cloathed with wood as it is about Hawkes Bay, but for the most part looks like our high Downs in England, and to all appearance well inhabited, for we saw several Villages as we run along shore, not only in the Vallies, but on the Tops and sides of the Hills, and Smokes in other places. The ridge of Mountains before mentioned extends to the Southward farther than we could see, and are every where Checquer'd with Snow. This night saw 2 Large fires up in the inland Country, a sure sign that it must be inhabited. At Noon Cape Kidnapper bore North 56 degrees West, distant 7 Leagues; latitude observed 39 degrees 52 minutes South.

Wednesday, 18th. Variable light winds and fine weather. At 4 a.m. Cape Kidnapper bore North 32 degrees West, distant 2 Leagues. In this situation had 62 fathoms; and when the said Cape bore West by North, distant 3 or 4 Leagues, had 45 fathoms; Midway between the Isle of Portland and Cape Kidnapper had 65 fathoms. At Noon the Isle of Portland bore North-East 1/2 East, distant 4 Leagues; latitude observ'd 39 degrees 34 minutes South.

Thursday, 19th. The first part had Gentle breezes at East and East-North-East; in the night, fresh Gales between the South and South-West; dark, Cloudy weather, with Lightning and rain. At 1/2 past 5 P.M. Tack'd and stood to the South-East: the Isle of Portland bore South-East, distant 3 Leagues. Soon after we Tacked a boat or Canoe came off from the Shore, wherein were 5 People. They came on board without shewing the least signs of fear, and insisted upon staying with us the whole night; indeed, there was no getting them away without turning them out of the Ship by force, and that I did not care to do; but to prevent them playing us any Trick I hoisted their Canoe up alongside. Two appear'd to be Chiefs, and the other 3 their Servants. One of the Chiefs seem'd to be of a free, open, and Gentle disposition; they both took great notice of everything they saw, and was very thankful for what was given them. The 2 Chiefs would neither Eat nor Drink with us, but the other 3 Eat whatever was offer'd them. Notwithstanding that these people had heard of the Treatment the others had meet with who had been on board before, yet it appear'd a little strange that they should place so much Confidence in us as to put themselves wholy in our power wether we would or no, especially as the others we had meet with in this bay had upon every occasion behaved in quite a different manner. At 11 brought too until daylight (the night being dark and rainy), then made sail. At 7 a.m. brought too under Cape Table, and sent away the Indian Canoe. At this Time some others were putting off from the Shore, but we did not wait their coming, but made sail to the Northward. At Noon the Northermost land in sight North 20 degrees East, and Young Nicks head, or the South point of Poverty Bay, West-Northerly, near 4 Leagues. Latitude observed 38 degrees 44 minutes 30 seconds South.

Friday, 20th. P.M. a fresh breeze at South-South-West; in the night, variable light breezes, with rain; A.M. a fresh breeze at South-West. At 3 p.m. passed by a remarkable head, which I called Gable end Foreland on account of the very great resemblance the white cliff at the very point hath to the Gable end of a House. It is made still more remarkable by a Spir'd Rock standing a little distance from it. This head land lies from Cape Table North 24 degrees East, distant 12 Leagues. Between them the Shore forms a Bay, wherein lies Poverty Bay, 4 Leagues from the former and 8 Leagues from the Latter. From Gable end Foreland the land trends North by East as far as we could see. The land from Poverty Bay to this place is of a moderate but very unequal height, distinguished by Hills and Vallies that are Cover'd with woods. We saw, as we run along shore, several Villages, cultivated lands, and some of the Natives. In the evening some Canoes came off to the Ship, and one Man came on board to whom we gave a few Trifles and then sent him away. Stood off and on until daylight, and then made sail in shore in order to look into 2 Bays that appear'd to our view about 2 Leagues to the Northward of the Foreland. The Southermost we could not fetch, but in the other we Anchor'd about 11 o'Clock in 7 fathoms, a black sandy bottom. The North point bore North-East 1/2 North, distant 2 Miles, and the South Point South-East by East, distant one Mile, and about 3/4 of a Mile from the Shore. This Bay is not so much Shelter'd from the Sea as I at first thought it was; but as the Natives, many of whom came about us in their Canoes, appear'd to be of a friendly disposition, I was willing to try if we could not get a little water on board, and to see a little into the Nature of the Country before we proceeded further to the Northward.

Saturday, 21st. We had no sooner come to an Anchor, as mentioned above, than perceiving 2 old Men in the Canoes, who from their Garbe appear'd to be Chiefs, these I invited on board, and they came without Hesitation. To each I gave about 4 Yards of linnen and a Spike Nail; the linnen they were very fond of, but the Nails they seem'd to set no Value upon. Tupia explain'd to them the reasons of our Coming here, and that we should neither hurt nor Molest them if they did but behave in the same peaceable manner to us;

indeed, we were under very little apprehension but what they would, as they had heard of what hapned in Poverty Bay. Between 1 and 2 p.m. I put off with the Boats mann'd and Arm'd in order to land to look for fresh Water, these 2 Men along with us; but the surf running very high, and it begun to blow and rain at the same time, I returned back to the Ship, having first put the 2 Chiefs into one of their Canoes. In the evening it fell moderate, and we landed and found 2 Small Streams of Fresh Water, and the Natives to all appearance very friendly and peaceable; on which account I resolved to Stay one day at least, to fill a little water and to give Mr. Banks an opportunity to Collect a little of the Produce of the Country. In the morning Lieutenant Gore went on shore to superintend the Watering with a Strong party of Men, but the getting the Casks off was so very difficult, on account of the Surf, that it was noon before one Turn came on board.

[At Tegadoo Bay, North Island, New Zealand.]

Sunday, 22nd. P.M. light breezes and Cloudy. About or a little after Noon several of the Natives came off to the Ship in their Canoes and began to Traffick with us, our people giving them George's Island Cloth for theirs, for they had little else to dispose of. This kind of exchange they seem'd at first very fond of, and prefer'd the Cloth we had got at the Islands to English Cloth; but it fell in its value above 500 p. ct. before night. I had some of them on board, and Shew'd them the Ship, with which they were well pleased. The same friendly disposition was observed by those on shore, and upon the whole they behaved as well or better than one could expect; but as the getting the Water from the Shore proved so very Tedious on account of the Surf, I resolved upon leaving this place in the morning, and accordingly, at 5 a.m., we weighed and put to Sea. This Bay is called by the Natives Tegadoo;* (* Anaura Bay.) it lies in the Latitude of 38 degrees 16 minutes South, but as it hath nothing to recommend it I shall give no discription of it. There is plenty of Wild Sellery, and we purchased of the Natives 10 or 15 pounds of sweet Potatoes. They have pretty large plantations of these, but at present they are scarce, it being too Early in the Season. At Noon the Bay of Tegadoo bore West 1/2 South, distant 8 Leagues, and a very high double peak'd Mountain some distance in land bore North-West by West. Latitude observed 38 degrees 13 minutes South; Wind at North, a fresh Gale.

Monday, 23rd. P.M. fresh Gales at North, and Cloudy weather. At 1 Tack'd and stood in shore; at 6 Sounded, and had 56 fathoms fine sandy bottom; the Bay of Tegadoo bore South-West 1/2 West, distance 4 Leagues. At 8 Tack'd in 36 fathoms, being then about 2 Leagues from land; stood off and on all night, having Gentle breezes. At 8 a.m., being right before the Bay of Tegadoo and about a League from it, some of the Natives came off to us and inform'd us that in a Bay a little to the Southward (being the same that we could not fetch the day we put into Tegadoo) was fresh Water and easey getting at it; and as the wind was now against us, and we gain'd nothing by beating to windward, I thought the time would be better spent in this Bay* (* Tolaga.) in getting on board a little water, and forming some Connections with the Natives, than by keeping the Sea. With this view we bore up for it, and sent 2 Boats in, Mann'd and Arm'd, to Examine the Watering Place, who returned about noon and conform'd the account the Natives had given. We then Anchor'd in 11 fathoms, fine sandy bottom; the North point of the Bay North by East and the South point South-East, and the watering place, which was in a Small Cove a little within the South point of the Bay, distance one Mile.

Tuesday, 24th. Winds Westerly and fine weather. This afternoon, as soon as the Ship was moor'd, I went ashore to Examine the watering place, accompanied by Mr. Banks and Dr. Solander. I found the Water good and the Place pretty Convenient, and plenty of Wood close to high Water Mark, and the Natives to all appearance not only very friendly but ready to Traffick with us for what little they had. Early in the morning I sent Lieutenant Gore ashore to Superintend the Cutting wood and filling of Water, with a Sufficient number of men for both purposes, and all the Marines as a Guard. After breakfast I went myself, and remain'd there the whole day; but before this Mr. Green and I took several observations of the Sun and Moon. The mean result of them gave 180 degrees 47 minutes West Longitude from the Meridian of Greenwich; but as all the observations made before exceeded these, I have laid down this Coast agreeable to the means of the whole. At noon I took the Sun's Meridian Altitude with the Astronomical Quadrant, and found the Latitude 38 degrees 22 minutes 24 seconds South.

Wednesday, 25th. Winds and weather as Yesterday. P.M. set up the Armourer's Forge to repair the Tiller braces, they being broke. By night we had got on board 12 Tons of Water and two or 3 Boats' loads of Wood, and this I looked upon to be a good day's work. The Natives gave us not the least disturbance, but brought us now and then different sorts of Fish out to the Ship and Watering place, which we purchased of them with Cloth, beads, etc.

Thursday, 26th. P.M. had the winds from between the South and South-West, fair weather; the remainder, rainy, dirty weather. Notwithstanding we continued getting on board Wood and Water.

Friday, 27th. Winds at South-West; first part rainy weather, the remainder fair. A.M. sent the Pinnace to drudge, but she met with no success; after this, I went and sounded the Bay. I made a Shift to land in 2 Places, the first time in the bottom of the bay, where I went a little way into the Country, but met with nothing extraordinary. The other place I landed at was at the North point of the Bay, where I got as much Sellery and Scurvy grass as loaded the Boat. This day we compleated our Water to 70 Tons, but not wood Enough.

Saturday, 28th. Gentle breezes Southerly and fine weather. Employ'd wooding, cutting, and making of Brooms, there being a Shrub here very fit for that purpose; and as I intended to sail in the morning some hands were employ'd picking of Sellery to take to Sea with us. This is found here in great plenty, and I have caused it to be boiled with Portable Soup and Oatmeal every morning for the people's breakfast; and this I design to continue as long as it will last, or any is to be got, and I look upon it to be very wholesome and a great Antiscorbutick.

[At Tolaga Bay, North Island, New Zealand.]

Monday, 29th. P.M. Gentle breezes with Thunder and Lightning up the Country; in the night had light Airs off the land and very foggy; in the forenoon had a gentle breeze at North-North-East and Clear weather. At 4 a.m. unmoor'd, and at 6 weigh'd and put to Sea. At Noon the bay sail'd from bore North 63 degrees West, distant 4 Leagues. This bay is called by the Natives Tolaga;* (* It still goes by this name.) it is moderately large, and hath in it from 13 to 8 and 7 fathoms, clean sandy bottom and good Anchorage, and is shelterd from all winds except those that blow from the North-East Quarter. It lies in the Latitude of 38 degrees 22 minutes South, and 4 1/2 Leagues to the Northward of Gable end Foreland. Off the South point lies a small but high Island, so near to the Main as not to be distinguished from it. Close to the North end of this Island, at the Entrance into the Bay, are 2 high Rocks; one is high and round like a Corn Stack, but the other is long with holes thro' it like the Arches of a Bridge. Within these rocks is the Cove, where we cut wood and fill'd our Water. Off the North point of the Bay is a pretty high rocky Island, and about a Mile without it are some rocks and breakers. The variation of the Compass is here 14 degrees 31 minutes East, and the Tide flows at full and change of the Moon about 6 o'Clock, and rises and falls upon a Perpendicular 5 or 6 feet, but wether the flood comes from the Southward or Northward I have not been able to determine.

During our stay in this bay we had every day more or less Traffick with the Natives, they bringing us fish, and now and then a few sweet Potatoes and several trifles which we deemd Curiosities; for these we gave them Cloth, Beads, Nails, etc. The Cloth we got at King George's Island and Ulietea, they valued more than anything we could give them, and as every one in the Ship were provided with some of this sort of Cloth, I suffer'd every body to purchase what ever they pleased without limitation; for by this means I knew that the Natives would not only sell but get a good Price for every thing they brought. This I thought would induce them to bring to Market whatever the Country afforded, and I have great reason to think that they did, yet it amounted to no more than what is above mentioned. We saw no 4 footed Animals, either Tame or Wild, or signs of any, except Dogs and Rats,* (* Cook's powers of observation are here evident. There were no other quadrupeds in New Zealand.) and these were very Scarce, especially the latter. The flesh of the former they eat, and ornament their clothing with their skins as we do ours with furs, etc. While we lay here I went upon some of the Hills in order to View the Country, but when I came there I could see but very little of it, the sight being interrupted by still higher hills. The Tops and ridges of the Hills are for the most part barren, at least little grows on them but fern; but the Valleys and sides of many of the Hills were luxuriously clothed with woods and Verdure and little Plantations of the Natives lying dispers'd up and down the Country. We found in the Woods, Trees of above 20 different sorts; Specimens of each I took on board, as all of them were unknown to any of us. The Tree which we cut for firing was something like Maple and yeilded a whitish Gum. There was another sort of a deep Yellow which we imagin'd might prove useful in dying. We likewise found one Cabage Tree* (* Palm.) which we cut down for the sake of the cabage. The Country abounds with a great Number of Plants, and the woods with as great a variety of beautiful birds, many of them unknown to us. The soil of both the hills and Valleys is light and sandy, and very proper for producing all kinds of Roots, but we saw only sweet potatoes and Yams among them; these they plant in little round hills, and have plantations of them containing several Acres neatly laid out and keept in good order, and many of them are fenced in with low paling which can only serve for Ornament.

Monday, 30th. P.M. little wind and cloudy weather. At 1 Tack'd and stood in shore; at 7 o'Clock Tolaga Bay bore West-North-West, distant one League. Tack'd and lay her head off; had it calm until 2 a.m., when a breeze sprung up at South-West, and we made Sail to the Northward. At 6, Gable end Foreland bore South-South-West, and Tolaga bay South-South-West 1/4 West, distance 3 Leagues. At 8, being about 2 Miles from the shore, some Canoes that were fishing came after the Ship; but we having a fresh of wind they could not come up with us, and I did not chuse to wait for them. At Noon, Latitude per observation 37 degrees 49 minutes South, a small Island lying off the Northernmost land in sight, bore North 16 degrees East, distant 4 Miles; course from Tolaga bay North by East 1/2 East, distance 13 Leagues. The Land from thence is of a moderate but unequal height, forming several small bays wherein are sandy beaches. Hazey, cloudy weather prevented us from seeing much of the inland country, but near the Shore we could see several Villages and Plantations of the Natives. Soundings from 20 to 30 fathoms.

[Off Cape Runaway, North Island, New Zealand.]

Tuesday, 31st. At half-past one p.m. hauled round the Island above mentioned, which lies East 1 Mile from the North-East point of the land. The lands from hence Trends North-West by West, and West-North-West, as far as we could see. This point of Land I have called East Cape, because I have great reason to think that it is the Eastermost land on this whole Coast; and for the same reason I have called the Island which lays off it, East Island. It is but of a small circuit, high and round, and appears white and barren. The Cape is of a moderate height with white cliffs, and lies in the Latitude of 37 degrees 42 minutes 30 seconds South, and Longitude 181 degrees 00 minutes West from the Meridian of Greenwich. After we had rounded the East Cape we saw, as we run along shore, a great number of Villages and a great deal of Cultivated land; and in general the country appear'd with more fertility than what we had seen before; it was low near the Sea, but hilly inland. At 8, being 8 leagues to the Westward of Cape East, and 3 or 4 miles from the shore, shortned sail and brought too for the night, having at this Time a fresh Gale at South-South-East and squally weather; but it soon fell moderate, and at 2 a.m. made Sail again to the South-West as the land now Trended. At 8 saw land which made like an Island bearing West. At the same time the South-Westermost part of the Main bore South-West. At 9, five Canoes came off to us, in one of which were upwards of 40 Men all Arm'd with Pikes, etc.; from this and other Circumstances it fully appear'd that they came with no friendly intentions; and I at this Time being very buisey, and had no inclination to stay upon deck to watch their Motions, I order'd a Grape shot to be fir'd a little wide of them. This made them pull off a little, and then they got together either to consult what to do or to look about them. Upon this I order'd a round shott to be fir'd over their heads, which frightend them to that degree that I believe they did not think themselves safe until they got ashore. This occasion'd our calling the Point of land off which this hapned, Cape Runaway. Latitude 37 degrees 32 minutes South, longitude 181 degrees 50 minutes West, and 17 or 18 Leagues to the Westward of East Cape. 4 Leagues to the Westward of East Cape is a bay which I have named Hicks's bay, because Lieutenant Hicks was the first who discover'd it.

[November 1769.]

Wednesday, 1st November. P.M., as we stood along shore (having little wind, and Variable), we saw a great deal of Cultivated land laid out in regular inclosures, a sure sign that the Country is both fertile and well inhabited. Some Canoes came off from the shore, but would not come near the Ship. At 8 brought to 3 Miles from the Shore, the land seen yesterday bearing West, and which we now saw was an Island, bore South-West,* (* This should evidently be North-West.) distant 8 leagues. I have named it White Island,* (* White Island is an active volcano. It was evidently quiescent at the time of the Endeavour passing.) because as such it always appear'd to us. At 5 a.m. made Sail along shore to the South-West, having little wind at East-South-East and Cloudy weather. At 8 saw between 40 and 50 Canoes in shore. Several of them came off to the Ship, and being about us some time they ventur'd alongside and sold us some Lobsters, Muscels, and 2 Conger Eales.

After these were gone some others came off from another place with Muscels only, and but few of these they thought proper to part with, thinking they had a right to everything we handed them into their Canoes without making any return. At last the People in one Canoe took away some linnen that was towing over the side, which they would not return for all that we could say to them. Upon this I fir'd a Musket Ball thro' the Canoe, and after that another musquet load with Small Shott, neither of which they minded, only pulled off a little, and then shook their paddles at us, at which I fir'd a third Musquet; and the ball, striking the Water pretty near them, they immediately apply'd their Paddles to another use; but after they thought themselves out of reach they got altogether, and Shook their Paddles again at us. I then gave the Ship a Yaw, and fir'd a 4 Pounder. This sent them quite off, and we kept on our course along shore, having a light breeze at East-South-East. At noon we were in the Latitude of 37 degrees 55 minutes, White Island bearing North 29 degrees West, distant 8 Leagues.

Thursday, 2nd. Gentle breezes from North-West round Northerly to East-South-East and fair weather. At 2 p.m. saw a pretty high Island bearing West from us, and at 5 saw more Islands and Rocks to the Westward of it. Hauld our wind in order to go without them, but, finding that we could not weather them before dark, bore up, and run between them and the Main. At 7 was close under the first Island, from whence a large double Canoe full of People came off to us. This was the first double Canoe we had seen in this Country. They staid about the Ship until it was dark, then left us; but not before they had thrown a few stones. They told us the name of the Island, which was Mowtohora.* (* Motuhora, called also Whale Island.) It is but of a small Circuit, but high, and lies 6 Miles from the Main. Under the South side is Anchorage in 14 fathoms. South-West by South from this Island on the Main land, seemingly at no great distance from the Sea, is a high round Mountain, which I have named Mount Edgcombe. It stands in the middle of a large Plain, which make it the more Conspicuous. Latitude 37 degrees 59 minutes South, Longitude 183 degrees 07 minutes West. In standing to the Westward we Shoalded our Water from 17 to 10 fathoms, and knowing that we were not far from some Small Islands and Rocks that we had seen before dark, after Passing of which I intended to have brought too for the night, but I now thought it more prudent to tack, and spend the Night under the Island of Mowtohora, where I knew there was no danger. And it was well we did, for in the morning, after we had made Sail to the Westward, we discovered Rocks ahead of us Level with and under the Water.* (* Rurima Rocks.) They lay 1 1/2 Leagues from the Island Mowtohora, and about 9 Miles from the Main, and North-North-East from Mount Edgecumbe. We passed between these Rocks and the Main, having from 7 to 10 fathoms. The double Canoe which we saw last night follow'd us to-day under Sail, and keept abreast of the Ship near an hour talking to Tupia, but at last they began to pelt us with stones. But upon firing one Musquet they dropt aStern and left us. At 1/2 past 10 Passed between a low flat Island and the Main, the distance from one to the other being 4 Miles; depth of Water 10, 12, and 15 fathoms. At Noon the flat Island* (* Motunau.) bore from North-East to East 1/2 North, distance 5 or 6 Miles; Latitude in per Observation 37 degrees 39 minutes South, Longitude 183 degrees 30 minutes West. The Main land between this and the Island of Mowtohara, which is 10 Leagues, is of a moderate height, and all a level, flat Country, pretty clear of wood and full of Plantations and Villiages. These Villiages are built upon Eminences Near the Sea, and are Fortified on the land side with a Bank and a Ditch, and Pallisaded all round. Besides this, some of them appear'd to have out-works. We have before now observed, on several parts of the Coast, small Villiages inclosed with Pallisades and works of this kind built on Eminences and Ridges of hills, but Tupia had all along told us that they were Mories, or places of worship; but I rather think they are places of retreat or strong hold where they defend themselves against the Attack of an Enemy, as some of them seem'd not ill design'd for that Purpose.* (* In the contests with the Maories in after years, these Pahs, or forts, proved to be no despicable defences.)

[In Bay of Plenty, North Island, New Zealand.]

Friday, 3rd. P.M. Fresh Gales at North-East by East and hazey weather. At 2 pass'd a small high Island lying 4 Miles from a high round head on the Main* (* The island was Moliti; the high round head was Maunganui, which marks the entrance to Tauranga harbour, a good port, where now stands a small town of the same name.) from this head the land Trends North-West as far as we could see, and appeared to be very rugged and hilly. The weather being very hazey, and the Wind blowing fresh on shore, we hauled off close upon a wind for the weathermost Island in sight, which bore from us North-North-East, distant 6 or 7 Leagues. Under this Island we spent the Night, having a fresh gale at North-East and North-East by East, and hazey weather with rain; this Island I have called the Mayor. At 7 a.m. it bore South 47 degrees East, distant 6 Leagues, and a Cluster of small Islands and Rocks bore North 1/2 East, distant one League. At the time had a Gentle breeze at East-North-East and clear weather. The Cluster of Islands and Rocks just mentioned we named the Court of Aldermen; they lay in the Compass of about half a League every way, and 5 Leagues from the Main, between which and them lay other Islands. The most of them are barren rocks, and of these there is a very great Variety, some of them are of as small a Compass as the Monument in London, and Spire up to a much greater height; they lay in the Latitude of 36 degrees 57 minutes, and some of them are inhabited. At Noon they bore South 60 degrees East, distant 3 or 4 Leagues, and a Rock like a Castle lying not far from the Main, bore North 40 degrees West, one League. Latitude observed 36 degrees 58 minutes South; Course and distance since

Yesterday noon is North-North-West 1/2 West, about 20 Leagues. In this Situation had 28 fathoms water, and a great many small Islands and Rocks on every side of us. The Main land appears here with a hilly, rugged, and barren surface, no Plantations to be seen, nor no other signs of its being well inhabited.

Saturday, 4th. The first and middle parts, little wind at East-North-East and Clear weather; the Latter had a fresh breeze at North-North-West and hazey with rain. At 1 p.m. 3 Canoes came off from the Main to the Ship, and after Parading about a little while they darted 2 Pikes at us. The first was at one of our Men as he was going to give them a rope, thinking they were coming on board; but the 2nd they throw'd into the Ship; the firing of one musquet sent them away. Each of these Canoes were made out of one large Tree, and were without any sort of Ornament, and the people in them were mostly quite naked. At 2 p.m. saw a large op'ning or inlet in the land, which we bore up for with an intent to come to an Anchor. At this time had 41 fathoms, which gradually decreased to 9 fathoms, at which time we were 1 1/2 Mile from a high Tower'd Rock lying near the South point of the inlet; the rock and the Northermost of the Court of Aldermen being in one bearing South 61 degrees East. At 1/2 past 7 Anchor'd in 7 Fathoms a little within the South Entrance of the Bay or inlet. We were accompanied in here by several Canoes, who stay'd about the Ship until dark; and before they went away they were so generous as to tell us that they would come and attack us in the morning; but some of them paid us a Visit in the night, thinking, no doubt, but what they should find all hands asleep, but as soon as they found their Mistake they went off. My reasons for putting in here were the hopes of discovering a good Harbour, and the desire I had of being in some convenient place to observe the Transit of Mercury, which happens on the 9th Instant, and will be wholy Visible here if the day is clear. If we be so fortunate as to obtain this observation, the Longitude of this place and Country will thereby be very accurately determined. Between 5 and 6 o'Clock in the morning several Canoes came off to us from all parts of the Bay; in them were about 130 or 140 People. To all appearances their first design was to attack us, being all Completely Arm'd in their way; however, this they never attempted, but after Parading about the Ship near 3 Hours, sometimes trading with us, and at other times Tricking of us, they dispersed; but not before we had fir'd a few Musquets and one great gun, not with any design to hurt any of them, but to shew them what sort of Weapons we had, and that we could revenge any insult they offer'd to us. It was observable that they paid but little regard to the Musquets that were fir'd, notwithstanding one ball was fir'd thro' one of their Canoes, but what Effect the great gun had I know not, for this was not fir'd until they were going away.

[At Mercury Bay, North Island, New Zealand.]

At 10, the weather Clearing up a little, I went with 2 Boats to sound the Bay and to look for a more convenient Anchoring place, the Master being in one Boat, and I in the other. We pull'd first over the North Shore, where some Canoes came out to meet us, but as we came near them they retir'd to the Shore and invited us to follow them, but seeing they were all Arm'd I did not think fit to Except of their Invitation; but after Trading with them out of the Boat for a few Minutes we left them and went towards the head of the Bay. I observed on a high Point a fortified Village, but I could only see a part of the works, and as I intend to see the whole, shall say no more about it at this time. After having fix'd upon an Anchoring place not far from where the Ship lay I return'd on board.

Sunday, 5th. Winds at North-North-West, Hazey weather with rain in the night. At 4 p.m. weigh'd and run in nearer the South shore and Anchor'd in 4 1/2 fathoms, a soft sandy bottom, the South point of the Bay bearing East, distant 1 Mile, and a River (into which the boats can go at low Water) South-South-East, distant 1 1/2 Miles.* (* The bight in which the Endeavour anchored is now known as Cook Bay.) In the morning the Natives came off again to the Ship, but their behaviour was very different to what it was Yesterday morning, and the little traffick we had with them was carried on very fair and friendly. Two came on board the Ship--to each I gave a Piece of English Cloth and some Spike Nails. After the Natives were gone I went with the Pinnace and Long boat into the River to haul the Sean, and sent the Master to sound the Bay and drudge for fish in the Yawl. We hauled the Sean in several places in the River, but caught only a few Mullet, with which we returned on board about Noon.

Monday, 6th. Moderate breezes at North-North-West, and hazey weather with rain in the night. P.M. I went to another part of the Bay to haul the Sean, but meet with as little Success as before; and the Master did not get above 1/2 a Bucket full of Shells with the Drudge. The Natives brought to the Ship, and sold to our People, small Cockles, Clams, and Mussels, enough for all hands. These are found in great plenty upon the Sand Banks of the River. In the morning I sent the Long boat to Trawl in the Bay, and one Officer with the Marines and a party of men to Cut wood and haul the Sean, but neither the Sean nor the Trawl meet with any success; but the Natives in some measure made up for this by bringing several Baskets of dry'd or ready dress'd fish; altho' it was none of the best I order'd it all to be bought up in order to encourage them to Trade.

Tuesday, 7th. The first part moderate and fair; the remainder a fresh breeze, northerly, with dirty, hazey, raining Weather. P.M. got on board a Long boat Load of Water, and Caught a dish of fish in the Sean. Found here a great Quantity of Sellery, which is boild every day for the Ship's Company as usual.

Wednesday, 8th. P.M. fresh breeze at North-North-West and hazey, rainy weather; the remainder a Gentle breeze at West-South-West and Clear Weather. A.M. heeld and Scrubb'd both sides of the Ship and Sent a Party of Men ashore to Cutt wood and fill Water. The Natives brought off to the Ship, and Sold us for Small pieces of Cloth, as much fish as served all hands; they were of the Mackrell kind, and as good as ever was Eat. At Noon I observ'd the Sun's Meridian Zenith distance, by the Astronomical Quadrant, which gave the Latitude 36 degrees 47 minutes 43 seconds South; this was in the River before mentioned, that lies within the South Entrance of the Bay.

Thursday, 9th. Variable light breezes and Clear weather. As soon as it was daylight the Natives began to bring off Mackrell, and more than we well know what to do with; notwithstanding I order'd all they brought to be purchased in order to encourage them in this kind of Traffick. At 8, Mr. Green and I went on shore with our Instruments to observe the Transit of Mercury, which came on at 7 hours 20 minutes 58 seconds Apparent time, and was observed by Mr. Green only.* (* Mr. Green satirically remarks in his Log, "Unfortunately for the seamen, their look-out was on the wrong side of the sun." This probably refers to Mr. Hicks, who was also observing. It rather seems, however, as if Cook, on this occasion, was caught napping by an earlier appearance of the planet than was expected.) I, at this time, was taking the Sun's Altitude in order to Ascertain the time. The Egress was observed as follows:--

By Mr. Green: Internal Contact at 12 hours 8 minutes 58 seconds Afternoon. External Contact at 12 hours 9 minutes 55 seconds Afternoon.

By myself: Internal Contact at 12 hours 8 minutes 45 seconds Afternoon. External Contact at 12 hours 9 minutes 43 seconds Afternoon.

Latitude observed at noon 36 degrees 48 minutes 28 seconds, the mean of this and Yesterday's observation gives 36 degrees 48 minutes 5 1/2 seconds South; the Latitude of the Place of Observation, and the Variation of the Compass was at this time found to be 11 degrees 9 minutes East. While we were making these observations 5 Canoes came alongside the Ship, 2 Large and 3 Small ones, in one were 47 People, but in the other not so many. They were wholy strangers to us, and to all appearance they came with a Hostile intention, being compleatly Arm'd with Pikes, Darts, Stones, etc.; however, they made no attempt, and this was very probable owing to their being inform'd by some other Canoes (who at this time were alongside selling fish) what sort of people they had to Deal with. When they first came alongside they begun to sell our people some of their Arms, and one Man offer'd to Sale a Haahow, that is a Square Piece of Cloth such as they wear. Lieutenant Gore, who at this time was Commanding Officer, sent into the Canoe a piece of Cloth which the Man had agreed to Take in Exchange for his, but as soon as he had got Mr. Gore's Cloth in his Possession he would not part with his own, but put off the Canoe from alongside, and then shook their Paddles at the People in the Ship. Upon this, Mr. Gore fir'd a Musquet at them, and, from what I can learn, kill'd the Man who took the Cloth; after this they soon went away. I have here inserted the account of this Affair just as I had it from Mr. Gore, but I must own it did not meet with my approbation, because I thought the Punishment a little too severe for the Crime, and we had now been long Enough acquainted with these People to know how to Chastise Trifling faults like this without taking away their Lives.

Friday, 10th. P.M., Gentle breezes and Variable; the remainder, a Strong breeze at East-North-East, and hazey weather. A.M., I went with 2 Boats, accompanied by Mr. Banks and the other Gentlemen into the River which Emptys itself into the head of the Bay, in order to Examine it; none of the Natives came off to the Ship this morning, which we think is owing to bad weather.

[Pahs in Mercury Bay, New Zealand.]

Saturday, 11th. Fresh Gales at East-North-East, and Cloudy, hazey weather with rain. Between 7 and 8 o'Clock p.m. I returnd on board from out the River, having been about 4 or 5 Miles up it, and could have gone much farther had the weather been favourable. I landed on the East side and went upon the Hills, from whence I saw, or at least I thought I saw, the head of the River. It here branched into several Channels, and form'd a Number of very low flat Islands, all cover'd with a sort of Mangrove Trees, and several places of the Shores of both sides the River were Cover'd with the same sort of wood. The sand banks were well stored with Cockles and Clams, and in many places were Rock Oysters. Here is likewise pretty plenty of Wild Fowl, such as Shags, Ducks, Curlews, and a Black bird, about as big as a Crow, with a long, sharp bill of a Colour between Red and Yellow; we also saw fish in the River, but of what sort I know not. The Country especially on the East side is barren, and for the most part destitute of wood, or any other signs of Fertility; but the face of the country on the other side looked much better, and is in many places cover'd with wood. We meet with some of the Natives and saw several more, and Smokes a long way inland, but saw not the least signs of Cultivation, either here or in any other part about the Bay, so that the inhabitants must live wholy on shell and other fish, and Fern roots, which they Eat by the way of Bread. In the Entrance of this river, and for 2 or 3 Miles up, it is very safe and Commodious Anchoring in 3, 4, and 5 fathoms, and Convenient places for laying a Ship aShore, where the Tide rises and falls about 7 feet at full and Change. I could not see whether or no any considerable fresh Water Stream came out of the Country into this river, but there are a number of small Rivulets which come from the Adjacent hills. [Pahs in Mercury Bay, New Zealand.] A little within the Entrance of the River on the East side is a high point or peninsula juting out into the River on which are the Remains of one of their Fortified towns. The Situation is such that the best Engineer in Europe could not have Chose a better for a Small Number of men to defend themselves against a greater; it is strong by Nature and made more so by Art. It is only Accessible on the land Side, and there have been cut a Ditch and a Bank raised on the inside. From the Top of the Bank to the Bottom of the Ditch was about 22 feet, and depth of the Ditch on the land side 14 feet; its breadth was in proportion to its depth, and the whole seem'd to have been done with great Judgment. There had been a row of Pickets on the Top of the Bank, and another on the outside of the Ditch; these last had been set deep in the ground and Sloping with their upper ends hanging over the Ditch. The whole had been burnt down, so that it is probable that this place had been taken and destroy'd by an Enemy. The people on this side of the Bay seem now to have no houses or fix'd habitations, but Sleep in the open Air, under Trees and in small Temporary shades; but to all appearance they are better off on the other side, but there we have not set foot. In the morning, being dirty rainy weather, I did not Expect any of the Natives off with fish, but thinking that they might have some ashore I sent a Boat with some Trade, who return'd about noon loaded with Oysters, which they got in the River which is abreast of the Ship, but saw no fish among the Natives.

Sunday, 12th. P.M. had Strong Gales at North-East, and hazey, rainy weather; A.M. a fresh breeze at North-West, and Clear weather. In the morning got on board a Turn of Water, and afterwards sent the Long boat into the River for Oysters to take to sea with us; and I went with the Pinnace and Yawl, accompanied by Mr. Banks and Dr. Solander, over to the North side of the Bay in order to take a View of the Country and the Fortified Village which stands there. We landed about a mile from it, and were meet by the inhabitants in our way thither, who, with a great deal of good nature and friendship, conducted us into the place and shew'd us everything that was there.

This village is built upon a high Promontory or point on the North side and near the head of the Bay. It is in some places quite inaccessible to man, and in others very difficult, except on that side which faced the narrow ridge of the hill on which it stands. Here it is defended by a double ditch, a bank and 2 rows of Picketing, the inner row upon the Bank; but not so near the Crown but what there was good room for men to Walk and handle their Arms between the Picketing and the inner Ditch. The outer Picketing was between the 2 Ditches, and laid sloping with their upper ends hanging over the inner Ditch. The Depth of this Ditch from the bottom to the Crown of the bank was 24 feet. Close within the inner Plcketing was erected by strong Posts a stage 30 feet high and 40 in length and 6 feet broad. The use of this stage was to stand upon to throw Darts at the Assailants, and a number of Darts lay upon it for that purpose. At right angles to this Stage and a few paces from it was another of the same Construction and bigness; this stood likewise within the Picketing, and was intended for the same use as the other--viz., to stand upon to throw stones and darts upon the Enemy as they advanc'd up the side of the Hill where lay the Main way into the place. It likewise might be intended to defend some little outworks and hutts that lay at the Skirts and on this side of the Hill. These outworks were not intended as advanced Posts, but for such of the Inhabitants to live in as had not room in the Main works, but had taken Shelter under it. Besides the works on the land side, above described, the whole Villiage was Pallisaded round with a line of pretty strong Picketing run round the Edge of the hill. The ground within having not been level at first, but laid Sloping, they had divided it into little squares and Leveled each of these. These squares lay in the form of an Amphitheatre, and were each of them Pallisaded round, and had communication one with another by narrow lanes and little gateways, which could easily be stoped up, so that if an Enemy had forced the outer Picketing he had several others to incounter before the place could be easily reduced, supposing them to defend everyone of the places one after another. The main way leading into this fortification was up a very steep part of the Hill and thro' a narrow passage about 12 feet long and under one of the Stages. I saw no door nor gate, but it might very soon have been barricaded up. Upon the whole I looked upon it to be very strong and well choose Post, and where a small number of resolute men might defend themselves a long time against a vast superior force, Arm'd in the manner as these People are. These seem'd to be prepared against a Siege, having laid up in store an immense quantity of Fern roots and a good many dry'd fish; but we did not see that they had any fresh Water nearer than a brook which runs close under the foot of a hill, from which I suppose they can at times get water, tho' besiged, and keep it in gouards until they use it. Under the foot of the point on which the Village stands are 2 Rocks, the one just broke off from the Main and other detatched a little from it. They are both very small, and more fit for Birds to inhabit than men; yet there are houses and places of defence on each of them, and about a Mile to Eastward of these is another of these small Fortified rocks, which communicates with the Main by a Narrow pathway, where there is a small Villiage of the Natives. Many works of this kind we have seen upon small Islands and Rocks and Ridges of hills on all parts of the Coast, besides a great number of Fortified towns, to all appearances Vastly superior to this I have described. From this it should seem that the People must have long and frequent Warrs, and must have been long accustomed to it, otherwise they never would have invented such strong holds as these, the Erecting of which must cost them immense labour, considering the Tools they have to work with, which are only made of Wood and Stone. It is a little strange that with such a Warlike People, as these undoubtedly are, no Omissive weapons are found among them, such as bows and Arrows, Slings, etc., things in themselves so easily invented, and are common in every other part of the world. The Arms they use are long spears or Lances, a Staff about 5 feet long. Some of these are pointed at one end like a Serjeant's Halberd, others are round and Sharp; the other ends are broad, something like the blade of an Oar. They have another sort about 4 1/2 feet long; these are shaped at one End like an Axe, and the other is made with a Sharp point. They have short Truncheons about a foot long, which they call Pattoo Pattoas; some made of wood, some of bone, and others of Stone. Those made of wood are Variously shaped, but those made of bone and Stone are of one shape, which is with a round handle, a broadish blade, which is thickest in the Middle and taper'd to an Edge all round. The use of these are to knock Men's brains out, and to kill them outright after they are wounded; and they are certainly well contrived things for this purpose. Besides these Weapons they Throw stones and Darts; the Darts are 10 or 12 feet long, are made of hard wood, and are barbed at one end. They handle all their Arms with great Agility, particularly their long Pikes or Lances, against which we have no weapon that is an equal match except a Loaded Musquet.

Monday, 13th. P.M., Gentle Breezes at North-West and Clear weather. After taking a Slight View of the Country and Loaded both boats with Sellery, which we found in Great plenty near the Sea beach, we return'd on board about 5 o'Clock. The Long boat at the same time return'd out of the River Loaded as deep as she could swim with Oysters. And now I intended to put to Sea in the morning if wind and weather will permit. In the night had the wind at South-East, with rainy, dirty, hazey weather, which continued all day, so that I could not think of Sailing, but thought myself very happy in being in a good Port. Samuel Jones, Seaman, having been confin'd since Saturday last for refusing to come upon deck when all hands were called, and afterwards refused to Comply with the orders of the officers on deck, he was this morning punished with 12 lashes and remited back to confinement.

Tuesday, 14th. Fresh Gales, Easterly, and rainy, Dirty weather.

Wednesday, 15th. In the evening I went in the Pinnace and landed upon one of the Islands that lies off of the South Head of the Bay, with a view to see if I could discover any sunken rocks or other Dangers lying before the Entrance of the Bay, as there was a pretty large swell at this Time. The Island we landed upon was very small, yet there were upon it a Village, the inhabitants of which received us very friendly. This little Village was laid out in small Oblong squares, and each pailisaded round. The Island afforded no fresh Water, and was only accessible on one side: from this I concluded that it was not choose for any Conveniency it could afford them, but for its Natural Strength.

[Sail from Mercury Bay, New Zealand.]

At 7 A.M. weigh'd, with a light breeze at West, and clear weather, and made Sail out of the Bay, steering North-East, for the Northermost of a Number of Islands lying off the North point of the Bay. These Islands are of Various extents, and lye Scattered to the North-West in a parallel direction with the Main as far as we could see. I was at first afraid to go within them, thinking that there was no safe Passage, but I afterwards thought that we might; and I would have attempted it, but the wind, coming to the North-West, prevented it, so that we were obliged to stand out to Sea. At Noon was in the Latitude of 36 degrees 4 minutes South. The Northermost Island, above mentioned, bore North, distant half a League; the Court of Aldermen, South-East by South, distant 6 Leagues; and the Bay Sail'd from, which I have named Mercury Bay, on account of the observation being made there, South-West by West, distant 6 Miles.

Mercury Bay* (* At the head of Mercury Bay is a small settlement called Whitianga.) lies in the Latitude of 36 degrees 47 minutes South, and the Longitude of 184 degrees 4 minutes West, from the Meridian of Greenwich. It lies in South-West between 2 and 3 Leagues. There are several Islands lying both to the Southward and Northward of it, and a Small high Island or Rock in the Middle of the Entrance. Within this Island the depth of water doth no were Exceed 9 or 8 fathoms; the best Anchorage is in a sandy Bay which lies just within the South head in 5 and 4 fathoms, bringing a high Tower Rock, which lies without the head, in one with the head, or just shut in behind it. Here it is very Convenient Wooding and Watering, and in the River are an immense quantity of Oysters and other small Shell fish; and this is the only thing it is remarkable for, and hath occasioned my giving it the Name of Oyster River. But the Snugest and Safest place for a Ship to lay in that wants to stay there any time is in the River at the head of the Bay, and where there is every conveniency the place can afford. To sail up and into it keep the South shore all the way on board. As we did not learn that the Natives had any name for this River, I have called it the River of Mangroves,* (* Still so called.) because of the great quantity of these Trees that are found in it. The Country on the South-East side of this River and Bay is very barren, producing little else but Fern, and such other plants as delight in a Poor Soil. The land on the North-West side is pretty well cover'd with wood, the Soil more fertile, and would no doubt produce the Necessarys of Life, was it Cultivated. However, this much must be said against it, that it is not near so Rich nor fertile as the lands we have seen to the Southward; and the same may be said of its inhabitants, who, although pretty numerous, are poor to the highest degree when Compar'd to others we have seen. They have no Plantations, but live only on Fern roots and fish; their Canoes are mean, and without ornament, and so are their Houses, or Hutts, and in general

- 202 -

everything they have about them. This may be owing to the frequent wars in which they are Certainly ingaged; strong proofs of this we have seen, for the people who resided near the place where we wooded, and who Slept every night in the Open Air, placed themselves in such a manner when they laid down to sleep as plainly shew'd that it was necessary for them to be always upon their Guard. They do not own Subjection to Teeratie, the Earadehi,* (* Cook did not realize that the New Zealanders were divided into independent tribes.) but say that he would kill them was he to come Among them; they confirm the Custom of Eating their Enemies, so that this is a thing no longer to be doubted. I have before observed that many of the People about this bay had no fix'd habitations, and we thought so then, but have since learnt that they have strong holds--or Hippas, as they call them-- which they retire to in time of danger.

We found, thrown upon the Shore in several places in this Bay, a quantity of Iron Sand, which is brought down out of the Country by almost every little fresh-water brook. This proves that there must be of that Ore not far inland. Neither of the Inhabitants of this Place, nor any other where we have been, know the use of Iron or set the least Value upon it, preferring the most Trifling thing we could give them to a Nail, or any sort of Iron Tools. Before we left this bay we cut out upon one of the Trees near the Watering Place the Ship's Name, date, etc., and, after displaying the English Colours, I took formal possession of the place in the Name of His Majesty.

[Off Cape Colville, North Island, New Zealand.]

Thursday, 16th. Fresh breezes between the North-West and South-West, and fair weather. At 1 P.M., having got within the Group of Islands which lies of the North head of Mercury Bay, hauld our wind to the Northward, and Kept plying to windward all the day between these Islands and some others laying to the Northward of them, with a View to get under the Main land, the Extream North-West point of which we could see, at Noon, bore West by North, distant 6 or 8 Leagues; Latitude in Per Observation 36 degrees 33 minutes South.

Note, in speaking of Mercury Bay, I had forgot to mention that the Mangrove Trees found there produce a resinous substance very much like Rosin. Something of this kind, I am told, is found in both the East and West Indies. We found it, at first, in small Lumps upon the Sea Beach, but afterwards found it sticking to the Mangrove Trees, and by that means found out from whence it came.

Friday, 17th. The fore and Middle parts had fresh Gales between the South-West and West by South, and Squally. Kept plying to windward in order to get under the land. At 6 A.M. fetched close under the lee of the Northernmost Island in sight, then Tackd and Stood to the Southward until

11, when we tack'd and Stood to the Northward. At this time the North head of Mercury Bay, or Point Mercury, bore South-East by East, distant 3 Leagues, being at this time between 2 and 3 Leagues from the Main land, and abreast of a place where there appear'd to be a Harbour;* (* Probably Waikawau Bay) but the heavy squalls which we had from the Land would not permit us to take a nearer View of it, but soon brought us under our Close reeft Topsails. At Noon Point Mercury bore South-East, distant 4 Leagues, and the weathermost point of the Main land in sight bore North 60 degrees West, distant 5 Leagues. Over the North-West side of Mercury Bay is a pretty high round hill, rising sloping from the Shore of the Bay. This hill is very conspicuous from where we now are.

Saturday, 18th. First part strong Gales at South-West and South-South-West, with heavy squalls: in the morning had Gentle breezes at South and South-East, towards noon had Whifling light Airs all round the Compass. Kept plying to windward under close Reeft Topsails until daylight, at which time we had got close under the Main, and the wind coming at South-East we made sail and steer'd North-West by West, as the land lays, keeping close in shore. At 6 we passed a small Bay* (* Charles Cove.) wherein there appear'd to be Anchorage, and pretty good Shelter from the Sea Winds, at the Entrance of which lies a Rock pretty high above water. 4 Miles farther to the West-North-West is a very Conspicuous promontory or point of land which we got abreast of about 7 o'Clock; it lies in the Latitude of 36 degrees 26 minutes South and North 48 degrees West, 9 Leagues from Point Mercury. From this point the Land trends West 1/2 South near one League, then South-South-East as far as we could see. Besides the Islands laying without us we could see land round by the South-West as far as North-West, but whether this was the Main or Islands was not possible for us at this Time to determine; the fear of loosing the Main land determin'd me to follow its direction. With this View we hauld round the point* (* Cape Colville.) and Steer'd to the Southward, but meeting with Whifling light Airs all round the Compass, we made but little progress untill noon, when we found ourselves by Observation in the Latitude of 36 degrees 29 minutes South; a small Island* (* Channel Island.) which lays North-West 4 Miles from the Promontory above-mentioned bore North by East, distant 6 1/2 Miles, being at this time about 2 Miles from the Shore. While we lay under the land 2 large Canoes came off to us; in one of them were 62 people; they staid about us some time, then began to throw stones into the Ship, upon which I fir'd a Musquet ball thro' one of the Canoes. After this they retir'd ashore.

Sunday, 19th. At 1 p.m. a breeze sprung up at East, which afterwards came to North-East, and with it we steer'd along shore South by East and South-South-East, having from 25 to 18 fathoms Water. At 1/2 past 7, having run 7 or 8 Leagues since Noon, we Anchor'd in 23 fathoms, not choosing to run any farther in the Dark, having the land on both sides of us forming the Entrance of a Streight, Bay or River, lying in South by East, for on that point of the Compass we could see no land. At daylight A.M., the wind being still favourable, we weighed and run under an Easy sail up the inlet, keeping nearest the East side. Soon after we had got under Sail 3 large Canoes came off to the Ship, and several of the people came on board upon the very first invitation; this was owing to their having heard of our being upon the Coast and the manner we had treated the Natives. I made each of those that came on board a small present, and after about an Hour's stay they went away well Satisfied. After having run 5 Leagues from the place where we Anchor'd last night our Depth of Water gradually decreased to 6 fathoms, and into less I did not choose to go, and as the wind blew right up the inlet and tide of flood, we came to an Anchor nearly in the middle of the Channell, which is here about 11 Miles over, and after this sent 2 Boats to sound, the one on one side and the other on the other side.

[At Frith of Thames, North Island, New Zealand.]

Monday, 20th. Moderate breezes at South-South-East and fair weather. At 2 p.m. the boats return'd from sounding, not having found above 3 feet more water than were we now lay; upon this I resolved to go no farther with the Ship but to examine the head of the Bay in the Boat, for as it appeard to run a good way inland, I thought this a good opportunity to see a little of the interior part of the Country and its produce. Accordingly at daylight in the morning I set out with the Pinnace and Long boat accompanied by Mr. Banks, Dr. Solander, and Tupia. We found the inlet end in a River, about 9 miles above the Ship, into which we Enter'd with the first of the flood, and before we had gone 3 Miles up it found the Water quite fresh. We saw a number of Natives and landed at one of their Villages, the inhabitants of which received us with open Arms. We made but a Short stay with them but proceeded up the river until near Noon, when finding the face of the country to continue pretty much the same, and no alteration in the Course or stream of the River or the least probability of seeing the end of it, we landed on the West side in order to take a View of the lofty Trees which Adorn its banks, being at this time 12 or 14 Miles within the Entrance, and here the Tide of Flood runs as strong as it does in the River Thames below bridge.

Tuesday, 21st. After Landing as above-mention'd, we had not gone a hundred yards into the woods before we found a Tree that girted 19 feet 8 inches, 6 feet above the ground, and having a Quadrant with me, I found its length from the root to the first branch to be 89 feet; it was as Streight as an Arrow and Taper'd but very little in proportion to its length, so that I judged that there was 356 Solid feet of timber in this Tree, clear of the branches. We saw many others of the same sort, several of which were Taller than the one we measured, and all of them very stout; there were likewise many other sorts of very Stout Timber Trees, all of them wholy unknown to any of us. We brought away a few specimens, and at 3 o'Clock we embarqued in order to return (but not before we had named this river the Thames,* (* The flourishing town of Thames now stands at the eastern entrance of the river: population nearly 5000. Gold is found in the vicinity.) on account of its bearing some resemblance to that River in England) on board with the very first of the Ebb. In our return down the river, the inhabitants of the Village where we landed in going, seeing that we return'd by another Channell, put off in their Canoes and met us and Trafficked with us in the most friendly manner immaginable, until they had disposed of the few Trifles they had. The tide of Ebb just carried us out of the narrow part of the River into the Sea reach, as I may call it, where meeting with the flood and a Strong breeze at North-North-West obliged us to come to a Grapnel, and we did not reach the Ship until 7 o'Clock in the A.M. Intending to get under Sail at high water the Long boat was sent to take up the Kedge Anchor, but it blow'd so strong that she could not reach the Buoy, and the gale increasing soon obliged us to vear away more Cable and Strike Top Gallant Yards.

Wednesday, 22nd. Winds at North-North-West. The A.M. fresh Gales and hazey with rain; the remainder, moderate and Clear. At 3 p.m. the Tide of Ebb making, we took up our Anchors and got under Sail and ply'd down the River until 8 o'Clock, when we again came to an Anchor in 7 fathoms, muddy bottom. At 3 a.m. weigh'd with the first of the Ebb and keept plying until the flood obliged us to anchor again. After this I went in the Pinnace over to the Western Shore, but found there neither inhabitants or anything else worthy of Note. At the time I left the Ship a good many of the Natives were alongside and on board Trafficking with our people for such Trifles as they had, and seem'd to behave as well as people could do, but one of them took the 1/2 hour glass out of the Bittacle, and was caught in the very fact, and for which Mr. Hicks, who was Commanding Officer, brought him to the Gangway and gave him a Dozen lashes with a Catt of nine Tails. The rest of the people seem'd not displeased at it when they came to know what it was for, and some old man beat the fellow after he had got into his Canoe; however, soon after this they all went away.

Thursday, 23rd. P.M. Gentle breezes at North-North-West and fair weather. Between 3 and 4 o'Clock got under Sail with the first of the Ebb and ply'd to windward until 9 when we anchor'd in 16 fathoms over upon the East shore. In the night had light Airs and Calm; at 3 A.M. weighed but had little or no wind until near noon, when a light breeze sprung up at North-North-West. At this time we were close under the West shore in 7 fathoms Water; Latitude 36 degrees 51 minutes South.

[Description of Frith of Thames, New Zealand.]

Friday, 24th. P.M., Fresh Gales and dark, Cloudy, squally weather, with Thunder, Lightning, and rain. Winds from the North-West to the South-West, and this last carried us by 7 o'Clock without the North-West point of the River, but the weather being bad and having land on all sides of us, and a Dark night coming on, I thought it most adviseable to Tack and stretch in under ye Point where we Anchor'd in 19 fathoms. At 5 a.m. weighed and made Sail to the North-West under our Courses and double Reef'd Topsails, the wind being at South-West by West and West-South-West, a strong Gale and Squally blowing right off the land, which would not permit us to come near it, so that from the time of our getting under Sail until' Noon (during which time we ran 12 Leagues) we had but a slight and distant View of the Coast and was not able to distinguish wether the points we saw were parts of the Main or Islands laying before it, for we never once lost sight of the Main Land.* (* The Endeavour was now in Hauraki Gulf and had passed the harbour where Auckland now stands, which is hidden behind a number of islands.) At noon our Latitude by observation was 36 degrees 15 minutes 20 seconds South, being at this time not above 2 Miles from a Point of Land on the Main and 3 1/2 Leagues from a very high Island* (* Little Barrier Island, now (1892) about to be made a reserve to protect native fauna.) which bore North-East by East of us; in this Situation had 26 fathoms Water. The farthest point we could see on the Main bore from us North-West, but we could see several small Islands laying to the Northward of that direction. The point of land we are now abreast off, I take to be the North-West Extremity of the River Thames, for I shall comprehend under that Name the Deep Bay we have been in for this week past, the North-East point of which is the Promontory we past on Saturday morning last, and which I have named Cape Colvill in honour of the Right hon'ble the Lord Colvill;* (* Cook had served under Rear Admiral Lord Colville in Newfoundland.) Latitude 36 degrees 26 minutes South; Longitude 184 degrees 27 minutes West. It rises directly from the Sea to a Considerable height, but what makes it most remarkable is a high Rock standing close to the pitch of the point, and from some points of view may be distinguished at a very great distance. From the South-West point of this Cape the river Extends itself in a direct line South by East, and is no where less than 3 Leagues broad until' you are 14 Leagues above the Cape, there it is at once Contracted to a Narrow stream. From this place it still continues the same South by East Course thro' a low flat Country or broad Valley that lies Parrallel with the Sea Coast, the End of which we could not see. The land on the East side of the Broadest part of this river is Tollerable high and hilly, that on the West side is rather low, but the whole is cover'd with woods and Verdure and looks to be pretty fertile, but we saw but a few small places that were Cultivated. About the Entrance of the narrow part of the River the land is mostly Cover'd with Mangroves and other Shrubs, but farther in are immense woods of as stout lofty timber as is to be found perhaps in any other part of the world. In many places the woods grow close upon the very banks of the River, but where it does not the land is Marshey such as we find about the Thames in England. We saw poles stuck up in many places in the River to set nets for Catching of fish; from this we immagin'd that there must be plenty of fish, but of what sort we know not for we saw none. The Greatest Depth of Water we found was 26 fathoms and decreaseth pretty gradually as you run up to 1 1/2 and 1 fathom. In the mouth of the fresh-water Stream or narrow part is 3 and 4 fathoms, but before this are sand banks and large flatts; Yet, I believe, a Ship of a Moderate draught of Water may go a long way up this River with a flowing Tide, for I reckon that the Tides rise upon a perpendicular near 10 feet, and is high water at the full and Change of the Moon about 9 o'Clock. Six Leagues within Cape Colvill, under the Eastern Shore, are several small Islands, these Islands together with the Main seem'd to form some good Harbours.* (* Coromandel Harbour.) Opposite to these Islands under the Western Shore lies some other Islands, and it appear'd very probable that these form'd some good Harbours likewise.* (* Auckland Harbour is one of them.) But even supposing there were no Harbours about this River, it is good anchoring in every part of it where the depth of Water is Sufficient, being defended from the Sea by a Chain of Large and Small Islands which I have named Barrier Isles, lying aCross the Mouth of it extending themselves North-West and South-East 10 Leagues. The South end of these Islands lies North-East 4 1/2 Leagues from the North-West point of the River, which I have named point Rodney; it lies West-North-West 9 leagues from Cape Colvill, Latitude 36 degrees 15 minutes; Longitude 184 degrees 58 minutes West. The Natives residing about this River do not appear to be very numerous considering the great Extent of Country; at least not many came off to the Ship at one Time, and as we were but little ashore ourselves we could not so well judge of their numbers. They are a Strong, well made, active People as any we have seen yet, and all of them Paint their Bodys with Red Oker and Oil from Head to foot, a thing that we have not seen before. Their Canoes are large, well built and Ornamented with Carved work in general as well as most we have seen.

Saturday, 25th. P.M., had fresh Gales at South-West, and Squally weather. We kept standing along Shore to the North-West, having the Main land on the one side and Islands on the other; our Soundings were from 26 to 12 fathoms. At 1/2 past 7 p.m. we Anchor'd in a Bay in 14 fathoms, sandy bottom. We had no sooner come to an Anchor than we caught between 90 and 100 Bream (a fish so called), this occasioned my giving this place the Name of Bream Bay.* (* Whangarei Bay.) The 2 points which forms this Bay lie North and South 5 Leagues from each other. The Bay is every where pretty broad and between 3 and 4 Leagues deep; at the bottom of it their appears to be a fresh water River.* (* Whangarei River. The district is very fertile. Coal mines are in the vicinity, and coal is exported.) The North head of the Bay, called Bream head, is high land and remarkable on account of several peaked rocks ranged in order upon the top of it; it lies in the Latitude 35 degrees 46 minutes South and North 41 degrees West, distant 17 1/2 Leagues from Cape Colvill. This Bay may likewise be known by some Small Islands lying before it called the Hen and Chickens, one of which is pretty high and terminates at Top in 2 peaks. The land between Point Rodney and Bream Head, which is 10 Leagues, is low and wooded in Turfs, and between the Sea and the firm land are white sand banks. We saw no inhabitants but saw fires in the Night, a proof that the Country is not uninhabited. At daylight A.M. we left the Bay and directed our Course along shore to the northward, having a Gentle breeze at South by West and Clear weather. A little after sunrise found the Variation to be 12 degrees 42 minutes Easterly. At Noon, our Latitude by observation was 36 degrees 36 minutes South; Bream head bore South distant 10 Miles; some small Islands (Poor Knights) at North-East by North distant 3 Leagues, and the Northermost land in sight bore North-North-West, being at this Time 2 miles from the Shore, and in this Situation had 26 fathoms; the land here about is rather low and pretty well cover'd with wood and seems not ill inhabited.

[Off Cape Brett, North Island, New Zealand.]

Sunday, 26th. P.M., Gentle breezes between the East-North-East and North, kept ranging along shore to the Northward. At the distance of 4 or 5 Miles off saw several Villages and some Cultivated lands; towards evening several Canoes came off to us, and some of the Natives ventur'd on board; to 2, who appear'd to be Chiefs, I gave presents. After these were gone out of the Ship, the others became so Troublesome that in order to get rid of them we were at the expence of 2 or 3 Musquet Balls, and one 4 pound Shott, but as no harm was intended them, none they received, unless they hapned to over heat themselves in pulling on shore. In the Night had variable light Airs, but towards morning had a light breeze at South, and afterward at South-East; with this we proceeded slowly to the Northward. At 6 a.m. several Canoes came off from the place where they landed last night, and between this and noon many more came from other parts. Had at one time a good many of the people on board, and about 170 alongside; their behaviour was Tolerable friendly, but we could not prevail upon them to Traffic with us. At noon, the Mainland Extending from South by East to North-West by West; a remarkable point of land bore West, distant 4 or 5 miles. Latitude Observed 35 degrees 11 minutes South.

Monday, 27th. P.M., Gentle breezes Easterly, and Clear weather. At 3 passed the point of land afore-mentioned, which I have named Cape Brett in honour of Sir Piercy.* (* Rear Admiral Sir Piercey Brett was one of the Lords of the Admiralty when the Endeavour sailed.) The land of this Cape is considerable higher than any part of the Adjacent Coast. At the very point of the Cape is a high round Hillock, and North-East by North, near one Mile from this is a small high Island or Rock with a hole pierced thro' it like the Arch of a Bridge, and this was one reason why I gave the Cape the above name, because Piercy seem'd very proper for that of the Island. This Cape, or at least some part of it, is called by the Natives Motugogogo; Latitude 35 degrees 10 minutes 30 seconds South, Longitude 185 degrees 25 minutes West. On the West side of Cape Brett is a large and pretty deep Bay* (* The Bay of Islands.) lying in South-West by West, in which there appear'd to be several small Islands. The point that forms the North-West entrance I have named Point Pocock; it lies West 1/4 North, 3 or 4 Leagues from Cape Brett. On the South-West side of this Bay we saw several Villages situated both on Islands and on the Main land, from whence came off to us several large Canoes full of People, but, like those that had been alongside before, would not Enter into a friendly Traffick with us, but would Cheat whenever they had an opportunity. The people in these Canoes made a very good appearance, being all stout well-made men, having their Hair--which was black--comb'd up and tied upon the Crown of their heads, and there stuck with white feathers; in each of the Canoes were 2 or 3 Chiefs, and the Habits of these were rather superior to any we had yet seen. The Cloth they wore was of the best sort, and cover'd on the outside with Dog Skins put on in such a manner as to look Agreeable enough to the Eye. Few of these people were Tattow'd or marked in the face, like those we have seen farther to the South, but several had their Backsides Tattow'd much in the same manner as the inhabitants of the Islands within the Tropics. In the Course of this day, that is this afternoon and Yesterday forenoon, we reckoned that we had not less than 400 or 500 of the Natives alongside and on board the ship, and in that time did not range above 6 or 8 Leagues of the Sea Coast, a strong proof that this part of the Country must be well inhabited. In the Evening, the Wind came to the Westward of North, and we Tack'd and stood off North-East until 11 o'Clock, when the wind coming more favourable we stood again to the Westward. At 8 a.m we were within a Mile of Groups of Islands lying close under the Mainland and North-West by West 1/2 West, distance 22 Miles from Cape Brett. Here we lay for near 2 Hours, having little or no wind. During this time several Canoes came off to the Ship, and 2 or 3 of them sold us some fish--Cavallys as they are called--which occasioned my giving the Islands the same name. After this some others began to Pelt us with Stones, and would not desist at the firing of 2 Musquet Balls thro' one of their Boats; at last I was obliged to pepper 2 or 3 fellows with small Shott, after which they retir'd, and the wind coming at North-West we stood off to Sea. At Noon, Cavally Islands bore South-West by South, distant 4 Miles; Cape Brett South-East, distant 7 Leagues, and the Westermost land in sight, making like Islands, bore West by North; Latitude in per Observation 34 degrees 55 minutes South.

Tuesday, 28th. A Fresh breeze from the Westward all this day, which being right in our teeth, we kept beating to windward with all the sail we could Crowd, but instead of Gaining we lost ground. A.M., being close in with the land to the Westward of the Bay, which lies on this side of Cape Brett, we saw at some distance inland 2 pretty large Villages Pallisaded in the same manner as others we have seen. At noon, Cape Brett South-East by East 1/2 East, distant 6 Leagues; Latitude observed 35 degrees 0 minutes South.

[At Bay of Islands, North Island, New Zealand.]

Wednesday, 29th. Fresh Gales at North-West and West-North-West, kept plying to Windward until 7 A.M., and finding that we lost ground every board we made, I thought I could not do better than to bear up for the Bay, which lies to the Westward of Cape Brett, it being at this Time not above 2 Leagues to Leeward of us, for by putting in there we should gain some knowledge of it, on the Contrary, by Keeping the Sea with a Contrary wind, we were sure of meeting with nothing new. These reasons induced me to bear away for the Bay,* (* The Bay of Islands.) and at 11 o'Clock we Anchor'd under the South-West side of one of the many Islands* (* Motu Arohia.) that line the South-East side of it, in 4 1/2 fathoms; but as we fell into this shoald water all at once, we Anchor'd sooner than was intended, and sent the Master with 2 Boats to sound, who found that we had got upon a Bank that spitted off from the North-West end of the Island, and that on the outside of it was 8 and 10 fathoms Water.

Thursday, 30th. P.M., had the winds Westerly, with some very heavy Showers of Rain. We had no sooner come to an Anchor than between 300 and 400 of the Natives Assembled in their Canoes about the Ship; some few were admitted on board, and to one of the Chiefs I gave a piece of Broad Cloth and distributed a few Nails, etc., among some others of them. Many of these People had been off to the Ship when we were at Sea, and seem'd to be very sencible of the use of Fire Arms, and in the Trade we had with them they behaved Tolerable well, but continued so not long, before some of them wanted to take away the Buoy,* (* The buoy on the anchor.) and would not desist at the firing of several Musquets until one of them was hurt by small Shott, after which they withdrew a small distance from the Ship, and this was thought a good opportunity to try what Effect a Great Gun would have, as they paid so little respect to a Musquet, and accordingly one was fir'd over their Heads. This, I believe, would have sent them quite off, if it had not been for Tupia, who soon prevail'd on them to return to the Ship, when their behaviour was such as gave us no room to suspect that they meant to give us any farther Trouble.

After the Ship was moved into Deeper Water I went with the Pinnace and Yawl, mann'd and Arm'd, and landed upon the Island, accompanied by Mr.

Banks and Dr. Solander. We had scarce landed before all the Canoes left the Ship and landed at different parts of the Island, and before we could well look about us we were surrounded by 2 or 300 People, and, notwithstanding that they were all Arm'd, they came upon us in such a confused, straggling manner that we hardly suspected that they meant us any harm; but in this we were very soon undeceived, for upon our Endeavouring to draw a line on the sand between us and them they set up the War dance, and immediately some of them attempted to seize the 2 Boats. Being disappointed in this, they next attempted to break in upon us, upon which I fir'd a Musquet loaded with small Shott at one of the Forwardest of them, and Mr. Banks and 2 of the Men fir'd immediately after. This made them retire back a little, but in less than a minute one of the Chiefs rallied them again. Dr. Solander, seeing this, gave him a peppering with small Shott, which sent him off and made them retire a Second time. They attempted to rally several times after, and only seem'd to want some one of resolution to head them; but they were at last intirely dispers'd by the Ship firing a few shott over their Heads and a Musquet now and then from us. In this Skirmish only one or 2 of them was Hurt with small Shott, for I avoided killing any one of them as much as Possible, and for that reason withheld our people from firing. We had observed that some had hid themselves in a Cave in one of the Rocks, and sometime after the whole was over we went Towards them. The Chief who I have mentioned to have been on board the Ship hapned to be one of these; he, his wife, and another came out to meet us, but the rest made off. Those 3 people came and sat down by us, and we gave them of such things as we had about us. After this we went to another part of the Island, where some of the inhabitants came to us, and were as meek as lambs. Having taken a View of the Bay from the Island and Loaded both Boats with Sellery, which we found here in great plenty, we return'd on board, and at 4 A.M. hove up the Anchor in order to put to Sea, with a light breeze at East, but it soon falling Calm, obliged us to come too again, and about 8 or 9 o'Clock, seeing no probability of our getting to Sea, I sent the Master to Sound the Harbour. But before this I order'd Matthew Cox, Henry Stevens, and Emanl Parreyra to be punished with a dozen lashes each for leaving their duty when ashore last night, and digging up Potatoes out of one of the Plantations.* (* Cook's care to deal fairly with natives is evinced by this punishment.) The first of the 3 I remitted back to Confinement because he insisted that there was no harm in what he had done. All this Forenoon had abundance of the Natives about the Ship and some few on board. We Trafficked with them for a few Trifles, in which they dealt very fair and friendly.

[December 1769.]

Friday, 1st December. Winds at North-North-West a Gentle breeze. At 3 p.m., the Boats having return'd from sounding, I went with them over to the

South side of the Harbour, and landed upon the Main, accompanied by Mr. Banks and Dr. Solander. We met with nothing new or remarkable. The place where we landed was in a small sandy Cove, where there are 2 small Streams of Fresh Water and Plenty of Wood for fuel. Here were likewise several little Plantations planted with Potatoes and Yams. The Soil and Natural produce of the Country was much the same as what we have hitherto met with. The people we saw behaved to us with great marks of friendship. In the evening we had Some very heavy showers of rain, and this brought us on board sooner than we intended. A.M., the wind being still contrary, I sent some people ashore upon the Island to cut Grass for our Sheep, in the doing of which the inhabitants gave them no sort of disturbance, and in the same friendly manner did those behave that were alongside the Ship. Punished Matthew Cox with 6 Lashes, and then dismiss'd him.

Saturday, 2nd. Winds at North-West and North. P.M. a Gentle breeze; the remainder Strong Gales and hazey, with much rain towards Noon. At 8 a.m. hoisted out the Long boat, and sent her ashore for water, and the Pinnace to haul the Sean; but they had not got well ashore before it began to blow and rain very hard. This occasioned them to return on board with one Turn of water and but a very few fish.

Sunday, 3rd. P.M., Strong Gales at North, with rain; the remainder Gentle breezes from the Westward. A.M., sent 2 Boats to sound the Harbour and one to haul the Sean, the latter of which met with very little Success.

Monday, 4th. Gentle breezes at North-West, West-North-West, and West; very fair weather. P.M., Mr. Banks, Dr. Solander, and myself landed upon one of the Islands* (* Probably Motu-Rua.) on the North side of the one the Ship lays under. This Island is about 3 Miles in Circuit, and hath upon it 40 or 50 Acres of Land cultivated and planted with roots; here are likewise several small streams of Excellent water. This Island, as well as most others in this Bay, seem to be well inhabited. At 4 a.m. sent the Long boat to the above Island for water and some hands to cut Grass, and at 9, I went with the Pinnace and Yawl over upon the Main, accompanied by Mr. Banks and Dr. Solander. In our way we passed by a point of land on which stood a Hippa or Fortified Village, the inhabitants of which waved us to come ashore, and accordingly we landed, which we had no sooner done than the People came about us with Quantitys of various sorts of fish, which we purchased of them for meer Trifles. After this they shew'd us the Village, which was a neat Compact place, and its situation well Choose. There were 2 or 3 more near unto this, but these we did not go to. We afterwards went a little way into the Country, and had some of the Natives along with us; we met with a good deal of Cultivated land, planted mostly with sweet potatoes. The face of the Country appear'd Green and pleasant, and the soil seem'd to be pretty rich and proper for Cultivation. The land is every where about this

Bay of a moderate height, but full of small Hills and Vallies, and not much incumbered with wood. We met with about 1/2 a dozen Cloth plants, being the same as the inhabitants of the Islands lying within the Tropics make their finest Cloth on. This plant must be very scarce among them, as the Cloth made from it is only worn in small pieces by way of Ornaments at their ears, and even this we have seen but very seldom. Their knowing the use of this sort of Cloth doth in some measure account for the extraordinary fondness they have shew'd for it above every other thing we had to give them. Even a sheet of white paper is of more value than so much English Cloth of any sort whatever; but, as we have been at few places where I have not given away more or less of the latter, it's more than probable that they will soon learn to set a value upon it, and likewise upon Iron, a thing not one of them knows the use of or sets the least value upon; but was European commodities in ever such Esteem among them, they have no one thing of Equal value to give in return, at least that we have seen.

Tuesday, 5th. P.M., had the winds at South-West and West-South-West, a fresh breeze. At 3 o'Clock we return'd on board, and after dinner Visited another part of the Bay, but met with nothing new. By the evening all our Empty Casks were fill'd with water, and had at the same time got on board a large quantity of Sellery, which is found here in great Plenty. This I still caused to be boild every morning with Oatmeal and Portable Soup for the Ship's Company's breakfast. At 4 a.m. weigh'd with a light breeze at South-East, but had Variable light Airs and sometimes Calm until near Noon, when a Gentle breeze sprung up at North. At this time we had not got out of the Bay; our Latitude by Observation was 35 degrees 9 minutes South. This Bay I have before observed, lies on the West side of Cape Brett: I have named it the Bay of Islands,* (* The principal settlement in the Bay of Islands is Russell. A little higher up the Waikare River, at Opua, coal obtained from mines in the vicinity is shipped. At Russell, then called Kororarika, the first settlement of missionaries was formed in 1814 by Samuel Marsden. Here also the Government of the Island was first established in 1840, but was soon removed to Auckland.) on account of the Great Number which line its shores, and these help to form Several safe and Commodious Harbours, wherein is room and Depth of Water sufficient for any number of Shipping. The one we lay in is on the South-West side of South-Westermost Island, that lies on the South-East side of the Bay. I have made no accurate Survey of this Bay; the time it would have requir'd to have done this discouraged me from attempting it; besides, I thought it quite Sufficient to be able to Affirm with Certainty that it affords a good Anchorage and every kind of refreshment for Shipping, but as this was not the Season for roots, we got only fish. Some few we Caught ourselves with hook and line and in the Sean, but by far the greatest part we purchased of the Natives, and these of Various sorts, such as Sharks, Stingrays, Breams, Mullet, Mackerel, and several other sorts. Their way of Catching them is the same as ours, viz., with Hook and line and Seans; of the last they have some prodidgious large made all of a Strong Kind of Grass. The Mackerel are in every respect the same as those we have in England, only some are larger than any I ever saw in any other Part of the World; although this is the Season for this fish, we have never been able to Catch one with hook and line. The inhabitants of this Bay are far more numerous than at any other place we have yet been in, and seem to live in friendship one with another, although it doth not at all appear that they are united under one head.* (* This district was found to be very populous when the missionaries came.) They inhabited both the Islands and the Main, and have a Number of Hippas, or Strong Holds, and these are all built in such places as nature hath in a great part fortified, and what she hath left undone the people themselves have finished. It is high water in this Bay at full and change of the Moon about 8 o'clock, and the tide at these times rises and falls upon a perpendicular 6 or 8 feet. It appears, from the few Observations I have been able to make of the Tides on the Sea-Coast, that the flood comes from the Southward, and I have lately had reasons to think that there is a current which comes from the Westward and sets along shore to the South-East or South-South-East, as the Land lays.

[Sail from Bay of Islands, New Zealand.]

Wednesday, 6th. P.M., had a Gentle breeze at North-North-West, with which we kept turning out of the Bay, but gain'd little or nothing; in the evening it fell little wind; at 10 o'Clock it was Calm. At this time the tide or Current seting the Ship near one of the Islands, where we were very near being ashore; but, by the help of our Boats and a light Air from the Southward, we got clear. About an hour after, when we thought ourselves out of all danger, the Ship struck upon a Sunken rock* (* Called Whale Rock, in Endeavour's chart.) and went immediately clear without receiving any perceptible damage. Just before the man in the Chains had 17 fathoms Water, and immediately after she struck 5 fathoms, but very soon Deepned to 20. This rock lies half-a-mile West-North-West from the Northermost or outermost Island that lies on the South-East side of the Bay. Had light Airs from the Land and sometimes Calm until 9 o'Clock a.m.; at this time we had got out of the Bay, and a breeze springing up at North-North-West, we stood out to Sea. At noon Cape Brett bore South-South-East 1/2 South, distant 10 miles. Latitude observed, 34 degrees 59 minutes South.

Thursday, 7th. P.M., a fresh breeze from the Westward and Clear weather. At 3 o'Clock took several Observations of the Sun and Moon; the mean result of them gives 185 degrees 36 minutes West Longitude from the Meridian of Greenwich. What winds we have had this 24 hours hath been against us, so that at Noon we had advanced but very little to the Westward.

Friday, 8th. Forepart of P.M. had a Gentle breeze at North-North-West, with which we stood in shore and fetched close under the Cavalle Islands. They are a Group of Small Islands lying close under the Main land, and 7 Leagues North 60 West from Cape Brett, and 3 1/2 Leagues from Point Rodney. From these Islands the Main land trends West by North. We were here Visited by several Canoes, and the People in them seem'd desirous of Trafficking with us, but at this time a breeze of wind sprung up at South, they could not keep up with the Ship, and I would not wait for them. The wind did not continue long at South before it veer'd to South-West and West, a light breeze. Found the Variation in the Evening to be 12 degrees 42 minutes East, and in the Morning 13 degrees East. Keept standing to the West-North-West and North-West until 10 A.M., at which time we tacked and stood in for the Shore, being about 5 Leagues off, and in this situation had 118 fathoms Water. At Noon Cape Brett bore South-East, distant 13 Leagues, and the Westermost land in sight bore West by South, being at this time about 4 Leagues from Land. Latitude in per Observation, 34 degrees 42 minutes South.

Saturday, 9th. P.M., had a Gentle Breeze at West, which in the Evening came to South and continued so all night; this by daylight brought us pretty well in with the land, 7 Leagues to the Westward of the Cavalle Isles, and where lies a deep Bay running in South-West by West and West-South-West, the bottom of which we could but just see, and there the land appear'd to be low and level, the 2 points which form the Entrance lie West-North-West and East-South-East 5 Miles from each other. This Bay I have named Doubtless Bay;* (* There is a small settlement called Mangonui in Doubtless Bay.) the wind not permitting us to look into this Bay we steer'd for the Westermost land we had in sight, which bore from us West-North-West, distant 3 Leagues, but before we got the length of it it fell calm, and continued so until 10 o'Clock, when a breeze sprung up at West-North-West, and with it we stood off North. While we lay becalm'd, several of the Natives came off to the Ship in 5 Canoes, but were fearful of venturing alongside. After these were gone, 6 more came off; these last came boldly alongside, and sold us fish of different sorts sufficient to give all hands a little.

At noon, the Cavalle Islands bore South-East by East, distant 8 Leagues, and the Entrance of Doubtless Bay South by West distant 3 Leagues, and the North-West Extremity of the Land in sight, which we judge to be the Main, bore North-West by West. Our Latitude by observation was 34 degrees 44 minutes South.

[Off Rangaunu Bay, North Island, New Zealand.]

Sunday, 10th. Had the winds from the Western board all this day, a Gentle breeze and clear weather. In the evening found the Variation to be 12 degrees

41 minutes East per Azimuth and 12 degrees 40 minutes by the Amplitude; in the morning we stood Close in with the Land, 7 Leagues to the westward of Doubtless Bay. Here the shore forms another large open Bay; the Bottom of this and Doubtless Bay cannot be far from each other, being to all appearance only seperated by a low neck of land from which juts out a Peninsula or head land, which I have named Knockle Point. West by South 6 Leagues from this point and about the Middle of the Bay is a high Mountain or Hill standing upon a desart shore, on which account we called it Mount Camel; Latitude 34 degrees 51 minutes; Longitude 186 degrees 50 minutes. In this Bay we had 24 and 25 fathoms Water, the bottom good for Anchorage, but their seems to be nothing that can induce Shipping to put into it for no Country upon Earth can look more barren than the land about this bay doth. It is in general low, except the Mountain just Mentioned, and the Soil to all appearance nothing but white sand thrown up in low irregular hills, lying in Narrow ridges parrallel with the shore; this occasioned me to name it Sandy Bay.* (* Rangaunu Bay.) The first ridge behind the Sea beach is partly cover'd with Shrubs, Plants, etc., but the second ridge hath hardly any green thing upon it, which induced me to think that it lies open to the Western Sea.* (* This is the fact.) As barren as this land appears it is not without inhabitants. We saw a Village on this Side of Mount Camel and another on the Eastern side of the Bay, besides 5 Canoes that were pulling off to the Ship, but did not come up with us. At 9 a.m. we tacked and stood to the Northward at Noon. Latitude in Per observation 34 degrees 38 minutes. The Cavalle Isles bore South-East by East, distant 13 Leagues; the Northern Extremity of the land in sight making like an Island bore North-West 1/4 North, distant 9 Leagues, and Mount Camel bore South-West by South, distant 6 Leagues. Tacked and stood in Shore.

Monday, 11th. Gentle breezes at North. M.d and pleasant weather. Keept plying all the day, but got very little to Windward; at Noon was in the Latitude of 34 degrees 32 minutes South, the Northermost inland set yesterday at noon bore North-West by West, distant 6 or 7 Leagues.

Tuesday, 12th. Moderate breezes of Wind between the North-West and North and Smooth Water, yet we gain'd very little in plying to Windward; at Noon Mount Camel bore South by West 1/4, distant 4 or 5 Leagues. Latitude observed 34 degrees 34 minutes South.

Wednesday, 13th. Fore part of P.M., Moderate breezes at North by West and fair weather; stood in shore until 5 O'Clock, at which time we tack'd and stood to the North-East being 2 Leagues to the Northward of Mount Camel and 1 1/2 Mile from shore, and this situation had 22 fathoms water. At 10 it began to blow and rain, which brought us under double Reeft Top sails; at 12 Tack'd and Stood to the Westward until 7 A.M. when we Tack'd and stood again to North-East, being at this time about a Mile to windward of the place where we tack'd last night. Soon after we Tack'd it came on to blow very hard at North-North-West with heavy squalls attended with rain, this brought us under our Courses and Split the Main Top sail in such a manner that it was necessary to unbend it and bring another to the Yard. At 10 it fell more moderate and we set the Top sails double reef'd. At Noon had strong Gales and hazey weather, Tack'd and stood to the Westward. No land in sight for the first time since we have been upon the Coast.

Thursday, 14th. Strong Gales at West and West-South-West with Squalls at times attended with Rain. At 1/2 past 3 P.M. Tack'd and stood to the Northward. A small Island lying off Knockle point, bore South 1/2 West, distant half a League. In the evening brought the Ship under her Courses, having first Split the Fore and Mizen Top sails; at Midnight wore and Stood to the Southward until 5 a.m., then Tack'd and stood to the North-West. At this time saw the land bearing South, distant 8 or 9 Leagues; by this we found we had fell very much to Leeward since Yesterday morning. Set the Top sails close Reeft and the people to dry and repair the Damaged Sails. At Noon a strong Gale and clear weather, Latitude observ'd 34 degrees 6 minutes South. Saw land bearing South-West being the same North-Westermost land we have seen before, and which I take to be the Northern Extremity of this Country, as we have now a large swell rowling in from the Westward which could not well be, was we covered by any land on that point of the Compass.* (* The Endeavour was now to the northward of the north point of New Zealand.)

[Off North Cape, New Zealand.]

Friday, 15th. Fresh Gales at South-West, and for the most part clear weather with a large Swell from the Westward. At 8 P.M. Tack'd and Stood to the South-East until 8 a.m., and then Tack'd and stood to the Westward with as much sail as the Ship could bear. At Noon we were in the Latitude of 34 degrees 10 minutes South, and Longitude 183 degrees 45 minutes West, and by Estimation about 15 Leagues from the Land notwithstanding we used our utmost Endeavours to keep in with it.

Saturday, 16th. Fresh breezes between the South by West and South-West. Clear weather with a Swell from the Westward. At 6 A.M. saw the land from the Mast Head bearing South-South-West. Got Top Gallant Yards up and set the Sail, unbent the Foresail to repair and brought another to the Yard. At Noon, Latitude observ'd 33 degrees 43 minutes South; Course made since Yesterday Noon North 60 degrees West; distance 56 Miles. The Land in sight bearing South by West, distant 14 Leagues.

Sunday, 17th. A Gentle breeze between the South-West by West and West with Clear weather. In standing in Shore sounded several times and had no ground with 90 fathoms of line. At 8 a.m. Tack'd in 108 fathoms 3 or 4 miles

- 218 -

from the Shore, being the same point of Land as we had to the North-West of us before we were blown off. At Noon it bore South-West, distant about 3 Miles. Mount Camel bore South by East, distant 11 Leagues, and the Westermost land in sight bore South 75 degrees West; Latitude observ'd 34 degrees 20 minutes South. The people at work repairing the Sails, the most of them having been Split in the late blowing weather.

Monday, 18th. Moderate breezes at West and West-North-West and Clear weather. At 4 p.m. Tack'd and stood in shore, in doing of which we meet with a Strong rippling, and the Ship fell fast to leeward, occasioned, as we thought, by a Current setting to the Eastward. At 8 Tack'd and stood off North until 8 a.m., when we Tack'd and stood in, being about 10 Leagues from the Land. At Noon the Point of Land we were near to yesterday at noon bore South-South-West, distant 5 Leagues. Latitude observed 34 degrees 8 minutes South.

Tuesday, 19th. The wind still continues at West. P.M., a moderate breeze and Clear weather. At 7 Tack'd in 35 fathoms; the point of land before mentioned bore North-West by North, distant 4 or 5 Miles, having not gained one inch to windward this last 24 hours, which is a great proof that there must be a Current setting to the Eastward.* (* This strong easterly current is now well known.) The Point of Land above mentioned I have called North Cape, judging it to be the Northermost Extremity of this Country. It lies in the Latitude of 34 degrees 22 minutes South and Longitude 186 degrees 55 minutes West from Greenwich,* (* This position is very correct.) and North 63 degrees West 31 Leagues from Cape Brett; it forms the North Point of Sandy Bay, and is a peninsula juting out North-East about 2 Miles, and Terminates in a Bluff head which is flatt at Top. The Isthmus which joins this head to the Mainland is very low, on which account the land off the Cape from several situations makes like an Island. It appears still more remarkable when to the Southward of it by the appearance of a high round Island at the South-East Point of the Cape; but this is likewise a deception, being a round hill join'd to the Cape by a low, narrow neck of Land; on the South-East side of the Cape there appears to be anchorage, and where ships must be covered from South-East and North-West winds. We saw a Hippa or Village upon the Cape and some few inhabitants. In the night had some Squalls attended with rain, which obliged us to take another Reef in our Topsails. At 8 a.m. Tack'd and stood in Shore, and being moderate loosed a Reef out of each Topsail and set the small sails. At noon we were in the Latitude of 34 degrees 2 minutes South, and being hazey over the land we did not see it.

Wednesday, 20th. P.M., Fresh breezes at West by North, and Clear weather. At 6 Tack'd and stood off, North Cape bore South, distant 3 or 4 Miles. At 4 a.m. Tack'd and stood in, Wind at West-North-West a fresh breeze, but at 9 it increased to a Strong Gale with heavy squalls attended with Thunder and

Rain, which brought us under our Courses. At 11 it Cleared up and the Wind came to West-South-West; we set the Topsails, double Reef'd and Tack'd and stood to the North-West. At Noon, a Stiff Gale and Clear weather; Latitude observed 34 degrees 14 minutes South. North Cape South-South-West, distant 3 Leagues.

Thursday, 21st. Fresh breezes at South-West and clear weather with a heavy swell first from the West, then from the South-West. At 8 a.m. loosed the 2nd Reef out of the Topsails; at noon clear weather, no land in sight. The North Cape bore South 25 degrees East, distant 24 Leagues. Latitude observed 33 degrees 17 minutes South.

Friday, 22nd. A moderate Gale at South by West and South-South-West and Cloudy weather. At 8 a.m. got up Top Gallant Yards and set the sails. At Noon Latitude observ'd 33 degrees 2 minutes South. Course and distant since Yesterday at Noon is North 69 1/2 West, 37 Miles. The North Cape bore South 39 degrees East, distant 38 Leagues.

Saturday, 23rd. Gentle breezes between the South by West and South-West, and Clear settled weather, with a swell from the South-West. Course and distance sailed since Yesterday at Noon is South 60 degrees East, 30 Miles. Latitude observed 33 degrees 17 minutes South. North Cape South 36 minutes East, distant 27 Leagues.

Sunday, 24th. Light Airs next to a Calm all this 24 Hours. At 7 p.m. saw the land from the Mast head bearing South 1/2 East; at 11 a.m. saw it again bearing South-South-East, distant 8 Leagues. At Noon Latitude observed 33 degrees 48 minutes South.

Monday, 25th. A Gentle breeze at South-East, the weather a little hazey. P.M., stood to the South-West. At 4 the land above mentioned bore South-East by South, distant 4 Leagues. It proves to be a small Island, which we take to be the 3 Kings discover'd by Tasman; there are several Smaller Islands or Rocks lying off the South-West end and one at the North-East end. It lies in the Latitude of 34 degrees 10 minutes South, and Longitude 187 degrees 45 minutes West and West 14 degrees North, 14 or 15 Leagues from the North Cape. At Midnight Tack'd and stood to the North-East until 6 a.m., then Tack'd and stood to the Southward. At Noon the Island of the 3 Kings bore East 8 degrees North, distant 5 or 6 Leagues. Latitude observed 34 degrees 12 minutes South, Longitude in 188 degrees 5 minutes West; variation per Azimuth taken this morning 11 degrees 25 minutes East.

Tuesday, 26th. Moderate breezes, Easterly and hazey weather; standing to the Southward close upon a wind. At Noon was in the Latitude of 35 degrees 10 minutes South and Longitude 188 degrees 20 minutes West. The island of the 3 Kings North 26 degrees West, distant 22 Leagues. In this situation had no land in sight, and yet by observation we are in the Latitude of the Bay of Islands, and by my reckoning but 30 Leagues to the Westward of the North Cape, from whence it appears that the Northern part of this land must be very narrow, otherwise we must have seen some part of the West side of it.

Wednesday, 27th. Winds at East. P.M., a fresh Gale, with which we stood to the Southward until 12 at Night, then Tack'd and Stood to the Northward. At 4 a.m. the wind began to freshen, and increased in such a manner that at 9 we were obliged to bring the Ship too under her Mainsail, it blowing at this time excessive hard with heavy Squalls attended with rain, and at the same time thick hazey weather. Course made good since Yesterday at Noon South-South-West 1/2 West, distance 11 Miles. Latitude in 35 degrees 19 minutes South, Longitude in 188 degrees 29 minutes West. The Island of the 3 Kings, North 27 degrees East, distant 77 Miles.

[Off North End of New Zealand.]

Thursday, 28th. The Gale continued without the least intermission until 2 a.m., when the wind fell a little and began to veer to the Southward and to the South-West where it fixed at 4, and we made Sail and steer'd East in for the Land under the Foresail and Mainsail, but was soon obliged to take in the latter as it began to blow very hard and increased in such a manner that by 8 o'Clock it was a meer Hurricane attended with rain and the Sea run prodidgious high. At this time we wore the Ship, hauld up the Topsail, and brought her too with her head to the North-West under a Reefed Mainsail, but this was scarcely done before the Main Tack gave way and we were glad to take in the Mainsail and lay too under the Mizen staysail and Ballanced Mizen, after which we reefd the Foresail and furl'd both it and the Mainsail. At Noon the Gale was a little abated, but had still heavy squalls attended with rain. Our Course made good to-day is North, a little Easterly, 29 miles; Latitude in per Account 34 degrees 50 minutes South; Longitude in 188 degrees 27 minutes West; the 3 Kings North 41 East; distant 52 Miles.

Friday, 29th. Winds at South-West and South-West by West. A very hard Gale with Squalls but mostly fair weather. At 7 p.m. wore and lay on the other Tack. At 6 a.m. loosed the Reef out of the Foresail and Set it and the Reefd Mainsail. At 11 unbent both Foresail and Mainsail to repair, and bent others and made Sail under them. At Noon Latitude observed 34 degrees 45 minutes South. Course and distance saild since yesterday East by North 29 miles.

Saturday, 30th. Winds at South-West. P.M., hard Gales with some Squalls attended with rain. A.M., more moderate and fair. At 8 p.m. wore and stood to the North-West until 5 a.m., then wore and stood to the South-East and being pretty moderate we set the Topsails close Reef'd, but the South-West

Sea runs so high that the Ship goes Bodily to leeward. At 6 saw the land bearing North-East distant about 6 Leagues which we judge to be the same as Tasman calls Cape Maria Van Dieman; at Noon it bore North-North-East 1/2 East and we could see the land extend to the East and Southward as far as South-East by East. Our Latitude by observation 34 degrees 50 minutes South.

Sunday, 31st. Fresh gales at South-West and South-West by South accompanied by a large Sea from the same Quarter. At 1 p.m. Tack'd and Stood to the North-West until 8, then stood to the South-East. At this time the Island of the 3 Kings bore North-West by West, distant 11 Leagues, and Cape Maria Van Diemen North by East. At Midnight wore and Stood to the North-West until 4 a.m., then wore and Stood to the South-East; at Noon our Latitude by observation was 34 degrees 42 minutes South. The land of Cape Maria Van Diemen bore North-East by North distant about 5 Leagues.

1770.

[January 1770.]

Monday, January 1st. P.M., fresh breezes at South-West by South and Squally, the remainder moderate breezes at South-West by South and South-West clear weather. At 7 p.m. Tack'd and stood to the Westward. At this time Mount Camel bore North 83 degrees East and the Northermost land or Cape Maria Van Diemen North by West, being distant from the Nearest Shore 3 Leagues; in this situation had 40 fathoms Water.

NOTE. Mount Camel doth not appear to lay little more than a Mile from the Sea on this Side* (* It is, in fact, about six miles, but the coast in front is so low that the mistake in estimation is very natural.) and about the same distance on the other, so that the land here cannot be above 2 or 3 Miles broad from Sea to Sea, which is what I computed when we were in Sandy Bay on the other side of the Coast. At 6 a.m. Tack'd and Stood to the Eastward, the Island of the 3 Kings North-West by North. At Noon Tack'd again and stood to the Westward, being in the Latitude of 34 degrees 37 minutes South; the Island of the 3 Kings bore North-West by North, distant 10 or 11 Leagues; and Cape Maria Van Diemen North 31 East, distant 4 1/2 Leagues; in this situation had 54 fathoms. I cannot help thinking but what it will appear a little strange that at this season of the Year we should be 3 Weeks in getting 10 Leagues to the Westward and 5 Weeks in getting 50 Leagues, for so long it is since we pass'd Cape Brett; but it will hardly be credited that in the midst of Summer and in the Latitude of 35 degrees South such a Gale of wind as we have had could have hapned which for its Strength and Continuance was such as I hardly was ever in before. Fortunately at this time we were a good distance from land, otherwise it would have proved fatal to us.* (* The north point of New Zealand is celebrated for bad weather.)

Tuesday, 2nd. Fresh breezes at South-South-West and West accompanied with a rowling Sea from the South-West. At 5 p.m. the wind Veering to the Westward we Tack'd and Stood to the Southward. At this time the North Cape bore East 3/4 North and was just open of a point that lies 3 Leagues West by South from it, being now well assured that it is the Northermost Extremity of this Country and is the East point of a Peninsula which Stretches out North-West and North-West by North 17 or 18 Leagues, and as I have before observed is for the most part low and narrow except its Extremity where the land is Tollerable high and Extends 4 or 5 Leagues every way. Cape Maria Van Diemen is the West point of the Peninsula and lies in the Latitude of 34 degrees 30 minutes South; Longitude 187 degrees 18 minutes West from Greenwich.* (* This is extraordinarily accurate, seeing that the ship was never close to the Cape, and the observations were all taken in bad weather. The latitude is exact, and the longitude is only three miles in error. The persistence with which Cook clung to this point until he could resume his exploration and examination of the coast is very characteristic of the man. He would not willingly miss a mile of it, nor did he.) From this Cape the Land Trends away South-East by South and South-East to and beyond Mount Camel, and is everywhere a barren shore affording no better prospect than what ariseth from white sand Banks. At 1/2 past 7 p.m. the Island of the 3 Kings bore North-West by North and Cape Maria Van Diemen North-East by East, distant 4 Leagues. At 5 a.m. Cape Maria Van Diemen bore North-North-East 1/2 East and Mount Camel East. At Noon was in the Latitude of 35 degrees 17 minutes and Cape Maria Van Diemen by judgment bore North distant 16 Leagues; having no land in sight, not daring to go near it as the wind blow'd fresh right on shore and a high rowling Sea from the Same Quarter, and knowing that there was no Harbour that we could put into in case we were Caught upon a lee shore.

Wednesday, 3rd. Winds at West-South-West and South-West; a fresh breeze and Squally, the remainder moderate with frequent Squalls attended with rain. In the evening shortned Sail and at Midnight Tack'd and made a Trip to the North-West until 2 a.m., then wore and stood to the Southward. At daylight made Sail and Edged away in order to make the Land; at 10 saw it bearing North-East and appeared to be high land; at Noon it extended from North to East-North-East distant, by Estimation, 8 or 10 Leagues, and Cape Maria Van Diemen bore North 2 degrees 30 minutes West, distant 33 Leagues. Our Latitude by observation was 36 degrees 2 minutes South. A high rowling swell from the South-West.

[Off Kaipara Harbour, North Island, New Zealand.]

Thursday, 4th. Winds at South-West and South-West by South; mostly a fresh Gale accompanied with a rowling sea from the same Quarter. Being desirous of taking as near a View of the coast as we could with safety we keept Edging in for it until 7 o'Clock p.m., being at this time 6 Leagues from the Land. We then hauld our wind to South-East and keept on that Course close upon the wind all night, sounding several times but had no ground with 100 and 110 fathoms. At 8 o'Clock a.m. was about 5 Leagues from the Land and a place which lies in the Latitude of 36 degrees 25 minutes that had the Appearance of a Bay or inlet bore East.* (* This was Kaipara Harbour, although, on a closer inspection, Cook thought he had been deceived. It is the largest harbour on this part of the coast. The town of Helensville stands on one of its arms.) In order to see more of this place we kept on our Course until 11 o'Clock when we were not above 3 Leagues from it, and then found that it was neither a Bay nor inlet, but low land bounded on each side by higher lands which caused the deception. At this time we Tack'd and stood to the North-West. At Noon we were between 3 and 4 Leagues from the Land and in the Latitude of 36 degrees 31 minutes and Longitude 185 degrees 50 minutes West. Cape Maria Van Diemen bore North 25 West, distant 44 1/2 Leagues. From this I form my judgment of the direction of this Coast, which is nearly South-South-East 3/4 East and North-North-West 3/4 West, and must be nearly a Strait Shore. In about the Latitude 35 degrees 45 minutes is some high land adjoining to the Sea; to the Southward of that the land is of a moderate heigth, and wears a most desolate and inhospitable aspect. Nothing is to be seen but long sand Hills, with hardly any Green thing upon them, and the great Sea which the prevailing Westerly winds impell upon the Shore must render this a very Dangerous Coast. This I am so fully sencible of, that was we once clear of it I am determined not to come so near Again, if I can possible avoid it, unless we have a very favourable wind indeed.* (* The mingled audacity and caution of Cook's navigation off this coast must awake the admiration of every seaman.)

Friday, 5th. Fresh gales at South-West with frequent Squalls attended with rain. The South-West swell still keeping up we stood to the North-West all this day with a prest Sail in order to get an Offing. At Noon True Course made good North 38 West, distance 102 Miles. Latitude in per Observation 35 degrees 10 minutes South. Cape Maria Van Diemen bore North 10 degrees East; distant 41 Miles.

Saturday, 6th. First part a fresh breeze at South-West by South; in the night had it at South. A.M., light Airs from the Southward next to a Calm, and Clear weather. Course made good to-day is North 76 West; distance 8 Miles; Latitude per Observation 35 degrees 8 minutes South.

Sunday, 7th. Variable light Airs and Sometimes Calm with Clear pleasant weather. At daylight saw the land which we took to be Cape Maria Van

Diemen bearing North-North-East, distant 8 or 9 Leagues. At Noon Latitude in per Observation 35 degrees 0 minutes South. Cape Maria Van Diemen bore North, distant 11 Leagues.

Monday, 8th. Gentle breezes at North-East and pleasant weather. At 6 p.m. saw the land bearing East, and sometime after saw a Turtle upon the Water. At Noon the land Extending from North to East, distant 5 or 6 Leagues, being the high land before mentioned and which it intersected in 2 places each having the appearance of a Bay or inlet, but I believe it is only low land.* (* These were Hokianga and False Hokianga.) Course and distance made good since Yesterday at Noon is South 33 East, 53 miles. Latitude per Observation 35 degrees 45 minutes South. Cape Maria Van Diemen North 25 West, distant 30 Leagues.

Tuesday, 9th. Gentle breezes between the North-East and North-West, Cloudy weather sailing along shore within sight of Land at Noon. Course and distance Sailed South 37 East, 69 Miles. Latitude in per Observation 36 degrees 39 minutes South; the place we were abreast of the 4th Instant, which we at first took for a Bay or Inlet* (* Kaipara.) bore North-East by North, distant 5 1/2 Leagues, and Cape Maria Van Diemen bore North 29 West, distant 47 Leagues.

[Off Kawhia Harbour, North Island, New Zealand.]

Wednesday, 10th. Winds at North-North-East and North, the first part a Gentle breeze, the remainder a fresh breeze and Cloudy with rain towards Noon. Continued a South-East Course until' 8 o'Clock p.m. at which time we had run 7 Leagues since Noon, and were between 3 and 4 Leagues from the Land which appear'd to be low and Sandy such as I have before Discribed, and we then steer'd South-East by East in a Parrallel direction with the Coast, our Depth of Water from 48 to 34 fathoms; a black sandy bottom; at daylight found ourselves between 2 and 3 Leagues from the land which was of a Moderate height and Cloathed with Wood and Verdure. At 7 o'Clock steer'd South by East and afterwards South by West, the land laying in that direction; at 9 was abreast of a Point of Land which rises sloping from the Sea to a Considerable height; it lies in the Latitude of 37 degrees 43 minutes South; I named it Woodyhead. South-West 1/2 West 11 Miles from this Head is a very small Island which we named Gannet Island, on account of the Great Number of these Birds we saw upon it. At Noon a high Craggy point bore East-North-East, distance 1 1/2 Leagues; this point I have named Albetross Point; it lies in the Latitude of 38 degrees 4 minutes South, and Longitude 184 degrees 42 minutes West, and from Woodyhead South 17 minutes West 7 Leagues. On the North side of it the shore forms a Bay wherein there appears to be anchorage and Shelter for Shipping against Southerly Winds;* (* Kawhia Harbour. There is a settlement here.) our

Course and distance saild since Yesterday at Noon is South 37 East, distance 69 Miles. Cape Maria Van Diemen bore North 30 West, distant 82 Leagues.

Thursday, 11th. At 1/2 past Noon the wind Shifted at Once from North-North-East to South-South-West with which we stood to the Westward until 4 p.m., then Tack'd and stood on Shore until' 7, when we again stood to the Westward having but little wind. At this Time Albetross Point bore North-East, distant near 2 Leagues, and the Southermost land in sight bore South-South-West 1/2 West being a very high Mountain and made very much like the Peak of Teneriff; in this Situation had 30 fathoms Water; had little wind all night; at 4 a.m. Tacked and stood in Shore, but it soon after fell Calm and being in 42 fathoms Water; the People caught about 10 or 12 Bream. At 11 a light breeze sprung up from the Westward and we made Sail to the Southward. At Noon was by Observation in the Latitude of 38 degrees 4 minutes South; Albetross Point bore due East, distant 5 or 6 Leagues.

Friday, 12th. Gentle breezes from between the North-West and North-North-East; Fore and Middle part Clear Weather; the Latter part dark and Cloudy; steering along shore South by West and South-South-West at the distance of 4 Leagues off. At 7 p.m. saw the top of the Peaked Mountain to the Southward above the Clouds bearing from us South; at the same time the Southermost land we had in Sight bore South by West. Took several Azimuths both in the Evening and the Morning which gave the Variation 14 degrees 15 minutes Easterly. At Noon had the winds very Variable with dark cloudy weather attended with excessive heavy Showers of rain; at this time we were about 3 Leagues from the Shore which lies under the Peaked Mountain before mentioned. This Peak we did not see, it being hid in the Clouds, but judged it to bear about South-South-East, and some very remarkable peaked Islands, lying under the Shore, bore East-South-East, distant 3 or 4 Leagues.

Saturday, 13th. Winds Variable. P.M., Cloudy weather. At 7 o'Clock sounded and had 42 fathoms water, being distant from the Shore between 2 and 3 Leagues and the Peaked Mountain as near as I could judge bore East. After it was Dark saw a fire upon the Shore, a sure sign that the Country is inhabited. In the night had some Thunder, Lightning, and Rain; at 5 a.m. saw for a few Minutes the Top of the Peaked Mountain above the Clouds bearing North-East. It is of a prodidgious height and its Top is cover'd with Everlasting Snow; it lies in the Latitude of 39 degrees 16 minutes South, and in the Longitude of 185 degrees 15 minutes West. I have named it Mount Egmont in honour of the Earl of Egmont.* (* The Earl of Egmont was First Lord of the Admiralty from 1763 to 1766. Mount Egmont is a magnificent conical mountain, surrounded on three sides by the sea, from which it rises to a height of 8300 feet.) This mountain seems to have a pretty large base and to rise with a Gradual Ascent to the Peak, and what makes it more

Conspicuous is its being situated near the Sea and in the Midst of a flat Country which afforded a very good Aspect, being Cloathed with Woods and Verdure. The shore under the foot of this Mountain forms a large Cape which I have named Cape Egmont; it lies South-South-West 1/2 West, 27 Leagues from Albetross Point. On the North-East side of the Cape lay 2 Small Islands near to a very remarkable Point of the Main that riseth to a good height in the very form of a Sugar Loaf. To the Southward of the Cape the Land tends away South-East by East and East-South-East, and seems to be every where a bold shore. At Noon had variable light Airs and Clear weather. Latitude observ'd 39 degrees 32 minutes South. Cape Egmont bore about North-East, and we were about 4 Leagues from the Shore in that direction; in this situation had 40 fathoms Water.

[In North Part of Cook's Strait.]

Sunday, 14th. P.M., had a Gentle Breeze at West. In the evening came to North-West by West and Continued so all night and blow'd a fresh breeze; we steer'd along shore East-South-East and South-East by East, keeping between 2 and 3 Leagues off. At 1/2 past 7 p.m. Saw for a few Minutes Mount Egmont which bore from us North 17 West, distant 10 Leagues. At 5 a.m. Steer'd South-East by South the land inclining more Southerly, but half an hour after we saw land bearing South-West by South which we hauld up for.* (* The north end of the South Island, New Zealand.) At this time the weather was squally attended with showers of rain. At noon had a Steady fresh breeze at West by North and Cloudy weather; the South-West Extremity of the Land in sight bore South 63 degrees West and some high land, which makes like an Island lying under the Main, bore South-South-East, distant 5 Leagues. The bottom of the Bay* (* This was the Northern part of Cook's Strait, but it was thought at the time to be a bay.) we are now in, and which bears from us South we cannot see, altho' it is very Clear in that Quarter. Our Latitude by Observation is 40 degrees 27 minutes South, Longitude 184 degrees 39 minutes West.* (* The western side of the North Island, which Cook took such trouble to follow, is 400 miles long, and is a most dangerous coast to explore, on account of the winds being mostly on shore. This prevented him from getting very close; and he missed the entrances to several harbours, such as the Manukau, the Waikato River, Whaingaroa, and others. No canoes were seen, as the coast is not favourable for such craft.)

Monday, 15th. Fore and Middle parts, fresh breezes between the West and North-West and fair weather. At 8 p.m. we were within 2 Leagues of the Land, we discover'd in the morning, having run 10 Leagues since Noon; the land seen then bearing South 63 degrees West bore now North 59 degrees West, distant 7 or 8 Leagues and makes like an Island. Between this land or Island and Cape Egmont is a very broad and Deep Bay or inlet the South-

West side of which we are now upon, and here the Land is of a Considerable height, distinguished by Hills and Valleys, and the Shore seems to form several Bays, into one of which I intend to go with the Ship in order to Careen her (she being very foul) and to repair some few defects, recruit our Stock of Wood, Water, etc. With this View we Keept plying on and off all Night, having from 80 to 63 fathoms Water; at daylight stood in for an inlet which runs in South-West.* (* Queen Charlotte's Sound, in the north-east part of the Middle Island.) At 8 a.m. we were got within the Entrance which may be known by a Reef of Rocks stretching off from the North-West point, and some rocky Islands lying off the South-East point. At 9 o'clock being little wind and Variable we were carried by the Tide or Current within 2 Cables length of the North-West Shore where we had 54 fathoms, but with the help of our Boats we got Clear, at this time we saw rise up twice near the Ship a Sea Lyon, the Head of which was Exactly like the head of the Male one described by Lord Anson. We likewise saw a Canoe with some of the Natives cross the Bay, and a Village situated upon a point of an Island, which lies 7 or 8 miles with the Entrance. At Noon we were the length of this Island, and being little wind had the Boats ahead Towing.

CHAPTER 6.
EXPLORATION OF MIDDLE ISLAND OF NEW ZEALAND.

[January 1770. In Queen Charlotte's Sound, New Zealand.]

TUESDAY, 16th. Variable light Airs and Clear settled weather. At 1 p.m. hauled close round the South-West end of the Island, on which stands the Village before mention'd, the inhabitants of which were all in Arms. At 2 o'Clock we anchor'd in a very Snug Cove,* (* Ship Cove, in Queen Charlotte's Sound.) which is on the North-West side of the Bay facing the South-West end of the Island in 11 fathoms; soft Ground, and moor'd with the Stream Anchor. By this time several of the Natives had come off to the Ship in their Canoes, and after heaving a few stones at us and having some Conversation with Tupia, some of them Ventur'd on board, where they made but a very short stay before they went into their Canoes again, and soon after left us altogether. I then went ashore in the bottom of the Cove, accompanied by most of the Gentlemen on board. We found a fine Stream of Excellent Water, and as to wood the land is here one intire forest. Having the Sean with us we made a few hauls and caught 300 pounds weight of different sorts of fish, which were equally distributed to the Ship's Company. A.M., Careen'd the Ship, scrubb'd and pay'd the Larboard side. Several of the Natives Visited us this Morning, and brought with them some stinking fish, which, however, I order'd to be bought up to encourage them in this kind of Traffick, but Trade at this time seem'd not to be their Object, but were more inclinable to Quarrel, and as the Ship was upon the Carreen I thought they might give us some Trouble, and perhaps hurt some of our people that were in the Boats alongside. For this reason I fir'd some small shott at one of the first Offenders; this made them keep at a proper distance while they stay'd, which was not long before they all went away. These people declared to us this morning, that they never either saw or heard of a Ship like ours being upon this Coast before. From this it appears that they have no Tradition among them of Tasman being here, for I believe Murtherers bay, the place where he anchor'd, not to be far from this place;* (* Tasman's Massacre Bay lies 70 miles to the West-North-West.) but this cannot be it from the Latitude, for I find by an Observation made this day at Noon that we are at an Anchor in 41 degrees 5 minutes 32 seconds South, which is 15 miles to the Southward of Murtherers Bay.* (* The bay in Queen Charlotte's Sound in which the Endeavour anchored, Ship Cove, lies 7 miles within the entrance on the western shore.)

Wednesday, 17th. Light Airs, Calm and pleasant weather. P.M., righted ship and got the other Side ready for heeling out, and in the Evening Haul'd the

Sean and caught a few fish. While this was doing some of us went in the pinnace into another Cove, not far from where the Ship lays; in going thither we meet with a Woman floating upon the Water, who to all appearance had not been dead many days. Soon after we landed we meet with 2 or 3 of the Natives who not long before must have been regaling themselves upon human flesh, for I got from one of them the bone of the Fore arm of a Man or Woman which was quite fresh, and the flesh had been but lately picked off, which they told us they had eat; they gave us to understand that but a few days before they had taken, Kill'd, and Eat a Boats Crew of their Enemies or strangers, for I believe they look upon all strangers as Enemies. From what we could learn the woman we had seen floating upon the Water was in this Boat and had been drowned in the fray. There was not one of us that had the least doubt but what these people were cannibals; but the finding this bone with part of the sinews fresh upon it was a stronger proof than any we had yet met with, and, in order to be fully satisfied of the truth of what they had told us, we told one of them that it was not the bone of a man, but that of a dog; but he, with great fervency, took hold of his Fore Arm, and told us again that it was that bone: and to convince us that they had eat the flesh he took hold of the flesh of his own Arm with his teeth and made Signs of Eating. A.M., Careen'd, Scrub'd, and pay'd the Starboard side of the Ship; while this was doing some of the Natives came alongside seemingly only to look at us. There was a woman among them who had her Arms, thighs, and Legs cut in several place's; this was done by way of Mourning for her Husband who had very lately been Kill'd and Eat by some of their Enemies as they told us and pointed towards' the place where it was done, which lay somewhere to the Eastward. Mr. Banks got from one of them a Bone of the fore Arm, much in the same state as the one before mentioned; and to show us that they eat the flesh, they bit and Naw'd the bone and draw'd it through their Mouths, and this in such a manner as plainly Shew'd that the flesh to them was a Dainty Bit.

Thursday, 18th. Winds mostly from the South-West; a gentle breeze and Clear settled weather. P.M., righted the Ship and sent on shore all or most of our empty Casks, and in the Morning the Coopers went about Trimming them, and the Carpenters went to work to Caulk the sides and to repair other defects in the Ship, while the seamen are Employ'd in the hold Cutting Wood, etc., etc. I made a little Excursion in the pinnace in order to take a View of the Bay, accompanied by Mr. Banks and Dr. Solander. We met with nothing remarkable, and as we were on the West side of the Bay where the land is so closely cover'd with wood that we could not penetrate into the country.

Friday, 19th. Winds and weather as yesterday, and the employment of the people the same. In the P.M. some of our people found in the Skirts of the

Wood 3 hip Bones of Men; they lay near to a Hole or Oven, that is a place where the Natives dress their Victuals; this Circumstance, trifling as it is, is still a further proof that these people eat human flesh. In the A.M. set up the Forge to repair the Braces of the Tiller and such other Iron work as was wanting. The Natives came alongside and sold us a quantity of large Mackrell for Nails, pieces of Cloth and paper, and in this Traffick they never once attempted to defraud us of any one thing but dealt as fair as people could do.

Saturday, 20th. Winds Southerly and fair, pleasant weather. Employ'd wooding, Watering, etc., and in the A.M. sent part of the Powder ashore to be Air'd. Some of the Natives brought alongside in one of their Canoes 4 of the heads of the Men they had lately kill'd; both the Hairy Scalps and Skin of the faces were on. Mr. Banks bought one of the 4, but they would not part with any of the other on any account whatever. The one Mr. Banks got had received a blow on the Temple that had broke the Skull. This morning I set out in the Pinnace accompanied by Mr. Banks and Dr. Solander, in order to Survey the West Coast of the Bay; we took our rout towards the head of the Bay, but it was near noon before we had got beyond the place we had been before.

Sunday, 21st. P.M., a Gentle breeze of Wind Southerly, the remainder light Airs and Calm with clear, settled weather. P.M., the people employ'd as usual, and at 8 o'Clock we return'd on board the Pinnace from surveying the bay, in the doing of which I met with an Excellent Harbour, but saw no inhabitants or any Cultivated land. In the A.M. after hauling the Sean for fish, I gave every body leave to go ashore at the Watering place to amuse themselves as they thought proper.

Monday, 22nd. P.M., and in the night had variable light Airs and Calms. A.M., had a fresh breeze Southerly and Cloudy weather. In the morning the people were set about the necessary business of the Ship, and I set out in the Pinnace accompanied by Mr. Banks and Dr. Solander, with a view of examining the head of the inlet, but after rowing between 4 and 5 Leagues up it, and finding no probability of reaching it, or even seeing the end,* (* The head of Queen Charlotte's Sound is 20 miles from where the Endeavour was lying.) the wind being against us and the day already half spent; we landed at Noon on the South-East side in order to try to get upon one of the Hills, to view the inlet from thence.

Tuesday, 23rd. P.M., Winds Southerly, a fresh breeze. Agreeable to what is mentioned above I took one hand with me and Climbed up to the Top of one of the Hills, but when I came there I was hindered from seeing up the inlet by higher hills, which I could not come at for impenetrable woods, but I was abundantly recompensed for the trouble I had in assending the Hill, for from it I saw what I took to be the Eastern Sea, and a Strait or passage from it into the Western Sea; a little to the Eastward of the Entrance of the inlet in which we now lay with the Ship. The Main land which lies on the South-East side of this inlet appeared to me to be a narrow ridge of very high hills, and to form a part of the South-West side of the Strait;* (* Cook's Strait, which divides the two islands of New Zealand.) the land on the opposite side seem'd to tend away East, as far as the Eye could see. To the South-East appeared an Open Sea, and this I took to be the Eastern. I likewise saw some Islands lying on the East side of the inlet, which before I had taken to be a part of the main land. As soon as I had desended the hill and we had refreshed ourselves, we set out in order to return to the Ship, and in our way passed through and Examin'd the Harbours, Coves, etc., that lay behind the Islands above mentioned. In this rout we met with an old Village in which were a good many Houses, but no Body had lived in them lately; we likewise saw another that was inhabited, but the day being so far spent, that we had not time to go to it, but made the best of our way to the Ship, which we reached between 8 and 9 o'Clock. In the night had much rain with Cloudy, Hazey weather, which continued by intervals until Noon.

Wednesday, 24th. P.M., had a fresh breeze southerly and cloudy weather. After dinner I employ'd myself in carrying on the survey of the place, and upon one of the Islands where I landed were a number of houses but no inhabitants, neither had any been there lately. In the morning the Gunner was sent ashore with the remainder of the powder to-day, and the Long boat was sent with a Gang of hands to one of the Islands to cut Grass for our Sheep, and the rest of the people were employ'd about the usual work of the Ship. This forenoon some of us visited the Hippa which is situated on the point of the Island mentioned on our first arrival;* (* Motuara.) the inhabitants of this place shew'd not the least dislike at our coming, but, on the contrary, with a great deal of seeming good nature shew'd us all over the place. We found among them some human bones, the flesh of which they told us they had eat; they likewise informed us that there was no passage into the Sea thro' this inlet, as I had imagined their was, because above where I was in the Boat it turn'd away to the Westward. Leaving these people, we Travelled to the other end of the Island, and there took Water and Crossed over upon the Main, where we met with several Houses that were at present, or had very lately been, inhabited, but we saw but very few of the inhabitants, and these were in their Boats fishing; after Viewing this place we returned on board to Dinner.

Thursday, 25th. Winds at North West, a Gentle breeze and fair weather. P.M. the Long boat having return'd with a Load of Grass, she was employ'd bringing on board Wood and Water, and the Caulkers having finished Caulking the Ship's sides (a thing they have been employ'd upon ever since we came here), they were pay'd with Tar. Early in the A.M. the Long boat was sent again for Grass, and return'd at Noon with a Load.

Friday, 26th. Gentle breezes and pleasant weather. In the P.M. I made a little Excursion in the pinnace along shore towards the Mouth of the inlet, accompanied by Mr. Banks and Dr. Solander. We found in a small Cove several of the Natives, of whom we purchased a quantity of fresh fish; and upon our return to the Ship found that the Sean had been equally as Successfull, which we generally haul morning and evening, and seldom fail of getting fish sufficient for all hands. In the A.M. I made an Excursion into one of the Bays which lye on the East side of the inlet, accompanied by Mr. Banks and Dr. Solander. Upon our landing we assended a very high hill, from which we had a full View of the passage I had before discovered, and the land on the opposite shore, which appeared to be about 4 Leagues from us; but as it was hazey near the Horizon we could not see far to the South-East. However, I had now seen enough of this passage to Convince me that there was the Greatest probability in the World of its running into the Eastern Sea, as the distance of that Sea from this place cannot Exceed 20 Leagues even to where we where. Upon this I resolved after putting to Sea to Search this passage with the Ship. We found on the Top of the Hill a parcel of loose stones, of which we built a Pyramid, and left in it some Musquet balls, small Shott, beads, and whatever we had about us that was likely to stand the test of Time; after this we descended the hill, and found along with Tupia and the boat's Crew several of the Natives, setting in the most free and friendly manner imaginable. Tupia always accompanies us in every Excursion we make, and proves of infinate Service. In our return to the Ship we visited the Hippa we had seen on Tuesday last, which is situated on a small Island, or rather a Rock. The inhabitants of this place invited us ashore with their usual Marks of Friendship, and shew'd us all over the place; which indeed was soon done, for it was very small, yet it contain'd a good number of people, and they had in it, Split and hanging up to dry, a prodidgious quantity of various sorts of small fish, a part of which they sold to us for such Trifles as we had about us.

Saturday, 27th. Fresh gales, Westerly. This day we got the Tiller properly secured, which hath been the Employment of the Armourers and part of the Carpenters since we Anchor'd at this place; the former in repairing and making new Iron work, and the Latter in fixing a Transom,* (* A transom is a curved piece of wood which supports the end of the tiller.) for the want of which the Tiller has often been in danger of being broke; the Iron braces that supply'd the want of a Transom have broke every time they have been repair'd. Coopers still employ'd repairing the Casks; some hands with the Long boat getting on board Stones to put into the bottom of the bread room to bring the Ship more by the Stern; while others were employ'd cutting wood, repairing the rigging, and fishing.

Sunday, 28th. Strong Gales westerly. P.M. fair and Cloudy, the remainder thick, hazey weather, with much rain.

Monday, 29th. Winds as yesterday. P.M. rainy weather, the remainder fair and Cloudy. Pretty early in the A.M. an old man, who had made us several visits upon our first Arrival here, came on board, and told us that one of our boats had fir'd upon and wounded 2 of their people, one of which was dead of his wounds. This affair hapned on Sunday was a week, and never before now came to my Knowledge; on that day the Master and 5 Petty officers desir'd to have a small boat to go a fishing; but instead of Keeping within the usual bounds and under the protection of the Ship, they went over to the Hippa on the Island, from which some of the inhabitants put off in 2 Canoes, as they thought to attack them; this Caused the Master to fire, and, according to the report of the old Man, wounded 2, one of which is since dead; but this last circumstance was soon after contradicted by another of the Natives, who Mr. Green and Tupia saw ashore, and I wish this last report may be true, because I find the reasons for firing upon them are not very Justifiable. This morning I went out to the Mouth of the Inlet and landed upon the West point, and from the Top of a pretty high hill which is there I had a view of this Coast to the North-West. The farthest land I could see in that Quarter was an Island* (* Stephens Island. Cape Stephens, off which it lies, forms the western termination of the strait, Cook's, between the two islands of New Zealand. The Coast between this and Cape Jackson, where Cook was standing, is thickly indented with inlets of great extent. The two Capes were named after the Secretaries of the Admiralty.) about 10 Leagues off, and lying pretty near the Main, and is the same as hath been before mentioned. Between this Island and the place where I was lay some other Islands close under the Shore, which forms several Bays, where there appears to be safe Anchorage for Shipping. After I had set the different points, etc., we Erected upon the Top of the Hill a Tower or Pile of Stones, in which we left a Piece of Silver Coin, some Musquet Balls, Beads, etc., and left flying upon it a piece of an old Pendant. After this we return'd to the Boat, and in our way to the Ship visited some of the Natives we met with along shore, and purchased of them a small quantity of fish.

Tuesday, 30th. Winds at North-West, Gentle breezes, and fair weather. Early in the A.M. a boat was sent to one of the Islands to get Sellery to boil for the People's breakfasts. While our people were gathering it near some empty huts about 20 of the Natives landed there--Men, Women, and Children. They had no sooner got out of their Canoe than 5 or 6 Women set down together, and cut and sacrificed themselves--viz., their Legs, Shins, Arms, and Faces, some with Shells, and others with pieces of Jaspar. So far as our people could understand them, this was done on account of their husbands being lately killed and devoured by their Enemies. While the women was performing this Ceremony, the Men went about repairing the Huts without showing the least Concern. The Carpenter went with part of his people into the Woods to cut and Square some Timber to saw into boards for the use of the Ship, and to prepare two Posts to be set up with inscriptions on them.

Wednesday, 31st. Little wind and Variable. In the P.M. the Carpenters having prepared the 2 Posts with inscriptions upon them, setting forth the Ship's Name, Month, and Year, one of them was set up at the Watering Place, on which was hoisted the Union flag; and in the Morning I took the other over to the Island which is known by the name of Motuouru, and is the one that lies nearest to the Sea; but before I attempted to set up the Post I went first to the Hippa, having Dr. Monkhouse and Tupia along with me. We here met with the old Man I have before spoke of. The first thing I did was to inquire after the Man said to be kill'd by our people, and the one that was wounded at the same time, when it did not appear to me that any such accidents had happened. I next (by means of Tupia) explain'd to the old Man and several others that we were Come to set up a Mark upon the Island, in order to shew to any ship that might put into this place that we had been here before. They not only gave their free Consent to set it up, but promised never to pull it down. I then gave every one a present of one thing or another; to the old man I gave Silver, three penny pieces dated 1763, and Spike Nails with the King's Broad Arrow cut deep in them; things that I thought were most likely to remain long among them. After I had thus prepared the way for setting up the post, we took it up to the highest part of the Island, and after fixing it fast in the ground, hoisted thereon the Union flag, and I dignified this Inlet with the name of Queen Charlotte's Sound, and took formal possession of it and the Adjacent lands in the Name and for the use of his Majesty. We then drank her Majesty's health in a Bottle of wine, and gave the Empty bottle to the old man (who had attended us up the hill), with which he was highly pleased. Whilst the Post was setting up we asked the old man about the Strait or Passage into the Eastern sea, and he very plainly told us there was a Passage, and as I had some Conjectures that the lands to the South-West of this Strait (which we are now at) was an Island, and not a Continent, we questioned the old Man about it, who said it consisted of two Wannuas, that is 2 lands or Islands that might be Circumnavigated in a few days, even in 4. This man spoke of 3 lands, the 2 above mentioned which he called Tovy-poinammu,* (* The two Wannuas were doubtless the peninsulas lying west of Queen Charlotte's Sound. The third was the North Island. Te Wai Pounamu (The Water of the Greenstone, of which the most prized weapons were made) is the native name of the Middle Island; but there must have been some confusion as to the possibility of getting round this in four days. The name of the North Island is Te Ika o Maui (The Fish of Maui), but is given by Cook as Aeheino Mouwe. It has been suggested (Rusden) that the name given to him was Tehinga o Maui (The Fishing of Maui), and imperfectly rendered.) which Signifies green Talk or Stone, such as they make their Tools or ornaments, etc., and for the third he pointed to the land on the East side of the Strait; this, he said, was a large land, and that it would take up a great many Moons to sail round it; this he called Aeheino Mouwe, a name many others before had called it by. That part which borders on the strait he called Teiria Whitte. After we had done our business upon the Island we returned on board, bringing the old Man along with us, who after dinner went ashore in a Canoe that came to attend upon him.

[February 1770.]

Thursday, February 1st. P.M. having compleated the Ship with wood, and filled all our water, the Boatswain was sent ashore with a party of Men to cut and make brooms, while others were Employ'd about the rigging, fishing, etc. In the night and the remainder of the day had a Strong Gale from the North-West, attended with very much rain.

Friday, 2nd. In the P.M. the Gale increased to a Storm, attended with rain and squalls, which came down in Excessive heavy gusts from off the high land, in one of which the hawser we had fast to the shore broke; this obliged us to let go another Anchor. Towards midnight the Gale moderated, and in the morning it fell Calm, and we took up the Sheet Anchor, looked at the best bower, and moored the ship again to the Shore. The heavy rain, which both fell and Continues to fall, hath caused the Brook we water'd at to overflow its banks, and carry away 10 small Casks we had Standing there full of Water, and notwithstanding we searched the whole Cove, we could not find one of them.

Saturday, 3rd. Winds Northerly, mostly fair weather. Very early in the A.M. sent the Long boat for Sellery to boil for the Ship's Company's breakfast, and as I intended sailing the first opportunity, I went over to the Hippa, which is on the East side of the sound, and purchased of the inhabitants a quantity of split and half dry'd fish, and such as I could get. While we were at this Hippa, Tupia made farther enquiry about the Lands and Strait, and these people confirm'd everything the old Man had before told us. About noon we took our leave of them, which some seem'd not sorry for; notwithstanding they sold us their fish very freely, there were some few among them who shew'd evident signs of disapprobation.

Sunday, 4th. Winds Northerly, a fresh breeze and fair weather. In the P.M., after returning from the Hippa, some of us made an Excursion along shore to the Northward, in order to Traffic with the Natives for fish, in which we had no great Success. In the evening got everything off from the Shore, designing to sail in the Morning, but the wind not permitting, we amused ourselves in fishing, collecting of shells, etc.

Monday, 5th. Winds and weather as Yesterday. In the A.M. Cast off the Hawser, hove short on the Bower, and carried out the Kedge Anchor, in order to warp the Ship out of the Cove. All the dry fish we have been able to procure from the Natives since we came here were this day divided amongst the Ship's Company.

Tuesday, 6th. At 2 p.m. hove up the Anchor, warped the Ship out of the Cove, and got under Sail, but it soon after falling little wind, and that very Variable, we anchor'd again a little above Motu-ouru. The old man, seeing us under sail, came on board to take his leave of us. Amongst other conversation that passed between him and Tupia, he was asked if either he or any of his Ancestors had ever seen or heard of any Ship like this being in these parts; to which question he answer'd in the Negative, but said that his Ancestors had told him that there came once to this place a small Vessel from a distant part, wherein were 4 Men that were all kill'd upon their landing; and being asked where this distant land lay, he pointed to the North, intimating that it would take up a great many days to go thither. Something of this land was mentioned by the People of the Bay of Islands, who said that some of their Ancestors had been there; but it is very clear to us that there knowledge of this land is only traditionary.* (* This was doubtless the tradition current among the Maoris, that their ancestors came from islands to the north. See Note below.) Had it Calm all night until 6 o'clock in the Morning, when a light breeze sprung up at North, and we got again under sail; but as the wind proved very unsteady, we got no farther than just without Motu-ouru by noon, but had a fair prospect of getting clear out of the Sound, which I shall next describe.

DESCRIPTION OF QUEEN CHARLOTTE'S SOUND.

The entrance of this Sound is situated in the Latitude of 41 degrees South and Longitude 184 degrees 45 minutes West, and near the middle of the South-West side of the Strait before mentioned. The land off the South-East head of the Sound called by the Natives, Koamaroo (off which lies 2 Small Islands and some rocks) makes the Narrowest part of the Strait. There stretcheth out 2 Miles North-East by North from the North-West head a reef of rocks, a part of which is above Water. This account of the 2 Heads will be found sufficient guide to know this sound, which is 3 Leagues broad at the Entrance, and lies in South-West by South-South-West, and West-South-West at least 10 Leagues, and is a collection of some of the finest harbours in the world, as will evidently appear from the plan which was taken with all the accuracy that time and Circumstances would admit. The Harbour or Cove in which we lay, called Ship Cove, is not inferior to any in the Sound, both in point of Security and other Conveniences. It lies on the West side of the Sound, and is the Southermost of 3 Coves lying within Motu-ouru, which Island bears East from it. You may sail into this Cove either between this last mentioned Island and the Isle Hamote, or Long Island, or between Motuouru and the West shore; in this last Channell are 2 Ledges of Rocks 3 fathoms under water, but they may be known by the Sea Weed which grows upon them. In sailing in or out of this sound with little wind attention must be had to the Tides, which flow 9 or 10 o'Clock full and Change of the Moon, and rises and falls upon a Perpendicular 7 or 8 feet. The flood comes in through the Strait from the South-East, and sets strong over upon the North-West Head and the reef laying off it; the Ebb sets with great rapidity to the South-East over upon the Islands and Rocks lying off the South-East Head. The Variation of the Compass from good observations we found to be 13 degrees 5 minutes East. The land about this Sound is of such height that we first saw it at the distance of 20 Leagues. It consists wholy of high hills and deep Valleys, well stored with a variety of excellent Timber, fit for all purposes except Ships' Masts, for which use it is too hard and heavy. The Sea abounds with a variety of fish, and in such plenty that, without going out of the Cove where we lay, we caught daily, what with the Sean, Hook, and Lines, quite sufficient for all hands, and upon our first arrival we found plenty of Shags and some few other Wild Fowls, which to people in our situation was fresh food not to be dispised. The Number of Inhabitants hardly exceeds 300 or 400 People. They live dispers'd along the Shore in search of their daily bread, which is fish and firn roots, for they Cultivate no part of the lands. Upon the appearance of danger they Retire to their Hippas or strongholds, for in this situation we found them, and they remain'd so for some days after. This people are poor when compared to many we have seen, and their Canoes are mean and without ornament. The little Traffick we had with them was wholy for fish, for we saw little else they had to dispose of. They had some knowledge of Iron, for they very readily took Nails in Exchange for fish, and sometimes Prefer'd them to anything else, which was more than the people of any other place would do. They were at first fond of Paper, but when they found it spoile by being wet they would not take it; nor did they set much value upon the cloth we got at George's Island, but shew'd an extraordinary fondness for English broad cloth and red Kersey, which shew'd them to be a more sensible People than many of their Neighbours. Besides the common dress, many of these People wore on their Heads round Caps made of Birds' feathers, which were far from being unbecoming.* (* Cook was not able to explore the whole of Queen Charlotte's Sound, which runs into the land for 25 miles. Towards the southern end is Picton, the port of Blenheim, the capital of the province of Marlborough.)

[In Cook's Strait, New Zealand.]

Wednesday, 7th. In the P.M. had a light breeze at North by West, with which we got out of the Sound and stood over to the Eastward, in order to get the Strait well open before the tide of Ebb Made. At 7 the 2 Small Islands which lies off Cape Koamaroo, or the South-East head of Queen Charlotte's Sound, bore East, distant 4 miles. At this time we had it nearly Calm, and the tide of Ebb making out, we were Carried by the Rapidity of the Stream in a very short time close upon one of the Islands,* (* The Brothers. There is now a lighthouse on this island.) where we narrowly escaped being dashed against the Rocks by bringing the Ship to an Anchor in 75 fathoms Water, with 150 fathoms of Cable out. Even this would not have saved us had not the Tide, which first set South by East, by meeting with the Island changed its direction to South-East, and carried us past the first point. When the Ship was brought up she was about 2 Cables' Lengths of the Rocks and in the Strength of the Stream, which set South-East at least 4 or 5 Knotts or miles per Hour. A little before 12 o'Clock the Tide abated, and we began to heave; by 3 the Anchor was at the bows, and having a light breeze at North-West, we made sail over for the Eastern Shore; but having the tide against us we made but little way. The wind afterwards freshned, and Came to North and North-East, with which and the tide of Ebb we were in a short time hurried thro' the narrowest part of the Strait, and then stood away for the Southermost land we had in sight, which bore from us South by West. Over this land appeared a Prodigious high Mountain,* (* The Kairoura Range, the summit of which is 9500 feet high.) the Summit of which was covered with snow. The narrowest part of the Strait we have passed lies between Cape Koamaroo on Tovy-poinammu and Cape Teerawhitte on Aeheino-mouwe; the distance from the one to the other I judged to be between 4 and 5 Leagues. And notwithstanding the strength of the Tides, now that is known, there is no great danger in passing it; in the doing of which I am of opinion that the North-East Shore is the safest to keep upon, for upon that side there appeared no danger, whereas on the other shore there are not only the Islands and Rocks lying off Cape Koamaroo, for I discover'd from the hill from which I had the Second View of the Strait, a Reef of Rocks stretching from these Islands 6 or 7 Miles to the Southward, and lay about 2 or 3 Miles off from the Shore. I shall not pretend here to assign limits to the length of this Strait; a view of the Chart will best illustrate that. About North 9 Leagues from Cape Teerawhitte, under the same shore, is a high remarkable Island, that may be distinctly seen from Queen Charlotte Sound, from which it lies North-East by East 1/4 East, distant 6 or 7 Leagues. I have called it Entry Isle, and was taken Notice of when we first past it on Sunday 14th of last Month. On the East side of Cape Teerawhitte the Land Trends away South-East by East about 8 Leagues, where it ends in a point, and is the Southermost land on Aeheinomouwe, which I have named Cape Pallisser in Honour of my worthy friend Capt. Pallisser.* (* Captain Palliser, afterwards

Sir Hugh, was Captain of the Eagle, Cook's first ship in the Royal Navy. He discovered Cook's talents, and was his warm friend throughout his life. Between Cape Teerawhitte and Cape Palliser is the entrance to Port Nicholson, wherein is situated Wellington, the capital of New Zealand. This entrance is, however, narrow, and Cook was never near enough to the land to discover it.) Latitude 41 degrees 34 minutes, Longitude 183 degrees 58 minutes, it bore from us this day at Noon South 79 degrees East, distant 12 or 13 Leagues, being then in the Latitude of 41 degrees 27 minutes South; at the same time Cape Koamaroo bore North 1/2 East, distant 7 or 8 Leagues. The Southermost point of land in sight bore South 16 degrees West, and the snowy Mountain South-West being about 3 Leagues from the shore and abreast of a Deep Bay or inlet called Cloudy bay, in the bottom of which appear'd low land cover'd with tall Trees.

Thursday, 8th. In the P.M. had a fresh breeze at North-North-East and Cloudy weather. At 3 o'Clock was abreast of the Southermost point of land set at Noon, which I named Cape Campbell, Latitude 41 degrees 42 minutes South, Longitude 184 degrees 47 minutes West, it lies South by West, distant 12 or 13 Leagues from Cape Koamaroo, and together with Cape Pallisser forms the Southern Entrance of the Straits; the Distance of the one to the other is 13 or 14 Leagues West by South and East by North. From this Cape we steer'd along Shore South-West by South until 8 o'Clock, when the wind died away; but an Hour after a fresh breeze sprung up at South-West, and we put the Ship right before it. The reason of my doing this was owing to a notion, which some of the Officers had just started, that Aeheinomouwe was not an Island; founding their opinion on a supposition that the land might extend away to the South-East from between Cape Turnagain and Cape Pallisser, there being a space of about 12 or 13 leagues which we had not seen. For my own part, I had seen so far into this Sea the first time I discover'd the Strait, together with many other Concurrent testimonies of its being an Island, that no such supposition ever enter'd my thoughts; but being resolved to clear up every doubt that might Arise on so important an Object, I took the opportunity of the Shifting of the Wind to Stand to the Eastward, and accordingly steer'd North-East by East all night. At 9 o'Clock A.M. we were abreast of Cape Pallisser, where we found the Land trend away North-East towards Cape Turnagain, which I reckon'd to be distant from us about 26 Leagues, but as the weather was hazey so that we could not see above 4 or 5 Leagues ahead, we Still kept standing to the North-East, with a light breeze at South. At Noon Cape Pallisser bore North 72 degrees West, distant 3 Leagues; our Latitude by account is 41 degrees 30 minutes South.

[Complete the Circuit of North Island, New Zealand.]

Friday, 9th. Gentle breezes at South and South-South-East, hazey Cloudy weather. In the P.M. 3 Canoes came off to the Ship, wherein were between

30 and 40 of the Natives, who had been pulling after us sometime. It appeared from the behaviour of these people that they had heard of our being upon the Coast, for they came alongside, and some of them on board the Ship, without shewing the least signs of fear. They were no sooner on board than they asked for Nails, but when Nails was given them they asked Tupia what they were, which was plain that they had never seen any before; yet they not only knowed how to ask for them, but know'd what use to make of them, and therefore must have heard of Nails, which they call Whow, the name of a Tool among them made generally of bone, which they use as a Chisel in making Holes, etc. These people asking so readily for Nails proves that their connections must extend as far North as Cape Kidnapper, which is 45 Leagues, for that was the Southermost place on this side the coast we had any Traffick with the Natives; and it is most probable that the inhabitants of Queen Charlotte's sound got the little knowledge they seem'd to have of Iron by the Connections they may have with the Teerawhitteans bordering upon them; for we have no reason to think that the inhabitants of any part of this land had the least knowledge of Iron before we came amongst them. After a short stay these people were dismissed with proper presents, and we continued our Course along shore to the North-East until 11 o'Clock A.M., when the weather clear'd up, and we saw Cape Turnagain bearing North by East 1/4 East, distant 7 Leagues. I then called the Officers upon deck, and asked them if they were now satisfied that this land was an Island; to which they answer'd in the Affirmative, and we hauled our wind to the Eastward.* (* The Endeavour had now completely circumnavigated the North Island of New Zealand, having spent four months in the exploration. That Cook had communicated his enthusiasm to his officers is evident; or, knowing his determination to leave nothing doubtful, they would not have started the idea that the North Island might not be really an island. The natural wish after so many months' absence from civilization must have been to get back to it, and to take things for granted that would otherwise delay their progress.) At Noon our Latitude by observation was 40 degrees 55 minutes South, which is 21 Miles to the Southward of Cape Turnagain, it bearing North by East, and Cape Pallisser by this day's run bears South 43 degrees West, 19 or 20 Leagues.

Saturday, 10th. Gentle breezes at South-East and Cloudy weather. At 4 P.M. Tack'd and stood South-West until 8 A.M., when being not above 3 or 4 Miles from the Shore we Tack'd, and stood off 2 hours, and then stood again to the South-West until noon, when being in the Latitude of 41 degrees 13 minutes South, and about 2 Miles from the Shore, the land of Cape Pallisser bearing South 53 degrees West, had 26 fathoms of water.

Sunday, 11th. P.M. had light breeze from the South-East. In the night it was Calm until 9 a.m., when a Gentle breeze sprung up at East-North-East, with which we made sail to the Southward, having a large swell rolling in from that Quarter. At Noon was in the Latitude of 41 degrees 6 minutes South, distant from the Shore 1 1/2 Leagues; a remarkable hillock,* (* Castle Point.) which stands close to the Sea, bore North 1/2 East, distance 4 Leagues. At this time 2 Canoes came alongside the Ship, with whom we had some little Traffic, and then dismissed them.

Monday, 12th. Most part of P.M. had a fresh breeze at North-East, which by sunset carried us the length of Cape Pallisser, and as the weather was clear I had an opportunity of Viewing the land of this Cape, which is of a height Sufficient to be seen in clear weather 12 or 14 Leagues, and is of a broken and hilly surface. Between the foot of the high land and the Sea is a border of low, flat land, off which lies some rocks, that appear above water. Between this Cape and Cape Turnagain the land near the shore is in many places low and flatt, and appear'd green and pleasant; but inland are many Hills. From Cape Pallisser to Cape Teerawhitte the land is tollerable high, making in Table-points, and the Shore forms 2 Bays; at least it appear'd so, for we were always too far off this part of the Coast to be particular.* (* The northern of these was the entrance to Port Nicholson, the harbour of Auckland.) The wind continued at North-East until 12 at Night, when it died away, and veer'd round to the West, and afterwards to South and South-South-East little wind, so that by noon we had advanced no farther than 41 degrees 52 minutes South Latitude. Cape Pallisser bearing North, distant 5 Leagues, and the Snowy mountain bore South 83 degrees West.

Tuesday, 13th. P.M. light Airs at South-East, the remainder Calm. At Noon found ourselves in the Latitude of 42 degrees 2 minutes South, Cape Pallisser bearing North 20 degrees East, distant 8 Leagues.

Wednesday, 14th. P.M. a fresh breeze sprung up at North-East, and we Steer'd South-West by West for the Southermost land we had in sight, which bore from us at sunset South 74 degrees West. At this time we found the Variation to be 15 degrees 4 minutes East. At 8 A.M. it fell Calm; at this time we had run 21 Leagues South 58 degrees West since Yesterday at noon, which brought us abreast of the high Snowy mountain, it bearing from us North-West in this direction. It lay behind a Mountainous ridge of nearly the same height, which riseth directly from the Sea, and runs Parrallel with the Shore, which lies North-East 1/2 North and South-West 1/2 South. The North-East end of the ridge takes its rise but a little way inland from Cape Campbell. These mountains are distinctly seen both from Cape Koamaroo and Cape Pallisser, being distant from the former South-West 1/2 South 22 Leagues, and from the Latter West-South-West 30 Leagues: but they are of a height sufficient to be seen at a much greater distance. By some on board they are thought to be much higher than the Peak of Teneriffe, which I cannot agree to; neither do I think them so high as Mount Egmont, on the

South-West Coast of Aeheinomouwe, founding my opinion on the summit of the Latter being almost wholy covered with Snow, whereas it only lies upon these in patches.* (* The highest peak of the Kaikoura Mountains, Mount Tapuaepuka, is 9500 feet high. It is therefore higher than Mount Egmont, but not so high as the Peak of Teneriffe. The snow lies thicker on the western side of New Zealand mountains, so Cook's parallel was fallacious. The Endeavour was now near the Kaikoura Peninsula, where a small town stands at the present day, the shipping port of an agricultural district.) At noon was in the Latitude of 42 degrees 34 minutes South; the Southermost land we had in sight bore South-West 1/2 West, and some low land that made like an Island lying close under the foot of the Ridge North-West by North, distant about 5 or 6 Leagues.

Thursday, 15th. In the P.M. 4 Double Canoes, in which were 57 Men, came off to the Ship; they kept at the distance of about a Stone's throw from us, and would not be prevailed upon to put alongside by all that Tupia could say to them. From this we concluded that they never had heard of our being upon the coast. At 8 p.m. a breeze sprung up at South-South-West, with which we Stretched off South-East, because some on board thought they saw land in that Quarter. We continued on this course until 6 A.M., at which time we had run 11 Leagues, but saw no land but that which we had left. Soon after this it fell calm, and continued so for an hour; then a light breeze sprung up at West, which afterwards veer'd to the North, and we stood to the Westward. At Noon our Latitude by Observation was 42 degrees 56 minutes South, and the High Land we were abreast of yesterday at Noon, North-North-West 1/2 West.

Friday, 16th. In the P.M. had a light breeze North-East, with which we steer'd West, edging in for the land, which was distant from us about 8 Leagues. At 7 o'Clock the Southermost Extream of the land in sight bore West-South-West, being about 6 Leagues from the Shore; soon after this it fell Calm, and continued so most part of the night, with sometimes light Airs from the land. At daylight we discover'd land bearing South by West, and seemingly detached from the Coast we were upon; at 8 o'Clock a breeze sprung up at North by East, and we steer'd directly for it. At Noon was in the Latitude of 43 degrees 19 minutes South; the Peak on the Snowy Mountains bore North 20 degrees East, distant 27 Leagues; the Southern Extremity we could see of that land bore West, and the land discover'd in the morning, making like an Island, extending from South-South-West to South-West by West 1/2 West, distant about 8 Leagues; our Course and distance sail'd since yesterday at Noon South-West by West, 43 Miles; Variation by this Morning's Amplitude 14 degrees 39 minutes East.

[Off Banks Peninsula, New Zealand.]

Saturday, 17th. P.M. stood to the Southward for the land above mention'd, with the wind at North, a fresh breeze and Clear weather. At 8 o'Clock we had run 11 Leagues since Noon, when the land extended from South-West by West to North by West, being distant from the nearest shore about 3 or 4 Leagues; in this situation had 50 fathoms, a fine sandy bottom. Soon after this it fell Calm, and continued so until 6 A.M., when a light breeze sprung up at North-West, which afterwards veer'd to North-East. At sun rise, being very Clear, we plainly discover'd that the last mentioned land was an Island by seeing part of the Land of Tovy-poenammu open to the Westward of it, extending as far as West by South. At 8 o'Clock the Extreams of the Island bore North 76 degrees West and North-North-East 1/2 East, and an opening that had the Appearance of a Bay or Harbour, lying near the South point North 20 degrees West, distant 3 or 4 Leagues, being in 38 fathoms, a brown Sandy bottom. This Island,* (* It is not an island, but a mountainous peninsula, still called after Mr. Banks, but from the lowness of the land it adjoins, looks like an island. On the north side is the fine harbour of Lyttelton, the port of Christchurch, a town of nearly 40,000 inhabitants. The harbour on the south side, that Cook saw, is Akaroa, a magnificent port.) which I have named after Mr. Banks, lies about 5 Leagues from the Coast of Tovy poenammu; the South point bears South 21 degrees West from the higher peak on the Snowy Mountain so often mention'd, and lies in the Latitude of 43 degrees 52 minutes South and in the Longitude of 186 degrees 30 minutes West, by observations made of the Sun and Moon this morning. It is of a circular figure, and may be about 24 Leagues in Compass; the land is of a height sufficient to be seen 12 or 15 Leagues, and of a very broken, uneven Surface, and hath more the appearance of barrenness than fertility. Last night we saw smoke up it, and this morning some people, and therefore must be inhabited. Yesterday Lieutenant Gore, having the Morning Watch at the time we first saw this Island, thought he saw land bearing South-South-East and South-East by East; but I, who was upon Deck at the same time, was very Certain that it was only Clouds, which dissipated as the Sun rose. But neither this, nor the running 14 Leagues to the South, nor the seeing no land to the Eastward of us in the Evening, could Satisfy Mr. Gore but what he saw in the morning was, or might be, land; altho' there was hardly a possibility of its being so, because we must have been more than double the distance from it at that time to what we were either last night or this morning, at both of which times the weather was Exceeding Clear, and yet we could see no land either to the Eastward or Southward of us. Notwithstanding all this, Mr. Gore was of the same opinion this morning; upon this I order'd the Ship to be wore, and to be steer'd East-South-East by Compass on the other Tack, the point on which he said the land bore at this time from us.* (* Another instance of the general desire to leave nothing unexplored.) At

Noon we were in the Latitude of 44 degrees 7 minutes South; the South point of Banks Island bore North, distant 5 Leagues.

Sunday, 18th. Gentle breezes at North and fair weather. P.M. stood East-South-East in search of Mr. Gore's imaginary land until 7 o'clock, at which time we had run 28 Miles since Noon; but seeing no land but that we had left, or signs of any, we bore away South by West, and continued upon that Course until Noon, when we found ourselves in the Latitude of 45 degrees 16 minutes South. Our Course and distance sail'd since Yesterday is South 8 minutes East, 70 Miles; the South point of Banks Island North 6 degrees 30 minutes West, distant 28 Leagues; Variation per Amplitude this Morning 15 degrees 30 minutes. Seeing no signs of Land, I thought it to no purpose standing any farther to the Southward, and therefore hauled to the Westward, thinking we were far enough to the Southward to weather all the land we had left; but this opinion was only founded on the information we had had from the Natives of Queen Charlotte's sound.* (* The ship was still 250 miles from the south point of New Zealand.)

Monday, 19th. P.M. had a Moderate breeze at North-North-West and North until 8 o'clock, when it fell little wind, and was very unsettled until 10, at which time it fix'd at South, and freshen'd in such a manner that before the morning it brought us under our close reeft Topsails. At 8 a.m. having run 28 Leagues upon a West by North 1/2 North Course, and now judging ourselves to be to the Westward of the Land of Tovy Poenammu, we bore away North-West with a fresh Gale at South. At 10 o'clock, having run 11 Miles upon this Course, we saw land extending from the South-West to the North-West at the distance of about 10 Leagues from us, which we hauled up for. At Noon our Latitude per observation was 44 degrees 38 minutes South; the South-East point of Banks Island bore North 59 degrees 30 minutes East, distant 30 Leagues, and the Main body of the land in sight West by North. Course and distance sail'd since Yesterday at Noon is North 66 degrees 45 minutes West, 96 Miles.

[Off Timaru, Middle Island, New Zealand.]

Tuesday, 20th. All P.M. had little wind, which veer'd round from South by East to North-North-East. Steer'd South-South-West, but got very little to the Southward on account of a head Sea. At 2 o'Clock sounded in 35 fathoms, fine sandy Bottom, being about 6 Leagues from the land. At 7 o'Clock the Extreams of the land extending from South-West by South to North by West, distant from the nearest shore 6 Leagues, depth of water 32 fathoms. At 12 o'Clock it fell Calm, and continued so until 4 A.M., when a fresh breeze sprung up at South by West, with which we stood in shore West by South, 4 Leagues, our Depth of Water from 32 to 13 fathoms. In this last Depth we Tack'd and Stood off, being about 3 Miles from the Shore, which lies nearly North and South, and is here very low and flatt, and continues so up to the skirts of the hills, which are at least 4 or 5 Miles inland. The whole face of the Country appears barren, nor did we see any signs of inhabitants.* (* This is a little south of Timaru, a rising town in a fertile district; so deceptive is appearance from the sea.) Latitude at Noon 44 degrees 44 minutes South; Longitude made from Banks' Island to this land 2 degrees 22 minutes West.

Wednesday, 21st. Wind at South. A fresh Gale at 2 p.m., being in 50 fathoms, and 12 Leagues from the land, we tack'd and stood in Shore until 8 o'Clock, when we Tack'd and Stood off until 4 a.m.; then Tack'd and Stood in, at 8 o'Clock being 10 Leagues from the Land; had 57 fathoms. At Noon, being in the Latitude 44 degrees 35 minutes, and 5 or 6 Leagues from the land, had 36 fathoms; notwithstanding we have Carried as much sail as the Ship could bear, it is apparent from the observed Latitudes that we have been drove 3 Leagues to leeward since Yesterday.

Thursday, 22nd. Moderate breezes between the South-East and South by West, and dark gloomy weather, with a Swell from the South-East plying to windward, keeping between 4 and 12 Leagues from the land; depth of water from 35 to 53 fathoms, fine sandy bottom. A great many Sea fowl and Grampusses about the Ship. In the A.M. Condemn'd 60 fathoms of the B.B. Cable,* (* B.B. stands for Best Bower, one of the principal cables. The hempen cables of those days were a continual cause of solicitude, and required great care.) and converted it into Junk; at Noon had no Observation, but by the land judged ourselves to be about 3 Leagues farther North than Yesterday.

Friday, 23rd. Winds Southerly, a Gentle breeze, and for the most part Cloudy weather. At sunset, the weather clearing up, presented to our View a high peaked Mountain* (* There are so many lofty mountains in this region that it is impossible to identify this. This ship was now no farther south than she had been five days earlier.) bearing North-West by North, and at the same time we saw the Land more Distincter than at any time we had before, extending from North to South-West by South, the inland parts of which appear'd to be high and Mountainous. We cannot tell yet whether or no this land joins to, or makes a part of, the land we have left; from the accounts received from the Natives of Queen Charlotte's sound it ought not, because if it did it must have been impossible for us to have sail'd round it in 4 Days; besides, the Mountains inland and the soundings off the Coast seem to indicate this Country to be more extensive than any they spoke of lying to the Southward. Having a large hollow swell from the South-East, which made me expect the Wind from the same quarter, we keept plying from 7 to 15 Leagues from the land, depth of Water 44 to 70 fathoms; at Noon our

Latitude, by Observation, was 44 degrees 40 minutes South; Longitude made from Banks's Island 1 degree 31 minutes West.

Saturday, 24th. Calm until 6 p.m., at which time a light breeze sprung up at East-North-East, with which we steer'd South-South-East all night, edging off from the Land because of a hollow swell which we had from the South-East; depth of water from 60 to 75 fathoms. At daylight the wind began to freshen, and before noon blowed a fresh Gale, and veer'd to North-North-East; at 8 a.m. Saw the land extending as far as South-West by South, which we steer'd directly for, and at Noon we were in the Latitude of 45 degrees 22 minutes South; the land in sight extending from South-West 1/2 South to North-North-West making high and hilly. Course and distance run since Yesterday at Noon is South 15 degrees West, 47 Miles. In the P.M., while we lay becalm'd, Mr. Banks, in a small Boat, shott 2 Port Egmont Hens, which were in every respect the same sort of Birds as are found in great Numbers upon the Island of Faro; they are of a very dark brown plumage, with a little white about the under side of their wings, and are as large as a Muscovy Duck. These were the first that we have seen since we arrived upon the Coast of this Country, but we saw of them for some days before we made land.

[Off Otago, Middle Island, New Zealand.]

Sunday, 25th. In the P.M. Steer'd South-West by South and South-West, edging in for the land, having the Advantage of a fresh Gale at North, which I was over desirous of making the most of, and by that means carried away the Maintop Gallant Mast and Foretopmast Steering Sail Boom; but these were soon replaced by others. Altho' we keept at no great Distance from the Shore, yet the weather was so Hazey that we could see nothing distinct upon the land, only that there were a ridge of Pretty high Hills lying Parrallel with, and but a little way from, the Sea Coast, which lies South by West and North by East, and seem'd to End in a high Bluff point to the Southward, which we run the length of by 8 o'Clock, when, being dark, and not knowing which way the Land Trended, we brought too for the night, having run 15 Leagues upon a South-West 1/2 West Course since Noon. The point bore at this time West, distant about 5 Miles, depth of Water 37 fathoms, the bottom small pebble stones. At 4 A.M. we made Sail, but by this time the Northerly wind was gone, and was succeeded by one from the Southward, which proved very Var'ble and unsteady. At day light the point above mention'd bore North, distant 3 Leagues, and we found that the land trended away from it South-West by West, as far as we could see. This point of land I have Named Cape Saunders, in Honour of Sir Charles* (* Admiral Sir Charles Saunders was First Lord of the Admiralty in 1766. He commanded the fleet at the capture of Quebec in 1759, in which Cook served.) (Latitude 45 degrees 55 minutes South; Longitude 189 degrees 4 minutes West). It requires no discription to know it by, the Latitude and the Angle made here by the Coast will be found quite sufficient; however, there is a remarkable saddle hill laying near the Shore, 3 or 4 Leagues South-West of the Cape. From 1 to 4 Leagues North of the Cape the Shore seem'd to form 2 or 3 Bays, wherein there appear'd to be Anchorage and Shelter from South-West, Westerly, and North-West winds.* (* One of these is Otago Harbour, where lies Dunedin, perhaps the most important commercial city in New Zealand.) I had some thoughts of bearing up for one of these places in the morning when the Wind came to South-West, but the fear of loosing time and the desire I had of pushing to the Southward, in order to see as much of the Coast as possible, or, if this land should prove to be an Island, to get round it, prevented me. Being not far from the Shore all this morning, we had an Opportunity of Viewing the Land pretty distinctly; it is of a Moderate height, full of Hills, which appear'd green and Woody, but we saw not the least signs of inhabitants. At Noon Cape Saunders bore North 30 degrees West, distant 4 Leagues. Latitude per Log, for we had no Observation, 46 degrees 0 minutes South.

Monday, 26th. In the P.M. had the wind Whifling all round the Compass, sometimes blowing a fresh Gale, and at other times almost Calm. At 5 o'Clock it fixed at West-South-West, and soon blow'd so hard as to put us past our Topsails, and to split the foresail all to pieces. After getting another to the Yard, we continued standing to the Southward under 2 Courses. At 1 A.M. the wind Moderating, set the Topsails with one Reef out; but soon after day light the Gale increased to a Storm, with heavy Squalls, attended with rain. This brought us again under our Courses, and the Main Topsail being Split we unbent it and bent another. At 6 o'Clock the Southermost land in sight bore West by North, and Cape Saunders bore North by West, distant 8 Leagues; at Noon it bore North 20 minutes West, distant 14 Leagues. Latitude observed 46 degrees 35 minutes.

Tuesday, 27th. A very hard gale at South-West by West, and West-South-West, with heavy squalls attended with Showers of rain, and a large hollow sea, without the least intermission the whole of this 24 Hours. We continued under our Courses from Noon until 7 P.M., when we handed the Mainsail, and lay too under the Foresail with the head to the Southward. Latitude at Noon 46 degrees 54 minutes; Longitude made from Cape Saunders 1 degree 24 minutes East.

Wednesday, 28th. Strong Gale at South-West, with a large Sea from the Same quarter. At 7 p.m. made sail under the Courses; at 8 a.m. set the Topsails close reefed. At Noon, being in the Latitude of 47 degrees 43 minutes South, and Longitude East from Cape Saunders 2 degrees 10 minutes, wore and stood to the Northward.

[March 1770.]

Thursday, March 1st. Winds between the South-West and North-North-West, a fresh gale. In the P.M. found the Variation to be 16 degrees 34 minutes East. At 8 Tack'd and Stood to the Southward, with the wind at West, which before the morning veer'd to North-West, accompanied with hazey weather and drizzling rain; at day light loosed a reef out of Each Topsail, and set some of the small sails. At Noon our Latitude by account was 47 degrees 52 minutes South, and Longitude made from Cape Saunders 1 degree 8 minutes East.

Friday, 2nd. Strong Gales from the West, with heavy Squalls, attended with showers of rain. In the P.M. Stood to the Southward till half-past 3, when being in the Latitude 48 degrees 0 minutes South and Longitude 188 degrees 00 minutes West, and seeing no Visible signs of Land, we Tack'd and Stood to the Northward, having a very large swell from the South-West by West. Soon after we tack'd we close reef'd the Topsails, and in the night were obliged to hand them, but at day light set them again. At Noon our Latitude by Observation was 46 degrees 42 minutes South, Cape Saunders bearing North 46 degrees West, distant 68 Miles.

Saturday, 3rd. P.M. Wind and weather as Yesterday. A.M. quite Moderate, yet the South-West swell continues, which makes me conjecture that there is no land near in that quarter. At Noon our Latitude was 46 degrees 42 minutes South, being East of Cape Saunders 1 degree 30 minutes.

Sunday, 4th. At 4 p.m. the Wind coming to the Northward we stood to the Westward with all the sail we could make. In the morning got up Topgallant yards, and set the sails; found the Variation to be 16 degrees 16 minutes East. Saw several Whales, Seals, and one Penguin; this bird was but Small of the sort, but seem'd to be such a one as we had never seen before. We have seen several Seals since we passed the Straits, but never saw one upon the whole Coast of Aeheinomouwe. We sounded both in the Night and the morning, but found no bottom with 150 fathoms Line; at Noon we saw Cape Saunders bearing North 1/2 West; our Latitude by observation was 46 degrees 31 minutes South.* (* The Endeavour had been blown off the land for seven days, and had barely recovered her position.)

[Off South Part of Middle Island, New Zealand.]

Monday, 5th. Most part of P.M. had a fresh breeze at North by East. Half past 1 saw Land bearing West by South, which we steer'd for; before dark we were within 3 or 4 Leagues of it, and seeing no land farther to the South we were in hopes this would prove the Southern point. At 7 shortned sail, and kept under an easy sail all night, standing to the West-South-West, having the wind at North-West, and North-North-West until 2 a.m., when it fell Calm, and soon after a breeze sprung up at South-East by South, and daylight coming on we made sail. During the whole night we saw a large fire upon

- 249 -

the land; a certain sign of its being inhabited. At 7 the Extreams of the land bore from North 38 degrees East to West 6 minutes South, being distant from the Shore about 3 Leagues. The land appear'd of a Moderate height, and not hilly. At 1/2 past 10 o'Clock the westermost land in sight bore West 1/2 North, distant 7 Leagues; at Noon had fresh Gales at South-South-East, and thick hazey weather with rain. Our Latitude by account was 46 degrees 50 minutes South, and Longitude made from Cape Saunders 1 degree 56 minutes West.* (* The ship was now off the south point of the Middle Island.)

Tuesday, 6th. P.M. Winds at South by East and South-East, and thick hazey weather until 3 o'clock, when it clear'd up, and we saw the land extending from North-East by North to North-West 1/2 North, and soon after low land, making like an Island, bearing West 1/2 South. Keeping on our Course to the West by South, we in 2 hours' time saw high land over the low, extending to the Southward as far as South-West by South; we could not see this land join to that to the Northward of us, there either being a total seperation, a deep Bay, or low land between them. At 8 o'Clock, being within 3 Leagues of the low land (which we now took to be an Island* (* Ruapuke Island.)), we Tack'd and stood to the Eastward, having the wind at South, which proved very unsettled all night; by which means, and a little bad management, I found the Ship in the morning considerably farther to the Eastward than I expected, and the wind afterwards coming to South-West and West-South-West, so that at noon we found ourselves much about the same place as we were Yesterday, our Latitude by observation being 46 degrees 50 minutes South, the land extending from North-East by East to West by North 1/2 North, the nearest part bearing North, distance 3 Leagues; the land to the South-West just in sight.

Wednesday, 7th. Light Airs in the South-West quarter. P.M. Clear weather, remainder dark and Cloudy. In the P.M. found the Variation per several Azimuths, and the Amplitude to be 15 degrees 10 minutes East, and by the Amplitude in the morning to be 15 degrees 56 minutes East. Stood to the South-East until 8 a.m., then tack'd and stood to the North-West; but it soon after fell Calm, and continued so until noon, when by our account we were in the Latitude of 47 degrees 6 minutes South, and had made 12 Miles Easting since Yesterday at Noon.

Thursday, 8th. Light Airs next to a Calm from South-South-East to North-East, with which we kept Steering to the South-West, but made but little way because of a swell which took us right ahead. At daylight A.M. we saw, or thought we saw, from the Masthead, the land which we have left to the Northward of us joined to that to the South-West of us; and at the same time we imagined we saw the land extend to the Southward as far as South-South-West; but after steering this Course until noon we discovered our Mistake, for there was no land to be seen to the Southward of West, which Course we now steer'd, being by observation in the Latitude of 47 degrees 12 minutes; Longitude made from Cape Saunders 2 degrees 2 minutes West.

[Off South Cape of New Zealand.]

Friday, 9th. P.M. Winds at North, a Gentle breeze and Clear weather. Stood to the Westward until sunset, at which time the Extreams of the land bore from North by East to West, distant about 7 or 8 Leagues; Depth of Water 55 fathoms; Variation by the Amplitude 16 degrees 29 minutes East. The wind now veer'd to the Westward, and as the weather was fine and Moonlight we kept standing close upon a Wind to the South-West all night. At 4 a.m. Sounded, and had 60 fathoms; at daylight we discover'd under our lee bow Ledges of Rocks, on which the Sea broke very high, extending from South by West to West by South, and not above 3/4 of a Mile from us; yet upon sounding we had 45 fathoms, a Rocky bottom. The wind being at North-West we could not weather the Ledge, and as I did not care to run to leeward, we tackt and made a Trip to the Eastward; but the wind soon after coming to the North enabled us to go clear of all. Our soundings in passing within the Ledge was from 35 to 47 fathoms, a rocky bottom. This Ledge lies South-East, 6 Leagues from the Southermost part of the Land, and South-East by South from some remarkable hills which stand near the Shore. These rocks are not the only dangers that lay here, for about 3 Leagues to the Northward of them is another Ledge of Rocks, laying full 3 Leagues from the land, whereon the Sea broke very high. As we passed these rocks in the night at no great distance, and discover'd the others close under our Lee at daylight, it is apparent that we had a very fortunate Escape. I have named them the Traps, because they lay as such to catch unweary Strangers.* (* The dangerous Traps lie south and east of the South Island of New Zealand. The Endeavour had now at last got to the southward of the land. There is a small but high rock farther south, the Snares, that Cook did not sight this voyage.) At Noon our Latitude per observation was 47 degrees 26 minutes South; Longitude made from Cape Saunders 3 degrees 4 minutes West, the land in sight--which has very much the appearance of an Island* (* South or Stewart Island.)--extending North-East by North to North-West by West, distant from the Shore about 4 or 5 Leagues; the Eastermost ledge of rocks bore South-South-East, distant 1 1/2 Leagues; and Northermost North-East 1/2 East, 3 Leagues. This land is of a moderate height, and has a very barren Aspect; not a Tree to be seen upon it, only a few Small Shrubs. There were several white patches, on which the sun's rays reflected very strongly, which I take to be a kind of Marble such as we have seen in many places of this Country, particularly to the Northward.

Saturday, 10th. P.M. Moderate breezes at North-West by North and North with which we stood close upon a Wind to the Westward. At sunset the

Southermost point of land, which I afterwards named South Cape,* (* South Cape is the southern point of Stewart Island. Cook's position for it is wonderfully exact.) and which lies in the Latitude of 47 degrees 19 minutes South, Longitude 192 degrees 12 minutes West from Greenwich, bore North 38 degrees East, distant 4 Leagues, and the Westermost land in sight bore North 2 degrees East. This last was a small Island, lying off the point of the Main.* (* Long Island, which lies, with others, on the west side of Stewart Island.) I began now to think that this was the Southermost land, and that we should be able to get round it by the West, for we have had a large hollow swell from the South-West ever since we had the last gale of wind from that Quarter, which makes one think there is no land in that direction. In the Night it began to blow, so that at or before daylight we were brought under our 2 Courses; but at 8 a.m. it fell moderate, and we set the Topsails close Reeft, and the Mizn and Mizn Staysail being split, we unbent them and bent others. At Noon, the wind Coming at West, we Tackt and stood to the Northward, having no land in sight; our Latitude by observation was 47 degrees 33 minutes South, Longitude West from the South Cape 0 degrees 59 minutes.

Sunday, 11th. Winds between the West and North-West, a fresh Gale, and Clear weather. Stood away North-North-East close upon a wind without seeing any land until 2 A.M., when we discover'd an Island bearing North-West by North, distant 4 or 5 Leagues. Two hours after this we saw the Land ahead, upon which we Tackt and stood off until 6 o'Clock; then stood in, in order to take a nearer View of it. At 11, being about 3 Leagues from the land, and the wind seem'd to incline on Shore, we Tackt and stood off to the Southward. And now we thought that the land to the Southward, or that we have been sailing round these 2 days past, was an Island, because there appeared an Open Channell between the North part of that land and the South part of the other in which we thought we saw the Small Island we were in with the 6th Instant; but when I came to lay this land down upon paper from the several bearings I had taken, it appeared that there was but little reason to suppose it an Island. On the contrary, I hardly have a doubt but what it joins to, and makes a part of, the Mainland,* (* Cook was deceived, as Stewart is an island.) the Western extremity of which bore at Noon North 59 degrees West, and the Island seen in the Morning* (* This was called by Cook Solander Island.) South 59 degrees West, distant 5 Leagues. Latitude observed 46 degrees 24 minutes South, Longitude 192 degrees 49 minutes West. It is nothing but a barren rock of about a Mile in Circuit, remarkably high, and lies full 5 Leagues from the Main. The shore of the Main lies nearest East by South and West by North, and forms a large open bay, in which there is no appearance of a Harbour or other place of safety for shipping against South-West and Southerly winds. The face of the Country bears a very rugged Aspect, being full of high craggy hills, on the Summits of which were several patches of Snow. However, the land is not wholy barren; we could see wood, not only in the Valleys, but on several of the Hills; but we saw no signs of inhabitants.

Monday, 12th. Fresh Gales between the West and North-West; latter part squally, with rain. Stood to the South-West by South until 11 a.m., at which time the wind shifted to the South-West by West. We wore, and stood to the North-North-West, being then in the Latitude of 47 degrees 40 minutes South, and Longitude 193 degrees 50 minutes West, having a Hollow Sea from the South-West.

Tuesday, 13th. Strong Gale between the South-West by West and South-South-West, with a large Hollow sea from the same Quarter. In the P.M. had frequent Squalls, with Showers of rain; in the night had several very heavy squalls, attended with Showers of Hail, which obliged us to take in our Topsails. During the night steer'd North-North-West until 6 a.m., when, seeing no land, we steer'd North by East, and set the Main Topsail, single reeft. At 8 set the Foretopsail, single reeft, and loosed all the Reefs out of the Maintopsail, and Steer'd North-East by East 1/2 East in order to make the land. At 10 saw it bearing East-North-East, and appeared to be very high; but, being hazey over it, we could see nothing distinct neither now nor at Noon, when, by Observation, we were in the Latitude of 46 degrees 0 minutes South. Course and distance Sailed since Yesterday North 5 degrees West, 96 Miles. Longitude made from the South Cape 1 degree 40 minutes West.

[Off the New Zealand Sounds.]

Wednesday, 14th. In the P.M. had a fresh Gale from the Southward, attended with Squalls. At 2 it Clear'd up over the land, which appeared high and Mountainous. At 1/2 past 3 double reeft the Topsails, and hauld in for a Bay, wherein their appear'd to be good Anchorage, and into which I had thought of going with the Ship; but after standing in an hour, we found the distance too great to run before dark, and it blow'd too hard to attempt it in the night, or even to keep to Windward; for these reasons we gave it up, and bore away along shore. This bay I have named Dusky Bay. It lies in the Latitude of 45 degrees 47 minutes South; it is about 3 or 4 Miles broad at the Entrance, and seems to be full as deep. In it are several Islands, behind which there must be Shelter from all winds, provided there is a Sufficient Depth of Water.* (* Dusky Bay is one of the remarkable inlets known now as the New Zealand Sounds. They are very deep, narrow fiords, running into the high mountains, that here come close to the shore, and are much visited now for the sake of the grandeur of the scenery. Cook visited and surveyed Dusky Bay in his next voyage. The Endeavour had nearly as much tempestuous weather in rounding the south end of New Zealand as she had off the North Cape; but

Cook managed to get a very fair idea of the coast, notwithstanding, by dint of perseverance.) The North point of this bay, when it bears South-East by South, is very remarkable, there being off it 5 high peaked rocks, standing up like the 4 fingers and thumb of a Man's hand; on which account I have named it Point Five Fingers. The land of this point is farther remarkable by being the only Level land near it, and extends near 2 Leagues to the Northward. It is pretty high, wholy cover'd with wood, and hath very much the Appearance of an Island, by its aspect being so very different from the Land behind it, which is nothing but barren rocky Mountains. At Sunset the Southermost Land in sight bore due South, distant 5 or 6 Leagues; and as this is the Westermost point of land upon the whole Coast I have called it West Cape. It lies about 3 Leagues to the Southward of the bay above-mentioned, in the Latitude of 45 degrees 54 minutes South, and Longitude 193 degrees 17 minutes West. The land of this Cape seems to be of a moderate height next the Sea, and hath Nothing remarkable about it that we could see, Except a very White Clift 2 or 3 Leagues to the Southward of it. The land to the Southward of Cape West trends away towards the South-East; to the Northward of it it Trends North-North-East and North-East. At 7 o'Clock brought the Ship too under the Foresail, with her head off Shore, having a fresh Gale at South by East. At Midnight it moderated, and we wore and lay her head in shore until 4 a.m.; then made Sail, and Steer'd along shore North-East 1/2 North, having a moderate breeze at South-South-East. At Noon we were by observation in the Latitude 45 degrees 13 minutes South; Course and distance sailed since Yesterday North 41 degrees East, 62 Miles; Longitude made from Cape West 0 degrees 29 minutes East, being at this time about 1 1/2 Leagues from Shore. Sounded, and had no ground with 70 fathoms Line. A little before Noon we passed a little Narrow opening in the land, where there appear'd to be a very Snug Harbour,* (* Doubtful Sound, another of the fiords mentioned in note above.) form'd by an Island, in the Latitude of 45 degrees 16 minutes South; inland, behind this Opening, were Mountains, the summits of which were Cover'd with Snow that seem'd to have fallen lately, and this is not to be wondered at, for we have found it very cold for these 2 days past. The land on each side the Entrance of this Harbour riseth almost perpendicular from the Sea to a very considerable Height; and this was the reason why I did not attempt to go in with the Ship, because I saw clearly that no winds could blow there but what was right in or right out, that is, Westerly or Easterly; and it certainly would have been highly imprudent in me to have put into a place where we could not have got out but with a wind that we have lately found to blow but one day in a Month. I mention this because there was some on board that wanted me to harbour at any rate, without in the least Considering either the present or future Consequences.

Thursday, 15th. Clear weather, Winds at South-West and South-West by South, a Gentle breeze, except in the night, when we had variable light Airs and Calm. In the evening, being about 2 Leagues from the land, we sounded, but had no ground with 103 fathoms. Variation per Azimuth 14 degrees East, per Amplitude 15 degrees 2 minutes East. With what wind we had we made the best of our way along shore to the North-East, keeping at the distance of 2 or 3 Leagues off from the Land. At Noon we were in the Latitude of 44 degrees 47 minutes, having run only 12 Leagues upon a North-East 1/4 North Course since Yesterday at Noon; Longitude made from Cape West 1 degree 3 minutes East.

Friday, 16th. Winds at South-West; a fresh breeze and Clear. Steer'd along shore North-East 1/4 East until 6 p.m., when we Shortned Sail, and brought too for the Night. Variation per Azimuth 13 degrees 48 minutes East. At 4 A.M. made sail, and Stood in for the land. At daylight saw the appearance of an inlet into the land; but upon a nearer approach found that it was only a deep Valley, bounded on each side by high lands, upon which we bore away North-East 1/4 East along shore, keeping about 4 or 5 miles off. At Noon the Northermost point of land in sight bore North 60 degrees East, distant 10 Miles; Latitude per Observation 44 degrees 5 minutes; Longitude made from Cape West 2 degrees 8 minutes East.

Saturday, 17th. Continued our Course along shore, having in the P.M. the advantage of a fresh Gale at South-West. At 2, past by the point aforementioned, which is of a Moderate height, with deep Red Clifts, down which falls 4 Small streams of Water, on which account it is named Cascades Point. Latitude 44 degrees 0 minutes South; Longitude 2 degrees 20 minutes East from Cape West. From this point the land at first Trends North 76 degrees East, but afterwards more to the Northward East-North-East, 8 Leagues. From this point and near the Shore lies a small low Island, which bore from us South by East, distant 1 1/2 Leagues. At 7 o'Clock we Shortned sail, and brought too under the Topsails, with her head off Shore, having 33 fathoms, and fine sandy bottom. At 10, had 50 fathoms, and at 12, wore in 65 fathoms, having drove about 5 Miles North-North-West since we brought too. Two hours after this had no ground with 140 fathoms; which shews that the soundings extend but a little way from the land. From 2 to 8 a.m. had it Calm and hazey, with drizzling rain, at which time a breeze sprung up at South-West, with which we steer'd along shore North-East by East 1/4 East, keeping about 3 Leagues from the land. At Noon had no Observation, being Hazey with rain. Our run since Yesterday at Noon is North-East by East, 55 Miles; Longitude from Cape West 3 degrees 12 minutes East.

[Off West Coast of Middle Island, New Zealand.]

Sunday, 18th. In the P.M. had a fresh breeze at South-West by West, attended with drizzling rain. At 8, being about 3 Leagues from the land, shortned sail, and brought too, having run 10 Leagues North-East by East since noon; at this time had 44 fathoms, and 2 hours before had 17 fathoms, fine sandy bottom, being then about 1 League from the land. Had it Calm the most part of the Night, and until 10 a.m., when a light breeze sprung up at South-West by West. We Made sail along shore North-East by North, having a large swell from the West-South-West, which had risen in the Night. At Noon Latitude in per Observation 43 degrees 4 minutes South; Course and distance sail'd since Yesterday is North 54 degrees East, 54 Miles; Longitude made from Cape West 4 degrees 12 minutes East. The Mountains and some of the Vallies we observed this morning were wholy cover'd with Snow, part of which we suppos'd to have fallen in the P.M. and fore part of the Night, at the time that we had rain--and yet the weather is not Cold.* (* They did not see Mount Cook, 12,300 feet high, and the highest mountain in New Zealand; no doubt the summit was in the clouds.)

Monday, 19th. In the P.M. had a fresh breeze at South-West by West and West-South-West, which we made the most of until 6, when we shortned sail, and at 10 brought too, and sounded 115 fathoms, judging ourselves to be about 5 Leagues from the land. At midnight it fell little wind, on which account we made sail. At 8 a.m. the wind veer'd to the North-West by North, with which we stood to the North-East close upon a wind until noon, at which time we Tack'd, being about 3 Leagues from the land, and by Observation in the Latitude of 42 degrees 8 minutes and Longitude from Cape West 5 degrees 5 minutes East* (* The Endeavour had passed the mouth of the Grey River, the district of the great coalfields of New Zealand.) Course and distance run since Yesterday at Noon North 35 degrees East, 68 Miles; Depth of Water 65 fathoms, the land extending from North-East by North to South-South-West.

Tuesday, 20th. Fresh Gales at North-West by North and North by West. P.M. fair weather; the remainder hazey, with rain, and Squall, which brought us under close Reeft Topsails. Stood to the Westward until 2 a.m., when we made a Trip to the Eastward, and afterwards stood to the Westward until Noon, when, by our reckoning, we were in the Latitude of 42 degrees 23 minutes South. Course and distance sail'd South 74 degrees West, 54 Miles; Longitude made from Cape West 5 degrees 55 minutes East. Tack'd and stood to the Eastward.

Wednesday, 21st. In the P.M. had a fresh Gale at North by West, attended with rain until 6, when the Wind shifted to South and South-South-West, and continued to blow a fresh Gale, with which we steer'd North-East by North until 6 A.M., at which time we haul'd in East by North in order to make the land which we saw soon after. At Noon our Latitude per Account was 41 degrees 37 minutes, and Longitude from Cape West 5 degrees 42 minutes East; Course and distance sail'd since Yesterday North 60 degrees East, 92 miles. At this time we were not above 3 or 4 Leagues from the land, but being very foggy upon it we could see nothing distinct, and as we had not much wind, and a prodigious swell rowling in upon the Shore from the West-South-West, I did not think it safe to go nearer.

Thursday, 22nd. In the P.M. had a Gentle breeze from the South-South-West, with which we steer'd along shore North-East until 8, when being about 2 or 3 Leagues from shore we sounded, and had 34 fathoms, upon which we haul'd off North-West by North until 11, then brought too, having at this time 64 fathoms. At 4 a.m. made sail to the North-East, wind at South-South-West, a light breeze. At 8 the wind veer'd to the Westward, and soon after fell Calm; at this time we were about 3 or 4 Miles from the Shore, and in 54 fathoms, having a large swell from the West-South-West rowling Obliquely upon the Shore, which put me under a good deal of Apprehension that we should be obliged to Anchor; but by the help of a light Air now and then from the South-West quarter we were Enabled to keep the Ship from driving much nearer the shore. At Noon the Northermost land in sight bore North-East by East 1/4 East, distant 8 or 10 Leagues; our Latitude by account was 40 degrees 55 minutes South, Longitude from Cape West 6 degrees 35 minutes East; Course and distance sail'd since Yesterday at Noon North 36 degrees East, 42 Miles; very foggy over the Land.

[Off Cape Farewell, Middle Island, New Zealand.]

Friday, 23rd. Light Airs from the Southward, at intervals Calm, the fore part hazey, the remainder clear, pleasant weather. At Noon our Latitude, by observation, 40 degrees 36 minutes 30 seconds South, Longitude from Cape West 6 degrees 52 minutes East; the Eastermost point of Land in sight* (* Cape Farewell, the north point of the Middle Island.) bore East 10 degrees North, distant 7 Leagues, and a bluff head or point we were abreast of yesterday at Noon, off which lay some rocks above Water, bore South 18 degrees West, distant 6 Leagues. This point I have named Rocks Point, Latitude 40 degrees 55 minutes South. Having now nearly run down the whole of this North-West Coast of Tovy Poenammu, it is time I should describe the face of the Country as it hath at different times appeared to us. I have mentioned on the 11th Instant, at which time we were off the Southern part of the Island, that the land seen then was rugged and mountainous; and there is great reason to believe that the same ridge of Mountains extends nearly the whole length of the Island from between the Westermost Land seen that day and the Eastermost seen on the 13th. There is a space of about 6 or 8 Leagues of the sea Coast unexplored, but the Mountains inland were Visible enough. The land near the Shore about Cape West is rather low, and riseth with a gradual assent up to the foot of the

Mountains, and appear'd to be mostly covered with wood. From Point Five Fingers down to the Latitude of 44 degrees 20 minutes there is a narrow ridge of Hills rising directly from the Sea, which are Cloathed with wood; close behind these hills lies the ridge of Mountains, which are of a Prodidgious height, and appear to consist of nothing but barren rocks, covered in many places with large patches of Snow, which perhaps have lain there since the Creation. No country upon Earth can appear with a more rugged and barren Aspect than this doth; from the Sea for as far inland as the Eye can reach nothing is to be seen but the Summits of these rocky Mountains, which seem to lay so near one another as not to admit any Vallies between them. From the Latitude of 44 degrees 20 minutes to the Latitude 42 degrees 8 minutes these mountains lay farther inland; the Country between them and the Sea consists of woody Hills and Vallies of Various extent, both for height and Depth, and hath much the Appearance of Fertility. Many of the Vallies are large, low, and flatt, and appeared to be wholy covered with Wood; but it is very probable that great part of the land is taken up in Lakes, Ponds, etc., as is very common in such like places. From the last mentioned Latitude to Cape Farewell, afterwards so Called, the land is not distinguished by anything remarkable; it rises into hills directly from the Sea, and is covered with wood. While we were upon this part of the Coast the weather was foggy, in so much that we could see but a very little way inland; however, we sometimes saw the Summits of the Mountains above the fogg and Clouds, which plainly shew'd that the inland parts were high and Mountainous, and gave me great reason to think that there is a Continued Chain of Mountains from the one End of the Island to the other.* (* This is, to a great extent, the case.)

Saturday, 24th. In the P.M. had a Gentle breeze at South-West, which by Dark run us the length of the Eastern Point set at Noon, and not knowing what Course the land took on the other side, we brought too in 34 fathoms about one League from the land. At 8, it falling little wind, we fill'd and stood on until 12, at which time we brought too until 4 a.m., then made Sail. At daylight we saw low land extending from the above point to the East-South-East as far as the Eye could reach, the Eastern Extremity of which appear'd in round Hillocks; by this time the wind had veer'd to the Eastward, which obliged us to ply to windward. At Noon the point above mention'd bore South-West by South, distant 16 miles; Latitude observ'd 40 degrees 19 minutes South. This point I afterwards named Cape Farewell, for reasons which will be given in their proper place.

Sunday, 25th. Winds Easterly; towards Noon had little winds and hazey, with rain. Made several trips, but gain'd nothing to Windward, so that at Noon our Situation was nearly as Yesterday.

Monday, 26th. At 3 p.m. the wind came to North, and we Steer'd East-South-East with all the Sail we could set until dark, when we shortned sail until the morning, having thick Misty weather. All Night we keept the lead going continually, and had from 37 to 48 fathoms. At day light we saw the land bearing South-East by East, and an Island laying near it bearing East-South-East, distant 5 Leagues. This I knew to be the Island* (* Stephens Island.) seen from the Entrance of Queen Charlotte's sound, from which it bears North-West by North, Distant 9 Leagues. At Noon it bore South-East, distant 4 or 5 miles, and the North-West head of Queen Charlotte's sound bore South-East by South, distant 10 1/2 Leagues; Latitude ohserv'd 43 degrees 33 minutes South.

[In Admiralty Bay, Middle Island, New Zealand.]

Tuesday, 27th. Fresh breeze of Wind Westerly, and hazey, Misty weather, with Drizling rain. As we have now Circumnavigated the whole of this Country, it is time for me to think of quitting it; but before I do this it will be necessary to compleat our Water first, especially as we have on board above 30 Tons of Casks empty, and knowing that there is a Bay between the above-mentioned Island and Queen Charlotte's sound, wherein no doubt there is Anchorage and convenient Watering places. Accordingly, in the P.M. we hauled round the Island and into the bay,* (* Admiralty Bay.) leaving 3 more Islands* (* Rangitoto Islets.) on our Starboard hand, which lay close under the West Shore 3 or 4 Miles within the Entrance. As we run in we keept the lead going, and had from 40 to 12 fathoms. At 6 we Anchor'd in 11 fathoms, Muddy bottom, under the West Shore, in the Second Cove within the fore-mentioned Island. At daylight I took a Boat and went to look for a Watering place, and a proper birth to moor the Ship in, both of which I found convenient enough. After the Ship was moor'd I sent an Officer ashore to Superintend the Watering, and the Carpenter with his Crew to cut wood, while the Long boat was employed carrying on shore Empty Casks.

Wednesday, 28th. Winds Westerly, which in the A.M. blow'd a fresh Gale, attended with rain. Employ'd getting on board Wood and Water and fishing; in the Latter we were pretty Successfull.

Thursday, 29th. In the P.M. had a Strong Gale from the Westward. A.M. Variable light Airs from the Eastward and hazey rainy weather the whole day; which, however, did not prevent us getting on board Wood and Water.

Friday, 30th. Winds at South-East, a moderate breeze; the first and middle part dark, Hazey weather, with rain; the latter, fair. In the A.M., as the wind seem'd to be settled at South-East, and having nearly compleated our Water, we warped the Ship out of the Cove in order to have room to get under Sail. Before this was done it was Noon, at which time I went away in the Pinnace, in order to examine the Bay, and to Explore as much of it as the little time I had would Admit.

Saturday, 31st. In the P.M., after rowing a League and a half or 2 Leagues up the Bay, I Landed upon a point of Land on the West side, where, from an Eminency, I could see this Western Arm of the Bay run in South-West by West, about 5 Leagues farther, yet did not see the Head of it. There appeared to be several other inlets, or at least small bays, between this and the North-West head of Queen Charlotte's sound, in every one of which I make no doubt but what there is Anchorage and Shelter for Shipping, as they are partly cover'd from the Sea wind by these Islands that lay without them.* (* There is a maze of inlets and harbours between Admiralty Bay and Queen Charlotte's Sound, a distance of 20 miles.) The land about this bay, at least what I could see of it, is of a very hilly, uneven Surface, and appears to be mostly cover'd with wood, Shrubs, Firns, etc., which renders Travelling both difficult and Fatiguing. I saw no inhabitants, neither have we seen any since we have been in this bay, but met with several of their Huts, all of which appear'd to have been at least 12 Months deserted.

Upon my return to the Ship, in the Evening, I found the Water, etc., all on board, and the Ship ready for Sea; and being now resolv'd to quit this Country altogether, and to bend my thought towards returning home by such a rout as might Conduce most to the Advantage of the Service I am upon, I consulted with the Officers upon the most Eligible way of putting this in Execution. To return by the way of Cape Horn was what I most wished, because by this rout we should have been able to prove the Existance or Non-Existance of a Southern Continent, which yet remains Doubtfull; but in order to Ascertain this we must have kept in a higher Latitude in the very Depth of Winter, but the Condition of the Ship, in every respect, was not thought sufficient for such an undertaking. For the same reason the thoughts of proceeding directly to the Cape of Good Hope was laid aside, especially as no discovery of any Moment could be hoped for in that rout. It was therefore resolved to return by way of the East Indies by the following rout: upon Leaving this Coast to steer to the Westward until we fall in with the East Coast of New Holland, and then to follow the direction of that Coast to the Northward, or what other direction it might take us, until we arrive at its Northern extremity; and if this should be found impracticable, then to Endeavour to fall in with the Land or Islands discovered by Quiros.* (* Quiros, a Spanish navigator, discovered in 1605 Espiritu Santo, the northern island of the New Hebrides, which he supposed to be a part of a great southern continent. Cook, in his second voyage, thoroughly explored the New Hebrides group; and for some of the islands his charts are still the only guide.)

With this view, at daylight we got under Sail and put to Sea, having the Advantage of a fresh Gale at South-East and Clear weather. At Noon the Island, which lies off the North-West point of the Bay, bore East 9 degrees

South, distant 10 Miles; our Latitude, by Observation, was 40 degrees 35 minutes South. This bay I have named Admiralty Bay; the North-West point Cape Stephens, and the East Point Jackson, after the 2 Secretarys.* (* The two secretaries of the Admiralty, Philip Stephens and George Jackson, both of whom showed great appreciation of Cook.) It may always be known by the Island above mentioned, which is pretty high, and lies North-East, 2 Miles from Cape Stephens; Latitude 40 degrees 37 minutes South; Longitude 185 degrees 6 minutes West. Between this Island and Cape Farewell, which is West by North and East by South, distant 14 or 15 Leagues from each other, the Shore forms a large deep Bay, the bottom of which we could hardly see in sailing in a Strait line from the one Cape to the other; but it is not at all improbable but what it is all lowland next the Sea, as we have met with less water here than on any other part of the Coast at the same distance from Land; however, a Bay there is, and is known on the Chart by the Name of Blind Bay, but I have reason to believe it to be Tasman's Murderers' Bay.* (* Blind Bay is now also known as Tasman Bay, and Massacre Bay is supposed to be a smaller bay in it, on the north-western side.)

Before I quit this land altogether I shall give a short general discription of the Country, its inhabitants, their manners, Customs, etc., in which it is necessary to observe that many things are founded only on Conjecture, for we were too short a time in any one place to learn much of their interior policy, and therefore could only draw conclusions from what we saw at different times.

[Description of New Zealand.]

SOME ACCOUNT OF NEW ZEALAND.

Part of the East* (* This should be West Coast.) Coast of this Country was first discovered by Abel Tasman in 1642, and by him called New Zeland; he, however, never landed upon it; probably he was discouraged from it by the Natives killing 3 or 4 of his People at the first and only place he Anchor'd at. This country, which before now was thought to be a part of the imaginary Southern Continent, consists of 2 large Islands, divided from each other by a Strait or Passage of 4 or 5 Leagues broad. They are situated between the Latitude of 34 and 48 degrees South, and between the Longitude of 181 and 194 degrees West from the Meridian of Greenwich. The situation of few parts of the world are better determin'd than these Islands are, being settled by some hundreds of Observations of the Sun and Moon, and one of the Transit of Mercury made by Mr. Green, who was sent out by the Royal Society to observe the Transit of Venus.

The Northermost of these Islands, as I have before observed, is called by the Natives Aeheinomouwe and the Southermost Tovy Poenammu. The former name, we were well assured, comprehends the whole of the Northern Island; but we were not so well satisfied with the latter whether it comprehended the whole of the Southern Islands or only a part of it. This last, according to the Natives of Queen Charlotte's Sound, ought to consist of 2 Islands, one of which at least we were to have sail'd round in a few days; but this was not verify'd by our own Observations. I am inclinable to think that they know'd no more of this land than what came within the Limits of their sight.* (* As before remarked, the natives at Queen Charlotte's Sound doubtless were speaking of the large peninsula and the islands which lie west of the Sound. There is a spot at the isthmus where canoes could be hauled over.) The Chart* (* See copy of this chart.) which I have drawn will best point out the figure and Extent of these Islands, the situation of the Bays and Harbours they contain, and the lesser Islands lay about them.

And now I have mentioned the Chart, I shall point out such places as are drawn with sufficient accuracy to be depended upon and such as are not, beginning at Cape Pallisser and proceed round Aeheinomouwe by the East Cape, etc. The Coast between these 2 Capes I believe to be laid down pretty accurate, both in its figure and the Course and distance from point to point; the opportunities I had and the methods I made use on to obtain these requisites were such as could hardly admit of an Error. From the East Cape to Cape Maria Van Diemen, altho' it cannot be perfectly true, yet it is without any very Material error; some few places, however, must be excepted, and these are very Doubtfull, and are not only here, but in every other part of the Chart pointed out by a Pricked or broken line. From Cape Maria Van Diemen up as high as the Latitude of 36 degrees 15 minutes we seldom were nearer the Shore than from 5 to 8 Leagues, and therefore the line of the Sea Coast may in some places be erroneous. From the above Latitude to nearly the Length of Entry Island we run along and near the shore all the way, and no circumstance occurd that made me liable to commit any Material error. Excepting Cape Teerawhitte, we never came near the Shore between Entry Island and Cape Pallisser, and therefore this part of the coast may be found to differ something from the truth; in Short, I believe that this Island will never be found to differ Materially from the figure I have given it, and that the Coast Affords few or no Harbours but what are either taken notice of in this Journal, or in some Measure pointed out in the Chart; but I cannot say so much for Tovy Poenammu. The Season of the Year and Circumstance of the Voyage would not permit me to spend so much time about this Island as I had done at the other, and the blowing weather we frequently met with made it both dangerous and difficult to keep upon the Coast. However, I shall point out the places that may be Erroneous in this as I have done in the other. From Queen Charlotte's sound to Cape Campbell, and as far to the South-West as the Latitude 43 degrees, will be found to be pretty Accurate; between this Latitude and the Latitude 44 degrees 20 minutes the coast is very Doubtfully laid down, a part of which we hardly, if at all, saw. From this last mentioned Latitude to Cape Saunders we were generally at too great a distance to be Particular, and the weather at the same time was unfavourable. The Coast, as it is laid down from Cape Saunders to Cape South, and even to Cape West, is no doubt in many places very erroneous, as we hardly were ever able to keep near the Shore, and were sometimes blown off altogether. From the West Cape down to Cape Farewell, and even to Queen Charlotte's sound, will in most places be found to differ not much from the truth.* (* Cook's open and plain statement as to the comparative accuracy of different parts of his chart is much to be commended. It has been too much the fashion with first explorers to leave such matters to be discovered by the student. But the astonishing accuracy of his outline of New Zealand must be the admiration of all who understand the difficulties of laying down a coast; and when it is considered that this coastline is 2400 miles in extent, the magnitude of the task will be realised by everybody. Never has a coast been so well laid down by a first explorer, and it must have required unceasing vigilance and continual observation, in fair weather and foul, to arrive at such a satisfactory conclusion; and with such a dull sailer as the Endeavour was, the six and a half months occupied in the work must be counted as a short interval in which to do it.)

[Animals, Timber, etc., New Zealand.]

Mention is likewise made in the Chart of the appearance or aspect of the face of the Country. With respect to Tovy Poenammu, it is for the most part very Mountainous, and to all appearance a barren Country. The people in Queen Charlotte's sound--those that came off to us from under the Snowy Mountain, and the five we saw to the South-West of Cape Saunders--were all the inhabitants, or Signs of inhabitants, we saw upon the whole Island; but most part of the Sea Coast of Aeheinomouwe, except the South-West side, is well inhabited; and although it is a hilly, Mountainous Country, yet the very Hills and Mountains are many of them cover'd with wood, and the Soil of the plains and Valleys appear'd to be very rich and fertile, and such as we had an opportunity to examine we found to be so, and not very much incumber'd with woods.

It was the Opinion of every body on board that all sorts of European grain, fruit, Plants, etc., would thrive here; in short, was this Country settled by an industrious people they would very soon be supplied not only with the necessaries, but many of the Luxuries, of Life. The Sea, Bays, and Rivers abound with a great Variety of Excellent Fish, the most of them unknown in England, besides Lobsters, which were allowed by every one to be the best they ever had eat. Oysters and many other sorts of shell fish all Excellent in their kind. Sea and Water Fowls of all sorts are, however, in no great plenty; those known in Europe are Ducks, Shags, Gannets, and Gulls, all of which were Eat by us, and found exceeding good; indeed, hardly anything came Amiss to us that could be Eat by Man. Land fowl are likewise in no great plenty, and all of them, except Quails, are, I believe, unknown in Europe; these are exactly like those we have in England. The Country is certainly destitute of all sorts of beasts, either wild or tame, except dogs and Rats; the former are tame, and lived with the people, who breed and bring them up for no other purpose than to Eat, and rats are so scarce that not only I, but many others in the Ship, never see one. Altho' we have seen some few Seals, and once a Sea Lion upon this Coast, yet I believe they are not only very scarce,* (* There are a good many seals round the southern part of New Zealand, and a regular fishery is now established on Stewart Island. Cook saw nothing of the few natives that occupied the southern parts of the Island.) but seldom or ever come ashore; for if they did the Natives would certainly find out some Method of Killing them, the Skins of which they no doubt would preserve for Cloathing, as well as the Skins of Dogs and birds, the only Skins we ever saw among them. But they must sometimes get Whales, because many of the Patta Pattoas are made of the bones of some such fish, and an Ornament they wear at their breast (on which they set great Value), which are supposed to be made of the Tooth of a Whale; and yet we know of no method or instrument they have to kill these Animals.

In the woods are plenty of Excellent Timber, fit for all purposes except Ships' Masts; and perhaps upon a Close Examination some might be found not improper for that purpose. There grows spontainously everywhere a kind of very broad-bladed grass, like flags of the Nature of Hemp,* (* The New Zealand flax (Phormium Tenax) is now a considerable article of commerce. It furnishes a very strong fibre, and is made into rope, etc.) of which might be made the very best of Cordage and Canvas, etc. There are 2 sorts, one finer than the other; of these the Natives make Cloth, rope, Lines, netts, etc. Iron Ore is undoubtedly to be found here, particularly about Mercury Bays, where we found great quantities of Iron sand; however, we met with no Ore of any Sort, neither did we ever see any sort of Metal with the Natives. We met with some stones at Admiralty Bay that appear'd to be Mineral in some degree, but Dr. Solander was of Opinion that they contain'd no Sort of Metal* (* Gold and coal have been found in New Zealand in large quantities. Gold at Otago and Hokatika in the South Island, and at Thames in the North. The coalfields round the Grey River are enormous, and have no doubt a great future; and this useful mineral is also found in the Bay of Islands, and other places in the North Island. Other metals, as copper, silver, antimony, have also been found and worked.) The white stone we saw near the South Cape and some other parts to the Southward, which I took to be a kind of Marble, such as I had seen on one of the Hills I was upon in Mercury Bay, Mr. Banks--I afterwards found--was of Opinion that they were Mineral to the highest degree; he is certainly a much better Judge of these things than I am, and therefore I might be mistaken in my opinion, which was only founded on what I had before seen not only in this Country, but in other parts where I have been; and at the same time I must observe we were not less than 6 or 8 Leagues from the Land, and nearer it was not possible for us at that time to come without running the Ship into Apparent Danger. However, I am no Judge how far Mineral can be distinguished as such; certain it is that in Southern parts of this Country there are whole Mountains of Nothing Else but stone, some of which, no doubt, may be found to contain Metal.

Should it ever become an object of settling this Country, the best place for the first fixing of a Colony would be either in the River Thames or the Bay of Islands; for at either of these places they would have the advantage of a good Harbour, and by means of the former an Easy Communication would be had, and settlements might be extended into the inland parts of the Country. For a very little trouble and Expence small Vessels might be built in the River proper for the Navigation thereof. It is too much for me to assert how little water a Vessel ought to draw to Navigate this River, even so far up as I was in the Boat; this depends intirely upon the Depth of Water that is upon the bar or flat that lay before the narrow part of the River, which I had not an opportunity of making myself acquainted with, but I am of Opinion that a Vessel that draws not above 10 or 12 feet may do it with Ease. So far as I have been able to Judge of the Genius of these people it does not appear to me to be at all difficult for Strangers to form a settlement in this Country; they seem to be too much divided among themselves to unite in opposing, by which means, and kind and Gentle usage, the Colonists would be able to form strong parties among them.

The Natives of this Country are a Strong, rawboned, well made, Active People, rather above than under the common size, especially the Men; they are of a very dark brown colour, with black hair, thin black beards, and white teeth, and such as do not disfigure their faces by tattowing, etc., have in general very good features. The Men generally wear their Hair long, Coomb'd up, and tied upon the Crown of their Heads; some of the women were it long and loose upon their Shoulders, old women especially; others again were it crop'd short. Their coombs are made some of bones, and others of Wood; they sometimes Wear them as an Ornament stuck upright in their Hair. They seem to enjoy a good state of Health, and many of them live to a good old Age.* (* The Maoris were remarkable for longevity, and for health and strength in old age.) Many of the old and some of the Middle aged Men have their faces mark'd or tattow'd with black, and some few we have seen who have had their buttocks, thighs, and other parts of their bodies marked, but this is less common. The figures they mostly use are spirals, drawn and connected together with great nicety and judgement. They are so exact in the application of these Figures that no difference can be found between the one side of the face and the other, if the whole is marked, for some have only one side, and some a little on both sides; hardly any but the old Men have the whole tattow'd. From this I conclude that it takes up some time, perhaps Years, to finish the Operation, which all Who have begun may not have perseverance enough to go through, as the manner in which it must be done must certainly cause intollerable pain, and may be the reason why so few are Marked at all--at least I know no other. The Women inlay the Colour of Black under the skins of their lips, and both sexes paint their faces and bodies at times more or less with red Oker, mixed with fish Oil.

[Clothing of New Zealanders.]

Their common Cloathing are very much like square Thrumb'd Matts, that are made of rope Yarns, to lay at the doors or passages into houses to clean ones shoes upon. These they tie round their necks, the Thrumb'd side out, and are generally large enough to cover the body as low as the knee; they are made with very little Preparation of the broad Grass plant before mentioned. Beside the Thrumb'd Matts, as I call them, they have other much finer cloathing, made of the same plant after it is bleached and prepared in such a Manner that it is as white and almost as soft as flax, but much stronger. Of this they make pieces of cloth about 5 feet long and 4 broad; these are wove some pieces close and others very open; the former are as stout as the strongest sail cloth, and not unlike it, and yet it is all work'd or made by hand with no other Instrument than a Needle or Bodkin. To one end of every piece is generally work'd a very neat border of different colours of 4 or 6 inches broad, and they very often Trim them with pieces of Dog Skin or birds' feathers. These pieces of Cloth they wear as they do the other, tying one End round their Necks with a piece of string, to one end of which is fixed a Needle or Bodkin made of Bone, by means of which they can easily fasten, or put the string through any part of the Cloth; they sometimes wear pieces of this kind of Cloth round their Middles, as well as over their Shoulders. But this is not common, especially with the Men, who hardly ever wear anything round their Middles, observing no sort of Decency in that respect; neither is it at all uncommon for them to go quite Naked without any one thing about them besides a belt round their waists, to which is generally fastened a small string, which they tye round the prepuse; in this manner I have seen hundreds of them come off to and on board the Ship, but they generally had their proper Cloathing in the boat along with them to put on if it rain'd, etc. The Women, on the other hand, always wear something round their Middle; generally a short, thrumbd Matt, which reaches as low as their Knees. Sometimes, indeed, I have seen them with only a Bunch of grass or plants before, tyed on with a piece of fine platting made of sweet-scented grass; they likewise wear a piece of cloth over their Shoulders as the Men do; this is generally of the Thrum kind. I hardly ever saw a Woman wear a piece of fine cloth. One day at Talago I saw a strong proof that the Women never appear naked, at least before strangers. Some of us hapned to land upon a small Island where several of them were Naked in the Water, gathering of Lobsters and shell fish; as soon as they saw us some of them hid themselves among the Rocks, and the rest remain'd in the Sea until they had made themselves Aprons of the Sea Weed; and even then, when they came out to us, they shew'd Manifest signs of Shame, and those who had no method of hiding their nakedness would by no means appear before us.

The Women have all very soft Voices, and may by that alone be known from the Men. The Making of cloth and all other Domestick work is, I believe, wholy done by them, and the more Labourious work, such as building Boats, Houses, Tilling the ground, etc., by the Men. Both men and women wear ornaments at their Ears and about their Necks; these are made of stone, bone, Shells, etc., and are variously shaped; and some I have seen wear human Teeth and finger Nails, and I think we were told that they did belong to their deceased friends. The Men, when they are dressed, generally wear 2 or 3 long white feathers stuck upright in their Hair, and at Queen Charlotte's sound many, both men and women, wore Round Caps made of black feathers.

[War Practices of New Zealanders.]

The old men are much respected by the younger, who seem to be govern'd and directed by them on most Occasions. We at first thought that they were united under one head or Chief, whose Name is Teeratu; we first heard of him in Poverty Bay, and he was own'd as Chief by every one we met with from Cape Kidnappers to the Northward and Westward as far as the Bay of Plenty, which is a great extent of territories for an Indian Prince. When we were upon the East Coast they always pointed inland to the Westward for the place of his residence, which I believe to be in the Bay of Plenty, and that those Hippas or fortified Towns are Barrier Towns either for or against him; but most likely the former, and if so, may be the utmost Extent of his Dominions to the Westwards, for at Mercury bay they did not own him as their Prince, nor no where else either to the Westward or Southward, or any other single person; for at whatever place we put in at, or whatever people we spoke with upon the Coast, they generally told us that those that were at a little distance from them were their Enemies; from which it appear'd to me that they were very much divided into Parties, which make war one with another, and all their Actions and behaviour towards us tended to prove that they are a brave, open, war-like people, and void of Treachery.

Whenever we were Visited by any number of them that had never heard or seen anything of us before they generally came off in the largest Canoe they had, some of which will carry 60, 80, or 100 people. They always brought their best Cloaths along with them, which they put on as soon as they came near the Ship. In each Canoe were generally an old Man, in some 2 or 3; these used always to direct the others, were better Cloathed, and generally carried a Halbard or Battle Axe in their hands, or some such like thing that distinguished them from the others. As soon as they came within about a Stone's throw of the Ship they would there lay, and call out, "Haromoi harenta a patoo ago!" that is, "Come here, come ashore with us, and we will kill you with our patoo patoos!" and at the same time would shake them at us. At times they would dance the War dance, and other times they would trade with and talk to us, and Answer such Questions as were put to them with all the Calmness imaginable, and then again begin the War Dance, shaking their Paddles, Patoo patoos, etc., and make strange contortions at the same time. As soon as they had worked themselves up to a proper pitch they would begin to attack us with Stones and darts, and oblige us, wether we would or no, to fire upon them. Musquetry they never regarded unless they felt the Effect; but great Guns they did, because they threw stones farther than they could Comprehend. After they found that our Arms were so much superior to theirs, and that we took no advantage of that superiority, and a little time given them to reflect upon it, they ever after were our very good friends; and we never had an instance of their attempting to surprize or cut off any of our people when they were ashore; opportunity for so doing they must have had at one time or another.

It is hard to account for what we have every where been told, of their Eating their Enemies killed in Battle, which they most Certainly do; Circumstances enough we have seen to Convince us of the Truth of this. Tupia, who holds this Custom in great aversion, hath very often Argued with them against it, but they have always as streniously supported it, and never would own that it was wrong. It is reasonable to suppose that men with whom this custom is found, seldom, if ever, give Quarter to those they overcome in battle; and if so, they must fight desperately to the very last. A strong proof of this supposition we had from the People of Queen Charlotte's sound, who told us, but a few days before we Arrived that they had kill'd and Eat a whole boat's crew. Surely a single boat's crew, or at least a part of them, when they found themselves beset and overpowered by numbers would have surrender'd themselves prisoners was such a thing practised among them. The heads of these unfortunate people they preserved as Trophies; 4 or 5 of them they brought off to shew to us, one of which Mr. Banks bought, or rather forced them to sell, for they parted with it with the utmost reluctancy, and afterwards would not so much as let us see one more for any thing we could offer them.

In the Article of Food these People have no great Variety; Fern roots, Dogs, Fish, and wild fowl is their Chief diet, for Cocos, Yams, and Sweet Potatoes is not Cultivated every where. They dress their Victuals in the same Manner as the people in the South Sea Islands; that is, dogs and Large fish they bake in a hole in the ground, and small fish, birds, and Shell fish, etc., they broil on the fire. Fern roots they likewise heat over the fire, then beat them out flat upon a stone with a wooden Mallet; after this they are fit for Eating, in the doing of which they suck out the Moist and Glutinous part, and Spit out the Fibrous parts. These ferns are much like, if not the same as, the mountain ferns in England.

They catch fish with Seans, Hooks and line, but more commonly with hooped netts very ingeniously made; in the middle of these they tie the bait, such as Sea Ears, fish Gutts, etc., then sink the Nett to the bottom with a stone; after it lays there a little time they haul it Gently up, and hardly ever without fish, and very often a large quantity. All their netts are made of the broad Grass plant before mentioned; generally with no other preparation than by Splitting the blade of the plant into threads. Their fish hooks are made of Crooked pieces of Wood, bones, and Shells.

WAR CANOE OF NEW ZEALAND.

[New Zealand Canoes, Houses, etc.]

The people shew great ingenuity and good workmanship in the building and framing their boats or Canoes. They are long and Narrow, and shaped very much like a New England Whale boat. Their large Canoes are, I believe, built wholy for war, and will carry from 40 to 80 or 100 Men with their Arms, etc. I shall give the Dimensions of one which I measured that lay ashore at Tolago. Length 68 1/2 feet, breadth 5 feet, and Depths 3 1/2, the bottom sharp, inclining to a wedge, and was made of 3 pieces hollow'd out to about 2 Inches or an Inch and a half thick, and well fastned together with strong platting. Each side consisted of one Plank only, which was 63 feet long and 10 or 12 Inches broad, and about 1 1/4 Inch thick, and these were well fitted and lashed to the bottom part. There were a number of Thwarts laid a Cross and Lashed to each Gunwale as a strengthening to the boat. The head Ornament projected 5 or 6 feet without the body of the Boat, and was 4 feet high; the Stern Ornament was 14 feet high, about 2 feet broad, and about 1 1/2 inch thick; it was fixed upon the Stern of the Canoe like the Stern post of a Ship upon her Keel. The Ornaments of both head and Stern and the 2 side boards were of Carved Work, and, in my opinion, neither ill design'd nor executed. All their Canoes are built after this plan, and few are less than 20 feet long. Some of the small ones we have seen with Outriggers, but this is not Common. In their War Canoes they generally have a quantity of Birds' feathers hung in Strings, and tied about the Head and stern as Additional Ornament. They are as various in the heads of their Canoes as we are in those of our Shipping; but what is most Common is an odd Design'd Figure of a man, with as ugly a face as can be conceived, a very large Tongue sticking out of his Mouth, and Large white Eyes made of the Shells of Sea Ears. Their paddles are small, light, and neatly made; they hardly ever make use of sails, at least that we saw, and those they have are but ill contrived, being generally a piece of netting spread between 2 poles, which serve for both Masts and Yards.

The Houses of these People are better calculated for a Cold than a Hot Climate; they are built low, and in the form of an oblong square. The framing is of wood or small sticks, and the sides and Covering of thatch made of long Grass. The door is generally at one end, and no bigger than to admit of a man to Creep in and out; just within the door is the fire place, and over the door, or on one side, is a small hole to let out the Smoke. These houses are 20 or 30 feet long, others not above half as long; this depends upon the largeness of the Family they are to contain, for I believe few familys are without such a House as these, altho' they do not always live in them, especially in the summer season, when many of them live dispers'd up and down in little Temporary Hutts, that are not sufficient to shelter them from the weather.

The Tools which they work with in building their Canoes, Houses, etc., are adzes or Axes, some made of a hard black stone, and others of green Talk. They have Chiszels made of the same, but these are more commonly made of Human Bones. In working small work and carving I believe they use mostly peices of Jasper, breaking small pieces from a large Lump they have for that purpose; as soon as the small peice is blunted they throw it away and take another. To till or turn up the ground they have wooden spades (if I may so call them), made like stout pickets, with a piece of wood tied a Cross near the lower end, to put the foot upon to force them into the Ground. These Green Talk Axes that are whole and good they set much Value upon, and never would part with them for anything we could offer.* (* The weapons of greenstone, found in the South Islands, were much prized. This hard material required years to shape into a mere, or short club, and these were handed down from father to son as a most valuable possession.) I offer'd one day for one, One of the best Axes I had in the Ship, besides a number of Other things, but nothing would induce the owner to part with it; from this I infer'd that good ones were scarce among them.

Diversions and Musical instruments they have but few; the latter Consists of 2 or 3 sorts of Trumpets and a small Pipe or Whistle, and the former in singing and Dancing. Their songs are Harmonious enough, but very doleful to a European ear. In most of their dances they appear like mad men, Jumping and Stamping with their feet, making strange Contorsions with every part of the body, and a hideous noise at the same time; and if they happen to be in their Canoes they flourish with great Agility their Paddles, Pattoo Pattoos, various ways, in the doing of which, if there are ever so many boats and People, they all keep time and Motion together to a surprizing degree. It was in this manner that they work themselves to a proper Pitch of Courage before they used to attack us; and it was only from their after behaviour that we could tell whether they were in jest or in Earnest when they gave these Heivas, as they call them, of their own accord, especially at our first coming into a place. Their signs of Friendship is the waving the hand or a piece of Cloth, etc.

We were never able to learn with any degree of certainty in what manner they bury their dead; we were generally told that they put them in the ground; if so it must be in some secret or by place, for we never saw the least signs of a burying place in the whole Country.* (* The burying places were kept secret. The body was temporarily buried, and after some time exhumed; the bones were cleaned, and hidden in some cave or cleft in the rocks. As bones were used by enemies to make implements, it was a point to keep these depositories secret, to prevent such desecration.) Their Custom of mourning for a friend or relation is by cutting and Scarifying their bodys, particularly their Arms and breasts, in such a manner that the Scars remain indelible, and, I believe, have some signification such as to shew how near related the deceased was to them.

[Maori and Tahiti Words.]

With respect to religion, I believe these people trouble themselves very little about it; they, however, believe that there is one Supream God, whom they call Tawney,* (* Probably Tane-mahuta, the creator of animal and vegetable life. The Maori does not pray.) and likewise a number of other inferior deities; but whether or no they worship or Pray to either one or the other we know not with any degree of certainty. It is reasonable to suppose that they do, and I believe it; yet I never saw the least Action or thing among them that tended to prove it. They have the same Notions of the Creation of the World,

Mankind, etc., as the people of the South Sea Islands have; indeed, many of their notions and Customs are the very same. But nothing is so great a proof of their all having had one Source as their Language, which differ but in a very few words the one from the other, as will appear from the following specimens, which I had from Mr. Banks, who understands their Language as well, or better than, any one on board.

English.	New Zealand.	South Sea Islands.
A Chief	Eareete	Eare
A Man	Taata	Taata
A Woman	Ivahina	Ivahine
The Head	Eupo	Eupo
,, Hair	Macauve	—
,, Ear	Terringa	Terrea
,, Forehead	Erai	Erai
,, Eyes	Matu	Matu
,, Cheek	Paparinga	Paparea
,, Nose	Ahewh	Ahew
,, Mouth	Hangoutou	Outou
,, Chinn	Ecouwai	—
,, Teeth	Hennihu	Nihio
,, Arm	Haringaringu	Rema
,, Finger	Maticara	Maneow
,, Belly	Ateraboo	Oboo
,, Naval	Apeto	Peto
Come here	Haromai	Haromai
Fish	Heica	Eyca
A Lobster	Kooura	Tooura
Coccos	Taro	Taro
Sweet Potatoes	Cumala	Cumala
Yamms	Tuphwhe	Tuphwhe
Birds	Mannu	Mannu
The Wind	Mebaw	Mattai
A Thief	Amootoo	Teto
To examine	Mataketake	Mataibai
To sing	Eheivà	Heivà
Bad	Keno	Eno
Trees	Oratou	Eraou
Grand Father	Toubouna	Toubouna
Friend	—	Tio
No	Kaoura	Oure
Number 1	Tahai	Tahai
2	Rua	Rua
3	Torou	Torou
4	Ha	Hea
5	Rema	Remo
6	Ono	Ono
7	Etu	Hetu
8	Wharou	Wharou
9	Iva	Hyva
10	Angahourou	Ahourou
What do you call this or that?	Owy Terra	Owy Terra

[Speculations on a Southern Continent.]

There are some small difference in the Language spoke by the Aeheinomoweans and those of Tovy Poenammu; but this differance seem'd to me to be only in the pronunciation, and is no more than what we find between one part of England and another. What is here inserted as a Specimen is that spoke by the People of Aeheinomouwe. What is meant by the South Sea Islands are those Islands we ourselves Touched at; but I gave it that title because we have always been told that the same Language is universally spoke by all the Islanders, and that this is a Sufficient proof that both they and the New Zelanders have had one Origin or Source, but where this is even time perhaps may never discover.

It certainly is neither to the Southward nor Eastward, for I cannot perswaide myself that ever they came from America; and as to a Southern Continent, I do not believe any such thing exist, unless in a high Latitude. But as the Contrary opinion hath for many Years prevail'd, and may yet prevail, it is necessary I should say something in support of mine more than what will be directly pointed out by the Track of this Ship in those Seas; for from that alone it will evidently appear that there is a large space extending quite to the Tropick in which we were not, or any other before us that we can ever learn for certain. In our route to the Northward, after doubling Cape Horn, when in the Latitude of 40 degrees, we were in the Longitude of 110 degrees; and in our return to the Southward, after leaving Ulietea, when in the same Latitude, we were in the Longitude of 145 degrees; the differance in this Latitude is 35 degrees of Longitude. In the Latitude of 30 degrees the differance of the 2 Tracks is 21 degrees, and that differance continues as low as 20 degrees; but a view of the Chart will best illustrate this.

Here is now room enough for the North Cape of the Southern Continent to extend to the Northward, even to a pretty low Latitude. But what foundation have we for such a supposition? None, that I know of, but this, that it must either be here or no where. Geographers have indeed laid down part of Quiros' discoveries in this Longitude, and have told us that he had these signs of a Continent, a part of which they have Actually laid down in the Maps; but by what Authority I know not. Quiros, in the Latitude of 25 or 26 degrees South, discover'd 2 Islands, which, I suppose, may lay between the Longitude of 130 and 140 degrees West. Dalrymple lays them down in 146 degrees West, and says that Quiros saw to the Southward very large hanging Clouds and a very thick Horizon, with other known signs of a Continent. Other accounts of their Voyage says not a word about this; but supposing this to be true, hanging Clouds and a thick Horizon are certainly no signs of a Continent--I have had many proofs to the Contrary in the Course of this Voyage; neither do I believe that Quiros looked upon such things as known signs of land, for if he had he certainly would have stood to the Southward, in order to have satisfied himself before he had gone to the Northward, for no man seems to have had discoveries more at heart than he had. Besides this, this was the ultimate object of his Voyage.* (* It is conjectured that what Quiros saw was Tahiti, but his track on this voyage is very vague. There are certainly no islands in the latitude given except Pitcairn.) If Quiros was in the Latitude of 26 degrees and Longitude 146 degrees West, then I am certain that no part of the Southern Continent can no where extend so far to the Northward as the above mentioned Latitude. But the Voyage which seems to thrust it farthest back in the Longitude I am speaking of, viz., between 130 and 150 degrees West, is that of Admiral Roggeween, a Dutchman, made in 1722, who, after leaving Juan Fernandes, went in search of Davis's Island; but not finding it, he ran 12 degrees more to the West, and in the Latitude of 28 1/2 degrees discover'd Easter Island. Dalrymple and some others have laid it down in 27 degrees South and 106 degrees 30 minutes West, and supposes it to be the same as Davis's Isle, which I think cannot be from the Circumstance of the Voyage; on the other hand Mr. Pingre, in his Treatise concerning the Transit of Venus, gives an extract of Roggeween's Voyage and a map of the South Seas, wherein he places Easter Island in the Latitude of 28 1/2 degrees South, and in the Longitude of 123 degrees West* (* Easter Island is in longitude 110 degrees West, and is considered identical with Davis' Island.) his reason for so doing may be seen at large in the said Treatise. He likewise lays down Roggeween's rout through those South Seas very different from any other Author I have seen; for after leaving Easter Island he makes him to steer South-West to the height of 34 degrees South, and afterwards West-North-West. If Roggeween really took this rout, then it is not probable that there is any Main land to the Northward of 35 degrees South. However, Mr. Dalrymple and some Geographers have laid down Roggeween's track very different from Mr. Pingre. From Easter Isle they have laid down his Track to the North-West, and afterwards very little different from that of La Maire; and this I think is not probable, that a man who, at his own request, was sent to discover the Southern Continent should take the same rout thro' these Seas as others had done before who had the same thing in View; by so doing he must be Morally certain of not finding what he was in search of, and of course must fail as they had done. Be this as it may, it is a point that cannot be clear'd up from the published accounts of the Voyage, which, so far from taking proper notice of their Longitude, have not even mentioned the Latitude of several of the Islands they discover'd, so that I find it impossible to lay down Roggeween's rout with the least degree of accuracy.* (* Roggeween's track is still unknown.)

But to return to our own Voyage, which must be allowed to have set aside the most, if not all, the Arguments and proofs that have been advanced by different Authors to prove that there must be a Southern Continent; I mean to the Northward of 40 degrees South, for what may lie to the Southward of that Latitude I know not. Certain it is that we saw no Visible signs of Land, according to my Opinion, neither in our rout to the Northward, Southward, or Westward, until a few days before we made the Coast of New Zeland. It is true we have often seen large flocks of Birds, but they were generally such as are always seen at a very great distance from land; we likewise saw frequently peices of Sea or Rock Weed, but how is one to know how far this may drive to Sea. I am told, and that from undoubted Authority, that there is Yearly thrown up upon the Coast of Ireland and Scotland a sort of Beans called Oxe Eyes, which are known to grow no where but in the West Indies;

and yet these 2 places are not less than 1200 Leagues asunder. Was such things found floating upon the Water in the South Seas one would hardly be perswaided that one was even out of sight of Land, so apt are we to Catch at everything that may at least point out to us the favourite Object we are in persuit of; and yet experiance shews that we may be as far from it as ever.

Thus I have given my Opinion freely and without prejudice, not with any View to discourage any future attempts being made towards discovering the Southern Continent; on the Contrary, as I think this Voyage will evidently make it appear that there is left but a small space to the Northward of 40 degrees where the grand object can lay. I think it would be a great pity that this thing, which at times has been the Object of many Ages and Nations, should not now be wholy be clear'd up; which might very Easily be done in one Voyage without either much trouble or danger or fear of Miscarrying, as the Navigator would know where to go to look for it; but if, after all, no Continent was to be found, then he might turn his thoughts towards the discovery of those Multitude of Islands which, we are told, lay within the Tropical regions to the South of the Line, and this we have from very good Authority, as I have before hinted. This he will always have in his power; for, unless he be directed to search for the Southern lands in a high Latitude, he will not, as we were, be obliged to go farther to the Westward in the Latitude of 40 degrees than 140 or 145 degrees West, and therefore will always have it in his power to go to George's Island, where he will be sure of meeting with refreshments to recruit his people before he sets out upon the discovery of the Islands.* (* Cook carried out this programme in his second voyage, when he set at rest for ever the speculation regarding the Southern Continent.) But should it be thought proper to send a Ship out upon this Service while Tupia lives, and he to come out in her, in that case she would have a prodidgious Advantage over every ship that hath been upon discoveries in those Seas before; for by means of Tupia, supposing he did not accompany you himself, you would always get people to direct you from Island to Island, and would be sure of meeting with a friendly reception and refreshment at every Island you came to. This would enable the Navigator to make his discoveries the more perfect and Compleat; at least it would give him time so to do, for he would not be Obliged to hurry through those Seas thro' any apprehentions of wanting Provisions.

[Tupia's List of Islands.]

I shall now add a list of those Islands which Tupia and Several others have given us an account of, and Endeavour to point out the respective Situations from Otaheite, or George's Island; but this, with respect to many of them, cannot be depended upon. Those marked thus (*) Tupia himself has been at, and we have no reason to doubt his Veracity in this, by which it will appear that his Geographical knowledge of those Seas is pretty Extensive; and yet I must observe that before he came with us he hardly had an Idea of any land being larger than Otaheite.

Name of the Islands N.E. Quarter.	Bearings from Otaheite.	Name of the Islands N.E. Quarter.	Bearings from Otaheite.
Oopate Ooura Teohcoa Oryvoa Ohevapato	Between the N. and N.N.E.	Whareva Whatteruro Tetioo Tetineohva Terouwhah	N.E.
Otaah Ohevaroa Temanno Ootta	N.N.E. to N.E. by N.	Whaoa Whaterretaah Whaneanea	N.N.E.
		Ohevatoutua	E. by N.
S.E. Quarter.			
Moutou Toomitoaroaro ‡Tennowhammeatane Ohitetamaruire Ouropoe	S. to S.E.	**N.W. Quarter.** ‡Tethuroa Oonnah Obaha Maataah	N. by W.
‡Mytea or Oznaburg Isld. Ohevanue Ohirotah	E.S.E. and E.		
S.W. Quarter.		‡Huiheine ‡Ulietea ‡Otaha ‡Bolabola ‡Tubai	Between the N. and W.
‡Imao or York Island ‡Tapooamanue or Saunders Island	W. by S. and W.S.W.		

Name of the Islands S.W. Quarter.	Bearings from Otaheite.	Name of the Islands N.W. Quarter.	Bearings from Otaheite.
‡Manua ‡Honue ‡Ohiteroa		‡Maurua Opoopooa Opopatea	Between the N. and W.
Onawhaa Otaohoera Opooroo Ooonow Teorooromatiwhatea ‡Teatowhite Oheavie	Between the S. and S.W.	‡Whennuaouda ‡Motehea ‡Oourio ‡Orurutu ‡Oateea	
Pooromathetua Teamoorohete Ohetotarive Ohetotareva Ohitetoutoumi	Between the S.W. and W.S.W.	Oahooahoo Oweha Orotuma Tenuna Orevavie	Between the N. by W. and W.
‡Mooenatayo Tetupatunaeo Ohiteteutenatu Ohitepoto	W.	Toutepa Orarathoa Oryvavai Oahourou	

The above list* was taken from a Chart of the Islands drawn by Tupia's own hands. (* This list is hopeless. With the exception of the Society Group (Huiheine, and the names that follow), Imao (Eimeo), Tapooamanuo, Tethuroa, and Ohiteroa, all lying near Tahiti, none can be recognised. Those north and east are no doubt names of the Paumotu Group, low coral islands, disposed in rings round lagoons, whose innumerable names are very little known to this day, and very probably the Tahitians had their own names for them.) He at one time gave us an account of near 130 Islands, but in his Chart he laid down only 74; and this is about the number that some others of the Natives of Otaheite gave us an account of; but the account taken by and from different people differ sencibly one from another both in names and numbers. The first is owing to the want of rightly knowing how to pronounce the names of the Islands after them; but be this as it may, it is very certain that there are these number of Islands, and very Probably a great many more, laying some where in the Great South Sea, the greatest part of which have never been seen by any European.

[Historical Notes on New Zealand.]

NOTES ON NEW ZEALAND.

As already stated by Cook in the Journal, New Zealand was first discovered by Abel Tasman, a Dutch navigator, in the year 1642. Sailing from Tasmania, he sighted the northern part of the Middle island, and anchored a little east of Cape Farewell in Massacre (Golden) Bay, so called by him because the Maoris cut off one of his boats, and killed three of the crew.

Tasman never landed anywhere, but coasted from Massacre Bay along the western side of the North Island to the north point. He passed outside the Three Kings, and thence away into the Pacific, to discover the Friendly Group.

No European eye again sighted New Zealand until Cook circumnavigated and mapped the islands.

The warlike character of the natives is well shown in this Journal. On nearly every occasion they either made, or attempted to make, an attack, even on the ships, and in self-defence firearms had constantly to be used. Nevertheless, Cook's judgment enabled him to inaugurate friendly relations in most places where he stopped long enough to enable the natives to become acquainted with the strangers.

It was not so with other voyagers. De Surville, a Frenchman, who called at Doubtless Bay very shortly after Cook left it, destroyed a village, and carried off a chief. Marion de Fresne was, in 1772, in the Bay of Islands, killed by the natives, with sixteen of his people, and eaten, for violation of some of their customs, and illtreatment of some individuals.

Other outrages followed, committed on both sides, and it is no wonder that, though Cook represented the advantages of the island for colonization, it was not considered a desirable place in which to settle. The cannibalism of the Maoris especially made people shy of the country.

Intermittent communication took place between New Zealand and the new Colony of New South Wales, and at last, in 1814, Samuel Marsden, a clergyman of the Church of England, who had seen Maoris in New South Wales, landed in the Bay of Islands with other missionaries. This fearless and noble-minded man obtained the confidence of the Maoris, and a commencement of colonization was made.

It was not, however, until 1840 that the New Zealand Company was formed to definitely colonize. They made their station at Wellington.

In the same year Captain Hobson, R.N., was sent as Lieutenant-Governor. Landing first at the Bay of Islands, he transferred his headquarters to the Hauraki Gulf in September 1840, where he founded Auckland, which remained the capital until 1876, when the seat of Government was transferred to Wellington.

The North Island, in which all these occurrences took place, contained by far the greater number of the natives, and it seems strange now that the first efforts to settle were not made in the Middle Island, which has proved equally suitable for Europeans, and where the difficulties of settlement, from the existence of a less numerous native population, were not so great. It is not necessary here to follow the complicated history of New Zealand in later years, which unfortunately comprises several bloody wars with the Maoris.

The present prosperous condition of this great colony is well known, but it has not been effected without the rapid diminution of the natives, who have met with the fate of most aborigines in contact with Europeans, especially when the former were naturally bold and warlike.

The Maoris have retained the tradition of the original arrival of their race in a fleet of canoes from a country called Hawaiki, which is by some supposed to be Hawaii in the Sandwich Group. As we have seen, the language was practically the same as that of Tahiti, and there is no doubt that they came from some of the Polynesian islands. The date of the immigration is supposed to be the fifteenth century.

Each canoe's crew settled in different parts of the North Island, and were the founders of the different great tribes into which the New Zealanders were divided. The more celebrated canoes were the Arawa, Tainui, Aotea, Kuruhaupo, Takitumu, and others.

The Arawa claimed the first landing, and the principal idols came in her. One of these is now in the possession of Sir George Grey. A large tribe on the east coast still bears the name of Arawa, and her name, that of the Tainui, and other of the canoes, are now borne by some of the great steamships that run to New Zealand.

Cook, in the voyage with which we have to deal, completely examined the whole group. His pertinacity and determination to follow the whole coast is a fine instance of his thoroughness in exploration. No weather nor delay daunted him, and the accuracy with which he depicted the main features of the outline of the islands is far beyond any of the similar work of other voyagers. It is true that he missed in the south island many of the fine harbours that have played such an important part in the prosperity of the Colony; but when we consider the narrowness of their entrances, and the enormous extent of the coast line which he laid down in such a short time, this is not astonishing.

His observations on the natives and on the country display great acuteness of observation, and had the settlers displayed the same spirit of fair treatment and respect for the customs of the natives, much of the bloody warfare that has stained the annals of the Colony might have been averted; though it is scarcely possible that with such a high-spirited race the occupation of the islands, especially the North island, where the majority of the Maoris were, could have taken place without some disturbances.

New Zealand now contains 630,000 Europeans, and 41,000 Maoris. Its exports are valued at 10,000,000 pounds, and the imports at 6,250,000 pounds. There are 2000 miles of railways open. Such is the result of fifty years of colonization in a fertile and rich island, the climate of which may be described as that of a genial England.

CHAPTER 7.
PASSAGE FROM NEW ZEALAND TO NEW HOLLAND.

[April 1770. From New Zealand to Australia.]

SUNDAY, 1st April. In the P.M. had a moderate breeze at East, which in the Night Veer'd to the North-East, and was attended with hazey, rainy weather. I have before made mention of our quitting New Zeland with an intention to steer to the Westward, which we accordingly did, taking our departure from Cape Farewell in the Latitude of 40 degrees 30 minutes South and Longitude 185 degrees 58 minutes West from Greenwich, which bore from us at 5 p.m. West 18 degrees North, distance 12 Miles. After this we steer'd North-West and West-North-West, in order to give it a good berth, until 8 o'Clock a.m., at which time we steered West, having the Advantage of a fresh Gale at North by East. At Noon our Latitude by account was 40 degrees 12 minutes South, Longitude made from Cape Farewell 1 degree 11 minutes West.

Monday, 2nd. In the P.M. had a moderate Gale at North, with thick hazey weather, attended with rain. At 8 it fell little wind, and Veer'd to West-South-West, at which time we Tack'd. At Midnight the wind came to South-South-West, and increased to a brisk gale with fair Cloudy weather, which we made the most of as soon as it was daylight. At Noon our Latitude, by Observation, was 40 degrees 0 minutes, and Longitude made from Cape Farewell 2 degrees 31 minutes West.

Tuesday, 3rd. Cloudy weather; Winds at South-West and South-South-West, a fresh Gale, with which we made our Course good North-West by West, and distance run from Yesterday at Noon to this day at Noon 38 1/2 Leagues. Latitude, by observation, 38 degrees 56 minutes South; Longitude made from Cape Farewell 4 degrees 36 minutes West.

Wednesday, 4th. Had a steady brisk Gale at South-South-West with some flying showers of rain and large hollow Sea from the Southward. In the P.M. unbent the Maintopsail to repair, and brought another to the Yard and set it close reefed. At Noon our Latitude, by Observation, was 37 degrees 56 minutes South; Course and distance since Yesterday at Noon North 60 degrees West, 122 Miles; Longitude made from Cape Farewell 6 degrees 54 minutes West.

Thursday, 5th. Fresh Gales at South, which in the A.M. veer'd to South-East by South. At Noon our Latitude, by observation, was 37 degrees 23 minutes South, Longitude made from Cape Farewell 9 degrees 10 minutes West;

Course and distance sail'd since Yesterday at Noon North 73 degrees 15 minutes West, 37 Leagues.

Friday, 6th. Winds between the South by East and South-East, with a Continued swell from the South-South-West. At Noon our Latitude in per Observation 37 degrees 18 minutes South; Course and distance sail'd since Yesterday at Noon North 85 degrees West, 58 Miles. Longitude made from Cape Farewell 10 degrees 35 minutes West.

Saturday, 7th. Gentle breezes at North-East, which in the A.M. Veer'd to North-West. In the P.M. found the Variation by the Mean of several Azimuths to be 13 degrees 50 minutes East, being then in the Latitude of 37 degrees 23 minutes South, and Longitude 196 degrees 44 minutes West. In the A.M. Punished Jno. Bowles, Marine, with 12 lashes for refusing to do his duty when order'd by the Boatswain's Mate and Serjeant of Marines. At Noon Latitude per Observation 37 degrees 35 minutes South, Longitude made from Cape Farewell 11 degrees 34 minutes West; Course and distance run since Yesterday noon South 70 degrees 15 minutes West, 50 Miles.

Sunday, 8th. Gentle breezes from the North-West and North. In the P.M. found the Variation to be 13 degrees 56 minutes East. At Noon Latitude in per Observation 38 degrees 0 minutes South, Longitude made from Cape Farewell 13 degrees 2 minutes West; Course and distance sail'd since Yesterday noon South 70 degrees 15 minutes West, 74 Miles.

Monday, 9th. Gentle breezes at North-West; pleasant weather and a Smooth Sea. In the A.M. saw a Tropic Bird, which, I believe, is uncommon in such high Latitudes. At Noon Latitude observ'd 38 degrees 29 minutes South, Longitude made from Cape Farewell 14 degrees 45 minutes West; Course and distance sail'd since Yesterday noon South 70 degrees 15 minutes West, 86 Miles.

Tuesday, 10th. Gentle breezes at North-West by North, and clear settled weather. In the A.M. found the Variation, by the Amplitude, to be 11 degrees 25 minutes East, and by Azimuth 11 degrees 20 minutes. At Noon the observed Latitude was 38 degrees 51 minutes South, and Longitude made from Cape Farewell 16 degrees 45 minutes; Longitude in 202 degrees 43 minutes West; Course and distance sail'd since Yesterday noon South 76 degrees 45 minutes West, 96 Miles.

Wednesday, 11th. Gentle breezes from the North-West, and pleasant weather, with some few showers of rain. In the A.M. found the Variation to be 13 degrees 48 minutes East, which is 2 1/2 degrees more than it was yesterday, altho' I should have expected to have found it less, for the observations were equally good. At Noon Latitude in 39 degrees 7 minutes South, Longitude made from Cape Farewell 17 degrees 23 minutes; and

Course and distance sail'd since Yesterday noon South 62 degrees West, 34 Miles.

Thursday, 12th. Calm, with now and then light Airs from the North-East and North-West; cloudy weather, but remarkably warm, and so it hath been for some days past. At Noon we were in the Latitude of 39 degrees 11 minutes, and Longitude from Cape Farewell 17 degrees 35 minutes West; Course and distance sail'd since Yesterday noon South 66 degrees West, 10 Miles.

Friday, 13th. Light Airs next to a Calm, with Clear pleasant weather; what little wind we had was from the North-West quarter. In the Course of this day found the Variation to be 12 degrees 27 minutes East, being at Noon, by observation, in the Latitude of 39 degrees 23 minutes South, and Longitude 204 degrees 2 minutes West; Course and distance since Yesterday noon South 62 degrees West, 26 Miles, and Longitude made from Cape Farewell 18 degrees 4 minutes West.

Saturday, 14th. Calm serene weather, with sometimes light Airs from the Northward. At sun set found the Variation to be 11 degrees 28 minutes East, and in the Morning to be 11 degrees 30 minutes East. The Spritsail Topsail being wore to rags, it was condemn'd as not fit for its proper use, and Converted to repair the 2 Top Gallant Sails, they being of themselves so bad as not to be worth the Expence of new Canvas, but with the help of this sail may be made to last some time longer. At Noon Latitude in 39 degrees 25 minutes South, Longitude made from Cape Farewell 18 degrees 21 minutes West; Course and distance since Yesterday noon South 18 degrees West, 13 Miles.

Sunday, 15th. In the P.M. had light Airs at North, which in the A.M. increased to a fresh Gale, with which we made the best of our way to the Westward, and by noon had run since yesterday upon a South 86 degrees 15 minutes West Course, 79 Miles. Latitude in, by Observation, 39 degrees 30 minutes South, and Longitude made from Cape Farewell 20 degrees 2 minutes West. Some flying fish seen this day.

Monday, 16th. Fresh Gales at North-North-West, with Cloudy, hazey weather. In the P.M. saw an Egg Bird, and yesterday a Gannet was seen; these are Birds that we reckon never to go far from land. We kept the lead going all night, but found no soundings with 100 and 130 fathoms line. At noon we were in the Latitude of 39 degrees 40 minutes South, and had made 22 degrees 2 minutes of Longitude from Cape Farewell; course and distance sail'd since Yesterday at Noon South 82 degrees West, 108 Miles.

Tuesday, 17th. At 2 p.m. the wind came to West-South-West, at which time we Tack'd and stood to the North-West. Before 5 o'Clock we were obliged to close reef our Topsails, having a Strong gale, with very heavy squalls; about this time a Small land bird was seen to pearch upon the rigging. We sounded, but had no ground with 120 fathoms of line. At 8 o'Clock we wore and stood to the Southward until 12 at Night, then wore and stood to the North-West until 4 a.m., when we again stood to the Southward, having a fresh Gale at West-South-West, attended with Squalls and dark hazey unsettled weather until 9; at which time it fell little wind, and the weather soon after Clear'd up, which, a little after 11, gave us an Opportunity of taking several observations of the Sun and Moon, the Mean result of which gave 207 degrees 56 minutes West Longitude from the Meridian of Greenwich. From these observations the Longitude of the Ship at Noon was 207 degrees 58 minutes, and by the Log 208 degrees 20 minutes, the difference being only 22 minutes; and this Error may as well be in the one as the other. Our Latitude at Noon was 39 degrees 36 minutes South, the Longitude made from Cape Farewell 22 degrees 22 minutes West.

Wednesday, 18th. Winds Southerly, a hard gale, with heavy squalls, attended with Showers of rain and a great Sea from the same Quarter. At 3 p.m. Close reeft the Topsails, handed the Main and Mizen Topsail, and got down Top Gallant Yards. At 6 the Gale increased to such a height as to oblige us to take in the Foretopsail and Mainsail, and to run under the Foresail and Mizen all night; Sounding every 2 hours, but found no ground with 120 fathoms. At 6 a.m. set the Mainsail, and soon after the Foretopsail, and before Noon the Maintopsail, both close reeft. At Noon our Latitude by observation was 38 degrees 45 minutes South, Longitude from Cape Farewell 23 degrees 43 minutes West; and Course and distance run since Yesterday noon North 51 degrees West, 82 Miles. Last night we saw a Port Egmont Hen, and this morning 2 More, a Pintado bird, several Albetrosses, and black sheer Waters. The first of these birds are Certain signs of the nearness of land; indeed we cannot be far from it. By our Longitude we are a degree to the Westward of the East side of Van Diemen's Land, according to Tasman, the first discoverer's, Longitude of it, who could not err much in so short a run as from this land to New Zeland; and by our Latitude we could not be above 50 or 55 Leagues to the Northward of the place where he took his departure from.

CHAPTER 8.
EXPLORATION OF EAST COAST OF AUSTRALIA.

[April 1770.]

THURSDAY, 19th. In the P.M. had fresh Gales at South-South-West and Cloudy Squally weather, with a large Southerly Sea; at 6 took in the Topsails, and at 1 A.M. brought too and Sounded, but had no ground with 130 fathoms of line. At 5, set the Topsails close reef'd, and 6, saw land* (* The south-east coast of Australia. See chart.) extending from North-East to West, distance 5 or 6 Leagues, having 80 fathoms, fine sandy bottom. We continued standing to the Westward with the Wind at South-South-West until 8, at which time we got Topgallant Yards a Cross, made all sail, and bore away along shore North-East for the Eastermost land we had in sight, being at this time in the Latitude of 37 degrees 58 minutes South, and Longitude of 210 degrees 39 minutes West. The Southermost point of land we had in sight, which bore from us West 1/4 South, I judged to lay in the Latitude of 38 degrees 0 minutes South and in the Longitude of 211 degrees 7 minutes West from the Meridian of Greenwich. I have named it Point Hicks, because Lieutenant Hicks was the first who discover'd this Land. To the Southward of this point we could see no land, and yet it was clear in that Quarter, and by our Longitude compared with that of Tasman's, the body of Van Diemen's land ought to have bore due South from us, and from the soon falling of the Sea after the wind abated I had reason to think it did; but as we did not see it, and finding the Coast to trend North-East and South-West, or rather more to the Westward, makes me Doubtfull whether they are one land or no.* (* Had not the gale on the day before forced Cook to run to the northward, he would have made the north end of the Furneaux Group, and probably have discovered Bass Strait, which would have cleared up the doubt, which he evidently felt, as to whether Tasmania was an island or not. The fact was not positively known until Dr. Bass sailed through the Strait in a whale-boat in 1797. Point Hicks was merely a rise in the coast-line, where it dipped below the horizon to the westward, and the name of Point Hicks Hill is now borne by an elevation that seems to agree with the position.) However, every one who compares this Journal with that of Tasman's will be as good a judge as I am; but it is necessary to observe that I do not take the Situation of Vandiemen's from the Printed Charts, but from the extract of Tasman's Journal, published by Dirk Rembrantse. At Noon we were in the Latitude of 37 degrees 50 minutes and Longitude of 210 degrees 29 minutes West. The extreams of the Land extending from North-West to East-North-East, a remarkable point, bore North 20 degrees East, distant 4 Leagues. This point rises to a round hillock very much like the Ramhead going into Plymouth sound, on which account I called it by the same name; Latitude 37 degrees 39 minutes, Longitude 210 degrees 22 minutes West. The Variation by an Azimuth taken this morning was 8 degrees 7 minutes East. What we have as yet seen of this land appears rather low, and not very hilly, the face of the Country green and Woody, but the Sea shore is all a white Sand.

Friday, 20th. In the P.M. and most part of the night had a fresh Gale Westerly, with Squalls, attended with Showers of rain. In the A.M. had the Wind at South-West, with Severe weather. At 1 p.m. saw 3 Water Spouts at once; 2 were between us and the Shore, and one at some distance upon our Larboard Quarter. At 6, shortned sail, and brought too for the Night, having 56 fathoms fine sandy bottom. The Northermost land in sight bore North by East 1/2 East, and a small Island* (* Gabo Island.) lying close to a point on the Main bore West, distant 2 Leagues. This point I have named Cape Howe* (* Cape Howe, called after Admiral Earl Howe, is the south-east point of Australia. The position is almost exact.); it may be known by the Trending of the Coast, which is North on the one Side and South-West on the other. Latitude 37 degrees 28 minutes South; Longitude 210 degrees 3 minutes West. It may likewise be known by some round hills upon the main just within it. Having brought too with her head off Shore, we at 10 wore, and lay her head in until 4 a.m., at which time we made sail along shore to the Northward. At 6, the Northermost land in sight bore North, being at this time about 4 Leagues from the Land. At Noon we were in the Latitude of 36 degrees 51 minutes South and Longitude of 209 degrees 53 minutes West, and 3 Leagues from the land. Course sail'd along shore since Yesterday at Noon was first North 52 degrees East, 30 miles, then North by East and North by West, 41 Miles. The weather being clear gave us an opportunity to View the Country, which had a very agreeable and promising aspect, diversified with hills, ridges, plains, and Valleys, with some few small lawns; but for the most part the whole was covered with wood, the hills and ridges rise with a gentle slope; they are not high, neither are there many of them.

[Off Cape Dromedary, New South Wales.]

Saturday, 21st. Winds Southerly, a Gentle breeze, and Clear weather, with which we coasted along shore to the Northward. In the P.M. we saw the smoke of fire in several places; a Certain sign that the Country is inhabited. At 6, being about 2 or 3 Leagues from the land, we shortned Sail, and Sounded and found 44 fathoms, a sandy bottom. Stood on under an easey sail until 12 o'Clock, at which time we brought too until 4 A.M., when we made sail, having then 90 fathoms, 5 Leagues from the land. At 6, we were abreast of a pretty high Mountain laying near the Shore, which, on account of its figure, I named Mount Dromedary (Latitude 36 degrees 18 minutes South, Longitude 209 degrees 55 minutes West). The shore under the foot of the Mountain forms a point, which I have named Cape Dromedary, over which is a peaked hillock. At this time found the Variation to be 10 degrees 42 minutes East. Between 10 and 11 o'Clock Mr. Green and I took several Observations of the Sun and Moon, the mean result of which gave 209 degrees 17 minutes West Longitude from the Meridian of Greenwich. By observation made yesterday we were in the Longitude 210 degrees 9 minutes. West 20 minutes gives 209 degrees 49 minutes the Longitude of the Ship to-day at noon per yesterday's observation, the Mean of which and to-day's give 209 degrees 33 minutes West, by which I fix the Longitude of this Coast. Our Latitude at Noon was 35 degrees 49 minutes South; Cape Dromedary bore South 30 degrees West, distant 12 Leagues. An Open Bay* (* Bateman Bay.) wherein lay 3 or 4 Small Islands, bore North-West by West, distant 5 or 6 Leagues. This Bay seem'd to be but very little Shelter'd from the Sea Winds, and yet it is the only likely Anchoring place I have yet seen upon the Coast.

Sunday, 22nd. In the P.M. had a Gentle breeze at South by West with which we steer'd along shore North by East and North-North-East at the distance of about 3 Leagues. Saw the smoke of fire in several places near the Sea beach. At 5, we were abreast of a point of land which, on account of its perpendicular Clifts, I call'd Point Upright; Latitude 35 degrees 35 minutes South; it bore from us due West, distant 2 Leagues, and in this Situation had 31 fathoms, Sandy bottom. At 6, falling little wind, we hauld off East-North-East; at this time the Northermost land in sight bore North by East 1/2 East, and at midnight, being in 70 fathoms, we brought too until 4 A.M., at which time we made sail in for the land, and at daylight found ourselves nearly in the same Place we were at 5 o'Clock in the evening, by which it was apparent that we had been drove about 3 Leagues to the Southward by a Tide or Current in the night. After this we steer'd along shore North-North-East, having a Gentle breeze at South-West, and were so near the Shore as to distinguish several people upon the Sea beach. They appeared to be of a very dark or black Colour; but whether this was the real Colour of their skins or the Cloathes they might have on I know not. At Noon we were by Observation in the Latitude of 35 degrees 27 minutes and Longitude 209 degrees 23 minutes; Cape Dromedary bore South 28 degrees West, distance 15 Leagues. A remarkable peak'd hill laying inland, the Top of which looked like a Pigeon house, and occasioned my giving it that name, bore North 32 degrees 33 minutes West, and a small low Island, laying close under the Shore, bore North-West, distance 2 or 3 Leagues; Variation of the Compass 9 degrees 50 minutes East. When we first discover'd this Island in the morning I was in hopes, from its appearance, that we should have found Shelter for the Ship behind it; but when we came to approach it near I did not think that there was even security for a Boat to land. But this, I believe, I should have attempted had not the wind come on Shore, after which I did not think it safe to send a Boat from the Ship, as we had a large hollow Sea from the South-East rowling in upon the land, which beat every where very high upon the Shore; and this we have had ever since we came upon the Coast. The land near the Sea coast still continues of a moderate height, forming alternately rocky points and Sandy beaches; but inland, between Mount Dromedary and the Pigeon house, are several pretty high Mountains, 2 only of which we saw but what were covered with Trees, and these lay inland behind the Pigeon House, and are remarkably flat a Top, with Steep rocky clifts all round them. As far as we could see the Trees in this Country hath all the appearance of being stout and lofty. For these 2 days past the observed Latitude hath been 12 or 14 Miles to the Southward of the Ship's account given by the Log, which can be owing to nothing but a Current set to the Southward.

Monday, 23rd. In the P.M. had a Gentle breeze at East, which in the night veer'd to North-East and North. At 1/2 past 4 P.M., being about 5 Miles from the Land, we Tack'd and stood off South-East and East until 4 A.M., at which time we Tack'd and stood in, being then about 9 or 10 Leagues from the land. At 8, it fell little wind, and soon after Calm. At Noon we were by Observation in the Latitude of 35 degrees 38 minutes and about 6 Leagues from the land, Mount Dromedary bearing South 37 degrees West, distant 17 Leagues, and the Pidgeon house North 40 degrees West; in this situation had 74 fathoms.

Tuesday, 24th. In the P.M. had Variable light Airs and Calms until 6 o'Clock, at which time a breeze sprung up at North by West; at this time we had 70 fathoms Water, being about 4 or 5 Leagues from the land, the Pidgeon house bearing North 40 degrees West, Mount Dromedary South 30 degrees West, and the Northermost land in sight North 19 degrees East. Stood to the North-East until Noon, having a Gentle breeze at North-West, at which time we Tack'd and stood to the Westward, being then, by observation, in the Latitude of 35 degrees 10 minutes South and Longitude 208 degrees 51 minutes West. A point of land which I named Cape St. George, we having discovered it on that Saint's day, bore West, distant 19 Miles, and the Pidgeon house South 7 degrees West, the Latitude and Longitude of which I found to be 35 degrees 19 minutes South and 209 degrees 42 minutes West. In the morning we found the Variation to be, by the Amplitude, 7 degrees 50 minutes East, by several Azimuths 7 degrees 54 minutes East.

[Off Jervis Bay, New South Wales.]

Wednesday, 25th. In the P.M. had a fresh breeze at North-West until 3 o'Clock, at which time it came to West, and we Tack'd and stood to the Northward. At 5 o'Clock, being about 5 or 6 Leagues from the land, the Pidgeon house bearing West-South-West, distant 9 Leagues, sounded and had 86 fathoms. At 8, being very squally, with lightning, we close reef'd the Topsails and brought too, being then in 120 fathoms. At 3 A.M. made sail again to the Northward, having the advantage of a fresh Gale at South-West. At Noon we were about 3 or 4 Leagues from the land and in the Latitude of 34 degrees 22 minutes and Longitude 208 degrees 36 minutes West. Course and distance sail'd since Yesterday noon is North by East 49 Miles. In the Course of this day's run we saw the Smoke of fire in several places near the Sea beach. About 2 Leagues to the Northward of Cape St. George the Shore seems to form a bay,* (* Jervis Bay, a very fine port, but little use has been made of it up to the present time.) which appear'd to be shelter'd from the North-East winds; but as we had the wind it was not in my power to look into it, and the appearance was not favourable enough to induce me to loose time in beating up to it. The North point of this bay, on account of its Figure, I nam'd Long Nose. Latitude 45 degrees 4 minutes South, 8 Leagues to the Northward of this, is a point which I call'd Red Point; some part of the Land about it appeared of that Colour (Latitude 34 degrees 29 minutes South, Longitude 208 degrees 49 minutes West). A little way inland to the North-West of this point is a round hill, the top of which look'd like the Crown of a Hatt.

Thursday, 26th. Clear, serene weather. In the P.M. had a light breeze at North-North-West until 5, at which time it fell Calm, we being then about 3 or 4 Leagues from the land and in 48 fathoms. Variation by Azimuth 8 degrees 48 minutes East, the extreams of the land from North-East by North to South-West by South. Saw several smokes along shore before dark, and 2 or 3 times a fire. In the Night we lay becalm'd, driving in before the Sea, until one o'Clock A.M., at which time we got a breeze from the land, with which we steer'd North-East, being then in 38 fathoms water. At Noon it fell little Wind, and veer'd to North-East by North, we being then in the Latitude of 34 degrees 10 minutes and Longitude 208 degrees 27 minutes West, and about 5 Leagues from the land, which extended from South 37 degrees West to North 1/2 East. In this Latitude are some White Clifts, which rise perpendicular from the Sea to a moderate height.

Friday, 27th. Var'ble light Airs between the North-East and North-West, clear pleasant weather. In the P.M. stood off Shore until 2, then Tackt and Stood in till 6, at which time we tack'd and stood off, being then in 54 fathoms and about 4 or 5 miles from the land, the Extreams of which bore from South, 28 degrees West to North 25 degrees 30 minutes East. At 12 we tack'd and stood in until 4 A.M., then made a Trip off until day light, after which we stood in for the land; in all this time we lost ground, owing a good deal to the Variableness of the winds, for at Noon we were by Observation in the Latitude of 34 degrees 21 minutes South, Red Point bearing South 27 degrees West, distant 3 Leagues. In this Situation we were about 4 or 5 Miles from the land, which extended from South 19 degrees 30 minutes West to North 29 degrees East.

Saturday, 28th. In the P.M. hoisted out the Pinnace and Yawl in order to attempt a landing, but the Pinnace took in the Water so fast that she was obliged to be hoisted in again to stop her leakes. At this time we saw several people a shore, 4 of whom where carrying a small Boat or Canoe, which we imagin'd they were going to put in to the Water in order to Come off to us; but in this we were mistaken. Being now not above 2 Miles from the Shore Mr. Banks, Dr. Solander, Tupia, and myself put off in the Yawl, and pull'd in for the land to a place where we saw 4 or 5 of the Natives, who took to the Woods as we approached the Shore; which disappointed us in the expectation we had of getting a near View of them, if not to speak to them. But our disappointment was heightened when we found that we no where could effect a landing by reason of the great Surf which beat everywhere upon the shore. We saw haul'd up upon the beach 3 or 4 small Canoes, which to us appeared not much unlike the Small ones of New Zeland. In the wood were several Trees of the Palm kind, and no under wood; and this was all we were able to observe from the boat, after which we return'd to the Ship about 5 in the evening.* (* The place where Cook attempted to land is near Bulli, a place where there is now considerable export of coal. A large coal port, Wollongong, lies a little to the southward.) At this time it fell Calm, and we were not above a Mile and a half from the Shore, in 11 fathoms, and within some breakers that lay to the Southward of us; but luckily a light breeze came off from the Land, which carried us out of danger, and with which we stood to the Northward. At daylight in the morning we discover'd a Bay,* (* Botany Bay.) which appeared to be tollerably well shelter'd from all winds, into which I resolved to go with the Ship, and with this View sent the Master in the Pinnace to sound the Entrance, while we kept turning up with the Ship, having the wind right out. At noon the Entrance bore North-North-West, distance 1 Mile.

[At Anchor, Botany Bay, New South Wales.]

Sunday, 29th. In the P.M. wind Southerly and Clear weather, with which we stood into the bay and Anchored under the South shore about 2 miles within the Entrance in 5 fathoms, the South point bearing South-East and the North point East. Saw, as we came in, on both points of the bay, several of the Natives and a few hutts; Men, Women, and Children on the South Shore abreast of the Ship, to which place I went in the Boats in hopes of speaking with them, accompanied by Mr. Banks, Dr. Solander, and Tupia. As we approached the Shore they all made off, except 2 Men, who seem'd resolved to oppose our landing. As soon as I saw this I order'd the boats to lay upon their Oars, in order to speak to them; but this was to little purpose, for neither us nor Tupia could understand one word they said. We then threw them some nails, beads, etc., a shore, which they took up, and seem'd not ill pleased with, in so much that I thought that they beckon'd to us to come ashore; but in this we were mistaken, for as soon as we put the boat in they again came to oppose us, upon which I fir'd a musquet between the 2, which had no other Effect than to make them retire back, where bundles of their darts lay, and one of them took up a stone and threw at us, which caused my firing a Second Musquet, load with small Shott; and altho' some of the shott struck the man, yet it had no other effect than making him lay hold on a Target. Immediately after this we landed, which we had no sooner done than they throw'd 2 darts at us; this obliged me to fire a third shott, soon after which they both made off, but not in such haste but what we might have taken one; but Mr. Banks being of Opinion that the darts were poisoned, made me cautious how I advanced into the Woods. We found here a few small hutts made of the Bark of Trees, in one of which were 4 or 5 Small Children, with whom we left some strings of beads, etc. A quantity of Darts lay about the Hutts; these we took away with us. 3 Canoes lay upon the beach, the worst I think I ever saw; they were about 12 or 14 feet long, made of one piece of the Bark of a Tree, drawn or tied up at each end, and the middle keept open by means of pieces of Stick by way of Thwarts. After searching for fresh water without success, except a little in a Small hole dug in the Sand, we embarqued, and went over to the North point of the bay, where in coming in we saw several people; but when we landed now there were nobody to be seen. We found here some fresh Water, which came trinkling down and stood in pools among the rocks; but as this was troublesome to come at I sent a party of men ashore in the morning to the place where we first landed to dig holes in the sand, by which means and a Small stream they found fresh Water sufficient to Water the Ship. The String of Beads, etc., we had left with the Children last night were found laying in the Hutts this morning; probably the Natives were afraid to take them away. After breakfast we sent some Empty Casks a shore and a party of Men to cut wood, and I went myself in the Pinnace to sound and explore the Bay, in the doing of which I saw some of the Natives; but they all fled at my Approach. I landed in 2 places, one of which the people had but just left, as there were small fires and fresh Muscles broiling upon them; here likewise lay Vast heaps of the largest Oyster Shells I ever saw.

Monday, 30th. As Soon as the Wooders and Waterers were come on board to Dinner 10 or 12 of the Natives came to the watering place, and took away their Canoes that lay there, but did not offer to touch any one of our Casks that had been left ashore; and in the afternoon 16 or 18 of them came boldly up to within 100 yards of our people at the watering place, and there made a stand. Mr. Hicks, who was the Officer ashore, did all in his power to intice them to him by offering them presents; but it was to no purpose, all they seem'd to want was for us to be gone. After staying a Short time they went away. They were all Arm'd with Darts and wooden Swords; the darts have each 4 prongs, and pointed with fish bones. Those we have seen seem to be intended more for striking fish than offensive Weapons; neither are they poisoned, as we at first thought. After I had return'd from sounding the Bay I went over to a Cove on the North side of the Bay, where, in 3 or 4 Hauls with the Sean, we caught about 300 pounds weight of Fish, which I caused to be equally divided among the Ship's Company. In the A.M. I went in the Pinnace to sound and explore the North side of the bay, where I neither met with inhabitants or anything remarkable. Mr. Green took the Sun's Meridian Altitude a little within the South Entrance of the Bay, which gave the Latitude 34 degrees 0 minutes South.

[May 1770.]

Tuesday, May 1st. Gentle breezes, Northerly. In the P.M. 10 of the Natives again visited the Watering place. I, being on board at this time, went immediately ashore, but before I got there they were going away. I follow'd them alone and unarm'd some distance along shore, but they would not stop until they got farther off than I choose to trust myself. These were armed in the same manner as those that came Yesterday. In the evening I sent some hands to haul the Saine, but they caught but a very few fish. A little after sunrise I found the Variation to be 11 degrees 3 minutes East. Last night Forby Sutherland, Seaman, departed this Life, and in the A.M. his body Was buried ashore at the watering place, which occasioned my calling the south point of this bay after his name. This morning a party of us went ashore to some Hutts, not far from the Watering place, where some of the Natives are daily seen; here we left several articles, such as Cloth, Looking Glasses, Coombs, Beads, Nails, etc.; after this we made an Excursion into the Country, which we found diversified with Woods, Lawns, and Marshes. The woods are free from underwood of every kind, and the trees are at such a distance from one another that the whole Country, or at least great part of it, might be Cultivated without being obliged to cut down a single tree. We found the Soil every where, except in the Marshes, to be a light white sand, and produceth a quantity of good Grass, which grows in little Tufts about as big as one can hold in one's hand, and pretty close to one another; in this manner the Surface of the Ground is Coated. In the woods between the Trees Dr. Solander had a bare sight of a Small Animal something like a Rabbit, and we found the Dung of an Animal* (* This was the kangaroo.) which must feed upon Grass, and which, we judge, could not be less than a Deer; we also saw the Track of a Dog, or some such like Animal. We met with some Hutts and places where the Natives had been, and at our first setting out one of them was seen; the others, I suppose, had fled upon our Approach. I saw some Trees that had been cut down by the Natives with some sort of a Blunt instrument, and several Trees that were barqued, the bark of which had been cut by the same instrument; in many of the Trees, especially the Palms, were cut steps of about 3 or 4 feet asunder for the conveniency of Climbing them. We found 2 Sorts of Gum, one sort of which is like Gum Dragon, and is the same, I suppose, Tasman took for Gum lac; it is extracted from the largest tree in the Woods.

Wednesday, 2nd. Between 3 and 4 in the P.M. we return'd out of the Country, and after Dinner went ashore to the watering place, where we had not been long before 17 or 18 of the Natives appeared in sight. In the morning I had sent Mr. Gore, with a boat, up to the head of the Bay to drudge for Oysters; in his return to the Ship he and another person came by land, and met with these people, who followed him at the Distance of 10 or 20 Yards. Whenever Mr. Gore made a stand and faced them they stood also, and notwithstanding they were all Arm'd, they never offer'd to Attack him; but after he had parted from them, and they were met by Dr. Monkhouse and one or 2 more, who, upon making a Sham retreat, they throw'd 3 darts after them, after which they began to retire. Dr. Solander, I, and Tupia made all the haste we could after them, but could not, either by words or Actions, prevail upon them to come near us, Mr. Gore saw some up the Bay, who by signs invited him ashore, which he prudently declined. In the A.M. had the wind in the South-East with rain, which prevented me from making an Excursion up the head of the bay as I intended.

Thursday, 3rd. Winds at South-East, a Gentle breeze and fair weather. In the P.M. I made a little excursion along the Sea Coast to the Southward, accompanied by Mr. Banks and Dr. Solander. At our first entering the woods we saw 3 of the Natives, who made off as soon as they saw us; more of them were seen by others of our people, who likewise made off as soon as they found they were discover'd. In the A.M. I went in the Pinnace to the head of the bay, accompanied by Drs. Solander and Monkhouse, in order to Examine the Country, and to try to form some Connections with the Natives. In our way thither we met with 10 or 12 of them fishing, each in a Small Canoe, who retir'd into Shoald water upon our approach. Others again we saw at the first place we landed at, who took to their Canoes, and fled before we came near them; after this we took Water, and went almost to the head of the inlet, were we landed and Travel'd some distance in land. We found the face of the Country much the same as I have before described, but the land much richer for instead of sand I found in many places a deep black soil, which we thought was Capable of producing any kind of grain. At present it produceth, besides Timber, as fine Meadow as ever was seen; however, we found it not all like this, some few places were very rocky, but this, I believe, to be uncommon. The stone is sandy, and very proper for building, etc. After we had sufficiently examin'd this part we return'd to the Boat, and seeing some Smoke and Canoes at another part we went thither, in hopes of meeting with the people, but they made off as we approached. There were 6 Canoes and 6 small fires near the Shore, and Muscles roasting upon them, and a few Oysters laying near; from this we conjectured that there had been just 6 people, who had been out each in his Canoe picking up the Shell fish, and come a Shore to eat them, where each had made his fire to dress them by. We tasted of their Cheer, and left them in return Strings of beads, etc. The day being now far spent, we set out on our return to the Ship.

Friday, 4th. Winds northerly, serene weather. Upon my return to the Ship in the evening I found that none of the Natives had Appear'd near the Watering place, but about 20 of them had been fishing in their Canoes at no great distance from us. In the A.M., as the Wind would not permit us to sail, I sent out some parties into the Country to try to form some Connections with the Natives. One of the Midshipmen met with a very old man and Woman and 2 Small Children; they were Close to the Water side, where several more were in their Canoes gathering of Shell fish, and he, being alone, was afraid to make any stay with the 2 old People least he should be discovr'd by those in the Canoes. He gave them a bird he had Shott, which they would not Touch; neither did they speak one word, but seem'd to be much frightned. They were quite Naked; even the Woman had nothing to cover her nudities. Dr. Monkhouse and another Man being in the Woods, not far from the watering place, discover'd 6 more of the Natives, who at first seem'd to wait his coming; but as he was going up to them he had a dart thrown at him out of a Tree, which narrowly escaped him. As soon as the fellow had thrown the dart he descended the Tree and made off, and with him all the rest, and these were all that were met with in the Course of this day.

Saturday, 5th. In the P.M. I went with a party of Men over to the North Shore, and while some hands were hauling the Sean, a party of us made an Excursion of 3 or 4 Miles into the Country, or rather along the Sea Coast. We met with nothing remarkable; great part of the Country for some distance inland from the Sea Coast is mostly a barren heath, diversified with Marshes and Morasses. Upon our return to the Boat we found they had caught a great number of small fish, which the sailors call leather Jackets on account of their having a very thick skin; they are known in the West Indies. I had sent the Yawl in the morning to fish for Sting rays, who returned in the Evening with upwards of four hundred weight; one single one weigh'd 240 pounds Exclusive of the entrails. In the A.M., as the wind Continued Northerly, I sent the Yawl again a fishing, and I went with a party of Men into the Country, but met with nothing extraordinary.

[Description of Botany Bay, New South Wales.]

Sunday, 6th. In the evening the Yawl return'd from fishing, having Caught 2 Sting rays weighing near 600 pounds. The great quantity of plants Mr. Banks and Dr. Solander found in this place occasioned my giving it the Name of Botany Bay.* (* The Bay was at first called Stingray Bay. The plan of it at the Admiralty is called by this name, and none of the logs know Botany Bay. It seems probable that Cook finally settled on the name after the ship left, and when Banks had had time to examine his collections. A monument was erected in 1870 near the spot, on the southern side, where Cook first landed. Botany Bay was intended to be the site where the first settlement of convicts should be made, but on the arrival of Captain Phillip, on January 18th, 1788, he found it so unsuited for the number of his colony that he started in a boat to examine Broken Bay. On his way he went into Port Jackson, and immediately decided on settling there. On the 25th and 26th the ships went round, and Sydney was founded.) It is situated in the Latitude of 34 degrees 0 minutes South, Longitude 208 degrees 37 minutes West. It is capacious, safe, and Commodious; it may be known by the land on the Sea Coast, which is of a pretty even and moderate height, Rather higher than it is inland, with steep rocky Clifts next the Sea, and looks like a long Island lying close under the Shore. The Entrance of the Bay lies about the Middle of this land. In coming from the Southward it is discover'd before you are abreast of it, which you cannot do in coming from the Northward; the entrance is little more than a Quarter of a Mile broad, and lies in West-North-West. To sail into it keep the South shore on board until within a small bare Island, which lies close under the North Shore. Being within that Island the deepest of Water is on that side, 7, 6 and 5 fathoms a good way up; there is Shoald Water a good way off from the South Shore--from the inner South Point quite to the head of the harbour; but over towards the North and North-West Shore is a Channell of 12 or 14 feet at low Water, 3 or 4 Leagues up, to a place where there is 3 or 4 fathoms; but there I found very little fresh Water. We Anchor'd near the South Shore about a Mile within the Entrance for the Conveniency of Sailing with a Southerly wind and the getting of Fresh Water; but I afterwards found a very fine stream of fresh Water on the North shore in the first sandy Cove within the Island, before which the Ship might lay almost land locked, and wood for fuel may be got everywhere. Although wood is here in great plenty, yet there is very little Variety; the bigest trees are as large or larger than our Oaks in England, and grows a good deal like them, and Yields a reddish Gum; the wood itself is heavy, hard, and black like Lignum Vitae. Another sort that grows tall and Strait something like Pines--the wood of this is hard and Ponderous, and something of the Nature of America live Oak. These 2 are all the Timber trees I met with; there are a few sorts of Shrubs and several Palm Trees and Mangroves about the Head of the Harbour. The Country is woody, low, and flat as far in as we could see, and I believe that the Soil is in general sandy. In the Wood are a variety of very beautiful birds, such as Cocatoos, Lorryquets, Parrots, etc., and crows Exactly like those we have in England. Water fowl is no less plenty about the head of the Harbour, where there is large flats of sand and Mud, on which they seek their food; the most of these were unknown to us, one sort especially, which was black and white, and as large as a Goose, but most like a Pelican.* (* Most probably the Black and White or Semipalmated Goose, now exterminated in these parts.) On the sand and Mud banks are Oysters, Muscles, Cockles, etc., which I believe are the Chief support of the inhabitants, who go into Shoald Water with their little Canoes and peck them out of the sand and Mud with their hands, and sometimes roast and Eat them in the Canoe, having often a fire for that purpose, as I suppose, for I know no other it can be for. The Natives do not appear to be numerous, neither do they seem to live in large bodies, but dispers'd in small parties along by the Water side. Those I saw were about as tall as Europeans, of a very dark brown Colour, but not black, nor had they woolly, frizled hair, but black and lank like ours. No sort of Cloathing or Ornaments were ever seen by any of us upon any one of them, or in or about any of their Hutts; from which I conclude that they never wear any. Some that we saw had their faces and bodies painted with a sort of White Paint or Pigment. Altho' I have said that shell fish is their Chief support, yet they catch other sorts of fish, some of which we found roasting on the fire the first time we landed; some of these they strike with Gigs,* (* A fishing implement like a trident.) and others they catch with hook and line; we have seen them strike fish with gigs, and hooks and lines are found in their Hutts. Sting rays, I believe, they do not eat, because I never saw the least remains of one near any of their Hutts or fire places. However, we could know but very little of their Customs, as we never were able to form any Connections with them; they had not so much as touch'd the things we had left in their Hutts on purpose for them to take away. During our stay in this Harbour I caused the English Colours to be display'd ashore every day, and an inscription to be cut out upon one of the Trees near the Watering place, setting forth the Ship's Name, Date, etc. [Off Port Jackson, New South Wales.]Having seen everything this place afforded, we, at daylight in the morning, weigh'd with a light breeze at North-West, and put to Sea, and the wind soon after coming to the Southward we steer'd along shore North-North-East, and at Noon we were by observation in the Latitude of 33 degrees 50 minutes South, about 2 or 3 Miles from the Land, and abreast of a Bay, wherein there appear'd to be safe Anchorage, which I called Port Jackson.* (* Cook having completed his water at Botany Bay, and having many hundreds of miles of coast before him, did not examine Port Jackson, the magnificent harbour in which Sydney, the capital of New South Wales, now lies. His chart gives the shape of what he could see very accurately, but the main arm of the harbour is hidden from the sea. He named the bay after Mr. (afterwards Sir George) Jackson, one of the Secretaries of the Admiralty. This fact is recorded on a tablet in the Bishop Stortford Church to the memory of Sir George Duckett, which name Sir George had assumed in later years. This interesting evidence was brought to light by Sir Alfred Stephen, Lieutenant-Governor of New South Wales, and puts an end to the legend which was long current, that Port Jackson was named after a sailor who first saw it. There was, moreover, no person of the name of Jackson on board.) It lies 3 leagues to the Northward of Botany Bay. I had almost forgot to mention that it is high water in this Bay at the full and change of the Moon about 8 o'Clock, and rises and falls upon a Perpendicular about 4 or 5 feet.

Monday, 7th. Little wind, Southerly, and Serene pleasant Weather. In the P.M. found the Variation by several Azimuths to be 8 degrees East; at sunset the Northermost land in sight bore North 26 degrees East; and some broken land that appear'd to form a bay bore North 40 degrees West, distant 4 Leagues. This Bay I named Broken bay,* (* The Hawkesbury River, the largest on the east coast of Australia, runs into Broken Bay.) Latitude 33 degrees 36 minutes South. We steer'd along shore North-North-East all night at the distance of about 3 Leagues from the land, having from 32 to 36 fathoms, hard sandy bottom. A little after sun rise I took several Azimuths with 4 Needles belonging to the Azimuth Compass, the mean result of which gave the Variation of 7 degrees 56 minutes East. At Noon we were by observation in the Latitude of 33 degrees 22 minutes South, and about 3 Leagues from the land, the Northermost part of which in sight bore North 19 degrees East. Some pretty high land which projected out in 3 bluff Points, and occasioned my calling it Cape 3 Points (Latitude 33 degrees 33 minutes South), bore South-West, distant 5 Leagues; Longitude made from Botany Bay 0 degrees 19 minutes East.

Tuesday, 8th. Variable Light Airs and Clear weather. In the P.M. saw some smooks upon the Shore, and in the Evening found the Variation to be 8 degrees 25 minutes East; at this time we were about 2 or 3 Miles from the land, and had 28 fathoms Water. Our situation at Noon was nearly the same as Yesterday, having advanced not one Step to the Northward.

Wednesday, 9th. Winds northerly; most part a fresh breeze, with which we stood off Shore until 12 at Night. At the distance of 5 Leagues from the land had 70 fathoms, at the distance of 6 Leagues 80 fathoms, which is the Extent of the Soundings, for at the Distance of 10 Leagues off we had no ground with 150 fathoms. Stood in Shore until 8 o'Clock A.M., and hardly fetched Cape Three Points; having a little wind at North-West by North, we tack'd, and stood off until Noon, at which Time we Tack'd with the wind at North-North-East, being then in the Latitude of 33 degrees 37 minutes South, Cape Three Points bearing North West by West, distance 4 Leagues.

Thursday, 10th. In the P.M., had the wind at North-East by North, with which we stood in Shore until near 4 o'Clock, when we Tack'd in 23 fathoms

Water, being about a Mile from the land, and as much to the Southward of Cape 3 Points. In the night the wind veer'd to North-West and West, and in the morning to South-West. Having the advantage of a light Moon, we made the best of our way along shore to the Northward. At Noon we were by observation in the Latitude of 32 degrees 53 minutes South, and Longitude 208 degrees 0 minutes West, and about 2 Leagues from the land, which extended from North 41 degrees East to South 41 degrees West. A small round rock or Island,* (* Nobby Head, at the entrance of Newcastle Harbour, formed by the Hunter River. Newcastle is the great coal port of New South Wales. It has a population of 20,000, and exports 1,500,000 tons of coal in the year.) laying close under the land, bore South 82 degrees West, distance 3 or 4 Leagues. At sunrise in the Morning found the Variation to be 8 degrees East. In the Latitude of 33 degrees 2 minutes South, a little way inland, is a remarkable hill, that is shaped like the Crown of a Hatt, which we past about 9 o'Clock in the forenoon.

[Off Cape Hawke, New South Wales.]

Friday, 11th. Winds Southerly in the day, and in the night Westerly; a Gentle breeze and Clear weather. At 4 P.M. past, at the distance of one Mile, a low rocky point which I named Point Stephens (Latitude 32 degrees 45 minutes); on the North side of this point is an inlet which I called Port Stephens* (* Called after Mr. Stephens, one of the Secretaries to the Admiralty. It is a large and fine harbour.) (Latitude 32 degrees 40 minutes; Longitude 207 degrees 51 minutes), that appear'd to me from the Masthead to be shelter'd from all Winds. At the Entrance lay 3 Small Islands, 2 of which are of a Tolerable height, and on the Main, near the shore, are some high round hills that make at a distance like Islands. In passing this bay at the distance of 2 or 3 miles from the Shore our soundings were from 33 to 27 fathoms; from which I conjectured that there must be a sufficient depth of Water for Shipping in the bay. We saw several smokes a little way in the Country upon the flat land; by this I did suppose that there were Lagoons which afforded subsistance for the Natives, such as shell-fish, etc., for we as yet know nothing else they have to live upon. At 1/2 past 5, the Northermost land in sight bore North 36 degrees East, and Point Stephens South-West, distant 4 Leagues, at which time we took in our Steerings,* (* Studding sails.) and run under an Easey sail all night until 4 A.M., when we made all sail; our soundings in the night were from 48 to 62 fathoms, at the distance of between 3 and 4 Leagues from the land. At 8 we were abreast of a high point of Land, which made in 2 Hillocks; this point I called Cape Hawke* (* After Admiral Sir Edward Hawke, First Lord of the Admiralty.) (Latitude 32 degrees 14 minutes South, Longitude 207 degrees 30 minutes West). It bore from us at this time West distant 8 Miles, and the same time the Northermost land in sight bore North 6 degrees East, and appear'd high and like an Island. At Noon this land bore

North 8 degrees East, the Northermost land in sight North 13 degrees East, and Cape Hawke South 37 degrees West. Latitude in per Observation 32 degrees 2 minutes South, which was 12 Miles to the Southward of that given by the Log, which I do suppose to be owing to a Current setting that way. Course and distance sail'd since Yesterday at Noon was first North-East by East, 27 Miles, then North 10 degrees East, 37 Miles; Longitude in 207 degrees 20 minutes West; Variation per morning Amplitude and Azimuth 9 degrees 10 minutes East.

Saturday, 12th. Winds Southerly, a Gentle breeze in the P.M. As we run along Shore we saw several smokes a little way in land from the Sea, and one upon the Top of a hill, which was the first we have seen upon elevated ground since we have been upon the Coast. At sunset we were in 23 fathoms, and about a League and a half from the land, the Northermost part of which we had in sight bore North 13 degrees East; and 3 remarkable large high hills lying Contigious to each other, and not far from the shore, bore North-North-West. As these Hills bore some resemblance to each other we called them the 3 Brothers. We steer'd North-East by North all Night, having from 27 to 67 fathoms, from 2 to 5 and 6 Leagues from the Land, and at day light we steer'd North for the Northermost land we had in sight. At noon we were 4 Leagues from the Land, and by observation in the Latitude of 31 degrees 18 minutes South, which was 15 miles to the Southward of that given by the Log. Our Course and distance made good since Yesterday noon was North 24 degrees East, 48 miles. Longitude 206 degrees 58 minutes West; several smokes seen a little way in land.

Sunday, 13th. In the P.M. stood in shore with the Wind at North-East until 6, at which time we Tack'd, being about 3 or 4 miles from the land, and in 24 fathoms. Stood off shore with a fresh breeze at North and North-North-West until midnight, then Tack'd, being in 118 fathoms and 8 Leagues from the Land. At 3 a.m. the wind veer'd to the Westward, and we Tack'd and stood to the Northward. At noon we were by Observation in the Latitude of 30 degrees 43 minutes South, and Longitude 206 degrees 45 minutes West, and about 3 or 4 Leagues from the Land, the Northermost part of which bore from us North 13 degrees West; and a point or head land, on which were fires that Caused a great Quantity of smoke, which occasioned my giving it the name of Smokey Cape, bore South-West, distant 4 Leagues; it is moderately high land. Over the pitch of the point is a round hillock; within it 2 others, much higher and larger, and within them very low land (Latitude 30 degrees 51 minutes, Longitude 206 degrees 5 minutes West). Besides the smoke seen upon this Cape we saw more in several places along the Coast. The observed Latitude was only 5 Miles to the Southward of the Log.

Monday, 14th. At the P.M. it fell Calm, and continued so about an hour, when a breeze sprung up at North-East, with which we stood in shore until

6 o'Clock, when, being in 30 fathoms and 3 or 4 Miles from the land, we Tack'd, having the wind at North-North-West. At this time Smoky Cape bore South 3/4 degrees West, distant about 5 Leagues, and the Northermost land in sight North 1/4 degrees East. At 8 we made a Trip in shore for an hour; after this the wind came off Shore, with which we stood along shore to the Northward, having from 30 to 21 fathoms, at the distance of 4 or 5 Miles from the Land. At 5 A.M. the Wind veer'd to North, and blow'd a fresh breeze, attended with Squalls and dark cloudy weather. At 8 it began to Thunder and Rain, which lasted about an Hour, and then fell Calm, which gave us an opportunity to sound, and found 86 fathoms, being about 4 or 5 Leagues from the Land; after this we got the wind Southerly, a fresh breeze and fair weather, and we Steer'd North by West for the Northermost land we had in sight. At noon we were about 4 Leagues from the land, and by observation in the Latitude of 30 degrees 22 minutes South, which was 9 Miles to the Southward of that given by the Log. Longitude in 206 degrees 39 minutes West, and Course and distance made good since Yesterday Noon North 16 degrees East, 22 miles; some Tolerable high land near the Shore bore West. As I have not mentioned the Aspect of the Country since we left Botany Bay, I shall now describe it as it hath at different times appear'd to us. As we have advanced to the Northward the land hath increased in height, in so much that in this Latitude it may be called a hilly Country; but between this and Botany Bay it is diversified with an agreeable variety of Hills, Ridges, and Valleys, and large plains all Cloathed with wood, which to all appearance is the same as I have before mentioned, as we could discover no Visible alteration in the Soil. Near the shore the land is in general low and Sandy, except the points which are rocky, and over many of them are pretty high hills, which at first rising out of the Water appear like a Island.

Tuesday, 15th. Fresh Gales at South-West, West-South-West, and South-South-West. In the P.M. had some heavy Squalls, attended with rain and hail, which obliged us to close reef our Topsails. Between 2 and 4 we had some small rocky Islands* (* The Solitary Islands.) between us and the land; the Southermost lies in the Latitude of 30 degrees 10 minutes, the Northermost in 29 degrees 58 minutes, and about 2 Leagues or more from the land; we sounded, and had 33 fathoms about 12 Miles without this last island. At 8 we brought too until 10, at which time we made sail under our Topsails. Having the Advantage of the Moon we steer'd along shore North and North by East, keeping at the distance of about 3 Leagues from the land having from 30 to 25 fathoms. As soon as it was daylight we made all the sail we could, having the Advantage of a fresh Gale and fair weather.* (* During the night the entrance of the Clarence River, now the outlet for the produce of a large and rich agricultural district, was passed, and in the morning that of the Richmond River, which serves a similar purpose.) At 9, being about a League from the Land, we saw upon it people and Smoke in Several places. At noon we were by observation in the Latitude of 28 degrees 39 minutes South, and Longitude 206 degrees 27 minutes West; Course and distance saild since Yesterday at Noon North 6 degrees 45 minutes East, 104 Miles. A Tolerable high point of land bore North-West by West, distant 3 Miles; this point I named Cape Byron* (* Captain John Byron was one of Cook's predecessors in exploration in the Pacific, having sailed round the World in H.M.S. Dolphin, in company with the Tamar, in 1764 to 1766.) (Latitude 28 degrees 37 minutes 30 seconds South, Longitude 206 degrees 30 minutes West). It may be known by a remarkable sharp peaked Mountain lying in land North-West by West from it. From this point the land Trends North 13 degrees West. Inland it is pretty high and hilly, but near the Shore it is low; to the Southward of the Point the land is low, and Tolerable level.

[Off Point Danger, New South Wales.]

Wednesday, 16th. Winds Southerly, a fresh Gale, with which we steer'd North along shore until sunset, at which time we discover'd breakers ahead, and on our Larboard bow, being at this time in 20 fathoms, and about 5 miles from the land. Haul'd off East until 8, at which time we had run 8 Miles, and had increased our Depth of Water to 44 fathoms. We then brought too with her head to the Eastward, and lay on this Tack until 10 o'Clock, when, having increased our Soundings to 78 fathoms, we wore and lay with her head in shore until 5 o'Clock a.m., when we made Sail. At daylight we were surprized by finding ourselves farther to the Southward than we were in the evening, and yet it had blown strong all night Southerly. We now saw the breakers again within us, which we passed at the distance of about 1 League; they lay in the Latitude of 28 degrees 8 minutes South, and stretch off East 2 Leagues from a point under which is a small Island; their situation may always be found by the peaked mountain before mentioned, which bears South-West by West from them, and on their account I have named it Mount Warning. It lies 7 or 8 Leagues in land in the Latitude of 28 degrees 22 minutes South. The land is high and hilly about it, but it is Conspicuous enough to be distinguished from everything else. The point off which these shoals lay I have named Point Danger;* (* Point Danger is the boundary point on the coast between New South Wales and Queensland.) to the Northward of it the land, which is low, Trends North-West by North; but we soon found that it did not keep that direction long before it turn'd again to the Northward. At Noon we were about 2 Leagues from the land, and by observation in the Latitude of 27 degrees 46 minutes, which was 17 Miles to the Southward of the Log; Longitude 206 degrees 26 minutes West. Mount Warning bore South 20 degrees West, distant 14 Leagues; the Northermost land in sight bore North. Our Course and distance made good since yesterday North 1 degree 45 minutes West, 53 miles.

[Off Moreton Bay, Queensland.]

Thursday, 17th. Winds Southerly, mostly a fresh breeze, with which in the P.M. we steer'd along shore North 3/4 East, at the distance of about 2 Leagues off. Between 4 and 5 we discover'd breakers on our Larboard bow; our Depth of Water at this time was 37 fathoms. At sunset the Northermost land in sight bore North by West, the breakers North-West by West, distant 4 Miles, and the Northermost land set at Noon, which form'd a Point, I named Point Lookout, bore West, distant 5 or 6 Miles (Latitude 27 degrees 6 minutes).* (* There is some mistake in this latitude. It should be 27 degrees 26 minutes.) On the North side of this point the shore forms a wide open bay, which I have named Morton's Bay,* (* James, Earl of Morton, was President of the Royal Society in 1764, and one of the Commissioners of Longitude.) in the Bottom of which the land is so low that I could but just see it from the Topmast head. The breakers I have just mentioned lies about 3 or 4 Miles from Point Lookout; at this time we had a great Sea from the Southward, which broke prodigious high upon them. Stood on North-North-East until 8, when, being past the breakers, and having Deepned our water to 52 fathoms, we brought too until 12 o'Clock, then made sail to the North-North-East. At 4 A.M. we sounded, and had 135 fathoms. At daylight I found that we had in the night got much farther to the Northward and from the Shore than I expected from the Course we steer'd, for we were at least 6 or 7 Leagues off, and therefore hauled in North-West by West, having the Advantage of a Fresh Gale at South-South-West. The Northermost land seen last night bore from us at this time South-South-West, distant 6 Leagues. This land I named Cape Morton, it being the North point of the Bay of the same Name (Latitude 26 degrees 56 minutes South, Longitude 206 degrees 28 minutes). From Cape Morton the Land Trends away West, further than we could see, for there is a small space where we could see no land; some on board where of opinion that there is a River there because the Sea looked paler than usual. Upon sounding we found 34 fathoms fine white sandy bottom, which alone is Sufficient change, the apparent Colour of Sea Water, without the Assistance of Rivers. The land need only to be low here, as it is in a Thousand other places upon the Coast, to have made it impossible for us to have seen it at the distance we were off. Be this as it may, it was a point that could not be clear'd up as we had the wind; but should any one be desirous of doing it that may come after me, this place may always be found by 3 Hills which lay to the Northward of it in the Latitude of 26 degrees 53 minutes South. These hills lay but a little way inland, and not far from Each other; they are very remarkable on account of their Singular form of Elivation, which very much resembles Glass Houses,* (* The Glass houses form a well-known sea mark on entering Moreton Bay, as the name is now written. Brisbane, the capital of Queensland, stands on the river of the same name, which falls into Moreton Bay.) which occasioned my giving them that Name. The Northermost of the 3 is the highest and largest. There are likewise several other peaked hills inland to the Northward of these, but they are not near so remarkable. At Noon we were by Observation in the Latitude of 26 degrees 28 minutes South, which was 10 Miles to the Northward of the Log; a Circumstance that hath not hapned since we have been upon the Coast before. Our Course and distance run since Yesterday noon was North by West 80 Miles, which brought us into the Longitude of 206 degrees 46 minutes. At this time we were about 2 or 3 Leagues from the land, and in 24 fathoms Water; a low bluff point, which was the Southern point of an open Sandy bay,* (* Laguna Bay. The point is called Low Bluff.) bore North 52 degrees West, distant 3 Leagues, and the Northermost point of land in sight bore North 1/4 East. Several Smokes seen to-day, and some pretty far inland.

Friday, 18th. In steering along shore at the distance of 2 Leagues off our Soundings was from 24 to 32 fathoms Sandy bottom. At 6 P.M. the North point set at Noon bore North 1/4 West; distant 4 Leagues; at 10 it bore North-West by West 1/2 West, and as we had seen no land to the Northward of it we brought too, not knowing which way to steer, having at this time but little wind, and continued so for the most part of the night. At 2 P.M. we made sail with the wind at South-West, and at daylight saw the land extending as far as North 3/4 East. The point set last night bore South-West by West, distant 3 or 4 Leagues; I have named it Double Island Point, on account of its figure (Latitude 25 degrees 58 minutes South, Longitude 206 degrees 48 minutes West). The land within this point is of a moderate and pretty equal height, but the point itself is of such an unequal Height that it looks like 2 Small Islands laying under the land; it likewise may be known by the white Clifts on the North side of it. Here the land trends to the North-West, and forms a large open bay,* (* Wide Bay.) in the bottom of which the land appear'd to be very low, in so much that we could but just see it from the Deck. In crossing the mouth of this bay our Depth of Water was from 30 to 32 fathoms, a white sandy bottom. At Noon we were about 3 Leagues from the Land, and in the Latitude of 25 degrees 34 minutes South, Longitude 206 degrees 45 minutes West; Double Island Point bore South 3/4 West, and the Northermost land in sight North 3/4 East. The land hereabouts, which is of a moderate height, appears more barren than any we have yet seen on this Coast, and the Soil more sandy, there being several large places where nothing else is to be seen; in other places the woods look to be low and Shrubby, nor did we see many signs of inhabitants.

Saturday, 19th. In the P.M. had Variable light Airs, and Calms; in the night had a light breeze from the land, which in the A.M. veer'd to South-West and South-South-West. In the evening found the Variation to be 8 degrees 36 minutes East, and in the Morning 8 degrees 20 minutes; as we had but little wind we keept to the Northward all night, having from 23 to 27 fathoms fine sandy bottom, at the Distance of 2 or 3 Leagues from the Land. At Noon we were about 4 Miles from it, and by observation in the Latitude of 25 degrees 4 minutes, and in this situation had but 13 fathoms; the Northermost land in Sight bore North 21 degrees West, distant 8 Miles; our Course and distance saild since yesterday at Noon was North 13 degrees 15 minutes East, 31 Miles.

[Off Sandy Cape, Queensland.]

Sunday, 20th. Winds Southerly, Gentle breezes. At 10 p.m. we passed, at the distance of 4 Miles, having 17 fathoms, a black bluff head or point of land, on which a number of the Natives were Assembled, which occasioned my naming it Indian Head; Latitude 25 degrees 0 minutes North by West, 4 Miles from this head, is another much like it. From this last the land Trends a little more to the Westward, and is low and Sandy next the Sea, for what may be behind it I know not; if land, it must be all low, for we could see no part of it from the Mast head. We saw people in other places besides the one I have mentioned; some Smokes in the day and fires in the Night. Having but little wind all Night, we kept on to the Northward, having from 17 to 34 fathoms, from 4 Miles to 4 Leagues from the Land, the Northermost part of which bore from us at daylight West-South-West, and seem'd to End in a point, from which we discover'd a Reef stretching out to the Northward as far as we could see, being, at this time, in 18 fathoms; for we had, before it was light, hauld our Wind to the Westward, and this course we continued until we had plainly discover'd breakers a long way upon our Lee Bow, which seem'd to Stretch quite home to the land. We then Edged away North-West and North-North-West, along the East side of the Shoal, from 2 to 1 Miles off, having regular, even Soundings, from 13 to 7 fathoms; fine sandy bottom. At Noon we were, by Observation, in the Latitude of 24 degrees 26 minutes South, which was 13 Miles to the Northward of that given by the Log. The extream point of the Shoal we judged to bear about North-West of us; and the point of land above-mentioned bore South 3/4 West, distant 20 Miles. This point I have named Sandy Cape,* (* Sandy Cape is the northern point of Great Sandy Island. A long narrow channel separates the latter from the mainland, and opens at its northern end into Harvey Bay, a great sheet of water 40 miles across. This channel is now much used by the coasting trade, as it avoids the long detour round Breaksea Spit, a most dangerous shoal.) on account of 2 very large white Patches of Sand upon it. It is of a height Sufficient to be seen 12 Leagues in Clear weather (Latitude 24 degrees 46 minutes, Longitude 206 degrees 51 minutes West); from it the Land trends away West-South-West and South-West as far as we could see.

Monday, 21st. In the P.M. we kept along the East side of the Shoal until 2, when, judging there was water for us over, I sent a Boat a Head to sound, and upon her making the Signal for more than 5 fathoms we hauld our wind and stood over the Tail of it in 6 fathoms. At this time we were in the Latitude of 24 degrees 22 minutes South, and Sandy Cape bore South 1/2 East, distant 8 Leagues; but the Direction of the Shoal is nearest North-North-West and South-South-East. At this time we had 6 fathoms; the boat which was not above 1/4 of a mile to the Southward of us had little more than 5 fathoms. From 6 fathoms we had the next Cast, 13, and then 20 immediately, as fast as the Man could heave the Lead; from this I did suppose that the West side of the Shoal is pretty steep too, whereas on the other side we had gradual Soundings from 13 to 7 fathoms. This Shoal I called Break Sea Spit, because now we had smooth water, whereas upon the whole Coast to the Southward of it we had always a high Sea or swell from the South-East. At 6, the Land of Sandy Cape extending from South 17 degrees East to South 27 degrees East, distance 8 Leagues; Depth of Water, 23 fathoms, which depth we keept all Night, as we stood to the Westward with light Airs from the Southward; but between 12 and 4 A.M. we had it Calm, after which a Gentle breeze sprung up at South, with which we still keept on upon a Wind to the Westward. At 7 we Saw from the Masthead the Land of Sandy Cape bearing South-East 1/2 East, distance 12 or 13 Leagues. At 9, we discover'd from the Mast head land to the Westward, and soon after saw smooke upon it. Our depth of Water was now decreased to 17 fathoms, and by Noon to 13, at which time we were by observation in the Latitude of 24 degrees 28 minutes South, and about 7 Leagues from the Land, which extended from South by West to West-North-West. Longitude made from Sandy Cape 0 degrees 45 minutes West.

For these few days past we have seen at times a sort of Sea fowl we have no where seen before that I remember; they are of the sort called Boobies. Before this day we seldom saw more than 2 or 3 at a time, and only when we were near the land. Last night a small flock of these birds passed the Ship and went away to the North-West, and this morning from 1/2 an hour before sun rise to half an hour after, flights of them were continually coming from the North-North-West, and flying to the South-South-East, and not one was seen to fly in any other direction. From this we did suppose that there was a Lagoon, River, or Inlet of Shallow Water to the Southward of us, where these birds resorted to in the day to feed, and that not very far to the Northward lay some Island, where they retir'd too in the night.

Tuesday, 22nd. In the P.M. had a Gentle breeze at South-East, with which we stood in for the land South-West until 4, when, being in the Latitude of 24 degrees 36 minutes South, and about 2 Leagues from land, in 9 fathoms, we bore away along shore North-West by West; at the same time we could see the land extending to the South-South-East about 8 Leagues. Near the Sea the land is very low, but inland are some moderately high hills, and the whole appeared to be thickly Cloathed with wood. In running along shore we shoalded our Water from 9 to 7 fathoms, and at one time had but 6 fathoms, which determined me to Anchor for the Night, and accordingly at 8 o'Clock we came too in 8 fathoms, fine gravelly bottom, about 5 miles from the land. This evening we saw a Water Snake, and 2 or 3 evenings ago one lay under the Ship's Stern some time; this was about 1 1/2 Yards in length, and was the first we had seen. At 6 A.M. weighed with a Gentle breeze Southerly, and Steer'd North-West 1/4 West, edging in for the land until we got Within 2 Miles of it, having from 7 to 11 fathoms; we then steer'd North-North-West as the land laid. At Noon we were by Observation in the Latitude of 24 degrees 19 minutes South; Longitude made from Sandy Cape 1 degree 14 minutes West.

[At Anchor. Bustard Bay, Queensland.]

Wednesday, 23rd. Continued our Course alongshore at the distance of about 2 Miles off, having from 12 to 9, 8 and 7 fathoms, until 5 o'Clock, at which time we were abreast of the South point of a Large open Bay,* (* Bustard Bay.) wherein I intended to Anchor. Accordingly we hauld in Close upon a Wind, and sent a boat ahead to sound; after making some Trips we Anchored at 8 o'Clock in 5 fathoms, a Sandy bottom. The South point of the bay bore East 3/4 South, distant 2 Miles; the North point North-West 1/4 North, about 2 Miles from the shore, in the bottom of the bay. Last night, some time in the Middle watch, a very extraordinary affair hapned to Mr. Orton, my Clerk. He having been drinking in the evening, some Malicious person or persons in the Ship took Advantage of his being Drunk, and cut off all the Cloaths from off his back; not being satisfied with this, they some time after went into his Cabin and cut off a part of both his Ears as he lay a Sleep in his Bed. The person whom he suspected to have done this was Mr. Magra, one of the Midshipmen; but this did not appear to me. Upon enquiry, however, as I had been told that Magra had once or twice before this in their drunken Frolicks cut off his cloaths, and had been heard to say (as I was told) that if it was not for the Law he would Murder him, these things consider'd, induced me to think that Magra was not Altogether innocent. I therefore for the present dismiss'd him the Quarter deck, and Suspended him from doing any duty in the Ship, he being one of those Gentlemen frequently found on board King's Ships that can very well be spared; besides, it was necessary in me to show my immediate resentment against the person on whom the suspicion fell, least they should not have stop'd here. With respect to Mr. Orton, he is a man not without faults; yet from all the inquiry I could make, it evidently appear'd to me that so far from deserving such Treatment, he had not designed injuring any person in the Ship; so that I do--and shall always--look upon him as an injured man. Some reasons, however, might be given why this misfortune came upon him, in which he himself was in some measure to blame; but as this is only conjecture, and would tend to fix it upon some people in the Ship, whom I would fain believe would hardly be guilty of such an Action, I shall say nothing about it, unless I shall hereafter discover the Offenders, which I shall take every method in my power to do, for I look upon such proceedings as highly dangerous in such Voyages as this, and the greatest insult that could be offer'd to my Authority in this Ship, as I have always been ready to hear and redress every complaint that have been made against any Person in the Ship.* (* This history of Mr. Orton's misadventure is omitted from the Admiralty copy. It is an illustration of the times to note that the fact of Orton having got drunk does not seem to call for the Captain's severe censure. In these days, though the practical joker receives punishment, the drunkard would certainly come in for a large share also.)

In the A.M. I went ashore with a party of men in order to Examine the Country, accompanied by Mr. Banks and the other Gentlemen; we landed a little within the South point of the Bay, where there is a Channel leading into a large Lagoon. The first thing that I did was to sound and examine the Channell, in which I found 3 fathoms, until I got about a Mile up it, where I met with a Shoal, whereon was little more than one fathom; being over this I had 3 fathoms again. The Entrance into this Channell lies close to the South point of this Bay, being form'd on the East by the Shore, and on the West by a large Spit of sand; it is about a 1/4 of a Mile broad, and lies in South by West; here is room for a few Ships to lay very secure, and a small Stream of Fresh Water. After this I made a little excursion into the Woods while some hands made 3 or 4 hauls with the Sean, but caught not above a dozen very small fish. By this time the flood was made, and I imbarqued in the Boats in order to row up the Lagoon; but in this I was hindred by meeting everywhere with Shoal Water. As yet we had seen no people, but saw a great deal of Smook up and on the West side of the Lagoon, which was all too far off for us to go by land, excepting one; this we went to and found 10 Small fires in a very small Compass, and some Cockle Shells laying by them, but the people were gone. On the windward or South side of one of the fires was stuck up a little Bark about a foot and a half high, and some few pieces lay about in other places; these we concluded were all the covering they had in the Night, and many of them, I firmly believe, have not this, but, naked as they are, sleep in the open air. Tupia, who was with us, observed that they were Taata Eno's; that is, bad or poor people. The Country is visibly worse than at the last place we were at; the soil is dry and Sandy, and the woods are free from underwoods of every kind; here are of the same sort of Trees as we found in Bottany Harbour, with a few other sorts. One sort, which is by far the most Numerous sort of any in the Woods, grow Something like birch; the Bark at first sight looks like birch bark, but upon examination I found it to be very different, and so I believe is the wood; but this I could not examine, as having no axe or anything with me to cut down a Tree. About the Skirts of the Lagoon grows the true Mangrove, such as are found in the West Indies, and which we have not seen during the Voyage before; here is likewise a sort of a palm Tree, which grows on low, barren, sandy places in the South Sea Islands. All, or most of the same sort, of Land and Water fowl as we saw at Botany Harbour we saw here; besides these we saw some Bustards, such as we have in England, one of which we kill'd that weighed 17 1/2 pounds, which occasioned my giving this place the Name of Bustard Bay (Latitude 24 degrees 4 minutes, Longitude 208 degrees 22 minutes West); we likewise saw some black and white Ducks. Here are plenty of small Oysters sticking to the Rocks, Stones, and Mangrove Trees, and some few other shell fish, such as large Muscles, Pearl Oysters, Cockels, etc. I measured the perpendicular height of the last Tide, and found it to be 8 foot above low water mark, and from the time of low water to-day I found that it must be high Water at the full and Change of the Moon at 8 o'Clock.

Thursday, 24th. In the P.M. I was employ'd ashore in the Transactions before related; at 4 a.m. we weighed with a Gentle breeze at South, and made sail out of the Bay. In standing out our soundings were from 5 to 15 fathoms; when in this last Depth we were abreast of the North Point, and being daylight we discover'd breakers stretching out from it about North-North-East, 2 or 3 miles; at the Outermost point of them is a Rock just above Water. In passing these rocks at the distance of 1/2 a mile we had from 15 to 20 fathoms; being past them, we hauld along shore West-North-West for the farthest land we had in sight. At Noon we were by Observation in the Latitude of 23 degrees 52 minutes South; the North part of Bustard Bay bore South 62 degrees East, distance 10 miles, and the Northermost land in sight North 60 degrees West. Longitude in 208 degrees 37 minutes West, distance from the nearest shore 6 Miles; in this situation had 14 fathoms water.

[Off Cape Capricorn, Queensland.]

Friday, 25th. In the P.M. had it calm until 5, when a light breeze sprung up at South-East, and we steer'd North-West as the land lay until 10, then brought too, having had all along 14 and 15 fathoms. At 5 A.M. we made sail; at daylight the Northermost point of the Main bore North 70 degrees West, and soon after we saw more land making like Islands, bearing North-West by North; at 9 we were abreast of the point, distant from it 1 mile; Depth of Water 14 fathoms. I found this point to lay directly under the Tropic of Capricorn, and for that reason call it by that Name. Longitude 209 degrees 0 minutes West. It is of a Moderate height, and looks white and barren, and may be known by some Islands which lie to the North-West of it, and some small Rocks one League South-East from it; on the West side of the Cape there appeared to be a Lagoon. On the 2 Spits which form the Entrance were a great Number of Pelicans; at least, so I call them. The most northermost land we could see bore from Cape Capricorn North 24 degrees West, and appeared to be an Island;* (* Hummocky Island.) but the Main land Trended West by North 1/2 North, which Course we steer'd, having from 15 to 16 fathoms and from 6 to 9, a hard sandy bottom. At Noon our Latitude by Observation was 23 degrees 24 minutes South; Cape Capricorn bore South 60 degrees East, distance 2 Leagues; a small Island North by East 2 Miles. In this Situation had 9 fathoms at the distance of 4 Miles from the Main land, which is here low and Sandy next the Sea, except the points which are moderately high and rocky; in land the Country is hilly, and affords but a very indifferent prospect.* (* Between Bustard Bay and Cape Capricorn is Port Curtis, in which stands the small town of Gladstone. Cape Capricorn is the eastern point of Curtis Island, and to the northward is Keppel Bay, into which falls the Fitzroy River. Up the latter, 35 miles from the sea, is Rockhampton, the second largest town of Queensland. All this coast is encumbered with shoals, outside of which Cook had so far prudently kept. To seaward begins the long chain of islands and reefs known as the Great Australian Barrier, which stretches up to Torres Straits. Cook was unaware of their existence, as they were out of sight, but he became painfully acquainted with them later, where the reefs approach the land, and make navigation along the coast anxious work; but he here began to get into difficulties with the shoals which stretch off the coast itself.)

Saturday, 26th. In the P.M. light breezes at East-South-East, with which we stood to the North-West until 4 o'Clock, when it fell calm, and soon after we Anchored in 12 fathoms. Cape Capricorn bearing South 54 degrees East, distant 4 Leagues, having the Main land and Islands in a manner all around us. In the night we found the tide to rise and fall near 7 feet, and the flood to set to the Westward and Ebb to the Eastward; which is quite the reverse to what we found it when at Anchor to the Eastward of Bustard Bay. At 6 a.m. we weigh'd with the Wind at South, a Gentle breeze, and stood away to the North-West, between the Outermost range of Islands* (* The Keppel Islands.) and the Main land, leaving several small Islands between us and the Latter, which we passed Close by. Our soundings was a little irregular, from 12 to 4 fathoms, which caused me to send a Boat ahead to sound. At noon we were about 3 Miles from the Main, about the same distance from the Islands without us; our Latitude by Observation was 23 degrees 7 minutes South, and Longitude made from Cape Capricorn 18 Miles West. The Main land in this Latitude is tolerable high and Mountainious; and the Islands which lay off it are the most of them pretty high and of a Small Circuit, and have more the appearance of barrenness than fertility. We saw smookes a good way in land, which makes me think there must be a River, Lagoon, or Inlet, into the Country, and we passed 2 places that had the Appearance of such this morning; but our Depth of Water at that Time was too little to haul in for them, where I might expect to meet with less.

Sunday, 27th. We had not stood on to the Northward quite an hour before we fell into 3 fathoms, upon which I anchor'd, and Sent away the Master with 2 Boats to sound the Channell, which lay to Leeward of us between the Northermost Island and the Main Land, which appear'd to me to be pretty broad; but I suspected that it was Shoal, and so it was found, for the Master reported to me upon his return that he found in many places only 2 1/2 fathoms, and where we lay at Anchor we had only 16 feet, which was not 2 feet more than the Ship drew.* (* This was between Great Keppel Island and the Main. There is a mass of shoals here.) In the Evening the wind veer'd to East-North-East, which gave us an opportunity to stretch 3 or 4 miles back the way we Came before the Wind Shifted to South, and obliged us again to Anchor in 6 fathoms. At 5 o'Clock in the A.M. I sent away the Master with 2 Boats to search for a Passage out between the Islands, while the Ship got under sail. As soon as it was light the Signal was made by the boats of their having found a Passage, upon which we hoisted in the Boats, and made sail to the Northward as the land lay; soundings from 9 to 15 fathoms, having still Some small Islands without us.* (* The ship passed out between Great Keppel Island and North Keppel Island.) At noon we were about 2 Leagues from the Main Land, and by observation in the Latitude of 22 degrees 53 minutes South, Longitude made from Cape Capricorn 0 degrees 20 minutes West. At this time the Northermost point of Land we had in sight bore North-North-West, distance 10 Miles; this point I named Cape Manyfold, from the Number of high Hills over it; Latitude 22 degrees 43 minutes South; it lies North 20 degrees West, distant 17 Leagues from Cape Capricorn. Between them the shore forms a large Bay, which I call'd Keppel Bay, and the Islands which lay in and Off it are known by the same name; in this Bay is good Anchorage, where there is a sufficient depth of Water; what refreshment it may afford for Shipping I know not.* (* As before mentioned, the Fitzroy River falls into Keppel Bay, and forms a good harbour, though much encumbered with sand banks.) We caught no fish here, notwithstanding we were at Anchor; it can hardly be doubted but what it afforded fresh Water in several places, as both Mainland and Islands are inhabited. We saw smokes by day and fires in the night upon the Main, and people upon one of the Islands.

[Off Cape Townshend, Queensland.]

Monday, 28th. Winds at South-South-East, a fresh breeze. At 3 o'Clock in the P.M. we passed Cape Manifold, from which the Land Trends North-North-West. The land of this Cape is tolerable high, and riseth in hills directly from the Sea; it may be known by 3 Islands laying off it, one near the Shore, and the other 2 Eight Miles out at Sea; the one of these is low and flat, and the other high and round.* (* Peak and Flat Islands.) At 6 o'Clock we shortned sail and brought too; the Northermost part of the Main we had in sight bore North-West, and some Islands lying off it bore North 31 degrees West; our soundings since Noon were from 20 to 25 fathoms, and in the Night 30 and 34 fathoms. At day light we made Sail, Cape Manifold bearing South by East, distance 8 Leagues, and the Islands set last night in the same directions, distance from us 4 Miles. The farthest point of the Main bore North 67 degrees West, distant 22 Miles; but we could see several Islands to the Northward of this direction.* (* The easternmost of the Northumberland Islands.) At 9 o'Clock we were abreast of the above point, which I named Cape Townshend* (* Charles Townshend was Chancellor of the Exchequer 1767.) (Latitude 22 degrees 13 minutes, Longitude 209 degrees 48 minutes West); the land of this Cape is of a moderate and pretty even height, and is more barren than woody. Several Islands lay to the Northward of it, 4 or 5 Leagues out at Sea. 3 or 4 Leagues to the South-East the Shore forms a bay,* (* Shoalwater Bay, a large inlet.) in the bottom of which there appeared to be an inlet or Harbour to the Westward of the Coast, and Trends South-West 1/2 South; and these form a very large Bay, which turns away to the Eastward, and probably communicates with the Inlet above mentioned, and by that Means makes the land of the Cape an Island. As soon as we got round the Cape we hauld our wind to the Westward in order to get within the Islands which lay scatter'd up and down in this bay in great number, and extend out to Sea as far as we could see from the Masthead; how much farther will hardly be in my power to determine; they are as Various in their height and Circuit as they are numerous.* (* The Northumberland islands, a very extensive group.) We had not stood long upon a Wind before we meet with Shoal Water, and was obliged to Tack about to avoid it; after which I sent a boat ahead, and we bore away West by North, leaving many small Islands, Rocks, and Shoals between us and the Main, and a number of Large Islands without us; soundings from 14 to 17 fathoms, Sandy Bottom. A little before noon the boat made the Signal for meeting with Shoal Water, upon which we hauld close upon a Wind to the Eastward, but suddenly fell into 3 1/4 fathoms water, upon which we immediately let go an Anchor, and brought the Ship up with all sails standing, and had then 4 fathoms Coarse sandy bottom. We found here a strong Tide setting to the North-West by West 1/2 West, at the rate of between 2 and 3 Miles an Hour, which was what Carried us so quickly upon the Shoal. Our Latitude by Observation was 22 degrees 8 minutes South; Cape Townshend bore East 16 degrees South, distant 13 Miles, and the Westermost part of the Main Land in sight West 3/4 North, having a number of Islands in sight all round us.* (* The ship was on the Donovan Shoal in Broad Sound Channel.)

Tuesday, 29th. Fresh gales between the South-South-East and East-South-East, Hazey weather, with some showers of rain. In the P.M., having sounded about the Ship, and found that their was Sufficient Water for her over the Shoal, we at 3 o'clock weigh'd and made Sail, and stood to the Westward as the Land lay, having first sent a boat ahead to sound. At 6 we Anchor'd in 10 fathoms, Sandy bottom, about 2 Miles from the Main Land, the Westermost part of which bore West-North-West, having still a Number of Islands in sight a long way without us. At 5 a.m. I sent away the Master with 2 Boats to sound the Entrance of an inlet, which bore from us West, distance about 1 League, into which I intended to go with the Ship to wait a few days, until the Moon increased, and in the meantime to examine the Country. By such time as we had got the Ship under Sail the Boats made the Signal for Anchorage, upon which we stood in with the Ship, and Anchor'd in 5 fathoms, about a League within the Entrance of the inlet, which we judged to be a River running a Good way inland, as I observed the Tides to flow and Ebb something considerable.* (* It is in reality a narrow channel which runs into Broad Sound.) I had some thoughts of laying the Ship a Shore to Clean her bottom. With this view both the Master and I went to look for a Convenient place for that purpose, and at the same time to look for fresh Water, not one drop of which we could find, but met with several places where a Ship might be laid ashore with safety.

[At Anchor, Thirsty Sound.]

Wednesday, 30th. In the P.M. I went again in search of Fresh Water, but had no better success than before; wherefore I gave over all thoughts of laying the Ship a Shore, being resolved to spend as little time as possible in a place that was likely to afford us no sort of refreshment. But as I had observed from the Hills the inlet to run a good way in, I thought this a good time to penetrate into the Country to see a little of the inland parts. Accordingly I prepared for making that Excursion in the morning, but the first thing I did was to get upon a pretty high Hill, which is at the North-West entrance of the inlet, before Sunrise, in order to take a view of the Sea Coast and Islands, etc., that lay off it, and to take their bearings, having the Azimuth Compass with me for that purpose, the Needle of which differ'd from its True position something very considerable, even above 30 degrees, in some places more, and in other less, for I try'd it in several places. I found it differ in itself above 2 points in the space of about 14 feet. The loose stones which lay upon the Ground had no effect upon the Needle; I therefore concluded that it must be owing to Iron Ore upon the Hill, visible signs of which appeared not only here, but in several other places. As soon as I had done here I proceeded up the inlet. I set out with the first of the flood, and long before high water got about 8 Leagues up it; its breadth thus far was from 2 to 4 or 5 Miles upon a South-West by South direction; but here it spread every way, and formed a Large lake, which communicated with the Sea to the North-West. I not only saw the Sea in this direction, but found the tide of flood coming strong in from the North-West. I likewise observ'd an Arm of this Lake extending to the Eastward, and it is not at all improbable but what it Communicates with the Sea in the bottom of the bay, which lies to the Westward of Cape Townshend.* (* This is exactly what it does.) On the South side of the Lake is a ridge of pretty high hills, which I was desirous of going upon; but as the day was far spent and high water, I was afraid of being bewilder'd among the Shoals in the night, which promised to be none of the best, being already rainy, dirty weather, and therefore I made the best of my way to the Ship. In this little Excursion I saw only 2 people, and those at a distance, and are all that we have seen in this place, but we have met with several fire places, and seen smokes at a distance. This inlet, which I have named Thirsty Sound, by reason we could find no fresh Water, lies in the Latitude of 22 degrees 05 minutes South, and Longitude 210 degrees 24 West; it may be known by a Group of small Islands Laying under the shore from 2 to 5 Leagues North-West from it.* (* Barren Islands.) There is likewise another Group of Islands laying right before it between 3 and 4 Leagues out at Sea.* (* Duke Islands.) Over each of the Points that form the Entrance is a pretty high, round Hill; that on the North-West is a Peninsula, surrounded by the Sea at high water; the distance from the one to the other is about 2 Miles bold to both Shores. Here is good Anchoring in 7, 6, 5, and 4 fathoms water, and very Convenient places for laying a Ship ashore, where at Spring Tides the tides doth not rise less than 16 or 18 feet, and flows at full and Change of the Moon about 11 o'Clock. We met with no fresh water, or any other kind of refreshments whatever; we saw 2 Turtle, but caught none, nor no sort of Fish or wild fowl, except a few small land birds. Here are the same sort of Water Fowl as we saw in Botany Bay, and like them, so shy that it is hardly possible to get within shott of them. No signs of Fertility is to be seen upon the Land; the Soil of the up lands is mostly a hard, redish Clay, and produceth several sorts of Trees, such as we have seen before, and some others, and clear of all underwoods. All the low lands are mostly overrun with Mangroves, and at Spring tides overflow'd by the Sea; and I believe in the rainy Seasons here are large land floods, as we saw in many places Gullies, which seem'd to have been made by torrents of Water coming from the Adjacent hills, besides other Visible signs of the Water having been a Considerable height above the Common Spring Tides. Dr. Solander and I was upon a rising Ground up the inlet, which we thought had at one time or another been overflow'd by the Sea, and if so great part of the Country must at that time been laid under Water. Up in the lakes, or lagoons, I suppose, are shell fish, on which the few Natives subsist. We found Oysters sticking to most of the Rocks upon the Shore, which were so small, as not to be worth the picking off.* (* Cook was very unfortunate in his landing here. The channel is at the end of a long headland between two bays, Shoalwater Bay and Broad Sound, and was a very unlikely place either to find water or get any true idea of the country.)

Thursday, 31st. Winds Southerly and South-East; Dark, Hazey weather, with rain. In the P.M., finding no one inducement to stay longer in this place, we at 6 a.m. Weighed and put to Sea, and stood to the North-West, having the Advantage of a fresh breeze at South-South-East. We keept without the Group of Islands which lay in Shore, and to the North-West of Thirsty Sound, as there appear'd to be no safe passage between them and the Main; at the same time we had a number of Islands without us extending out to Sea as far as we could see; as we run in this direction our depth of Water was 10, 8 and 9 fathoms.* (* The ship passed between the Duke Islands and the maze of reefs and islands lying North-West of Thirsty Sound.) At Noon the North-West point of Thirsty Sound, which I have named Pier head, bore South 36 degrees East, distant 5 Leagues; the East point of the other inlet, which Communicates with the former, as I have before mentioned, bore South by West, distance 2 1/2 Leagues, the Group of Islands above mentioned laying between us and the point. The farthest part of the Main in sight, on the other side of the inlet, bore North-West; our Latitude by Observation was 21 degrees 53 minutes South.

[June 1770.]

Friday, June 1st. At 1/2 an hour After Noon, upon the Boat we had ahead sounding making the Signal for Shoal Water, we hauld our wind to the North-East, having at that time 7 fathoms; the Next cast 5, and then 3, upon which we let go an Anchor, and brought the Ship up. The North-West point of Thirsty Sound, or Pier Head, bore South-East, distance 6 Leagues, being Midway between the Islands which lies off the East point of the Western inlet and 3 Small Islands directly without them,* (* The shoal is now known as Lake Shoal. The three Islands are the Bedwell Islands.) it being now the first of the flood which we found to set North-West by West 1/2 West. After having sounded about the Shoal, on which we found not quite 3 fathoms, but without it deep water, we got under Sail, and hauld round the 3 Islands just mentioned, and came to an Anchor under the Lee of them in 15 fathoms, having at this time dark, hazey, rainy weather, which continued until 7 o'Clock a.m., at which time we got again under sail, and stood to the North-West with a fresh breeze at South-South-East and fair weather, having the Main land in Sight and a Number of Islands all round us, some of which lay out at Sea as far as we could See. The Western Inlet before mentioned, known in the Chart by the Name of Broad Sound, we had now all open. It is at least 9 or 10 Leagues wide at the Entrance, with several Islands laying in and before, and I believe Shoals also, for we had very irregular Soundings, from 10 to 5 and 4 fathoms. At Noon we were by Observation in the Latitude of 21 degrees 29 minutes South, and Longitude made from Cape Townshend 59 degrees West. A point of Land, which forms the North-West Entrance into Broad Sound, bore from us at this Time West, distance 3 Leagues; this Cape I have named Cape Palmerston* (* Henry Viscount Palmerston was a Lord of the Admiralty, 1766 to 1778.) (Latitude 21 degrees 27 minutes South,

Longitude 210 degrees 57 minutes West). Between this Cape and Cape Townshend lies the Bay of Inlets, so named from the Number of Inlets, Creeks, etc., in it.* (* The name Bay of Inlets has disappeared from the charts. Cook applied it to the whole mass of bays in this locality, covering over 60 miles. A look at a modern chart causes amazement that Cook managed to keep his ship off the ground, as the whole sea in his track is strewed with dangers.)

[Off Cape Hillsborough, Queensland.]

Saturday, 2nd. Winds at South-South-East and South-East, a gentle breeze, with which we stood to the North-West and North-West by North, as the land lay, under an easey Sail. Having a boat ahead, found our Soundings at first were very irregular, from 9 to 4 fathoms; but afterwards regular, from 9 to 11 fathoms. At 8, being about 2 Leagues from the Main Land, we Anchor'd in 11 fathoms, Sandy bottom. Soon after this we found a Slow Motion of a Tide seting to the Eastward, and rode so until 6, at which time the tide had risen 11 feet; we now got under Sail, and Stood away North-North-West as the land lay. From the Observations made on the tide last Night it is plain that the flood comes from the North-West; whereas Yesterday and for Several days before we found it to come from the South-East. This is neither the first nor second time that we have observed the same thing, and in my Opinion easy accounted for; but this I shall do in another place. At sun rise we found the Variation to be 6 degrees 45 minutes East. In steering along shore between the Island and the Main, at the Distance of 2 Leagues from the Latter, and 3 or 4 from the former, our soundings were Regular, from 12 to 9 fathoms; but about 11 o'Clock we were again embarrassed with Shoal Water,* (* Blackwood Shoals.) but got clear without letting go an Anchor; we had at one time not quite 3 fathoms. At Noon we were about 2 Leagues from the Main land, and about 4 from the Islands without us; our Latitude by Observation was 20 degrees 56 minutes South, Longitude made from Cape Palmerston 16 degrees West; a pretty high Promontory, which I named Cape Hillsborough,* (* Earl of Hillsborough was the First Secretary of State for the Colonies, and President of the Board of Trade when the Endeavour sailed.) bore West 1/2 North, distant 7 Miles. The Main Land is here pretty much diversified with Mountains, Hills, plains, and Vallies, and seem'd to be tollerably Cloathed with Wood and Verdure. These Islands, which lay Parrallel with the Coast, and from 5 to 8 or 9 Leagues off, are of Various Extent, both for height and Circuit; hardly any Exceeds 5 Leagues in Circuit, and many again are very small.* (* The Cumberland Islands. They stretch along the coast for 60 miles.) Besides the Chain of Islands, which lay at a distance from the Coast, there are other Small Ones laying under the Land. Some few smokes were seen on the Main land.

Sunday, 3rd. Winds between the South by East and South-East. A Gentle breeze and Clear weather. In the P.M. we steer'd along shore North-West 1/2 West, at the distance of 2 Leagues from the Main, having 9 and 10 fathoms regular soundings. At sun set the furthest point of the Main Land that we could distinguish as such bore North 48 degrees West; to the Northward of this lay some high land, which I took to be an Island, the North West point of which bore North 41 degrees West; but as I was not sure that there was a passage this way, we at 8 came to an Anchor in 10 fathoms, muddy bottom. 2 hours after this we had a tide setting to the Northward, and at 2 o'clock it had fallen 9 Feet since the time we Anchored. After this the Tide began to rise, and the flood came from the Northward, which was from the Islands out at Sea, and plainly indicated that there was no passage to the North-West; but as this did not appear at day light when we got under Sail, and stood away to the North-West until 8, at this time we discover'd low land, quite a Cross what we took for an Opening between the Main and the Islands, which proved to be a Bay about 5 or 6 Leagues deep. Upon this we hauld our wind to the Eastward round the Northermost point of the Bay, which bore from us at this time North-East by North, distance 4 Leagues. From this point we found the Main land trend away North by West 1/2 West, and a Strait or Passage between it and a Large Island* (* Whitsunday Island.) or Islands laying in a Parrallel direction with the Coast; this passage we Stood into, having the Tide of Ebb in our favour. At Noon we were just within the Entrance, and by observation in the Latitude of 20 degrees 26 minutes South; Cape Hillsborough bore South by East, distant 10 Leagues, and the North point of the Bay before mentioned bore South 19 degrees West, distance 4 Miles. This point I have named Cape Conway* (* General H.S. Conway was Secretary of State 1765 to 1768.) (Latitude 20 degrees 30 minutes, Longitude 211 degrees 28 minutes), and the bay, Repulse Bay, which is formed by these 2 Capes. The greatest and least depth of Water we found in it was 13 and 8 fathoms; every where safe Anchoring, and I believe, was it properly examined, there would be found some good Harbour in it, especIally on the North Side within Cape Conway, for just within the Cape lay 2 or 3 Small Islands, which alone would shelter that side of the Bay from the South-East and Southerly winds, which seem to be the prevailing or Trade Winds. Among the many islands that lay upon this Coast there is one more Remarkable than the rest,* (* Probably Blacksmith Island.) being of a Small circuit, very high and peaked, and lies East by South, 10 Miles from Cape Conway at the South end of the Passage above mention'd.

[In Whitsunday Passage, Queensland.]

Monday, 4th. Winds at South-South-East and South-East, a Gentle breeze and Clear weather. In the P.M. Steerd thro' the passage* (* Whitsunday Passage. The aspect of the shores is very pleasing.) which we found from 3 to 6 or 7 Miles broad, and 8 or 9 Leagues in length, North by West 1/2 West and South by East 1/2 East. It is form'd by the Main on the West, and by Islands on the East, one of which is at least 5 Leagues in length. Our Depth of Water in running thro' was between 25 and 20 fathoms; everywhere good Anchorage; indeed the whole passage is one Continued safe Harbour, besides a Number of small Bays and Coves on each side, where ships might lay as it where in a Bason; at least so it appear'd to me, for I did not wait to Examine it, as having been in Port so lately, and being unwilling to loose the benefit of a light Moon. The land, both on the Main and Islands, especially on the former, is Tolerably high, and distinguished by Hills and Vallies, which are diversified with Woods and Lawns that looked green and pleasant. On a Sandy beach upon one of the Islands we saw 2 people and a Canoe, with an outrigger, which appeared to be both Larger and differently built to any we have seen upon the Coast. At 6 we were nearly the length of the North end of the Passage; the North Westermost point of the Main in sight bore North 54 degrees West, and the North end of the Island North-North-East, having an open Sea between these 2 points. [This passage I have named Whitsundays Passage, as it was discover'd on the day the Church commemorates that Festival, and the Isles which form it Cumberland Isles, in honour of His Royal Highness the Duke of Cumberland.* (* Henry Frederick, Duke of Cumberland, was a younger brother of George III.)] We kept under an Easey Sail and the Lead going all Night, having 21, 22, and 23 fathoms, at the distance of 3 Leagues from the land. At daylight A.M. we were abreast of the point above mentioned, which is a lofty promontory; that I named Cape Gloucester* (* William Henry, Duke of Gloucester and Edinburgh, a younger brother of George III.) (Latitude 19 degrees 57 minutes South, Longitude 211 degrees 54 minutes West). It may be known by an Island which lies out at Sea North by West 1/2 West, 5 or 6 Leagues from it; this I called Holbourn Isle.* (* Admiral Francis Holbourne commanded the fleet in North America in which Cook served in 1757.) There are also Islands laying under the Land between it and Whitsundays Passage. On the West side of the Cape the Land Trends away South-West and South-South-West, and forms a deep bay. The Sand in the bottom of this bay I could but just see from the Masthead; it is very low, and is a Continuation of the same low land as is at the bottom of Repulse Bay. Without Waiting to look into this bay, which I called Edgcumbe Bay,* (* In Port Denison, on the western side of Edgcumbe Bay, is the rising town of Bowen, the port of an agricultural district. There is good coal in the vicinity. Captain G. Edgcumbe commanded the Lancaster in the fleet in North America in 1758 in which Cook served. Afterwards Earl of Mount Edgcumbe.) we continued our Course to the Westward for the Westermost land we had in sight which bore from us West by North 1/2 North, and appeared very high. At Noon we were about 3 Leagues from the Land, and by observation in the Latitude of 19 degrees 47 minutes South, Cape Gloucester bearing South 63 degrees East, distant 7 1/2 Leagues.

Tuesday, 5th. Winds between the South and East, a Gentle breeze, and Serene weather. At 6 a.m. we were abreast of the Western point of Land above mentioned, distant from it 3 Miles, which I have named Cape Upstart, because being surrounded with low land it starts or rises up singley at the first making of it (Latitude 19 degrees 39 minutes South, Longitude 212 degrees 32 minutes West); it lies West-North-West 14 Leagues from Cape Gloucester, and is of a height sufficient to be seen 12 Leagues; but it is not so much of a Promontory as it appears to be, because on each side of it near the Sea is very low land, which is not to be seen unless you are pretty well in with the Shore. Inland are some Tolerable high hills or mountains, which, like the Cape, affords but a very barren prospect. Having past this Cape, we continued standing to the West-North-West as the land lay, under an easey Sail, having from 16 to 10 fathoms, until 2 o'Clock a.m., when we fell into 7 fathoms, upon which we hauled our wind to the Northward, judging ourselves to be very near the land; as so we found, for at daylight we were little more than 2 Leagues off. What deceived us was the Lowness of the land, which is but very little higher than the Surface of the Sea, but in the Country were some hills. At noon we were in 15 fathoms Water, and about 4 Leagues from the land. Our Latitude by Observation was 19 degrees 12 minutes South; Cape Upstart bore 38 degrees 30 minutes East, distant 12 Leagues. Course and distance sail'd since Yesterday noon North 48 degrees 45 minutes, 53 Miles. At and before Noon some very large smokes were Seen rise up out of the low land. At sun rise I found the Variation to be 5 degrees 35 minutes Easterly; at sun set last night the same Needle gave near 9 degrees. This being Close under Cape Upstart, I judged that it was owing to Iron ore or other Magnetical Matter Lodged in the Earth.

[Off Cleveland Bay, Queensland.]

Wednesday, 6th. Light Airs at East-South-East, with which we Steer'd West-North-West as the Land now lay; Depth of Water 12 and 14 fathoms. At Noon we were by Observation in the Latitude of 19 degrees 1 minute South, Longitude made from Cape Gloucester 1 degree 30 minutes West; Course and distance saild since Yesterday noon West-North-West, 28 Miles. In this situation we had the Mouth of a Bay all open extending from South 1/2 East to South-West 1/2 South, distance 2 Leagues. This bay, which I named Cleveland Bay,* (* In Cleveland Bay is Townsville, the largest town in Northern Queensland. Population 12,000.) appeared to be about 5 or 6 Miles in Extent every way. The East point I named Cape Cleveland, and the West, Magnetical Head or Island, as it had much the appearance of an Island; and the Compass did not traverse well when near it. They are both Tolerable high, and so is the Main Land within them, and the whole appeared to have the most rugged, rocky, and barren Surface of any we have yet seen. However, it is not without inhabitants, as we saw smoke in several places in the bottom of the bay. The Northermost land we had in sight at this time bore North-West; this we took to be an Island or Islands, for we could not trace the Main land farther than West by North.

Thursday, 7th. Light Airs between the South and East, with which we steer'd West-North-West, keeping the Main land on board, the outermost part of which at sun set bore from us West by North; but without this lay high land, which we took to be Islands. At daylight A.M. we were the Length of the Eastern part of this Land, which we found to Consist of a Group of Islands* (* Palm Islands.) laying about 5 Leagues from the Main. We being at this time between the 2, we continued advancing Slowly to the North-West until noon, at which time we were by observation in the Latitude of 18 degrees 49 minutes, and about 5 Leagues from the Main land, the North-West part of which bore from us North by West 1/2 West, the Island extending from North to East; distance of the nearest 2 Miles. Cape Cleveland bore South 50 degrees East, distant 18 Leagues. Our Soundings in the Course of this day's Sail were from 14 to 11 fathoms.

Friday, 8th. Winds at South-South-East and South; first part light Airs, the remainder a Gentle breeze. In the P.M. we saw several large smokes upon the Main, some people, Canoes, and, as we thought, Cocoa Nut Trees upon one of the Islands; and, as a few of these Nutts would have been very acceptable to us at this Time, I sent Lieutenant Hicks ashore, with whom went Mr. Banks and Dr. Solander, to see what was to be got. In the Meantime we keept Standing in for the Island with the Ship. At 7 they returned on board, having met with Nothing worth Observing. The Trees we saw were a small kind of Cabbage Palms. They heard some of the Natives as they were putting off from the Shore, but saw none. After the Boat was hoisted in we stood away North by West for the Northermost land we had in sight, which we were abreast of at 3 o'Clock in the Morning, having passed all the Islands 3 or 4 hours before. This point I have named Point Hillock,* (* Point Hillock is the east point of Hinchinbrook Island, which is separated from the main by a narrow and tortuous channel.) on account of its Figure. The Land of this point is Tolerable high, and may be known by a round Hillock or rock that appears to be detached from the point, but I believe it joins to it. Between this Cape and Cape Cleveland the shore forms a Large bay, which I named Hallifax bay;* (* The Earl of Halifax was Secretary of State 1763 to 1765.) before it lay the Groups of Islands before mentioned, and some others nearer the Shore. These Islands shelter the Bay in a manner from all Winds, in which is good Anchorage. The land near the Shore in the bottom of the bay is very low and Woody; but a little way back in the Country is a continued ridge of high land, which appear'd to be barren and rocky. Having passed

Point Hillock, we continued standing to the North-North-West as the land Trended, having the Advantage of a light Moon. At 6 a.m. we were abreast of a point of Land which lies North by West 1/2 West, 11 Miles from Point Hillick; the Land between them is very high, and of a craggy, barren surface. This point I named Cape Sandwich;* (* Earl of Sandwich was First Lord of the Admiralty 1763.) it may not only be known by the high, craggy land over it, but by a small Island which lies East one Mile from it, and some others about 2 Leagues to the Northward of it. From Cape Sandwich the Land trends West, and afterwards North, and forms a fine, Large Bay, which I called Rockingham Bay;* (* The Marquis of Rockingham was Prime Minister 1765 to 1766.) it is well Shelter'd, and affords good Anchorage; at least, so it appear'd to me, for having met with so little encouragement by going ashore that I would not wait to land or examine it farther, but continued to range along Shore to the Northward for a parcel of Small Islands* (* The Family Islands.) laying off the Northern point of the Bay, and, finding a Channel of a Mile broad between the 3 Outermost and those nearer the Shore, we pushed thro'. While we did this we saw on one of the nearest Islands a Number of the Natives collected together, who seem'd to look very attentively upon the Ship; they were quite naked, and of a very Dark Colour, with short hair. At noon we were by observation in the Latitude of 17 degrees 59 minutes, and abreast of the North point of Rockingham Bay, which bore from us West 2 Miles. This boundry of the Bay is form'd by a Tolerable high Island, known in the Chart by the Name of Dunk Isle; it lays so near the Shore as not to be distinguished from it unless you are well in with the Land. At this time we were in the Longitude of 213 degrees 57 minutes. Cape Sandwich bore South by East 1/2 East, distant 19 Miles, and the northermost land in sight North 1/2 West. Our depth of Water in the Course of this day's Sail was not more than 16, nor less than 7, fathoms.* (* About here the Great Barrier Reefs begin to close in on the land. Cook kept so close to the latter that he was unconscious as yet of their existence; but he was soon to find them.)

[Anchored near Cape Grafton, Queensland.]

Saturday, 9th. Winds between the South and South-East, a Gentle breeze, and Clear weather, with which we steer'd North by West as the land lay, the northern extream of which at sunset bore North 25 degrees West. We kept on our Course under an Easey sail all night, having from 12 to 16 fathoms, at the distance of about 3 or 4 Leagues from the Land. At 6 a.m. we were abreast of Some small Islands, which we called Frankland Isles, that lay about 2 Leagues from the Mainland, the Northern Point of which in sight bore North by West 1/2 West; but this we afterwards found to be an Island,* (* Fitzroy Island.) tolerable high, and about 4 Miles in Circuit. It lies about 2 Miles from the Point on the Main between which we went with the ship, and were in the Middle of the Channell at Noon, and by observation in the Latitude of 16 degrees 55 minutes, where we had 20 fathoms of water. The point of land we were now abreast of I called Cape Grafton* (* The Duke of Grafton was Prime Minister when Cook sailed.) (Latitude 16 degrees 55 minutes South, Longitude 214 degrees 11 minutes West); it is Tolerable high, and so is the whole Coast for 20 Leagues to the southward, and hath a very rocky surface, which is thinly cover'd with wood. In the night we saw several fires along shore, and a little before noon some people.

Sunday, 10th. After hauling round Cape Grafton we found the land trend away North-West by West; 3 Miles to the Westward of the Cape is a Bay, wherein we Anchor'd, about 2 Miles from the Shore, in 4 fathoms, owsey bottom. The East point of the Bay bore South 74 degrees East, the West point South 83 degrees West, and a Low green woody Island laying in the Offing bore North 35 degrees East. The Island lies North by East 1/2 East, distance 3 or 4 Leagues from Cape Grafton, and is known in the Chart by the Name of Green Island. As soon as the Ship was brought to an Anchor I went ashore, accompanied by Mr. Banks and Dr. Solander; the first thing I did was to look for fresh Water, and with that View rowed out towards the Cape, because in the bottom of the bay was low Mangrove land, and little probability of meeting with any there. But the way I went I found 2 Small streams, which were difficult to get at on account of the Surf and rocks upon the Shore. As we came round the Cape we saw, in a sandy Cove, a small stream of Water run over the beach; but here I did not go in the boat because I found that it would not be Easey to land. We hardly advanced anything into the Country, it being here hilly, which were steep and rocky, and we had not time to Visit the Low lands, and therefore met with nothing remarkable. My intention was to have stay'd here at least one day, to have looked into the Country had we met with fresh water convenient, or any other Refreshment; but as we did not, I thought it would be only spending of time, and loosing as much of a light Moon to little purpose, and therefore at 12 o'Clock at night we weighed and stood away to the North-West, having at this time but little wind, attended with Showers of rain.* (* In the next bay west of where Cook anchored is Cairns, a small but rising town in the centre of a sugar-growing district.) At 4 the breeze freshned at South by East, with fair weather; we continued steering North-North-West 1/2 West as the Land lay, having 10, 12, and 14 fathoms, at a distance of 3 Leagues from the Land. At 11 we hauld off North, in order to get without a Small Low Island* (* Low Isles. There is now a lighthouse on them.) which lay about 2 Leagues from the Main; it being about high Water, about the time we passed it, great part of it lay under water. About 3 Leagues to the North Westward of this Island, close under the Main land, is another Island,* (* Snapper Island.) Tolerable high, which bore from us at Noon North 55 degrees West, distant 7 or 8 Miles; we being at this time in the Latitude of 16 degrees 20 minutes South, Cape Grafton bore South 29 degrees East, distant 40 Miles, and the Northermost point of Land in Sight North 20 degrees West, and in this Situation had 15 fathoms Water. The Shore between Cape Grafton and the above Northern point forms a large but not very deep Bay, which I named Trinity Bay, after the day on which it was discover'd; the North point Cape Tribulation, because here began all our Troubles. Latitude 16 degrees 6 minutes South, Longitude 214 degrees 39 minutes West.

[The Ship Aground on Endeavour Reef.]

Monday, 11th. Wind at East-South-East, with which we steer'd along shore North by West at the distance of 3 or 4 Leagues off, having from 14 to 10 and 12 fathoms water. Saw 2 Small Islands in the Offing, which lay in the Latitude of 16 degrees 0 minutes South, and about 6 or 7 Leagues from the Main. At 6 the Northermost land in sight bore North by West 1/2 West, and 2 low, woody Islands,* (* Hope Islands.) which some took to be rocks above Water, bore North 1/2 West. At this time we shortened Sail, and hauld off shore East-North-East and North-East by East, close upon a Wind. My intention was to stretch off all Night as well to avoid the danger we saw ahead as to see if any Islands lay in the Offing, especially as we now begun to draw near the Latitude of those discover'd by Quiros, which some Geographers, for what reason I know not, have thought proper to Tack to this land. Having the advantage of a fine breeze of wind, and a clear Moon light Night in standing off from 6 until near 9 o Clock, we deepned our Water from 14 to 21 fathoms, when all at once we fell into 12, 10 and 8 fathoms. At this time I had everybody at their Stations to put about and come to an Anchor; but in this I was not so fortunate, for meeting again with Deep Water, I thought there could be no danger in standing on.* (* The ship passed just northward of Pickersgill Reef.) Before 10 o'Clock we had 20 and 21 fathoms, and Continued in that depth until a few minutes before 11, when we had 17, and before the Man at the Lead could heave another cast, the Ship Struck and stuck fast. Immediately upon this we took in all our Sails, hoisted out the Boats and Sounded round the Ship, and found that we had got upon the South-East Edge of a reef of Coral Rocks, having in some places round the Ship 3 and 4 fathoms Water, and in other places not quite as many feet, and about a Ship's length from us on the starboard side (the Ship laying with her Head to the North-East) were 8, 10, and 12 fathoms. As soon as the Long boat was out we struck Yards and Topmast, and carried out the Stream Anchor on our Starboard bow, got the Coasting Anchor and Cable into the Boat, and were going to carry it out in the same way; but upon my sounding the 2nd time round the Ship I found the most water a Stern, and therefore had this Anchor carried out upon the Starboard Quarter, and hove upon it a very great Strain; which was to no purpose, the Ship being quite fast, upon which we went to work to lighten her as fast as possible, which seem'd to be the only means we had left to get her off. As we went ashore about the Top of High Water we not only started water, but threw overboard our Guns, Iron and Stone Ballast, Casks, Hoop Staves, Oil Jarrs, decay'd Stores, etc.; many of these last Articles lay in the way at coming at Heavier. All this time the Ship made little or no Water. At 11 a.m., being high Water as we thought, we try'd to heave her off without Success, she not being afloat by a foot or more, notwithstanding by this time we had thrown overboard 40 or 50 Tuns weight. As this was not found sufficient we continued to Lighten her by every method we could think off; as the Tide fell the ship began to make Water as much as two pumps could free: at Noon she lay with 3 or 4 Streakes heel to Starboard; Latitude observed 15 degrees 45 minutes South.

Tuesday, 12th. Fortunately we had little wind, fine weather, and a smooth Sea, all this 24 Hours, which in the P.M. gave us an Opportunity to carry out the 2 Bower Anchors, one on the Starboard Quarter, and the other right a Stern, got Blocks and Tackles upon the Cables, brought the falls in abaft and hove taught. By this time it was 5 o'Clock p.m.; the tide we observed now begun to rise, and the leak increased upon us, which obliged us to set the 3rd Pump to work, as we should have done the 4th also, but could not make it work. At 9 the Ship righted, and the Leak gain'd upon the Pumps considerably. This was an alarming and, I may say, terrible circumstance, and threatened immediate destruction to us. However, I resolv'd to risque all, and heave her off in case it was practical, and accordingly turn'd as many hands to the Capstan and Windlass as could be spared from the Pumps; and about 20 Minutes past 10 o'Clock the Ship floated, and we hove her into Deep Water, having at this time 3 feet 9 Inches Water in the hold. This done I sent the Long boat to take up the Stream Anchor, got the Anchor, but lost the Cable among the Rocks; after this turn'd all hands to the Pumps, the Leak increasing upon us.

A mistake soon after hapned, which for the first time caused fear to approach upon every man in the Ship. The man that attended the well took the Depth of water above the Ceiling; he, being relieved by another who did not know in what manner the former had sounded, took the Depth of water from the outside plank, the difference being 16 or 18 inches, and made it appear that the leak had gained this upon the pumps in a short time. This mistake was no sooner cleared up than it acted upon every man like a Charm; they redoubled their vigour, insomuch that before 8 o'clock in the morning they gained considerably upon the leak.* (* The circumstance related in this paragraph is from the Admiralty copy.) We now hove up the Best Bower, but found it impossible to save the small Bower, so cut it away at a whole Cable; got up the Fore topmast and Foreyard, warped the Ship to the South-East, and at 11 got under sail, and stood in for the land, with a light breeze at East-South-East. Some hands employ'd sewing Oakham, Wool, etc., into a Lower Steering sail to fother the Ship; others employ'd at the Pumps, which still gain'd upon the Leak.

[Fothering the Ship.]

Wednesday, 13th. In the P.M. had light Airs at East-South-East, with which we keept edging in for the Land. Got up the Maintopmast and Mainyard, and having got the Sail ready for fothering of the Ship, we put it over under the Starboard Fore Chains, where we suspected the Ship had suffer'd most, and soon after the Leak decreased, so as to be keept clear with one Pump with ease; this fortunate circumstance gave new life to every one on board.

It is much easier to conceive than to discribe the satisfaction felt by everybody on this occasion. But a few minutes before our utmost Wishes were to get hold of some place upon the Main, or an island, to run the Ship ashore, where out of her Materials we might build a Vessel to carry us to the East Indies; no sooner were we made sencible that the outward application to the Ship's bottom had taken effect, than the field of every Man's hopes inlarged, so that we thought of nothing but ranging along Shore in search of a Harbour, when we could repair the Damages we had sustained.* (* The foregoing paragraph is from the Admiralty copy. The situation was indeed sufficiently awkward. When it is considered that the coast was wholly unknown, the natives decidedly hostile, the land unproductive of any means of subsistence, and the distance to the nearest Dutch settlements, even if a passage should be found south of New Guinea, 1500 miles, there was ample cause for apprehension if they could not save the ship. Knowing what we now know, that all off this coast is a continuous line of reefs and shoals, Cook's action in standing off might seem rash. But he knew nothing of this. There was a moon; he reduced sail to double reefed topsails with a light wind, as the log tells us, and with the cumbrous hempen cables of the day, and the imperfect means of heaving up the anchor, he was desirous of saving his men unnecessary labour. Cook was puzzled that the next tide did not, after lightening the ship, take him off; but it is now known that on this coast it is only every alternate tide that rises to a full height, and as he got ashore nearly at the top of the higher of the two waters he had to wait twenty-four hours until he got a similar rise. Lucky was it for them that the wind was light. Usually at this season the trade wind is strong, and raises a considerable sea, even inside the Barrier. Hawkesworth or Banks makes the proposition to fother the ship emanate from Mr. Monkhouse; but it is scarcely to be supposed that such a perfect seaman as Cook was not familiar with this operation, and he merely says that as Mr. Monkhouse had seen it done, he confided to him the superintendence of it, as of course the Captain had at such a time many other things to do than stand over the men preparing the sail. In 1886 the people of Cooktown were anxious to recover the brass guns of the Endeavour which were thrown overboard, in order to place them as a memento in their town; but they could not be found, which is not altogether surprising.) In justice to the Ship's Company, I must say that no men ever behaved better than they have done on this occasion; animated by the behaviour of every Gentleman on board, every man seem'd to have a just sence of the Danger we were in, and exerted himself to the very utmost. The Ledge of Rocks, or Shoal, we have been upon, lies in the Latitude of 15 degrees 45 minutes, and about 6 or 7 Leagues from the Main land; but this is not the only Shoal that lay upon this part of the Coast, especially to the Northward, and one which we saw to the Southward, the tail of which we passed over when we had the uneven Soundings 2 hours before we Struck. A part of this Shoal is always above Water, and looks to be white Sand; part of the one we were upon was dry at low Water, and in that place consists of Sand and stones, but every where else Coral Rocks. At 6 we Anchored in 17 fathoms, about 5 or 6 Leagues from the land, and one from the Shoal. At this time the Ship made about 15 Inches Water per hour. At 6 a.m. weigh'd and stood to the North-West, edging in for the land, having a Gentle breeze at South-South-East. At 9 we past close without 2 small low Islands, laying in the Latitude of 15 degrees 41 minutes, and about 4 Leagues from the Main; I have named them Hope Islands, because we were always in hopes of being able to reach these Islands. At Noon we were about 3 Leagues from the Land, and in the Latitude of 15 degrees 37 minutes South; the Northermost part of the Main in sight bore North 30 degrees West, and the above Islands extending from South 30 degrees East to South 40 degrees East. In this situation had 12 fathoms water and several sandbanks without us. The Leak now decreaseth, but for fear it should break out again we got the Sail ready fill'd for fothering; the manner this is done is thus: We Mix Oacham and Wool together (but Oacham alone would do), and chop it up Small, and then stick it loosely by handfulls all over the Sail, and throw over it Sheep dung or other filth. Horse Dung for this purpose is the best. The Sail thus prepared is hauld under the Ship's bottom by ropes, and if the place of the Leak is uncertain, it must be hauld from one part of her bottom to another until one finds the place where it takes effect. While the Sail is under the Ship the Oacham, etc., is washed off, and part of it carried along with the water into the Leak, and in part stops up the hole. Mr. Monkhouse, one of my Midshipmen, was once in a Merchant Ship which Sprung a Leak, and made 48 Inches Water per hour; but by this means was brought home from Virginia to London with only her proper crew; to him I gave the direction of this, who executed it very much to my satisfaction.

[In Endeavour River, Queensland.]

Thursday, 14th. P.M., had a Gentle breeze at South-East by East. Sent the Master, with 2 Boats as well, to sound ahead of the Ship, as to look out for a Harbour where we could repair our defects, and put the Ship on a proper

Trim, both of which she now very much wanted. At 3 saw an Opening that had the appearance of a Harbour; stood off and on while the Boats were examining it, who found that there was not a sufficient depth of Water for the Ship. By this time it was almost sun set, and seeing many shoals about us we Anchored in 4 fathoms about 2 miles from the Shore, the Main land extending from North 1/2 East to South by East 1/2 East. At 8 o'clock the Pinnace, in which was one of the Mates, return'd on board, and reported that they had found a good Harbour* (* Cook Harbour, Endeavour River.) about 2 Leagues to leeward. In consequence of this information we, at 6 a.m., weigh'd and run down to it, first sending 2 Boats ahead to lay upon the Shoals that lay in our way; and notwithstanding this precaution, we were once in 3 fathoms with the Ship. Having pass'd these Shoals, the Boats were sent to lay in the Channell leading into the Harbour. By this time it begun to blow in so much that the Ship would not work, having missed stays Twice; and being entangled among Shoals, I was afraid of being drove to Leeward before the Boats could place themselves, and therefore Anchoredd in 4 fathoms about a Mile from the Shore, and then made the Signal for the Boats to come on board, after which I went myself and Buoy'd the Channell, which I found very narrow, and the Harbour much smaller than I had been told, but very convenient for our Purpose. At Noon Latitude observed 15 degrees 26 minutes South. [Note. This day I restor'd Mr. Magra to his Duty, as I did not find him guilty of the crimes laid to his charge.]

Friday, 15th. A fresh Gale at South-East and Cloudy weather, attended with Showers of Rain. In the Night, as it blow'd too fresh to break the Ship loose to run into the Harbour, we got down the Topgallant yards, unbent the Mainsail, and some of the Small sails; got down the Foretopgallant mast, and the Jibb Boom and Spritsailyard in, intending to lighten the Ship Forward as much as possible, in order to lay her ashore to come at the Leak.

Saturday, 16th. Strong Gales at South-East, and Cloudy, hazey weather, with Showers of Rain. At 6 o'Clock in the A.M. it moderated a little, and we hove short, intending to get under sail, but was obliged to desist, and veer away again; some people were seen ashore to-day.

Sunday, 17th. Most part strong Gales at South-East, with some heavy showers of rain in the P.M. At 6 a.m., being pretty moderate, we weigh'd and run into the Harbour, in doing of which we run the Ship ashore Twice. The first time she went off without much Trouble, but the Second time she Stuck fast; but this was of no consequence any farther than giving us a little trouble, and was no more than what I expected as we had the wind. While the Ship lay fast we got down the Foreyard, Foretopmast, booms, etc., overboard, and made a raft of them alongside.

Monday, 18th. Fresh Gales and Cloudy, with Showers of Rain. At 1 p.m. the Ship floated, and we warped her into the Harbour, and moor'd her alongside of a Steep Beach on the South side; got the Anchors, Cables, and all the Hawsers ashore. In the A.M. made a Stage from the Ship to the Shore, Erected 2 Tents, one for the Sick, and the other for the Stores and Provisions; Landed all the empty Casks and part of the Provisions, and sent a boat to haul the Sean, which return'd without Success.

Tuesday, 19th. Fresh Gales at South-East and Cloudy weather, with frequent showers of Rain. P.M., landed all the Provisions and Part of the Stores; got the Sick ashore, which amounted, at this time, to 8 or 9, afflicted with different disorders, but none very dangerously ill. This afternoon I went upon one of the highest Hills over the Harbour, from which I had a perfect View of the inlet or River, and adjacent country, which afforded but a very indifferent prospect. The Low lands near the River is all over run with Mangroves, among which the salt water flows every tide, and the high land appear'd to be barren and Stoney. A.M., got the 4 remaining Guns out of the hold, and mounted them on the Quarter Deck; got a spare Anchor and Stock ashore, and the remaining part of the Stores and ballast that were in the Hold; set up the Forge, and set the Armourer and his Mate to work to make Nails, etc., to repair the Ship.

Wednesday, 20th. Winds at South-East, a fresh breeze, Fore and Middle parts rainy, the Latter fair. This day got out all the Officers' stores and the ground Tier of Water, having now nothing in the Fore and Main Hold But the Coals and a little Stone ballast.

Thursday, 21st. P.M., landed the Powder, got out the stone ballast, wood, etc., which brought the Ship's Draught of water to 8 feet 10 inches Forward, and 13 feet abaft. This I thought, by trimming the Coals aft, would be sufficient, as I find the Tides will rise and fall upon a Perpendicular 8 feet at Spring tides; but after the Coals was trimm'd away from over the Leak we Could hear the Water come Gushing in a little abaft the Foremast about 3 feet from her Keel. This determin'd me to clear the hold intirely; accordingly very early in the Morning we went to work to get out the Coals, which was Employment for all hands.

[Ship Beached in Endeavour River.]

Friday, 22nd. Winds at South-East, fair weather. At 4 p.m., having got out most of the Coals, cast loose the Ship's moorings, and warped her a little higher up the Harbour to a place I had pitched upon to lay her ashore to stop the Leak; draught of water Forward 7 feet 9 inches and abaft 13 feet 6 inches. At 8, being high water, hauld her bow close ashore, but Keept her stern afloat, because I was afraid of Neaping her,* (* I.e., Having her so far on shore that they could not heave her off at Neap tide.) and yet it was necessary to lay the whole of her as near the ground as possible.* (* The town of Cooktown now stands where the Endeavour was beached, and the (as near as can be judged) exact spot is marked by a monument.) At 2 a.m. the Tide left her, which gave us an Opportunity to Examine the Leak, which we found to be at her Floor Heads, a little before the Starboard Fore Chains; here the Rocks had made their way thro' 4 planks, quite to, and even into the Timbers, and wounded 3 more. The manner these planks were damaged--or cut out, as I may say--is hardly credible; scarce a Splinter was to be seen, but the whole was cut away as if it had been done by the Hands of Man with a blunt-edge Tool. Fortunately for us the Timbers in this place were very close; other wise it would have been impossible to have saved the Ship, and even as it was it appeared very extraordinary that she made no more water than what she did. A large peice of Coral rock was sticking in one Hole, and several peices of the Fothering, small stones, etc., had made its way in, and lodged between the Timbers, which had stopped the Water from forcing its way in in great Quantities. Part of the Sheathing was gone from under the Larboard bow, part of the False Kiel was gone, and the remainder in such a Shatter'd Condition that we should be much better off if it was gone also; her Forefoot and some part of her Main Kiel was also damaged, but not Materially. What damage she may have received abaft we could not see, but believe not much, as the Ship makes but little water, while the Tide Keeps below the Leak forward. At 9 the Carpenters went to work upon the Ship, while the Armourers were buisy making Bolts, Nails, etc.

Saturday, 23rd. Winds South Easterly, a fresh Gale and fair weather. Carpenters employed Shifting the Damaged planks as long as the tide would permit them to work. At low water P.M. we examined the Ship's bottom under the Starboard side, she being dry as far aft as the After-part of the Fore Chains; we could not find that she had received any other damage on this side but what has been mentioned. In the morning I sent 3 Men into the Country to shoot Pidgeons, as some of these birds had been seen flying about; in the evening they return'd with about 1/2 a Dozen. One of the Men saw an Animal something less than a greyhound; it was of a Mouse Colour, very slender made, and swift of Foot.* (* Kangaroo.) A.M., I sent a Boat to haul the Sean, who return'd at noon, having made 3 Hauls and caught only 3 fish; and yet we see them in plenty Jumping about the harbour, but can find no method of catching them.

Sunday, 24th. Winds and weather as Yesterday. P.M., the Carpenters finished the Starboard side, and at 9 heeld the Ship the other way, and hauld her off about 2 feet for fear of Neaping. In the A.M. they went to work repairing the Sheathing under the Larboard bow, where we found 2 planks cut about half thro'. Early in the morning I sent a party of Men into the Country under the direction of Lieutenant Gore to seek for refreshments; they return'd about noon with a few Palm Cabbages and a Bunch or 2 of wild Plantains; these last were much Smaller than any I had ever seen, and the Pulp full of small Stones; otherwise they were well tasted. I saw myself this morning, a little way from the Ship, one of the Animals before spoke off; it was of a light mouse Colour and the full size of a Grey Hound, and shaped in every respect like one, with a long tail, which it carried like a Grey hound; in short, I should have taken it for a wild dog but for its walking or running, in which it jump'd like a Hare or Deer. Another of them was seen to-day by some of our people, who saw the first; they described them as having very small Legs, and the print of the Feet like that of a Goat; but this I could not see myself because the ground the one I saw was upon was too hard, and the length of the Grass hindered my seeing its legs.* (* These kangaroos were the first seen by Europeans. The name was obtained from the natives by Mr. Banks.)

Monday, 25th. At low water in the P.M. While the Carpenters were buisey in repairing the Sheathing and plank under the Larboard bow I got people to go under the Ship's bottom, to examine all her Larboard side, she only being dry Forward, but abaft were 9 feet water. They found part of the Sheathing off abreast of the Mainmast about her floor heads, and a part of one plank a little damaged. There were 3 people who went down, who all agreed in the same Story; the Master was one, who was positive that she had received no Material Damage besides the loss of the Sheathing. This alone will be sufficient to let the worm into her bottom, which may prove of bad consequence. However, we must run all risque, for I know of no method to remedy this but by heaving her down, which would be a work of Emence Labour and time, if not impractical in our present situation.

The Carpenters continued hard at work under her bottom until put off by the Tide in the evening, and the morning Tide did not Ebb out far enough to permit them to work upon her, for here we have only one Tolerable low and high tide in 24 Hours. A.M., a party of Men were employ'd ashore filling water, while others were employ'd overhauling the rigging.

Tuesday, 26th. Fair weather, a South-East wind, and a fresh Gale; at low Water P.M. the Carpenters finished under the Larboard bow and every other place the tide would permit them to come at. Lashed some Casks under the Ship's bows in order to help to float her, and at high water in the Night attempted to heave her off, but could not, she not being afloat partly owing to some of the Casks not holding that were Lashed under her. A.M., employed getting more Casks ready for the same purpose; but I am much afraid that we shall not be able to float her now the Tides are Taking off.

Wednesday, 27th. A fresh breeze of Wind at South-East and Cloudy weather. P.M., lashed 38 empty Butts under the Ship's Bottom in order to float her off, which proved ineffectual, and therefore gave over all hopes of getting her off until the Next spring tides. At daylight we got a Considerable weight of sundry Articles from Aft forward to ease the Ship; the Armourer at work at the Forge repairing Iron work, etc., Carpenters caulking and Stocking one of the Spare Anchors, Seamen employ'd filling of Water and overhauling the rigging, and I went in the pinnace up the Harbour, and made several hauls with the Sean, but caught only between 20 and 30 pound of fish, which were given to the sick and such as were weak and Ailing.

Thursday, 28th. Fresh breezes and Cloudy. All hands employ'd as Yesterday.

Friday, 29th. Wind and weather as Yesterday, and the employment of the People the same, Lieutenant Gore having been 4 or 5 miles in the Country, where he met with nothing remarkable. He saw the footsteps of Men, and likewise those of 3 or 4 sorts of wild beasts, but saw neither Man nor beast. Some others of our people who were out Yesterday on the North side of the River met with a place where the Natives have just been, as their fires was then burning; but they saw nobody, nor have we seen one since we have been in port. In these excursions we found some Wild Yamms or Cocos growing in the Swampy grounds, and this Afternoon I sent a Party of Men to gather some. The Tops we found made good greens, and eat exceedingly well when Boil'd, but the roots were so bad that few besides myself could eat them. This night Mr. Green and I observ'd an Emersion of Jupiter's first Satellite, which hapned at 2 hours 58 minutes 53 seconds in the A.M.; the same Emersion hapnd at Greenwich, according to Calculation, on the 30th at 5 hours 17 minutes 43 seconds A.M. The differance is 14 hours 18 minutes 50 seconds, equal to 214 degrees 42 minutes 30 seconds of Longitude,* (* This was an excellent observation. The true longitude is 214 degrees 45 minutes.) which this place is West of Greenwich, and its Latitude 15 degrees 26 minutes South. A.M., I sent some hands in a Boat up the River to haul the Sean, while the rest were employ'd about the rigging and sundry other Dutys.

Saturday, 30th. Moderate breezes at South-East, and clear serene weather. P.M., the Boat returned from hauling the Sean, having caught as much fish as came to a pound and a half a Man. A.M., I sent her again to haul the Sean, and some hands to gather greens, while others were employ'd about the rigging, etc., etc. I likewise sent some of the Young Gentlemen to take a plan of the Harbour, and went myself upon the hill, which is near the South point to take a view of the Sea.* (* Grassy Hill.) At this time it was low water, and I saw what gave me no small uneasiness, which were a Number of Sand Banks and Shoals laying all along the Coast; the innermost lay about 3 or 4 Miles from the Shore, and the outermost extended off to Sea as far as I could see without my glass, some just appeared above water.* (* These were the innermost reefs of the Great Barrier. There is a tolerably clear passage about 8 miles wide between them and the shore, though this has some small shoals in it.) The only hopes I have of getting clear of them is to the Northward, where there seems to be a Passage, for as the wind blows constantly from the South-East we shall find it difficult, if not impractical, to return to the Southward.

[July 1770.]

Sunday, 1st July. Gentle breezes at South-East, and Cloudy weather, with some Gentle Showers in the morning. P.M., the People return'd from hauling the Sean, having caught as much fish as came to 2 1/2 pound per Man, no one on board having more than another. The few Greens we got I caused to be boil'd among the pease, and makes a very good Mess, which, together with the fish, is a great refreshment to the people. A.M., a party of Men, one from each Mess, went again a fishing, and all the rest I gave leave to go into the Country, knowing that there was no danger from the Natives. To-day at Noon the Thermometer in the Shade rose to 87 degrees, which is 2 or 3 Degrees higher than it hath been on any day before in this place.

Monday, 2nd. Ditto weather. P.M., the fishing-party caught as much fish as came to 2 pounds a Man. Those that were in the Country met with nothing New. Early in the A.M. I sent the Master in the pinnace out of the Harbour, to sound about the Shoals in the Offing and to look for a Channel to the Northward. At this time we had a breeze of wind from the land, which continued till about 9. What makes me mention this is, that it is the first Land breeze we have had since we have been in this River. At low water lashed empty Casks under the Ship's bows, being in some hopes of floating her the next high Water, and sent some hands a fishing, while others were employ'd in refitting the Ship.

Tuesday, 3rd. Winds at South-East, Fore and Middle part gentle breeze, the remainder a fresh gale. In the evening the fishing Party return'd, having got as much fish as came to 2 pounds a Man. At high water we attempted to heave the Ship off, but did not succeed. At Noon the Master return'd, and reported he had found a passage out to Sea between the Shoals, which passage lies out East-North-East or East by North from the River mouth. He found these Shoals to Consist of Coral Rocks; he landed upon one, which drys at low Water, where he found very large cockles* (* Tridacna.) and a Variety of other Shell fish, a quantity of which he brought away with him. He told me that he was 5 Leagues out at Sea, having at that distance 21 fathoms water, and judg'd himself to be without all the Shoals, which I very much doubted.* (* Cook was right. The shoals extend for four leagues farther.) After this he came in Shore, and Stood to the Northward, where he met with a Number of Shoals laying a little distance from the Shore. About 9 in the evening he landed in a Bay about 3 Leagues to the Northward of this Place, where he disturbed some of the Natives, whom he supposed to be at supper; they all fled upon his approach, and Left him some fresh Sea Eggs, and a fire ready lighted behind them; but there was neither House nor Hut near. Although these Shoals lay within sight of the Coast, and abound very much with Shell fish and other small fish, which are to be caught at Low water in holes in the Rocks, yet the Natives never visit them, for if they did we must have seen of these Large shells on shore about their fire places. The reason I do suppose is, that they have no Boats that they dare Venture so far out at Sea in.* (* Nevertheless the natives do get out to the islands which lie farther from the shore than these reefs, as Cook himself afterwards found.)

Wednesday, 4th. Strong gales at South-East and fair weather. P.M., the fishing party return'd with the usual success; at High water hove the ship Afloat. A.M., employ'd trimming her upon an even Kiel, intending to lay her ashore once more, to come at her bottom under the Larboard Main Chains.

Thursday, 5th. Strong breezes at South-East and fair weather. P.M. Warped the Ship over, and at high Water laid her ashore on the Sandbank on the South side of the River, for I was afraid to lay her broad side to the Shore where she lay before, because the ground lies upon too great a decent, and she hath already received some Damage by laying there these last Niep Tides, at least she still makes water.

[At Anchor, Endeavour River.]

Friday, 6th. Ditto weather. At low water in the P.M. had hardly 4 feet water under the Ship; yet could not repair the Sheathing that was beat off, the place being all under water. One of the Carpenter's crew, a Man I could trust, went down and Examin'd it, and found 3 Streakes of the Sheathing gone about 7 or 8 feet long, and the Main Plank a little rubbed; this account agrees with the report of the Master and others that were under her bottom before. The Carpenter, who I look upon to be well skill'd in his profession, and a good judge in these matters, was of Opinion that this was of little consequence; and as I found that it would be difficult, if not impractical, for us to get under her bottom to repair it, I resolved to spend no more time about it. Accordingly at high water hove her off, and moor'd her alongside the beach, where the Stores, etc., lay, and in the A.M. got everything in readiness for taking them on board, and at the same time got on board 8 Tuns of Water, and stow'd in the ground Tier in the after Hold. In the Morning Mr. Banks and Lieutenant Gore with 3 Men went in a small Boat up the Harbour, with a View to stay 2 or 3 days to try to Kill some of the Animals we have seen about this place.

Saturday, 7th. Fresh breezes at South-East and fair weather. Employ'd getting on board Coals, Ballast, etc., and caulking the Ship; a work that could not be done while she lay aground. The Armourer and his Mate are Still employ'd at the Forge making and repairing sundry Articles in the Iron way.

Sunday, 8th. Gentle breeze and South-East, and clear weather. Early I sent the Master in a Boat out to Sea to sound again about the Shoals, because the account he had given of the Channell before mentioned was to me by no means Satisfactory; likewise sent some hands to haul the Sean, who caught near 80 pounds of fish; the rest of the people I gave leave to go into the Country.

Monday, 9th. In the Day Ditto Winds, but in the night Calm. P.M., Mr. Gore and Mr. Banks return'd, having met with nothing remarkable; they were about 3 or 4 Leagues up in the Country without finding hardly any Variation either in the Soil or Produce. In the Evening the Master return'd, having been several Leagues out at Sea, and at that Distance off saw Shoals without him, and was of opinion there was no getting out to Sea that way. In his return he touched upon one of the Shoals, the same as he was upon the first time he was out; he here saw a great number of Turtle, 3 of which he Caught weighing 791 pounds. This occasion'd my sending him out again this morning provided with proper gear for Striking them, he having before nothing but a Boat Hook. Carpenters, Smiths, and Coopers at their respective Employments, and the Seamen employed getting on board stones, ballast, etc. This day all hands feasted upon Turtle for the First time.* (* As they had had nothing fresh but a little fish for four months, and scarcely any meat since they left the Society Islands, eleven months before, we can imagine that this was a feast.)

Tuesday, 10th. Winds and weather as yesterday. Employ'd hoisting on board and stowing away the ground Tier of Water. P.M., saw 7 or 8 of the Natives on the South side of the River, and 2 of them came down upon the Sandy point opposite the Ship; but as soon as I put off in a Boat in order to speak with them they run away as fast as they could. At 11 Mr. Banks, who had gone out to Sea with Mr. Molineux, the Master, return'd in his own Small Boat, and gave but a Very bad account of our Turtlecatchers. At the time he left them, which was about 6 o'Clock, they had not got one, nor were they likely to get any; and yet the Master was so obstinate that he would not return,* (* This seems rather hard upon the Master.) which obliged me to send Mr. Gore out in the Yawl this morning to order the Boat and People in, in Case they could not be employ'd there to some Advantage. In the A.M. 4 of the Natives came down to the Sandy point on the North side of the Harbour, having along with them a small wooden Canoe with Outriggers, in which they seem'd to be employed striking fish, etc. Some were for going over in a Boat to them; but this I would not suffer, but let them alone without seeming to take any Notice of them. At length 2 of them came in the Canoe so near the Ship as to take some things we throw'd them. After this they went away, and brought over the other 2, and came again alongside, nearer than they had done before, and took such Trifles as we gave them; after this they landed close to the Ship, and all 4 went ashore, carrying their Arms with them. But Tupia soon prevailed upon them to lay down their Arms, and come and set down by him, after which most of us went to them, made them again some presents, and stay'd by them until dinner time, when we made them understand that we were going to eat, and asked them by signals to go with us; but this they declined, and as soon as we left them they went away in their Canoe. One of these Men was something above the Middle Age, the other 3 were young; none of them were above 5 1/2 feet high, and all their Limbs proportionately small. They were wholy naked, their Skins the Colour of Wood soot, and this seem'd to be their Natural Colour. Their Hair was black, lank, and cropt short, and neither wooly nor Frizled; nor did they want any of their Fore Teeth, as Dampier has mentioned those did he saw on the Western side of this Country. Some part of their Bodys had been painted with red, and one of them had his upper lip and breast painted with Streakes of white, which he called Carbanda. Their features were far from being disagreeable; their Voices were soft and Tunable, and they could easily repeat any word after us, but neither us nor Tupia could understand one word they said.

Wednesday, 11th. Gentle land and Sea breezes. Employed Airing the Bread, stowing away water, Stores, etc. In the night the Master and Mr. Gore returned with the Long Boat, and brought with them one Turtle and a few Shell fish; the Yawl Mr. Gore left upon the Shoal with 6 Men to endeavour to strike more Turtle. In the morning 4 of the Natives made us another Short Visit; 3 of them had been with us the preceeding day, the other was a stranger. One of these men had a hole through the Bridge* (* The cartilage of the nostril.) of his nose, in which he stuck a peice of Bone as thick as my finger. Seeing this we examin'd all their Noses, and found that they had all holes for the same purpose; they had likewise holes in their Ears, but no Ornaments hanging to them; they had bracelets on their Arms made of hair, and like Hoops of small Cord. They sometimes may wear a kind of fillet about their Heads, for one of them had applied some part of an old shirt which I had given them to this use.

Thursday, 12th. Winds and weather as Yesterday, and the Employment of the People the same. At 2 A.M. the Yawl came on board, and brought 3 Turtle and a large Skeat, and as there was a probability of succeeding in this kind of fishery, I sent her out again after breakfast. About this time 5 of the Natives came over and stay'd with us all the Forenoon. There were 7 in all-- 5 Men, 1 Woman, and a Boy; these 2 last stay'd on the point of Land on the other side of the River about 200 Yards from us. We could very clearly see with our Glasses that the Woman was as naked as ever she was born; even those parts which I always before now thought Nature would have taught a woman to Conceal were uncovered.

Friday, 13th. Gentle breezes from the South-East in day, and Calm or light Airs from the Land in the Night. Employ'd taking on board water, Stores, etc. At Noon the Yawl return'd with one Turtle and a large Sting ray.

Saturday, 14th. Gentle breezes at South-East and Hazey weather. In the P.M. compleated our water; got on board all the Bread, and part of our Stores; in the evening sent the Turtlers out again. A.M., employ'd getting on board stone ballast and Airing the spare Sails. Mr. Gore, being in the Country, shott one of the Animals before spoke of; it was a small one of the sort, weighing only 28 pound clear of the entrails; its body was ----* (* Blank in manuscript.) long; the head, neck, and Shoulders very Small in proportion to the other parts. It was hair lipt, and the Head and Ears were most like a Hare's of any Animal I know; the Tail was nearly as long as the body, thick next the Rump, and Tapering towards the End; the fore Legs were 8 Inches long, and the Hind 22. Its progression is by Hopping or Jumping 7 or 8 feet at each hop upon its hind Legs only, for in this it makes no use of the Fore, which seem to be only design'd for Scratching in the ground, etc. The Skin is cover'd with a Short, hairy furr of a dark Mouse or Grey Colour. It bears no sort of resemblance to any European animal I ever saw; it is said to bear much resemblance to the Jerboa, excepting in size, the Jerboa being no larger than a common rat.

Sunday, 15th. Gentle breezes at South-East and East. P.M., got on board the Spare Sails and sundry other Articles. In the A.M., as the people did not work upon the Ship, one of the Petty Officers was desirous of going out to Catch Turtles. I let him have the Pinnace for that purpose, and sent the Long boat to haul the Sean, who caught about 60 fish.

Monday, 16th. Fore and Latter parts gentle breezes at East-North-East; in the night had light Airs and Calm. In the evening the Yawl came in with 4 Turtle and a Large Sting ray, and soon after went out again; but the Pinnace did not return as I expected. A.M., employ'd getting on board Cables; at the same time I went upon one of the high hills on the North side of the River, from which I had an extensive view of the inland Country, which consisted of hills, Valleys, and Large plains, agreeably diversified with Woods and Lawns.

Tuesday, 17th. Wind at South-East, a fresh breeze; people employed as yesterday setting up the rigging. In the evening the Pinnace returned with 3 Turtles, 2 of which the Yawl caught and sent in. At 7 hours 41 minutes 17 seconds p.m. observ'd the first Satellite of Jupiter to Emerge, and the same Emersion hapned at Greenwich at 10 hours 00 minutes 52 seconds in the a.m.; the difference is 14 hours 19 minutes 35 seconds equal to 214 degrees 53 minutes 45 seconds of Longitude. The observation made on the 29th of last Month gave 214 degrees 42 minutes 30 seconds; the mean is 214 degrees

48 minutes 7 1/2 seconds, which this place is West of Greenwich.* (* As before mentioned, the true longitude is 214 degrees 45 minutes.)

Wednesday, 18th. Wind at East-South-East, a Gentle breeze. P.M., I sent the Master and one of the Mates in the Pinnace to the Northward to look for a Channell that way clear of the Shoal. Mr. Banks, Dr. Solander, and myself took a turn into the woods on the other side of the water, where we met with 5 of the Natives; and although we had not seen any of them before, they came to us without showing any signs of fear. 2 of these wore Necklaces made of Shells, which they seem'd to Value, as they would not part with them. In the evening the Yawl came in with 3 Turtle, and early in the A.M. she went out again. About 8 we were Visited by several of the Natives, who now became more familiar than ever. Soon after this Mr. Banks and I went over to the South* (* This should be North.) side of the River, and Travel'd 6 or 8 miles along shore to the Northward, where we ascended a high hill, from whence I had an extensive view of the Sea Coast; it afforded us a melancholy prospect of the difficulties we are to encounter, for in whatever direction we looked it was cover'd with Shoals as far as the Eye could see; after this we return'd to the Ship without meeting with anything remarkable, and found several of the Natives on board. At this time we had 12 tortoise or Turtle upon our Decks, which they took more Notice of than anything Else in the Ship, as I was told by the officers, for their Curiosity was Satisfied before I got on board, and they went away soon after.

Thursday, 19th. Gentle breezes and fair weather. Employ'd getting everything in readyness for Sea. A.M., we were Visited by 10 or 11 of the Natives; the most of them came from the other side of the Harbour, where we saw 6 or 7 more, the most of them Women, and, like the men, quite naked. Those that came on board were very desirous of having some of our Turtles, and took the liberty to haul 2 of them to the Gangway to put over the side; being disappointed in this, they grew a little Troublesome, and were for throwing every thing overboard they could lay their hands upon. As we had no Victuals dress'd at this time, I offer'd them some bread to Eat, which they rejected with Scorn, as I believe they would have done anything else excepting Turtle;* (* No doubt, in the native view, the turtle belonged to them, and they considered the strangers had annexed their property.) soon after this they all went ashore, Mr. Banks, myself, and 5 or 6 of our people being their at same time. Immediately upon their Landing one of tbem took a Handful of dry grass and lighted it at a fire we had ashore, and before we well know'd what he was going about he made a larger Circuit round about us, and set fire to the grass in his way, and in an instant the whole place was in flames. Luckily at this time we had hardly anything ashore, besides the Forge and a Sow with a litter of young Pigs, one of which was scorched to Death in the fire. As soon as they had done this they all went to a place where some of our people were washing, and where all our nets and a good deal of linnen were laid out to dry; here with the greatest obstinacy they again set fire to the grass, which I and some others who were present could not prevent, until I was obliged to fire a Musquet load with small Shott at one of the Ring leaders, which sent them off. As we were apprised of this last Attempt of theirs we got the fire out before it got head, but the first spread like wild fire in the Woods and grass. Notwithstanding my firing, in which one must have been a little hurt, because we saw a few drops of blood on some of the linnen he had gone over, they did not go far from us; for we soon after heard their Voices in the woods, upon which Mr. Banks and I and 3 or 4 more went to look for them, and very soon met them coming toward us. As they had each 4 or 5 Darts, and not knowing their intention, we seized upon 6 or 7 of the first darts we met with. This alarm'd them so much that they all made off, and we follow'd them for near 1/2 a Mile, and then set down and called to them, and they stop'd also; after some little unintelligible conversation had passed they laid down their darts, and came to us in a very friendly manner. We now return'd the Darts we had taken from them, which reconcil'd everything. There were 4 Strangers among them that we had not seen before, and these were interduced to us by name by the others; the Man which we supposed to have been Struck with small Shott was gone off, but he could not be much hurt as he was at a great distance when I fir'd. They all came along with us abreast of the Ship, where they stay'd a short time, and then went away, and soon after set the woods on fire about a Mile and a half or two Miles from us.

Friday, 20th. Fresh breezes at South-East and Cloudy weather. P.M., got everything on board the Ship, new berth'd her, and let her swing with the tide. In the night the Master return'd with the pinnace, and reported that there was no safe Passage for the Ship to the Northward at low water. A.M., I went and Sounded and buoy'd the Bar, being now ready to put to sea the first opportunity.

Saturday, 21st. Strong breezes at South-East and Cloudy weather. P.M., sent a Boat to haul the Sean, which return'd with as much fish as came to 1 3/4 pounds per Man; the Yawl return'd with only one Turtle, which was caught in the Net, for it blew too hard for the Boat to strike any. In the morning I sent her out again, but she was obliged to return, not being able to get to Windward. The Carpenters employ'd in repairing the Boats and overhauling the Pumps, and as the Wind would not permit us to sail, I sent the Boatswain with some hands ashore to make rope, and a petty Officer with 2 Men to gather Greens for the Ship's Company.

Sunday, 22nd. Fresh breezes at South-East and East-South-East. Employ'd as Yesterday. A.M., the weather would not permit us to Sail; sent the Turtlers out again. In opening of one to-day we found sticking thro' both Shoulder bones a wood Harpoon, or Turtle Peg, 15 Inches long, bearded at the end, such as we have seen among the Natives; this proves to a Demonstration that they strike Turtle, I suppose at the Time they come ashore to lay their Eggs, for they certainly have no boat fit to do this at Sea, or that will carry a Turtle, and this Harpoon must have been a good while in, as the wound was quite heal'd up.

Monday, 23rd. Fresh breezes in the South-East quarter, which so long as it continues will confine us in Port. Yesterday, A.M., I sent some people in the Country to gather greens, one of which stragled from the rest, and met with 4 of the Natives by a fire, on which they were broiling a Fowl, and the hind leg of one of the Animals before spoke of. He had the presence of mind not to run from them (being unarm'd), least they should pursue him, but went and set down by them; and after he had set a little while, and they had felt his hands and other parts of his body, they suffer'd him to go away without offering the least insult, and perceiving that he did not go right for the Ship they directed him which way to go.

Tuesday, 24th. Winds and weather continues. The Seamen employ'd making ropes, Caulking the Ship, Fishing, etc.

Wednesday, 25th. Fresh gales at South-East and fair weather. In the evening the Yawl came in, having not been able to Strike one Turtle on account of the blowing weather, nor can we catch much fish with the Sean in the Harbour.

Thursday, 26th. Winds and weather as Yesterday. Such people as can be spared from the necessary Dutys of the Ship are employ'd fishing and gathering greens and other refreshments.

Friday, 27th. Very fresh Gales at South-East by South and fair weather. A.M., caught as much fish as served 3/4 pounds a man, and Mr. Gore shott one of the Animals before spoke of, which weighed 80 pounds and 54 pounds, exclusive of the entrails, Skin, and head; this was as large as the most we have seen.

Saturday, 28th. Winds and weather as above, without the least Variation the whole of the 24 hours. The Carpenters finish'd caulking the Ship.

Sunday, 29th. Winds at South-East, a fresh breeze until 5 a.m., at which time it fell calm, and soon after had a light breeze from the land. Upon this I sent a Boat to see what water was upon the bar (it being 2 hours Ebb), and hove up the Anchor in order to put to Sea; but upon the return of the Boat came too again, as there were only 13 feet water on the Bar, which was 6 Inches less water than what the Ship Draw'd. After this I sent the Yawl to look for Turtle, as those we had got before were nearly all expended. About 8 the Sea breeze set in again, which put an end to our Sailing this day; after which I sent the Pinnace to haul the Sean; she return'd with only 20 pounds of Fish.

Monday, 30th. Winds at South-East, a fresh Gale and fair weather in the P.M., the remainder Hazey, with rain, but the winds, tho more moderate, keept in the South-East quarter.

Tuesday, 31st. Fresh Gales at South-East, and hazey with rain all P.M. and most part of the Night. At 2 a.m. I had thoughts of trying to Warp the Ship out of the Harbour, but upon my going first out in a Boat I found it blow too fresh for such an Attempt.

[August 1770.]

Wednesday, 1st August. Strong Gales from the South-East, with Squalls attended with Rain. P.M., the Yawl came in with 2 Rays, which together weighed 265 pounds; it blow'd too hard all the time they were out for striking Turtle. Carpenters employ'd overhauling the Pumps, all of which we find in a state of decay; and this the Carpenter says is owing to the Sap having been left in, which in time has decay'd the sound wood. One of them is quite useless, and was so rotten when hoisted up as to drop to peices. However, I cannot complain of a Leaky Ship, for the most water She makes is not quite an Inch an Hour.

Thursday, 2nd. Winds and weather as yesterday, or rather more Stormy; we have now no Success in the Sein fishing, hardly getting above 20 or 30 pounds a day.

Friday, 3rd. Strong breezes, and hazey until 6 a.m., when it moderated, and we unmoor'd, hove up the Anchor, and began to Warp out; but the Ship tailing upon the Sand on the North side of the River, the Tide of Ebb making out, and a fresh breeze setting in, we were obliged to desist and moor the Ship again just within the Barr.

Saturday, 4th. In the P.M., having pretty moderate weather, I order'd the Coasting Anchor and Cable to be laid without the barr, to be ready to warp out by, that we might not loose the least opportunity that might Offer; for laying in Port spends time to no purpose, consumes our Provisions, of which we are very Short in many Articles, and we have yet a long Passage to make to the East Indies through an unknown and perhaps dangerous Sea; these Circumstances consider'd, make me very Anxious of getting to Sea. The wind continued moderate all night, and at 5 a.m. it fell calm; this gave us an opportunity to warp out. About 7 we got under sail, having a light Air from the Land, which soon died away, and was Succeeded by the Sea breezes from South-East by South, with which we stood off to Sea East by North, having the Pinnace ahead sounding. The Yawl I sent to the Turtle bank to take up the Net that was left there; but as the wind freshen'd we got out before her, and a little After Noon Anchor'd in 15 fathoms water, Sandy bottom, for I did not think it safe to run in among the Shoals until I had well view'd them at low Water from the Mast head, that I might be better Able to Judge which way to Steer; for as yet I had not resolved whether I should beat back to the Southward round all the Shoals, or seek a Passage to the Eastward or Northward, all of which appeared to be equally difficult and dangerous. When at Anchor the Harbour sail'd from bore South 70 degrees West, distant 4 or 5 Leagues; the Northermost point of the Main land we have in sight, which I named Cape Bedford* (* Probably after John, 4th Duke, who had been First Lord of the Admiralty, 1744 to 1747.) (Latitude 15 degrees 17 minutes South, Longitude 214 degrees 45 minutes West), bore North 20 degrees West, distant 3 1/2 Leagues; but we could see land to the North-East of this Cape, which made like 2 high Islands;* (* Direction Islands.) the Turtle banks bore East, distant one Mile. Latitude by Observation 15 degrees 23 minutes South; our depth of Water, in standing off from the land, was from 3 1/2 to 15 fathoms.

[Description of Endeavour River.]

I shall now give a Short description of the Harbour, or River, we have been in, which I named after the Ship, Endeavour River. It is only a small Barr Harbour or Creek, which runs winding 3 or 4 Leagues in land, at the Head of which is a small fresh Water Brook, as I was told, for I was not so high myself; but there is not water for Shipping above a Mile within the barr, and this is on the North side, where the bank is so steep for nearly a quarter of a Mile that ships may lay afloat at low water so near the Shore as to reach it with a stage, and is extreamly Convenient for heaving a Ship down. And this is all the River hath to recommend it, especially for large Shipping, for there is no more than 9 or 10 feet Water upon the Bar at low water, and 17 or 18 feet at high, the Tides rises and falling about 9 feet at spring Tide, and is high on the days of the New and full Moon, between 9 and 10 o'Clock. Besides, this part of the Coast is barrocaded with Shoals, as to make this Harbour more difficult of access; the safest way I know of to come at it is from the South, Keeping the Main land close on board all the way. Its situation may always be found by the Latitude, which hath been before mentioned. Over the South point is some high Land, but the North point is formed by a low sandy beach, which extends about 3 Miles to the Northward, then the land is again high.

The refreshments we got here were Chiefly Turtle, but as we had to go 5 Leagues out to Sea for them, and had much blowing weather, we were not over Stocked with this Article; however, what with these and the fish we caught with the Sean we had not much reason to Complain, considering the Country we were in. Whatever refreshment we got that would bear a Division I caused to be equally divided among the whole Company, generally by weight; the meanest person in the Ship had an equal share with myself or any one on board, and this method every commander of a Ship on such a Voyage as this ought ever to Observe. We found in several places on the Sandy beaches and Sand Hills near the Sea, Purslain and beans, which grows on a Creeping kind of a Vine. The first we found very good when boiled, and the latter not to be dispised, and were at first very serviceable to the Sick; but the best greens we found here was the Tarra, or Coco Tops, called in the West Indies Indian Kale,* (* Colocasia Macrorhiza.) which grows in most Boggy Places; these eat as well as, or better, than Spinnage. The roots, for want of being Transplanted and properly Cultivated, were not good, yet we could have dispensed with them could we have got them in any Tolerable plenty; but having a good way to go for them, it took up too much time and too many hands to gather both root and branch. The few Cabage Palms we found here were in General small, and yielded so little Cabage that they were not worth the Looking after, and this was the Case with most of the fruit, etc., we found in the woods.

Besides the Animals which I have before mentioned, called by the Natives Kangooroo, or Kanguru, here are Wolves,* (* Probably Dingos.) Possums, an Animal like a ratt, and snakes, both of the Venemous and other sorts. Tame Animals here are none except Dogs, and of these we never saw but one, who frequently came about our Tents to pick up bones, etc. The Kanguru are in the greatest number, for we seldom went into the Country without seeing some. The land Fowls we met here, which far from being numerous, were Crows, Kites, Hawkes, Cockadores* (* Cockatoos.) of 2 Sorts, the one white, and the other brown, very beautiful Loryquets of 2 or 3 Sorts, Pidgeons, Doves, and a few other sorts of small Birds. The Sea or Water fowl are Herns, Whisling Ducks, which perch and, I believe, roost on Trees; Curlews, etc., and not many of these neither. Some of our Gentlemen who were in the Country heard and saw Wild Geese in the Night.

The Country, as far as I could see, is diversified with Hills and plains, and these with woods and Lawns; the Soil of the Hills is hard, dry, and very Stoney; yet it produceth a thin Coarse grass, and some wood. The Soil of the Plains and Valleys are sandy, and in some places Clay, and in many Parts very Rocky and Stoney, as well as the Hills, but in general the Land is pretty well Cloathed with long grass, wood, Shrubs, etc. The whole Country abounds with an immense number of Ant Hills, some of which are 6 or 8 feet high, and more than twice that in Circuit. Here are but few sorts of Trees besides the Gum tree, which is the most numerous, and is the same that we found on the Southern Part of the Coast, only here they do not grow near so large. On each side of the River, all the way up it, are Mangroves, which Extend in some places a Mile from its banks; the Country in general is not badly water'd, there being several fine Rivulets at no very great distance from one another, but none near to the place where we lay; at least not in the Dry season, which is at this time. However we were very well supply'd with water by springs which were not far off.* (* Cooktown, which now stands on the Endeavour River, is a thriving place, and the northernmost town on this coast. It has some 2000 inhabitants, and is the port for a gold mining district. A deeper channel has now been dredged over the bar that gave Cook so much trouble, but it is not a harbour that will admit large vessels.)

[At Anchor, Off Turtle Reef, Queensland.]

Sunday, 5th. In the P.M. had a Gentle breeze at South-East and Clear weather. As I did not intend to weigh until the morning I sent all the Boats to the Reef to get what Turtle and Shell fish they could. At low water from the Mast head I took a view of the Shoals, and could see several laying a long way without this one, a part of several of them appearing above water; but as it appear'd pretty clear of Shoals to the North-East of the Turtle Reef, I came to a Resolution to stretch out that way close upon a wind, because if we found no Passage we could always return back the way we went. In the Evening the Boats return'd with one Turtle, a sting ray, and as many large Clams as came to 1 1/2 pounds a Man; in each of these Clams were about 20 pounds of Meat; added to this we Caught in the night several Sharks. Early in the morning I sent the Pinnace and Yawl again to the Reef, as I did not intend to weigh until half Ebb, at which time the Shoals began to appear. Before 8 it came on to blow, and I made the Signal for the Boats to come on Board, which they did, and brought with them one Turtle. We afterwards began to heave, but the wind Freshening obliged us to bear away* (* To veer cable, i.e., pay out more cable, in order to hold the ship with the freshening wind.) again and lay fast.

Monday, 6th. Winds at South-East. At 2 o'Clock p.m. it fell pretty Moderate, and we got under sail, and stood out upon a wind North-East by East, leaving the Turtle Reef to windward, having the Pinnace ahead sounding. We had not stood out long before we discovered shoals ahead and on both bows. At half past 4 o'Clock, having run off 8 Miles, the Pinnace made the Signal for Shoal water in a place where we little Expected it; upon this we Tack'd and Stood on and off while the Pinnace stretched farther to the Eastward, but as night was approaching I thought it safest to Anchor, which we accordingly did in 20 fathoms water, a Muddy bottom. Endeavour River bore South 52 degrees West; Cape Bedford West by North 1/2 North, distant 5 Leagues; the Northermost land in sight, which made like an Island, North; and a Shoal, a small, sandy part of which appear'd above water, North-East, distance 2 or 3 Miles. In standing off from this Turtle Reef to this place our soundings were from 14 to 20 fathoms, but where the Pinnace was, about a Mile farther to the East-North-East, were no more than 4 or 5 feet of water, rocky ground; and yet this did not appear to us in the Ship. In the morning we had a strong Gale from the South-East, that, instead of weighing as we intended, we were obliged to bear away more Cable, and to Strike Top Gallant yards.

Tuesday, 7th. Strong Gales at South-East, South-East by South, and South-South-East, with cloudy weather at Low water in the P.M. I and several of the Officers kept a look out at the Mast head to see for a Passage between the Shoals; but we could see nothing but breakers all the way from the South round by the East as far as North-West, extending out to Sea as far as we could see. It did not appear to be one continued Shoal, but several laying detached from each other. On the Eastermost that we could see the Sea broke very high, which made one judge it to be the outermost; for on many of those within the Sea did not break high at all, and from about 1/2 flood to 1/2 Ebb they are not to be seen, which makes the Sailing among them more dangerous, and requires great care and Circumspection, for, like all other Shoals, or Reefs of Coral Rocks, they are quite steep too. Altho' the most of these Shoals consist of Coral Rocks, yet a part of some of them is sand. The Turtle Reef and some others have a small Patch of Sand generally at the North end, that is only cover'd at high water. These generally discover themselves before we come near them. Altho' I speak of this as the Turtle Reef, yet it is not to be doubted but what there are Turtle upon the most of them as well as this one. After having well viewed our situation from the Mast Head, I saw that we were surrounded on every side with Dangers, in so much that I was quite at a loss which way to steer when the weather will permit us to get under sail, for to beat back to the South-East the way we came, as the Master would have had me done, would be an endless peice of work, as the winds blow constantly from that Quarter, and very Strong, without hardly any intermission;* (* The south-east trade wind blows home on this coast very strong from about June to October. Though the Barrier Reef prevents any great sea from getting up, the continuance of this wind is a great nuisance for a sailing ship from many points of view though from others it is an advantage.) on the other hand, if we do not find a passage to the Northward we shall have to come back at last. At 11 the Ship drove, and obliged us to bear away to a Cable and one third, which brought us up again; but in the morning the Gale increasing, she drove again. This made us let go the Small Bower Anchor, and bear away a whole Cable on it and 2 on the other; and even after this she still kept driving slowly, until we had got down Top gallant Masts, struck Yards and Top masts close down, and made all snug; then she rid fast, Cape Bedford bearing West-South-West, distant 3 1/2 Leagues. In this situation we had Shoals to the Eastward of us extending from the South-East by South to the North-North-West, distant from the nearest part of them about 2 Miles.

Wednesday, 8th. Strong gales at South-South-East all this day, in so much that I durst not get up Yards and Topmasts.

Thursday, 9th. In the P.M., the weather being something moderate, we got up the Top masts, but keept the Lower yards down. At 6 in the morning we began to heave in the Cable, thinking to get under sail; but it blow'd so fresh, together with a head sea, that we could hardly heave the ship a head, and at last was obliged to desist.

[Off Cape Flattery, Queensland.]

Friday, 10th. Fresh Gales at South-South-East and South-East by South. P.M., the wind fell so that we got up the small Bower Anchor, and hove into a whole Cable on the Best Bower. At 3 in the morning we got up the Lower Yards, and at 7 weighed and stood in for the Land (intending to seek for a passage along Shore to the northward), having a Boat ahead sounding; depth of water as we run in from 19 to 12 fathoms. After standing in an hour we edged away for 3 Small Islands* (* Now called the Three Isles.) that lay North-North-East 1/2 East, 3 Leagues from Cape Bedford. To these Islands the Master had been in the Pinnace when the Ship was in Port. At 9 we were abreast of them, and between them and the Main, having another low Island between us and the latter, which lies West-North-West, 4 Miles from the 3 Islands. In this Channell had 14 fathoms water; the Northermost point of the Main we had in sight bore from us North-North-West 1/2 West, distant 2 Leagues. 4 or 5 Leagues to the North-East of this head land appeared 3 high Islands,* (* The Direction Islands.) with some smaller ones near them, and the Shoals and Reefs without, as we could see, extending to the Northward as far as these Islands. We directed our Course between them and the above headland, leaving a small Island* (* The Two Isles. Cook had now got among the numerous islands and reefs which lie round Cape Flattery. There are good channels between them, but they are very confusing to a stranger. Cook's anxiety in his situation can well be imagined, especially with his recent disaster in his mind.) to the Eastward of us, which lies North by East, 4 Miles from the 3 Islands, having all the while a boat ahead sounding. At Noon we were got between the head Land and the 3 high Islands, distant from the former 2, and from the latter 4 Leagues; our Latitude by observation was 14 degrees 51 minutes South. We now judged ourselves to be clear of all Danger, having, as we thought, a Clear, open Sea before us; but this we soon found otherwise, and occasioned my calling the Headland above mentioned Cape Flattery (Latitude 14 degrees 55 minutes South, Longitude 214 degrees 43 minutes West). It is a high Promontory, making in 2 Hills next the sea, and a third behind them, with low sandy land on each side; but it is better known by the 3 high Islands out at Sea, the Northermost of which is the Largest, and lies from the Cape North-North-East, distant 5 Leagues. From this Cape the Main land trends away North-West and North-West by West.

Saturday, 11th. Fresh breezes at South-South-East and South-East by South, with which we steer'd along shore North-West by West until one o'Clock, when the Petty Officer at the Masthead called out that he saw land ahead, extending quite round to the Islands without, and a large reef between us and them; upon this I went to the Masthead myself. The reef I saw very plain, which was now so far to windward that we could not weather it, but what he took for Main land ahead were only small Islands, for such they appeared to me; but, before I had well got from Mast head the Master and some others went up, who all asserted that it was a Continuation of the Main land, and, to make it still more alarming, they said they saw breakers in a Manner all round us. We immediately hauld upon a wind in for the Land, and made the Signal for the Boat, which was ahead sounding, to come on board; but as she was well to leeward, we were obliged to edge away to take her up, and soon after came to an Anchor under a point of the Main in 1/4 less 5* (* The nautical manner of expressing four and three-quarters.) fathoms, about a Mile from the Shore, Cape Flattery bearing South-East, distant 3 1/2 Leagues. After this I landed, and went upon the point, which is pretty high, from which I had a View of the Sea Coast, which trended away North-West by West, 8 or 10 Leagues, which was as far as I could see, the weather not being very clear. I likewise saw 9 or 10 Small, Low Islands and some Shoals laying off the Coast, and some large Shoals between the Main and the 3 high Islands, without which, I was now well assured, were Islands, and not a part of the Mainland as some had taken them to be. Excepting Cape Flattery and the point I am now upon, which I have named point Lookout, the Main land next the sea to the Northward of Cape Bedford is low, and Chequer'd with white sand and green Bushes, etc., for 10 or 12 Miles inland, beyond which is high land. To the northward of Point Lookout the shore appear'd to be shoal and flat some distance off, which was no good sign of meeting with a Channell in with the land, as we have hitherto done. We saw the footsteps of people upon the sand, and smoke and fire up in the Country, and in the evening return'd on board, where I came to a resolution to visit one of the high Islands in the Offing in my Boat, as they lay at least 5 Leagues out at Sea, and seem'd to be of such a height that from the Top of one of them I hoped to see and find a Passage out to sea clear of the Shoals. Accordingly in the Morning I set out in the Pinnace for the Northermost and largest of the 3, accompanied by Mr. Banks. At the same time I sent the Master in the Yawl to Leeward, to sound between the Low Islands and the Main. In my way to the Island I passed over a large reef of Coral Rocks and sand, which lies about 2 Leagues from the Island; I left another to leeward, which lays about 3 Miles from the Island. [On Lizard Island, Queensland.] On the North part of this is a low, sandy Isle, with Trees upon it; on the reef we pass'd over in the Boat we saw several Turtle, and Chased one or Two, but caught none, it blowing too hard, and I had no time to spare, being otherways employ'd. I did not reach the Island until half an hour after one o'Clock in the P.M. on

Sunday, 12th, when I immediately went upon the highest hill on the Island,* (* Lizard Island.) where, to my Mortification, I discover'd a Reef of Rocks laying about 2 or 3 Leagues without the Island, extending in a line North-West and South-East, farther than I could see, on which the sea broke very high.* (* This was the outer edge of the Barrier Reefs.) This, however, gave one great hopes that they were the outermost shoals, as I did not doubt but what I should be able to get without them, for there appeared to be several breaks or Partitions in the Reef, and Deep Water between it and the Islands. I stay'd upon the Hill until near sun set, but the weather continued so Hazey all the time that I could not see above 4 or 5 Leagues round me, so that I came down much disappointed in the prospect I expected to have had, but being in hopes the morning might prove Clearer, and give me a better View of the Shoals. With this view I stay'd all night upon the Island, and at 3 in the Morning sent the Pinnace, with one of the Mates I had with me, to sound between the Island and the Reefs, and to Examine one of the breaks or Channels; and in the mean time I went again upon the Hill, where I arrived by Sun Rise, but found it much Hazier than in the Evening. About Noon the pinnace return'd, having been out as far as the Reef, and found from 15 to 28 fathoms water. It blow'd so hard that they durst not venture into one of the Channels, which, the Mate said, seem'd to him to be very narrow; but this did not discourage me, for I thought from the place he was at he must have seen it at disadvantage. Before I quit this Island I shall describe it. It lies, as I have before observed, about 5 Leagues from the Main; it is about 8 Miles in Circuit, and of a height sufficient to be seen 10 or 12 Leagues; it is mostly high land, very rocky and barren, except on the North-West side, where there are some sandy bays and low land, which last is covered with thin, long grass, Trees, etc., the same as upon the Main. Here is also fresh Water in 2 places; the one is a running stream, the water a little brackish where I tasted it, which was close to the sea; the other is a standing pool, close behind the sandy beach, of good, sweet water, as I daresay the other is a little way from the Sea beach. The only land Animals we saw here were Lizards, and these seem'd to be pretty Plenty, which occasioned my naming the Island Lizard Island. The inhabitants of the Main visit this Island at some Seasons of the Year, for we saw the Ruins of Several of their Hutts and heaps of Shells, etc. South-East, 4 or 5 Miles from this Island, lay the other 2 high Islands, which are very small compared to this; and near them lay 3 others, yet smaller and lower Islands, and several Shoals or reefs, especially to the South-East. There is, however, a clear passage from Cape Flattery to those Islands, and even quite out to the outer Reefs, leaving the above Islands to the South-East and Lizard Island to the North-West.

Monday, 13th. At 2 P.M. I left Lizard Island in order to return to the Ship, and in my way landed upon the low sandy Isle mentioned in coming out. We found on this Island* (* Eagle Island.) a pretty number of Birds, the most of them sea Fowl, except Eagles; 2 of the Latter we shott and some of the others; we likewise saw some Turtles, but got none, for the reasons before mentioned. After leaving Eagle Isle I stood South-West direct for the Ship, sounding all the way, and had not less than 8 fathoms, nor more than 14. I had the same depth of Water between Lizard and Eagle Isle. After I got on board the Master inform'd me he had been down to the Islands I had directed him to go too, which he judged to lay about 3 Leagues from the Main, and had sounded the Channel between the 2, found 7 fathoms; this was near the Islands, for in with the Main he had only 9 feet 3 Miles off, but without the Islands he found 10, 12, and 14 fathoms. He found upon the islands piles of turtle shells, and some finns that were so fresh that both he and the boats' crew eat of them. This showed that the natives must have been there lately. After well considering both what I had seen myself and the report of the Master's, I found by experience that by keeping in with the Mainland we should be in continued danger, besides the risk we should run in being lock'd in with Shoals and reefs by not finding a passage out to Leeward. In case we persever'd in keeping the Shore on board an accident of this kind, or any other that might happen to the ship, would infallibly loose our passage to the East India's this Season,* (* In November the wind changes to the North-West, which would have been a foul wind to Batavia.) and might prove the ruin of both ourselves and the Voyage, as we have now little more than 3 Months' Provisions on board, and that at short allowance. Wherefore, after consulting with the Officers, I resolved to weigh in the morning, and Endeavour to quit the Coast altogether until such time as I found I could approach it with less danger. With this View we got under sail at daylight in the morning, and stood out North-East for the North-West end of Lizard Island, having Eagle Island to windward of us, having the pinnace ahead sounding; and here we found a good Channell, wherein we had from 9 to 14 fathoms. At Noon the North end of Lizard Island bore East-South-East, distant one Mile; Latitude observed 14 degrees 38 minutes South; depth of water 14 fathoms. We now took the pinnace in tow, knowing that there were no dangers until we got out to the Reefs.* (* From the 13th to the 19th the language used in Mr. Corner's copy of the Journal is quite different from that of the Admiralty and the Queen's, though the occurrences are the same. From internal evidences, it appears that Mr. Corner's copy was at this period the first written up, and that Cook amended the phrases in the other fair copies.)

[Pass Outside Barrier Reef, Queensland.]

Tuesday, 14th. Winds at South-East, a steady gale. By 2 P.M. we got out to the outermost reefs, and just fetched to Windward of one of the openings I had discover'd from the Island; we tacked and Made a short trip to the South-West, while the Master went in the pinnace to examine the Channel, who soon made the signal for the Ship to follow, which we accordingly did, and in a short time got safe out. This Channel* (* Now known as Cook's Passage.) lies North-East 1/2 North, 3 Leagues from Lizard Island; it is about one-third of a Mile broad, and 25 or 30 fathoms deep or more. The moment we were without the breakers we had no ground with 100 fathoms of Line, and found a large Sea rowling in from the South-East. By this I was well assured we were got with out all the Shoals, which gave us no small joy, after having been intangled among Islands and Shoals, more or less, ever since the 26th of May, in which time we have sail'd above 360 Leagues by the Lead without ever having a Leadsman out of the Chains, when the ship was under sail; a Circumstance that perhaps never hapned to any ship before, and yet it was here absolutely necessary. I should have been very happy to have had it in my power to have keept in with the land, in order to have explor'd the Coast to the Northern extremity of the Country, which I think we were not far off, for I firmly believe this land doth not join to New Guinea. But this I hope soon either to prove or disprove, and the reasons I have before assign'd will, I presume, be thought sufficient for my leaving the Coast at this time; not but what I intend to get in with it again as soon as I can do it with safety. The passage or channel we now came out by, which I have named, ----* (* Blank in MS.) lies in the Latitude of 14 degrees 32 minutes South; it may always be found and known by the 3 high Islands within it, which I have called the Islands of Direction, because by their means a safe passage may be found even by strangers in within the Main reef, and quite into the Main. Lizard Island, which is the Northermost and Largest of the 3, Affords snug Anchorage under the North-West side of it, fresh water and wood for fuel; and the low Islands and Reefs which lay between it and the Main, abound with Turtle and other fish, which may be caught at all Seasons of the Year (except in such blowing weather as we have lately had). All these things considered there is, perhaps, not a better place on the whole Coast for a Ship to refresh at than this Island. I had forgot to mention in its proper place, that not only on this Island, but on Eagle Island, and on several places of the Sea beach in and about Endeavour River, we found Bamboos, Cocoa Nutts, the seeds of some few other plants, and Pummice-stones, which were not the produce of the Country. From what we have seen of it, it is reasonable to suppose that they are the produce of some lands or Islands laying in the Neighbourhood, most likely to the Eastward, and are brought hither by the Easterly trade winds. The Islands discover'd by Quiros lies in this parrallel, but how far to the Eastward it's hard to say; for altho' we found in most Charts his discoveries placed as far to the West as this country yet from the account of his Voyage, compared with what we ourselves have seen, we are Morally certain that he never was upon any part of this Coast.* (* The Island of Espiritu Santo, in the New Hebrides, which Quiros discovered, lies 1200 miles to the eastward, and New Caledonia, from which these objects might equally have come, is 1000 miles in the same direction.) As soon as we had got without the Reefs we Shortened sail, and hoisted in the pinnace and Long boat, which last we had hung alongside, and then stretched off East-North-East, close upon a wind, as I did not care to stand to the Northward until we had a whole day before us, for which reason we keept making short boards all night. The large hollow sea we have now got into acquaints us with a Circumstance we did not before know, which is that the Ship hath received more Damage than we were aware of, or could perceive when in smooth Water; for now she makes as much water as one pump will free, kept constantly at work. However this was looked upon as trifling to the Danger we had lately made an Escape from. At day light in the morning Lizard Island bore South by West, distant 10 Leagues. We now made all the sail we could, and stood away North-North-West 1/2 West, but at 9 we steer'd North-West 1/2 North, having the advantage of a Fresh Gale at South-East; at Noon we were by observation in the Latitude of 13 degrees 46 minutes South, the Lizard Island bore South 15 degrees East, distant 58 Miles, but we had no land in sight.

Wednesday, 15th. Fresh Trade at South-East and Clear weather. At 6 in the evening shortned sail and brought too, with her head to the North-East. By this time we had run near 12 Leagues upon a North-West 1/2 North Course since Noon. At 4 a.m. wore and lay her head to the South-West, and at 6 made all Sail, and steer'd West, in order to make the land, being fearful of over shooting the passage, supposing there to be one, between this land and New Guinea. By noon we had run 10 Leagues upon this Course, but saw no land. Our Latitude by observation was 13 degrees 2 minutes South, Longitude 216 degrees 00 minutes West, which was 1 degree 23 minutes to the West of Lizard Island.

[Ship in Danger, Outside Barrier Reef.]

Thursday, 16th. Moderate breezes at East-South-East and fair weather. A little after Noon saw the Land from the Mast head bearing West-South-West, making high; at 2 saw more land to the North-West of the former, making in hills like Islands; but we took it to be a Continuation of the Main land. An hour after this we saw a reef, between us and the land, extending away to the Southward, and, as we thought, terminated here to the Northward abreast of us; but this was only on op'ning, for soon after we saw it extend away to the Northward as far as we could distinguish anything. Upon this we hauld close upon a Wind, which was now at East-South-East, with all the sail we could set. We had hardly trimm'd our sails before the wind came to East by North, which made our weathering the Reef very doubtful, the Northern point of which in sight at sun set still bore from us North by West, distant about 2 Leagues. However, this being the best Tack to Clear it, we keept standing to the Northward, keeping a good look out until 12 at night, when, fearing to run too far upon one Course, we tack'd and stood to the southward, having run 6 Leagues North or North by East since sun set; we had not stood above 2 Miles to the South-South-East before it fell quite Calm. We both sounded now and several times before, but had not bottom with 140 fathoms of line.* (* The description which follows, of the situation of the ship, and the occurrences until she was safely anchored inside the Barrier Reef, is from the Admiralty copy, as it is much fuller than that in Mr. Corner's.) A little after 4 o'clock the roaring of the surf was plainly heard, and at daybreak the Vast foaming breakers were too plainly to be seen not a mile from us, towards which we found the ship was carried by the Waves surprisingly fast. We had at this time not an air of Wind, and the depth of water was unfathomable, so that there was not a possibility of anchoring. In this distressed Situation we had nothing but Providence and the small Assistance the Boats could give us to trust to; the Pinnace was under repair, and could not immediately be hoisted out. The Yawl was put in the Water, and the Longboat hoisted out, and both sent ahead to tow, which, together with the help of our sweeps abaft, got the Ship's head round to the Northward, which seemed to be the best way to keep her off the Reef, or at least to delay time. Before this was effected it was 6 o'clock, and we were not above 80 or 100 yards from the breakers. The same sea that washed the side of the ship rose in a breaker prodidgiously high the very next time it did rise, so that between us and destruction was only a dismal Valley, the breadth of one wave, and even now no ground could be felt with 120 fathom. The Pinnace was by this time patched up, and hoisted out and sent ahead to Tow. Still we had hardly any hopes of saving the ship, and full as little our lives, as we were full 10 Leagues from the nearest Land, and the boats not sufficient to carry the whole of us; yet in this Truly Terrible Situation not one man ceased to do his utmost, and that with as much Calmness as if no danger had been near. All the dangers we had escaped were little in comparison of being thrown upon this reef, where the Ship must be dashed to pieces in a Moment. A reef such as one speaks of here is Scarcely known in Europe. It is a Wall of Coral Rock rising almost perpendicular out of the unfathomable Ocean, always overflown at high Water generally 7 or 8 feet, and dry in places at Low Water. The Large Waves of the Vast Ocean meeting with so sudden a resistance makes a most Terrible Surf, breaking Mountains high, especially as in our case, when the General Trade Wind blows directly upon it. At this Critical juncture, when all our endeavours seemed too little, a Small Air of Wind sprung up, but so small that at any other Time in a Calm we should not have observed it. With this, and the Assistance of our Boats, we could observe the Ship to move off from the Reef in a slanting direction; but in less than 10 Minutes we had as flat a Calm as ever, when our fears were again renewed, for as yet we were not above 200 Yards from the Breakers. Soon after our friendly Breeze visited us again, and lasted about as long as before. A Small Opening was now Seen in the Reef about a 1/4 of a Mile from us, which I sent one of the Mates to Examine. Its breadth was not more than the Length of the Ship, but within was Smooth Water. Into this place it was resolved to Push her if Possible, having no other Probable Views to save her, for we were still in the very Jaws of distruction, and it was a doubt wether or no we could reach this Opening. However, we soon got off it, when to our Surprise we found the Tide of Ebb gushing out like a Mill Stream, so that it was impossible to get in. We however took all the Advantage Possible of it, and it Carried us out about a 1/4 of a Mile from the breakers; but it was too Narrow for us to keep in long. However, what with the help of this Ebb, and our Boats, we by Noon had got an Offing of 1 1/2 or 2 Miles, yet we could hardly flatter ourselves with hopes of getting Clear, even if a breeze should Spring up, as we were by this time embay'd by the Reef, and the Ship, in Spite of our Endeavours, driving before the Sea into the bight. The Ebb had been in our favour, and we had reason to Suppose the flood which was now made would be against us. The only hopes we had was another Opening we saw about a Mile to the Westward of us, which I sent Lieutenant Hicks in the Small Boat to Examine. Latitude observed 12 degrees 37 minutes South, the Main Land in Sight distant about 10 Leagues.

[Pass Again Inside Barrier Reef.]

Friday, 17th. While Mr. Hicks was Examining the opening we struggled hard with the flood, sometime gaining a little and at other times loosing. At 2 o'Clock Mr. Hicks returned with a favourable Account of the Opening. It was immediately resolved to Try to secure the Ship in it. Narrow and dangerous as it was, it seemed to be the only means we had of saving her, as well as ourselves. A light breeze soon after sprung up at East-North-East, with which, the help of our Boats, and a Flood Tide, we soon entered the Opening, and was hurried thro' in a short time by a Rappid Tide like a Mill race, which kept us from driving against either side, though the Channel was not more than a 1/4 of a Mile broad, having 2 Boats ahead of us sounding.* (* This picture of the narrow escape from total shipwreck is very graphic. Many a ship has been lost under similar circumstances, without any idea of anchoring, which would often save a vessel, as it is not often that a reef is so absolutely steep; but that Cook had this possibility in his mind is clear. As a proof of the calmness which prevailed on board, it may be mentioned that when in the height of the danger, Mr. Green, Mr. Clerke, and Mr. Forwood the gunner, were engaged in taking a Lunar, to obtain the longitude. The note in Mr. Green's log is: "These observations were very good, the limbs of sun and moon very distinct, and a good horizon. We were about 100 yards from the reef, where we expected the ship to strike every minute, it being calm, no soundings, and the swell heaving us right on.") Our depth of water was from 30 to 7 fathoms; very irregular soundings and foul ground until we had got quite within the Reef, where we Anchor'd in 19 fathoms, a Coral and Shelly bottom. The Channel we came in by, which I have named Providential Channell, bore East-North-East, distant 10 or 12 Miles, being about 8 or 9 Leagues from the Main land, which extended from North 66 degrees West to South-West by South.

It is but a few days ago that I rejoiced at having got without the Reef; but that joy was nothing when Compared to what I now felt at being safe at an Anchor within it. Such are the Visissitudes attending this kind of Service, and must always attend an unknown Navigation where one steers wholy in the dark without any manner of Guide whatever. Was it not from the pleasure which Naturly results to a man from his being the first discoverer, even was it nothing more than Land or Shoals, this kind of Service would be insupportable, especially in far distant parts like this, Short of Provisions and almost every other necessary. People will hardly admit of an excuse for a Man leaving a Coast unexplored he has once discovered. If dangers are his excuse, he is then charged with Timerousness and want of Perseverance, and at once pronounced to be the most unfit man in the world to be employ'd as a discoverer; if, on the other hand, he boldly encounters all the dangers and Obstacles he meets with, and is unfortunate enough not to succeed, he is then Charged with Temerity, and, perhaps, want of Conduct. The former of these Aspersions, I am confident, can never be laid to my Charge, and if I am fortunate to Surmount all the Dangers we meet with, the latter will never be brought in Question; altho' I must own that I have engaged more among the Islands and Shoals upon this Coast than perhaps in prudence I ought to have done with a single Ship* (* Cook was so impressed with the danger of one ship alone being engaged in these explorations, that in his subsequent voyages he asked for, and obtained, two vessels.) and every other thing considered. But if I had not I should not have been able to give any better account of the one half of it than if I had never seen it; at best, I should not have been able to say wether it was Mainland or Islands; and as to its produce, that we should have been totally ignorant of as being inseparable with the other; and in this case it would have been far more satisfaction to me never to have discover'd it. But it is time I should have done with this Subject, which at best is but disagreeable, and which I was lead into on reflecting on our late Dangers.

In the P.M., as the wind would not permit us to sail out by the same Channel as we came in, neither did I care to move until the pinnace was in better repair, I sent the Master with all the other Boats to the Reef to get such refreshments as he could find, and in the meantime the Carpenters were repairing the pinnace. Variations by the Amplitude and Azimuth in the morning 4 degrees 9 minutes Easterly; at noon Latitude observed 12 degrees 38 minutes South, Longitude in 216 degrees 45 minutes West. It being now about low water, I and some other of the officers went to the Masthead to see what we could discover. Great part of the reef without us was dry, and we could see an Opening in it about two Leagues farther to the South-East than the one we came in by; we likewise saw 2 large spots of sand to the Southward within the Reef, but could see nothing to the Northward between it and the Main. On the Mainland within us was a pretty high promontary, which I called Cape Weymouth (Latitude 12 degrees 42 minutes South, Longitude 217 degrees 15 minutes); and on the North-West side of this Cape is a Bay, which I called Weymouth Bay.* (* Viscount Weymouth was one of the Secretaries of State when the Endeavour sailed.)

Saturday, 18th. Gentle breezes at East and East-South-East. At 4 P.M. the Boats return'd from the Reef with about 240 pounds of Shell-fish, being the Meat of large Cockles, exclusive of the Shells. Some of these Cockles are as large as 2 Men can move, and contain about 20 pounds of Meat, very good. At 6 in the morning we got under sail, and stood away to the North-West, as we could not expect a wind to get out to Sea by the same Channel as we came in without waiting perhaps a long time for it, nor was it advisable at this time to go without the Shoals, least we should by them be carried so far off the Coast as not to be able to determine wether or no New Guinea joins to or makes a part of this land. This doubtful point I had from my first coming upon the Coast, determined, if Possible, to clear up; I now came to a fix'd resolution to keep the Main land on board, let the Consequence be what it will, and in this all the Officers concur'd. In standing to the North-West we met with very irregular soundings, from 10 to 27 fathoms, varying 5 or 6 fathoms almost every Cast of the Lead. However, we kept on having a Boat ahead sounding. A little before noon we passed a low, small, sandy Isle, which we left on our Starboard side at the distance of 2 Miles. At the same time we saw others, being part of large Shoals above water, away to the North-East and between us and the Main land. At Noon we were by observation in the Latitude of 12 degrees 28 minutes South, and 4 or 5 Leagues from the Main, which extended from South by West to North 71 degrees West, and some Small Islands extending from North 40 degrees West to North 54 degrees West, the Main or outer Reef seen from the Masthead away to the North-East.

[Amongst Shoals off Cape Grenville.]

Sunday, 19th. Gentle breezes at South-East by East and Clear wether. At 2 P.M., as we were steering North-West by North, saw a large shoal right ahead, extending 3 or 4 points on each bow, upon which we haul'd up North-

North-East and North-East by North, in order to get round to North Point of it, which we reached by 4 o'clock, and then Edged away to the westward, and run between the North end of this Shoal and another, which lays 2 miles to the Northward of it, having a Boat all the time ahead sounding. Our depth of Water was very irregular, from 22 to 8 fathoms. At 1/2 past 6 we Anchor'd in 13 fathoms; the Northermost of the Small Islands mentioned at Noon bore West 1/2 South, distant 3 Miles. These Islands, which are known in the Chart by the name of Forbes's Isles,* (* Admiral John Forbes was a Commissioner of Longitude in 1768, and had been a Lord of the Admiralty from 1756 to 1763.) lay about 5 Leagues from the Main, which here forms a moderate high point, which we called Bolt head, from which the Land trends more westerly, and is all low, sandy Land, but to the Southward it is high and hilly, even near the Sea. At 6 A.M. we got under sail, and directed our Course for an Island which lay but a little way from the Main, and bore from us at this time North 40 degrees West, distant 5 Leagues; but we were soon interrupted in our Course by meeting with Shoals, but by the help of 2 Boats ahead and a good lookout at the Mast head we got at last into a fair Channel, which lead us down to the Island, having a very large Shoal on our Starboard side and several smaller ones betwixt us and the Main land. In this Channel we had from 20 to 30 fathoms. Between 11 and 12 o'Clock we hauld round the North-East side of the Island, leaving it between us and the Main from which it is distant 7 or 8 Miles. This Island is about a League in Circuit and of a moderate height, and is inhabited; to the North-West of it are several small, low Islands and Keys, which lay not far from the Main, and to the Northward and Eastward lay several other Islands and Shoals, so that we were now incompassed on every side by one or the other, but so much does a great danger Swallow up lesser ones, that these once so much dreaded spots were now looked at with less concern. The Boats being out of their Stations, we brought too to wait for them. At Noon our Latitude by observation was 12 degrees 0 minutes South, Longitude in 217 degrees 25 minutes West; depth of Water 14 fathoms; Course and distance sail'd, reduced to a strait line, since yesterday Noon is North 29 degrees West, 32 Miles. The Main land within the above Islands forms a point, which I call Cape Grenville* (* George Grenville was First Lord of the Admiralty for a few months in 1763, and afterwards Prime Minister for two years.) (Latitude 11 degrees 58 minutes, Longitude 217 degrees 38 minutes); between this Cape and the Bolt head is a Bay, which I Named Temple Bay.* (* Richard Earl Temple, brother of George Grenville, was First Lord of the Admiralty in 1756.) East 1/2 North, 9 Leagues from Cape Grenville, lay some tolerable high Islands, which I called Sir Charles Hardy's Isles;* (* Admiral Sir C. Hardy was second in command in Hawke's great action in Quiberon Bay, 1759.) those which lay off the Cape I named Cockburn Isles.* (* Admiral George Cockburn was a Commissioner of Longitude and Comptroller of the Navy when Cook left

England. Off Cape Grenville the Endeavour again got into what is now the recognised channel along the land inside the reefs.)

[Nearing Cape York, Queensland.]

Monday, 20th. Fresh breezes at East-South-East. About one P.M. the pinnace having got ahead, and the Yawl we took in Tow, we fill'd and Steer'd North by West, for some small Islands we had in that direction. After approaching them a little nearer we found them join'd or connected together by a large Reef; upon this we Edged away North-West, and left them on our Starboard hand, steering between them and the Island laying off the Main, having a fair and Clear Passage; Depth of Water from 15 to 23 fathoms. At 4 we discover'd some low Islands and Rocks bearing West-North-West, which we stood directly for. At half Past 6 we Anchor'd on the North-East side of the Northermost, in 16 fathoms, distant from the Island one Mile. This Isle lay North-West 4 Leagues from Cape Grenville. On the Isles we saw a good many Birds, which occasioned my calling them Bird Isles. Before and at Sunset we could see the Main land, which appear'd all very low and sandy, Extends as far to the Northward as North-West by North, and some Shoals, Keys, and low sandy Isles away to the North-East of us. At 6 A.M. we got again under sail, with a fresh breeze at East, and stood away North-North-West for some low Islands* (* Boydong Keys.) we saw in that direction; but we had not stood long upon this Course before we were obliged to haul close upon a wind in Order to weather a Shoal which we discover'd on our Larboard bow, having at the same time others to the Eastward of us. By such time as we had weathered the Shoal to Leeward we had brought the Islands well upon our Leebow; but seeing some Shoals spit off from them, and some rocks on our Starboard bow, which we did not discover until we were very near them, made me afraid to go to windward of the Islands; wherefore we brought too, and made the signal for the pinnace, which was a head, to come on board, which done, I sent her to Leeward of the Islands, with Orders to keep along the Edge off the Shoal, which spitted off from the South side of the Southermost Island. The Yawl I sent to run over the Shoals to look for Turtle, and appointed them a Signal to make in case they saw many; if not, she was to meet us on the other side of the Island. As soon as the pinnace had got a proper distance from us we wore, and stood After her, and run to Leeward of the Islands, where we took the Yawl in Tow, she having seen only one small Turtle, and therefore made no Stay upon the Shoal. Upon this Island, which is only a Small Spott of Land, with some Trees upon it, we saw many Hutts and habitations of the Natives, which we supposed come over from the Main to these Islands (from which they are distant about 5 Leagues) to Catch Turtle at the time these Animals come ashore to lay their Eggs. Having got the Yawl in Tow, we stood away after the pinnace North-North-East and North by East to 2 other low

Islands, having 2 Shoals, which we could see without and one between us and the Main. At Noon we were about 4 Leagues from the Main land, which we could see Extending to the Northward as far as North-West by North, all low, flat, and Sandy. Our Latitude by observation was 11 degrees 23 minutes South, Longitude in 217 degrees 46 minutes West, and Course and distance sail'd since Yesterday at Noon North 22 degrees West, 40 Miles; soundings from 14 to 23 fathoms. But these are best seen upon the Chart, as likewise the Islands, Shoals, etc., which are too Numerous to be Mentioned singly.* (* It is very difficult to follow Cook's track after entering Providential Channel to this place. The shoals and islands were so confusing that their positions are very vaguely laid down on Cook's chart. It is easy to imagine how slow was his progress and tortuous his course, with a boat ahead all the time constantly signalling shallow water. Nothing is more trying to officers and men.)

Tuesday, 21st. Winds at East by South and East-South-East, fresh breeze. By one o'Clock we had run nearly the length of the Southermost of the 2 Islands before mentioned, and finding that we could not well go to windward of them without carrying us too far from the Main land, we bore up, and run to Leeward, where we found a fair open passage. This done, we steer'd North by West, in a parrallel direction with the Main land, leaving a small Island between us and it, and some low sandy Isles and Shoals without us, all of which we lost sight of by 4 o'Clock; neither did we see any more before the sun went down, at which time the farthest part of the Main in sight bore North-North-West 1/2 West. Soon after this we Anchor'd in 13 fathoms, soft Ground, about five Leagues from the Land, where we lay until day light, when we got again under sail, having first sent the Yawl ahead to sound. We steer'd North-North-West by Compass from the Northermost land in sight; Variation 3 degrees 6 minutes East. Seeing no danger in our way we took the Yawl in Tow, and made all the Sail we could until 8 o'Clock, at which time we discover'd Shoals ahead and on our Larboard bow, and saw that the Northermost land, which we had taken to be a part of the Main, was an Island, or Islands,* (*Now called Mount Adolphus Islands.) between which and the Main their appeared to be a good Passage thro' which we might pass by running to Leeward of the Shoals on our Larboard bow, which was now pretty near us. Whereupon we wore and brought too, and sent away the Pinnace and Yawl to direct us clear of the Shoals, and then stood after them. Having got round the South-East point of the Shoal we steer'd North-West along the South-West, or inside of it, keeping a good lookout at the Masthead, having another Shoal on our Larboard side; but we found a good Channel of a Mile broad between them, wherein were from 10 to 14 fathoms. At 11 o'Clock, being nearly the length of the Islands above mentioned, and designing to pass between them and the Main, the Yawl, being thrown a stern by falling in upon a part of the Shoal, She could not get over. We brought the Ship too, and Sent away the Long boat (which we had a stern, and rigg'd) to keep in Shore upon our Larboard bow, and the Pinnace on our Starboard; for altho' there appear'd nothing in the Passage, yet I thought it necessary to take this method, because we had a strong flood, which carried us on end very fast, and it did not want much of high water. As soon as the Boats were ahead we stood after them, and got through by noon, at which time we were by observation in the Latitude of 10 degrees 36 minutes 30 seconds South. The nearest part of the Main, and which we soon after found to be the Northermost,* (* Cape York, the northernmost point of Australia.) bore West southerly, distant 3 or 4 Miles; the Islands which form'd the passage before mentioned extending from North to North 75 degrees East, distant 2 or 3 Miles. At the same time we saw Islands at a good distance off extending from North by West to West-North-West, and behind them another chain of high land, which we likewise judged to be Islands.* (* The islands around Thursday Island.) The Main land we thought extended as far as North 71 degrees West; but this we found to be Islands. The point of the Main, which forms one side of the Passage before mentioned, and which is the Northern Promontory of this Country, I have named York Cape, in honour of his late Royal Highness, the Duke of York.* (* Edward Augustus, Duke of York and Albany, was a brother of George III.) It lies in the Longitude of 218 degrees 24 minutes West, the North point in the Latitude of 10 degrees 37 minutes South, and the East point in 10 degrees 41 minutes. The land over and to the Southward of this last point is rather low and very flatt as far inland as the Eye could reach, and looks barren. To the Southward of the Cape the Shore forms a large open bay, which I called Newcastle bay, wherein are some small, low Islands and shoals, and the land all about it is very low, flatt, and sandy. The land on the Northern part of the Cape is rather more hilly, and the shore forms some small bays, wherein there appear'd to be good Anchorage, and the Vallies appear'd to be tolerably well Cloathed with wood. Close to the East point of the Cape are 3 small Islands, and a small Ledge of rocks spitting off from one of them. There is also an Island laying close to the North Point. The other Islands before spoke of lay about 4 Miles without these; only two of them are of any extent. The Southermost is the largest, and much higher than any part of the Main land. On the North-West side of this Island seem'd to be good Anchorage, and Vallies that to all appearance would afford both wood and fresh Water. These Isles are known in the Chart by the name of York Isles.* (* Now called Mount Adolphus Islands.) To the Southward and South-East of them, and even to the Eastward and Northward, are several low Islands, rocks, and Shoals. Our depth of Water in sailing between them and the Main was 12, 13, and 14 fathoms.* (* In this channel is the dangerous rock on which the steamship Quetta was wrecked, with such terrible loss of life, in 1890. By the Endeavour's track she must have passed very near it.)

[Land upon Possession Island.]

Wednesday, 22nd. Gentle breezes at East by South and clear weather. We had not steer'd above 3 or 4 Miles along shore to the westward before we discover'd the land ahead to be Islands detached by several Channels from the main land; upon this we brought too to Wait for the Yawl, and called the other Boats on board, and after giving them proper instructions, sent them away again to lead us thro' the Channell next the Main, and as soon as the Yawl was on board made sail after them with the Ship. Soon after we discover'd rocks and Shoals in this Channell, upon which I made the Signal for the boats to lead thro' the next Channel to the Northward* (* This led to Endeavour Strait, but the recognised track is the channel farther north.) laying between the Islands, which they accordingly did, we following with the Ship, and had not less than 5 fathoms; and this in the narrowest part of the Channel, which was about a Mile and a 1/2 broad from Island to Island. At 4 o'Clock we Anchor'd about a Mile and a 1/2 or 2 Miles within the Entrance in 6 1/2 fathoms, clear ground, distance from the Islands on each side of us one Mile, the Main land extending away to the South-West; the farthest point of which we could see bore from us South 48 degrees West, and the Southermost point of the Islands, on the North-West side of the Passage, bore South 76 degrees West. Between these 2 points we could see no land, so that we were in great hopes that we had at last found out a Passage into the Indian seas; but in order to be better informed I landed with a party of men, accompanied by Mr. Banks and Dr. Solander, upon the Islands which lies at the South-East point of the Passage. Before and after we Anchor'd we saw a Number of People upon this Island, Arm'd in the same manner as all the others we have seen, Except one man, who had a bow and a bundle of Arrows, the first we have seen upon this Coast. From the appearance of the people we expected they would have opposed our landing; but as we approached the shore they all made off, and left us in peaceable possession of as much of the Island as served our purpose. After landing I went upon the highest hill, which, however, was of no great height, yet no less than twice or thrice the height of the Ship's Mastheads; but I could see from it no land between South-West and West-South-West, so that I did not doubt but there was a passage. I could see plainly that the lands laying to the North-West of this passage were compos'd of a number of Islands of Various extent, both for height and Circuit, ranged one behind another as far to the Northward and Westward as I could see, which could not be less than 12 or 14 Leagues.

Having satisfied myself of the great Probability of a passage, thro' which I intend going with the Ship, and therefore may land no more upon this Eastern coast of New Holland, and on the Western side I can make no new discovery, the honour of which belongs to the Dutch Navigators, but the Eastern Coast from the Latitude of 38 degrees South down to this place, I am confident, was never seen or Visited by any European before us; and notwithstanding I had in the Name of his Majesty taken possession of several places upon this Coast, I now once More hoisted English Colours, and in the Name of His Majesty King George the Third took possession of the whole Eastern coast from the above Latitude down to this place by the Name of New Wales,* (* The Admiralty copy, as well as that belonging to Her Majesty, calls it New South Wales. The island where the ceremony was performed was named on Cook's chart Possession Island, and is still so called.) together with all the Bays, Harbours, Rivers, and Islands, situated upon the said Coast; after which we fired 3 Volleys of small Arms, which were answer'd by the like number from the Ship.

This done, we set out for the Ship, but were some time in getting on board on account of a very Rapid Ebb Tide, which set North-East out of the Passage. Ever since we came in amongst the Shoals this last time we have found a Moderate Tide; the flood setting to the North-West and Ebb to the South-East; at this place is high water at full and change of the moon, about 1 or 2 o'Clock, and riseth and falleth upon a perpendicular about 10 or 12 feet. We saw upon all the Adjacent Lands and Islands a great number of smokes--a certain sign that they are inhabited--and we have daily seen smokes on every part of the Coast we have lately been upon. Between 7 and 8 o'Clock a.m. we saw several naked people, all or most of them Women, down upon the beach picking up Shells, etc.; they had not a single rag of any kind of Cloathing upon them, and both these and those we saw yesterday were in every respect the same sort of People we have seen everywhere upon the Coast. 2 or 3 of the Men we saw Yesterday had on pretty large breast plates, which we supposed were made of pearl Oyster Shells; this was a thing, as well as the Bow and Arrows, we had not seen before. At low water, which hapned about 10 o'Clock, we got under sail, and stood to the South-West, with a light breeze at East, which afterwards veer'd to North by East, having the Pinnace ahead; depth of Water from 6 to 10 fathoms, except in one place, were we passed over a Bank of 5 fathoms. At Noon Possession Island, at the South-East entrance of the Passage, bore North 53 degrees East, distant 4 Leagues; the Western extream of the Main land in sight South 43 degrees West, distant 4 or 5 Leagues, being all exceeding low. The South-West point of the largest Island* (* Prince of Wales Island.) on the North-West side of the passage bore North 71 degrees West, distant 8 Miles; this point I named Cape Cornwall (Latitude 10 degrees 43 minutes South, Longitude 218 degrees 59 minutes West),* (* This longitude is 70 minutes too far west, and one of the worst given in the Journal. There were no observations, and the dead reckoning among the shoals was difficult to keep.) and some low Islands lying about the Middle of the Passage, which I called Wallace's Isles, bore West by South 1/2 South, distance about 2 Leagues. Our Latitude by Observation was 10 degrees 46 minutes South.

[In Endeavour Strait, Torres Strait.]

Thursday, 23rd. In the P.M. had little wind and Variable, with which and the Tide of Flood we keept advancing to the West-North-West; depth of Water 8, 7, and 5 fathoms. At 1/2 past 1 the pinnace, which was ahead, made the Signal for Shoal Water, upon which we Tackt and sent away the Yawl to sound also, and then Tack'd again, and stood after them with the Ship; 2 hours after this they both at once made the Signal for having Shoal water. I was afraid to stand on for fear of running aground at that time of the Tide, and therefore came to an Anchor in 1/4 less 7 fathoms, sandy ground. Wallice's Islands bore South by West 1/2 West, distant 5 or 6 Miles, the Islands to the Northward extending from North 73 degrees East to North 10 degrees East, and a small island* (* Booby Island.) just in sight bearing North-West 1/2 West. Here we found the flood Tide set to the Westward and Ebb to the Contrary. After we had come to Anchor I sent away the Master with the Long boat to sound, who, upon his return in the evening, reported that there was a bank stretching North and South, upon which were 3 fathoms Water, and behind it 7 fathoms. We had it Calm all Night and until 9 in the morning, at which time we weigh'd, with a light breeze at South-South-East, and steer'd North-West by West for the Small Island above mentioned, having first sent the Boats ahead to sound; depth of Water 8, 7, 6, 5, 4, and 3 fathoms when upon the Bank,* (* The Endeavour Strait is now little used, on account of this great bank, which nearly bars its western part. There is, however, deeper water than Cook found, a few miles to the southward; but it is just the difficulty of finding this narrow pass, so far from land, and the fact that there is a deep though narrow channel north of Prince of Wales Island, that has caused it to be abandoned. The passage of Torres Strait is, however, still an anxious bit of navigation.) it being now the last Quarter Ebb. At this time the most Northermost Islands we had in sight bore North 9 degrees East; the South-West point of the largest Islands on the North-West side of the Passage, which I named Cape Cornwall, bore East; distant 3 Leagues. This bank, at least so much as we sounded, extends nearly North and South, how far I cannot say; its breadth, however, is not more than 1/4 or at most 1/2 a Mile. Being over the Bank, we deepned our water to a 1/4 less 7 fathoms, which depth we carried all the way to the small Island ahead, which we reached by Noon, at which time it bore South, distant near 1/2 a Mile; depth of Water 5 fathoms. The most northermost land we had in sight (being part of the same Chain of Islands we have had to the Northward of us since we entered the Passage) bore North 71 degrees East; Latitude in, by Observation, 10 degrees 33 minutes South, Longitude 219 degrees 22 minutes West. In this situation we had no part of the Main land in sight. Being now near the island, and having but little wind, Mr. Banks and I landed upon it, and found it to be mostly a barren rock frequented by Birds, such as Boobies, a few of which we shott, and occasioned my giving it the name of Booby Island.* (* Booby Island is now the great landmark for ships making Torres Strait from the westward. There is a light upon it.) I made but very short stay at this Island before I return'd to the Ship; in the meantime the wind had got to the South-West, and although it blow'd but very faint, yet it was accompanied with a Swell from the same quarter. This, together with other concuring Circumstances, left me no room to doubt but we had got to the Westward of Carpentaria, or the Northern extremity of New Holland, and had now an open Sea to the Westward; which gave me no small satisfaction, not only because the danger and fatigues of the Voyage was drawing near to an end, but by being able to prove that New Holland and New Guinea are 2 separate Lands or Islands, which until this day hath been a doubtful point with Geographers.* (* Luis Vaez de Torres, commanding a Spanish ship in company with Quiros in 1605, separated from his companion in the New Hebrides. He afterwards passed through the Strait separating New Guinea from Australia, which now bears his name. This fact, however, was little known, as the Spaniards suppressed all account of the voyage; and though it leaked out later, the report was so vague that it was very much doubted whether he had really passed this way. On most charts and maps of the period, New Guinea was shown joined to Australia, and to Cook the establishment of the Strait may fairly be given. Only the year before Bougainville, the French navigator, who preceded Cook across the Pacific, and who was steering across the Coral Sea on a course which would have led him to Lizard Island, abandoned his search in that direction, after falling in with two reefs to the eastward of the Barrier, because he feared falling amongst other shoals, and had no faith whatever in the reports of the existence of Torres Strait. Had he persevered, he would have snatched from Cook the honour of the complete exploration of Eastern Australia, and of the verification of the passage between it and New Guinea. Bougainville paid dearly for his caution, as he found that retracing his steps against the trade wind, in order to pass eastward and northward of New Guinea, occupied such a weary time, that he and his people were nearly starved before they reached a place of refreshment.)

[Description of Endeavour Strait.]

The North-East entrance of this passage or Strait lies in the Latitude of 10 degrees 27 minutes South, and in the Longitude of 218 degrees 36 minutes West from the Meridian of Greenwich.* (* As before mentioned, this longitude is over a degree in error. The sun was not available for lunars until the 24th August, and the first was observed on the 25th, when the ship was at Booby Island; but the result is not recorded in Mr. Green's log. Mr. Green was at this time ill. The latitude is a clerical error for 10.37, which Cook's chart shows, and is nearly correct.) It is form'd by the Main, or the northern extremity of New Holland, on the South-East, and by a Congeries of Islands to North-West, which I named Prince of Wales's Islands. It is very Probable that the Islands extend quite to New Guinea;* (* This conjecture was very near the truth. The whole of Torres Strait is obstructed by either islands or reefs that leave very little passage.) they are of Various Extent both for height and Circuit, and many of them seem'd to be indifferently well Cloath'd with wood, etc., and, from the smokes we saw, some, if not all of them, must be inhabited. It is also very probable that among these Islands are as good, if not better, passages than the one we have come thro', altho' one need hardly wish for a better, was the access to it from the Eastward less dangerous; but this difficulty will remain until some better way is found out than the one we came, which no doubt may be done was it ever to become an object to be looked for.* (* It is the western and not the eastern approach of Endeavour Strait that forms the difficulty, now the locality has been charted, for vessels of deeper draught than the Endeavour; though for small craft, as Cook says, you can hardly wish for a better.) The northern Extent of the Main or outer reef, which limit or bounds the Shoals to the Eastward, seems to be the only thing wanting to Clear up this point; and this was a thing I had neither time nor inclination to go about, having been already sufficiently harrass'd with dangers without going to look for more.* (* The east coast of Australia, which Cook had now followed from end to end, is 2000 miles in extent. He took four months over it, much less time than he had given to New Zealand; but this is easily accounted for. His people were getting worn out, and he was haunted by fears of not getting off the coast before the North-West monsoon set in, which would have been a foul wind for him in getting from Torres Straits to Batavia, and his provisions were running short. Besides this, there was the grave doubt whether Australia and New Guinea were really separated. If this turned out to be false, there was a long round to make, back to the eastern extremity of the latter, and the voyage to Batavia would have been infinitely extended. Considering these circumstances, Cook's exploration of the coast was wonderful, and the charts attached to this book attest the skill and unwearied pains taken in mapping it from such a cursory glance. He only stopped at four places: Botany Bay, Bustard Bay, Thirsty Sound, and the Endeavour River; and from the neighbourhood of these, with the view obtained as he coasted along, he had to form his opinion of the country--an opinion, as we shall see, singularly correct.)

This passage, which I have named Endeavour Straits, after the Name of the Ship, is in length North-East and South-West 10 Leagues, and about 5 leagues broad, except at the North-East entrance, where it is only 2 Miles broad by reason of several small Islands which lay there, one of which, called Possession Island, is of a Moderate height and Circuit; this we left between us and the Main, passing between it and 2 Small round Islands, which lay North-West 2 Miles from it. There are also 2 Small low Islands, called Wallice's Isles,* (* These are probably called after Captain Wallis, who made a voyage across the Pacific in the Dolphin in 1767, and discovered Tahiti.) laying in the Middle of the South-West entrance, which we left to the southward; the depth of Water we found in the Straits was from 4 to 9 fathoms. Every where good Anchorage, only about 2 Leagues to the Northward of Wallice's Islands is a Bank, whereon is not more than 3 fathoms at low Water, but probable there might be found more was it sought for. I have not been particular in describing this Strait, no more than I have been in pointing out the respective Situations of the Islands, Shoals, etc., on the Coast of New Wales; for these I refer to the Chart, where they are deliniated with all the accuracy that Circumstances would admit of.

With respect to the Shoals that lay upon this Coast I must observe, for the benefit of those who may come after me, that I do not believe the one 1/2 of them are laid down in my Chart; for it would be Absurd to suppose that we Could see or find them all. And the same thing may in some Measure be said of the Islands, especially between the Latitude of 20 and 22 degrees, where we saw Islands out at Sea as far as we could distinguish any thing. However, take the Chart in general, and I believe it will be found to contain as few Errors as most Sea Charts which have not undergone a thorough correction.* (* Cook's pride in his chart is well justified, as its general accuracy is marvellous, when one considers that he simply sailed along the coast. The great feature of this shore, however--the Barrier Reef--only appears on it at its northern end, where its approach to the land caused Cook to make such unpleasant acquaintance with it. See charts.) The Latitude and Longitude of all, or most of, the principal head lands, Bays, etc., may be relied on, for we seldom fail'd of getting an Observation every day to correct our Latitude by, and the Observation for settling the Longitude were no less Numerous, and made as often as the Sun and Moon came in play; so that it was impossible for any Material error to creep into our reckoning in the intermediate times. In justice to Mr. Green,* (* From this phrase, and from various remarks in Mr. Green's own log, it would appear that Mr. Green was not very easy to get on with; but there is no doubt of his unwearied zeal in astronomical observations.) I must say that he was indefatigable in making and calculating these observations, which otherwise must have taken up a great deal of my time, which I could not at all times very well spare; not only this, but by his instructions several of the petty Officers can make and calculate these observations almost as well as himself. It is only by such Means that this method of finding the Longitude at Sea can be put into universal practice; a Method that we have generally found may be depended upon within 1/2 a degree, which is a degree of Accuracy more than sufficient for all Nautical purposes. Would Sea Officers once apply themselves to the making and calculating these Observations they would not find them so very difficult as they at first imagine, especially with the Assistance of the Nautical Almanack and Astronomical Ephemeris, by the help of which the

Calculation for finding the Longitude takes up but little more time than that of an Azimuth for finding the Variation of the Compass; but unless this Ephemeris is Published for some time to come, more than either one or 2 Years, it can never be of general use in long Voyages, and in short Voyages it's not so much wanted.* (* The "Nautical Almanac" was first published for 1767. That for 1770 was not published until 1769; but it seems probable that Cook either had proof sheets, or the manuscript calculations.) Without it the Calculations are Laborious and discouraging to beginners, and such as are not well vers'd in these kind of Calculations.

[Account of New South Wales Coast.]

SOME ACCOUNT OF NEW WALES.* (* Called in Admiralty and the Queen's Copy New South Wales. It would appear that for this part of the voyage Mr. Corner's copy was the first written, and that Cook's first idea was to christen the country New Wales.)

In the Course of this Journal I have at different times made mention of the Appearance or Aspect of the face of the Country, the Nature of the Soil, its produce, etc. By the first it will appear that to the Southward of 33 or 34 degrees the land in general is low and level, with very few Hills or Mountains; further to the Northward it may in some places be called a Hilly, but hardly anywhere can be called a Mountainous, Country, for the Hills and Mountains put together take up but a small part of the Surface in Comparison to what the Planes and Valleys do which intersect or divide these Hills and Mountains. It is indifferently well water'd, even in the dry Seasons, with small brooks and Springs, but no great Rivers, unless it be in the Wet Season, when the low lands and Vallies near the Sea, I do suppose, are mostly laid under Water. The Small Brooks may then become large Rivers; but this can only happen with the Tropick. It was only in Thirsty Sound that we could find no fresh Water, and that no doubt was owing to the Country being there very much intersected with Salt Creeks and Mangrove land.

The low land by the Sea, and even as far in land as we were, is for the most part friable, loose, sandy Soil yet indifferently fertile, and Cloathed with woods, long grass, shrubs, plants, etc. The Mountains or Hills are checquer'd with woods and Lawns; some of the Hills are wholy cover'd with Flourishing Trees; others but thinly, and the few that are upon them are small, and the spot of Lawns or Savannahs are rocky and barren, especially to the Northward, where the Country did not afford or produce near the Vegetation that it does to the Southward, nor were the Trees in the Woods half so tall and stout. The Woods do not produce any great variety of Trees; there are only 2 or 3 sorts that can be called Timber. The largest is the gum Tree, which grows all over the country; the wood of this Tree is too hard and ponderous for most common uses. The Tree which resembles our Pines I saw nowhere in perfection but in Botany Bay; this wood, as I have before observed, is something of the same Nature as American Live Oak; in short, most of the large Trees in this Country are of a hard and ponderous nature, and could not be applied to many purposes. Here are several sorts of the Palm kind, Mangrove, and several other sorts of small Trees and Shrubs quite unknown to me, besides a very great number of Plants hitherto unknown; but these things are wholy out of my way to describe, nor will this be of any loss, since not only plants, but every thing that can be of use to the Learned World will be very accurately described by Mr. Banks and Dr. Solander. The Land naturally produces hardly anything fit for Man to eat, and the Natives know nothing of Cultivation. There are, indeed, growing wild in the wood a few sorts of Fruit (the most of them unknown to us), which when ripe do not eat amiss, one sort especially, which we called Apples, being about the size of a Crab Apple it is black and pulpey when ripe, and tastes like a Damson; it hath a large hard stone or Kernel, and grows on Trees or Shrubs.* (* The Black Apple, or Sapota Australis.)

In the Northern parts of the Country, as about Endeavour River, and probably in many other places, the Boggy or watery Lands produce Taara or Cocos,* (* A species of Taro, Colocasia macrorhiza.) which, when properly cultivated, are very good roots, without which they are hardly eatable; the Tops, however, make very good greens.

Land Animals are scarce, so far as we know confin'd to a very few species; all that we saw I have before mentioned. The sort which is in the greatest Plenty is the Kangooroo or Kanguru, so called by the Natives; we saw a good many of them about Endeavour River, but kill'd only 3, which we found very good Eating. Here are likewise Lizards, Snakes, Scorpions, Centapees, etc., but not in any plenty. Tame Animals they have none but Dogs, and of these we saw but one, and therefore must be very scarce, probably they eat them faster than they breed them; we should not have seen this one had he not made us frequent Visits while we lay in Endeavour River.

The land Fowls are Bustards, Eagles, Hawks, Crows, such as we have in England, Cockatoes of 2 sorts, White and Brown, very beautiful Birds of the Parrot kind, such as Lorryquets, etc., Pidgeons, Doves, Quails, and several sorts of smaller birds. The Sea and Water Fowls are Herons, Boobies, Noddies, Guls, Curlews, Ducks, Pelicans, etc., and when Mr. Banks and Mr. Gore where in the Country, at the head of Endeavour River, they saw and heard in the Night great numbers of Geese. The Sea is indifferently well stocked with fish of Various sorts, such as Sharks, Dog-fish, Rockfish, Mullets, Breams, Cavallies, Mack'rel, old wives, Leather Jackets, Five Fingers,* (* Old wives are Enoploxus Armatus; Leather jackets, Monacanthus; Five fingers, Chilodactylus.) Sting rays, Whip rays, etc., all excellent in their kind. The Shell fish are Oysters of 3 or 4 sorts, viz., Rock

Oysters and Mangrove Oysters, which are small, Pearl Oysters and Mud Oysters; these last are the best and Largest I ever saw. Cockles and Clams of several sorts, many of those that are found upon the Reefs are of a prodigious size, Craw fish, Crabs, Muscles, and a variety of other sorts. Here are also upon the Shoals and Reefs great Numbers of the finest Green Turtle in the world, and in the River and Salt Creeks are some Aligators.

[Australian Natives.]

The Natives of this Country are of a middle Stature, streight Bodied and Slender limb'd; their Skins the Colour of Wood soot, their Hair mostly black, some Lank and others curled; they all wear it Cropt Short; their Beards, which are generally black, they likewise crop short, or Singe off. There features are far from being disagreeable, and their Voices are soft and Tunable. They go quite Naked, both Men and Women, without any manner of Cloathing whatever; even the Women do not so much as cover their privities, altho' None of us was ever very near any of their Women, one Gentleman excepted, yet we are all of us as well satisfied of this as if we had lived among them. Notwithstanding we had several interviews with the Men while we lay in Endeavour River, yet, wether through Jealousy or disregard, they never brought any of their women along with them to the Ship, but always left them on the Opposite side of the River, where we had frequent Opportunities viewing them thro' our Glasses. They wear as Ornaments, Necklaces made of Shells, Bracelets, or Hoops, about their Arms, made mostly of Hair Twisted and made like a Cord Hoop; these they wear tight about the upper parts of their Arms, and some have Girdles made in the same manner. The Men wear a bone, about 3 or 4 Inches long and a finger's thick, run thro' the Bridge* (* The cartilage of the nostril. Banks mentions that the bluejackets called this queer ornament the "spritsail yard.") of their Nose; they likewise have holes in their Ears for Ear Rings, but we never saw them wear any; neither are all the other Ornaments wore in Common, for we have seen as many without as with them. Some of these we saw on Possession Island wore breast plates, which we supposed were made of Mother of Pearl Shells. Many of them paint their Bodies and faces with a Sort of White paste or Pigment; this they apply different ways, each according to his fancy.

Their offensive weapons are Darts; some are only pointed at one end, others are barb'd, some with wood, others with Stings of rays, and some with Sharks' Teeth, etc.; these last are stuck fast on with Gum. They throw the Darts with only one hand, in the doing of which they make use of a piece of wood about 3 feet long, made thin like the blade of a Cutlass, with a little hook at one End to take hold of the End of the dart, and at the other end is fix'd a thin piece of bone about 3 or 4 Inches long; the use of this is, I believe, to keep the dart steady, and to make it quit the hand in a proper direction. By the helps of these throwing sticks, as we call them, they will hit a mark at the Distance of 40 or 50 yards, with almost, if not as much, Certainty as we can do with a Musquet, and much more so than with a ball.* (* The invention of these throwing sticks, and of the Boomerang, is sufficient to prove the intelligence of the Australian aborigines.) These throwing sticks we at first took for wooden swords, and perhaps on some occasions they may use them as such; that is, when all their darts are expended. Be this as it may, they never Travel without both them and their Darts, not for fear of Enemies, but for killing of Game, etc., as I shall show hereafter. There defensive weapons are Targets, made of wood; but these we never saw used but once in Botany Bay.

I do not look upon them to be a warlike people; on the contrary, I think them a Timerous and inoffensive race, no ways inclined to Cruelty, as appear'd from their behaviour to one of our people in Endeavour River, which I have before mentioned, neither are they very numerous. They live in small parties along by the Sea Coast, the banks of Lakes, Rivers, Creeks, etc. They seem to have no fixed habitation, but move about from place to place like wild beasts in search of Food, and, I believe, depend wholy upon the Success of the present day for their Subsistance. They have wooden fish Gigs, with 2, 3, or 4 prongs, each very ingeniously made, with which they strike fish. We have also seen them strike both fish and birds with their Darts. With these they likewise kill other Animals; they have also wooden Harpoons for striking Turtle, but of these I believe they get but few, except at the seasons they come ashore to lay. In short, these people live wholy by fishing and hunting, but mostly by the former, for we never saw one Inch of Cultivated land in the whole Country. They know, however, the use of Taara, and sometimes eat them; we do not know that they Eat anything raw, but roast or broil all they eat on slow small fires. Their Houses are mean, small Hovels, not much bigger than an Oven, made of Peices of Sticks, Bark, Grass, etc., and even these are seldom used but in the Wet seasons, for in the daytimes we know they as often sleep in the Open Air as anywhere else. We have seen many of their Sleeping places, where there has been only some branches or peices of Bark, grass, etc., about a foot high on the Windward side.

[Australian Canoes.]

Their Canoes are as mean as can be conceived, especially to the Southward, where all we saw were made of one peice of the Bark of Trees about 12 or 14 feet long, drawn or Tied together at one end. As I have before made mention, these Canoes will not Carry above 2 people, in general there is never more than one in them; but, bad as they are, they do very well for the purpose they apply them to, better than if they were larger, for as they draw but little water they go in them upon the Mud banks, and pick up Shell fish, etc., without going out of the Canoe. The few Canoes we saw to the Northward were made out of a Log of wood hollow'd out, about 14 feet long and very narrow, with outriggers; these will carry 4 people. During our whole stay in Endeavour River we saw but one Canoe, and had great reason to think that the few people that resided about that place had no more; this one served them to cross the River and to go a Fishing in, etc. They attend the Shoals, and flatts, one where or another, every day at low water to gather Shell fish, or whatever they can find to eat, and have each a little bag to put what they get in; this bag is made of net work. They have not the least knowledge of Iron or any other Metal that we know of; their working Tools must be made of Stone, bone, and Shells; those made of the former are very bad, if I may judge from one of their Adzes I have seen.

Bad and mean as their Canoes are, they at Certain seasons of the Year (so far as we know) go in them to the most distant Islands which lay upon the Coast, for we never landed upon one but what we saw signs of People having been there before. We were surprized to find Houses, etc., upon Lizard Island, which lies 5 Leagues from the nearest part of the Main; a distance we before thought they could not have gone in their Canoes.

The Coast of this Country, at least so much of it as lays to the Northward of 25 degrees of Latitude, abounds with a great Number of fine bays and Harbours, which are Shelter'd from all winds; but the Country itself, so far as we know, doth not produce any one thing that can become an Article in Trade to invite Europeans to fix a settlement upon it. However, this Eastern side is not that barren and miserable country that Dampier and others have described the Western side to be. We are to consider that we see this country in the pure state of nature; the Industry of Man has had nothing to do with any part of it, and yet we find all such things as nature hath bestow'd upon it in a flourishing state. In this Extensive Country it can never be doubted but what most sorts of Grain, Fruit, roots, etc., of every kind would flourish here were they once brought hither, planted and Cultivated by the hands of Industry; and here are Provender for more Cattle, at all seasons of the Year, than ever can be brought into the Country.* (* It says a good deal for Cook's penetration that he wrote like this, for the coast of Australia is not promising, especially in the dry season; and coming as he did from the more apparently fertile countries of Tahiti and New Zealand, Australia must have appeared but a barren land.) When one considers the Proximity of this Country with New Guinea, New Britain, and several other Islands which produce Cocoa Nutts and many other fruits proper for the support of man, it seems strange that they should not long ago be Transplanted here; by its not being done it should seem that the Natives of this Country have no commerce with their Neighbours, the New Guineans.* (* The climate is too dry for the cocoanut palm.) It is very probable that they are a different people, and speak a different Language. For the advantage of such as want to Clear up this point I shall add a small Vocabulary of a few Words in the New Holland Language which we learnt when in Endeavour River.* (* The languages of the different tribes differ very much. This results from the continual state of war in which they live, as they have no communication the one with the other.)

COLUMN 1: ENGLISH. COLUMN 2: NEW HOLLAND.

The Head : Whageegee. The Hair of the head : Morye or More. The Eyes : Meul. The Ears : Melea. The Lips : Yembe or Jembi. The Teeth : Mulere or Moile. The Chinn : Jaeal. The Beard : Waller. The Tongue : Unjar. The Nose : Bonjoo. The Naval : Toolpoor or Julpur. The Penis : Keveil or Kerrial. The Scrotum : Coonal or Kunnol. The Arms : Aw or Awl. The Hand : Marigal. The Thumb : Eboorbalga. The Fore, Middle and Ring fingers : Egalbaiga. Little Finger : Nakil or Eboonakil. The Thighs : Coman. The Knees : Ponga. The Legs : Peegoorgo. The Feet : Edamal. The Nails : Kolke or Kulke. A Stone : Walba. Sand : Joo'wal, Yowall, or Joralba. A Rope or Line : Goorgo or Gurka. Fire : Maianang or Meanang. The Sun : Galan or Gallan. The Sky : Kere or Kearre. A Father : Dunjo. A Son : Jumurre. A Man : Bamma or Ba ma. A Dog : Cotta or Kota. A Lorryquet : Perpere or Pier-pier. A Cocatoo : Wanda. Male Turtle : Poonja or Poinja. Female : Mamingo. A great Cockle : Moenjo or Moingo. Cocos Yams : Maracotu (?). A Canoe : Maragan.

[Australian Natives.]

From what I have said of the Natives of New Holland they may appear to some to be the most wretched People upon Earth; but in reality they are far more happier than we Europeans, being wholy unacquainted not only with the Superfluous, but with the necessary Conveniences so much sought after in Europe; they are happy in not knowing the use of them. They live in a Tranquility which is not disturbed by the Inequality of Condition. The earth and Sea of their own accord furnishes them with all things necessary for Life. They covet not Magnificient Houses, Household-stuff, etc.; they live in a Warm and fine Climate, and enjoy every wholesome Air, so that they have very little need of Cloathing; and this they seem to be fully sencible of, for many to whom we gave Cloth, etc., left it carelessly upon the Sea beach and in the Woods, as a thing they had no manner of use for; in short, they seem'd to set no Value upon anything we gave them, nor would they ever part with anything of their own for any one Article we could offer them. This, in my opinion, Argues that they think themselves provided with all the necessarys of Life, and that they have no Superfluities.* (* The native Australians may be happy in their condition, but they are without doubt among the lowest of mankind. Confirmed cannibals, they lose no opportunity of gratifying their love of human flesh. Mothers will kill and eat their own children, and the women again are often mercilessly illtreated by their lords and masters. There are no chiefs, and the land is divided into sections, occupied by families, who consider everything in their district as their own. Internecine war exists between the different tribes, which are very small. Their treachery, which is unsurpassed, is simply an outcome of their savage ideas, and in their eyes is a form of independence which resents any intrusion on THEIR land, THEIR wild animals, and THEIR rights generally. In their untutored state they therefore consider that any method of getting rid of the invader is proper. Both sexes, as Cook observed, are absolutely nude, and lead a wandering life, with no fixed abode, subsisting on roots, fruits, and such living things as they can catch. Nevertheless, although treated by the coarser order of colonists as wild beasts to be extirpated, those who have studied them have formed favourable opinions of their intelligence. The more savage side of their disposition being, however, so very apparent, it is not astonishing that, brought into contact with white settlers, who equally consider that they have a right to settle, the aborigines are rapidly disappearing.)

I shall conclude the account of this Country with a few observations on the Currents and Tides upon the Coast, because I have mentioned in the Course of this Journal that the latter hath sometimes set one way and sometimes another, which I shall Endeavour to account for in the best manner I can. From the Latitude of 32 degrees, or above downwards to Sandy Cape in the Latitude of 24 degrees 46 minutes, we constantly found a Current setting to the Southward at the rate of 10 or 15 Miles per Day, more or less, according to the distance we were from the land, for it runs stronger in shore than in the Offing. All this time I had not been able to satisfy myself whether the flood-tide came from the Southward, Eastward, or Northward, but judged it to come from the South-East; but the first time we anchor'd upon the coast, which was in the Latitude of 24 degrees 30 minutes, and about 10 Leagues to the South-East of Bustard Bay, we found there the flood to come from the North-West. On the Contrary, 30 Leagues further to the North-West, on the South side of Keppel Bay, we found the Flood to come from the East, and at the Northern part of the said Bay we found it come from the Northward, but with a much Slower Motion than the Easterly Tide. Again, on the East side of the Bay of Inlets we found the flood to set strong to the Westward as far as the Op'ning of Broad sound, but on the North side of that sound the flood come with a Slow motion from the North-West; and when at Anchor before Repulse bay we found the flood to come from the northward. We need only admit the flood tide to come from the East or South-East, and then all these seeming Contradictions will be found to be conformable to reason and experience. It is well known that where there are deep Inlets, large Creeks, etc., into low lands, that it is not occasioned by fresh water Rivers; there is a very great indraught of the Flood Tide, the direction of which will be determin'd according to the possition or direction of the Coast which forms the Entrance into such Inlets; and this direction the Tide must follow, let it be ever so contrary to their general Course out at Sea, and where the Tides are weak, as they are in general upon this Coast, a large Inlet will, if I may so call it, attract the Flood tide for many Leagues. Any one need only cast an Eye over the Chart to be made sencible of what I have advanced. To the Northward of Whitsundays Passage there are few or no large Inlets, and consequently the Flood sets to the Northward or North-West, according to the direction of the Coast, and Ebb the Contrary; but this is to be understood at a little distance from land, or where there is no Creeks or Inlets, for where such are, be they ever so small, they draw the flood from the Southward, Eastward, and Northward, and, as I found by experience, while we lay in Endeavour River.* (* Cook's reasoning on the course of the flood stream is quite sound.) Another thing I have observed upon the Tides which ought to be remarked, which is that there is only one high Tide in 24 Hours, and that is the night Tide. On the Spring Tides the difference between the perpendicular rise of the night and day Tides is not less than 3 feet, which is a great deal where the Tides are so inconsiderable, as they are here.* (* This difference in the heights of consecutive tides is termed the diurnal inequality. It results from the tide wave being made up of a large number of undulations, some caused by the moon, some by the sun; some occurring twice a day, others only once. It occurs in all parts of the world, but is inconspicuous on the coasts of Europe. In Australia it is very marked, and occasions the night tides to be the highest at one time of the year, when the Endeavour was on the coast, and the day tides at the other. There are places on the east coast of Australia where the range of the tide is very great, but Cook did not anchor at any of them.) This inequality of the Tide I did not observe till we run ashore; perhaps it is much more so to the Northward than to the Southward. After we had got within the Reefs the second time we found the Tides more considerable than at any time before, except in the Bay of Inlets. It may be owing to the water being confin'd in Channels between the Shoals, but the flood always set to the North-West to the extremity of New Wales, from thence West and South-West into the India Seas.

[Historical Notes, East Coast of Australia.]

HISTORICAL NOTES ON THE EAST COAST OF AUSTRALIA.

PREVIOUS to Cook's visit no European, so far as is known, had ever sighted the East Coast of Australia, or, as it was then called, New Holland. The Dutch had examined and mapped the shores from the Gulf of Carpentaria on the north round by the west to Van Dieman's Land or Tasmania, but had not decided whether the latter was a part of the mainland or no. Dampier, in 1699, had the intention of passing south to explore the unknown eastern shore, but never carried it out, confining his attention to the northern part of the west coast, with which, and with good reason, he was not favourably impressed.

On all maps of the time, the east coast, from Tasmania to the north, was shown as a dotted and more or less straight line, Tasmania being joined at the south, and generally New Guinea at the north.

There is indeed one manuscript known as the Dauphin's Map, a copy of which is in the British Museum, of the date of about 1540, which shows a certain amount of the north-east coast, and has been thought by some to prove that some one had visited it. But an inspection of it shows that it is far more probably a case of imaginative coast drawing, such as occurs in other places in the same map, and in many others of the same and later dates, and there is certainly no record of any voyage to this coast.

After Cook's exploration it remained unvisited until 1788, when, owing mainly to Banks' influence, Botany Bay was pitched upon as a convict settlement, and a squadron, consisting of H.M.S. Sirius, the Supply brig, 3 storeships, and 6 transports, under the command of Captain Arthur Phillip, R.N., which had sailed from England on May 13th, 1787, arrived in that bay on January 18th, 1788, but immediately moved into Port Jackson, where the settlement of Sydney was formed.

The early history of the Colony was one of struggle and starvation, and it was many years before any prosperity was attained. In 1839 the deportation of convicts ceased, but it was not until 1851, when gold was found, that free settlers in any large number came to the Colony.

Queensland, formerly the northern part of New South Wales, was formed a separate Colony in 1859.

A white population of about 1,500,000 now inhabits the eastern part of Australia, first explored by Cook, and their numbers are rapidly increasing.

Although the products of the Colonies are mainly agricultural and mineral, a very large proportion of this population are in the large towns.

Sydney contains 230,000, Newcastle 20,000, Brisbane 55,000, Rockhampton 13,000.

Wool, one of the staple products, is obtained from some 80,000,000 sheep, which, as Cook foresaw, have thriven well; and with 8,000,000 head of cattle supply another export in the shape of frozen meat. Coal and other minerals employ a large number of people, and the total value of exports amounts to about 24,000,000 pounds.

The uninhabited shores and untracked seas of Cook's time, only 120 years ago, are thus now teeming with life and trade; and it is no wonder that the name of the great explorer is more venerated, and the memory of his deeds is more fresh, in the Colonies than in the Mother country that sent him forth to find new fields for British enterprise.

CHAPTER 9.
FROM TORRES STRAIT TO BATAVIA.

[August 1770.]

FRIDAY, 24th. In the P.M. had light Airs from the South-South-West, with which, after leaving Booby Island, as before mentioned, we steer'd West-North-West until 5 o'clock, when it fell Calm, and the Tide of Ebb which sets to the North-East soon after making, we Anchor'd in 8 fathoms soft sandy bottom, Booby Island bearing South 50 degrees East, distant 5 miles; Prince of Wales Isles extending from North-East by North to South 55 degrees East. There appear'd to be an open clear passage between these Islands extending from North 64 degrees East to East by North. At 1/2 past 5 in the morning in purchasing* (* Weighing the anchor.) the Anchor, the Cable parted about 8 or 10 fathoms from the Anchor; I immediately order'd another Anchor to be let go, which brought the ship up before she had drove a cable's length from the Buoy; after this we carried out a Kedge, and warped the ship nearer to it, and then endeavour'd to sweep the Anchor with a Hawser, but miss'd it, and broke away the Buoy rope.* (* The kedge is a small anchor. Sweeping is dragging the middle of a rope, or hawser, held at the two ends from two boats some distance apart, along the bottom, with the object of catching the fluke of the anchor as it lies on the bottom, and so recovering it. It is a long and wearisome operation if the bottom is uneven. Cook, however, having already lost one of his large anchors, could not afford to leave this without an effort.) We made several Attempts afterwards, but did not succeed. While the Boats were thus employed we hove up the Kedge Anchor, it being of no more use. At Noon Latitude observed 10 degrees 30 minutes South. Winds at North-East, a fresh breeze; the Flood Tide here comes from the same Quarter.

Saturday, 25th. Winds at North-East and East-North-East, a gentle breeze. Being resolv'd not to leave the Anchor behind while there remain'd the least probability of getting of it, after dinner I sent the Boats again to sweep for it first with a small line, which succeeded, and now we know'd where it lay we found it no very hard matter to sweep it with a Hawser. This done, we hove the Ship up to it by the same Hawser, but just as it was almost up and down the Hawser slip'd, and left us all to do over again. By this time it was dark, and obliged us to leave off until daylight in the morning, when we sweep'd it again, and hove it up to the bows, and by 8 o'Clock weigh'd the other anchor, got under sail, and stood away North-West, having a fresh breeze at East-North-East. At Noon we were by observation in the Latitude of 10 degrees 18 minutes South, Longitude 219 degrees 39 minutes West, having no land in sight, but about 2 miles to the Southward of us lay a Shoal,* (* Cook Reef.) on which the Sea broke, and I believe a part of it dry. At low Water it extended North-West and South-East, and might be about 4 or 5 Leagues in Circuit; depth of Water at this time and since we weigh'd 9 fathoms.

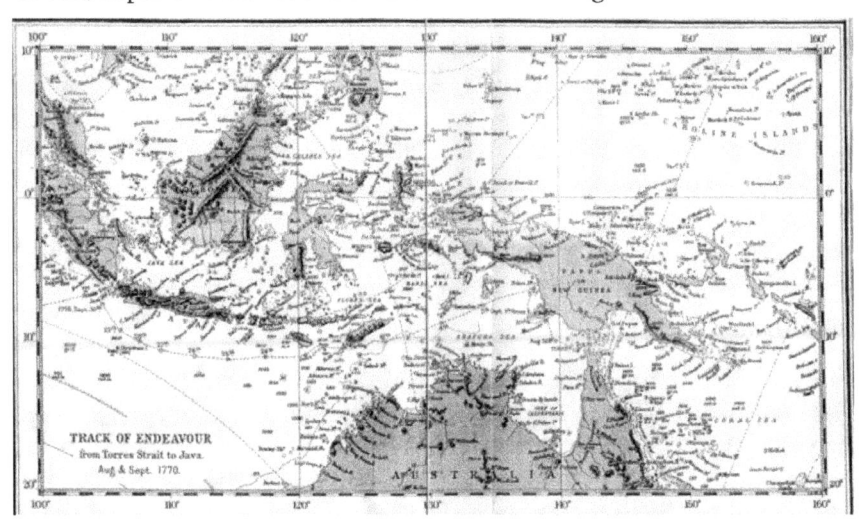

**TRACK OF ENDEAVOUR FROM TORRES STRAIT TO JAVA.
AUGUST AND SEPTEMBER 1770.**

Sunday, 26th. Fresh breezes at East in standing to the North-West. We began to Shoalden our water from 9 to 7 fathoms, and at 1/2 past one, having run 11 Miles since Noon, the boat which was a head made the signal for Shoal Water, immediately upon which we let go an Anchor, and brought the Ship up with the sails standing as the boats was but a little way ahead, having but just relieved the Crew, and at same time we saw from the Ship Shoal Water* (* Cook Shoal.) in a manner all round us, and both wind and Tide setting upon it. We lay in 6 fathoms with the Ship, but upon sounding about her found hardly 2 fathoms, a very rocky bottom, not much above 1/2 a cable's length from us from the east round by the North and West as far as South-West, so that there was no way to get clear but the way we came. This was one of the many Fortunate Escapes we have had from Shipwreck, for it was near high water, and there run a short cockling sea that would soon have bulged the Ship had she struck. These Shoals that lay a fathom or 2 under Water are the most dangerous of any, for they do not shew themselves until you are close upon them, and then the water upon them looks brown like the reflection of dark clouds. Between 3 and 4 the Ebb began to make, when I sent the Master to sound to the Southward and South Westward, and in the meantime, as the Ship tended,* (* Swung to the tide.) hove up the Anchor, and with a little Sail stood to the Southward and afterwards edged away to the Westward, and got once more out of danger, where at sun set we

Anchor'd in 10 fathoms Sandy bottom. Having a fresh of wind at East-South-East, at 6 o'clock in the morning we weighed and stood West, with a fresh of wind at East, having first sent a boat ahead to sound. I did intend to have steer'd North-West until we had made the Coast of New Guinea, designing if Possible to touch upon that Coast, but the meeting with these Shoals last night made me Alter the Course to West, in hopes of meeting with fewer dangers and deeper Water; and this we found, for by Noon we had deepned our water gradually to 17 fathoms, and this time we were by observation in the Latitude of 10 degrees 10 minutes South, Longitude 220 degrees 12 minutes West. Course and distance sail'd since yesterday at noon North 76 degrees West, 11 Leagues, no land in sight.

[Off South Coast of New Guinea.]

Monday, 27th. Fresh breezes between the East by North and East-South-East, with which we steer'd West until sun set; depth of Water from 27 to 23 fathoms. We now Reef'd the Topsails, shortened Sail, and hoisted in the pinnace and Long boat up alongside, and afterwards kept upon a Wind all night under our Topsails, 4 hours on one Tack and four hours on the other; depth of Water 25 fathoms, very even soundings. At daylight made all the Sail we could, and steer'd West-North-West until 8 o'clock, then North-West; at Noon we were by Observation in the Latitude of 9 degrees 56 minutes South, Longitude 221 degrees 00 minutes West; Variation 2 degrees 30 minutes East. Course and distance sail'd since yesterday at Noon North 73 degrees 33 minutes West, 49 miles.

Tuesday, 28th. Fresh breezes at East and East by South and fair weather. Continued a North-West Course until sun set, at which time we shortned sail, and haul'd close upon a Wind to the Northward; depth of Water 21 fathoms. At 8 Tack'd and stood to the Southward until 12, then stood to the Northward under little Sail until daylight, sounding from 25 to 17 fathoms; Shoalding as we stood to the Northward. At this time we made sail and steer'd North in order to make the land of New Guinea; from the time of our making sail until noon the depth of Water gradually decreased from 17 to 12 fathoms, a stony and shelly bottom. We were now by Observation in the Latitude of 8 degrees 52 minutes South, which is in the same Parrallel as the Southern parts of New Guinea as it is laid down in the Charts; but there are only 2 points so far to the South, and I reckon we are a degree to the Westward of both, and for that reason do not see the Land which trends more to the Northward. Our Course and distance sail'd since Yesterday is North-North-West, 69 Miles; Longitude in 221 degrees 27 minutes West. The Sea in many places is here cover'd with a kind of a brown scum, such as Sailors generally call spawn; upon our first seeing it it alarm'd us, thinking we were among Shoals, but we found the same depth of Water were it was as in other places; neither Mr. Banks nor Dr. Solander could tell what it was, altho' they had of it to Examine.

Wednesday, 29th. Continued standing to the Northward, with a fresh gale at East by South and South-East until 6 o'clock, having very irregular and uncertain soundings from 24 to 7 fathoms. At 4 we made the Land from the Mast head, bearing North-West by North, and which appear'd to be very low. At 6 it extended from West-North-West to North-North-East, distant 4 or 5 Leagues. At this time hauld close upon a wind to the Eastward until 7 o'clock, then Tack'd and stood to the Southward until 12, at which time we wore and stood to the Northward until 4, then lay her Head off until daylight, when we again saw the Land, and stood North-North-West directly for it, having a fresh gale at East by South. Our Soundings in the night were from 17 to 5 fathoms, very irregular, without any sort of Rule with respect to our distance from the Land. At 1/2 past 6 a small low island, laying about a League from the Main, bore North by West, distant 5 miles; this island lays in the Latitude of 8 degrees 13 minutes South, Longitude 221 degrees 25 minutes West. I find it laid down in the Charts by the Name of St. Bartholomew or Whermoysen. We now steer'd North-West by West, West-North-West, West by North, West by South, and South-West by West, as we found the land to lay, having a Boat ahead of the Ship sounding; depth of water from 5 to 9 fathoms. When in 7, 8 or 9 fathoms we could but just see the Land from the Deck; but I did not think we were at above 4 Leagues off, because the land is exceeding low and level, and appeared to be well cover'd with wood; one sort appeared to us to be Cocoa Nutt Trees. By the Smookes we saw in different parts as we run along shore we were assured that the Country is inhabited. At Noon we were about 3 Leagues from the land, the Westermost part of which that we could see bore South 79 degrees West; our Latitude by Observation was 8 degrees 19 minutes South, Longitude 221 degrees 44 minutes West. The Island, St. Bartholomew, bore North 74 degrees East, distant 20.* (* The ship was now off the south coast of New Guinea, and near what is known as Princess Marianne Strait, which separates Frederick Henry Island from the main island. All this coast is very shallow, but very imperfectly charted to the present day.)

Thursday, 30th. Fresh breezes at South-East, East-South-East, and East by South. After steering South-West by West, 6 miles, we discover'd on our Starboard bow and ahead a Strong appearance of Shoal Water, and by this time we had Shoald our water from 10 to 5 fathoms; upon which I made the Pinnace Signal to Edge down to it, but she not going far enough, we sent the Yawl to sound in it, and at the same time hauld off close upon a Wind, with the Ship until 4, at which time we had run 6 Miles, but did not depen our water anything. We then Edged away South-West, 4 Miles more, but finding still Shoal Water we brought too, and call'd the Boats on board by Signal, hoisted them in, and then hauld off close upon a wind, being at this time about 3 or 4 Miles from the Land. The Yawl found only 3 fathoms water in the place where I sent her to sound, which place I weather'd about 1/2 a mile. Between 1 and 2 we passed a Bay or Inlet, before which lies a small Island that seems to Shelter it from the Southerly winds; but I very much doubt their being Water behind it for Shipping. I could not attempt it because the South-East Trade wind blows right in, and we have not as yet had any land breezes. We stretched off to Sea until 12 o'Clock, at which time we were 10 and 11 Leagues from the Land, and had depen'd our Water to 29 fathoms; we now tack'd and stood in until 4 o'Clock, when, being in 6 1/2 fathoms, we tack'd and lay her head off until day light, at which time we saw the land bearing North-West by West, distant about 4 Leagues. We now made sail and steer'd West-South-West, and then West by South, but coming into 54 fathoms we hauld off South-West until we depen'd our Water to 8 fathoms; we then keept away West by South and West, having 9 fathoms and the Land just in sight from the Deck, which we judged not above 3 or 4 Leagues off, as it is everywhere exceeding low. At Noon we were by Observation in the Latitude of 8 degrees 38 minutes South, Longitude 222 degrees 34 minutes West. St. Bartholomew Isle bore North 69 degrees East, distant 74 Miles.

[Off Cape Walsche, New Guinea.]

Friday, 31st. Between 12 and 1 in the P.M. Steer'd North-North-West, in which time we Shoalded our Water from 8 to 5 1/2, which I thought was little enough, and therefore keept away again West, and soon depen'd it to 7 fathoms, which depth we keept until 6, having the land just in sight from the Deck. At this time the Western Extream bore North, distant about 4 Leagues, and Seem'd to end in a point and turn away to the Northward; we took it to be Point St. Augustine or Walsche Caep, Latitude 8 degrees 24 minutes South, Longitude 222 degrees 55 minutes West.* (* This position is correct. Mr. Green had been assiduously observing lunars, and it appears strange that the error of the position of the north point of Australia was not discovered; but doubtless the discrepancy was put down to current.) We now shortned sail and hauld off South-South-West and South by West, having the wind at South-East and South-East by East, a Gentle breeze; we stood off 16 Miles, having from 7 to 27 fathoms, deepning gradually as we run off. At midnight we Tacked and stood in until daylight, at which time we could see no land, and yet we had only 5 1/2 fathoms. We now Steer'd North-West, having the same deepth of Water until near 9 o'Clock, when we began to Depen our Water to 6 1/2 and 7 fathoms. By this I thought that we were far Enough to the Westward of the Cape, and might haul to the Northward with Safety, which we now did, having the Wind at North-East by East, a light breeze. By Noon we had increased our Water to 9 fathoms, and were by Observation in the Latitude of 8 degrees 10 minutes South, which was 10

Miles to the Northward of that given by the Log; by which I conjectur'd that we had meet with a strong Current setting round the Cape, not only to the Northward, but to the Westward also, otherwise we ought to have seen the Land, which we did not.

[September 1770.]

Saturday, 1st September. In the P.M. and most part of the night had a fresh breeze from the South-East with which we keept standing in for the land North-East and East-North-East, close upon a wind, until half past 6, when we Anchor'd in 4 1/2 fathoms, soft muddy bottom, as we have every were found upon the Coast. About an hour before we Anchor'd we saw the land from the Mast head extending from the East by North to South-South-East, all very low; at the time we Anchor'd we found a small drean* (* Drain.) of a Tide setting away to the North-West, which continued until 2 in the morning, when the Water had fell 9 feet or better. This Tide of Ebb was then succeeded by the Flood, which came from the South-West; yet we did not find the Water to rise much upon a perpendicular, or else the greatest fall of the Tide had not been well attended to in the night, for at 6, when we got under sail, we had no more than 3 fathoms under the ship, and yet we could not see the land from the Deck. After getting under sail we stood to the Northward with a light breeze at East, and deepned our Water by noon to 10 fathoms, having the Land just in sight from the Mast head to the South-East. At this time we were in the Latitude of 7 degrees 39 minutes South, Longitude 222 degrees 42 minutes West; Port St. Augustine bore South 10 degrees West, distant 15 Leagues.

Sunday, 2nd. In the P.M. had Calm until 2, when a light breeze sprung up at North by East, and we stood in for the Land East by North until 5, at which time we got the wind from the South-West, a light breeze, with which we steer'd North-East, edging in for the land, having it in sight from the Deck, and which I judged to be about 3 or 4 Leagues off, being very low land. Found the Variation to be 2 degrees 34 minutes East, and a little before 8 o'Clock, having but little wind, we Anchor'd in 7 fathoms, soft Muddy bottom. In the Afternoon and evening we saw several Sea Snakes, some of which the people in the Boat alongside took up by hand. At daylight in the Morning we got under sail, and stood away to the North-North-East, having a fresh gale at East, which by noon brought us into the Latitude of 7 degrees 14 minutes South, Longitude 222 degrees 30 minutes West; Depth of Water 13 fathoms. Course and distance sail'd since Yesterday Noon is North 24 degrees East, 27 Miles, having at this time no land in sight, for the Land, according to the Charts, trends more Easterly than the Wind would permit us to sail.

Monday, 3rd. Steer'd North by East, with a fresh breeze at East by North until 7 in the Evening, when the wind came to South-East by South, with which we keept standing to the Eastward close upon a wind all Night, having from 17 to 10 fathoms pretty even Soundings. At daylight we saw the land extending from North by East to South-East, distant about 4 Leagues. We still keept standing in for it, having the advantage of a fresh gale at East-South-East and East by South, until near 9, when, being about 3 or 4 Miles off, and in 3 fathoms, we brought too and I went ashore in the pinnace, accompanied by Mr. Banks and Dr. Solander, having a mind to land once in this Country before we quit it Altogether, which I now am determin'd to do without delay; for I found that it is only spending time to little purpose, and carrying us far out of our way, staying upon this Coast, which is so shallow that we can hardly keep within sight of land.

[Land in New Guinea.]

At the time we put off from the Ship we saw not the least sign of inhabitants; but we had no sooner landed than we saw the print of Men's feet fresh upon the sand, and a little way farther we found a small Shed or Hutt, about which lay green shells of Cocoa Nutts. By this we were well assured that the inhabitants were not far off; nay, we thought we heard their Voices in the woods, which were so close and thick that we did not think it safe to venture in, for fear of an Ambuscade, as we had only a Boat's crew with us, a part of which were left to look after the boat, which lay about a 1/4 of a Mile from the Shore. We therefore took a walk upon the Sea beach, but had not gone above 200 Yards before we were attack'd by 3 or 4 Men, who came out of the woods a little before us, but upon our firing upon them they retir'd. Finding that we could not search the Country with any degree of Safety, we return'd to the boat, and was followed by 60, or, as some thought, about 100, of the Natives, who had advanced in small parties out of the woods; but they suffer'd us to go to our boats without giving us any trouble. We had now time to view them attentively; we thought them to be about the size and Colour of the New Hollanders, with short, Cropt Hair, and quite naked like them. I thought these of a lighter Colour; but that may be owing to a whitish Pigment with which we thought their bodies were painted, because some appeared darker than others.

Their Arms were ordinary darts of about 4 feet long, made of a kind of reed, and pointed at one end with hard wood; but what appear'd more extraordinary to us was something they had which caused a flash of fire or Smoak, very much like the going off of a pistol or small Gun, but without any report. The deception was so great that the people in the Ship actually thought that they had fire Arms; indeed, they seem'd to use these things in imitation of such, for the moment the first man we saw made his appearance he fir'd off one of these things, and while we lay looking at them in the boat

4 or 5 would let them off all at once, which had all the appearance in the world of Volleys of Small Arms; but I am confident that nothing came from them but smook, but by what means this was done, or what purpose it answer'd, we were not able to Guess. I thought the Combustable matter was contain'd in a reed or piece of small Bamboo, which they gave a Swing round in the hand and caused it to go off.* (* The natives carry hollow canes with burning tinder for making fires.)

This place lies in the Latitude of 6 degrees 15 minutes South, about 65 Leagues to the North-East of Point St. Augustine, or Walsche Caep, and is near to what is called in the Charts by the long name of Cape de la Colta de St. Bonaventura.* (* Cook's landing place in New Guinea, on the western side of this great island, was on a part of the coast scarcely known to this day. It is in the part of the island claimed by the Dutch. Cook's insatiable desire to explore is well shown in this digression from his course to Batavia.) The land is very low, like every other part of the Coast we have seen here; it is thick and Luxuriously cloathed with woods and Verdure, all of which appear Green and flourishing. Here were Cocoa nutt Trees, Bread Fruit Trees, and Plantain Trees, but we saw no fruit but on the former, and these were small and Green; the other Trees, Shrubs, Plants, etc., were likewise such as is common in the South Sea Islands and in New Holland.

Upon my return to the Ship we hoisted in the boat and made sail to the Westward, with a design to leave the Coast altogether. This, however, was contrary to the inclination and opinion of some of the Officers, who would have had me send a Party of Men ashore to cut down the Cocoa Nutt Trees for the sake of the Nutts; a thing that I think no man living could have justified, for as the Natives had attacked us for meer landing without taking away one thing, certainly they would have made a Vigerous effort to have defended their property; in which case many of them must have been kill'd, and perhaps some of our own people too, and all this for 2 or 300 Green Cocoa Nutts, which, when we had got them, would have done us little service; besides nothing but the utmost necessity would have obliged me to have taken this method to come at refreshments.

It's true I might have gone farther along the Coast to the Northward and Westward until we had found a place where the Ship could lay so near the Shore as to cover the people with her Guns when landed; but it is very probable that before we had found such a place we should have been carried so far to the West as to have been obliged to have gone to Batavia by the way of the Moluccas, and on the North side of Java, where we were all utter Strangers. This I did not think was so safe a Passage as to go to the South of Java and thro' the Straits of Sunda, the way I propose to myself to go. Besides, as the Ship is leakey, we are not yet sure wether or no we shall not be obliged to heave her down at Batavia; in this case it becomes the more necessary that we should make the best of our way to that place, especially as no new discovery can be Expected to be made in these Seas, which the Dutch have, I believe, long ago narrowly examin'd, as appears from 3 Maps bound up with the French History of Voyages to the Terra Australis, published in 1756,* (* De Brye's Voyages.) which Maps, I do suppose, by some means have been got from the Dutch, as we found the Names of many of the places are in that Language.

It should likewise seem from the same Maps that the Spaniards and Dutch have at one time or another circumnavigated the whole of the Island of New Guinea, as the most of the Names are in these 2 Languages; and such part of the Coast as we were upon I found the Chart tolerable good, which obliges me to give some Credit to all the rest, notwithstanding we neither know by whom or when they were taken, and I always understood, before I had a sight of these Maps, that it was unknown whether or no New Holland and New Guinea was not one continued land, and so it is said in the very History of Voyages these Maps are bound up in. However, we have now put this wholy out of dispute; but, as I believe, it was known before, tho' not publicly, I claim no other Merit than the Clearing up of a doubtful point. Another doubtfull point I should have liked to have clear'd up, altho' it is of very little, if of any Consequence, which is, whether the Natives of New Holland and those of New Guinea are, or were, Original, one People, which one might well suppose, as these 2 Countrys lay so near to each other, and the intermediate space fill'd up with Islands. On the other hand, if these 2 people have or ever had any friendly communication with Each other it seems strange, as I have before observed, that they should not have transplanted from New Guinea over to New Holland Cocoa Nutts, Bread fruit, Plantains, etc., etc., all very useful Articles for the support of Man, that We never saw grow in the latter, and which we have now seen in the former. La Maire hath given us a Vocabulary of Words spoken by the People of New Britain (which before Dampier's time was taken to be a part of New Guinea), by which it appears that the people of New Britain speak a very different Language from those of New Holland. Now should it be found that the Natives of New Britain and those of New Guinea have had One Origin, and speak the same Language, it will follow, of Course, that the New Hollanders are a different People from both.* (* In the north of Australia the natives are distinctly allied to the Papuans, but on the east of the continent they are of a type of their own, and speak many different languages.)

[Off South-west Coast of New Guinea.]

Tuesday, 4th. Stood to the Westward all this day, having at first a moderate breeze Southerly, which afterwards freshned and Veered to South-East and East-South-East. We kept on sounding all the time, having from 14 to 30 fathoms not regular, but sometimes more and sometimes less. At noon we were in 14 fathoms; by observation in the Latitude of 6 degrees 44 minutes South, Longitude 223 degrees 51 minutes West. Course and distance sail'd since Yesteday Noon South 76 minutes West, 120 Miles.

Wednesday, 5th. Winds at East by South and South-East by East, a fresh gale and Clear weather, with which were run 118 Miles upon a South 69 degrees 15 minutes West Course, which at Noon brought us into the Latitude of 7 degrees 25 minutes South, Longitude 225 degrees 41 minutes West; depth of Water 28 fathoms, having been in soundings the whole of this day's run, generally between 10 and 20 fathoms. At half an hour past one in the Morning we past by a small low Island, which bore from us at that time North-North-West, distant 3 or 4 Miles; depth of Water 14 fathoms, and at daylight we discover'd another low Island extending from North-North-West and North-North-East, distant 2 or 3 Leagues. I believe I should have landed upon this Island to have known its produce, as it did not appear to be very small, had not the wind blown too fresh for such an undertaking, and at the time we passed the Island we had only 10 fathoms Water, a rocky bottom; I was therefore afraid of running down to leeward for fear of meeting with Shoal Water and foul ground. These Islands have no place on the Charts, unless they are the Arrow Isles, which, if they are, they are laid down much too far from New Guinea. I found the South part of these to lay in the Latitude 7 degrees 6 minutes South, Longitude 225 degrees 0 minutes West.* (* These were probably Karang and Ennu Islands, two outliers of the Arru Islands.)

Thursday, 6th. A steady fresh gale at East by South and clear weather, with which we steer'd West-South-West. At 7 in the Evening we took in the small Sails, reefd the Topsails, and sounded, having 50 fathoms; we still keept West-South-West all night, going at the rate of 4 1/2 Miles an hour. At 10 had 42 fathoms; at 11, 37; and at 12 o'Clock 45; 1 o'Clock 49; and at 3, 120; after which we could get no ground. In the evening we caught 2 Boobies, which settled upon the rigging, and these were the first of the kind we have caught in this manner the voyage, altho' I have heard of them being caught this way in great numbers. At daylight, in the Morning, we made all the sail we could, and at 10 o'Clock saw land extending from North-North-West to West by North, distant 5 or 6 League. At Noon it bore from North to West about the same distance; our Latitude by observation was 8 degrees 15 minutes South, Longitude 227 degrees 47 minutes West. This land is of an even and moderate height, and by our run from New Guinea ought to be a part of the Arrow Isles;* (* This was the southern part of the Tenimber Islands.) but it lays a degree farther to the South than any of these Islands are laid down in the Charts. We sounded, but had no ground, with 50 fathoms of Line.

[Remarks on Charts.]

Friday, 7th. As I was not able to satisfy myself from any Chart what land it was we saw to Leeward of us, and fearing it might trend away more Southerly, and the weather being hazey so that we could not see far, we steer'd South-West, which Course by 4 o'Clock run us out of sight of the land; by this I was assured that no part of it lay to the Southward of 8 degrees 15 minutes South. We continued standing to the South-West all night under an Easey sail, having the advantage of a fresh gale at South-East by East and East-South-East, and clear moon light; we sounded every hour, but had no bottom with 100 and 120 fathoms of line. At daylight in the Morning we steer'd West-South-West, and afterwards West by South, which by Noon brought us into the Latitude of 9 degrees 30 minutes South, and Longitude 229 degrees 34 minutes West, and by our run from New Guinea ought to be in sight of Wessels Isle, which, according to the Chart is laid down about 20 or 25 Leagues from the coast of New Holland; but we saw nothing, by which I conclude that it is wrong laid down; and this is not to be wonder'd at when we consider that not only these Islands, but the lands which bound this Sea have been discover'd and explored by different people and at different times, and compiled and put together by others, perhaps some Ages after the first discoveries were made. Navigation formerly wanted many of these helps towards keeping an Accurate Journal which the present Age is possessed of; it is not they that are wholy to blame for the faultiness of the Charts, but the Compilers and Publishers, who publish to the world the rude Sketches of the Navigator as Accurate surveys, without telling what authority they have for so doing; for were they to do this we should then be as good or better judge than they, and know where to depend upon the Charts, and where not. Neither can I clear Seamen of this fault; among the few I have known who are Capable of drawing a Chart or Sketch of a Sea Coast I have generally, nay, almost always, observed them run into this error. I have known them lay down the line of a Coast they have never seen, and put down Soundings where they never have sounded; and, after all, are so fond of their performances as to pass the whole off as Sterling under the Title of a Survey Plan, etc. These things must in time be attended with bad Consequences, and cannot fail of bringing the whole of their works in disrepute.* (* Cook had good reason for writing thus, and being himself scrupulously honest and careful, he felt this scamped work to be a disgrace to seamen.) If he is so modest as to say, Such and such parts, or the whole of his plan is defective, the Publishers or Vendures will have it left out, because they say it hurts the sale of the work; so that between the one and the other we can hardly tell when we are possessed of a good Sea Chart until we ourselves have proved it.

Saturday, 8th. Winds Easterly, with a high Sea from the same Quarter. Our Course and distance sail'd this 24 Hours is South 86 degrees 30 minutes West,

102 Miles; Latitude in 9 degrees 36 minutes South, Longitude 231 degrees 17 minutes West.

Sunday, 9th. Light Airs and Clear weather the most part of this 24 Hours. In the evening found the Variation by several Azimuths to be 0 degrees 12 minutes West, and by the Amplitude 0 degrees 5 minutes West. At Noon we were by observation in the Latitude of 9 degrees 46 minutes South, Longitude 232 degrees 7 minutes West. Course and distance sail'd since yesterday at Noon South 78 degrees 45 minutes West, 52 Miles. For these 2 days past we have steer'd due West, and yet we have by observation made 16 Miles Southing--6 Miles Yesterday and 10 to-day; from which it should seem that there is a Current setting to the Southward and Westward withall, as I should suppose.

Monday, 10th. Light Airs Easterly, except in the morning, when we had it at North; at sunset found the Variation to be 0 degrees 2 minutes West, at the same time saw, or thought we saw, very high land bearing North-West, and in the Morning saw the same appearances of land in the same Quarter, which left us no room to doubt but what it was land, and must be either the Island of Timor land or Timor, but which of the 2 I cannot as yet determine.* (* This was Timor. What Cook calls Timor land is probably Timor Laut, another name for the principal island of the Tenimber Group.) At Noon we were by Observation in the Latitude of 10 degrees 1 minute South, which was 15 Miles to the Southward of that given by the Log. Longitude in per Observation 233 degrees 27 minutes West.

Tuesday, 11th. Variable light Airs and Clear weather. Steer'd North-West, in order to discover the Land plainer until 4 in the morning, at which time the wind came to North-West and West, with which we stood to the Southward until 9 o'Clock, when we Tack'd and stood North-West, having the wind at West-South-West. At sun rise in the morning we could see the land extend from West-North-West to North-East; at noon we could see it extend to the Westward as far as West by South 1/2 South, but no farther to the Eastward than North by East. We were now well assured that this was part of the Island of Timor, in consequence of which the last Island we saw must have been Timor land, the South part of which lies in the Latitude of 8 degrees 15 minutes South, Longitude 228 degrees 10 minutes, whereas in the Charts the South Point is laid down in Latitude 9 degrees 30 minutes. It is possible that the Land we saw might be some other Island; but then I cannot see how we could have miss'd seeing Timor land, soposing it to be right laid down in Latitude, as we were never to the Southward of 9 degrees 30 minutes; for my design was to have made that Island, and to have landed upon it to have seen what it produced, as it is (according to the Charts) a large Island, and not settled by the Dutch that I ever heard off. We were now in the Latitude of 9 degrees 37 minutes, Longitude 233 degrees 54 minutes West by observation of the Sun and Moon, and Yesterday we were by Observation in 233 degrees 27 minutes West. The difference is 27 minutes, which is exactly the same as what the Log gave; this, however, is a degree of accuracy in observation that is seldom to be expected.

[Off South Coast of Timor.]

Wednesday, 12th. Winds between the South and West, a light breeze and Clear weather in the P.M.; stood in shore until 8 o'Clock, then Tack'd and stood off, being about 6 Leagues from the Land, which at dark extend from South-West 1/2 West to North-East; at this time we sounded and had no ground with 140 fathoms of line, being not above 4 Leagues from the Land. At 12 o'Clock we Tack'd and stood in, having but little wind, and continued so until noon, at which time we were by Observation in Latitude 9 degrees 36 minutes South; the Log this 24 Hours gave 18 Miles Westing, but it did not appear by the land that we had made so much. We saw several Smoaks upon the Land by day, and fires in the Night.

Thursday, 13th. Stood in shore, with a light breeze at South by West until 1/2 past 5 o'Clock in the P.M., when, being a Mile and a 1/2 from the Shore, and in 16 fathoms, we tack'd and stood off. At this time the Extreams of the Land extended from North-East by East to West by South 1/2 South; this last was a low point, distant from us about 3 Leagues. We were right before a small Creek or Inlet into the low land, which lies in the Latitude of 9 degrees 34 minutes South. Probably it might be the same as Dampier went into in his Boat, for it did not seem to have depth of Water sufficient for anything else. In standing in shore we sounded several times, but found no soundings until we got within 2 1/2 Miles of the Shore, where we had 25 fathoms, soft bottom. We stood off Shore until 12 o'Clock, with the wind at South, then Tack'd and stood to the Westward 2 Hours, when the wind veer'd to the South-West and West-South-West, and then we stood to the Southward. In the Morning found the Variation to be 1 degree 10 minutes West by the Amplitude, and by the Azimuth 1 degree 27 minutes West; at Noon we were by Observation in the Latitude of 9 degrees 45 minutes South, Longitude 234 degrees 12 minutes West, and about 6 or 7 Leagues from the land, which extended from North 31 degrees East to West-South-West 1/2 West. Winds at South-South-West, a Gentle breeze.

Friday, 14th. Light Land and Sea breezes; the former we had from West by North, and only a few hours in the morning, the latter we had from the South-South-West and South. With these winds we advanced but slowly to the Westward. At Noon we were about 6 or 7 Leagues from the Land, which extended from North by East to South 78 degrees West; our Latitude by Observation was 9 degrees 54 minutes South. Course and Distance sail'd since Yesterday noon South 68 degrees West, 24 Miles. We saw several

Smoakes ashore in the P.M., and fires in the night, both upon the Low land and up in the Mountains.

Saturday, 15th. In the P.M. had the Sea breezes at South-South-West and South, with which we stood to the Westward until 8 o'Clock, when being about 3 Leagues from the Land, and having very little wind, we tack'd and lay her Head off Shore. At 11 o'Clock we got the Land wind at North by West, with which we steer'd South-West by West along shore, keeping about 4 or 5 Miles from the Land on which in the morning we saw several Houses, Plantations, etc. At 9 o'Clock we got the wind at North-East by East, a light breeze; at Noon we were about 2 Leagues from the Land, which extended as far to the Southward as South-West by West; our Latitude by observation was 10 degrees 1 minute South. Course and Distance sail'd since Yesterday at Noon South 78 degrees 45 minutes West, 36 Miles.

Sunday, 16th. Light breezes from the North-East by East, with clear weather, except in the morning, when we had it cloudy, with a few small Showers of Rain. Steer'd along shore South-West and South-West by West until 6 o'Clock in the morning, when we steer'd West-South-West, and at 9, West, at which time we saw the Island Rotte right ahead. At Noon we were in the Latitude of 10 degrees 39 minutes, Longitude 235 degrees 57 minutes; the South end of Timor bore North-North-West, distant 5 or 6 Leagues; the Island of Rotte extending from South 75 degrees West to North 67 degrees West, and the Island of Anaboa as Dampier calls it, or Seman* (* Semao. This island lies off the Dutch settlement of Koepang or Concordia in Timor; but Cook was right in supposing he would have received but a cold reception there. The Dutch discouraged any visits at their outlying settlements. Rotte is a large island lying off the south-west end of Timor.) as it is called in the Charts, which lies of the South end of Timor, bore North-West. Course and distance sail'd since Yesterday noon South 55 degrees 15 minutes West, 67 Miles. Dampier, who has given us a large and, so far as I know, an Accurate discription of the Island of Timor, says that it is 70 Leagues long and 16 Broad, and that it lies North-East and South-West. I found the East side to lie nearest North-East by East and South-West by West, and the South end to lie in the Latitude 10 degrees 23 minutes South, Longitude 236 degrees 5 minutes West from Greenwich. We run about 45 Leagues along the East side, which I observed to be free from Danger, and, excepting near the South end, the Land which bounds the Sea is low for 2, 3, or 4 Miles inland, and seem'd in many places to be intersected with Salt Creeks. Behind the low land are Mountains, which rise one above another to a considerable height. We continually saw upon it smoakes by day and fires by night, and in many places houses and plantations. I was strongly importuned by some of my Officers to go to the Dutch settlement at Concordia, on this Island, for refreshments; but this I refused to comply with, knowing that the Dutch look upon all

Europeans with a Jealous Eye that come among these Islands, and our necessities were not so great as to oblige me to put into a place where I might expect to be but indifferently treated.

[Anchor at Savu.]

Monday, 17th. Winds Easterly, with which we steer'd West-North-West until 2 o'Clock, when being pretty near the North end of Rotte, we hauled up North-North-West, in order to go between it and Anaboa. After steering 3 Leagues upon this Course we edged away North-West by West, and by 6 we were clear of all the Islands; at this time the South part of Anaboa, which lies in the Latitude of 10 degrees 15 minutes South, bore North-East, distant 4 Leagues, and the Island of Rotte extending as far to the Southward as South 36 degrees West. The North End of this Island and the South end of Timor lies North 1/2 East and 1/2 West, distant about 3 or 4 Leagues from each other. At the West end of the Passage between Rotte and Anaboa are two Small Islands; the one lays near the Rotte shore and the other off the South-West point of Anaboa; there is a good Channel between the 2 of 5 or 6 Miles broad, which we came thro'. Being now clear of the Islands we steer'd a West course all night until 6 a.m., when we unexpectedly saw an Island* (* Savu. An island about twenty miles in length. It is but little visited or known by others than the Dutch to this day.) bearing West-South-West, for by most of the Maps we had on board we were to the Southward of all the Islands that lay between Timor and Java; at least there were none laid down so near Timor in this Latitude by almost one half, which made me at first think it a new discovery; but in this I was mistaken. We now steer'd directly for it, and by 10 o'Clock were close in with the North side, where we saw Houses, Cocoa Nutt Trees, and a Flock of Cattle grazing; these were Temptations hardly to be withstood by people in our situation, especially such as were but in a very indifferent State of Health, and I may say mind too, for in some this last was worse than the other, since I refused to touch at the Island of Timor, whereupon I thought I could not do less than to try to procure some refreshments here, as there appeared to be plenty.* (* Cook's utter indifference as to what he eat or drank made him regard privations in the matter of food with an equanimity which was not shared by the rest of his companions.) With this View we hoisted out the Pinnace, in which I sent Lieutenant Gore in shore to see if there were any Convenient place to land, sending some trifles along with him to give to the Natives in case he saw any. Mr. Gore landed in a small sandy cove near to some Houses, and was met on the beach by 8 or 10 of the people, who from both their behaviour and what they had about them shew'd that they had Commerce with Europeans; upon Mr. Gore's returning with this report, and likewise that there was No Anchorage for the Ship, I sent him away with both money and goods to try to purchase some refreshments, while we keept standing on and off with the

Ship. At Noon we were about a Mile from the Shore of the Island, which extends from South-East to West-North-West, Latitude 10 degrees 27 minutes, Longitude 237 degrees 31 minutes West.

Tuesday, 18th. As soon as Mr. Gore landed he was meet on the beach by several people, both Horse and Foot, who gave him to understand that there was a Bay to Leeward where we could Anchor, and likewise get refreshments. Upon Mr. Gore's return with this intelligence we bore away for the Bay, in which we Anchor'd at 7 o'Clock in 38 fathoms Water, Clean sandy bottom. About a Mile from Shore the North point of the Bay bore North 30 degrees East, 2 1/2 Miles, and the South point or West end of the Island bore South 63 degrees West. Two hours before we Anchor'd we saw Dutch Colours hoisted in a Village which stands about a Mile inland, and at day light in the Morning the same Colours were hoisted on the beach abreast of the Ship. By this I was no longer in doubt but what here was a Dutch settlement, and accordingly sent Lieutenant Gore on shore to wait upon the Governor, or chief person residing here, to acquaint him with the reasons that induced us to touch at this Island. Upon Mr. Gore's landing we could perceive that he was received by a Guard of the Natives, and not Dutch Troops, and Conducted up to the Village where the Colours were hoisted last night. Some time after this I received a message from him, acquainting me that he was there with the king of the Island, who had told him that he could not supply him with anything without leave from the Dutch Governor, who resided at another part of the Island, but that he had sent to acquaint him of our Arrival and request.

[At Anchor. Savu.]

Wednesday, 19th. At 2 P.M. the Dutch Governor, and king of this part of the Island, with his attendance, came on board with Mr. Gore (he having left 2 Gentlemen ashore as Hostages). We entertained them at Dinner in the best Manner we could, gave them plenty of good Liquor, made them some considerable presents, and at their going away Saluted them with 9 Guns. In return for these favours they made many fair Promises that we should be immediately supplied with everything we wanted at the same price the Dutch East India Company had it; and that in the morning Buffaloes, Hogs, Sheep, etc., should be down on the beach for us to look at, and agree upon a price. I was not at all at a loss for Interpreters, for both Dr. Solander and Mr. Sporing understood Dutch enough to keep up a Conversation with the Dutchman, and several of the Natives could speak Portuguese, which language 2 or 3 of my people understood. In the morning I went on shore, accompanied by Mr. Banks and several of the Officers and Gentlemen, to return the King's Visit; but my Chief Business was to see how well they would perform their Promises in regard to the things I wanted. We had not been long ashore before we found that they had promised more than they ever intended to perform; for, instead of finding Buffaloes upon the beach, we did not so much as see one, or the least preparations making for bringing any down, either by the Dutch Factor or the King. The former pretended he had been very ill all night, and told us that he had had a letter from the Governor of Concordia in Timor, acquainting him that a ship (meaning us) had lately passed that Island, and that if she should touch at this, and be in want of anything, he was to supply her; but he was not to suffer her to make any stay, nor to distribute, or leave behind her to be distributed, any valuable presents to the inferior Natives. This we looked upon to be Afection that hardly answer'd any purpose, unless it was leting us see how the Dutch had insinuated themselves into favour with these people, which never could be his intention. However, both he and the King still promised we should have what we wanted, but pretended the Buffaloes were far in the Country, and could not be brought down before night. With these excuses we were obliged to be satisfied. The King gave us a dinner of boil'd Pork and Rice, served up in Baskets after their manner, and Palm wine to drink; with this, and some of our own Liquor, we fair'd Tolerable well. After we had dined our Servants were called in to pertake of what remain'd, which was more than they could Eat.

Thursday, 20th. We stay'd at the King's Pallace all the Afternoon, and at last were obliged to return on board without doing anything farther than a promise of having some Buffaloes in the morning; which we had now no great reason to rely on. In the morning I went on shore again, and was showed one small Buffaloe, which they asked 5 Guineas for. I offer'd 3, which the man told me he would gladly take, and sent a Message to the king to let him know what I had offer'd. The Messenger soon return'd, and let me know that I could not have it under 5 Guineas; and this I refused to give, knowing it was not worth one fifth part of the money. But this, my refusal, had like to have overset all we had before done, for soon after about 100 Men, some Arm'd with Musquets, others with Lances, came down to the Landing Place. Besides the officer that commanded this party, there came along with them a Man who spoke Portuguese, and I believe was born of Portuguese Parents. This man is here (as we afterwards Understood) as an Assistant to the Dutch Factor. He deliver'd to me the King's order, or rather those of the Dutch Factor, the purport of which was that we were to stay no longer than this day, pretending that the people would not trade with us because we wanted their provisions for nothing, etc.; whereas the Natives shew'd the greatest inclination imaginable to supply us with whatever they had, and were far more desirous of goods than money, and were, before this man came, selling us Fowls and Syrup as fast as they could bring these things down. From this and other Circumstances we were well Assured that this was all the Dutchman's doing, in order to extort from us a sum of Money to put into his own pocket. There hapned to be an old Raja at this time upon the beach, whose Interest I had secured in the Morning by presenting him with a Spy-glass; this man I now took by the hand, and presented him with an old broad sword. This effectually secured him in our Interest, for the Moment he got it he began to flourish it over the old Portuguese, and made him and the Officer commanded the party to sit down at his back side. Immediately after this trade was restored again for Fowls, etc., with more Spirit than ever; but before I could begin a Trade for Buffaloes, which was what we most wanted, I was obliged to give 10 Guineas for 2, one of which weigh'd only 160 pounds. After this I bought 7 more at a more reasonable price, one of which we lost after he was paid for. I might now have purchased as many as I pleased, for they now drove them down to the Water side by Herds; but having got as many as I well know'd what to do with, and likewise a number of Fowls, and a large quantity of Syrup, I resolved to make no longer stay.

Friday, 21st. We got under sail, and stood away to the Westward along the North side of the Island, and another smaller Island, which lies farther to the Westward, which last bore from us at Noon South-South-East, distant 2 Leagues.

[Description of Savu.]

Before we proceed any further it will be proper in this place to say something of the Island we have been last at, which is called by the Natives Savu. The Middle of it lies in about the Latitude of 10 degrees 35 minutes South, Longitude 237 degrees 30 minutes West. It may be about 8 Leagues in length from East to West, but of what breadth I know not, because I only saw the North side. There are, as I am told, 3 Bays where Ships can Anchor; the best is on the South-West side of the South-East point; the one we lay in, called Seba, lies on the North-West side of the Island. This bay is very well sheltered from the South-East Trade wind, but lays wholy open to the North-West. The Land of this Island which bounds the Sea is, in general, low, but in the Middle of the Island are Hills of a moderate height, and the whole is agreeably diversified with woods and Lawns, which afford a most pleasing prospect from the Sea. We were told that the Island is but indifferently water'd in the dry Season, especially towards the latter end of it, at which time there is no running Stream upon the whole Island, only small Springs, which are all at a distance from the Sea side. The dry seasons commences in March or April, and ends in November; the remaining 3 or 4 Months they have Westerly winds with rain, and this the time their Crops of Rice, Calivances, and Indian Corn are brought forth, which are Articles that this Island produceth.

They also breed a great Number of Cattle, viz., Buffaloes, Horses, Hogs, Sheep, and Goats. Many of the former are sent to Concordia, where they are kill'd and salted, in order to be sent to the more Northern Islands, which are under the Dominion of the Dutch. Sheep and Goats' flesh is dried upon this Island, packed up in Bales, and sent to Concordia for the same purpose. The Dutch resident, from whom we had this information, told us that the Dutch at Concordia had lately behaved so ill to the Natives of Timor that they were obliged to have recourse to this Island and others Adjacent for provisions for their own subsistance, and likewise Troops (Natives of this Island) to assist the Dutch against those of Timor. Besides the above productions, here are an Emmence Number of Palm Trees, from which is extracted the Palm Wine, as it is called, a very sweet, agreeable, cooling Liquor. What they do not immediately use they boil down and make Syrup or Sugar of, which they keep in Earthen Jarrs. Here are likewise Cocoa Nutts, Tamerind Trees, Limes etc., but in no great plenty; Indico, Cotton, and Cinnamon, sufficient to serve the Natives; these last Articles, we were told, the Dutch discourage the growth of.

The Island is divided into 5 Kingdoms, which have lived in Peace and Amity with each other for these hundred Years. At present the whole Island is partly under the direction of the Dutch East India Company, who have a Resident or Factor who constantly lives here, without whose leave the Natives are not to supply any other Nation with anything whatever; but the whole produce of the Island, besides what serves themselves, is in a manner the property of the Company. The Company by way of a Tribute oblige them to raise and pay Annually a certain quantity of Rice, Indian Corn, and Callivances, for which the Company makes Each of the Kings a yearly present of a Cask of Arrack, and some other Trifles; the live stock, Sheep and Goats' flesh, etc., they pay for in goods. The small Islands which lie about a League to the Westward of this pays Annually a Certain quantity of Arica Nutts, which is almost the only produce of that Island.

The Island of Rotte is upon the same footing as this of Savu; both these Islands, and the 3 Solors, belong to the Government of Concordia. From what we could learn of the Island of Timor, it seems to be much upon the same footing as it was in Dampier's time, which is that the Dutch possess little more of that Island than what lies under the Command of the Fort Concordia; the rest is in possession either of the Native Indians or the Portuguese. We were likewise told that the Island of Ende belongs to the Portuguese; that the principal settlement is at Larentucha, where there is a Fort and a good Harbour. We were told that the Concordia, on the Island Timor, is a free Port for Ships of any nation to touch at, where they would not only be supplied with refreshments, but Naval Stores also. Trading ships might probably meet with a good reception, but Kings' ships, I am perswaided, would be looked upon as Spys. For my own part was I only in want of refreshments, and obliged to touch at any of these Islands, I should prefer going to a Portuguese settlement before any of the Dutch, and when I was solicited by the Officers to call at Timor, I proposed going to one of the Portuguese settlements; but this Mr. Hicks made some Objections to, which was sufficient for me to lay it aside, as I had not the least inclination to touch any where till we arriv'd at Batavia, for my falling in with Savu was more chance and not design.

But to return to this Island, the Natives of which are of a Dark brown Colour, with long lank Hair; their Cloathing is a peice of Calicoe or other Cotton Cloath wrapped about their Middle; the better sort have another peice, which they wear over their Shoulders, and the most of them wear Turbands or Handkercheifs tyed round their Heads. They Eat of all the Tame Animals they have got, viz., Hogs, Horses, Buffaloes, Cocks and Hens, Dogs, Catts, Sheep and Goats, and are esteem'd much in the same order, as I have mentioned; that is, their Hog flesh, which is certainly as good as any in the world, they prefer before anything else; next to Hogs, Horses, and so on. Fish is not esteem'd by them, and is only eat by the common or poor people, who are allowed little else of meat kind.

They have a Custom among them, that whenever a king dies all the Cattle, etc., that are upon his Estate are kill'd, with which the Successor makes a feast, to which is invited all the principal people of the Island, who stay until all is consumed; after this they every one, according to his Abilities, make the young King a present, by which means he gets a fresh stock, which he is obliged to Husband for some time. The other principal men make also feasts, which are as extraordinary as these, for they seldom end so long as the giver has got anything left alive upon his Estate. They are said to be a people of good Morals, Virtuous and Chaste, each man having only one wife, which he keeps for life; Fornication and Adultry is hardly known among them. When a great Man marrys he makes presents to all his Wife's relations of European and other Foreign commodities to the value of 100 Rix Dollars. This Custom the Dutch East India Company find it to their Interest to incourage. They speak a Language peculiar to themselves, into which the Dutch have caus'd the new Testament to be Translated, and have introduced it, with the use of letters and writing, among them. By this means several hundred of them have been converted to Christianity; the rest are some heathens, and others of no religion at all, and yet they all stick up to the strict rules of Morality. They all, both Men and Women, Young and Old, Chew of the Beetle Leaf, Areca Nutts, and a sort of white lime, which I believe is made from Coral stone; this has such an effect upon the Teeth that very few, even of the Young people, have hardly any left in their Heads, and those they have are as black as Ink. Their houses are built on posts about 4 feet from the Ground; we asked the reason why they built them so, and was told that it was only

Custom; they are, however, certainly the Cooler for it. They are thatched with Palm Leaves, and the Floors and sides are boarded.

The man who resides upon this Island in behalf of the Dutch East India Company is a German by birth. His name is Johan Christopher Lange. It is hard to say upon what footing he is here. He is so far a Governor that the Natives dare do nothing without his consent, and yet he can transact no sort of business with Foreigners either in his own or that of the Company's name; nor can it be a place of either Honour or Profit. He is the only white man upon the Island, and has resided there ever since it has been under the direction of the Dutch, which is about 10 Years. He is allowed 50 Slaves (Natives of the Island) to attend upon him. These belong to, and are Maintained by, the Company. He goes the Circuit of the Island once in 2 Months; but on what account he did not tell us. When he makes these rounds he carries with him a certain quantity of Spirit to treat the great men with, which, he says, he is obliged to look well after, otherwise they would steal it and get drunk; and yet, at another time, he told us that he never knew a theft committed in the Island; but some of the Natives themselves contradicted him in this by stealing from us an Axe. However, from their behaviour to us in general I am of opinion that they are but seldom guilty of these Crimes. This going round the Island once in Two Months is most likely to see that the Natives make the necessary preparations for fulfilling their engagements with the Dutch, and to see that the Large Boats or small Vessels are taken proper care of, which the Dutch keep in all the Bays of this Island in order to collect and carry the grain, etc., to the Ship which comes Annually here. They are likewise employed in carrying cattle, grain, etc., to Timor; and, when not wanted, they are hauled aShore into Houses or Sheds built on purpose. As I have mentioned Slaves, it is necessary to observe that all the great men have Slaves which are the Natives of the Island. They can dispose of them one to another, but cannot sell them to go out of the Island. The price of a Slave is a good, large, fatt Hogg, Horse, etc. I have before mentioned that many of the people can speak Portuguese, but hardly any one Dutch. From this it is probable that this Island was formerly under the Jurisdiction of the Portuguese, tho' the Dutch Government never own'd as much, but said that the Dutch had Traded here these hundred years past.* (* This account of the economy of Savu is a good example of Cook's powers of observation. He was only four days at the island, and yet gives us a good idea of the place and its inhabitants.)

[Sail from Savu.]

Saturday, 22nd. Winds at South-South-East, South-East, and East; a gentle breeze, which we steer'd West-South-West by Compass. At 4 o'Clock we discover'd a small low Island* (* Dama Island.) bearing South-South-West, distant 3 Leagues. The Island hath no place in any of our Charts: Latitude 10 degrees 47 minutes South, Longitude 238 degrees 28 minutes West. At Noon we were in the Latitude of 11 degrees 9 minutes South, Longitude 239 degrees 26 minutes West. Course and distance sail'd since yesterday noon, South 63 West, 67 miles.

Sunday, 23rd. Winds Easterly; a moderate breeze, which by noon brought us into the Latitude of 11 degrees 10 minutes South, Longitude 240 degrees 48 minutes West. Course and distance saild since yesterday at noon is West, 8 miles.

Monday, 24th. Winds at East and South-East; a moderate breeze, and fine, pleasant weather. In the evening found the Variation to be 2 degrees 44 minutes West. At noon our Latitude was 11 degrees 8 minutes South, Longitude 242 degrees 13 minutes West. Since we have been clear of the Islands we have had constantly a swell from the Southward which I do not suppose is owing to the winds blowing anywhere from thence, but to the Sea, being so determined by the portion of the Coast of New Holland.

Tuesday, 25th. Moderate breezes at South-East, and clear, pleasant weather. At Noon our Latitude was 11 degrees 13 minutes South, and Longitude 244 degrees 41" West.

Wednesday, 26th. Winds and weather as yesterday. At Noon Latitude in 11 degrees 10 minutes, Longitude 245 degrees 41" West.

Thursday 27th. Winds at South-South-East; a fresh breeze. In the evening found the variation to be 3 degrees 10 minutes West. At noon we were in the Longitude of 247 degrees 42 minutes West, and Latitude 10 degrees 47 minutes, which is 25 Miles to the Northward of the Log, which I know not how to account for.

Friday 28th. Winds at South-South-East and South-East; a fresh breeze and Cloudy, with some Showers of rain. At Noon Latitude observed 10 degrees 51 minutes South, which is agreeable to the Logg, Longitude in 250 degrees 9 minutes, West.

Saturday, 29th. Moderate breeze at South-East and clear pleasant weather, Steer'd North-West all this day, in order to make the land of Java. At Noon we were by Observation in the Latitude of 9 degrees 31 minutes South and Longitude 251 degrees 40 minutes West.

Sunday, 30th. Fresh gales and fair weather. In the A.M. I took into my possession the Officers', Petty Officers' and Seamen's Log Books and Journals, at least all that I could find, and enjoin'd every one not to divulge where they had been.* (* These logs are now in the Public Record Office. Mr. Green's log ends on the 2nd October. Not being an officer, Cook doubtless overlooked it at first. This log should by rights have been returned to Mr. Green, but as he died shortly after leaving Batavia, it has found its way, with the others, to the Record Office.) At noon our Course and distance sail'd since Yesterday at noon, is North 20 degrees West, 126 Miles, which brought us into the Latitude of 7 degrees 34 minutes South and Longitude 252 degrees 23 minutes West.

[October 1770. Enter Sunda Strait.]

Monday, 1st October. First and latter parts fresh breezes at South-East and fair weather; the Middle squally with Lightning and rain. At 7 p.m., being then in the Latitude of Java head, and not seeing any land, assured us that we had got too far to the Westward; upon which we hauld up East-North-East, having before Steerd North by East. At 12 o'Clock saw the Land bearing East, Tack'd, and stood to the South-West until 4, then stood again to the Eastward, having very unsettled squally weather which split the Main Topsail very much, and obliged us to bend the other; many of our Sails are now so bad that they will hardly stand the least puff of Wind. At 6 o'Clock Java head, on the West end of Java, bore South-East by East, distant 5 Leagues; soon after this saw Princes Island, bearing East 1/2 South. At 10 o'Clock saw the Island of Cracatoa* (* The great eruption, and consequent destruction of the larger part of this island in 1883, will be remembered. It lies in the centre of Sunda Strait.) bearing North-East, distant 7 Leagues; Princes Island extending from South 53 degrees East to South by West, distant 3 Leagues. Course and distance saild since Yesterday at Noon is North 24 degrees 30 minutes East, 70 Miles. Latitude in per Observation, 6 degrees 29 minutes South, Longitude 251 degrees 54 minutes; but either our Longitude must be erroneous or the Straits of Sunda must be faltily laid down in all Books and Charts; but this no doubt we shall have an opportunity to settle.* (* Cook's longitude was in error nearly three degrees. No lunars had been taken since they left Savu, and there is a current running westward. It is a good example of the error of dead reckoning, even with the most careful of navigators.)

Tuesday, 2nd. In the P.M., had the wind at South-South-East, South-East by South and South-South-East, with which we stood to the Eastward close upon a wind. At 6 o'Clock the Hill on Princes Island bore South-West by South, and Cracatoa Island, North 10 Miles; in this situation had 58 fathoms, standing still to the Eastward. At 8 o'Clock had 52 fathoms, muddy bottom, at 10 23 fathoms. By 4 in the morning we fetched close in with the Java shore in 15 fathoms, then steer'd along shore. At 5 it fell Calm, which continued with some Variable light Airs until noon, at which time Anger Point bore North-East, distant 1 League, and Thwart-the-way Island North. In the morning I sent a Boat ashore to try to get some fruits for Tupia, who is very ill, and, likewise, to get some grass, etc., for the Buffaloes we have still left. The Boats return'd with only 4 Cocoa Nutts, a small bunch of Plantains, which they purchased of the Natives for a Shilling, and a few Shrubs for the Cattle.

Wednesday, 3rd. Soon after 12 o'Clock it fell quite Calm, which obliged us to Anchor in 18 fathoms, Muddy bottom, about 2 Miles from shore, where we found a strong Current setting to the South-West. Not long before we Anchor'd we saw a Dutch Ship laying off Anger Point, on board which I sent Mr. Hicks to enquire after News.* (* It will be recollected that the Endeavour was now two years and two months from England, without the slightest chance of any news from home. We can imagine the anxiety and excitement on board on thus approaching civilisation, though they had no prospect of personal letters. With the frequent communication of modern times, we can scarcely realise such circumstances, and should certainly consider them as an exceeding hardship.) Upon his return he inform'd me that there were 2 Dutch Ships from Batavia, one bound for Ceylon, and the other to the Coast of Mallabar, besides a small Fly-boat or Packet, which is stationed here to carry all Packets, Letters, etc., from all Dutch Ships to Batavia; but it seems more Probable that she is stationed here to examine all Ships that pass and repass these Straits. We now first heard the agreeable news of His Majesty's Sloop The Swallow being at Batavia about 2 Years ago.* (* The Swallow, Captain Cartaret, had sailed with the Dolphin in 1766, but separated from her on emerging from the Strait of Magellan. The Dolphin had reached England some months before Cook sailed, but nothing had been heard of the Swallow, and fears were entertained of her loss.) At 7 o'Clock a breeze sprung up at South-South-West, with which we weighed and stood to the North-East between Thwart-the-way Island and the Cap:* (* Thwart-the-Way is an island that lies right across the fairway of Sunda Strait. The Cap is another smaller island that lies North-East of it.) soundings from 18 to 26 fathoms. We had but little Wind all night, and having a Strong Current against us, we got no further by 8 o'Clock in the morning than under Bantam Point. At this time the wind came to North-East, and obliged us to Anchor in 22 fathoms about 2 Miles from the Shore. The above point bore North-East by East, distant 1 League. Here we found a strong Current setting to the North-West. In the morning we saw the Dutch packet standing after us, but after the wind Shifted to the North-East she bore away. One of the Dutch Captains told Mr. Hicks yesterday that the Current sets constantly to the South-Westward, and that it would continue to set so for a Month or Six Weeks longer.

[In Sunda Strait.]

Thursday, 4th. In the P.M. had the wind at North-East by North, which obliged us to lay fast. About 6 o'Clock in the evening one of the Country Boats came alongside in which was the Commander of the Packet before mentioned; he seem'd to have 2 Motives for coming, one to take an account of the Ship, and the other to sell us refreshments, for in the Boat were Turtle, Fowls, Birds, etc., all of which they held at a pretty high Price, and had brought to a bad market, as our Savu stock was not all expended. I gave a Spanish Dollar for a small Turtle which weighed only 36 pounds. With respect to the Ship, he wanted to know her name, the Captain's, the place we came last from and were bound, as I would not see him myself. I order'd that no account should be given him from whence we came; but Mr. Hicks, who wrote the Ship's name down in his book, put down from Europe. Seeing this he expressed some surprise, and said that we might write down what we pleased, for it was of no other use than for the information of such of our Country men as might pass these Streights. At 7 o'Clock a light breeze sprung up at South-South-East, with which we got under sail. At 1 A.M. Anchor'd again, having not wind to stem the Current which we found to run 3 Knotts; at 2 o'Clock we weighed again, but, finding that we lost ground, we were obliged to Anchor in 18 fathoms, the Island Pulo Morack, which lies close under the Shore 3 Miles to the Westward of Bantam Point: bore South-East by South, distance 1 1/2 miles. Latitude observed, 5 degrees 55 minutes South.

Friday, 5th. At 5 in the P.M. we weighed with a light breeze at South-West by South, which continued not long before it fell Calm, and obliged us to Anchor again. At 1 o'Clock we weigh'd with the Land wind at South-South-East, which died away in the Morning, and the Current running strong against us we Anchor'd in 17 fathoms. A little before this, a Proe came alongside, wherein was a Dutch Officer who came upon the same business as the other. He sent me down a printed paper in English containing 9 Articles or Questions, of which this is a Copy.

"The Commanders and Officers of the Ships where this Paper may be presented, will be pleased to answer on the following Questions: viz., 1. "To what Nation the Ship belongs, and its Name. 2. "If it comes from Europe or any other place. 3. "From what place it lastly departed from. 4. "Where unto design'd to go. 5. "What, and how many, ships of the Dutch Company by departure from the last shore there lay'd, and their names. 6. "If one or more of these ships in Company with this is departed for this or any other place. 7. "If during the Voyage any particularity is hapned or seen. 8. "If not any ships in Sea, or the Streights of Sunda have seen or Hail'd in, and which. 9. "If any other News worth Attention at the place from whence the Ship lastly departed or during the vogage is hapned.

"Batavia in the Castle, the By Order of the Governor General and the Counselors of India.

"J. BRANDER BUNGL, Sect."

The first and fourth of these Questions I only answer'd, which when the Officer saw, he made use of the very same words the other had done before, viz.: that we might write what we pleased, for it was of no consequence, etc., and yet he immediately said that he must send that very paper away to Batavia by water, and that it would be there by to-morrow noon, which shows that the Governor and Counselors of India look upon such papers to be of some consequence. Be this as it may, my reason for taking notice of it in this Journal, is because I am well inform'd that it is but of very late years that the Dutch have taken upon them to examine all Ships that pass these Streights. At 10 o'Clock we weigh'd with a light breeze at South-West, but did little more than stem the Current. At Noon, Bantam Point* (* Bantam Point, now called St. Nicholas Point, is the north-west point of Java, and forms the north-eastern extreme of Sunda Strait.) and Pula Baba, in one bearing East by North, distant from the Point 1 1/2 Mile. Latitude observed, 5 degrees 53 minutes South.

Saturday, 6th. At 2 o'Clock P.M., finding we could not stem the Current, we anchor'd, with the Kedge Anchor, under Bantam Point, where we lay until 9, at which time Current made Slowly to the Eastward, and at the same time a light breeze springing up, we weigh'd and stood to the East until 10 o'Clock in the A.M., when the Current oblig'd us again to Anchor in 22 fathoms, Pula Baba bearing East by South 1/2 South, distant 3 or 4 Miles. Our sounding from Bantam Point to this place was from 36 to 22 fathoms.

Sunday 7th. Light Air from the Southward with frequent Calms. At 6 o'Clock P.M., weighed with a light breeze at South-South-West, which was not sufficient to stem the current, and was therefore obliged to come too again, in 15 fathoms. At 10 o'Clock weighed again and stood to the Eastward with the Wind at South-South-East. At 11 A.M., Anchor'd in 21 fathoms, the West end of Wapping Island bore South, distant 3 Miles, and the Thousand Islands North by East 1/2 East, distant 3 or 4 Miles. Found the Current still set to the Westward.

Monday, 8th. Had it Calm until 4 in the P.M., when we got the Sea breeze at North-East very faint, with which we weighed and stood to the Eastward, past Wapping Island, and the first Island to the Eastward of it. Falling little wind we were carried by the Current between this last Island and the 2nd Island, to the Eastward of Wapping Island, where we were obliged to Anchor in 30 fathoms, being very near a ledge of Rocks which spitted out from one of the Islands. At 1/2 past 2 o'Clock in the A.M., weighed with the land wind at South and stood out clear of the shoal, where we were again obliged to come to an Anchor, having Variable light winds attended with Thunder and rain. At 5 o'Clock the weather being fair, and a light breeze at South, we weighed, but making little or no way against the Current, we soon came too again, in 28 fathoms, near a small Island not laid down in the Charts; Pulo

Pare* (* Wapping Island is now known as Hoorn, and Pulo Pare as Agenietan Islands. They lie, among many others, to the north-west of Batavia Roads.) bore East-North-East, distant 6 or 7 Miles. While we lay here a Proe came alongside, where in were 2 Malays, who sold us 3 Turtles, weighing 147 pounds, for a Spanish Dollar. Some on board thought them dear, but I thought they were cheap, founding my Judgment on the price the two Dutchmen that were on board before set upon those they had, one of which we paid a Dollar for, that weighed only 36 pounds.

Tuesday, 9th. A little past Noon weigh'd with a light breeze at North-East, and stood to the Eastward until 5 o'Clock, when, not being able to weather Pulo Pare, we Anchor'd in 30 fathoms, the said Island extending from South-East to South-South-West, distant 1 Mile. At 10 got the land wind at South, with which we weighed and stood to the East-South-East all night; depth of water, from 30 to 22 fathoms, and from 22 to 16 fathoms. When we Anchor'd at 10 o'Clock in the A.M. to wait for the Sea breeze, the Island of Edam bore South-West by West, distant 6 or 7 Miles. At Noon we weighed and stood in for Batavia Road, having the advantage of the Sea breeze at North-North-East.

[Arrival at Batavia.]

Wednesday, 10th, according to our reckoning, but by the people here Thursday, 11th. At 4 o'Clock in the P.M. Anchor'd in Batavia road, where we found the Harcourt Indiaman from England, 2 English Country Ships,* (* A country ship is a vessel under the English flag, but belonging to a port in English possessions abroad.) 13 Sail of large Dutch Ships, and a number of small Vessels. As soon as we Anchor'd* (* The Endeavour took nine days, and had to anchor fifteen times, in getting from Java Head, at the entrance of Sunda Strait, to Batavia, a distance of 120 miles.) I sent Lieutenant Hicks a shore to acquaint the Governor of our Arrival, and to make an excuse for not Saluting; as we could only do it with 3 Guns I thought it was better let alone.

[At Batavia.]

The Carpenter now deliver'd me in the defects of the ship, of which the following is a copy:--

"The Defects of His Majesty's Bark Endeavour, Lieutenant James Cook, Commander.

"The Ship very leaky (as she makes from 12 to 6 Inches water per hour), occasioned by her Main Kiel being wounded in many places and the Scarfe of her Stem being very open. The false Kiel gone beyond the Midships (from Forward and perhaps further), as I had no opportunity of seeing for the water when hauld ashore for repair. Wounded on her Starboard side under the

Main Chains, where I immagine is the greatest leakes (but could not come at it for the water). One pump on the Starboard side useless, the others decayed within 1 1/2 Inch of the bore, otherwise Masts, Yards, Boats, and Hull in pretty good condition.

"Dated in Batavia Road,

"this 10th of October, 1770.

"J. SATTERLY."

Previous to the above, I had consulted with the Carpenter and all the other Officers concerning the Leake, and they were all unanimously of Opinion that it was not safe to proceed to Europe without first seeing her bottom; accordingly I resolved to apply for leave to heave her down at this place, and, as I understood that this was to be done in writing, I drew up the following request to be presented to the Governor, etc., etc.:--

"Lieutenant James Cook, commander of His Brittannick Majesty's Bark Endeavour, Requests of the Right Hon'ble Petrus Albertus Van der Parra, Governor-General, etc., etc., etc., the Indulgence of the following Articles, viz.:

"Firstly, That he may be allow'd a proper and convenient place to heave down and repair His Brittannick Majesty's Ship under his command.

"Secondly, That he may have leave to purchase such few Trifling Naval stores as he may be in want of.

"Thirdly, That he may be permitted daily to purchase such provisions as he may want; also such an Additional quantity as may enable him to proceed on his passage home to England.

"Dated on board His Brittannick Majesty's Bark Endeavour, in Batavia Road, the 11th October, 1770.

"JAMES COOK."

In the morning I went on shore myself and had the foregoing request Translated into Dutch by a Scotch Gentleman, a Merchant here.

Friday, 12th. At 5 o'clock P.M. I was introduced to the Governor-General, who received me very politely and told me that I should have every thing I wanted, and that in the Morning my request should be laid before the Council where I was desir'd to attend.

About 9 o'clock in the Evening we had much rain, with some very heavy Claps of Thunder, one of which carried away a Dutch Indiaman's Main Mast by the Deck, and split it, the Maintopmast and Topgallantmast all to shivers. She had had an Iron Spindle at the Maintopgallant Mast head which had first attracted the Lightning. The ship lay about 2 Cable lengths from us, and we were struck with the Thunder at the same time, and in all probability we should have shared the same fate as the Dutchman, had it not been for the Electrical Chain which we had but just before got up; this carried the Lightning or Electrical matter over the side clear of the Ship. The Shock was so great as to shake the whole ship very sencibly. This instance alone is sufficient to recommend these Chains to all Ships whatever, and that of the Dutchman ought to Caution people from having Iron Spindles at their Mast heads.* (* No instance is known of ships fitted with properly constructed lightning conductors having received any damage.)

[At Batavia.]

In the morning I went on shore to the Council Chamber and laid my request before the Governour and Council, who gave me for answer that I should have every thing I wanted.

Saturday, 13th. Received on board a Cask of Arrack and some Greens for the Ship's Company.

Sunday, 14th. Early this morning a ship sail'd from hence for Holland by which I had just time to write 2 or 3 lines to Mr. Stephens, Secretary of the Admiralty, to acquaint him of our Arrival, after which I went on shore and waited upon the Shabander, who has the direction of the Town, Port, etc., to get an order to the Superintendent at Onrust to receive us at that Island, but this, I was told, would not be ready before Tuesday next. Received from the Shore Fresh Beef and Greens for the Ship's Company.

Monday, 15th. Fresh Sea and land breezes and fair weather. I had forgot to mention, that upon our arrival here I had not one man upon the Sick List; Lieut. Hicks, Mr. Green, and Tupia were the only people that had any complaints occasioned by a long continuance at Sea.* (* This was an achievement indeed, and Cook records it in this simple observation. Of the many ships which had arrived at Batavia after voyages across the Pacific, none but had come to an anchor with crews decimated and enfeebled through scurvy. Hawksworth mentions, probably on the authority of Banks, that when passing Torres Straits there were several incipient cases of this disease in the Endeavour. The fresh provisions obtained at Savu probably dissipated these symptoms, if they were symptoms; but Mr. Perry, the surgeon, in his report, given in the Introduction, distinctly states that there were no cases after leaving Tahiti.)

Tuesday, 16th. Finding, by a strict inquiry, that there were no private person or persons in the place that could at this time advance me a sufficient sum of money to defray the charge I might be at in repairing and refitting the Ship--at least, if there were any, they would be afraid to do it without leave from the Governor--wherefore I had nothing left but to apply to the Governor himself, and accordingly drew up the following request, which I laid before the Governor and Council this morning, in consequence of which the Shebander had orders to supply me with what money I wanted out of the Company's Treasure:--

"Lieutenant James Cook, Commander of His Brittannick Majesty's Bark the Endeavour, begs leave to represent to His Excellency the Right Honourable Petrus Albertus Van der Parra, Governor-General, etc., etc., That he will be in want of a Sum or Sums of Money in order to defray the Charge he will be at in repairing and refiting His Brittannick Majesty's Ship at this place; which sum or sums of money he is directed by his Instructions, and empower'd by his commission, to give Bills of Exchange on the respective Offices which Superintend His Brittannick Majesty's Navy.

"The said Lieutenant James Cook Requests of His Excellency, That he will be pleased to order him to be supply'd with such sum or sums of money, either out of the Company's Treasure, or permit such private persons to do it as may be willing to advance money for Bills of Exchange on the Honourable and Principal Officers and Commissioners of His Brittannick Majesty's Navy, the Commissioners for Victualling His Majesty's Navy, and the Commissioners for taking care of the Sick and Hurt.

"Dated on board His Brittannick Majesty's Bark the Endeavour, in Batavia Road, the 16th of October, 1770.

"JAMES COOK."

Wednesday, 17th. In the P.M. I waited upon the Superintendent of Onrust, with an order from the Shebander, to receive us at that Island, but this order, the Superintendent told me, was not sufficient to impower him to give me the conveniences and assistance I wanted, and when I came to call upon the Shebander, I found this mistake was owing to the word "heave down" being wrong translated; this Circumstance, trifling as it is, will cause a delay of some days, as it cannot be set to rights until next Council day, which is not till Friday.

Thursday, 18th. In the P.M. received on board 2 live Oxen, 150 Gallons of Arrack, 3 Barrels of Tar, and one of Pitch; at daylight in the A.M. took up our Anchor and run down to Onrust.

At 9 Anchor'd in 7 fathoms off Coopers Island, which lies close to Onrust. There are wharfs at both of these Islands, and ships land there stores, sometimes on the one and sometimes on the other, but it is only at Onrust where the proper conveniences are for heaving down. Soon after we Anchor'd I went on shore to the Officer of the Yard, to see if they could not allow us some place to land our stores, but this could not be granted without orders.

Friday, 19th. In the P.M. I sent a Petty Officer to Mr. Hicks, who Lodges ashore at Batavia for the recovery of his health, with orders to desire him to wait upon the Shebander, in order to get the necessary orders respecting us dispatched to this place as soon as possible.

Saturday, 20th. Employ'd unrigging the ship, etc.

Sunday, 21st. In the P.M. orders came down to the Officers of the yard to comply with everything I wanted, but we could not yet get a Wharfe to land our Stores, they being all taken up by shipping.

Monday, 22nd. In the A.M. two ships went from the Wharfes at Coopers Island, when we prepared to go along side one of them.

FACSIMILE OF TUESDAY, 23RD OCTOBER, 1770.

Tuesday, 23rd. In the P.M. hauled along side one of the Wharfes, in order to take out our stores, etc., after which the Ship is to be deliver'd into the Charge of the proper Officers at Onrust, who will (as I am inform'd) heave her down, and repair her, with their own people, while ours must stand and look on, who, if we were permitted, could do every thing wanting to the Ship ourselves.* (* Here Mr. Corner's copy of the Journal ends abruptly. The record for the next day explains the reason, and there is no doubt that this was the copy of the Journal sent home. The Queen's copy ends on 10th October. The remainder of the Journal is taken from the Admiralty copy.)

[Reports Sent Home from Batavia.]

Wednesday, 24th. Employ'd clearing the Ship, having a Store House to put our Stores, etc., in. In the P.M. I went up to Town in order to put on board the first Dutch Ship that Sails, a pacquet for the Admiralty containing a Copy of my Journal, a Chart of the South Sea, another of New Zeeland, and one of the East Coast of New Holland. In the morning the General, accompanied by the Water Fiscall, some of the Council, and the Commodore, each in their respective Boats, went out into the Road on board the oldest Captain, in order to appoint him Commodore of the Fleet, ready to Sail for Holland. The Ships was drawn up in 2 Lines, between which the General past to the new Commodore's Ship, which lay the farthest out. Each ship as he passed and repassed gave him 3 Cheers, and as soon as he was on board, and the Dutch Flag Hoisted at the Main Topmast Head, the other Commodore Saluted him with 21 Guns, and immediately after Struck his Broad Pendant, which was again hoisted as soon as the General left the other Ship; he was then Saluted with 17 Guns by the new made Commodore, who now hoisted a Common Pendant. This Ceremony of appointing a Commodore over the Grand Fleet, as they call it, we were told is Yearly perform'd. I went out in my Boat on purpose to see it, accompanied by Mr. Banks and Dr. Solander, because we were told it was one of the Grandest sights Batavia afforded; that may be too, and yet it did not recompense us for our trouble. I thought that the whole was but ill conducted, and the Fleet appear'd to be very badly mann'd. This fleet consists of 10 or 12 stout Ships; not only these, but all or most of their other Ships are pierced for 50 Guns, but have only their upper Tier mounted, and these are more by half than they have men to fight.

Thursday, 25th. In the evening I sent the Admiralty Packet on board the Kronenburg, Captain Fredrick Kelger, Commodore, who, together with another Ship, sails immediately for the Cape, where she waits for the remainder of the Fleet.*

(* The following letter to the Secretary of the Admiralty (now in Public Record Office) was also dispatched:--

"To Philip Stephens, Esq.

"Sir,

"Please to acquaint my Lords Commissioners of the Admiralty that I left Rio de Janeiro the 8th of December, 1768, and on the 16th of January following arrived in Success Bay in Straits La Maire, where we recruited our Wood and Water; on the 21st of the same month we quitted Straits La Maire, and arrived at George's Island on the 13th of April. In our Passage to this Island I made a far more Westerly Track than any Ship had ever done before; yet it was attended with no discovery until we arrived within the Tropick, where we discovered several Islands. We met with as Friendly a reception by the Natives of George's Island as I could wish, and I took care to secure ourselves in such a manner as to put it out of the power of the whole Island to drive us off. Some days preceeding the 3rd of June I sent Lieutenant Hicks to the Eastern part of this Island, and Lieutenant Gore to York Island, with others of the Officers (Mr. Green having furnished them with Instruments), to observe the Transit of Venus, that we may have the better Chance of succeeding should the day prove unfavourable; but in this We were so fortunate that the observations were everywhere attended with every favourable Circumstance. It was the 13th of July before I was ready to quitt this Island, after which I spent near a month in exploring some other Islands which lay to the Westward, before we steer'd to the Southward. On the 14th of August we discovered a small Island laying in the Latitude of 22 degrees 27 minutes South, Longitude 150 degrees 47 minutes West. After quitting this Island I steered to the South, inclining a little to the East, until we arrived in the Latitude 40 degrees 12 minutes South, without seeing the least signs of Land. After this I steer'd to the Westward, between the Latitude of 30 and 40 degrees until the 6th of October, on which day we discovered the East Coast of New Zeland, which I found to consist of 2 large Islands, extending from 34 to 48 degrees of South Latitude, both of which I circumnavigated. On the 1st of April, 1770, I quitted New Zeland, and steer'd to the Westward, until I fell in with the East Coast of New Holland, in the Latitude of 30 degrees South. I coasted the shore of this Country to the North, putting in at such places as I saw Convenient, until we arrived in the Latitude of 15 degrees 45 minutes South, where, on the night of the 10th of June, we struck upon a Reef of Rocks, were we lay 23 Hours, and received some very considerable damage. This proved a fatal stroke to the remainder of the Voyage, as we were obliged to take shelter in the first Port we met with, were we were detain'd repairing the damage we had sustain'd until the 4th of August, and after all put to Sea with a leaky Ship, and afterwards coasted the Shore to the Northward through the most dangerous Navigation that perhaps ever ship was in, until the 22nd of same month, when, being in the Latitude of 10 degrees 30 minutes South, we found a Passage into the Indian Sea between the Northern extremity of New Holland and New Guinea. After getting through the Passage I stood for the Coast of New Guinea, which we made on the 29th; but as we found it absolutely necessary to heave the Ship down to Stop her leaks before we proceeded home, I made no stay here, but quitted this Coast on the 30th of September, and made the best of my way to Batavia, where we Arrived on the 10th instant, and soon after obtained leave of the Governor and Council to be hove down at Onrust, where we have but just got alongside of the Wharf in order to take out our Stores, etc.

"I send herewith a copy of my Journal, containing the Proceedings of the whole Voyage, together with such Charts as I have had time to Copy, which I judge will be sufficient for the present to illustrate said Journal. In this Journal I have with undisguised truth and without gloss inserted the whole

Transactions of the Voyage, and made such remarks and have given such discriptions of things as I thought was necessary in the best manner I was Capable off. Altho' the discoverys made in this Voyage are not great, yet I flatter myself they are such as may Merit the Attention of their Lordships; and altho' I have failed in discovering the so much talked of Southern Continent (which perhaps do not exist), and which I myself had much at heart, yet I am confident that no part of the Failure of such discovery can be laid to my charge. Had we been so fortunate not to have run a shore much more would have been done in the latter part of the Voyage than what was; but as it is, I presume this Voyage will be found as compleat as any before made to the South Seas on the same account. The plans I have drawn of the places I have been at were made with all the Care and accuracy that time and Circumstances would admit of. Thus far I am certain that the Latitude and Longitude of few parts of the World are better settled than these. In this I was very much assisted by Mr. Green, who let slip no one opportunity for making of Observations for settling the Longitude during the whole Course of the Voyage; and the many Valuable discoveries made by Mr. Banks and Dr. Solander in Natural History, and other things useful to the learned world, cannot fail of contributing very much to the Success of the Voyage. In justice to the Officers and the whole Crew, I must say they have gone through the fatigues and dangers of the whole Voyage with that cheerfulness and Allertness that will always do Honour to British Seamen, and I have the satisfaction to say that I have not lost one Man by sickness during the whole Voyage. I hope that the repairs wanting to the Ship will not be so great as to detain us any length of time. You may be assured that I shall make no unnecessary delay either here or at any other place, but shall make the best of my way home. I have the Honour to be with the greatest respect,

"Sir,

"Your most Obedient Humble Servant,

"(Signed) JAMES COOK.

"Endeavour Bark, at Onrust, near Batavia, the 23rd of October, 1770."

"Although the discoveries made in this voyage are not great." In these modest words does Cook describe his work. I read them to mean that with his love of accuracy he did not wish to claim his explorations of New Zealand and the East Coast of Australia as discoveries, as it was already known that lands existed there; but seeing how little was known, and how completely he did his work, there are but few men who would have refrained from classing them, as indeed he truly might have, as discoveries.)

Friday, 26th. Set up the Ship's Tent for the reception of the Ship's Company, several of them begin to be taken ill, owing, as I suppose, to the extream hot weather.

[Heaving down at Batavia.]

Saturday, 27th. Employed getting out Stores, Ballast, etc.

Sunday, 28th. Employ'd as above.

Monday, 29th, Tuesday, 30th, Wednesday, 31st. Employ'd clearing the Ship.

[November 1770.]

Thursday, November 1st. Got every thing out of the Ship, and all clear for going alongside of the Carreening, but about Noon I received a message from the Officer at Onrust acquainting me that they could not receive us there until they had first despatched the Ships bound to Europe, which were down here taking in pepper.

Friday, 2nd, Saturday, 3rd, Sunday, 4th. Employ'd overhauling the rigging, and making rope, making and repairing Sails.

Monday, 5th. Clear, hot sultry weather. In the A.M. transported the ship over to Onrust, alongside one of the Carreening Wharfs.

Tuesday, 6th. In the A.M. the officers of the Yard took the Ship in hand, and sent on board a number of Carpenters, Caulkers, Riggers, Slaves, etc., to make ready to heave down.

Wednesday, 7th. Employ'd getting ready to heave down in the P.M. We had the misfortune to loose Mr. Monkhouse, the Surgeon, who died at Batavia of a Fever after a short illness, of which disease and others several of our people are daily taken ill, which will make his loss be the more severely felt; he was succeeded by Mr. Perry, his mate, who is equally as well skilled in his profession.

Thursday, 8th. In the night had much Thunder, Lightning, and Rain; during the day fair weather, which gave us time to get everything in readiness for heaving down.

Friday, 9th. In the P.M. hove the Larboard side of the Ship, Kiel out, and found her bottom to be in a far worse condition than we expected; the false kiel was gone to within 20 feet of the Stern post, the main Kiel wounded in many places very considerably, a great quantity of Sheathing off, and several planks much damaged, especially under the Main Channell near the Kiel, where 2 planks and a 1/2, near 6 feet in length, were within 1/8th of an inch of being cutt through; and here the worms had made their way quite into the timbers, so that it was a matter of surprise to every one who saw her bottom how we had kept her above water, and yet in this condition we had sailed some hundreds of Leagues, in as dangerous a Navigation as in any part of the World, happy in being ignorant of the continual danger we were in. In the evening righted the Ship, having only time to patch up some of the worst places to prevent the water getting in in large quantitys for the present. In the morning hove her down again, and most of the Carpenters and Caulkers in the Yard (which are not a few) were set to work upon her Bottom, and at the same time a number of Slaves were employ'd bailing the water out of the Hold. Our people, altho' they attend, were seldom called upon; indeed, by this time we were so weakned by sickness that we could not muster above 20 Men and Officers that were able to do duty, so little should we have been able to have hove her down and repair'd her ourselves, as I at one time thought us capable of.

Saturday, 10th. In the P.M. we were obliged to righten the ship before night, by reason of her making water in her upper works faster than we could free; it made it necessary to have her weather works inside and out caulked, which before was thought unnecessary.

Sunday, 11th. In the A.M., having caulked her upper works, hove out the Larboard side again, which a number of Workmen were employ'd repairing.

Monday, 12th. In the P.M. finished the Larboard side, and in the A.M. began to get ready to heave out the other.

Tuesday, 13th. This day they hove the Starboard side Kiel out, which we found very little damaged, and was therefore soon done with.

Wednesday, 14th. Employ'd clearing the Ship of the Carreening gear, her bottom being now thoroughly repair'd, and very much to my satisfaction. In justice to the Officers and Workmen of this Yard, I must say that I do not believe that there is a Marine Yard in the World where work is done with more alertness than here, or where there are better conveniences for heaving Ships down both in point of safety and despatch. Here they heave down by 2 masts, which is not now Practised by the English; but I hold it to be much safer and more expeditious than by heaving down by one mast; a man must not only be strongly bigotted to his own customs, but in some measure divested of reason, that will not allow this, after seeing with how much ease and safety the Dutch at Onrust heave down their largest ships.

Thursday, 15th. In the A.M. transported the Ship from Onrust to Cooper's Island, and moored her alongside the Wharf.

Friday, 16th. Employ'd taking in Coals and Ballast; sent one of the decay'd Pumps up to Batavia to have a new one made by it.

Saturday, 17th, Sunday, 18th, Monday, 19th, Tuesday, 20th, Wednesday, 21st, Thursday, 22nd, Friday, 23rd, Saturday, 24th, Sunday, 25th. Employ'd rigging the Ship, getting on board Stores and Water, which last we have sent from Batavia at the rate of Six shillings and 8 pence a Leager, or 150 Gallons. We are now become so sickly that we seldom can muster above 12 or 14 hands to do duty.

Monday, 26th. In the night had much rain, after which the Westerly Monsoons set in, which blow here generally in the night from the South-West or from the land, in the day from the North-West or North.

Tuesday, 27th, Wednesday, 28th, Thursday, 29th, Friday, 30th, [December 1770.] Saturday, December 1st, Sunday, 2nd, Monday, 3rd, Tuesday, 4th, Wednesday, 5th, Thursday, 6th, Friday, 7th. Employ'd getting on board Stores, Provisions, Water, rigging the Ship, repairing and bending the Sails. On the last of these days, having got all the Sick on board, and every other thing from the Island, we hauled off from the Wharfe with a design to run up to Batavia road, but the Wind proving scant obliged us to lay at anchor.

[At Batavia.]

Saturday, 8th. Fresh breezes Westerly, and fair weather. At 10 A.M. weigh'd and run up to Batavia road, where we anchor'd in 4 1/2 fathoms water.

Sunday, 9th. First and latter parts ditto weather, middle squally with rain. In the P.M. sent on shore a Boat load of empty casks, and at the same time went myself in order to forward the things we wanted, and in the evening sent on board the new Pump, with some other stores that were immediately wanting.

Monday, 10th. For the most part Squally, with rain; the people employ'd scraping the paint work.

Tuesday, 11th, Wednesday, 12th, Thursday, 13th, Friday, 14th. For the most part of these days fair weather. Employ'd taking on board Provisions and Water; this last is put on board at 5 shillings a Leager or 150 Gallons.

Saturday, 15th. In the P.M. anchor'd here the Earl of Elgin, Captain Cooke, an English East India Company Ship from Madras, bound to China, but having lost her passage, put in here to wait for the next Season.

Sunday, 16th, Monday, 17th. Employ'd taking on board Provisions; Scraping and Painting the Ship.

Tuesday, 18th. Gentle breezes and fair weather. Anchored here the Phoenix, Captain Black, an English Country Ship from Bencoolen.

Wednesday, 19th, Thursday, 20th, Friday, 21st, Saturday, 22nd, Sunday, 23rd, Monday, 24th. Fresh breezes, and for the most part fair weather. Completed taking on board Provisions, Water, etc., and getting the Ship ready for sea.

Tuesday, 25th. Having now compleatly refitted the ship, and taken in a sufficient quantity of Provisions of all kinds, I this afternoon took leave of the General, and such others of the principal Gentlemen as I had any connection with, all of whom upon every occasion gave me all the assistance I required. A small dispute, however, now hapned between me and some of the Dutch Naval Officers about a Seaman that had run from one of the Dutch Ships in the Road, and enter'd on board mine; this man the General demanded as a Subject of Holland, and I promised to deliver him up provided he was not an English Subject, and sent the necessary orders on board for that purpose. In the morning the Commodore's Captain came and told me that he had been on board my ship for the man, but that the Officer had refused to give him up, alledging that he was an Englishman, and that he, the Captain, was just then come from the General to demand the man of me as a Deanish Subject, he standing upon their Ship's books as born at Elsinore. I told him that I believed there must be some mistake in the General's message, for I apprehended he would not demand a Deanish Seaman from me who had committed no other crime than preferring the English Service before that of the Dutch; but to convince him how unwilling I was to disoblige any one concerned, I had sent orders on board to deliver the man to him in case he was found to be a Foreigner; but as that was not done I suspected that the man was a Subject of England, and if I found him to be such I was resolved to keep him. Soon after this I received a letter from Mr. Hicks, which I carried to the Shabander, and desired that it might be shewn to the General, and at the same time to acquaint him that, after my having such unanswerable proof of the man's being an English Subject, as was mentioned in that letter, it was impossible for me to deliver him up. After this I heard no more about it.

Wednesday, 26th. In the P.M. myself, Mr. Banks, and all the Gentlemen came on board, and at 6 a.m. weigh'd and came to sail with a light breeze at South-West. The Elgin Indiaman saluted us with 3 cheers and 13 Guns, and soon after the Garrison with 14, both of which we return'd. Soon after this the Sea breeze set in at North by West, which obliged us to Anchor just without the Ships in the Road. The number of Sick on board at this time amounts to 40 or upwards, and the rest of the Ship's Company are in a weakly condition, having been every one sick except the Sailmaker, an old Man about 70 or 80 years of age; and what is still more extraordinary in this man is his being generally more or less drunk every day. But notwithstanding this general sickness, we lost but 7 men in the whole: the Surgeon, 3 Seamen, Mr. Green's Servant, and Tupia and his Servant, both of which fell a sacrifice to this unwholesome climate before they had reached the object of their wishes. Tupia's death, indeed, cannot be said to be owing wholy to the unwholesome air of Batavia; the long want of a Vegetable Diet, which he had all his life before been used to, had brought upon him all the Disorders attending a Sea life. He was a shrewd, sensible, ingenious man, but proud and obstinate, which often made his situation on board both disagreeable to himself and those about him, and tended much to promote the diseases which put a Period to his Life.* (* It is rather curious that Cook does not here record his sense of the value of Tupia's services as interpreter, which he has before alluded to in the Journal. There is no doubt that his presence on board when the ship was in New Zealand was the greatest advantage, affording a means of communication with the natives, which prevented the usual gross misunderstandings which arise as to the object of the visit of an exploring ship. Without him, even with Cook's humane intention and good management, friendly relations would have been much more difficult to establish.)

[Description of Batavia.]

Batavia is a place that hath been so often visited by Europeans, and so many accounts of it extant, that any discription I could give would seem unnecessary; besides, I have neither abilities nor materials sufficient for such an undertaking, for whoever gives a faithful account of this place must in many things contradict all the Authors I have had an opportunity to consult; but this task I shall leave to some abler hand, and only take notice of such things that seem to me necessary for Seamen to know.

The City of Batavia is situated on a low flatt near the Sea, in the Bottom of a large Bay of the same name, which lies on the North side of Java, about 8 Leagues from the Straits of Sunda; it lies in 6 degrees 10 minutes South Latitude, and 106 degrees 50 minutes East Longitude from the Meridian of Greenwich, settled by Astronomical Observations made on the spot by the Reverend Mr. Mohr, who has built a very ellegant Observatory, which is as well furnished with Instruments as most in Europe. Most of the Streets in the City have canals of water running through them, which unite into one Stream about 1/2 a mile before they discharge themselves into the Sea; this is about 100 feet broad, and is built far enough out into the Sea to have at its entrance a sufficient depth of Water to admit Small Craft, Luggage boats, etc. The communication between the Sea and the City is by this Canal alone, and this only in the day; for it is shut up every night by a Boom, through which no Boats can pass from about 6 o'clock in the evening to between 5 and 6 the next morning. Here stands the Custom house, where all goods, either imported or exported, pay the Customary Dutys; at least, an Account is here taken of them, and nothing can pass without a Permit, wether it pays duty or no. All kinds of refreshments, Naval Stores, and Sea Provisions are to be had here; but there are few Articles but what bear a very high Price, especially if you take them of the Company, which you are obliged to do if you want any Quantity; that is, of such Articles as they monoplie to themselves, which are all manner of Naval Stores and Salted Provisions.

The Road of Batavia, or place where Shipping Anchor, lies right before the City, and is so large as to contain any number of Shipping. You anchor with the Dome of the Great Church, bearing about South in 7, 6, or 5 fathoms water, about 1 1/2 or 2 miles from the Shore; and nearer you cannot come with Large Ships, by reason of a Mud bank which lines all the Shore of the Bay. The ground that you Anchor in is of such a nature that the Anchors buries themselves so deep that it is with difficulty they are got out; for this reason Ships always lays at Single Anchor, being in no manner of danger of fouling them. You lay apparently open to the winds from the North-West to the East-North-East; but the Sea that is caused by these winds is a good deal broke before it reaches the Road by the small Islands and Shoals without. These Shoals have all of them either Buoys or Beacons upon them; but if these Guides should be moved, there is a very good Chart of this Bay and the Coast of Java as far as the Straits of Sunda, bound up in the English East India Pilot, sold by Mount & Page. In this Chart everything seems to be very accurately delineated.

Fresh water and wood for fuel must be purchased here. The water is put on board the Ship in the Road at a Spanish Dollar, or 5 shillings a Leager, containing 150 Gallons; but if sent to Onrust, which is one League from the Road, it cost a Duccatoon, or 6 shillings 8 pence. The supplying shipping with water, especially Foreigners, is a perquisite of the Commodore, who is always an Officer in the State's Service, but acts here under the Company. He takes care to tell you that the Water is very good, and will keep sweet at Sea; whereas everybody else tells you that it is not so.

Be this as it will, Batavia is certainly a place that Europeans need not covet to go to; but if necessity obliges them, they will do well to make their stay as short as possible, otherwise they will soon feel the effects of the unwholesome air of Batavia, which, I firmly believe, is the Death of more Europeans than any other place upon the Globe of the same extent. Such, at least, is my opinion of it, which is founded on facts. We came in here with as healthy a Ship's Company as need go to Sea, and after a stay of not quite 3 months left it in the condition of an Hospital Ship, besides the loss of 7 men; and yet all the Dutch Captains I had an opportunity to converse with said that we had been very lucky, and wondered that we had not lost half our people in that time.* (* Batavia bears an evil reputation for health to this day; but it must be remembered that the Endeavour lay there during the rainy or most unhealthy season.)

CHAPTER 10.
BATAVIA TO CAPE OF GOOD HOPE.

[December 1770.]

THURSDAY, 27th. Moderate breezes at West and North-West, with fair weather. At 6 a.m. weighed, and stood out to Sea; at Noon the Island of Edam bore North by East, distant 3 miles.

Friday, 28th. Winds variable between the North and West. At 6 in the Evening anchored in 13 fathoms, Edam Island bearing East, distant 1 1/2 miles. At day light in the morning weighed again, and kept plying to windward between Edam and Duffin's Island, but gained very little owing to the variableness of the winds.

Saturday, 29th. In the P.M. anchored in 12 fathoms water in the Evening until daylight, when we got again under Sail, with the wind at West-South-West, and stood out North-West for the Thousand Islands. Before noon the wind veer'd to North-West, and we endeavour'd to turn through between Pulo Pare and Wapping Island.

Sunday, 30th. After making a short trip to the North-East, we tacked, and weather'd Pulo Pare, and stood in for the Main, having the wind at North-West, a fresh breeze. We fetched Maneaters Island (a small island laying under the Main midway between Batavia and Bantam) after making a trip to the North-East, and finding that we lost ground, we stood in shore again and anchored in 13 fathoms, the above mentioned Island bearing South-West by West, distant 1 mile, and in one with Bantam Hill. At 7 A.M. weighed, with the wind at West-South-West, and stood to the North-West, and weather'd Wapping Island, having the current in our favour.

Monday, 31st. At 1 P.M. the wind veer'd to the Northward; we tack and stood to the Westward, and weather'd Pulo Baby. In the Evening Anchor'd between this Island and Bantam Bay, the Island bearing North, distant 2 miles, and Bantam Point West; at 5 a.m. weighed with the wind at West by South, which afterwards proved variable; at noon Bantam Point South-West 1/2 West, distant 3 Leagues.

JANUARY, 1771.

Tuesday, 1st. In the P.M. stood over for the Sumatra Shore, having the wind at South-South-West, a fresh breeze, and the current in our favour; but this last shifted and set to the Eastward in the Evening, and obliged us to Anchor in 30 fathoms, under the Islands which lay off Verekens point, which point constitutes the narrowest part of the Straits of Sunda. Here we found the current set to the South-West the most part of the night; at 5 a.m. weigh'd with the wind at North-West, and stood to the South-West between the Island Thwart-the-way and Sumatra; the wind soon after coming to the westward we stood over for the Java Shore. At noon the South point of Peper Bay bore South-West by South, and Anger Point North-East 1/2 East, distant 2 Leagues; tacked and stood to the North-West.

Wednesday, 2nd. First and middle parts fresh breezes at South-West, and fair the remainder, squally with rain; plying to windward between Cracatoa and the Java shore without gaining anything.

Thursday, 3rd. In the P.M. had it very squally, with heavy showers of rain; at 1/2 past 7 anchor'd in 19 fathoms, Cracatoa Island South-West, distance 3 Leagues. In the morning came to sail, having very squally variable weather; at Noon Cracatoa West 2 Leagues.

Friday, 4th. Most part of these 24 hours squally, rainy weather, winds variable between the North-North-West and South-South-West; at 5 p.m. anchor'd in 28 fathoms water, Cracatoa West, distant 3 miles. Some time after the wind veer'd to North-West, with which we got under sail, but the wind dying away we advanced but little to the South-West before noon, at which time Princes Island bore South-West, distance 8 or 9 Leagues.

Saturday, 5th. Had fresh breezes at South-West, with squally, rainy weather until the evening, when it clear up, and the wind veer'd to South and South-East, with which we stood to the South-West all night. In the morning the wind veer'd to North-East, which was still in our favour; at noon Princes Island bore West 1/2 South, distant 3 Leagues.

[At Anchor. Princes Island, Sunda Strait.]

Sunday, 6th. At 3 o'clock in the P.M. anchor'd under the South-East side of Princes Island in 18 fathoms water, in order to recruit our wood and water, and to procure refreshments for the people, which are now in a much worse state of health than when we left Batavia. After coming to an anchor I went on shore to look at the watering place, and to speak with the Natives, some of whom were upon the Beach. I found the watering place convenient, and the water to all appearance good, Provided proper care is taken in the filling of it. The Natives seemed inclined to supply us with Turtle, Fowls, etc.; Articles that I intended laying in as great a stock as possible for the benefit of the Sick, and to suffer every one to purchase what they pleased for themselves, as I found these people as easy to traffick with as Europeans. In the morning sent the Gunner ashore with some hands to fill water, while others were empboy'd putting the whole to rights, sending on shore Empty Casks, etc. Served Turtle to the Ship's Company. Yesterday was the only Salt meat day they have had since our arrival at Java, which is now near 4 months.

Monday, 7th. From this day till Monday 14th we were employ'd wooding and watering, being frequently interrupted by heavy rains. Having now compleated both we hoisted in the Long boat, and made ready to put to Sea, having on board a pretty good stock of refreshments, which we purchased of the natives, such as Turtle, Fowls, Fish, two species of Deer, one about as big as a small sheep, the other no bigger than a Rabbit; both sorts eat very well, but are only for present use, as they seldom lived above 24 hours in our possession. We likewise got fruit of several sorts, such as Cocoa Nutts, plantains, Limes, etc. The Trade on our part was carried on chiefly with money (Spanish Dollars); the natives set but little value upon any thing else. Such of our people as had not this Article traded with Old Shirts, etc., at a great disadvantage.

[Batavia to Capetown.]

Tuesday, 15th. Had variable light airs of wind, with which we could not get under sail until the morning, when we weighed with a light breeze at North-East, which was soon succeeded by a calm.

Wednesday, 16th. Had it calm all P.M., which at 5 o'clock obliged us to Anchor under the South Point of Princes Island, the said Point bearing South-West by West, distance 2 miles. At 8 o'clock in the A.M. a light breeze sprung up at North, with which we weigh'd and stood out to Sea. At noon Java Head bore South-East by South, distance 2 Leagues, and the West Point of Princes Island North-North-West, distance 5 Leagues; Latitude Observed 6 degrees 45 minutes South. Java Head, from which I take my departure, lies in the Latitude of 6 degrees 49 minutes South, and Longitude 255 degrees 12 minutes West from the Meridian of Greenwich, deduced from several Astronomical Observations made at Batavia by the Reverend Mr. Mohr.* (* The true longitude of Java Head is 254 degrees 49 minutes West.)

Thursday, 17th. Little wind and fair at 6 p.m. Java head bore East-North-East, distant 4 or 5 Leagues; at 6 a.m. it bore North-North-East, 12 Leagues. Wind North-East; course South 27 degrees 15 minutes West; distance 48 miles; latitude 7 degrees 32 minutes South; longitude 255 degrees 35 minutes West.

Friday, 18th. Light Airs and Calms, with Showers of Rain. Wind Variable; course South-West 1/2 South; distance 30 miles; latitude 7 degrees 55 minutes South; longitude 255 degrees 54 minutes West.

Saturday, 19th. For the most part of these 24 hours had little wind and fair weather. Wind Westerly; course South 3 degrees East; distance 53 miles; latitude 8 degrees 48 minutes South; longitude 255 degrees 51 minutes West.

Sunday, 20th. Light Airs and Calms, with some Showers of Rain. Saw 2 Sail in the North-West Quarter standing to the South-West; one of them shew'd

Dutch Colours. Wind North Westerly; course South 44 degrees West; distance 36 miles; latitude 9 degrees 14 minutes South; longitude 256 degrees 15 minutes West.

Monday, 21st. First part Little wind, the remainder a Gentle breeze; the 2 Sail in sight. Wind Easterly; course South 57 degrees West; distance 58 miles; latitude 9 degrees 46 minutes South; longitude 257 degrees 5 minutes West.

Tuesday, 22nd. Little wind and fair weather. Wind South-Westerly; course North 10 degrees West; distance 17 miles; latitude 9 degrees 29 minutes South; longitude 257 degrees 8 minutes West.

Wednesday, 23rd. Ditto weather; a swell from the Southward, and which we have had ever since we left the Straits of Sunda. Wind Ditto; course East Southerly; distance 18 miles; latitude 9 degrees 30 minutes South; longitude 256 degrees 50 minutes West.

Thursday, 24th. First part Light Airs, the remainder Calm. In the A.M. died John Trusslove, Corporal of Marines, a man much esteem'd by every body on board. Many of our people at this time lay dangerously ill of Fevers and Fluxes. We are inclinable to attribute this to the water we took in at Princes Island, and have put lime into the Casks in order to purifie it. Wind South-West by South to South-South-East; course South; distance 4 miles; latitude 9 degrees 34 minutes South; longitude 256 degrees 50 minutes West.

Friday, 25th. Light Airs and Calms; hot, sultry weather. Departed this life Mr. Sporing, a Gentleman belonging to Mr Banks's retinue. Wind Variable and Calms; course South 30 degrees East; distance 12 miles; latitude 9 degrees 44 minutes South; longitude 256 degrees 44 minutes West.

Saturday, 26th. First part little wind, the remainder calm and very hot; set up the Topmast Rigging, and clear'd ship between Decks, and wash her with Vinegar. Wind South Westerly; course South-East; distance 17 miles; latitude 9 degrees 56 minutes South; longitude 256 degrees 32 minutes West.

Sunday, 27th. Little wind, and sometimes calm. In the evening found the Variation to be 2 degrees 51 minutes West. Departed this life Mr. Sydney Parkinson, Natural History Painter to Mr. Banks, and soon after John Ravenhill, Sailmaker, a man much advanced in years. Wind Variable; course South 30 degrees West; distance 19 miles; latitude 10 degrees 12 minutes South; longitude 256 degrees 41 minutes West.

Monday, 28th. Moderate breezes, with some Squalls, attended with Showers of Rain. Wind West-North-West, North-East; course South 43 degrees West; distance 66 miles; latitude 11 degrees 0 minutes South; longitude 257 degrees 27 West.

Tuesday, 29th. Very variable weather; sometimes squally, with rain, other times little wind and calms. In the Night died Mr. Charles Green, who was sent out by the Royal Society to observe the Transit of Venus. He had long been in a bad state of health, which he took no care to repair, but, on the contrary, lived in such a manner as greatly promoted the disorders he had had long upon him; this brought on the Flux, which put a period to his life. Wind North Westerly; course South 40 degrees West; distance 74 miles; latitude 11 degrees 57 minutes South; longitude 258 degrees 15 minutes West.

Wednesday, 30th. First and Latter parts moderate breezes and Cloudy weather; the middle Squally, with rain, Thunder, and Lightning. Died of the Flux Samuel Moody and Francis Haite, 2 of the Carpenter's Crew. Wind Easterly; course South 40 degrees West; distance 67 miles; latitude 12 degrees 48 minutes South; longitude 258 degrees 59 minutes West.

Thursday, 31st. First part Moderate and fair, the remainder frequent Squalls, attended with Showers of Rain. In the course of this 24 Hours we have had 4 men died of the Flux, viz., John Thompson, Ship's Cook; Benjamin Jordan, Carpenter's Mate; James Nickolson and Archibald Wolf, Seamen; a melancholy proof of the calamitieous situation we are at present in, having hardly well men enough to tend the Sails and look after the Sick, many of whom are so ill that we have not the least hopes of their recovery. Wind East-South-East; course South-West; distance 80 miles; latitude 13 degrees 42 minutes South; longitude 259 degrees 55 minutes West.

[February 1771.]

Friday, February 1st. Fresh Gales, with flying showers of rain. Clean'd between Decks, and washed with Vinegar. Wind South-East by South; course South 58 1/2 degrees West; distance 119 miles; latitude 14 degrees 44 minutes South; longitude 261 degrees 40 minutes West.

Saturday, 2nd. A Fresh Trade, and mostly fair weather. Departed this life Daniel Roberts, Gunner's Servant, who died of the Flux. Since we have had a fresh Trade Wind this fatal disorder hath seem'd to be at a stand; yet there are several people which are so far gone, and brought so very low by it, that we have not the least hopes of their recovery. Wind East-South-East; course South 61 degrees West; distance 131 miles; latitude 15 degrees 48 minutes South; longitude 264 degrees 16 minutes West.

Sunday, 3rd. Ditto weather. In the Evening found the variation to be 2 degrees 56 minutes West. Departed this life John Thurman, Sailmaker's Assistant. Wind Ditto; course South 65 degrees West; distance 128 miles; latitude 16 degrees 40 minutes South; longitude 266 degrees 16 West.

Monday, 4th. A fresh Trade and hazey weather, with some Squalls, attended with Small Rain; unbent the Main Topsail to repair, and bent another. In the night died of the Flux Mr. John Bootie, Midshipman, and Mr. John Gathrey, Boatswain. Wind South-East; course South 69 degrees West; distance 141 miles; latitude 17 degrees 30 minutes South; longitude 268 degrees 32 minutes West.

Tuesday, 5th. A fresh Trade wind, and hazey, cloudy weather. Employ'd repairing Sails; appointed Samuel Evans, one of the Boatswain's Mates, and Coxswain of the Pinnace, to be Boatswain, in the room of Mr. Gathrey, deceased, and order'd a Survey to be taken of the Stores. Wind East by South; course West 15 degrees South; distance 141 miles; latitude 18 degrees 6 minutes South; longitude 270 degrees 54 minutes West.

Wednesday, 6th. A Fresh Trade wind and fair weather. In the night died Mr. John Monkhouse, Midshipman, and Brother to the late Surgeon. Wind South-East; course West 12 degrees South; distance 126 miles; latitude 18 degrees 30 minutes South; longitude 272 degrees 28 minutes West.

Thursday, 7th. Gentle Gales, with some Showers in the night. In the Evening found the variation to be 3 degrees 24 minutes West, and in the Morning I took several observations of the Sun and Moon, the mean result of which, carried on to Noon, gave 276 degrees 19 minutes West Longitude from Greenwich, which is 2 degrees to the Westward of that given by the Log; this, I believe, is owing to a following Sea, which I have not as yet allowed, for I judge it to be 6 miles a day since we have had the South-East Trade wind. Wind South-East; course South 75 degrees 15 minutes West; distance 110 miles; latitude 18 degrees 58 minutes South; longitude 274 degrees 20 minutes per Log, 276 degrees 19 minutes per Observation.

Friday, 8th. Winds as Yesterday; clear weather in the day, and Showrey in the Night. In the morning took Observations again of the Sun and Moon, the mean result of which, reduced to noon, gave 278 degrees 50 minutes West, which is 2 degrees 31 minutes West of Yesterday's Observation; the log gives 2 degrees 20 minutes. Wind South-East; course South 78 degrees West; distance 127 miles; latitude 19 degrees 24 minutes South; longitude 276 degrees 40 minutes per Log, 278 degrees 50 minutes per Observation.

Saturday, 9th. Gentle Gales and fair weather in the morning. Saw a Ship on our Larboard Quarter, which hoisted Dutch Colours. Wind South-East; course South 74 degrees 30 minutes West; distance 127 miles; latitude 19 degrees 58 minutes South.

Sunday, 10th. Fresh breezes and Hazey weather. Lost sight in the night of the Dutch Ship, she having out sail'd us. Wind South-East quarter; course

South 77 degrees 15 minutes West; distance 136 miles; latitude 20 degrees 28 minutes South; longitude 281 degrees 12 minutes West.

Monday, 11th. Winds and weather as Yesterday. Some hands constantly employ'd repairing Sails. Wind Ditto; course South 75 degrees West; distance 126 miles; latitude 20 degrees 58 minutes South; longitude 283 degrees 22 minutes West.

Tuesday, 12th. Gentle breezes and fair weather. At 7 a.m. died of the Flux, after a long and painful illness, Mr. John Satterly, Carpenter, a man much Esteem'd by me and every Gentleman on board. In his room I appoint George Nowell, one of the Carpenter's Crew, having only him and one more left. Wind South-South-East; course South 71 minutes West; distance 83 miles; latitude 21 degrees 25 minutes South; longitude 284 degrees 46 minutes West.

Wednesday, 13th. Weather as Yesterday. Employ'd Surveying the Carpenter's Stores and repairing Sails. Wind Ditto; course South 72 degrees 30 minutes West; distance 87 miles; latitude 21 degrees 51 minutes South; longitude 286 degrees 15 minutes West.

Thursday, 14th. Moderate breezes and Cloudy, with some Showers of Rain. Variation per Azimuth 4 degrees 10 minutes West. Died Alexander Lindsay, Seaman; this man was one of those we got at Batavia, and had been some time in India. Winds Ditto; course South 73 degrees 15 minutes West; distance 105 miles; latitude 22 degrees 21 minutes South; longitude 288 degrees 3 minutes West.

Friday, 15th. Ditto Weather. Died of the Flux Daniel Preston, Marine. Wind South-East by East; course South 81 degrees 15 minutes West; distance 123 miles; latitude 22 degrees 40 minutes; longitude 290 degrees 15 minutes West.

Saturday, 16th. A Fresh Trade and Cloudy weather. Employ'd repairing Sails, rigging, etc. Wind Ditto; course South 84 degrees West; distance 115 miles; latitude 22 degrees 52 minutes South; longitude 292 degrees 20 minutes West.

Sunday, 17th. Fresh Gales, with some Showers of rain. Variation per Azimuth 10 degrees 20 minutes Westerly. Wind South-East by South; course South 79 degrees 45 minutes West; distance 157 miles; latitude 23 degrees 20 minutes South; longitude 295 8 minutes West.

Monday, 18th. Fair and pleasant weather. Wind South-East by East; course South 75 degrees 30 minutes West; distance 148 miles; latitude 23 degrees 57 minutes South; longitude 297 degrees 46 minutes West.

Tuesday, 19th. Ditto weather. Wind South-East by East and South; course South 77 degrees West; distance 130 miles; latitude 24 degrees 26 minutes South; longitude 300 degrees 5 minutes West.

Wednesday, 20th. Fresh Gales and clear weather. Variation per Azimuth 12 degrees 15 minutes West. This morning the Carpenter and his Mate set about repairing the Long boat, being the first day they have been able to work since we left Princes Island. Wind South; course South 75 degrees 45 minutes West; distance 127 miles; latitude 24 degrees 57 minutes South; longitude 302 degrees 21 minutes West.

Thursday, 21st. First and middle parts fair weather; Latter Squally, attended with Showers of Rain. Between 2 and 3 o'Clock p.m. took several Observations of the Sun and Moon; the mean result of them gave 306 degrees 33 minutes West Longitude from Greenwich, which is 1 degree 55 minutes West of account, and corresponds very well with the last Observations, for at that time the Ship was 2 degrees 10 minutes West of account. In the Night died of the Flux Alexander Simpson, a very good Seaman. In the Morning punished Thomas Rossiter with 12 lashes for getting Drunk, grossly assaulting the Officer of the Watch, and beating some of the Sick. Wind South to East-South-East; course West by South; distance 126 miles; latitude 25 degrees 21 minutes South; longitude 304 degrees 39 minutes per Account, 306 degrees 34 minutes per Observation.

Friday, 22nd. Fresh Trade and fair weather. Nothing remarkable. Wind South-East by South; course South 70 degrees 45 minutes West; distance 133 miles; latitude 26 degrees 5 minutes South; longitude 306 degrees 59 minutes West, 308 degrees 54 minutes per Observation.

Saturday, 23rd. Ditto Winds and weather. Variation per Evening Amplitude 17 degrees 30 minutes West. Wind Ditto; course South 64 degrees 14 minutes West; distance 124 miles; latitude 26 degrees 59 minutes; longitude 309 degrees 6 minutes West, 311 degrees 28 minutes per Observation.

Sunday, 24th. Gentle breezes and fair weather. In the A.M. took the opportunity of a fine morning to stay the Main Mast, and set up the Topmast Rigging. Saw an Albatross. Wind Ditto; course South 66 degrees 45 minutes West; distance 117 miles; latitude 27 degrees 45 minutes South; longitude 311 degrees 7 minutes West, 313 degrees 41 minutes per Observation.

Monday, 25th. Gentle Gales, and fair weather. Variation per Evening Azimuth 24 degrees 20 minutes West, and by the Morning Amplitude 24 degrees West Longitude; by Observation of the [circle around a dot, sun] and [crescent, moon] is 3 degrees to the Westwarn of the Log, which shews that the Ship has gain'd upon the Log 1 degree 5 minutes in 3 Days, in which time we have always found the Observ'd Latitude to the Southward of that given by the Log. These Joint Observations proves that there must be a current setting between the South and West. Wind East by South; course South 58 degrees 30 minutes West; distance 122 miles; latitude 28 degrees 49 minutes South; longitude 313 degrees 6 minutes West, 316 degrees 6 minutes per Observation.

Tuesday, 26th. Fresh Gales. Variation by Azimuth in the Evening 26 degrees 10 minutes West. Wind South-East by East; course South 82 degrees West; distance 122 miles; latitude 29 degrees 6 minutes South; longitude 315 degrees 24 minutes West.

Wednesday, 27th. Ditto Gales and Cloudy. In the A.M. died of the Flux Henry Jeffs, Emanuel Parreyra, and Peter Morgan, Seamen; the last came Sick on board at Batavia, of which he never recover'd, and the other 2 had long been past all hopes of recovery, so that the death of these 3 men in one day did not in the least alarm us.* (* These were the last deaths directly attributable to the dysentery contracted at Batavia. Though always enjoying an unenviable reputation, Batavia seems to have had, this year, a more unhealthy season than usual. The Endeavour lost seven persons while at Batavia, and twenty-three after sailing up to this date.) On the contrary, we are in hopes that they will be the last that will fall a sacrifice to this fatal disorder, for such as are now ill of it are in a fair way of recovering. Wind East by South, East by North-North-East; course South 77 degrees 15 minutes West; distance 108 miles; latitude 29 degrees 30 minutes South; longitude 317 degrees 25 minutes West.

Thursday, 28th. Moderate breezes and fair weather until near 5 o'Clock in the A.M., when a heavy Squall from the South-West, attended with rain, took us all aback, and obliged us to put before the wind, the better to take in our Sails; but before this could be done the Foretopsail was split in several places. By 6 o'clock the Topsails and Mainsail were handed, and we brought too under the Foresail and Mizen; at 8 it fell more moderate, and we set the Mainsail, and brought another Foretopsail to the Yard; at Noon had strong Gales and Cloudy weather. Wind North-East by East, North, and South-West; course South 85 1/2 degrees West; distance 88 miles; latitude 29 degrees 37 minutes South; longitude 319 degrees 5 minutes West.

[March 1771.]

Friday, March 1st. Fresh Gales and Cloudy. Found the Bitts which secures the foot of the Bowsprit, loose; this obliged us to put before the wind until they were secured in the best manner our situation would admit; this done, we hauld our wind again to the Westward under the Courses and close Reef'd Topsails. Wind South-West to South by West; course South 86 degrees 45 minutes West; distance 71 miles; latitude 29 degrees 41 minutes South; longitude 320 degrees 26 minutes West.

Saturday, 2nd. First part fresh Gales and Cloudy; remainder little wind, with some few showers of rain; a Sea from the South-West. Wind Southerly; course South 60 degrees West; distance 80 miles; latitude 30 degrees 21 minutes South; longitude 321 degrees 46 minutes West.

Sunday, 3rd. First part little wind; remainder Gentle gales and clear weather, and the Sea pretty smooth. Wind North-East; course South 58 degrees 15 minutes West; distance 71 miles; latitude 31 degrees 1 minute South; longitude 323 degrees 2 minutes West.

Monday, 4th. In the P.M. had a moderate breeze, which continued until 5 o'clock in the A.M., when it fell calm, and soon after a breeze sprung up at South-West. In the Evening, and most part of the Night, the weather was dark and cloudy, with much Lightning to the Westward. Variation 25 degrees 35 minutes West. Winds North-East to South-West; course South 67 degrees 45 minutes West; distance 87 miles; latitude 31 degrees 54 minutes South; longitude 324 degrees 36 minutes West.

[Off Coast of Natal.]

Tuesday, 5th. Fresh Gales from the South-South-West, with squally, rainy weather, with which we stood to the Westward. In the evening some people thought they saw the appearance of land to the Northward; but this appear'd so improbable that I, who was not on deck at this time, was not acquainted with it until dark, when I order'd them to sound, but found no ground with 80 fathoms, upon which we concluded that no land was near. But daylight in the Morning proved this to be a mistake by shewing us the land at the distance of about 2 Leagues off. We had now the wind at South-East, blowing fresh right upon the land. When we made the land we were standing to the Westward; but, thinking the other the best tack to get off on, we wore, and hauld off to the Eastward, and by Noon had got an Offing of about 4 Leagues, the land at this time extending from North-East by North to West-South-West. This part of the Coast of Africa which we fell in with lies in about the Latitude of 32 degrees 0 minutes South, and Longitude 331 degrees 29 minutes West, and near to what is called in the Charts Point Nattall.* (* Natal.) It was a steep, craggy point, very much broke, and looked as if the high, craggy rocks were Islands. To the North-East of this point the land in General appear'd to rise, sloping from the Sea to a Moderate height; the Shore, alternately Rocks and Sands. About 2 Leagues to the North-East of the Point appear'd to be the mouth of a River, which probably may be that of St. Johns. At this time the weather was very hazey, so that we had but a very imperfect view of the land, which did not appear to great advantage. Wind South-South-West to South-East; course per Log North 31 degrees West; distance 32 miles; latitude 31 degrees 5 minutes South per Observation,

31 degrees 7 minutes per Reckoning; longitude 331 degrees 19 minutes per Observation, 324 degrees 56 minutes per Reckoning.

Wednesday, 6th. Moderate Gales, with hazey, rainy weather. Stood to the Eastward all the day, having the land in sight, which at 4 p.m. extended from North-East by North to South-West by West, distant 5 Leagues. At 6 in the Morning we could only see it at West distant 7 or 8 Leagues. At Noon found the Ship by Observation 90 Miles to the Southward of account. Thus far the current has carried us to the South since the last observation, which was only 2 days ago; but it is plain, from the position of the Coast, that we have been carried full as far to the West also, notwithstanding we have been standing all the time to the East-North-East* (* The ship was now in the Agulhas Current.) Wind Southerly; course South 54 degrees East; distance 37 miles; latitude 32 degrees 4 minutes South; 330 degrees 44 minutes per Observation, 323 degrees 36 minutes per Reckoning.

Thursday, 7th. Cloudy, hazey weather; winds varying between the South-West by South and South-East by South; a light breeze at 1 p.m. Tack'd, and stood to the Westward, land at North, distant about 8 Leagues. At 6 saw it extending from North by West to West by North, distant 5 or 6 Leagues; at 8 tack'd, and stood to the Eastward till 12; then again to the Westward, standing 4 hours on one tack, and 4 on the other. At Noon very cloudy; had no observation; saw the land extending from North by West to West by North. Wind Southerly; course South 156 degrees 5 minutes West; distance 72 miles; latitude 32 degrees 54 minutes South; longitude 331 degrees 56 minutes West per Observation, 323 degrees 54 per Reckoning.

Friday, 8th. In the P.M. stood to the Westward, with the wind at South by West until 4 o'clock; then again to the Eastward, having the land in sight, extending from North-North-East to West by North, distant 8 Leagues. At 12 the wind veer'd to the Eastward, and before Noon blow'd a fresh breeze, with which we steer'd South-West. At 7, the land extending from North-North-West to East-North-East, distant 10 or 12 Leagues, found the Variation by the Amplitude to be 28 degrees 30 minutes West, and by an Azimuth 28 degrees 8 minutes West. At Noon Latitude observ'd 34 degrees 18 minutes, which is 93 miles to the Southward of that given by the Log, or dead reckoning since the last observation. Wind Easterly; course South 39 1/2 degrees West; distance 109 miles; latitude 34 degrees 18 minutes South; longitude 333 degrees 19 minutes West per Observation, 324 degrees 23 minutes per Reckoning.

Saturday, 9th. A steady, fresh Gale, and settled weather. At 4 in the P.M. had high land in sight, bearing North-East by North. At Noon had little wind and clear weather; the observed Latitude 46 miles to the Southward of the Log, which is conformable to what has hapned the 4 preceeding days; and by Observation made of the Sun and Moon this morning found that the Ship had gain'd 7 degrees 4 minutes West of the Log since the last observation, 13 days ago. Wind Ditto; course South 65 degrees West; distance 210 miles; latitude 35 degrees 44 minutes South; longitude 337 degrees 6 minutes West per Observation, 326 degrees 53 minutes per Reckoning.

Sunday, 10th. In the P.M. had a light breeze at North-East until 4 o'clock, when it fell calm, and continued so until 11, at which time a breeze sprung up at West-North-West, with which we stood to the Northward. In the Morning found the Variation to be 22 degrees 46 minutes; at Noon the observ'd Latitude was 14 Miles to the Northward of the Log, which shews that the current must have shifted. Wind North-East Westerly; course North 17 degrees 15 minutes West; distance 55 miles; latitude 34 degrees 52 minutes South; longitude 337 degrees 25 minutes West per Observation, 327 degrees 12 minutes per Reckoning.

Monday, 11th. First part light Airs at West; the remainder had a fresh gale at South-East, with which we steer'd West and West-North-West, in order to make the Land, which was seen from the Deck at 10 A.M. At Noon it extended from North-East to North-West, distant 5 Leagues; the middle appear'd high and mountainous, and the two Extremes low. Took several Observations of the Sun and Moon, which gave the Longitude, reduced to Noon, as per Column. Wind Ditto South-East; course North 85 degrees West; distance 79 miles; latitude 34 degrees 45 minutes South; longitude 338 degrees 48 minutes West per Observation, 328 degrees 35 minutes per Reckoning.

[Off Cape Agulhas.]

Tuesday, 12th. In the P.M. had the wind at South-East and East, with which we steer'd along shore West and West-South-West. At 6 Cape Laguillas* (* L'Agulhas.) bore West, distance 3 Leagues. At 8, the wind being then at South, we tack'd and stood off, being about 2 Leagues from the Cape, which bore about West-North-West. In this Situation had 33 fathoms water; the Wind continued between South-West and South all night, in times very Squally, with rain. At 2 a.m. tacked to the Westward until near 8, when we again stood off Cape Laguillas, North-West, distance 2 or 3 Leagues. At 9 the weather clear'd up, and the wind fix'd at South by West. We tack'd, and stood to the Westward. At Noon Cape Laguillas bore North-East by North, distant 4 Leagues. The land of this Cape is very low and sandy next the Sea; inland it is of a moderate height. Latitude 34 degrees 50 minutes South, Longitude 339 degrees 23 minutes West, or 20 degrees 37 minutes East, deduced from Yesterday's Observations. Wind East-South-East Southerly; course South 69 degrees 30 minutes West; distance 37 miles; Latitude 34 degrees 58 minutes South; longitude 339 degrees 30 minutes per Observation, 329 degrees 17 minutes per Reckoning.

Wednesday, 13th. In the P.M., having the wind at South, we steer'd along shore West by South 1/2 South until 3 o'clock, when, finding this course carried us off from the land, we steer'd West by North; at 6 o'clock Cape Laguillas, or the high land over it, bore East by North 12 Leagues distance, and the westermost land in sight North-West 1/2 West. We continued a West by North course, with the wind at South-East until day light in the Morning, when we haul'd in North-West and North-West by North; at 8 the Cape of Good Hope North-West by North, and at 10 we were abreast of it, and distance off about 1 League or little more. We passed close without a rock, on which the Sea broke very high; it lies about a League right out to Sea from the Cape. After passing the Cape we kept along shore at the distance of about 1 League off, having a fresh Gale at South-East; at noon the Cape bore South-East, distance 4 Leagues. Latitude observed 34 degrees 15 minutes South, Longitude in, by our reckoning, corrected by the last observation, 341 degrees 7 minutes West, or 18 degrees 53 minutes East from Greenwich, by which the Cape lies in 34 degrees 25 minutes South Latitude, and 19 degrees 1 minute East Longitude from Greenwich, which nearly agrees with the observations made at the Cape Town by Messrs. Mason and Dixon in 1761; a proof that our observations have been well made, and that as such they may always be depended upon to a surprizing degree of accuracey. If we had had no such guide we should have found an error of 10 degrees 13 minutes of Longitude, or perhaps more to the East, such an effect the current must have had upon the ship.

Thursday, 14th. Winds at South-East, a fresh Gale, but as we approached the Lyons Tail or West point, Table Bay, we had flurries of wind from all Points of the Compass; this was occasioned by the high land, for clear of it the wind was still at South-East, and bbow'd so strong out of the Bay that we could not work the Ship in; we were therefore obliged to Anchor a good way without all the Ships at Anchor in the Road, in the whole 16 Sail, viz., 8 Dutch, 3 Danes, 4 French, a Frigate, and 3 Store Ships, and one English East Indiamen, who saluted us with 11 Guns; we returned 9. The Gale continued, which obliged us to lay fast all the morning.

Friday, 15th. Strong Gales at South-East all the Afternoon and most part of the Night, though in the Evening it fell a little moderate, which gave the Indiaman's Boat an opportunity to come on board us, with a Complement of a Basket of Fruit, etc,; she was the Admiral Pocock, Captain Riddell, homeward bound from Bombay. In the morning we got under sail, and stood into the Road, having variable light airs mostly from the Sea. A Dutch boat from the Shore came on board, in which were the Master Attendant and some other Gentlemen; the former directed us to a proper birth, where about

10 o'clock we anchored in 7 fathoms water, a Ouzey bottom; the Lyon Tail, or West point of the Bay, bore West-North-West, and the Castle South-West, distance 1 1/2 miles. I now sent a Petty Officer on shore to know if they would return our Salute, but before he return'd we Saluted, which was immediately return'd with the same number of Guns; after this I waited myself upon the Governour, who was pleased to tell me that I should have everything I wanted that the place afforded. My first care was to provide a proper place ashore for the reception of the Sick, for which purpose I order'd the Surgeon to look out for a House where they could be lodged and dieted. This he soon found, and agreed with the people of the house for 2 shillings a day per man; which I found was the customary Price and method of proceeding. I afterwards gave the Surgeon an order to superintend the whole.

[Remarks on Dysentery.]

Few remarks have hapned since we left Java Head that can be of much use to the Navigator, or any other Person, into whose hand this Journal may fall; such, however, as have occur'd I shall now insert. After our leaving Java head we were 11 days before we got the General South-East Trade wind, in which time we did not advance above 5 degrees to the South and 3 degrees to the West, having all the time Variable light Airs of Wind, interrupted by frequent Calms, the weather all the time hot and sultry, and the Air unwholesome, occasioned most probably by the Vast Vapours brought into these Latitudes by the Easterly Trade wind and Westerly Monsoons, both of which blow at this time of the Year in this Sea. The Easterly winds prevail as far as 12 or 10 degrees South, and the Westerly winds as far as 6 or 8 degrees; between them the winds are Variable, and I believe always more or less unwholesome, but to us it was remarkable from the Fatal Consequences that attended it, for whatever might be the cause of First bringing on the Flux among our people, this unwholesome Air had a Great share in it, and increased it to that degree that a Man was no sooner taken with it than he look'd upon himself as Dead. Such was the Despondency that reigned among the Sick at this time, nor could it be by any Means prevented, when every Man saw that Medicine, however skillfully Administered, had not the least effect. I shall mention what Effect only the immaginary approach of this disorder had upon one man. He had long tended upon the Sick, and injoyed a tolerable good State of Health; one morning, coming upon Deck, he found himself a little griped, and immediately began to stamp with his feet, and exclaim, "I have got the Gripes, I have got the Gripes; I shall die, I shall die!" In this manner he continued until he threw himself into a fit, and was carried off the Deck, in a manner, Dead; however he soon recover'd, and did very well.

We had no sooner got into the South-East Trade wind than we felt its happy Effect, tho' we lost several men after, but they were such as were brought so low and weak that there were hardly a possibility of there recovery; and yet some of them linger'd out in a State of Suspence a month after, who, in all Probability, would not have lived 24 Hours before this Change hapned. Those that were not so far gone remained in the same state for some time, and at last began to recover; some few, however, were seized with the disorder after we got into the Trade wind, but they had it but slightly, and soon got over it. It is worth remarking, that of all those who had it in its last stage only one man lived, who is now in a fair way of recovering; and I think Mr. Banks was the only one that was cured at the first Attack'd that had it to a great degree, or indeed at all, before we got into the South-East Trade, for it was before that time that his Cure was happily effected.

It is to be wished, for the good of all Seamen, and mankind in general, that some preventative was found out against this disease, and put in practice in Climates where it is common, for it is impossible to Victual and water a Ship in those Climates but what some one article or another, according to different Peoples opinions, must have been the means of bringing on the Flux. We were inclinable to lay it to the water we took in at Princes Island, and the Turtle we got their, on which we lived several days; but there seems to be no reason for this when we consider that all the Ships from Batavia this Year suffer'd by the same disorder as much as we have done, and many of them arrived at this place in a far worse State; and yet not one of the Ships took any water in at Princes Island. The same may be said of the Harcourt Indiaman, Captain Paul, who sail'd from Batavia soon after our arrival, directly for the Coast of Sumatra; we afterwards heard that she, in a very short time, lost by Sickness above 20 men; indeed, this seem to have been a year of General Sickness over most parts of India, the Ships from Bengal and Madrass bring Melancholly Accounts of the Havock made there by the united force of Sickness and famine.

Some few days after we left Java we saw, for 3 or 4 evenings succeeding one another, boobies fly about the ship. Now, as these birds are known to roost every night on land they seem'd to indicate that some Island was in our neighbourhood; probably it might be the Island Selam, which Island I find differently laid down in different Charts, both in Name and Situation.

The variation of the Compass off the West Coast of Java is about 3 degrees West, which Variation continues, without any sencible difference in the Common Track of Ships, to the Longitude of 288 degrees West, Latitude 22 degrees 0 minutes South. After this it begins to increase apace, in so much that in the Longitude of 295 degrees, Latitude 23 degrees, the Variation was 10 degrees 20 minutes West; in 7 degrees more of Longitude and one of Latitude it increased 2 degrees; in the same space farther to the West it increased 5 degrees; in the Latitude of 28 degrees and Longitude 314 degrees it was 24 degrees 20 minutes; in the Latitude 29 degrees and Longitude 317 degrees it was 26 degrees 10 minutes, and continued to be much the same for the space of 10 degrees farther to the West; but in the Latitude of 34 degrees, Longitude 333 degrees we observed it twice to be 28 1/4 degrees West; but this was the greatest Variation we observed, for in the Latitude of 35 1/2 degrees, Longitude 337 degrees, it was 24 degrees, and continued decreasing, so that of Cape Laguillas it was 22 degrees 30 minutes and in Table Bay it was 20 degrees 30 minutes West.

From what I have observed of the Current it doth not appear that they are at all considerable until you draw near the Meridian of Madagascar, for after we had made 52 degrees of Longitude from Java head we found, by observation, our Error in Longitude was only 2 degrees, and it was the same when we had made only 19 degrees. This Error might be owing partly to a Current setting to the Westward, or, what I thought most likely, that we did not make sufficient allowance for the set of the Sea before when we run, and, lastly, the assum'd Longitude of Java head might be wrong. If any Error lays there it Arises from the imperfection of the Charts I made use of in reducing the Longitude from Batavia to the above mentioned Head, for it cannot be doubted but the Longitude of Batavia is well Determined. After we had passed the Longitude of 307 degrees we began to find the Effects of the Westerly Currents, for in 3 days our Error in Longitude was 1 degree 5 minutes; its Velocity kept increasing as we got to the Westward, in so much that for 5 days successively, after we had made the land, we were drove to the South-West or South-West by West by the Currents not less than 20 Leagues a day; and this continued until we were within 60 or 70 Leagues of the Cape, where we found the Current to set sometimes one way and sometimes another, but mostly to the Westward.

After the Boobies above mentioned left us we saw no more birds till we got nearly abreast of Madagascar, where, in the Latitude of 27 3/4 degrees, we saw an Albatross. After that time we saw more of these birds every day, and in greater numbers, together with several other sorts; one sort about as big as a Duck, of a very Dark brown Colour, with a yellowish bill. The number of these birds increased upon us as we approached the Shore. As soon as we got into Soundings we saw Gannets, which we continued to see as long as we were on the Bank, which stretches off Laguillas 40 Leagues, and Extends along shore to the Eastward from Cape False, according to some charts, 160 Leagues; the Extent of this Bank is not well known, however, it is useful in directing Shipping when to haul in to make the land.

[At Anchor. Table Bay.]

Saturday, 16th. Variable light Airs all this day. Moor'd the Ship and Struck Yards and Topmast, and in the morning got all the Sick (28) ashore to Quarters provided for them, and got off fresh meat and Greens for the People on board.

Sunday, 17th. In the A.M. sail'd for England the Admiral Pocock, Captain Riddle, by whom I sent Letters to the Admiralty and Royal Society. About noon came on a hard, dry Gale from the South-East.

Monday, 18th. In the P.M. anchored in the offing an English Ship, which proved to be the Houghton Indiaman from Bengal. In the A.M. it fell moderate, and we began to water the Ship.

Tuesday, 19th. Variable Gentle breezes. All this day employ'd repairing Sails, Rigging, Watering, etc.

Wednesday, 20th. In the P.M. Sail'd the Houghton Indiaman, who saluted us with 11 Guns, which Complement we returned; this Ship, during her stay in India, lost by sickness between 30 and 40 men, and had at this time a good many down with the Scurvey. Other Ships suffer'd in the same proportion. Thus we find that Ships which have been little more than 12 months from England have suffer'd as much or more by Sickness than we have done, who have been out near 3 Times as long. Yet their sufferings will hardly, if att all, be mentioned or known in England; when, on the other hand, those of the Endeavour, because the Voyage is uncommon, will very probable be mentioned in every News Paper, and, what is not unlikely, with many Additional hardships we never Experienced; for such are the disposition of men in general in these Voyages that they are seldom content with the Hardships and Dangers which will naturally occur, but they must add others which hardly ever had existence but in their imaginations by magnifying the most Trifling accidents and circumstances to the greatest Hardships and unsurmountable dangers without the imediate interposition of Providence, as if the whole merit of the Voyage consisted in the Dangers and Hardships they underwent, or that real ones did not hapen often enough to give the mind sufficient anxiety. Thus Posterity are taught to look upon these Voyages as hazardous to the highest degree.

Thursday, 21st. Fine Pleasant Weather. Employ'd getting on board water, overhauling the rigging, and repairing Sails. Sail'd for Batavia a Dutch Ship.

Friday, 22nd, Saturday, 23rd, Sunday, 24th, Monday, 25th, Tuesday, 26th. Mostly Fine pleasant weather. On the 23rd compleated our water, after which I gave as many of the People leave to go on shore to refresh themselves as could be spared at one time.

Wednesday, 27th. Winds variable and clear. Pleasant weather. Sailed for Holland 4 Sail Dutch Ships.

Thursday, 28th, Friday, 29th. Ditto weather. Employ'd fixing new Topmast and Backstays, repairing Sails, etc.

Saturday, 30th. In the P.M. anchor'd here the Duke of Gloucester, English East India Ship from China. In the Evening a prodigious hard gale of wind came on at South-East, which continued till about 3 o'clock in the Morning. During the Gales the Table Mountains and Adjacent Hills were cap'd with Extraordinary while Clouds; the remainder of the Day light Airs and pleasant weather.

Sunday, 31st. Clear pleasant weather all this day. In the Morning we got on board a whole Ox, which we cut up and salted. I had eat ashore some of as good and Fat Beef as ever I eat in my life, and was told that I might have as good to salt; but in this I was very much disappointed. The one I got was thin and Lean, yet well taisted; it weighed 408 pounds.

[April 1771.]

Monday, April 1st. In the P.M. I observed a dark, dence haze like a Fog bank in the South-East Horizon, and which clouds began to gather over the Table Mountain; certain signs of an approaching gale from the same Quarter, which about 4 o'clock began to blow with great voialance, and continued more or less so the Remainder of these 24 Hours, the Table Mountain cap'd with White Clouds all the time. The weather dry and clear.

Tuesday, 2nd. First part fresh Gales at South-East, the remainder little wind and calms. In the P.M. sail'd for England the Duke of Gloucester Indiaman, who Saluted us at his departure. In the A.M. anchored here 2 Dutch Ships from Batavia, and a third at Anchor under Penguin Island in distress. Put on shore some Sick People.

Wednesday, 3rd. Fine, pleasant weather. Some people on shore on Liberty to refresh; the rest Employ'd repairing Sails and overhauling the Rigging.

Thursday, 4th. Ditto Weather. Employ'd Painting the Ship and paying her sides.

Friday, 5th. Var'ble light winds. Sail'd for Holland 3 Dutch Ships. Employ'd as above, and getting on board Provisions, etc.

Saturday, 6th. Gentle breezes, with some rain in the Night.

Sunday, 7th. Gentle breezes, and fine, pleasant weather; a Signal for some Ships being in the offing.

Monday, 8th. Gentle Breezes from the Westward. In the Night Anchor'd here the Europa, an English East Indiaman from Bengal, and in the Morning she saluted us with 11 Guns, which Complement we return'd.

Tuesday, 9th. Little wind at South-West, with Foggy, hazey weather. Employ'd making ready for Sea.

Wednesday, 10th. Gentle breezes at South-South-East and fair weather. Took on board 11 of our people from Sick Quarters.

Thursday, 11th. Ditto weather. Employ'd getting on board various Articles of Provisions from the Shore.

Friday, 12th. Wind at South-West, fair weather. Set up the Topmast rigging, and bent the Sails.

Saturday, 13th. Fresh breezes at South-West, and Cloudy, hazey weather, in the night Anchor'd here a Dutch Ship from Holland; she sail'd about 3 months ago in company with 2 more. The news brought by this Ship is that a War is dayley expected between England and Spain; Signals out for 4 or 5 Sail more being in the Offing, one of which is said to be a ship from England; took leave of the Gouvernour, intending to Sail to-morrow.

Sunday, 14th. Wind Westerly, gentle breezes. In the P.M. got all the Sick on board, many of whom are yet in a very bad state of health; 3 died here, but this loss was made up by the opportunity we had of compleating our full complement. In the morning unmoor'd and got ready for Sailing.

Monday, 15th. None of the Ships in the Offing are yet arrived. Desirous as we must be of hearing news from England, I detemmin'd not to wait the arrival of these Ships, but took the advantage of a breeze of wind from the West-South-West; weigh'd and stood out of the Bay, saluted with 13 Guns, which Complement was return'd both by the Castle and Dutch Commodore. The Europa Saluted us as we passed her, which we return'd. This Ship was to have sail'd with or before us, but not liking the opportunity she lay fast. At 5 in the Evening anchor'd under Penguin or Robin Island in 10 fathoms water, the Island extending from West-North-West to South-South-West, distant 1 1/2 or 2 miles.

In the Morning saw a Ship standing into Table Bay, under English Colours, which we took to be an Indiaman; at Noon Latitude observed 33 degrees 49 minutes South; Cape Town South 20 degrees East, distant 7 miles. As we could not Sail in the Morning for want of wind, I sent a Boat to the Island for a few Trifling Articles we had forgot to take in at the Cape, but the people on shore would not permit her to land, so that she return'd as she went, and I gave myself no further Trouble at it. Mr. Banks, who was in the Boat, was of opinion that it was owing to a mistake made respecting the rank of the Officer commanding the Boat; be this as it may, it seems probable that the Dutch do not admit of Strangers landing upon this Island least they should carry off some of those people which, for certain crimes, they Banish here for Life, as we were told was done by a Danish Ship a few years ago. But they might have a better reason for refusing our Boat to land, for it is not improbable but what there might be some English Seamen upon this Island whom they had sent from the Cape while we lay there, well knowing that if they came in my way I should take them on board; and this, I am told, is frequently done when any of His Majesty's Ships are in the Bay, for it is well known that the Dutch East India Ships are mostly mann'd by Foreigners.

[Remarks on Cape of Good Hope.]

The Cape of Good Hope hath been so often discribed by Authors, and is so well known to Europeans, that any discription I can give of it may appear unnecessary. However, I cannot help observing that most Authors, particularly the Author of Mr. Byron's voyage, have heightened the picture to a very great degree above what it will bear; so that a Stranger is at once struck with surprise and disappointment, for no Country we have seen this voyage affords so barren a prospect as this, and not only so in appearance, but in reality.

The land over the Cape which constitutes the Peninsula form'd by Table Bay on the North, and False Bay on the South, consists of high barren Mountains; behind these to the East, or what may be called the Isthmus, is a vast extensive plane, not one thousand part of which either is or can be cultivated. The Soil consists mostly of a light kind of Sea sand, producing hardly anything but heath; every inch of Ground that will bear Cultivation is taken up in Small Plantations, consisting of Vineyards, Orchards, Kitchen Gardens, etc. Hardly any 2 lay together, but are dispers'd from one another at some Distance. If we may judge from circumstances, the Interior Parts of this Country is not more fertile; that is, the fertile land bears a very small proportion to the whole. We were told that they have settlements 28 days' journey inland, which is computed at 900 English Miles, and thus far they bring Provisions to the Cape by land. It is also said that the Dutch Farmers are so dispers'd about the country that some have no neighbours within 4 or 5 days' Journeys of them. Admitting these to be facts, and it will at once appear that the Country in General cannot be very fertile, for it would be absurd to suppose that they would raise provisions at such an immence distance, where the trouble and expence of bringing them to Market must increase, in proportion, could it be done nearer. The Dutch assign another reason for being obliged to extend their Scattered Settlements so far in land; which is, they never disturb the Original native, but always leave them in peaceable possession of whatever lands they may have appropriated to their own use, which in some places is pretty Extensive, and that probably none of the worst, by which good Policy the new Settlers very seldom if ever meet with any Disturbance from the Natives; on the contrary, many of them become their Servants, and mix among them, and are useful members to Society.

Notwithstanding the many disadvantages this Country labours under, such is the industry, economy, and good management of the Dutch that not only the necessary, but all the Luxuries, of Life are raised here in as great abundance, and are sold as cheap, if not cheaper, then in any part of Europe, some few Articles excepted. Naval Stores, however, do not want for price any more here than they do at Batavia; these are only sold by the company, who have a certain fix'd exorbitant Price, from which they never deviate.

The inhabitants of the Cape Town are in General well bred and Extreamly Civil and Polite to all Strangers; indeed, it is their Interest so to do, for the whole Town may be considered as one great Inn fitted up for the reception of all Comers and goers. Upon the whole, there is perhaps not a place in the known World that can Equal this in Affording refreshments of all kinds to Shipping. The Bay is Capacious, pretty safe, and Commodious; it lies open to the North-West winds, which winds, we are told, very seldom blow very Strong,* (* In the winter months these winds are very strong, and make the anchorage in Table Bay anything but safe.) but sometimes sends in a Great Sea, for which reason Ships moor North-East and South-West, and in such a manner as to have an Open Hawse with North-West winds. The South-East winds blow frequently with great Violence; but as this is right out of the Bay it is attended with no danger. Near the Town is a wharfe built of wood, run out a proper Distance into the Sea for the Conveniency of landing and Shipping off goods. To this wharfe water is convey'd in pipes and by means of Cocks. Several Boats may fill water at one and the same time. The Company keeps several large Boats or Hoys to carry goods, provisions, water, etc., to and from Shipping, as well Strangers as their own. Fuel is one of the Scarcest articles they have, and is brought a long way out of the Country, and Consists of Roots of Trees, Shrubs, etc. Except a few English Oaks which they have planted, this Country is wholly destitute of wood, except at too great a distance to be brought to the Cape.* (* Since Cook's day large plantations have been made in the vicinity of Capetown.) In the Article Timber, Boards, etc., they are chiefly supply'd from Batavia.

3 of the winter months, viz., from the middle of May to the middle of August, the Dutch do not allow any of their Ships to lay in Table Bay, but oblige them to go into False Bay, where there is a very safe Harbour,* (* Simon's Bay, now the naval station, where there is a dockyard.) and every other Conveniency both for their own Shipping and Strangers, and where every produce of the Country can be had as cheap as at the Cape Town. The Dutch, I am told, never Deviate from this custom of sending their ships to False Bay at this Season of the Year, notwithstanding there had not a Gale of wind hapned for many years that would have put them in the least Danger in Table Bay.

Table Bay is defended by a Square Fort, situated on the East side of the Town, close to the Sea beach, together with several other out works and Batterys along the Shore of the Bay on each side of the Town. They are so situated as to be cannonaded by Shipping, and are in a manner defenceless against a superior land force. The Garrison at present consists of 800 regulars, besides Militia of the Country, which comprehend every man able to bear Arms. They can, by means of Signals, alarm the whole Country in a very short time, and then every man is immediately to repair to the Cape Town. The French at Mauritius are supply'd with large Quantitys of Provisions from the Cape, viz., Salted Beef, Biscuit, Flour, and wine. While we lay in the Bay 2 Store Ships belonging to the King, of the Burthen of 50 or 60 Gun Ships, and a Snow, sail'd for that Island Loaded with Provisions, besides a large (King's) Frigate we left in the Bay taking in her Cargo. The Provisions contracted for this Year by the French were Salt Beef, 500,000 pounds; Flour, 400,000 pounds; Biscuit, 400,000 pounds; and Wine, 1,200 Leagers.

CHAPTER 11.
CAPE OF GOOD HOPE TO ENGLAND.

[April 1771.]

TUESDAY, 16th. At 2 o'clock in the P.M. saw a large Ship behind the Island, under French Colours, standing into Table Bay; at 3 weigh'd with a Light breeze at South-East, and put to Sea; at 4 departed this Life Mr. Robert Molineux Master, a young man of good parts, but had unfortunately given himself up to Extravagancy and intemperance, which brought on disorders that put a Period to his Life. At 6 we had the Table Mountain and the Penguin Island in one bearing South-South-East, distant from the latter about 4 or 5 Leagues; had it calm most part of the night. In the morning a light breeze sprung up Southerly, with which we steer'd North-West; at noon we were by Observation in Latitude 33 degrees 30 minutes South. The Table Mountain bore South 54 degrees East, distant 14 Leagues. N.B. The Table Mountain lies directly over the Cape Town, from which last I take my departure; it lies in the Latitude of 33 degrees 56 minutes South, and Longitude 341 degrees 37 minutes West from Greenwich.

Wednesday, 17th. Fresh breezes and fair weather, with a swell from the South-West. Wind Southerly; course North 50 degrees West; distance 118 miles; latitude 32 degrees 14 minutes South, longitude 344 degrees 8 minutes West.

Thursday, 18th. Gentle breezes and clear weather. Swell as before. Wind Ditto; course North-West; distance 85 miles; latitude 31 degrees 14 minutes South, longitude 345 degrees 19 minutes West.

Friday, 19th. Little wind and Sometimes calm. Swell from the Southward. Wind South-East to North-West; course North 50 degrees West; distance 16 miles; latitude 31 degrees 14 minutes South, longitude 345 degrees 33 minutes West.

Saturday, 20th. Gentle breezes and Clear weather. Wind Westerly; latitude 29 degrees 40 minutes South, longitude 346 degrees 10 minutes West.

Sunday, 21st. A moderate trade wind and Pleasant weather. Wind Southerly; course North 54 degrees West; distance 100 miles; latitude 28 degrees 43 minutes South, longitude 347 degrees 42 minutes West.

Monday, 22nd. A Fresh Trade, and Pleasant weather. Exercised the People at Small Arms. Observations for Longitude with the Sun and Moon agree with the Log. Wind South-East; course North 50 degrees West; distance 118 miles; latitude 27 degrees 27 minutes South, longitude 349 degrees 24 minutes West.

Tuesday, 23rd. Gentle breezes, and Clear weather. Found the Variation in the Evening, by the Amplitude, to be 17 degrees 40 minutes West, and by Azimuth in the Morning 18 degrees 37 minutes. Employ'd repairing Boats and Sails. Exercis'd Great Guns and Small Arms. Wind South-East by South to West-South-West; course North 46 degrees West; distance 98 miles; latitude 26 degrees 19 minutes South, longitude 350 degrees 42 minutes West.

Wednesday, 24th. Ditto weather. Found the Variation to be 17 degrees 30 minutes West. Employ'd as yesterday. Wind West, West-North-West; course North 20 degrees West; distance 78 miles; latitude 25 degrees 6 minutes South, longitude 351 degrees 16 minutes West.

Thursday, 25th. First part, moderate and Clear; Middle, Squally, with Rain; Latter, fresh Gales and Cloudy. Employ'd as above. Wind North-West, South-West; course North 20' West; distance 105 miles; latitude 23 degrees 28 minutes South, longitude 351 degrees 52 minutes West.

Friday, 26th. Fresh Gales, and a large Swell from the Southward. Wind South-South-West, South-East by South; course North 50 degrees West; distance 168 miles; latitude 21 degrees 40 minutes South, longitude 354 degrees 12 minutes West.

Saturday, 27th. Fresh Gales and Cloudy. Employ'd repairing Sails. Wind South-East 1/2 South; course North 55 degrees West; distance 168 miles; latitude 20 degrees 4 minutes South, longitude 356 degrees 40 minutes West.

Sunday, 28th. Ditto weather. Variation per Azimuth 14 degrees West. Wind South-East; course North 56 degrees 30 minutes West; distance 152 miles; latitude 18 degrees 41 minutes South, longitude 358 degrees 54 minutes West.

Monday, 29th. Ditto Gales. Variation 13 degrees 53 minutes West. In the A.M. crossed the line of our first Meridian, viz., that of Greenwich, having now Circumnavigated the Globe in a West direction. Wind South-East; course North 53 degrees West; distance 136 miles; latitude 17 degrees 19 minutes South, longitude 0 degrees 50 minutes West.

Tuesday, 30th. Fresh Gales and Pleasant weather. Exercised the people at Great Guns and Small Arms. Wind South-East; course North 58 degrees West South, distance 126 miles; latitude 16 degrees 11 minutes South, longitude 2 degrees 42 minutes West.

[May 1771. At St. Helena.]

Wednesday, May 1st. Fresh Trade and Pleasant weather. At 6 A.M. saw the Island of St. Helena bearing West, distant 8 or 9 Leagues. At Noon Anchor'd in the Road, before James's Fort, in 24 fathoms water. Found riding here His

Majesty's Ship Portland and Swallow* (* This was not the same Swallow that preceded Cook in circumnavigation. She had been broken up.) Sloop, and 12 Sail of Indiaman. At our first seeing the Fleet in this Road we took it for granted that it was a War; but in this we were soon agreeably deceived. The Europa Indiaman Anchor'd here a little before us; she sail'd from the Cape 2 days after us, and brings an account the French Ship we saw standing into Table Bay was a French Man of War, of 64 Guns, bound to India, and that there were 2 more on their Passage. Wind South-East. At noon at Anchor in St. Helena Road.

Thursday, 2nd. Clear, Pleasant weather. In the P.M. moor'd with the Kedge Anchor, and in the A.M. received some few Officers' stores from the Portland. Wind Ditto. At noon at Anchor in St. Helena Road.

Friday, 3rd. Clear, Pleasant weather. Employ'd repairing Sails, overhauling the Rigging, etc. Wind South-East. At noon at Anchor in St. Helena Road.

Saturday, 4th. Little wind and pleasant weather. At 6 A.M. the Portland made the Signal to unmoor, and at Noon to Weigh, at which time the Ships began to get under Sail. Wind Ditto. At noon at Anchor in St. Helena Road.

Sunday, 5th. Gentle breezes and Clear weather. At 1 P.M. weigh'd, and stood out of the Road in company with the Portland and 12 Sail of Indiamen. At 6 o'clock James Fort, St. Helena, bore East 1/2 South, distant 3 Leagues. In the A.M. found the Variation to be 13 degrees 10 minutes West. Wind East by South; course North 50 degrees 30 minutes West; distance 71 miles; latitude 15 degrees 5 minutes South, longitude 6 degrees 46 minutes West.

Monday, 6th. Moderate breezes and Cloudy weather. Sailing in Company with the Fleet. Wind East-South-East; course North 47 1/2 degrees West; distance 122 miles; latitude 13 degrees 42 minutes South, longitude 8 degrees 27 minutes West.

Tuesday, 7th. Ditto Weather. In the A.M. found the Variation to be 12 degrees 5 minutes West. Exercised the people at Great Guns and Small Arms. Wind South-East; course North 46 degrees West; distance 137 miles; latitude 12 degrees 5 minutes South, longitude 10 degrees 9 minutes West.

Wednesday, 8th. A Steady breeze and Pleasant Weather. All the Fleet in Company. Wind South-East; course North 46 degrees 45 minutes West; distance 126 miles; latitude 10 degrees 39 minutes South, longitude 11 degrees 42 minutes West.

Thursday, 9th. Ditto Weather. In the Evening found the Variation to be 11 degrees 42 minutes West. Wind South-East by South; course North-West; distance 118 miles; latitude 9 degrees 16 minutes, longitude 13 degrees 17 minutes West.

Friday, 10th. At 6 in the A.M. saw the Island of Ascension bearing North-North-West, distant 7 Leagues. Made the Signal to speak with the Portland, and soon after Captain Elliott himself came on board, to whom I deliver'd a Letter for the Admiralty, and a Box containing the Ship's Common Log Books, and some of the Officers' Journals, etc. I did this because it seem'd probable that the Portland would get home before us, as we sail much heavier than any of the Fleet.* (* The Portland and the India fleet got home three days before the Endeavour.) At Noon the Island of Ascension bore East by South, distant 4 or 5 Leagues. By our Observations it lies in the Latitude of 7 degrees 54 minutes South, and Longitude of 14 degrees 18 minutes West. A North-West by North course by Compass, or North-West a little Westerly by the Globe from St. Helena, will bring you directly to this Island. Wind Ditto; course North-West; distance 120 miles; latitude 7 degrees 51 minutes South, longitude 14 degrees 32 minutes West.

Friday, 11th. A steady Trade wind and pleasant Weather. At 1/2 past 6 p.m. the Island of Ascension bore South-East 3/4 East, distant 11 or 12 Leagues. Sailing in Company with the Fleet. Wind Ditto; course North 42 degrees West, distance 117 miles; latitude 6 degrees 24 minutes South, longitude 15 degrees 51 minutes West.

Saturday, 12th. First and Middle parts a Steady breeze, and fair the Latter; light Squalls, with rain. Wind South-East by South to South-East by East; course North 31 degrees 15 minutes West; distance 123 miles; latitude 4 degrees 38 minutes South, longitude 16 degrees 54 minutes West.

Sunday, 13th. Gentle breezes and Clear Weather; hott and Sultry. Sailing in Company with the fleet. Variation 10 degrees West. Wind South-East by South; course North 32 1/2 degrees West; distance 119 miles; latitude 2 degrees 58 minutes South, longitude 17 degrees 58 minutes West.

Monday, 14th. Ditto Weather. Wind South-East by South; course North 32 1/2 degrees West; distance 109 miles; latitude 1 degree 26 minutes South, longitude 18 degrees 57 minutes West.

Tuesday, 15th. Little wind and hot, Sultry weather. In the P.M. observed, meerly for the sake of Observing, an Eclipse of the Sun. In the A.M. brought another Foretopsail to the Yard, the old one being quite wore out. Wind East-South-East; course North 32 1/2 degrees West; distance 85 miles; latitude 0 degrees 14 minutes South, longitude 19 degrees 43 minutes West.

Wednesday, 16th. Light breezes and fair weather. Variation 9 degrees 30 minutes West. Wind South-East by South; course North 31 degrees West; distance 71 miles; latitude 0 degrees 47 minutes North, longitude 20 degrees 20 minutes West.

Thursday, 17th. Ditto Weather. Sailing in Company with the Fleet. Wind Ditto; course North 31 degrees West; distance 61 miles; latitude 1 degree 39 minutes North, longitude 20 degrees 50 minutes West.

Saturday, 18th. First part ditto weather; remainder Squally, with Thunder and Rain. The observ'd Latitude is 14 Miles to the Northward of the Log. Sailing in Company with the Fleet. Wind South-South-East to East; course North 20 degrees West; distance 86 miles; latitude 3 degrees 0 minutes North, longitude 21 degrees 22 minutes West.

Sunday, 19th. Cloudy, unsettled weather, with some rain. In the A.M. found the Variation by the Amplitude and Azimuth 7 degrees 40 minutes West. Hoisted a Boat out, and sent on board the Houghton for the Surgeon, Mr. Carret, in order to look at Mr. Hicks, who is so far gone in a Consumption that his Life is dispair'd of. Observation at Noon 16 Miles to the Northward of the Log. Wind South-East to South by East; course North 20 degrees West; distance 98 miles; latitude 4 degrees 32 minutes North, longitude 21 degrees 58 minutes West.

[With India Fleet. Homeward Bound.]

Monday, 20th. Dark, cloudy, unsettled weather, with rain. At Noon the Observ'd Latitude was 27 Miles to the Northward of the Log. Sailing in Company with the Fleet. Wind Variable between the South and East; course North 19 degrees West; distance 70 miles; latitude 5 degrees 38 minutes North, longitude 22 degrees 21 minutes West.

Tuesday, 21st. Little wind, with some heavy showers of rain. At 2 p.m. had some Observations of the Sun and Moon, which gave the Longitude 24 degrees 50 minutes West, 2 degrees 28 minutes West of Account. In the morning it was Calm, and the Ships, being near one another, several of them had their Boats out to tow. We Observed the Portland to carry out a long Warp. I, being desirous to see the Machine they made use of, we hoisted out a Boat, and Mr. Banks, Dr. Solander, and myself went on board her, where we was show'd it. it was made of Canvas, in every respect like an Umbrello; its Circumference, if extended to a Circle, was 24 feet, tho' this was a Small one of the Sort; yet Captain Elliot told me that it would hold as much as 150 Men could haul. I was so well satisfied of the Utility of this Machine that I would not have delayed a moment in having one Made had not our Forge been render'd Useless by the loss of some of its parts. Winds Variable; course North 31 degrees West; distance 35 miles; latitude 6 degrees 8 minutes North, longitude 25 degrees 8 minutes West.

Wednesday, 22nd. Variable, unsettled weather, with rain. About 9 o'clock in the A.M. the Portland shorten'd Sail for the Sternmost Ships to come up. As we imagin'd, this gave us an Opportunity to get a Head of the Fleet, after which we made such sail as was necessary to keep in Company. Wind Variable; course North-North-West 3/4 West; distance 58 miles; latitude 6 degrees 58 minutes North, longitude 25 degrees 38 minutes West.

Thursday, 23rd. Little wind from the Eastward, with frequent showers of Rain, and hazey weather. The Fleet astern of us all this day. At Noon we Shortned Sail for them to come up, the headmost being about 2 Leagues off. Wind East to North-East; course North 25 degrees West; distance 56 miles; latitude 7 degrees 49 minutes North, longitude 26 degrees 2 minutes West.

Friday, 24th. First part Moderate breezes, and hazey, with rain; the latter, fresh breezes and fair. At 3 p.m., finding the Fleet to come fast up with us, we made all the Sail we could. Soon after it became hazey, and we lost sight of them until near 6, when it clear'd up a little, and we saw 3 Sail abreast of us, bearing East about 2 or 3 Miles' Distance; by this we saw that they not only kept a better wind, but out sail'd us upon a wind. It became again hazey, and we lost Sight of them, and notwithstanding we kept close upon a wind all night, with as much Sail out as we could bear, there was not one Sail in sight in the Morning. Wind North-East and North-North-East; course North 54 degrees West; distance 92 miles; latitude 8 degrees 42 minutes North, 27 degrees 18 minutes West.

Saturday, 25th. Moderate Trade Wind and Cloudy weather. Wind North-North-East; course North 50 degrees 15 minutes West; distance 92 miles; latitude 9 degrees 41 minutes North, longitude 28 degrees 30 minutes West.

Sunday, 26th. A Steady Trade and Cloudy Weather. About 1 o'Clock P.M. departed this Life Lieutenant Hicks, and in the Evening his body was committed to the Sea with the usual ceremonys. He died of a Consumption which he was not free from when we sail'd from England, so that it may be truly said that he hath been dying ever since, tho' he held out tolerable well until we got to Batavia. Wind North-East by North; course North 46 degrees West; distance 92 miles; latitude 20 degrees 47 minutes North, longitude 29 degrees 35 minutes West.

Monday, 27th. A Steady, fresh Trade and Cloudy weather. This day I gave Mr. Charles Clerk an order to act as Lieutenant in the room of Mr. Hicks, deceased, he being a Young Man extremely well qualified for that Station. Wind North-East; course North 39 degrees West; distance 103 miles; latitude 12 degrees 7 minutes North, longitude 30 degrees 40 minutes West.

Tuesday, 28th. A steady Trade and fair weather. Wind North Easterly; course North 40 degrees West; distance 108 miles; latitude 13 degrees 30 minutes North, longitude 31 degrees 51 minutes West.

Wednesday, 29th. Fresh Gales and Hazey. Wind Ditto; course North 31 1/2 degrees West; distance 128 miles; latitude 15 degrees 19 minutes North, longitude 33 degrees 2 minutes West.

Thursday, 30th. Ditto Gales and Cloudy. Fix'd a new maintopmast Backstay, the old one having broke several times. Wind Ditto; course North 31 degrees 15 minutes West; distance 124 miles; latitude 17 degrees 5 minutes North, longitude 34 degrees 9 minutes West.

Friday, 31st. Strong Gales and Cloudy in the Evening. Got down Top Gallant Yards, and in the Morning found the Variation 5 degrees 9 minutes West. Wind North-East and North-East by East; course North 39 1/2 degrees West; distance 136 miles; latitude 18 degrees 50 minutes North, longitude 35 degrees 40 minutes West.

[June 1771.]

Saturday, June 1st. Fresh Trade, and Cloudy weather. In the A.M. got up Top Gallant Yards. Wind North-East; course North 35 degrees West; distance 100 miles; latitude 20 degrees 12 minutes North, longitude 36 degrees 41 minutes West.

Sunday, 2nd. Moderate Gales and Clear weather. Variation 5 degrees 4 minutes West. Wind North-East to North-North-East; course North 49 degrees West; distance 104 miles; latitude 21 degrees 20 minutes North, longitude 38 degrees 5 minutes West.

Monday, 3rd. A Gentle Trade Wind, and Pleasant weather. Wind North-East; course North 44 degrees West; distance 85 miles; latitude 22 degrees 21 minutes North, longitude 39 degrees 9 minutes West.

Tuesday, 4th. Ditto weather. In the A.M. found the Variation to be 4 degrees 30 minutes West. Wind North-East; course North 34 degrees West; distance 91 miles; latitude 23 degrees 40 North, longitude 40 degrees 4 minutes West.

Wednesday, 5th. Gentle breezes, with some Showers of Small Rain. Wind Ditto; course North 52 degrees West; distance 83 miles; latitude 24 degrees 31 minutes North, longitude 41 degrees 11 minutes West.

Thursday, 6th. Ditto weather. In the A.M. found the Variation by the mean of the Amplitude and Azimuth to be 5 degrees 34 minutes West, and by Observation of the Sun and Moon found the Ship in Longitude 43 degrees 18 minutes West of Greenwich, 2 degrees 51 minutes West of the Log since the last Observations; this I judge to be owing to a Westerly Current. Wind East-North-East to East; course North 3/4 West; distance 90 miles; latitude 26 degrees 1 minute North, longitude, per Observation Sun and Moon, 43 degrees 18 minutes West.

Friday, 7th. Moderate breezes, and Cloudy. A.M., Variation per mean of 20 Azimuths 5 degrees 20 minutes West. Wind East-North-East; course North 15 degrees West; distance 84 miles; latitude 27 degrees 22 minutes North, longitude 43 degrees 42 minutes West.

Saturday, 8th. Moderate breezes and Pleasant weather. In the A.M. found the Variation to be 5 degrees 24 minutes West. By the Observation of the Sun and Moon the Longitude of the Ship at Noon was 43 degrees 42 minutes West. Wind Easterly; course North; distance 88 miles; latitude 28 degrees 50 minutes North, longitude 43 degrees 42 minutes West.

Sunday, 9th. Clear, pleasant weather and a Smooth Sea. In the A.M. found the Variation to be 7 degrees 33 minutes West. Some Tropick birds flying about the Ship; we have seen of these birds every day since we passed the Tropick. Wind Ditto; course North by West 1/2 West; distance 81 miles; latitude 30 degrees 11 minutes North, longitude 44 degrees 9 minutes West.

Monday, 10th. Little wind and Clear weather. Exercised the people at Small Arms. Wind Ditto; course North 30 degrees West; distance 71 miles; latitude 31 degrees 12 minutes North, longitude 44 degrees 50 minutes West.

Tuesday, 11th. Ditto weather. A Smooth Sea. Wind North-East by East; course North 18 minutes West; distance 67 miles; latitude 32 degrees 16 North, longitude 45 degrees 14 minutes West.

Wednesday, 12th. Light breezes and clear weather. Variation by the Amplitude in the Evening 7 degrees 0 minutes West, and by Azimuth in the Morning 6 degrees 55 minutes West. Exercised Great Guns and Small Arms. Wind East by South; course North-North-East; distance 48 miles; latitude 33 degrees 8 minutes North, longitude 44 degrees 53 minutes West.

Thursday, 13th. Little wind and pleasant weather. Found the Variation by the Amplitude in the Evening to be 8 degrees 23 minutes; in the Morning 8 degrees 15 minutes, and by Azimuth soon after 8 degrees 14 minutes West. Wind Ditto; Course North by East 1/2 East; distance 77 miles; latitude 34 degrees 14 minutes North, longitude 44 degrees 25 minutes West.

Friday, 14th. A Gentle Gale, and pleasant weather. In the A.M. saw 2 Turtle laying a Sleep upon the water. Wind East-South-East; course North 18 degrees East; distance 99 miles; latitude 35 degrees 48 minutes North, longitude 43 degrees 48 minutes West.

Saturday, 15th. Ditto Weather at Daylight. In the Morning saw a Sloop to Windward standing to the Eastward, which we run out of sight by Noon. Wind South-East; course North-East 1/2 East; distance 119 miles; latitude 37 degrees 2 minutes North, longitude 41 degrees 54 minutes West.

Sunday, 16th. A Steady breeze and pleasant weather, with some rain in the Night. At daylight in the Morning saw a Sail a head, which we came up and spoke with a little after 10 o'clock. She proved a Portoguee Ship from Rio de Janeiro, bound to Lisbon. Wind Ditto; course North-East 1/2 East; distance 119 miles; latitude 38 degrees 18 minutes North, longitude 40 degrees 38 minutes West.

Monday, 17th. Steady, Gentle Gales and pleasant weather. Variation in the Evening 9 degrees West. Wind South-South-East; course North 68 degrees East; distance 104 miles; latitude 38 degrees 57 minutes North, longitude 38 degrees 36 minutes West.

Tuesday, 18th. Little wind, and clear weather. At 2 p.m. found the Ship to be by Observation 1 degree 22 minutes to the Westward of Account carried on from the last Observation; in the Evening the Variation was 14 degrees 15 minutes West, and in the Morning 14 degrees 24 minutes. Wind South; course North 66 degrees East; distance 82 miles; latitude 39 degrees 52 minutes North, longitude 36 degrees 59 minutes West.

Wednesday, 19th. Fresh Gales and Cloudy. At 2 p.m. found by observation the same Error in our Longitude as Yesterday, which I have now corrected. The Longitude of this day is that resulting from Observation. At 10 A.M. saw a Sail a head, which we soon came up with, and sent a Boat on board. She was a Schooner from Rhoad Island out upon the Whale fishery. From her we learnt that all was peace in Europe, and that the America Disputes were made up; to confirm this the Master said that the Coat on his back was made in old England. Soon after leaving this Vessel we spoke another from Boston, and saw a third, all out on the same account. Wind South to South-West; course North 73 degrees East; distance 127 miles; latitude 40 degrees 9 minutes North, longitude 36 degrees 44 minutes West.

Thursday, 20th. Fresh Gales and Cloudy, with some Showers of rain. At day light in the Morning saw a Sail ahead standing to the East. A Swell from the North-North-West. Wind South-West, North-West, North; course North 80 1/2 degrees East; distance 121 miles; latitude 40 degrees 29 minutes North, longitude 33 degrees 10 minutes West.

Friday, 21st. Fresh Gales and Cloudy. In the P.M. saw a Sail astern standing to the South-East, and at 11 o'Clock A.M. saw from the Mast head 13 Sail of Stout Ships, which we took to be the East India Fleet. Wind Northerly; course East by North; distance 128 miles; latitude 40 degrees 33 minutes North, longitude 30 degrees 20 minutes West.

Saturday, 22nd. Fresh Gales, with Squalls, attended with rain. In the Evening had 14 Sail in sight, 13 upon our lee Quarter, and a Snow upon our lee Bow. In the Night split both Topgallant Sails so much that they were obliged to be unbent to repair. In the Morning the Carpenter reported the Maintopmast to be Sprung in the Cap, which we supposed hapned in the P.M., when both the Weather Backstays broke. Our Rigging and Sails are now so bad that something or another is giving way every day. At Noon had 13 Sail in sight, which we are well assured are the India Fleet, and are all now upon our Weather Quarter. Wind North to North-East; course North 81 degrees East; distance 114 miles; latitude 41 degrees 11 minutes, longitude 27 degrees 52 minutes West.

Sunday, 23rd. Fresh Gales and Squally, attended with Showers of rain. In the Evening all the Fleet were to Windward of us, and in the Morning not one was to be seen. Wind North-East by North to East-North-East; course South 69 1/2 degrees East; distance 80 miles; latitude 40 degrees 43 minutes North, longitude 26 degrees 13 minutes West.

Monday, 24th. First part, moderate breezes; remainder, Squally. At Noon Tack'd. Wind North-East to East-South-East; course South 82 degrees East; distance 64 miles; latitude 40 degrees 34 minutes North, longitude 24 degrees 49 minutes West.

Tuesday, 25th. First part and remainder a fresh breeze and Cloudy. Wind North-East to North-North-East; course South 85 degrees East; distance 58 miles; latitude 40 degrees 39 minutes North, longitude 23 degrees 33 minutes West.

Wednesday, 26th. First part, breezes; remainder, little wind. Wind North by East; course North 86 degrees 45 minutes East; distance 72 miles; latitude 40 degrees 43 minutes North, longitude 21 degrees 58 minutes West.

Thursday, 27th. Moderate breezes and Cloudy weather. Wind Westerly; course North 54 minutes East; distance 54 miles; latitude 41 degrees 14 minutes North, longitude 20 degrees 59 minutes West.

Friday, 28th. Fresh breezes, with Showers of Rain. Wind West to North-North-West; course North 38 degrees East; distance 123 miles; latitude 42 degrees 55 minutes North, longitude 19 degrees 18 minutes West.

Saturday, 29th. First part, little wind; remainder, Fresh Gales and Squally, with Showers of Rain. Wind South-West to West and North-East; course North 59 degrees 15 minutes East; distance 86 miles; latitude 43 degrees 39 minutes North, longitude 17 degrees 36 minutes West.

Sunday, 30th. Gentle breezes and fair weather. Variation in the Evening 18 degrees 30 minutes West, and in the Morning 19 degrees 30 minutes. Wind Northerly; course North 50 degrees 45 minutes East; distance 87 miles; latitude 44 degrees 34 minutes North, longitude 16 degrees 2 minutes West.

[July 1771.]

Monday, July 1st. Ditto weather. In the Night passed 2 Sail Standing to the South-West. Wind Ditto; course North 77 degrees 15 minutes East; distance 90 miles; latitude 44 degrees 54 minutes North, longitude 13 degrees 59 minutes West.

Tuesday, 2nd. Little wind and Cloudy, hazey weather. One Sail in Sight to the North-East. Wind Ditto; course East; distance 42 miles; latitude 45 degrees 54 minutes North, longitude 13 degrees 2 minutes West.

Wednesday, 3rd. Little wind and pleasant weather. At 9 A.M. found the Ship by Observation of the Sun and Moon 1 degree 14 minutes East of Account. Six Sail in Sight. Wind North and North-West; course North 56 degrees East; distance 54 miles; latitude 45 degrees 24 minutes North, longitude 11 degrees 59 minutes West per Log, 10 degrees 45 minutes per Observation.

Thursday, 4th. Gentle breezes and Cloudy weather. Variation per Azimuth and Amplitude in the Evening 21 degrees 25 1/2 West, and in the Morning 20 degrees 10 minutes West. Wind West, North, and North-East; course South 85 degrees East; distance 55 miles; latitude 45 degrees 29 minutes North, longitude 10 degrees 44 minutes West per Log, 9 degrees 27 minutes per Observation.

Friday, 5th. Little wind and Cloudy. At 1 P.M. spoke a Dutch Galliot bound to Riga. At 5 Tack't, and stood to the Westward till 8 a.m., then to the Eastward. Wind North-East; course North 50 degrees East; distance 8 miles; latitude 45 degrees 34 minutes North, longitude 10 degrees 32 minutes West per Log, 9 degrees 18 minutes per Observation.

Saturday, 6th. Gentle breezes and Cloudy. At 1 p.m. sent a Boat on board a Brig belonging to Boston, last from Gibraltar, and bound to Falmouth. Wind North-North-East; course North 72 degrees 30 minutes East; distance 37 miles; latitude 44 degrees 45 minutes North, longitude 9 degrees 42 minutes West per Log, 8 degrees 28 minutes per Observation.

Sunday, 7th. Gentle breezes and Clear weather. In the Evening found the Variation by the Amplitude to be 22 degrees 30 minutes West. At 9 A.M. Spoke a Brig from Liverpool bound to Porto, and some time after another from London, bound to the Granades. She had been 3 days from Scilly, and reckoned herself in the Longitude of about 10 minutes West, which was about 40 minutes to the Westward of what we found ourselves to-day by Observation. We learnt from this Vessel that no account had been received in England from us, and that Wagers were held that we were lost. It seems highly improbable that the Letters sent by the Dutch Ships from Batavia should not come to hand, as it is now 5 months since these Ships sail'd from the Cape of Good Hope. Wind North-North-East and North-West; course North 50 degrees East; distance 49 miles; latitude 46 degrees 16 minutes

North, longitude 9 degrees 39 minutes West per Account, 9 degrees 29 minutes per Observation.

Monday, 8th. Little wind and hazey weather. Swell from the Northward. Wind North-North-West to South-West; course North 46 degrees 45 minutes East; distance 43 miles; latitude 46 degrees 45 minutes North, longitude 8 degrees 54 minutes West.

Tuesday, 9th. Fore and middle parts a Gentle breeze, and thick, Foggy weather; remainder, a fresh Breeze and Cloudy. A swell from the North-North-West all day. Wind South Westerly; course North 21 degrees East; distance 100 miles; latitude 48 degrees 19 minutes North, longitude 8 degrees 1 minute West per Account, 8 degrees 7 minutes per Observation.

Wednesday, 10th. Pleasant breezes and Clear weather. At 6 o'Clock in the Morning sounded, and Struck ground in 60 fathoms Shells and Stones, by which I judged we were the length of Scilly Isles. At Noon we saw land from the Mast Head, bearing North, which we judged to be about the Land's End. Soundings 54 fathoms, Coarse, Grey Sand. Wind Westerly; course North 44 degrees East; distance 97 miles; latitude 49 degrees 29 minutes North, longitude 6 degrees 18 minutes West.

Friday, 11th. Steady fresh breezes and clear weather. At 2 in the P.M. saw the Lizardland, and at 6 o'clock the lighthouse bore North-West, distant 5 Leagues, we being at this time, by my reckoning, in the Longitude of 5 degrees 30 minutes West; soon after 2 Ships under their Topsails between us and the land, which we took for Men of War. At 7 o'clock in the morning the Start Point bore North-West by North, distant 3 Leagues, and at Noon we reckon'd ourselves about 5 Leagues short of Portland. This Forenoon a small cutter built vessel came under our Stern, and inquir'd after the India Fleet, which, they said, they were cruizing for and had not seen.

Friday, 12th. Winds at South-West, a fresh Gale, with which we run briskly up Channel. At 1/2 past 3 p.m. passed the Bill of Portland, and at 7 Peverell Point; at 6 a.m. passed Beachy head at the distance of 4 or 5 miles; at 10 Dungeness, at the distance of 2 miles, and at Noon we were abreast of Dover.

Saturday, 13th. At 3 o'clock in the P.M. anchor'd in the Downs, and soon after I landed in order to repair to London.

(Signed) JAMs COOK.

POSTCRIPT.

I HAVE made mention in Book 1st,* (* The Journal was written in thin books, afterwards bound together in England. The page given here is of this published copy.) page 76, of 2 Spanish Ships touching at Georges Island some months before our Arrival there. Upon our arrival at Batavia we were inform'd that 2 French Ships, commanded by the Sieur de Bougainville, had put in there about 2 years before us in their way home from the South Seas. We were told many Circumstances relating to the 2 Ships, all tending to prove beyond a doubt that they were the same 2 as were at George's Island as above mentioned, which we then conjectur'd to be Spaniards, being lead into that mistake by the Spanish Iron, etc., we saw among the Natives, and by Toobouratomita pitching upon the Colours of that Nation for those they wore, in which he might very easily be mistaken; but as to the Iron, etc., there might be no mistake, for we were told that either one or both of these Ships had put into the River de la Plata, where they disposed of all their European goods brought for that purpose, and purchased others to Trade with the Islanders in the South Sea; and I think we were told that they also touched upon the Spanish Main in the South Sea. As a proof of their having been trading with the Spaniards, Bougainville's Ship had on board a great Quantity of Spanish Dollars at the time she arrived at and left Batavia, some days after our arrival at the Cape of Good Hope. I was told by some French Officers, lately come from the Island Mauritius, that Orette, the Native of George's Island which Bougainville brought away with him, was now at the Maritius, and that they were going to fit out a Ship to carry him to his Native country, where they intend to make a Settlement; 100 Troops for that purpose were to go out in the same Ship. This account is confirmed by a French Gentleman we have on board, who has very lately been at the Maritius.* (* This intention was never carried out.) As I have no reason to doubt the truth of this account, it leads me to consider the rout that this Ship must take, which I think can be no other than that of Tasmans as far as the Coast of New Zeland; and if she fall in with that Coast to the Southward of Cape Farewell will very probably put into Admiralty Bay, or Queen Charlotte's sound, as Tasman's track will in some measure point out to her one or the other of these places. I think it is not likely she will venture through the Strait, even suppose she discovers it, but will follow Tasman's Track to the North Cape, where no doubt she will leave him, and follow the direction of the Coast to the South-East, as it will not be out of her way; by which means she will fall in with the most fertile part of that Country, and as they cannot know anything of the Endeavour's voyage, they will not hesitate a moment to declare themselves the first discoverers. Indeed, I cannot see how they can think otherwise, unless the Natives inform them to the contrary, which they may not choose to understand. The French Officers before spoke of would not allow that George's Island was first discover'd by the Dolphin, though no doubt Bougainville did; but it was not for the Interest of his Country, nor perhaps his own, to own it. Thus this Island, though of little value, may prove a Bone of Contention between the 2 Nations, especially if the French make a Settlement upon it, and the Dolphin's voyage, and this of ours, published by Authority to fix the prior right of discovery beyond disputes.

Now I am upon the Subject of discoveries, I hope it will not be taken amiss if I give it as my opinion that the most feasable method of making further discoveries in the South Sea is to enter it by the way of New Zeland, first touching and refreshing at the Cape of Good Hope; from thence proceed to the Southward of New Holland for Queen Charlotte's Sound, where again refresh Wood and water, taking care to be ready to leave that place by the latter end of September, or beginning of October at farthest, when you would have the whole Summer before you, and after getting through the Strait, might, with the prevailing Westerly Winds, run to the Eastward in as high a Latitude as you please, and if you meet with no lands would have time enough to get round Cape Horne before the Summer was too far spent; but if after meeting with no Continent, and you had other objects in view, then haul to the Northward, and after visiting some of the Islands already discovered, after which proceed with the trade wind back to the Westward in search of those before mentioned--thus the discoveries in the South Sea would be compleat.* (* This programme Cook carried out in his second voyage in the most complete manner possible.)